SPYING AND T

CW00402545

Richard J. Aldrich is a Professor of Inte... of Warwick. A regular commentator on ~~...~~ ...~~...~~ ...~~...~~ he has written for *The Times*, *Guardian* and *Daily Telegraph*. He is a prize-winning author of several books, including *The Hidden Hand* and *GCHQ*.

Rory Cormac is a Professor of International Relations at the University of Nottingham, specializing in secret intelligence and covert action. He is the author of *Disrupt and Deny* and *How To Stage A Coup*, and co-author, with Richard J. Aldrich, of *The Black Door*.

'This monumental book is really a history of the British secret services, focusing on the fascinating moments when this intersects with royal history... Authoritative and highly readable... As every page of this book attests, the royals have always been involved in secretly directing the affairs not just of this country but of many others.' Ben Macintyre, *The Times*, 'Book of the Week'

'Bizarre and disturbing episodes are revealed in this excellent history of the royal family's relationship with espionage... Through unbelievably thorough research – all of it fully referenced for grateful future scholars – they have compiled something comprehensive and compelling.' *Guardian*

'A fascinating history of royal espionage... The book, which stretches back to Elizabeth I and her spymaster Sir Francis Walsingham, has something of interest on pretty much every page.' Rowland White, *Sunday Times*

'Their mastery of a subject that is extensive both chronologically and in its geographical scope is assured and impressive... An intriguing alternative narrative of British royal history.' Matthew Dennison, *Sunday Telegraph*

'Aldrich and Cormac have written an important book. Packed with new material and fresh insights, it offers an original way of looking at royal history. It's also a very good read.' Jane Ridley, *Literary Review*

'[A] thorough and informed survey of how matters of high state have really worked – and work.' Alan Judd, *Spectator*

Also by Richard J. Aldrich & Rory Cormac

The Black Door: Spies, Secret Intelligence and
British Prime Ministers

Spying on the World: The Declassified Documents of the Joint
Intelligence Committee, 1936–2013 (*with Michael S. Goodman*)

Also by Richard J. Aldrich

GCHQ: The Fully Updated Centenary Edition

The Hidden Hand: Britain, America and Cold War
Secret Intelligence

Intelligence and the War Against Japan: Britain,
America and the Politics of Secret Service

Also by Rory Cormac

How To Stage A Coup: And Ten Other Lessons
from the World of Secret Statecraft

Disrupt and Deny: Spies, Special Forces and the Secret
Pursuit of British Foreign Policy

Confronting the Colonies: British Intelligence and
Counterinsurgency

SPYING
AND THE
CROWN

The Secret Relationship
Between British Intelligence
and the Royals

Richard J. Aldrich & Rory Cormac

Atlantic Books
London

First published in Great Britain in 2021 by Atlantic Books,
an imprint of Atlantic Books Ltd.

This paperback edition first published in Great Britain in 2022
by Atlantic Books.

Previously published as *The Secret Royals: Spying and the Crown,
from Victoria to Diana*

1 2 3 4 5 6 7 8 9

A CIP catalogue record for this book is available from the British Library.

Paperback ISBN: 978-1-78649-914-1
E-book ISBN: 978-1-78649- 913-4

Printed in Great Britain by Clays Ltd, Elcograf S.p.A.

Atlantic Books
An Imprint of Atlantic Books Ltd
Ormond House
26–27 Boswell Street
London
WC1N 3JZ

www.atlantic-books.co.uk

To Libby and Joanne – who are just the best!

CONTENTS

ILLUSTRATIONS

First section

Elizabeth I's 'Rainbow Portrait' (*Wikimedia Commons*)
Queen Victoria with her eldest daughter Vicky (*Private collection*)
George V and Tsar Nicholas II with their heirs (*Private collection*)
Rasputin (*Universal History Archive/Getty Images*)
Fridtjof Nansen (*Frum Museum*)
The police arrest the would-be assassin George McMahon (*Ernest Brooks/Getty Images*)
Edward, Wallis with Charles and Fern Bedaux (*US National Archives and Records Administration*)
The Windsors loose in Florida, 1941 (*US National Archives and Records Administration*)
Gray Phillips followed Edward with care in the 1940s (*Private collection*)
'Mouse' Fielden (*Private collection*)
The royal family inspect the 6th Airborne Division (© *IWM H 38612*)
George VI inspects a special forces raiding jeep (© *IWM H 19947*)
George VI inspects a landing craft (*Military Images/Alamy Stock Photo*)

Second section

George VI in Monty's caravan (© *IWM TR 2393*)
George VI and Princess Margaret (*Private collection*)
The Treetops Hotel in Kenya (*Private collection*)
Queen Elizabeth II and Marshall Tito (*AFP via Getty Images*)

John F. Kennedy, Mountbatten and Lyman Lemnizter (*JFK Library*)

Queen Elizabeth II with President Kwame Nkrumah in Ghana (*Kara University Library*)

Queen Elizabeth II and Anthony Blunt (*PA Images/Alamy Stock Photo*)

Ian Fleming with Sean Connery (*PictureLux/The Hollywood Archive/Alamy Stock Photo*)

Prince Charles at Cambridge University (© *Hulton-Deutsch Collection/Corbis via Getty Images*)

Prince Charles enjoys pistol practice in West Berlin (*INGA SA*)

Aftermath of the attempted kidnap of Princess Anne (*PA/Alamy Stock Photo*)

Queen Elizabeth II with Harold Wilson (*Ford Library*)

Queen Elizabeth II with the Shah of Iran (*PA/Alamy Stock Photo*)

Prince Charles eyes Idi Amin (*Keystone/Getty Images*)

Diana, Princess of Wales (*Tim Ockenden/Alamy Stock Photo*)

Queen Elizabeth II unveils a plaque to mark the centenary of GCHQ (*Niklas Halle'n/AFP via Getty Images*)

INTRODUCTION: 007

On Her Majesty's Secret Service.

Ian Fleming[1]

O N A BALMY summer evening in late July 2012 the world's most famous intelligence officer arrived at Buckingham Palace in an iconic black cab. Dressed in his trademark tuxedo, he skipped up the central red staircase and, flanked by the royal corgis, entered a gilded room. At a desk in the corner sat Queen Elizabeth II. She kept him waiting; he glanced at the clock and coughed politely.

'Good evening, Mr Bond,' she said, turning to face him. 'Good evening, your majesty,' he quietly responded.

James Bond followed her as she made her way down the stairs and headed towards a helicopter waiting on the lawn outside. Moments later, Agent 007 and the queen jumped from the helicopter in a dramatic parachute drop down towards the Olympic stadium in east London. The crowd gasped as they vanished from sight, before Elizabeth reappeared, wearing the same pink dress, in the royal box. The sequence formed the highlight of the Olympic Games opening ceremony.

Organized by the Oscar-winning director Danny Boyle and partly filmed in Buckingham Palace, this masterpiece of deception involved the real queen, stunt doubles and cameo roles for three royal corgis, Monty, Holly and Willow. In over fifty years of Bond feature films, the paths of 007 and the royal family have frequently crossed. Prince Charles visited the Bond set at Pinewood Studios to the west of

London in 2019. Photographs showed him inspecting the set and chatting to James Bond himself. More discreetly, producers borrowed some of the most striking interior designs featured in the iconic film *Goldfinger* from Princess Margaret's palace. The early 007 films were known for their conspicuous consumption, high fashion, exotic air travel and the latest designs. Margaret's abode fitted right in.

Few realize that these momentary connections are far from fantasy and instead capture a fleeting glance of Britain's most secret partnership – the British monarchy and their secret services.

Surprisingly, the queen, like her predecessors, is no stranger to the real secret service. Even before her coronation, the young Princess Elizabeth had met two Albanian agents near a hidden MI6 training camp on Malta. Sporting Thompson submachine guns and training on secret transmitters, they were preparing to overthrow the communist government in Tirana. Shortly after ascending the throne in 1952, the queen was discussing a troublesome Middle Eastern leader with officials. She quipped about assassinating him.

The queen knows more state secrets than any living person – and, unlike her prime ministers, she keeps them. The queen is a human library of intelligence history. She knew about the British nuclear weapons programme at a remarkably early stage. And she knew more about the Soviet mole, Anthony Blunt, still in her employment as Surveyor of the Queen's Pictures, than even the prime minister did. Later, she invited the CIA's head of operations to Buckingham Palace to ask him how 'my boys' were treating him. The senior CIA officer was surprised that Elizabeth knew about his real job at all.

The queen has spent time in the SAS 'Killing House' in Hereford where special forces hone their deadly skills. She stood unflinch-ing for the most part as operators trained with live ammunition for hostage rescue operations. Throughout her long reign, Elizabeth has met many heads of Britain's intelligence agencies. When Stella Rimington, the first publicly named leader of MI5, attended lunch at Buckingham Palace, the royal household helped her to escape via an inconspicuous exit in order to avoid the assembled reporters desperate to know what a monarch might say to a spy chief.

The royal family and the secret services have much in common. They are two of Britain's most important institutions. They are small and secretive, seen by many as 'the establishment'. They feature prominently in the popular imagination. They are heavily mythologized and often misunderstood.

THE SECRET ROYALS uncovers the remarkable relationship between the royal family and the intelligence community since the reign of Queen Victoria. It argues that modern intelligence grew out of persistent attempts to assassinate Victoria and then operated on a private and informal basis, drawing on close personal relationships between senior spies, the aristocracy and the monarchy. Moreover, it is a remarkable place where women rulers, rather more than men, are often playing the role of a royal 'M', standing at the centre of what has hitherto been assumed to be a masculine world.

Britain's spies are 'crown servants' and, since the accession of Victoria in 1837, they have served mostly women at the top. Early in her career, Margaret Thatcher reflected on the symbolic importance of the young Queen Elizabeth, noting that it would 'help to remove the last shreds of prejudice against women aspiring to the highest places'. Victoria does not seem to have shared her views, famously observing that 'Feminists ought to get a good whipping.'

The mid-Victorian era was a period of political upheaval: royal intelligence channels clashed with amateur equivalents used by nation states; royals with multiple nationalities faced increasing suspicion from politicians; and monarchs used private sources to bypass their own Cabinets and protect their dynastic interests. Victoria was often at odds with her own government, for example over issues of surveillance, and used private royal intelligence sources to support – but also outmanoeuvre – government policy. She acted as intelligence gatherer, analyst and, in modern jargon, 'consumer'. Her son, King Edward VII, had restricted access to intelligence when prince, largely because of fears of blackmail and poor security practices. Despite this, he tried to continue in a similar mould to Victoria when king, drawing on private family networks across the Continent.

In 1909, the first chief of MI6, Mansfield Cumming, proclaimed himself a servant of the king, not the prime minister. His successors' royal connections often allowed them to move more easily in the royal court than in the corridors of Whitehall. This reached its apotheosis before the Russian Revolution when MI6 intervened to try to save the Russian tsar, the king's cousin, from disaster. Afterwards, fearing a similar revolt in Britain, private networks provided King George V with intelligence on the loyalty of his own subjects.

In 1936, the dramatic abdication of Edward VIII formed a dangerous turning point. What originally started as family feuding over a romantic liaison with the American divorcee Wallis Simpson, escalated into a national security crisis. Fearing the couple's Nazi sympathies as well as domestic instability, British spies turned their attention towards Edward, creating profound dilemmas for intelligence officers who had previously been his drinking partners.

They worried about when and how to intervene. As fears grew, MI5 spied on the king himself, hiding in the bushes of Green Park near Buckingham Palace to access a telephone junction box and eavesdrop on his personal telephone calls. Even after the abdication, he remained a high priority target as spies reported back on his political views and on the less than salubrious company he kept, assessing him and his wife as 'fifth columnists'. Reading these surveillance reports on his activities, the Foreign Office complained of his 'fascist sympathies'. Sent away into a kind of Caribbean exile as governor of the Bahamas, the duke of Windsor was, bizarrely, both the recipient of secret service reports and under close surveillance by the same agencies.

During the Second World War, his brother and successor, King George VI, gradually restored trust between the secret world and the

House of Windsor. Although initially tarnished as an enthusiastic appeaser, George eventually acquired inside knowledge of the electronic 'Wizard War' that would gradually turn the tide against the Axis. The king knew all the secrets in the land, from radar research to incredibly sensitive decrypted Enigma material produced at Bletchley Park, and from secret black radio stations to the legendary D-Day deception masterminded by MI5.

He became involved in several Special Operations Executive escapades, enjoyed a personal tour of their gadgets and gizmos, and decorated numerous secret agents. The king maintained a keen interest until his death, after which the last copy of an eye-wateringly secret report on deception operations was found locked in his private despatch box by the queen.

In the 1950s, the young Queen Elizabeth II continued her father's fastidious interest in secret statecraft, from nuclear bunkers to weekly intelligence assessments. She was more than what the eminent constitutional historian Peter Hennessy called a 'gilded sponge', and, exercising her constitutional right to encourage, warn and be consulted, would raise an eyebrow knowingly at prime ministers and spymasters alike. On occasions, the Foreign Office would deploy her on subtle diplomacy. On other occasions, she made suggestions of her own, often about the fate of fellow monarchs.

This close relationship lasted through four decades of the Cold War. Then, in the early 1990s, Queen Elizabeth's private secretary, Sir Robert Fellowes, lunched at MI6's crumbling headquarters, Century House. This dilapidated tower block situated in a singularly unfashionable borough south of the river seemed to symbolize an uncertain future for the agency at the end of the Cold War. With the icy conflict clearly over, Elizabeth wanted to know if MI6 still had a purpose in this new world. What should he tell her? Gerry Warner, its second in command, replied: 'Please tell her it is the last penumbra of her empire.'[2]

THE SECRET ROYALS argues that the relationship between spies and royals has evolved into something rather unusual. It has moved from the informal and personal to something more formal with a real role for senior royals. In the last century, Stewart Menzies, chief of MI6, himself a stepson of the king's equerry, traded off rumours that he was an illegitimate son of another king. Now, the head of MI6 nominates its most brilliant officers for private awards from Prince Charles, who has long been fascinated by secret operations. In a dark world where life often hangs by a thread, these awards are the equivalent of a secret Victoria Cross – for acts of gallantry or ingenuity that we will never hear about. Intelligence agencies receive visits from Prince Charles in this role, signified by the flying of the royal ensign. Demonstrating the close relationship, Queen Elizabeth appointed a recent head of MI5, Andrew Parker, as lord chamberlain in 2021, a senior member of her royal household.

Monarchy has directly shaped intelligence. Attempts to assassinate Queen Victoria stimulated the creation and growth of Special Branch. Ever since, intelligence has maintained an important function of keeping the monarch alive. In return, intelligence has shaped monarchy. Discreet protection and early warning allowed kings and queens to remain accessible and visible in dangerous eras of war and terrorism.

Monarchy drove intelligence in other ways too. Access to intelligence enabled kings and queens to intervene in foreign and security policy. Royal marriages created important dynastic intelligence networks across the Continent providing sensitive information back to the palace. The high-level attendance at royal marriages and funerals made them a forerunner of the modern G-20 summit, with opportunities for diplomacy and espionage. It could even be argued that states' frustration at private royal channels and the dynastic interests they pursued helped spur the creation of more official national intelligence services across Europe.

In return, intelligence shaped monarchy. Tensions over secret information sat at the heart of debates about the role of the constitutional monarch in the nineteenth and twentieth centuries. Moreover, the competition between royal intelligence and that of the nation state formed part of a broader clash between dynastic and state interests during a period of revolutionary upheaval. In this sense, the relationship between intelligence and monarchy played a part in shaping the nationalism of the nineteenth century.

Much of this took place against a backdrop of war and insecurity. European wars of the nineteenth century allowed Queen Victoria to flex her royal networks, but those further away in places like Russia and the imperial frontiers led to her demanding greater intelligence coverage. The end of the First World War decimated the royal intelligence system but, by this time, state intelligence was becoming more institutionalized. Across Europe, royals were not only decimated but also disrespected; in the 1919 election, when Lloyd George campaigned on the slogan 'Hang the Kaiser' he was openly urging the lynching of the king's cousin. Even then, King George V maintained his own military intelligence network and found himself surrounded by those working for secret organizations. The Second World War salvaged and formalized the relationship between king and intelligence.

Secret intelligence moved seamlessly from dynastic and family politics to national security politics. Yet the monarch still maintains an important role. How kings and queens access and use intelligence directly affects their ability to exercise their constitutional rights – and ultimately their power. Famously, the Victorian essayist Walter Bagehot suggested that the crown's 'mystery is its life. We must not let in daylight upon magic.' Nowhere is this mystery more pronounced than in the relationship between the monarchy and the intelligence services. It is now possible to let a little daylight into the most secret rooms of the British state.

1

ELIZABETH I AND MODERN ESPIONAGE

'Do not tell secrets to those whose faith and silence
you have not already tested.'

Queen Elizabeth I, 1600[1]

AROUND 1600, THREE years before her death, a stunning painting of Queen Elizabeth I was commissioned. Known as the Rainbow Portrait, it still hangs in Hatfield House, the historic home of her advisers, the Cecils, on the northern edge of London. Her face is ageless and perfect. At the height of her powers, glorying in her defeat of the Spanish Armada a decade earlier, this image is rich with complex symbols and hidden meanings. Eyes and ears are embroidered all over Elizabeth's orange dress, warning that she sees and hears everything. The dominant theme is surveillance; it is all about spies and royals.[2]

The painting is more than a visible celebration of the triumph of Elizabeth's intelligence networks over many rebellions, plots and conspiracies. Her left arm sports the most cunning of all creatures, a vast jewelled snake. It symbolizes that intelligence is only powerful in the hands of those who understand its complexities, who know how to use it wisely, and who then have the courage to take timely action. In her right hand, she holds a rainbow, a symbol of peace: the ultimate prize of her statecraft. Elizabeth is perhaps saying that without her impressive spy network, without her skill in using intelligence and her capability in covert action, there could be no peace.[3]

In England, spies and royal statecraft were episodic and opportunistic partners.[4] Elizabeth was the first monarch who can claim to have presided over an organized intelligence community, perhaps reaching its apogee during the penultimate decade of the sixteenth century when she battled the Spanish Armada. Here, familiar tradecraft suddenly becomes apparent, including human espionage, codebreaking and interrogation, but also more complex 'dark arts' of covert action, double agents and even strategic deception. At first glance, all this seems strikingly modern. Indeed, the historian Stephen Budiansky argues that Elizabeth and her spymasters constitute 'the birth of modern espionage'.[5]

Yet in other ways, Elizabeth's spymasters are peculiar and distant. They relied on private endeavour and personal connections more than formal machinery. Some of her most loyal subjects went into debt, even bankruptcy, subsidizing this strange assemblage of subterranean activities only partly funded by the crown. Intelligence was sometimes run alongside family members from their own private houses – a rather vernacular form of espionage.[6]

Elizabeth's inner circle, including William Cecil, Francis Walsingham and the earl of Leicester, were all heavily involved in intelligence work. Espionage fascinated the queen, raising the question of how much she personally knew about these remarkable, and often competing, clandestine structures operating in her name. Was she an active intelligence manager, or else to what extent was she manoeuvred by competing courtiers who were spinning intelligence for their own ends? The Elizabethan spy network was impressive in its geographical and political range, but the hand of Elizabeth herself is often hard to trace.[7]

The Elizabethan age has been much celebrated and so has its supposedly modern spy system. But over the years we have been fed

an anachronism: the idea of a proto-modern collective and constitutional secret service, working largely for national security with
Elizabeth commanding her forces against the invading Spanish
Armada – a curiously Churchillian vision. One can almost imagine
her puffing a cigar and orating 'we shall fight them on the beaches'.[8]

Some see the ballooning intelligence bureaucracy as a successful
attempt to isolate Elizabeth from policymaking; as a shift to a more
constitutional form of government. Others have even suggested
that the privy council, by controlling the flow of intelligence,
became the practical head of the regime. In one historian's view,
the way her ministers dominated intelligence circulation diminished Elizabeth's power, pointing the way to something close to a
'monarchical republic'.[9]

This is misleading. Elizabeth was in personal control, engaged
in the everyday detail of spy craft, even setting out how particular agents should be rewarded – or how specific suspects might
be tortured. She did, however, seek plausible deniability when it
suited her.

Elizabeth had to engage directly because there was more than
one spy system. In fact, there were at least three rival intelligence
systems. Cecil, Leicester and Walsingham, while working together
to a degree, ran their own private networks with distinctive styles
and their own clientele. This reflected not only rivalry for privilege
and patronage, but also deep ideological divides over how to secure
the monarchy from subversion.[10]

Far from being a proto-modern intelligence community, these
networks competed at home and abroad, spying on each other and
even attempting to undermine each other's work.[11] What is curious
is how well this byzantine system, with Elizabeth at its head, worked,
despite the fact that intelligence was often a way of gaining favour or
smearing court rivals. Elizabeth needed all these spies, but she also
found them vexing. Walsingham, the most famous spymaster of the
era, was intense, puritanical, obsessive, even paranoid. Perhaps the
first to encapsulate the idea of worst-case analysis, he urged: 'There

is lesse daynger in fearinge to muche then to little.'[12] Elizabeth, as the old saying goes, needed to watch the watchers.

QUEEN ELIZABETH DID not inherit an intelligence community. Instead, it developed slowly during her first decade on the throne. Succeeding her half-sister in 1558, she enjoyed a decade of relative grace that ended with the arrival of Mary, Queen of Scots, in England. The following year, northern earls unsuccessfully tried to overthrow Elizabeth in favour of her rival, Mary. So began the Elizabethan era of secret intelligence.

The Northern Rebellion was superficially about tensions between Catholics and Protestants at court. Although Elizabeth tried to present a tolerant front, she marginalized important Catholic figures. They, along with several other nobles in the north, revolted in the summer of 1569. By November, several hundred knights assembled in County Durham; open rebellion had broken out. Even Pope Pius V weighed in, declaring Elizabeth a heretic and encouraging defiance.[13]

On 13 December, Elizabeth's forces arrived to meet them, and, within a week, the rebel leaders were on the run to Scotland. The rather short-lived revolt signalled the beginning of a long period of spy wars and, with the rebellion over, Elizabeth ramped up her intelligence capabilities. The Northern Rebellion shocked her, for it was not merely a conspiracy of northern barons but, in her mind at least, constituted a popular religious rising.

Elizabeth personally intervened in the reprisals. She asked for more executions of 'the meaner sort of rebels' as a deterrent, or, as she put it, for 'the terror of the others'.[14] Her agents executed no fewer than 750 of them. More importantly, Elizabeth, along with her closest advisers, had come to see the threat that Catholicism posed to her rule, and how it combined active external subversion with internal disloyalty. The Northern Rebellion not only transformed how Elizabeth understood her enemies, but also drew her towards new forms of intelligence operations, in particular the use of elaborate covert operations, even provocation and entrapment; much of it focused on her captive Catholic rival, Mary, Queen of Scots.[15]

IN 1571, THE somewhat fanciful Ridolfi Plot again underlined that Elizabeth was no mere bystander when it came to intelligence operations. Roberto Ridolfi was a gregarious Florentine banker based in London, who had links to the Cecils and even to the queen herself. Seemingly respectable, he travelled Europe on business without suspicion, moving effortlessly between Amsterdam, Rome and Madrid.

During his travels, Ridolfi quietly built up support for an invasion of eastern England which, he hoped, would stimulate a Catholic revolt. This would be followed by Thomas Howard, the duke of Norfolk, marrying Mary, who would then replace Elizabeth as queen.[16]

No less than her nemesis Elizabeth, Mary also delighted in the pantomime and paraphernalia of spy craft. An English prisoner for almost twenty years, she presided over an elaborate system of couriers, codes and encryption. She was a particularly zealous practitioner of the arcane art of invisible inks, encouraging contacts, 'under the pretext of sending me some books', to 'write in the blanks between the lines'.[17] Unfortunately for Mary, most of her correspondence, whether disguised by cyphers or invisible ink, was available to Elizabeth's spymasters throughout her captivity.

For Walsingham and Cecil, the Ridolfi Plot offered a wonderful chance to act against Norfolk, among the wealthiest men in the country. In April, they detained one of Mary's servants at Dover. An inspection of his luggage unearthed forbidden texts and enciphered letters. Later, deep in a dungeon inside the Tower of London, he was placed on the rack and blurted out enough to bring in one of Mary's closest advisers, the bishop of Ross, and the duke of Norfolk.[18] The rack was such a fearsome limb-dislocating device that often the mere sight of it caused brave men to buckle. Two of Norfolk's clerks were rounded up, each caught carrying gold to Mary's Scottish supporters. Offered a brief opportunity to inspect the rack that awaited him, the first, Robert Higford, quickly told all he knew.

The second clerk, William Barker, refused to confess and was duly tortured. He then revealed that secret documents were hidden in the roof tiles of one of Norfolk's houses. In this ingenious hiding place, Walsingham found a complete collection of papers connected with Ridolfi's mission, and nineteen remarkable letters to Norfolk from Mary and the bishop of Ross.[19]

All was not as it seemed, and even this stash of secret letters did not tell the full story. Ridolfi was effectively one of Elizabeth's own personal agents who had gone rogue. Like so many figures in the relatively benign first decade of her reign, he had felt safe enough to play all sides. Walsingham had worried about Ridolfi as early as 1569 and had even brought him in for interrogation. Although Ridolfi's house was turned upside down, Walsingham found nothing incriminating and duly released him. Elizabeth chose her words carefully when he was arrested.[20]

Because of his excellent mobility and contacts, the queen had in fact used him to secretly explore the chances of compromise with the Continent. As late as October 1570, she seems to have sent him on discreet diplomatic missions to Flanders. More remarkably, in March 1571, Ridolfi held a secret rendezvous with Elizabeth at Greenwich Palace, where he again offered his services. She gave him 'a very favourable passport' as her blessing, before despatching him on a secret mission to Rome. This was nothing less than Elizabeth's backdoor attempt at détente with the papacy. However, Elizabeth had misjudged him and, in urging Walsingham to let him loose, she had simply allowed the slippery Ridolfi to switch sides again.[21]

Farcical and fantastic though it was, there can be no doubt that the discovery of the Ridolfi Plot had important consequences. Indeed, it rearranged power politics within Elizabeth's regime: Cecil replaced the executed Norfolk to become the principal person in the Council; meanwhile, Walsingham briefly headed off to Paris, the world centre of espionage, where he refined his skills further.[22]

Walsingham's fabled spy system came on quite late, being established only in the mid-1570s, almost two decades after Elizabeth's accession. He built his network gradually, for his early lack of power and patronage slowed the development of his innovative approach to intelligence. Before rising to be senior principal secretary in 1576, he had lacked the necessary resources and was often little more than a courier between Cecil and his more old-fashioned elite spies of patronage. Walsingham was a relative late-comer, albeit rather more effective and ruthless.[23]

He became more hawkish than Cecil, advocating wider surveillance together with an aggressive, expansive and technical intelligence-based approach to countering subversion.[24]

He was more professional, employing people of any class so long as they had the special skills that were now required. He presided over a more scientific kind of spying. Codebreakers, such as Thomas Phelippes, became increasingly important. The supply of intelligence depended on a delicate dance between the talented cryptographers and moles deep in the embassies of France and Spain.

Elizabeth knew all about this. For example, she learnt in 1572 that there were spies in the French embassy who would 'remain quiet in place' providing access to secret documents.[25] She understood that these deep cover spies had become one of the primary methods of obtaining information during the middle part of her reign.[26]

ACROSS THE NORTH Sea, the Dutch Revolt against Spanish rule further stretched Elizabethan intelligence. When Dutch Protestants rose up in the mid-1560s, some asked Elizabeth for support. She expressed sympathy for the rebels and knew that Spanish victory would have challenged her Protestant supremacy and enabled King

Philip II of Spain to invade southeast England from Dutch deep-water ports. At the same time, she wished neither to provoke the powerful king nor to financially support an expensive insurgency.[27]

Her initial response was covert action. Elizabeth used a kind of performative secrecy to demonstrate the long reach of her secret services. In 1570, this was achieved through the abduction on the Continent of Dr John Story, underlining that, even abroad, traitors could not escape her wrath.

As a Catholic member of parliament, Story had strongly criticized Elizabeth and supported the Northern Rebellion. Elizabeth already knew that he was one of the foremost opponents of her ban on Catholic books and papist propaganda. Her spies then realized that he had been working for subversive underground Catholic movements. Tipped off about this discovery, and knowing he was in imminent peril, he escaped to the Spanish Netherlands, confident that King Philip would grant him asylum alongside some of the leaders of the Northern Rebellion.

He was wrong. Queen Elizabeth approved a successful operation to abduct him and bring him back to England for trial. On 1 June 1571, he was executed at Tyburn gallows by being hanged, drawn and quartered. Not only was this an early example of 'rendition to justice', but it also showcased Elizabeth's secret strength to her foreign counterparts.[28]

Meanwhile, and despite some initial success, Spain's heavy-handed response to the insurrection only inflamed local violence further. Elizabeth's advisers emphasized the importance of plausible deniability when supporting the rebels. As early as 1562, her ambassador to France argued 'the more expedicion and the more secrecie that is used in this, the better it will prove for all respectes. The Queen's majestie and you of her councel muste be ignorant of this matter.'[29]

Elizabeth approved a range of covert measures or, as Cecil put it, 'covert meanes' to aid the rebels. She turned a blind eye to the recruitment of English soldiers fighting alongside the local Protestants. She secretly sent William of Orange, leading the revolt, a few hundred soldiers alongside a subsidy of around 300,000 florins. The message was clear – if deniable. Zealous Protestants knew they were fighting with Elizabeth 'as it were but winking at their doings'.[30]

In 1578, the queen covertly and grudgingly sent a further one million florins – and a mercenary army. Although she loathed spending the money, she knew that covert action was less expensive and less provocative than open warfare. In 1581, with the situation continuing to deteriorate, she tried to work through the French, sending the duke of Anjou, her one-time suitor, secret financial assistance in his attempts to counter the Spanish. At numerous points, perhaps to maintain secrecy, Elizabeth fought to make sure that the Dutch cause was not taken up in the English parliament.[31] She had grown so used to covert operations that Walsingham accused her of finding it difficult 'to enter into the action otherwise than underhand'.[32]

All the while, Elizabeth attempted to present herself as neutral to Spain. She duplicitously tried to assure King Philip that she stood aloof from the rebels who had 'solicited [her] to take possession of Holland and Zealand' and that 'he never had such a friend as she had been'.[33]

ON THE DOMESTIC front, Walsingham enjoyed success in tackling subversion by launching elaborately offensive counter-intelligence operations. The Catholic plots of this era were certainly real, but they were often dreadfully naïve, allowing Walsingham to manipulate their efforts from the outset. In the past, the authorities would have swooped on any plotters immediately, but Walsingham's new approach to espionage involved playing a longer game to win bigger prizes. In the short term it allowed him to justify a more zealous anti-Catholic approach and in the long term it generated enough evidence to secure his ultimate ambition: Mary's execution.[34]

He enjoyed numerous intelligence successes using a combination of undercover agents inside foreign embassies, torture and intercepting communications, to protect Elizabeth and incriminate Mary.

Despite this, the queen's relations with him were never good. By equal turns she found him both indispensable and obnoxious. He was at the height of his powers between 1581 and 1586, rooted in Elizabeth's regime as a technical bureaucrat. Yet Elizabeth hesitated to give her favour with the same enthusiasm as she had to Cecil or to Leicester. Elizabeth nick-named Leicester her 'eyes' because she valued his watchfulness. She never tried to hide her opprobrium or hostility towards Walsingham. In March 1586, she even threw a slipper in his face when she discovered he had been downplaying the threat of the Spanish navy allegedly assembling at Lisbon in order to avoid resources being spared from the campaign in the Low Countries. Elizabeth knew that to allow Walsingham alone to control intelligence was to surrender too much power.[35]

JUST LIKE RIDOLFI, William Parry was another Elizabethan agent gone rogue. Over a period of three years he morphed from being a loyal spy for England into a spy willing to assassinate the queen herself.

Studying law but mired in debt, Parry joined Cecil's band of noble spies watching Catholics in Europe, but mostly with the hope of fleeing his creditors. Moving backwards and forwards between London and Rome, he passed intelligence over to Cecil, but was secretly drawn towards Catholicism. In 1580, when briefly in London, he assaulted one of his creditors and was sentenced to death. Elizabeth stepped in to pardon him, suggesting that he was still a valuable agent.

Two years later, on another sojourn to the Continent, Parry seems to have become a double agent, going over to the Catholic side and seeking approval in France and Italy for an assassination scheme. Returning to England in 1584, he sought to become an elaborate triple agent. He disclosed some of his dealings to the queen, claiming to have acted only to provide cover to Protestant espionage. Astonishingly, Elizabeth not only pardoned him, but also rewarded him with a seat in parliament and a sizeable income.

It was not enough. Still plagued by debts, Parry attempted to manufacture one more plot to be 'discovered' in the hope of yet greater rewards. He approached another conspirator, Sir Edmund Nevylle. The two plotters came up with diverse and creative ways to despatch Elizabeth, from riding up to her coach and shooting her at point blank range to killing her during a private audience. They settled upon stabbing her in a private garden in Whitehall Palace.

By February 1585, they were ready. Unfortunately for Parry, Nevylle started to have doubts and informed against his fellow conspirator. Regardless of whether or not Parry had actually intended to kill Elizabeth or whether he had intended to expose Nevylle and bolster his own standing, he quickly found himself in the Tower of London facing execution for high treason. He wrote a full confession to the queen and sent letters to Cecil and Leicester.[36] Perhaps in the hope of pardon, he pleaded guilty at his trial, but subsequently declared his innocence, insisting that his confession was a tissue of falsehoods.

The outcome of all this twisting was predictable. Parry was executed on 2 March in Westminster Palace Yard. On the scaffold he again declared his innocence and appealed to the queen for more lenient treatment of her Catholic subjects.

Also implicated was Thomas Morgan, an adviser to Mary. Walsingham swiftly arrested him, getting closer to the elusive prize of Mary herself. While Walsingham moved in on Mary, Cecil focused his attention on her allies. He placed ever greater numbers of spies within the French and Spanish embassies in order to better investigate the correspondence between Mary and these ambassadors.

THE BABINGTON PLOT of 1586, which led to the execution of Mary, formed one of the darker episodes in Elizabethan intelligence. The intricate scheme to counter it was so highly secret that Walsingham made 'none of my fellows here privy thereunto', except for Leicester.[37]

Anthony Babington was a recusant English gentleman who, like those before him, wanted to replace Elizabeth with Mary. Walsingham uncovered the plot and this time offensively used it to entrap, and finally remove, Mary. He created, and secretly controlled, a channel of communication to and from the unsuspecting Mary. She thought her incriminating letters were secure but Walsingham's agents, who had infiltrated her circle and helped establish the channel, ensured that they were decoded and made their way back to him.[38]

The deciphered messages implicating Mary piled up. Walsingham turned his evidence over to Cecil, a more impeccably respectable adviser and better placed to present the case against Mary to the queen. On 8 October 1586, faced with overwhelming evidence, Elizabeth gave her agreement to 'authorize them to use their discretion respecting the manner of first communicating with the queen of Scots; also in respect to any private interview with her if she should require it'. Mary was arrested and awaited trial for treason.[39]

Again, Elizabeth was in charge. Although she condemned Leicester and Walsingham as 'a pair of knaves', and distanced herself from the execution, her concern was more with the public spectacle than the private reality. She had explored the possibility of Mary's assassination, or perhaps being met with some unfortunate accident, several times. Walsingham understood the queen's views. In a letter to one of his contacts, he expressed Elizabeth's disappointment that 'you have not in all this time... found out some way to shorten the life of that queen'.[40]

MARY'S EXECUTION PRECEDED a wider round of international conflict. Elizabeth retaliated against King Philip by escalating support for the Dutch Revolt against Spain, as well as funding privateers to raid Spanish ships across the Atlantic. Spain had to respond and, by 1587, Walsingham's spies reported that the Armada was ready to sail.

As over a hundred Spanish ships prepared to depart, Elizabeth's attention turned to deception. For this she needed another kind of network. Cecil ran an alternative spy system based around English Catholics exiled on the Continent. Its main focus was Edward Stafford's embassy in Paris which competed with Walsingham's spy network, searching for Catholic intelligence that would benefit their patrons in policy debates back home.[41]

Stafford's mission in Paris infuriated Walsingham. He thought it was all too close to Catholicism and he was deeply suspicious that Stafford was selling secrets to Elizabeth's enemies. Meanwhile, Elizabeth and Cecil used Stafford, seemingly the voice of détente, as a channel of deception.

In early 1587, he supplied the Spanish with secrets about a forthcoming expedition by Francis Drake. The detail was remarkable, including the number of ships, who was commanding each vessel, their weaponry and most importantly their destinations. Few at court knew such things.

Stafford's leak, for which he was bribed the paltry sum of 5,200 crowns, constituted treason.[42] But Elizabeth and Cecil had deliberately mixed in false information alongside the accurate intelligence, suggesting the fleet's destination was either Lisbon or Cape St Vincent. The Spanish bought the deception and had no idea that Drake was actually headed for Cadiz to 'singe the King of Spain's beard'.[43] This was an intelligence triumph, even if the subsequent defeat of the Armada the following year owed more to fortuitous weather and circumstance.

ELIZABETH PERSONALLY STEERED intelligence. By the mid-1580s, the key meeting seems to have taken place at about 10 o'clock each day. Here, Walsingham briefed the queen in her private chamber, usually verbally, giving her the latest intelligence but also bringing documents for her to sign. He would then return often two or three times during the day, suggesting that Elizabeth was a hands-on and rather demanding intelligence consumer. Walsingham was in increasingly poor health and, as he noted, these meetings 'maketh me wery of my lief'.[44]

She knew who her star spies were. Indeed, they were sometimes encouraged to write accounts of their missions for her to read. Typically, Edward Burnham, one of Walsingham's agents, wrote the story of his operations in France. A racy read, it made both Burnham and Walsingham look good. The queen often granted them a personal pension, normally about £100 a year, in recognition of their special service.

One of the most important spies was Thomas Phelippes, whose codebreaking efforts were central to unravelling the Babington Plot. The queen promised him a position as clerk of the Duchy of Lancaster but to his dismay it never materialized. Walsingham's secretaries, who were also important to the espionage effort, were rewarded differently, usually with parliamentary seats.[45]

Elizabeth took a personal – and particularly ghoulish – interest in executions. She pressured Cecil to ensure that the deaths of Babington and his co-conspirators were especially nasty. They had, after all, committed 'horrible treason' and she wanted their public deaths to deter others by creating 'more terror'. Somewhat baffled, Cecil responded that the normal practice of hanging, drawing and quartering was surely 'as terrible as any other device could be'. But Elizabeth urged that their bodies be torn into little pieces afterwards. She also had them executed on specially constructed gallows at St-Giles-in-the-Fields, the place where the plot had first been concocted. She was determined to make her point.[46]

Elizabeth also seems to have taken a keen interest in interrogation techniques and corresponded personally with her chief torturers. The most fearsome was Richard Topcliffe, a zealous and persistent hunter of fugitive priests. A forensic reader of Catholic books, he might be regarded as a pioneer of 'open source' intelligence practice.[47] Rather like Walsingham, he was a free-booting, self-financed operator with his team of 'instruments', and, while he worked with both Cecil and Walsingham, he always considered himself the queen's personal servant and friend.

'You know who I am?' Topcliffe rhetorically asked his victims, revelling in his reputation. 'I am Topcliffe! No doubt you have often heard people talk about me?' A perverse sadist, he sometimes boasted to his prisoners of being physically intimate with the queen, almost certainly a bizarre fantasy, before following them to the gallows to observe 'God's butchery'. Undoubtedly, he knew the queen well and, as late as 1592, was writing to her about special techniques to be used on particular individuals. After he was imprisoned for extorting money from some of his wealthy victims, the queen had him quickly released.[48]

ELIZABETH'S INTELLIGENCE SYSTEM looked impressive, but it was deeply precarious. She oversaw a mess of competing networks, private interests and questionable loyalties. Most importantly, intelligence was desperately underfunded.

The queen was notoriously parsimonious, and spying was costly. She left poor Walsingham to bridge the gap personally. To help cover his costs, the queen granted him various sinecures, including the Duchy of Lancaster. The biggest earner was granted prior to the Babington Plot, a royal patent covering the customs of all the important western and northern ports from August 1585, bringing in an annual sum of £11,263. Walsingham kept more than half of this money. Elizabeth grudgingly recognized his professionalism, for while Cecil and Leicester spent their cash on impressive residences, Walsingham dutifully ploughed most of his income back into ever more elaborate systems of espionage.

Elizabeth did provide some money directly for espionage, but it was not remotely enough. She saw intelligence as a short-term panacea rather than the construction of a long-term system, still less a proto-modern intelligence community as some have suggested. In 1585, she allowed only £500, rising to £2,100 in 1586, as a response to the Babington Plot. The panic before the Spanish Armada represented a high-water mark at £2,800. But it was sharply cut soon afterwards.[49]

On his death in April 1590, Walsingham had large debts. Despite state subventions, his zealous spying activities had outrun his own resources. Moreover, because he had no male heirs, his personal system collapsed. By contrast, Cecil passed his old-style network of gentlemanly spies down to his son. With this change, Cecil's political pragmatism and softer approach had eventually triumphed over Walsingham's intense Protestantism.

Given the rapid collapse of Walsingham's intelligence system, it was perhaps just as well that Elizabeth's last decade was the quietest. The absence of top spies frustrated the queen, though, and she even turned to Thomas Phelippes, Walsingham's star codebreaker who had since ended up in debtors' prison. Both she and Cecil unfairly complained about the fact that, from his cell, he now seemed to take longer over his work.[50] Towards the end of her reign, one lawyer lamented that the ghost of Sir Francis Walsingham 'groaned to see England barren of serviceable intelligence'.[51]

2

POPISH PLOTS AND
PUBLIC PARANOIA

'every man who does not agree with me is a
traitor and a scoundrel'

George III[1]

EVEN BEFORE QUEEN Elizabeth died, an 'intelligence group' planned her succession. It consisted of half a dozen influential figures, including Robert Cecil, who corresponded secretly and identified each other only by a number. Childless, Elizabeth was succeeded in 1603 by James, the son of Mary, Queen of Scots. The new king, known as James I in England, kept the younger Cecil on as his first minister.[2] Robert Cecil had succeeded his father as Queen Elizabeth I's lord privy seal and remained in power during the first nine years of King James I's reign until his death. If there was any continuity with sixteenth-century espionage it was with the Cecils' network of gentlemanly spies.[3]

Over the following two and a half centuries, monarchs directly shaped the ebb and flow of secret intelligence. Some, like Elizabeth, enthused about spy craft; others showed little interest at all. James fell into the latter camp. He and his immediate successors surrounded themselves with pampered favourites and flamboyant chancers rather than intelligence professionals.[4] To be fair, he had less need for secret intelligence after rapidly signing a peace treaty with Spain. In an instant, many of the Catholic plots which plagued Elizabeth became impotent without Spanish support. Whether interested in intelligence or not, James and many of his successors preferred propaganda to a more professional use of espionage. Some would 'blow' hard-earned codebreaking successes to achieve a quick public victory; others would stoke conspiracy over facts.

THE GUNPOWDER PLOT of 1605 was an important exception: a Catholic plot that was far from impotent. Despite the king's disinterest in intelligence, Cecil maintained an active network of agents in the form of 'false priests' and continued to gather intelligence through embassies, but the days of Walsingham's ferocious surveillance were long past. King James received no hint of the plot. Although the plotters have been represented as anti-Protestant, they were perhaps even more anti-Scottish.[5]

Fortunately for the king, the plotters' ambition proved their downfall. They had hoped to accompany the assassination of James with an insurrection and widened their network accordingly to wealthy families in the Midlands, especially in Northamptonshire, whom they hoped would rise up in the wake of the attack. Uprisings are always difficult to conceal and, sure enough, some of these families worried for the safety of their relatives in parliament who might be literally sitting on top of the explosion. Relatives alerted relatives – and one such warning reached Cecil on 1 November. He took it to the king.

Unimpressed that the plot was so advanced, James took personal control of events. He was clearly capable of action. Five years earlier, he had responded with unprecedented ferocity against a conspiracy to overthrow him. Two aristocratic brothers had lured him to a country house at Perth under the pretence of having found a treasure trove. After dinner, when James went upstairs to bed, one of the brothers pulled out a knife, held James hostage and called for the other to join him. The king stuck his head out of the turret window and shouted, 'Murder! Treason!' His courtiers rushed up to find the first brother dead. The second pulled his own knife but was quickly killed. James had been personally duped and clearly lacked any intelligence of the plot. Afterwards, he confiscated their property and insisted that their dead bodies be hanged, drawn and quartered.[6]

Now, James did not want to make the same mistake again. Adopting a watch and wait strategy, he waited until 4 November to conduct the first search in the hope of catching the conspirators late in the preparations. All he found was a pile of firewood inside one of the cellars underneath parliament.

Still suspicious, James ordered a second search. It famously uncovered thirty-six barrels of gunpowder under the firewood and netted Guy Fawkes. Brave to the last, Fawkes told James to his face that he planned to blow him 'back to Scotland' and resisted giving up the names of his fellow conspirators despite being tortured in the Tower.

Nevertheless, Fawkes's network was rolled up; its leaders hunted, tortured and killed. Addressing parliament afterwards, James claimed personal credit for thwarting the plot and, although he had gone to some lengths to 'big' this up, it was not without foundation.[7]

The Gunpowder Plot was culturally important. By the 1620s, the population had been fed a constant diet of conspiracies for decades, contributing to an abiding climate of paranoia. If it was not Protestant stories about 'popish plots' then it was Catholic rumours of evil counsellors. These conspiracy theories reached their apogee in the early Stuart period with the mysterious demise of James.

The king had chosen George Villiers as his key adviser. Good-looking and swashbuckling, but a poor manager of political affairs, he was certainly no Walsingham.[8] When James grew ill and died in 1625, suspicion fell on the man who had administered his final treatment: Villiers. Courtiers whispered that he had poisoned the king to hasten the promotion of his friend and James's heir, King Charles I.[9]

Villiers' speedy rise, combined with the early death of some of his aristocratic rivals, increased suspicion further.[10] In a world where forensic science barely existed, the administration of poison was a popular tool of assassination. The conspiracy theory caught the tide of current fashion and gained credibility by complementing the popular narrative about Villiers and Prince Charles. The pair had grown close during James's reign, with Villiers even joining him in disguise on a secret mission to win the hand of the Spanish princess, thus sealing the king's policy of détente. They bonded closer when the mission failed, uniting them in a distaste for all things Spanish. The young pair excluded the ageing monarch, who increasingly lost interest in matters of state and became resentful and suspicious towards them.[11] Villiers was an opportunist and, conscious of his rapidly deteriorating relationship with James, joined Charles in pushing for war with Spain.[12]

Whatever the truth, the rumours would not go away. Factions across the political spectrum hated Villiers and seized upon the story. Print had become cheaper and, in the era of the political pamphlet, scandal sheets circulated far and wide. The conspiracy undermined the parliament of 1626 and almost certainly led to the assassination of Villiers two years later at the age of just thirty-five.[13]

The propaganda, whether true or not, had catastrophic consequences. At the beginning of the first English Civil War, parliamentarians skilfully exploited the belief that Charles I was an accessory to his father's death. It helped to discredit the king and would surface again during his trial. Indeed, it became almost a founding myth of Cromwell's republic, debated furiously by each faction down the decades.[14]

Elizabeth's complex competing spy empire was long gone, but this sea of rumour and propaganda was to some extent the backwash of her personal approach. She had stoked public paranoia about spies and plots to a remarkable degree and turned public executions into spectacles in the hope of creating more terror. It is not surprising that espionage, conspiracy and rumour, mixing myth and reality freely, featured so prominently in early Stuart England. This murky climate shaped how the king approached intelligence at the onset of civil war.

THE CIVIL WARS between royalists and parliamentarians – what is now often called the War of the Three Kingdoms – resulted in the defeat and execution of Charles I and the eventual restoration of his son, Charles II, interspersed by the temporary republican rule of Oliver Cromwell. The scale of death and destruction was remarkable, certainly well beyond that of the First World War, casting a long shadow that lasted more than a hundred years, shaping politics well into the middle of the eighteenth century.[15]

Like his father, Charles I did not embrace secret intelligence. In fact, his closest adviser openly expressed disdain for espionage, rejecting the use of spies and adamantly refusing to intercept the correspondence of Charles's opponents. Such underhand activity was too ungentlemanly. The king did maintain a secret service budget, but, as was often the way, he spent most of it on propaganda.[16] In a world where perceptions often mattered more than truth, Charles desperately lacked a Cecil, still less a Walsingham, to control and direct secret activities.[17] Even when underground networks of royalist exiles mobilized on the Continent, weaknesses in the king's organization and his reliance on inexperienced favourites fatally undermined their espionage capability.[18]

Parliamentary leaders also lacked a sophisticated intelligence system. Like Charles, they never recreated the complex edifice erected under Elizabeth. They did, entirely fortuitously however, recover one of its key elements: cryptography.

John Wallis, a Cambridge-educated mathematician, was accidentally drawn into the world of cryptography during a dinner party. A guest who happened to be a senior parliamentarian whipped out an intercepted letter written in cypher as a curious talking point. He asked, half in jest, whether Wallis could make anything of it. To his surprise, Wallis responded, 'Perhaps I might.' After dinner, he successfully deciphered the code.[19]

What it contained was sheer dynamite. Confirming the parliamentarians' worst fears and suspicions about Charles, the letter showed that he had been trying to raise an army of Catholic soldiers from Ireland to invade England, as well as negotiating help from French and Spanish mercenaries – all of them also Catholic. They published the letter widely, presumably blowing the ability to read the cypher in the process and again showing the seventeenth-century preference for propaganda over cryptography. Queen Elizabeth, who understood the value of codebreaking, would never have done this.

As the grip of the English parliamentarians tightened, royalists resorted to disguises and elaborate plots. Many of these failed but notably one did succeed: the fourteen-year-old duke of York, and future King James II, disguised himself as a girl and caught a boat to Europe. The king attempted secret escape plans of his own, but by contrast these failed.[20]

On 30 January 1649, Charles I was beheaded in London. Endless paranoia about plots, some far-fetched, finally seemed to be confirmed by deciphered letters in Charles's own hand. Britain was now ruled by a commonwealth, although committed royalists remained loyal to his exiled son, the future Charles II.

The new government appointed a head of foreign and domestic intelligence. Thomas Scot, a lawyer and fervent Protestant, was perhaps the first individual to replicate the professionalism of Walsingham for almost a century. He not only maintained agents inside the circles of Charles II on the Continent, but also employed Wallis as a successful codebreaker.[21] By contrast, the defeated royalists had to settle for the clandestine supporters of a defeated monarch. Their predicament was exacerbated by the perennial shortage of money. While collectively they failed to bring down Cromwell, they were brave, persistent and resilient. The republicans could never feel entirely safe.[22]

WHEN MONARCHY RETURNED under King Charles II, intelligence in Britain once again plunged into darkness. The new king's only real security interest was a passionate and persistent search for those involved in the death of his father. Instead of building on, or at least replicating, Cromwell's burgeoning intelligence system, Charles lured Thomas Scot with the false promise of a royal pardon. Scot soon found himself in the Tower but, instead of being tortured, he was offered a pardon in return for a list of his agents. He was cruelly deceived, for having given them up he then joined them on the scaffold. As the intelligence historian Christopher Andrew remarks, Scot is the only British intelligence chief ever to have been executed for treason.[23]

Charles II employed not so much an intelligence chief as a bounty hunter: George Downing. Emblematic of those who did well in these turbulent times, he was a chancer who had previously fought for Cromwell. The diarist Samuel Pepys, who characterized Downing's conduct as odious though useful to the king, called him 'a perfidious rogue' and remarked that 'all the world took notice of him for a most ungrateful villain for his pains'.[24]

Downing now turned on his former associates, creating spy rings to hunt them down. He successfully engineered the arrest, exfiltration and execution of three prominent regicides in Holland by enticing them out of hiding under the false pretence that they could meet their wives from England, whose company they sorely missed.[25]

Intelligence barely improved during the latter part of Charles's reign. Attempts to rebuild intelligence networks were stymied by a tiny budget, poor organization and above all the chaotic decision-making of Charles, who continued the Stuart tradition of using favourites as single emissaries without telling others in the circle of decision-making what they were up to. The only saving grace was the codebreaker John Wallis, who, like Downing, had switched sides and now worked for the king.[26]

Charles was marginally better at secret diplomacy. He took personal control of negotiations with France, using his sister as a top-secret channel of communication with King Louis, allegedly to gain support for his impending public declaration of Catholicism. It was a bizarre – and dangerous – move. The British public would have been furious, and, given the secrecy involved, Louis now had valuable material with which to blackmail Charles whenever he wanted to do so. Some historians think that Charles's purported conversion was an elaborate ruse to cement an alliance with France against the Dutch; others think it was sincere but short-lived. Charles did successfully sign secret treaties with the French, promising that war against the Dutch would follow his conversion. He even managed to dupe parliament that funds he requested for the navy would be used to counter the French, rather than the Dutch, threat. As people started to get wind of the real target, and real ally, Charles's supposed commitment to publicly converting unsurprisingly dwindled away.[27]

Royal networks had allowed for secret diplomacy, and raised the possibility of blackmail, behind the backs of their own governments and advisers. Charles would not be the last monarch to attempt to use private channels to outmanoeuvre ministers.

NONE OF ELIZABETH'S successors had invested in intelligence, which made the country susceptible to deception, fraud and manipulation. By the late 1670s, after more than a hundred years of real conspiracies, some ludicrous but some more serious, and with endless wars in the Netherlands and Scandinavia, Britain was rife with spy mania. Cheap printing presses and increased literacy made the latter part of the seventeenth century a period of growing pamphlet wars. Some 2,200 pamphlets were published between 1600 and 1715, many of them warning of fantastical and even supernatural conspiracies. This left monarchs vulnerable to one of the most damaging intelligence scams in history.[28]

The perpetrator was Titus Oates, a failing but bombastic Cambridge theology student who was perpetually shunted from college to college. Thereafter, as an Anglican priest, he again moved rapidly from house to house because of his annoying and unruly behaviour, especially towards women. Expelled by the Anglicans, he travelled to the Continent and entered a Jesuit seminary where he once more fought with his fellow students. Expelled again, he returned to London, claiming a PhD that he did not have, but with enough knowledge to whisper that the Jesuits had tried to use him as a secret agent.[29]

Already an improbable figure, all Oates needed was a fantastic narrative. He joined with a friend to write a treatise warning of a 'Popish Plot' to murder Charles II. Teams of Jesuit assassins were apparently already in London preparing to act. In October 1677, Oates found himself a star witness before the House of Commons.

He offered more bluster than facts, but the politicians and Charles's intelligence chief, Joseph Williamson, were taken in. Personally, Charles was not worried, but, in the paranoid panic that followed, the authorities rounded up and executed over twenty suspects, consigning many others to prison. Remarkably, the finger of suspicion even turned to Williamson, who found himself briefly in the Tower for being rather too lenient on Irish Catholic army officers. Only in 1685, some seven years later, as Charles was succeeded by his brother James II, did the country realize how badly they had been duped by this flamboyant fraudster. After casting out yet more improbable charges against prominent figures, Oates was now sentenced to life imprisonment.[30]

Titus Oates is often presented as a preposterous episode but it caused real panic. In retrospect, much of the story now appears humorous, yet it underlined important historical truths. Despite the considerable journey towards a more parliamentary government, the fate of monarchs as individuals really mattered. It fuelled an obsession with plots. England was still ruled by kings and their favourites; its course could be radically changed by the momentary use of poison, an assassin's dagger or a primitive pistol. In this atmosphere, horrible forms of public execution, which involved prolonged burning and slow dismemberment, were designed to deter plotters. Often, they failed to do so. Oates was a comic figure, but he pointed a finger towards a dangerous future.

KING JAMES II was not overthrown by assassins but by an invasion. He may have privately hoped of returning England to Catholicism, but a pantomime secrecy attended his dealings with France, and, coming shortly after the exposure of Charles's secret diplomacy, it caused huge anxiety at home. Publicly, he expressed a commitment to religious toleration, but many believed he was in league with France's powerful absolutist King Louis XIV and wished to take England in that direction. Historians are still divided about where the heart of James II really lay.[31]

The person most anxious about this was William of Orange in the Netherlands. A Catholic England would have left him isolated against France, Austria and Spain. William received excellent intelligence from his many supporters in England – but he hardly needed it. When his invasion force landed in Torbay, support for James evaporated overnight. James was allowed, perhaps even encouraged, to flee to France. William became the new king, reigning alongside his wife, James's daughter Mary, from the spring of 1689.

King William III was instrumental in developing Britain's ability to intercept and decode correspondence. He inherited the veteran codebreaker John Wallis, working the frail old man hard but paying him several productivity bonuses on top of a regular salary of £100 a year. Unfortunately, the king woefully misused Wallis's intelligence, again prioritizing propaganda and publicity over long-term intelligence gathering. Having uncovered an attempt by France to draw Poland into war with England, William publicized the decrypted despatches, embarrassing Louis XIV but also making Wallis's job much more difficult. Wallis continued his service into his early eighties, outliving the king.[32]

Despite 'blowing' Wallis's triumphs, William was the first monarch since Elizabeth to be truly adept at building an organized intelligence capability and took the first step towards forming a British Black Chamber for codebreaking, mirroring similar organizations on the Continent. Crucially, due to William's enthusiasm, it became a government profession not an amateur activity. Under the king's direction, Wallis had worked with two other Black Chambers in Europe, including those of the House of Hanover, distant relatives of William. While they regarded Wallis as superior, what the Continent had to offer was continuity.

Appropriately, two years after King George I, the first Hanoverian, ascended the throne, Britain acquired a proper Black Chamber. This secret government office, building on William's efforts, constituted the first physical equivalent to Government Communications Headquarters (GCHQ), Britain's current codebreaking centre. Demonstrating the importance of royal networks, George encouraged co-operation with the Hanoverian Black Chamber at Nienburg. George's Black Chambers enjoyed great success in intercepting and reading the correspondence of King Charles XII of Sweden. Charles was an exceptionally skilled military leader, a brilliant diplomat and, most worryingly for George, a close ally of the Jacobite rebels determined to restore the House of Stuart to the throne.[33]

With full access to their communications, George was furious at Swedish subversion. He arrested the Swedish ambassador, an unheard-of breach of protocol (Elizabeth had expelled two Spanish ambassadors for the same offence but never arrested them). Making the same mistake as his predecessors, and again prioritizing propaganda over espionage, he also published the secret letters. More than that, he trumpeted them across Europe in multiple translations. One can only imagine the collective howl of dismay from the codebreakers in Black Chambers on the Continent. Predictably, the Swedes changed their cyphers, making them much harder to break.

More importantly, European leaders became keenly aware that their letters might be intercepted and deciphered. It is likely that many became much more careful about what they wrote down.

With royal support, codebreaking had come of age as an organized business. Its chiefs were well rewarded and presided over professional assistants drafted into the trade, often via Oxford University. This was no longer an eccentric activity carried out by a single figure in debtors' prison. It was a long-standing institution competing with similar chambers in France, Austria, Russia and Prussia.[34]

The last blow to the Jacobite rebels was dealt not by the burgeoning British Black Chamber, but by a human spy. George II and his prime minister, Robert Walpole, personally gave approval for the recruitment of the most important spy of the mid-eighteenth century, a French diplomat called François de Bussy.[35]

Talent-spotted by the British ambassador in France, the extravagant Bussy lived well beyond his means and had outrageous debts. He was ripe for recruitment. By now George had a 'secret service' and he paid Bussy using its 'secret fund'. In return, Bussy faithfully supplied top-secret documents including material from Louis XV and his foreign minister. He then transferred to the French embassy in London where he climbed the ladder of promotion; he was thus able to provide all the details of French support for Bonnie Prince Charlie, the pretender to the Stuart throne, together with the names of his supporters. George's forces rounded them up.[36]

GEORGE III SUCCEEDED his father in 1760 and presided over an unprecedented period of peace in Europe. He could not enjoy it, though; neither could he afford to allow his inherited secret service to wither. Across the Atlantic, Britain faced its first colonial insurgency.

The American War of Independence was the culmination of an intellectual and political revolution. This was not surprising since some of the most successful Jacobean regicides had fled there – and become celebrities. Brought to a head by the lack of American representation in parliament and anger at direct taxes levied without consent, armed conflict between British regulars and colonial militiamen broke out in April 1775.

George III is often accused of obstinately trying to keep Britain at war with the revolutionaries in America, despite the opinions of his own ministers. However, more recent historians defend him: no king of that era would willingly surrender such an important colonial territory, especially one in which he was competing with France. Both parliament and the British people increasingly favoured the war, army recruitment ran at high levels, and political opponents were a small but vocal minority.

George, like many kings before him, was a poor intelligence consumer. His government had achieved a remarkable intelligence feat in recruiting a spy working alongside Benjamin Franklin, the American representative in Europe. Edward Bancroft, Franklin's assistant, was a world-class agent with access to superb intelligence. Rumour has it that, thanks to Bancroft, the Franco-American treaty was in George's hands just forty-eight hours after it was signed. However, George dismissed his reports as exaggerated or invented. He accused Bancroft of being a 'double spy' and wrongly warned 'no other faith can be placed in his intelligence, but that it suited his private views to make us expect the French Court means war'. Another agent even managed to switch an American diplomatic pouch, delivering its contents to the king and sending an empty decoy to its intended recipients. George remained unimpressed and mistrusting.[37]

By contrast, his opponent, George Washington, was a far superior intelligence consumer. 'There is nothing more necessary,' he once reflected, 'than good intelligence to frustrate a designing enemy, & nothing that requires greater pains to obtain.'[38] The Americans won the War of Independence in 1783, and Washington established a peacetime intelligence system on a huge scale shortly afterwards. Britain, on the other hand, stumbled blindly forward.

The French Revolution followed only a decade after events in America. Revolutions are particularly difficult to predict using intelligence. Therefore, the great revolutions of history, in France, Russia, China and more recently the Arab Spring, have been judged major intelligence failures insofar as few around the world anticipated their ferocity or capacity for long-term political change. They are hard to predict because no one is in charge. Despite the romantic idea of a heroic revolutionary leader as the vanguard of the people, revolutions are often less about plotters and conspirators and more about the implosion of the previous regime and the sentiment of masses. These things are hard to measure at a single point.[39]

The French Revolution burst onto the scene in 1789. George and his government failed to predict it, and then underestimated its significance. Despite the difficulties, Britain perhaps had less excuse than other countries, having executed its own monarch in the previous century, overturned another in the Glorious Revolution of 1688, and recently fought against the American Revolution.

What George III initially thought about the French Revolution was unrecorded. However, his ministers were delighted, seeing this as an inward collapse of a Great Power with which they had been at war intermittently for centuries. They expected a moderate progression towards a French constitutional monarchy, together with an abatement of their military activity in North America that continued to trouble Britain's remaining colonies including Canada.

But amid the accelerating turmoil in France, Britain enjoyed little intelligence on the unfolding revolution and George received few reports. Britain hoped for peace and watched at a distance, while France descended into civil war. With British intelligence rudderless and unable or unwilling to scheme, Paris increasingly viewed Austria, the homeland of Marie-Antoinette, not Britain, to be the centre of pro-royalist restoration plots.

The summer of 1792 marked the turning point in France. With Prussian armies advancing on Paris, public hysteria became intense, prompting the growth of a police state that was eagerly searching out enemies both foreign and domestic. Britain had now closed its embassy, reducing its undercover activity to almost nothing. A single agent, Captain George Monro, reported the September massacres in which paranoid mobs descended on the prisons to butcher those they suspected of being royalist spies, but sadly in most cases were merely debtors or common criminals.

On 21 January 1793, Monro reported in horrified tones the bloody execution of Louis XVI and then fled, fearing for his life. It was just as well, for France declared war on Britain a month later and descended into several years of even more intense spy-hunting paranoia and further waves of massacres known as the 'Reign of Terror'.[40]

Back home, George's government now feared revolutionary plots by republicans influenced by France. Although overseas intelligence was weak, the prime minister, William Pitt the Younger, expanded Britain's domestic secret capabilities by creating the Alien Office, which not only looked after immigration, but also security, forming effectively a late eighteenth-century equivalent to MI5.

Its leading light was William Wickham, an Oxford graduate and magistrate who had worked closely with the London police. Although the government accelerated secret service expenditure and passed emergency legislation granting special powers against treason and sedition, genuine plots were few and far between. Intelligence remained poorly led, though, failing to identify a French attack on Bristol in 1797, which was farcical yet still caused panic in London.

THE GREATEST THREAT to the king was not foreign spies or French-inspired republicans, but the rise of apocalyptic religious revolutionaries propelled by the social tumult of the times. Self-appointed prophets and preachers saw the massive wars in Europe and execution of the French king in millenarian terms, insisting that it had been biblically foretold in the books of Daniel and Revelations.

The European crisis, they insisted, pointed to the end of the world and the second coming of Christ.

George, who remained a popular monarch, felt naïvely untroubled by the threat of assassination. Two people suffering from mental illness did try to physically attack him; a third was committed to a lunatic asylum after publicly predicting that he would replace George on the throne. The king treated them all kindly.[41]

A more dangerous assault occurred in 1800. James Hadfield, an injured war veteran, shot at the king. Before being captured by the French, Hadfield was struck eight times on the head, a portion of his skull having been sliced off by a French sabre. After returning to England, he became involved in a millennialist movement and came to believe that the second coming would be advanced if he himself were killed by the British government. He therefore resolved to assassinate the king – and bring about his own judicial execution.

The king arrived at the Theatre Royal on Drury Lane on the evening of 15 May. As the audience rose to greet him, and the orchestra played the national anthem, Hadfield jumped out from his hiding place in the pit. He stood on a second-row seat, raised his arm, and fired a huge horse pistol at the royal box.

The leaden bullet passed less than eighteen inches above the king's head. A great suspense hung over the audience until they realized that the king was unhurt. A cry rose up: 'Seize the Villain! Shut all the doors!' The musicians secured the assassin and bundled him down below the stage.

George remained calm. He placed his opera glass to his eye and studied the scene without the slightest loss of composure. In fact, he seemed completely unperturbed by the attempt on his life, so much so that he actually slumbered during the interval.[42]

Remarkably, the incident at Drury Lane was not the only time that day when the king's life had been in danger. In the late morning, during a military field exercise in Hyde Park, a stray bullet injured a clerk standing near him. As the man who fired the shot could not be detected, authorities remained uncertain whether it had been intentional or not. When inevitably questioned about this earlier incident, Hadfield denied any involvement. Unsurprisingly, George's privy council thought it more likely to be a republican conspiracy at work.[43]

Hadfield was tried for high treason. His brother told the court that in the hot weather when the moon was full, he 'talked about Jesus Christ and proclaimed himself God'. In previous times, he would have been quickly and publicly executed. Instead, he was consigned to a mental hospital. He escaped, attempted to flee to France but was recaptured. His gentle treatment owed much to the fact that he was an injured veteran, a former prisoner of the French, and, at the time of the attack, a Chelsea pensioner.[44]

Although Hadfield was treated kindly, the assault on the king had important effects. Previously, assailants considered insane were simply discharged back into the community. Inspired by this case, parliament rushed through the Criminal Lunatics Act of 1800, which allowed such persons to be detained indefinitely.[45] Hadfield was not the last royal assailant to be detained for a long period under these special measures.

THE RELATIONSHIP BETWEEN monarchs and secret intelligence in the two centuries after the death of Queen Elizabeth I is a rather sorry story. Existing at the whims of kings and determined by royal patronage, intelligence was perennially underfunded and neglected. Too often kings put unsuitable favourites or political bounty hunters in charge. For every William III and George I who built up code-breaking capabilities and recognized the need for professionalism, there were more like James I, Charles I and George III who ranged from neglectful to disdainful. Even those who did value intelligence were woeful consumers, blowing valuable sources in a desperate attempt to publicly embarrass or discredit their rivals.

Indeed, propaganda and conspiracy all too often trumped facts. Audiences, from monarchs to rumourmongers, interpreted truths through their own prisms of ideology and religion. They relied on gut reactions as much as evidence. This created a difficult environment in which intelligence – pursuing objective reporting – had to operate at the best of times. Royal indifference often made it harder still.

During the nineteenth century a new monarchical landscape would emerge. Characterized by the creation of modern states and their secret services, together with the trappings of technology, including trains and the telegraph, the royal intelligence network still had a part to play. More than ever, monarchs provided secret back channels for diplomacy, while uneven and contested progress towards constitutional government seemed to make royals a yet more attractive target for the lone assassin or bomb-throwing anarchist. At the centre of this turbulent new world would be another female monarch who understood intelligence just as well as her Elizabethan predecessor. This was the inheritance of a young Queen Victoria.

Part I

THE RISE AND
FALL OF ROYAL
INTELLIGENCE

QUEEN VICTORIA: ASSASSINS
AND REVOLUTIONARIES

*'For a man to strike any women is most brutal, and I... think
this far worse than any attempt to shoot, which, wicked as it is, is
at least more comprehensible and more courageous.'*

Queen Victoria, 1854[1]

O N MATTERS OF espionage, Queen Victoria was decidedly un-
Victorian. Spying in nineteenth-century Britain was a dirty
word. Victoria's subjects thought it ungentlemanly; the kind of
unscrupulous activity undertaken by despots on the Continent. Yet
espionage was more than un-British; it was, so the argument went,
unnecessary and counterproductive. The British population, prosperous and content, had no reason to rebel, while the foreign policy
of splendid isolationism reduced the risk of war – and with it the
need for secret intelligence altogether. Espionage was problematic
in so far as spies, saboteurs and undercover surveillance generated
mistrust; and mistrust led to rebellion.[2]

In the wake of Wellington's resounding victory in the Napoleonic
Wars, Britain had few international worries for the first time in
centuries. One historian has described the mid-Victorian period as a
vast 'chasm of spylessness'.[3] The precursor to MI5 and MI6 was not
created until 1909, late in the reign of Victoria's successor, Edward

VII. During Victoria's reign domestic spying was limited; and the British state lacked a formal network of human spies overseas.

Personally, the queen was far less squeamish. But then Victoria was rather continental herself; she sat at the heart of a dense network of royal relatives spanning Europe. Her uncle was king of the Belgians, whose wife was the daughter of the French king. Victoria's own daughter married the crown prince of Prussia. By the end of her long reign, Victoria had royal relatives in Bulgaria, Denmark, Germany, Greece, the Netherlands, Romania, Russia and Spain.[4] They formed a transnational intelligence agency, and, in a world where the private and public seamlessly blurred, the queen often knew more about foreign powers than her own ministers did. She claimed to be unimpressed when her foreign office engaged in 'diplomatic intrigue, spying, &c', but in truth, she had her own sources and did not appreciate ministerial meddling.[5]

Although more absorbed in foreign and dynastic affairs, Victoria did develop a personal interest in domestic intelligence. The reason was simple: her ministers might have had the luxury of seeing virtue in Britain's lack of intelligence service, but they were not subjected to continuous threats of assassination, neither did they have to watch revolutionaries murder their relatives across the Continent. For any monarch, the stakes were dangerously high. The bearded bomb-throwing anarchist became a dominant theme as the century wore on, and their primary target was the crowned heads of Europe.

Intelligence, for Victoria, was about survival – both physically and dynastically. It was also decidedly ad hoc, and sometimes highly personal. She referred to letters from her daughter, Vicky, about Prussian intentions as 'intelligence', but they slipped seamlessly between political insight and family gossip. Victoria interpreted intelligence broadly: it ranged from secret reports sent from the Russian border to, rather bizarrely, news that her opera coach was ill and had to reschedule a lesson. To Victoria, all of this was 'intelligence'. Like more recent connoisseurs of 'open source', she knew that intelligence was simply useful and actionable information. It did not necessarily have to come from spies.

Victoria was only eighteen years old when she became queen in 1837. She had led a sheltered childhood, during which a rigid discipline had been instilled. The young queen, diminutive and inexperienced, was not entirely innocent of politics. Her uncle Leopold, king of the Belgians, tutored her in foreign affairs as a teenager and, after she became queen, emphasized the virtues of discretion in statecraft.[6] He also offered an early lesson in deception operations and how to take advantage of nascent counter-intelligence tradecraft. It was fairly standard practice, he counselled, for states to intercept, read and reseal letters. This could be cunningly exploited by writing the letters in such a way as to send a deliberate message – accurate or otherwise – to the intercepting state.[7]

The young queen revelled in her new role, enjoying the stark contrast to her highly constrained childhood. She had a great deal to learn and acquired a famously intimate and trusting relationship with her first prime minister, Lord Melbourne.

Victoria was stubborn, inquisitive and highly intelligent, with a keen eye for detail. She liked to know what was going on at home, overseas, and especially across her vast and growing empire. As she grew into the role, Victoria rarely hesitated to advise – or berate – her ministers for failing to keep her updated or for ignoring her warnings. Throughout her reign, she remained closely involved in the affairs of successive governments. She read papers, including Foreign Office despatches and Cabinet discussions, quickly and efficiently – and sharply rebuked ministers if ever they dared to withhold something.

Secret information, arriving through convoluted routes to land on the government's desk, often ended up on hers too. Early in her reign, for example, she found herself sitting alongside Melbourne in Buckingham Palace discussing the veracity of a single spy report. It concerned Russian military intentions and had come from a well-placed human source via the duke of Wellington, who continued to command the army and advise the queen as late as 1851. In the end, they thought its contents improbable, but the image of a queen and her prime minister poring over human intelligence together is a striking one.[8] She was quickly learning her craft and would go on to admonish ministers if they interpreted intelligence differently from her. More generally speaking, her red boxes rarely included formalized 'secret intelligence' – in the modern sense – because such agencies did not yet exist.

Victoria married Prince Albert of Saxe-Coburg and Gotha in 1840. Albert was handsome, hard-working and, like Victoria, disciplined. Above all he was hard-working, quickly learning about English history, law and the constitution. Although theirs was an arranged marriage, the affection between the young couple was clear. Despite this, the queen initially froze her new husband out of statecraft, secret or otherwise; much to Albert's frustration. 'I am only the husband,' he once complained to a friend, 'and not the master of the house!'

Things soon changed when Victoria became pregnant a few months later. The relentless red boxes of official papers continued to arrive at the palace and the exhausted queen reluctantly resorted to reading their contents to her eager husband. His influence grew, albeit informally, thereafter. At Albert's request, Lord Melbourne advised the queen to take political guidance from her husband and, upon leaving office, told her that he had 'formed the highest opinion of His Royal Highness's judgement, temper and discretion'. Victoria, he counselled, 'cannot do better than have recourse to it'. Melbourne's successor, Robert Peel, accordingly sent Albert nightly reports of parliamentary debates and Cabinet discussions. This was quite a turnaround: a year earlier, the queen had not allowed him a key to the red boxes, yet by 1844 he had become an unofficial private secretary. Eventually he gained his own key to those boxes carrying the most secret and sensitive affairs of state.[9]

For all their access to state secrets, Victoria and Albert's best intelligence did not come from these boxes. Instead, their vast web of relations provided unrivalled sources of inside information

– some of it highly sensitive – about foreign affairs. According to one senior official in Number 10, Queen Victoria selected the most intelligent member of each European royal family, and 'on any question, domestic or foreign, which arose, she obtained an opinion'.[10] Royal communication travelled securely through private messenger or diplomatic bags, and the queen felt confident in her sources: shared blood was more reliable than some perfidious secret agent working for money.[11] As a result, Victoria and Albert knew a great deal more about German, and broader continental, affairs than the Foreign Office did. And Albert convinced the queen that foreign policy peculiarly came within the sovereign's province.[12] Knowledge was power, however, and the dynastic intelligence system soon came into conflict with that of the modern nation state at home and abroad.

IF INTELLIGENCE WAS about survival then Victoria's personal safety should have been the highest priority. Even in the first decade of her reign, plenty of malcontents, from Irish terrorists to loners with a grudge, wanted the young queen dead. Yet domestic intelligence, necessary to unearth plots and conspiracies, barely existed. Formed in 1829, the Metropolitan Police was a fairly new organization at the start of Victoria's reign. It did not acquire a small detective department until 1842. By then, the queen had survived three separate assassination attempts.

The first unfolded dramatically on 10 June 1840. In the early evening, Victoria and Albert left the garden gate of Buckingham Palace in a carriage. All of a sudden, as they headed towards Constitution Hill, Victoria 'was deafened by the loud report of a pistol'. 'Our carriage,' she recalled that night, 'involuntarily stopped.'[13]

On the path beside them, she and Albert saw 'a little man', his arms 'folded over his breast, a pistol in each hand'. Less than thirty seconds later, the assailant aimed again. The queen ducked and 'another shot', as she described it, 'equally loud instantly followed'.[14] He adopted the classic highwayman's pose, something he had been perfecting, steadying his left hand on his right forearm, and zoning in on his target.[15]

'My God!' Albert exclaimed as the gun fired. Catching his composure, he turned to his young wife. 'Don't be alarmed.' She assured him she was 'not the least frightened', and, as police eventually seized the assailant, Albert ordered the driver to carry on as if nothing had happened. In the background, onlookers chanted: 'Kill him! Kill him!'[16] In the confusion the gathering crowd first turned on the brave bystanders who had wrestled the pistols from a certain Edward Oxford. Anxious to claim responsibility he shouted: 'It was I who fired: it was me.' The crowd then turned on Oxford. But it was unnecessary as he had no wish to run away – instead he stood with a beaming smile – taking full credit. Police constables from A Division, who looked after royal protection, now arriving at the scene, had difficulty preventing the crowd from attacking him.[17]

The queen was morbidly fascinated by the incident. Over the following days, she examined a nearby wall looking for bullet marks, spoke at length with the prime minister about the specific bullet used and the height and direction it travelled, and inspected the pistols that, in her words, 'might have <u>finished</u> <u>me</u> <u>off</u> & perhaps Albert too'.[18] She fiercely disputed the home secretary's assessment that the pistols were not in fact loaded.[19]

Victoria asked to be kept updated about the unfolding investigation. Melbourne soon told her that police had arrested Oxford for high treason, and intriguingly added that letters about a secret society named 'Young England', with 400 members, had been unearthed at his house. Each member was supposedly required to have a hidden 'brace of pistols, a sword, a rifle and a dagger'. It seemed like an elaborate conspiracy to overthrow the monarchy and the government. The French ambassador observed that these appeared to be a poor emulation of the 'great secret societies' that had existed on the Continent.[20]

Oxford was only eighteen, but looked several years younger. Under interrogation, he alleged that the king of Hanover, who would have assumed the throne had Victoria died, and Lord Palmerston, the foreign secretary, were members of 'Young England'. These wild allegations were quickly dismissed, and a jury found Oxford guilty but insane.

It was all a figment of his imagination.[21] The real driving force for Oxford had been an addiction to 'penny dreadful novels'. He was fascinated by the highwayman Jack Sheppard, and his favourite reading included a book called *The Bravo of Venice*, which featured a figure who rises to prominence by becoming the 'King of the Assassins'.[22] He followed James Hadfield, George III's millenarian would-be assassin, into long-term institutional confinement. Was Oxford really mad rather than malevolent? The queen was sceptical and talked with Melbourne 'of the jury being bad'.[23]

The press speculated wildly about Oxford's connections to either the Chartists, a working-class male suffrage movement for political reform, who had recently triggered riots in Birmingham, or else ultra-right underground movements. In fact, Oxford was a lone operator. The real political significance was to trigger a vast and spontaneous outburst of popular support for the queen and her new husband. For days, huge crowds surrounded the palace, thrilled to see her going about her duties with no obvious additional protection.

Undoubtedly, Oxford was deranged. Witnesses testified to a long history of instability, characterized by maniacal fits of laughing and crying, since early childhood. When questioned by the home secretary, he again erupted in hysterical laughter, which discomforted everyone present.[24]

Fascinatingly, once confined, Oxford met up with another would-be royal assassin. It was something of an elite club. Oxford would eventually join Hadfield at Bethlem Hospital. Hadfield was momentarily filled with hope when Victoria had been crowned queen, expecting that his long service to the nation as a soldier in Wellington's army would count for something. He petitioned her to release him and make him a Chelsea pensioner. But Victoria was now alert to the danger of lunatics and chose to keep him contained.[25]

It was undoubtedly convenient for the authorities to find Oxford insane. Lacking intelligence capacity, the police would have struggled to uncover and penetrate such a secret society had one existed. Besides, the state's limited surveillance capabilities were focused on the growing Chartist movement. Lone wolf attacks against the monarch were a more difficult proposition altogether. The queen was protected on state occasions by plain clothes officers, plucked from the uniformed police to monitor suspicious characters in the crowds.[26] These arrangements were clearly insufficient. Nor were they improved – and they needed to be.

On 29 May 1842, Albert heard 'a trigger snap' as he and Victoria returned to Buckingham Palace. A short swarthy man had stepped out from the crowd and aimed to fire. The bumbling police failed even to notice the incident. No one around him appeared to have noticed at all. Albert kept the matter highly secret, telling only the prime minister and those immediately concerned with the queen's safety.[27] Peel hurried to the palace and the two walked in the gardens, discussing what to do next.

The following day, Albert and Victoria took matters into their own hands and launched a daring operation to flush out the assailant.[28] They repeated the same route, albeit this time travelling a little more quickly and ensuring that undercover police lurked at every corner.[29] Victoria decided that she could expose the lives of her gentlemen, but not her ladies, so kept the ladies in waiting out of the line of fire.[30] Constantly looking over her shoulder, she unsurprisingly felt 'agitated and excited'.[31] Albert 'looked behind every tree', she later recalled, 'and I cast my eyes round in search of the rascal's face'.

Constable William Trounce of A Division had been observing a suspicious character in the same area for about thirty minutes. But as the royals approached, patriotic feelings overcame his limited undercover training. Instead of watching his suspect, he bizarrely stood smartly to attention and saluted. Meanwhile, his suspect, the same man as before, stepped forward and shot his pistol at a range of seven yards.[32] This time, the police caught him. His name was John Francis, a twenty-two-year-old Londoner. He was initially detained in the same cell that Oxford had occupied two years before.[33]

Despite the mishaps, Victoria was remarkably impressed with the whole operation and the secrecy with which she had carried it out.[34] Again she pressed ministers for details.[35] Francis was tried for high treason and sentenced to death, but this was later commuted to transportation on the grounds that his pistol was not loaded.[36] Victoria and Albert naturally both argued for better security, and also lobbied for a change in the law to better protect the monarchy.[37]

Two days after the Francis verdict, the home secretary told her of yet another assassination attempt.[38] Enough was enough. The prime minister, Robert Peel, rushed to Albert to discuss protective measures. He and the queen promoted a legislative solution, believing that such attempts would continue so long as the law allowed assailants only to be charged with high treason, a cumbersome procedure.[39] Under intense pressure from the palace, parliament passed a Treason Act just nine days afterwards, which introduced a new crime of intending to wound or alarm the sovereign, punishable by transportation, imprisonment or whipping.[40]

More importantly, less than a month later, the police established a small eight-man 'Detective Department', albeit this was as much to appease public fears amid a recent murder spree as to protect the monarch. It had already existed in embryo within A Division, widely considered the Metropolitan Police's elite district, and they had already been called away to conduct what were essentially Special Branch tasks against the Chartists in Birmingham two years before. Now they had an excuse to move forward more brazenly. Tasked by the Home Office, it cultivated ad hoc informants to gather intelligence on subversive individuals and groups. Surveillance focused predominantly on the Chartists and on foreign nationals who had recently arrived in Britain. All the while, detectives consciously tried to avoid accusations of French-style authoritarian political policing with its undercover agents.[41]

In the early nineteenth century, Peel's police force had been regarded with suspicion as a civilian army of 'bludgeon men'. But the newly formed Detective Department had some unlikely allies. Charles Dickens was fascinated by this new development and wrote several press pieces praising them. Remarkably, he incorporated them into his latest novel, *Bleak House*. The first fictional detective, 'Mr Bucket', was closely modelled on a real detective-inspector, Charles Field. Some police officers worked closely with journalists to create what have been called 'pseudo-autobiographies of professional men'. As the century wore on, novelists, drawing on the public fascination with the science of forensics, conjured up the image of a new intelligence-driven policeman. Not all of them were men. One of the first fictional detectives was Ruth Trail of 'Secret Intelligence' whose office door boasted a brass plaque that read 'Secret Agent'.[42]

With this slowly changing public mood, the Victorian era saw the beginnings of modern state surveillance. The introduction of the penny black stamp made the postal service affordable for the average person, dramatically increasing the opportunities for state interception. Mushrooming bureaucracies, from the growth of the census to the blossoming library system, also offered a sort of indirect surveillance that earlier societies had not experienced. Public health bureaucracies began to keep comprehensive files on ordinary citizens for the first time, crime being closely associated with disease in the popular imagination.[43] Such activity might have helped the police keep order and prevent conspiracies, but not everyone was impressed. Royal fears that ordinary members of the public might obtain unseemly glimpses into the private lives of the elite formed an early counterweight against these developments.[44] Moreover, undercover police and indirect surveillance simply failed to prevent further assassination attempts.

In January 1843, Albert received 'intelligence', as Victoria put it, that one of Peel's personal secretaries had been shot. The bullet, she recorded in graphic detail, 'had passed through the ribs but had been extracted, — no vital part had been touched, & it was hoped he would do well'. She and Albert looked awkwardly across the dinner table, where, by coincidence, the victim's brother sat blissfully unaware of what had happened. Albert gently broke the news to him after dinner.[45] The next day, Peel revealed a further secret to the queen: the assassin had intended to kill Peel himself, and, in a case of mistaken identity, thought he had succeeded. Victoria was horrified.[46] Peel promised to send her all the latest intelligence, no matter how seemingly insignificant.[47]

The victim, Edward Drummond, died from his wounds five days later. Sadly, Drummond was related to Spencer Perceval, the only British prime minister to be assassinated, and they were eventually buried in the same family tomb in Charlton in Kent.[48] The queen's temperature rose further when the attacker, Daniel McNaughton, was acquitted on the grounds of insanity. '*What* security is there left now!' she thundered. 'Something ought to be done,' Victoria demanded of the prime minister, 'to alter the law, which is indeed very defective.'[49]

The very next day, debate opened in parliament.[50] She continued to keep up the pressure on the prime minister, and, three months later, the House of Lords announced new rules to change how jurors would be instructed regarding insanity. From then on, every man was to be presumed sane, leaving it for the defence to prove that, when committing the act, he, through 'disease of the mind', either did not know what he was doing or did not know that it was wrong.

In the background, dramatic events abroad helped drive the change. Passions were building towards another round of momentous revolutions on the Continent in 1848. In France, politics, rather than mentally disturbed assassins, fuelled rising violence against royalty. Many of the assailants subscribed to an underlying anarchist philosophy, believing that by killing the king they would unhinge the entire establishment and trigger a major change in the established social order. The most inventive was Giuseppe

Fieschi, who had created a primitive form of machine gun for his formidable attack in 1835. As King Louis Philippe rode through Paris to inspect his national guard, Fieschi unleashed no fewer than twenty-five loaded guns bound together on a wooden frame. Eighteen people around the king were exterminated, while half of Freschi's own face was blown off. Yet the king survived and, emulating Victoria's famous courage under fire, he rode on to review his troops as if nothing had happened.[51]

Victoria had successfully changed the law on mental health. Despite developments on the Continent, her demands for increased security did not have the same impact. The prime minister assured her that 'every precaution possible' would be taken to keep her and Albert safe on state occasions, but naïvely comforted her by saying that he had 'walked home every night from the House of Commons, and, notwithstanding frequent menaces and intimations of danger, he has not met with any obstructions'.[52] Prince Albert personally designed an armoured parasol – made out of chain mail – to protect the queen, but it was rather heavy and she never used it.[53]

Victoria faced at least a further five assassination attempts over her reign. Another took place in May 1849, when William Hamilton, a refugee from the Irish famine, shot at her with an unloaded and home-made gun. Once again this took place at Constitution Hill, which was rapidly becoming assassination alley for the royal family. The queen's escorts spotted a man with a gun and called for the coach to stop, providing him with a perfect target. There was a flash and a loud roar. A crowd fell on him rapidly, shouting, 'Tear him to pieces!' and 'Kill him at once!', but detectives from A Division quickly hauled him away for interrogation.[54] Under the new act, he was tried, with royal approval, of misdemeanour, rather than high treason, and sentenced to seven years' transportation.[55]

A year later, another man stepped from a crowd and struck Victoria with his walking stick, knocking her unconscious momentarily. This was another monumental lapse of royal security, and, as the queen staggered to her feet nursing a swollen eye, the public leapt on the assailant. This attack angered Victoria more than all the others. She thought it 'by far the most disgraceful & cowardly thing that has ever been done'. Hitting a woman with a stick was judged 'far worse than an attempt to shoot, which, wicked as it is, is at least more comprehensible & more courageous'.[56] He faced the same punishment as the Irishman and was transported to Australia.[57]

IN SPRING 1844, amid assassination attempts and the tentative growth of undercover policing and state surveillance, Britain's one long-standing and most professional intelligence success story, one that had been quietly nurtured since the Civil War, now faced a major scandal.

The protagonist was Giuseppe Mazzini: an Italian nationalist who had taken refuge in London after being chased across Europe following a string of failed insurrections and sentenced to death in absentia. In 1831, he had founded 'Young Italy', an underground movement designed to unite his country that, two years later, had 60,000 members. This was the movement that the fantasist and would-be assassin Edward Oxford had tried to emulate. After a number of failed insurrections, he was exiled to London, where he ran his movement from the British Museum. Sitting among scholars and novelists, he wrote to agents across Europe and North America agitating for a unified Italian republic.

Early in 1844, a friend called at his house in a state of distress. Two of his associates, Emilio Bandiera and his brother Attilio, had been seized shortly after arriving in Naples and executed. How had the Neapolitan police managed to find them so quickly? This increased Mazzini's existing suspicions that someone was tampering with his mail. After yet another failed uprising, this time in southern Italy, Mazzini accused the British government of intercepting his mail and tipping off the local authorities.[58] Specifically, Mazzini accused the government of 'post-office espionage'. Setting out to prove it, he carefully placed poppy seeds, strands of hair and grains of sand into envelopes, sealing them with wax, and posting them to himself. Sure enough, they arrived sealed, but without their tell-tale contents.

As word spread, members of parliament now feared their own letters were being opened. The scandal caused outrage in parliament and instigated a broader debate about spying. What difference, one MP asked furiously, was there between 'a government breaking the seal of his letter in the Post Office, and the government employing a spy to poke his ear to the keyhole?' These underhand practices were 'singularly abhorrent to the genius of the English people'.[59]

Parliamentary anger caught the national mood. Britain prided itself on being the most open of democratic powers, and the philosopher Jeremy Bentham had recently popularized the notion that secrecy was an 'instrument of conspiracy' deployed by tyrants.[60] Here, in the absence of poppy seeds, surveillance and security collided with newfound ideals of liberty and privacy, driven by cheap, secure correspondence and a feeling that the home was a private space in which the state had no business.[61]

Soon, James Graham, the home secretary, was nicknamed 'Fouché' by the press, after Joseph Fouché, Napoleon's notorious minister of police famous for his system of political spies. Meanwhile, Mazzini became an overnight celebrity and household name. Yet Queen Victoria was unmoved. Sympathizing with her royal relatives across Europe who faced violent republican revolutionaries, she maintained her more pragmatic attitude to security. She was also unsurprised by the exposés, having become an experienced reader of intercepted letters herself.

Before 1844, Victoria had enjoyed access to an impressive range of intercepts. She found some 'most impertinent', others 'curious', while some simply made her laugh.[62] They offered rich insight into the French court,[63] German politics,[64] Russian-German relations,[65] and the implications of the Spanish civil war for its monarchy.[66] Victoria found them fascinating, recording how she would discuss 'people <u>knowing things</u>' with her prime minister.[67] Some were particularly sensitive: one intercept was a letter written by her own uncle, King Leopold, criticizing her government;[68] another batch contained some 'violent letters' by that 'old foolish Sir Robert Gardiner', a former general whom she had inherited as an assistant in her own court.[69] In some cases, Victoria not only saw the raw intercepts but acted as an intelligence analyst. She used her encyclo-paedic knowledge of the intricate power structures in Europe to help her government interpret the royal material.

Albert shared his wife's pragmatism. When some of his own correspondence later fell into French hands, he reacted simply by saying that 'if people have spies to open and read letters, they must expect to see what they may not like'.[70]

Therefore, when the Mazzini affair erupted, Victoria just could not understand the hysteria. She believed that the home secretary 'must have, in moments of difficulty', the ability to intercept letters. She was disappointed that the government lost the subsequent debate and expressed surprise that Melbourne, with whom she was still in close touch despite his having left office, 'condemned the practice'.[71] And she did have some right to be surprised at his purported squeamish-ness: Melbourne had once forwarded reams of foreign intercepts to the palace. Admittedly, this time with Mazzini, the state had targeted British communications, an altogether more controversial target.

Victoria's views were at odds with those of her subjects. Her dynastic sympathies, fear of revolutionaries and loathing of republi-canism help explain this. Surveillance of Mazzini was instigated at the request of Austria, which, at the time, owned large parts of Italy and was roundly repressive. This raised the thorny issue of national sovereignty and spying at the request of a foreign state. The philoso-pher Thomas Carlyle angrily wrote that while Englishmen had no interest in the affairs of the Austrian emperor, 'it is a question vital to us that sealed letters in an English post-office be, as we all fancied they were, respected as things sacred'. An editorial in *The Times* agreed that such activity 'cannot be English, any more than masks, poisons, sword-sticks, secret signs and associations, and other such dark inventions'.[72]

The queen had a clear interest in maintaining those monarchies that radicals like Mazzini were trying to overthrow. Surveillance mattered more to the crown than to parliament. But parliament won. After a lengthy inquiry, the government was forced to admit that a secret department of the Post Office had existed for two centuries. In 1655, after the English Civil War, Oliver Cromwell had appointed a postmaster general to intercept letters of monarchists suspected of plotting against his regime. With a warrant, this Secret Office and Deciphering Branch had the power to intercept mail.

Ministers tried to fudge the outcome. They kept the law the same, hoping to leave it a 'mystery whether or not this power is exercised'. This, the inquiry hoped, would 'deter the evil-minded from applying the Post to improper use'. In practice, the Peel government closed down the Deciphering Branch and the Secret Office of the Post Office altogether. Britain seemingly lost the ability to intercept and decipher letters.[73] The operatives, which still included relatives of Edward Willes, who had created the institution more than a century before, were quietly pensioned off with money from a secret fund.[74] It was, according to the historian Christopher Andrew, a 'turning point in intelligence history'.[75]

The following year, the queen discussed the issue with Robert Peel again. She maintained that the power to open letters was necessary, but agreed it should not be abused. The issue of secretly resealing them was more controversial, but again the queen was in favour. She argued that if this were 'not done and letters merely stopped, without being resealed before being forwarded, then hardly any information could be obtained'. Intriguingly, the queen added that the Post Office was not the best institution to conduct such secret activity anyway. Instead, she thought that the Foreign Office did it 'in a far more secret manner'; a practice she was relieved had not fallen under the recent investigation and perhaps pointing to a yet more secret office.[76]

The government did continue to watch Mazzini closely, although he wrote in code after the 1844 scandal. A few years later, the prime minister told Victoria that the authorities still hoped to 'shut' him 'up for a time', but despite keeping him under surveillance they were struggling to catch him doing anything actually illegal.[77] A decade after the scandal, the French king impressed Victoria with his detailed knowledge of secret societies and told her that he too had failed to 'get at' Mazzini, but vented 'if I catch him, I will embalm him'. Victoria listened sympathetically, knowing full well that her own ministers had been soft on the revolutionary a decade earlier.[78] A European royal club was closing in on revolutionaries and they had found their mark.

Despite the closure of the Deciphering Branch, British authorities, probably through the Foreign Office, still intercepted Mazzini's mail twenty years after the scandal. For thirty years, he skipped across the Continent, creating insurrections and then returning to the safety of the British Museum when things got too hot. Thus, the queen still had periodic access to what he penned. The aim, as ever, was to gather intelligence on his revolutionary network. Victoria was relieved, for example, when intercepts showed that Giuseppe Garibaldi, the nationalist republican and contributor to Italian unification, was leaving London. She noted that they clearly revealed him to be a 'tool' of Mazzini.[79]

THE MAZZINI AFFAIR reflected the thorny broader issue of British attitudes towards European political exiles and put the queen in a difficult position. Amid great political upheaval on the Continent, dissidents fled fierce crackdowns on rebellion and insurrection. Taking advantage of Britain's liberal asylum policy, which starkly contrasted with the authoritarianism across the Channel, many found a home in London.

In nineteenth-century Britain, the position regarding refugees and exiles was remarkably liberal. Everyone was welcome, ranging from overturned monarchs and routed royalists to the leaders of failed revolutionary bands and escaped political prisoners. Between 1823 and 1900, not a single refugee was expelled. While refugees in Europe faced draconian treatment, foreigners who fled to Britain could reside in freedom. An act permitting deportation was introduced in 1848, but was scrapped five years later, never having been used. Yet behind the scenes, Victoria was pursuing a secret battle to put an end to this political openness.[80]

This was because these refugees, from Mazzini to Karl Marx, turned nineteenth-century Britain into a petri dish of radical political ideas. Often, they were at odds with each other. Mazzini declared Marx to be an authoritarian who was filled with the hatred rather than the love of mankind, while Marx responded that the veteran Italian nationalist was 'an everlasting old ass'.[81] Nevertheless, here dissident groups could organize, plot attacks and print material to be smuggled back to the Continent. Unsurprisingly, foreign governments continuously pressured Britain to deport these subversives for trial, but Victoria's government possessed neither the means nor the inclination to place so many dissidents under surveillance.[82] Victoria, who empathized with the European monarchs and abhorred republicanism, found herself caught between dynasty and country.

In 1844, the year of the Mazzini affair, the home secretary, James Graham, met police chiefs to discuss how to keep track of foreign nationals more effectively. Around the same time, detectives at Scotland Yard did place some refugees under surveillance.[83] The leading detective in this controversial field was Jonathan Sanders, who, fluent in French, could easily pass himself off as a refugee. Throughout the 1850s, he reported the mood among neighbourhoods that had become hotbeds of radicalism and monitored meetings at political clubs popular with foreign dissidents. More often than not his investigations concluded that these groups posed little real threat beyond drunken cries of 'Death to the Aristocrats'.[84] All the while, politicians and members of the public complained about alleged spying on political activity. Even though he sympathised with the dissidents' liberal ideals, Palmerston, the foreign secretary, was forced to defend the principle of surveillance in the House of Commons.[85] The queen would have approved.

After 1848, the situation became more serious, when democratic revolutions swept across Europe, existentially challenging monarchical rule. They began in southern Europe and spread to around fifty nations, including France, Austria, the Netherlands, Denmark and Hungary. Tens of thousands of people died in the violence that followed. British politicians were in two minds, on the side of those rebelling against authoritarian governments, yet fearing their own radicals at home, the Chartists. Although unsettling, the overall effect was to leave Britain without a serious strategic competitor in Europe, allowing the country to focus on imperial expansion. Therefore, Britain's official position was procrastination and a pragmatic neutrality, hoping no single state would gain the upper hand and quietly admiring the chaos in the capitals of its European competitors.

Nevertheless, Victoria was understandably agitated. Reading report after report from well-placed relatives describing murder across the Continent, she worried about the ease with which the revolutions were unfolding. Although it pleased the queen, Britain's initial response was small: a new law would make treasonable language a punishable felony.[86] She continued to worry, and soon found herself at odds with parts of her own government about how to intervene. Whether to place radicals under surveillance at home or even whether to launch covert actions abroad in support of them became contentious issues.

In September 1848, Palmerston approved a covert operation to support Sicilian rebels in their uprising against the king of Naples. Running counter to British professions of neutrality, the government allowed stocks of arms from the War Office to be sold on to the rebels via a British arms manufacturer.[87] Palmerston neglected to tell the queen, who was livid when *The Times* broke the story early the following year. Victoria was 'startled' to learn that 'this <u>was done</u> and <u>sanctioned</u> by Lord Palmerston!!'[88]

The queen was particularly furious because, despite the supposed neutrality, her sympathies throughout the revolutions lay with monarchs. To make matters worse, she and Albert had earlier said that *if* Sicily did become independent, they would rather it be under a monarchy than a republic. She felt that Palmerston had deliberately misrepresented this view by letting his colleagues believe that the crown supported the rebels.[89]

After the *Times* exposé, Victoria knew her government could not plausibly deny the operation; neither could they defend it. Britain would therefore have to apologize. She detested having to do so, viewing it as a humiliating affront. From her own sources, she knew that leaders across Europe assumed Britain was covertly supporting rebellion.[90] In damage limitation mode, Victoria and Albert pushed – unsuccessfully – for Palmerston's resignation.[91] Britain abandoned support for the Sicilians, after which rather predictably Neapolitan forces quickly regained control of the island.[92]

The Sicilian case was not a one-off. At the same time, Victoria and Palmerston had been at loggerheads about the latter's sympathy for Sardinian attempts to drive Austria out of northern Italy. Once again, Palmerston was prepared to offer secret assistance to the rebels.[93]

Meanwhile, foreign governments continued to persuade the British to spy on prominent political exiles. To achieve this, they regularly sent intelligence to monarch and ministers alike exaggerating the threat. This included intelligence from Prussia stating that Karl Marx was plotting to assassinate the queen,[94] and a stream of alarmist warnings about the terrorist threat to the 1851 Great Exhibition held in London – the most ridiculous of which involved revolutionaries disguised as trees.[95] Victoria astutely paid little notice of 'absurd reports of dangers of every kind and sort', and instead lavished praise on Albert for his role in organizing the event. He had proved wrong all of those 'mischievous' people who up until midnight on the day the exhibition opened 'maintained something dreadful would happen!'[96]

The queen was more worried about revolutionaries plotting against monarchs abroad. In October 1851, she implored Palmerston not to meet a leading Hungarian nationalist, Lajos Kossuth, who was touring the country and making inflammatory speeches.[97] She knew from her own correspondence that foreign governments, watching closely, were deeply unimpressed by Britain's lack of empathy with the public order problems they faced. Palmerston's intention to meet Kossuth encapsulated this neatly. As a result, and 'disgusted' by the whole spectacle, she stretched her constitutional powers to the limit and was on the verge of demanding Palmerston's resignation.[98] Eventually, under pressure from Cabinet as well as the crown, Palmerston acquiesced and resigned, but the episode left Victoria with a bitter taste.[99] The eventual breaking point had been Palmerston's support for French revolutionaries, which annoyed even his most supportive Cabinet colleagues. Albert was delighted and wrote to his relatives: 'Give a rogue a rope and he will hang himself'.[100]

Although Kossuth only stayed in Britain for three weeks, the government kept him under surveillance afterwards, hoping to catch him doing something illegal. Only eighteen months later, Queen Victoria was pleased when, after a successful intelligence operation, Albert told her that a rocket factory suspected to have been under Kossuth's direction had been seized and 800 rockets confiscated.[101]

The queen feared Kossuth was the tip of a republican iceberg. Her sources on the Continent warned her of 'rumours of plots directed from London' aiming for 'the assassination of all Monarchs'.[102] She learnt, among other things, that European leaders believed Britain planned to 'destroy the Austrian Empire' and that London had become a menagerie of revolutionaries 'kept to be let occasionally loose on the Continent to render its quiet and prosperity impossible'.[103] Victoria did not believe them all, but she was supportive of the underlying issue. Monarchs had a right to respect and loyalty;

any hint of insubordination should not be encouraged.[104] After hearing of violence in Vienna, she thought of all 'her dear ones' stuck in 'the possession of the mob'. The queen did not mince her words: 'these horrible Republicans should be exterminated'.[105]

In short, Britain was a reservoir of rebellious ideas in the mid-nineteenth century. Victoria's European counterparts begged her to intervene against the government's lenient policy on protecting revolutionaries.[106] Yet the queen felt powerless: parliament would do little in terms of deportation or even surveillance.[107] This led to frequent clashes with Palmerston who was much more sympathetic to the nationalism unfolding on the Continent. She had feared Palmerston was withholding information from her about his own meddling in foreign affairs and, drawing on her royal intelligence networks, worried that his hectoring of foreign monarchs was making Britain unpopular in Europe.[108]

Frustrated by the experience, Victoria successfully blocked the appointment of Lord Clarendon as Palmerston's successor as foreign secretary in 1851. Her rationale was instructive: she thought him too fond of 'diplomatic intrigue' and 'spying'.[109] When a new prime minister, Lord Derby, took office shortly afterwards, she wasted little time in warning him against the dangers of 'Diplomatists and Agents' and the harm that 'intrigue' had done to Britain's international reputation as the revolutions had played out.[110] She relied on her own dynastic network to keep her updated and opposed secret activity conducted by her ministers that undermined European monarchism. Intelligence was fine; so long as it suited the queen's interests.

Accordingly, Victoria was pleased when Palmerston, back as home secretary, discovered 'some incendiary papers' printed for Mazzini and Kossuth. They finally constituted a crime that could be prosecuted, although another minister dampened expectations by warning that the 'detective Police were very inefficient'. She would have been equally pleased by the new foreign secretary's suggestion that 'there were many little services we might render' to the Austrian government giving them notice of the movements of 'these danger-ous Refugees'.[111]

The surveillance issue climaxed in 1858. On the night of 14 January, an Italian revolutionary and one-time follower of Mazzini, Felice Orsini, attempted to assassinate the French emperor, hoping to trigger a revolution that would spread to Italy. Orsini and a couple of accomplices threw three hand grenades at the emperor and his wife as they attended the Paris opera. He missed his target but killed numerous bystanders. Such an attack was not unusual in this period and Victoria quickly received reams of telegrams bringing her the latest intelligence from Paris and providing gory details.[112]

Orsini's London connections proved more troubling. After a dramatic and daring escape from an Austrian prison in 1855, he had fled to London and published popular accounts of his adven-tures. Orsini's plot to kill the emperor was hatched in London and the bomb, which bore his name, was made in Birmingham. Unsurprisingly, the French authorities quickly accused the Foreign Office of having turned a blind eye to his activities and demanded that Britain restrict the right to asylum.[113]

Although annoyed at the criticisms of her country, Victoria accepted the point.[114] She agreed that 'were similar assassins to be tolerated in France & came over to attempt to do something against us here, the whole British nation would demand instant repara-tion'.[115] Accordingly, she supported surveillance of Orsini's former lodgings and moves to make conspiracy to murder abroad a felony. Both responses would have involved stepping up the intelligence effort against refugees.

Detectives quickly investigated Orsini's old neighbourhood. The task fell to Jonathan Sanders, specializing in surveillance of foreign nationals. Unfortunately, witnesses saw him rummaging around without a warrant, thereby causing unwelcome publicity and criti-cism.[116] The inflammatory incident undermined Sanders' careful attempts not to give credence to accusations that the government used political espionage, French-style.

The second response, a bill making conspiracy to murder abroad a felony, was less successful still. The following month, the government dramatically fell after losing a parliamentary vote on this contentious issue. In an ironic twist, the outgoing prime minister was none other than Lord Palmerston, now trying to curb, rather than encourage, continental rebellion.[117] This time, the queen had nothing but sympathy and tried to convince him not to resign. She was particularly frustrated by Palmerston's opponents, writing with disdain about how Orsini had been a regular house guest of Thomas Gibson, the member of parliament who had dramatically censured the government.[118] For now, Palmerston, whose views on revolutions had so frustrated Victoria, was out of office. The queen was relieved that his successor, Lord Derby, had 'behaved remarkably well on the Conspiracy Bill'.[119] The new foreign secretary, the earl of Malmesbury, told the queen that 'letters from *private* sources' in France now indicated that criticism of Britain would subside.[120]

IN THE FIRST two decades of her reign, Victoria had been an intelligence gatherer, analyst and consumer. She learnt quickly and understood intelligence broadly, encouraging her extensive dynastic network to send her insights on European attitudes and intentions. As she grew in confidence, she clashed with her governments about sensitive issues of surveillance and covertly supporting rebels, which placed her in a difficult position. She demanded secret material and berated ministers if ever they kept things from her. Still fairly inexperienced, though, she often felt powerless to change things directly. Thereafter, the rise of Germany, a country to which she held great affinity, in the 1860s served only to increase the tension between monarchical and state intelligence. And again, Victoria had all the best-placed intelligence sources. She now grew more confident to use them to outmanoeuvre her governments.

QUEEN VICTORIA'S SECRETS: WAR AND THE RISE OF GERMANY

'It is evident the whole is a Prussian intrigue'

Queen Victoria, 1866[1]

RULING FROM THE very public location of Buckingham Palace, Queen Victoria sat at the pinnacle of a vast private intelligence network spanning the European continent. Victoria's network frustrated her ministers, but it proved useful on many occasions. Intelligence now became a battleground in the broader European struggle for modern nation states. Here, Victoria's intelligence allowed her to stretch her powers to the limit, influence Cabinet, and even help prevent war.

Britain and France had a tense and complex relationship in the 1850s. The French resented Britain's provocatively welcoming attitude towards European dissidents; the British resented French despotism with all its illiberal penumbrae of shadowy police spies and political surveillance. At the same time, the two rivals joined forces to prevent Russia from exploiting the demise of the Ottoman Empire and gaining access to the strategically important Mediterranean.

The Crimean War, fought in the Balkans, Black Sea and the Baltic between 1853 and 1856, pitted Britain, France and the Ottoman Empire against Imperial Russia. Unfortunately for Victoria, Russia was an intelligence black hole. Three factors explain this: first, Britain still had no organized intelligence service – nor even a proper military intelligence department; second, even though the invention of the telegraph drastically sped up communication, gaps in the network caused lengthy delays in information reaching London; and third, the queen's royal intelligence network proved less useful on political affairs in the Russian capital so far away where less European nobility circulated.

Although there was little to go on, the queen impatiently demanded updates. She tried to keep a close eye on diplomatic manoeuvrings in the run-up to hostilities, but much of what reached the palace was confused and contradictory. In August 1853, after the Russian tsar had sent troops towards the Balkans, Victoria gratefully received what she called 'very satisfactory telegraphic intelligence' from the prime minister, Lord Aberdeen, that Russia had accepted a peaceful resolution.[2] After the Ottomans scuppered this, she became increasingly alarmed at reports coming from the region.[3] Victoria's cousin, the duke of Cambridge, special emissary to the queen from Constantinople, informed her of the 'wretched' state of the Turkish military. Meanwhile, her pro-Turkish ambassador in Constantinople deliberately interpreted any Russian communications he could get his hands on as evidence of Russian aggression. It took weeks for their letters to arrive at Buckingham Palace, creating much confusion.[4] The queen grew impatient.

Aberdeen promised that there was 'very little chance' of a Russian attack. Accordingly, Victoria approved the despatch of a naval fleet to Turkey that autumn on the assumption that it would not see action. This 'intelligence', as she called it, proved entirely wrong.[5] British commanders set sail lacking basic information about the remote region's terrain and climate, let alone secret intelligence about Russian intentions or battle plans. Staggeringly, they did not even own a proper map.[6]

Back home, newspapers claimed to have unmasked a spy of an entirely different kind. In January 1854, rumours began to circulate that Prince Albert was a Russian agent. The prince had been part of British public life for well over a decade, but remained a constitutional anomaly. As a proud German, he had never entirely fitted in. Newspapers now peddled innuendo questioning his loyalty. They accused him of orchestrating foreign relations with German princes behind ministers' backs and of thwarting any British policy that undermined his own interests. Prussia, one of the most prominent German states, supported the tsar because of inter-marriage and, at a time of international tension, accusations unfairly extended to Albert being a Russian spy.[7]

Victoria was livid and thought the attacks 'abominable'. In combative mood, she expressed 'intense indignation' to her government.[8] Consoling her, Lord Aberdeen said that very few people shared these views and that he had received some information about the origins of the attacks.[9] Although he stopped short of saying what this information was, rumours circulated that the French had covertly planted the anti-Albert articles as part of a propaganda operation to undermine British sympathies towards Germany.[10] Interestingly, the queen had heard that 'Russian intrigue', as she described it, was very active in Paris, where agents were trying to prevent the French from joining the war effort.[11]

Whatever the cause, thousands of gullible Londoners assembled at the Tower of London, wildly believing that Albert was about to be imprisoned for treason. 'One word more about the credulity of the public,' Albert wrote to a friend on 24 January 1854. 'You will scarcely believe that my being committed to the Tower was believed all over the country – nay, even "that the Queen had been arrested!"' The prime minister was forced to publicly extoll Albert's 'unimpeachable loyalty to the Crown and Country' before the attacks subsided.[12]

In truth, Albert was both busy and patriotic. He was lobbying ministers with enough letters to now fill some fifty volumes in the Royal Archives. He drew up detailed plans to raise a force of 15,000 foreigners to fight in the conflict with Russia. The government politely declined.[13] Despite her intelligence and over ten years of experience with world affairs, Victoria felt out of her depth with military matters and the war increased Albert's influence; it now became commonplace for him to meet with the prime minister alone. Though very much in love, Victoria and Albert were also engaged in a power struggle. Albert acquired more of Victoria's government work as her pregnancies forced her to step aside. Victoria was grateful for the support, but she deeply resented being robbed of her powers as queen.[14]

As war in Crimea intensified, improvements in the telegraph network dramatically decreased the amount of time it took for information to reach London from the theatre. In spring 1854 it took around five days; a year later it took only a few hours.[15] Unfortunately, there was still little intelligence to report. 'If only there was more news from the front,' the queen complained. 'If only one knew the details.' She demanded that the secretary of state for war tell her everything. He had little to tell.[16]

Most of the reporting came from newspapers. The new position of 'war correspondent', sending back detailed updates at the same speed as diplomatic reporting, infuriated senior soldiers. One effectively accused *The Times* of treason, complaining that the Russians no longer needed spies for they could read all about British developments in the newspaper.[17] He had a point: the tsar did indeed exclaim that 'we have no need of spies, we have *The Times*'.[18] The royal couple, although always eager for information, prized secrecy above all else. Victoria was 'much disgusted' with the journalists; Albert melodramatically feared that 'soon there will not be room enough in the same country for both the Monarchy and *The Times*'.[19]

Sometimes the queen did successfully beat the press to sensitive material from Crimea. In March 1854, her royal messenger brought secret intelligence from the British consul at St Petersburg. It was so sensitive that he had not dared put it on paper. Once safely inside Buckingham Palace, he told Victoria about Russian preparations to lay new forms of explosives, which could be detonated remotely, underneath ice sheets. The Russians, he continued, planned to entice the British fleet into icy northern waters off the coast of St Petersburg, which became a forgotten theatre of the Crimean War, before attacking from the rear.[20] His intelligence was improbable, but it was hurriedly despatched to the naval forces that had left for the Baltic earlier in the month.

The Crimean theatre was more significant. Here, by the middle of 1854, Charles Cattley, a multilingual British diplomat with long experience of the region, began to improvise a military intelligence department. Indeed, Cattley had grown up in Russia and his family was still there, forcing him to adopt a cover name to ensure their safety.[21] The foreign secretary, Lord Clarendon, was so impressed that he told the queen straight away about Cattley's methods, sources and intelligence. Cattley, Clarendon eagerly recounted, had gained valuable intelligence on enemy morale, learning that Russian soldiers did not want to fight. 'We curse that old tyrant and brute Nicholas,' they had told him, 'for dragging us from our homes.' The queen listened intently. She thought it 'pretty strong language'.[22]

Early the following year, the duke of Newcastle, secretary of state for war, told Queen Victoria that Cattley had taken charge of a nascent 'department of intelligence'.[23] His sources included Polish deserters, Russian forces and Muslim Crimean Tartars. He was willing to conduct interrogations, but, so desperate were the conditions on the ground, he gained much of his intelligence by simply providing food and warm shelter. He also ran several 'Tartar' spies.

As a result, Cattley tracked Russian troop movements and provided invaluable intelligence for operational planning. His main contribution was professional order of battle reports on the numbers and movements of the enemy; it made a considerable difference in battles across the theatre.

Unfortunately, the success was short-lived; Cattley died of cholera in 1855.[24] So important was his intelligence that Queen Victoria herself described his death as 'such a serious loss'.[25] Shortly afterwards, she grew frustrated that 'with the head of the Intelligence

Department dead', Britain now had 'no means left' whereby 'to gather information or keep up secret correspondence' with sources.[26]

Perhaps the most vexing aspect of the war for Victoria was the lack of secrecy. With the arrival of the telegraph and aggressive war reporting it was impossible to hide the weak progress. Led by gentlemen who knew little of modern warfare, equipped with obsolete weapons and often short of ammunitions, soldiers died mostly of dysentery and pneumonia. They were more at danger from their own side than from the enemy, who were no more competent. Dissatisfaction with the running of the war increased and, in January 1855, parliament appointed a select committee to probe this. Aberdeen resigned and was replaced by Palmerston, the royal couple's least favourite minister. It was no surprise that both Albert and Victoria had hated the frank and fearless war reporting of *The Times*.

Despite the setback, Victoria was determined to maintain as good an understanding of events in Crimea as possible. She developed an impressive grasp of allied positions, personally signed the commission of every officer, and wrote encouraging letters to generals in the field.[27] 'You never saw anyone,' the secretary of state for war told the commander in the region, 'so entirely taken up with military affairs as she is.'[28] On 18 April 1855, Windsor Castle hosted a one-day war council attended by Albert.[29] A few days later, Victoria joined in a less formal discussion, describing it as 'one of the most interesting things I ever was present at'.[30] Her persistent pestering of ministers had paid off, placing her well inside the loop. In September, she received 'with deep emotion, the welcome intelligence of the fall of Sebastapol', the capital of Crimea and perhaps the final phase of the war.[31]

British victory was achieved in early 1856, and the queen found out in the most curious manner. Just before midnight on 16 January, as she was about to go to bed, secret news of a peace settlement arrived via the king of Prussia. It left Victoria 'astounded and indeed startled'. Oddly, although the telegram was not written in code and the king had openly signed his name, he begged her not to mention him as the source.[32] The deal was still a secret. She and Albert decided that the operators along the whole line of the telegraph must have already read the king's message and so, against his wishes, passed on both its content and provenance to the foreign secretary.[33]

Victoria was more sceptical than her Prussian counterpart about whether this deal would actually result in a *bona fide* peace settlement and, sure enough, it was a slow process. The following month Clarendon tried to update her about various diplomatic setbacks, but, once again, Victoria had already heard the 'intelligence', as she called it, through her private channels.[34] Both sides eventually signed a peace agreement in March 1856, denying Russia access to a warm-water port in the south and returning occupied territory to the Ottoman Empire. Victoria was unimpressed with the final deal, but begrudgingly accepted it.[35]

In fact, Albert and Victoria were busy developing their own 'northern' strategy focused on the Baltic. British intelligence was better there and they were convinced that they could defeat Russia's famous Kronstadt fortress, repeating Anglo-French success against an island fort off the coast of Finland two years earlier. They were hoping for more spoils and more victories. So, on 11 March 1856, Victoria wrote in her diary, 'I own that peace rather sticks in my throat, and so it does in that of the <u>whole</u> nation'.[36] Some twenty thousand British troops had died and yet, with Russia finally on the ropes, the war had been allowed to end prematurely due to French pressure. Russia soon ignored the more restrictive parts of the peace treaty.[37]

PRUSSIA HAD FRUSTRATED Victoria throughout the Crimean War. She accused the king, who had oscillated between supposed neutrality and support for the tsar, of falling victim to 'Russian intrigues'.[38] How she would have loved a source close to the Prussian government, especially as Prussia would become increasingly significant to European intrigues over the following decades. The end of the Crimean War left France as the dominant continental land power, sparking a chain of events leading to the unification of Germany in 1871.

Princess Victoria, known affectionately as Vicky, was Queen Victoria's eldest child. Close to both her parents, but her father in particular, Vicky was a bright and precocious child, who, at eleven years old, had escorted the crown prince of Prussia, nine years her senior, around the Great Exhibition. She was fourteen when they met again at Balmoral. Victoria and Albert hoped that a marriage between the two would cement relations between London and Berlin, perhaps encouraging a more liberal Prussia in the process. Vicky married Crown Prince Frederick, known to the family as Fritz, in January 1858.

Married to the heir, the young princess had an instant place at the heart of the Prussian court. Vicky became an outstandingly well-placed source of intelligence. She sent over four thousand letters back to her mother, often full of sensitive details about state affairs. The value of this was not lost on her parents and, before his death in 1861, Albert regularly looked to her for intelligence, supplementing his own German contacts. In 1859, when Prussia mobilized against France, it was Vicky who provided the best material, including military plans.[39]

Vicky was a foreigner in a strange court. Her split loyalties put her in a difficult position and she suffered similar problems to her father. Like Albert, she faced accusations of being a spy; unlike Albert, she actually was sending sensitive information back to her homeland. Victoria warned her eldest daughter, soon after marrying Fritz, about spies in the palace and on one occasion berated her for sending a sensitive letter by unsecured post rather than private messenger.[40] Otto von Bismarck, the ambitious minister president of Prussia, was under no illusions. To him, Vicky was nothing less than an English agent, and he interpreted her intimacy with Queen

Victoria as potentially treasonous.[41] As his influence grew, Bismarck sought to freeze her out.

Vicky not only provided intelligence but also acted as an agent of influence. As Albert's favourite child and protégé, she promoted her father's vision of a more liberal Germany against the thoroughly autocratic style of the emperor. Highly educated and fluent in several languages, she was up to date on the latest social and political theories. She eventually read the works of Karl Marx to ensure that she had a proper understanding of socialism, but such behaviour did not find favour in the Prussian court. Marx had been exiled from Germany in 1849 because of his ideas and was living in London, alongside Mazzini and other rebels.[42]

In July 1863, someone leaked letters between Fritz and his father, the king of Prussia, to the newspapers. They revealed Fritz's opposition to the king's high-handed rule. The mole was none other than Vicky herself. It was a secretive attempt to undermine the king and covertly influence Prussia in a more liberal direction.[43] *The Times* praised Vicky's liberal values and her support for the prince's protests against Prussia's slide towards tyranny.

The leaks infuriated the king; but they infuriated Bismarck even more and he quickly accused Fritz of being too indiscreet with his wife. The king, he counselled opportunistically, should no longer trust his son.[44] Meanwhile, Vicky gave her mother the inside track on the fallout from what she 'will have no doubt seen' in the newspapers.[45] A few weeks later she wrote: 'I send you *all the papers* so that you may see what Fritz has done, said, and written!'[46] Bismarck had a point.

The so-called Schleswig-Holstein question, the status of two small duchies in northern Europe, presented another opportunity for Vicky to provide useful intelligence to her demanding mother. The death of her father three years earlier had made her reporting from Germany even more important.

With both countries claiming rights over the duchies, war broke out between Denmark and Prussia in February 1864. The causes were painfully intricate, combining Prussian nationalist aspirations, the succession of the Danish monarchy, and Danish violation of a treaty signed after the first Schleswig-Holstein war in 1852. 'The Schleswig-Holstein question,' Lord Palmerston, the prime minister, famously quipped, 'is so complicated, only three men in Europe have ever understood it. One was Prince Albert, who is dead. The second was a German professor who became mad. I am the third and I have forgotten all about it.'

After refreshing his memory, Palmerston intended to intervene in support of Denmark. Queen Victoria's natural sympathies lay with the Germans, and, desperate to avoid war with Prussia, she insisted her ministers tone down their threats in defence of Denmark.[47] There were problems for Vicky too. The previous year, her brother Bertie, heir to the throne, had married Princess Alexandra of Denmark instead of a German woman and the public blamed Vicky for encouraging this. Now that war had broken out between Prussia and Denmark, many suspected her of supporting the Danish on behalf of her new sister-in-law, although in fact, like her mother, she supported the Germans.

At the start of February, as German troops crossed into Schleswig, the foreign secretary, John Russell, continued to agitate for intervention to help the Danes. Victoria countered that neither France nor Russia would support him. Not trusting the queen's advice, Russell double-checked via his own intelligence channels and found St Petersburg open to a naval demonstration. The queen was furious. As the Germans marched north, Palmerston and Russell pressed for naval forces to be sent to the Baltic to defend Copenhagen. The queen refused – and received Cabinet backing.[48] Once again Palmerston and Victoria were at odds and they were effectively running rival intelligence networks to promote their opposing policies.

Vicky's intelligence proved invaluable in helping the queen rebuff calls for British intervention. Throughout February 1864, she sent bundles of sensitive material on intentions, progress of battles, weather conditions, and even letters written by her husband's aide-de-camp.[49] She continually updated her mother on the animosity between Britain and Prussia, which, she thought, was 'kept up by foolish trifles which could be avoided'. The meddling queen used these insights to prevent a rupture of British-Prussian relations.[50]

Another source of royal intelligence came from Laurence Oliphant. A celebrated mystic, author and traveller, Oliphant was a freelance amateur who had already undertaken intelligence missions in Italy and Poland.[51] When Queen Victoria's sister-in-law, the duchess of nearby Coburg, asked to have an 'able agent' sent to Schleswig-Holstein to send back intelligence on attitudes towards its monarchy, Oliphant was the obvious candidate.[52] He spent time in the duchies and then with Vicky in Prussia, before reporting back to the queen in person at Windsor Castle and updating her on likely outcomes of the crisis. He warned that Bismarck clearly wanted to 'get the Duchies for Prussia', but wrongly predicted that 'his rule could not last long'. Bismarck's power actually grew and he remained in place till 1890.[53]

As war continued, Vicky warned her mother about rising tensions after 'absurd, unjust, rude and violent attacks' against Prussia in the British press.[54] A few days later, Queen Victoria again told Russell to tone down his rhetoric which could 'only be taken by Austria and Prussia as implying a threat'.[55] Attempting to undercut rival channels of intelligence so as to increase her own influence, Vicky criticized information Britain had gathered through diplomatic channels. She told Queen Victoria that the ambassador in Berlin 'knows no German and understands nothing whatever of German affairs'. He was, she continued, 'continually misinformed' and picked 'up his information from bad sources, such as other silly diplomatists who understand nothing at all'.[56] In June 1864, Vicky wrote a particularly alarming letter, telling her mother that the British ambassador had 'spoken of our going to war with Prussia!' This, Queen Victoria concluded sharply, 'is not at all right'.[57]

The queen augmented these insights from the Continent with sources closer to home. Throughout the crisis, she used Lord Granville as a 'special observer' inside the Cabinet. A former foreign secretary, he now attended Cabinet as lord president of the council, a role which brought him into regular contact with the monarch. Granville discreetly reported individual ministers' opinions back to the palace without their knowledge, allowing Victoria insight into the arguments and factions inside government. The queen also used Granville, alongside her private secretary, to influence Cabinet members against Russell and Palmerston.[58]

It is impossible to determine the decisiveness of Queen Victoria's interventions, but the outcomes matched her preferences. Rejecting the wishes of both the prime minister and the foreign secretary, her government eventually decided against military intervention. In August 1864, Denmark ceded Schleswig and Holstein to Prussia and Austria. The queen's victory came at a price. The press criticized her for overstepping the monarch's constitutional role and being soft on Germany. After loyally defending her in parliament, John Russell warned the queen that her relatives in Germany had 'allowed rumours to go forth' that she supported the Germans over the Danes. Victoria was 'most indignant' at being called out.[59] She had now been on the throne for over a quarter of a century. As the years had turned into decades, she had grown more confident and wilier. Not only did she berate her ministers and demand to know everything that was going on, she also intrigued against them and even tried to outmanoeuvre them.

Queen Victoria now received more and more intelligence from Prussia about Bismarck's growing power. The queen of Prussia told her bluntly that her husband was 'under the influence of a clever, unprincipled man, who has virtually changed him'.[60] As his influence grew, Bismarck tried to isolate Vicky and Fritz, even placing spies in their household to monitor their contacts and conversations. Secrets were not shared with them. While the flow of intelligence to Queen Victoria continued, its quality inevitably diminished. Vicky was playing a dangerous game and Lady Ponsonby, wife of the queen's private secretary, worried for her safety, confiding: 'I don't think the Queen realizes what an extraordinary state of things exists in Germany in the way of espionage and intrigue.'[61]

IN EARLY MARCH 1866, Princess Vicky's private secretary sent a stark warning to Buckingham Palace. Otto von Bismarck intended to provoke a war with Austria; his plan of achieving German unification through violence, or blood and iron as he famously stated, would triumph over the hesitance of the Prussian king. Underlining the importance of royal intelligence, the British ambassador in Berlin could only confirm that a secret meeting between ministers and military officers had in fact taken place. The experienced British minister in Frankfurt confessed to being 'utterly in the dark'.[62]

Vicky's intelligence was accurate. Bismarck was indeed agitating for war so as to challenge Austria for leadership of the German confederation. He found pretext in a dispute over the administration of Schleswig and Holstein, which Prussia and Austria had run jointly since the war in 1864. Intelligence would be crucial in determining the outbreak and timing of the war. The future of Europe was at stake.

To determine its response, Britain needed to know first whether Bismarck had the ability to carry Prussia with him and second whether Prussia and Austria were interpreting each other's military preparations as defensive or offensive. Britain, still without a military intelligence department, still less an intelligence community, had yet to work out that Bismarck was deliberately misinterpreting Austrian manoeuvres as offensive, and that he had enough influence to persuade the king to send troops to the southern border.[63] Victoria turned to her own trusted intelligence sources.

The queen received a flood of letters from royal houses across Germany warning that war was becoming more likely.[64] She had developed an impressive network: in addition to Vicky's access, the duke of Coburg boasted of 'confidential and trustworthy' contacts in Vienna and Berlin keeping him up to date with 'the most secret proceedings'.[65] These royal communications soon bypassed official government channels, frustrating Bismarck and the British foreign secretary, Lord Clarendon, alike.[66] The Prussian court asked Victoria to mediate, but she was dissuaded by Vicky's warning that Bismarck, 'the wicked man', was determined to 'pin' the king to war and 'paralyse any intervention from elsewhere'.[67]

Vicky's position placed a great deal of pressure on her. In one letter she hurriedly wrote: 'I am not supposed to know anything contained in the Despatches, but as I did hear this I thought I would tell you.' Fearful of Prussian spies and not trusting British diplomats either, she now wanted to increase the security of their communications by using coded cyphers to which even the Foreign Office would not have access.[68] The queen had first seen a new 'deciphering machine', as she called it, three years earlier and thought it 'very curious'.[69] She now knew that this contraption was increasingly important in securing communications. Meanwhile, Clarendon grew frustrated that the queen rarely consulted him or asked him for information.[70]

Warned off mediation, Queen Victoria instead sought to drive a wedge between the Prussian king and Bismarck. She hoped not only to avoid war but to unify Germany as a liberal ally of Britain, just as Albert had always wanted. Victoria told the king that Bismarck had betrayed his confidence by revealing their private conversations.[71] Without consulting her ministers, she warned him in strong terms of Bismarck's ambition and deception: 'You are deceived, you are made to believe that you are to be attacked, and I your true friend and sister hear your honoured name attacked and abused, for the faults and recklessness of others – or rather more of <u>one man</u>.'[72] She insisted her message be hand-delivered to the king in order to avoid Bismarck's spies.[73]

Victoria assessed incoming contradictory intelligence astutely. While Vicky provided intelligence on Prussian mobilization, her mother received reports from Germany that 'only Bismarck' wanted war 'and was pushing the King of Prussia into it'; that Prussia would disarm if Austria disarmed first; and that Austrian defensive manoeuvres had raised hopes of peace.[74] At the same time, she understood Bismarck's influence and intentions, noting 'Prussian intrigue' colouring assessments of Austrian intentions.[75] She continued to think 'the deluded' king had misread the situation in blaming Austria for imaginary offences.[76] Fearing war, she pressed for some sort of intervention.

By contrast, diplomats in the Foreign Office clung onto the wishful assumption that Germany was heading irreversibly towards liberalism. They failed to properly understand Bismarck, pointing to his unpopularity with large sections of the population, especially in the south. As late as May 1866, Clarendon predicted that war would not break out because of a lack of domestic support.[77] Accordingly, diplomats advocated strict neutrality and refused to get involved in continental quarrels.[78]

For all her intelligence sources, the queen had little influence as Cabinet persistently blocked her requests for intervention, including joining an alliance with Austria and France, to prevent war. She continued to push for some sort of remonstrance, but reluctantly acquiesced. All the while, she expressed strong opinions, shaped by her own intelligence sources and dynastic interests.[79] This was one battle that Victoria lost. War broke out in the middle of June 1866 and ended with Prussian victory seven weeks later.

As the dust settled, the queen continued to press the importance of a 'strong united liberal Germany' as a 'most useful ally' to Britain. She used her outstanding sources to try to shape policy in her favour. Arguing against a policy of isolationism, she told the incoming foreign secretary that she would share 'any private intelligence which she may receive' to shed light on the present state of feeling.[80] Or rather, she would selectively share any intelligence that backed up her stance. The delicate balance of power on the Continent had been disturbed; senior diplomats in the Foreign

Office now assessed that a war between Prussia and France was inevitable.[81]

BISMARCK'S DRAMATIC ASCENDANCY made Princess Vicky nervous. She was well aware of having sent piles of state secrets to Queen Victoria and, fearing they might fall into the hands of Bismarck's spies, asked her mother to burn them. The queen refused: the intelligence was too important for her personal diplomacy.[82]

The build-up to the Franco-Prussian War of 1870 was mostly about European dynasties and royal marriages. So it is all the more surprising that it was marked by a royal intelligence failure. Bismarck plotted to put a Prussian prince on the vacant Spanish throne, so as to extend his influence, humiliate France and potentially provoke war. From Berlin, Queen Victoria's sources in the royal court informed her of wider developments – but they had no idea of Bismarck's detailed role: that he had been secretly scheming for six months.[83]

Vicky naïvely informed her mother merely of a Spanish invitation for a Prussian prince to take the throne. This in itself, she emphasized, was '*most profoundly secret*': the French could not find out.[84] When the initial offer was turned down, Vicky wrongly told her mother that 'all thoughts about Spain are entirely given up'.[85] Her husband, Crown Prince Fritz, later updated that 'fresh communications were opened'. He made no mention of Bismarck's insistence on them.[86]

When the news broke, the French – with some justification – were outraged by what they saw as a Prussian plot to humiliate France and provoke war. It took a great deal of diplomacy and royal letter-writing to calm tensions and convince the Prussian candidate to withdraw. Drawing on her continental sources, Victoria assumed the matter was settled.[87] She was wrong. Paris now demanded future guarantees from the king of Prussia that the candidature would never be renewed.[88]

The king politely refused, but in doing so presented Bismarck with another opportunity to provoke the French. Without the king's knowledge, he edited the Prussian response to French demands. Although careful not to fabricate anything, Bismarck did deliberately give the impression that the French had been more aggressive than was actually the case and the king brusquer in his reply. He quickly sent his edited version to the press and, posing as the injured party, sat back to watch the fallout. Both nations began to mobilize.[89]

Victoria's otherwise excellent network across Germany lacked access to the real centre of power: Bismarck. Accordingly, the queen and her government possessed little knowledge about what was really going on. She did not know about Bismarck's role in either the controversy over the Spanish throne or the edited telegram. A decade later, Vicky was still telling her mother that Bismarck, despite being 'the most mischievous and dangerous person alive', did 'not fan the flame' of the Franco-Prussian War.[90] This intelligence failure contributed to Britain's complacent response to the Spanish crisis.[91] Unaware of Bismarck's role, and influenced by Vicky and by close relatives serving in the German army, Queen Victoria blamed what she saw as the despotic and corrupt government in Paris: it was the 'infatuated French who seem only bent on finding a pretext to go to war'.[92]

This was surprising, for the queen had been convinced, just four years earlier, that Bismarck was the 'sole author' of the 1866 war.[93] So this was also an intelligence assessment failure by Victoria. Perhaps her long-standing suspicion of the French, alongside the lack of sources on Bismarck, affected her judgement. Either way, Victoria prided herself on being well-enough informed to influence European politics through her personal diplomacy. In this instance she failed miserably, and it was not until the eventual declaration of war that the foreign secretary started to point the finger towards Bismarck.[94] Even then, however, Vicky still insisted that France had forced Prussia into hostilities against her will.[95]

Bismarck's propaganda successfully turned British public opinion against the French – and perpetuated his victim status. Shortly after the outbreak of war, he told the Belgian minister in Berlin that France had previously offered to exchange south Germany for Belgium. This alarmed King Leopold II, who quickly fired off an angry letter to Victoria about French desire to 'dominate the world'.[96] The very next day, *The Times* published a draft treaty from 1866 – although Bismarck was careful not to reveal the date – between France and Prussia, in which Paris had made similar territorial demands.[97]

The queen, lacking intelligence on Bismarck, did not know what to make of it: 'people doubted it being genuine', she wrote, or 'at best some did, others, were greatly alarmed'.[98] The ambassador to Berlin verified its authenticity, and the queen reacted with outrage towards the French just as Bismarck had intended.[99] Victoria then asked Vicky whether taking Belgium had been Napoleon's idea, as Bismarck implied, or Prussia's. Again, Vicky was unsure, responding simply that she never trusted Bismarck.[100]

Victoria had been played, and she continued to blame the French for the war. When one British diplomat in Germany accurately reported Bismarck's role in the run-up to war, the queen's private secretary dismissed it, again preferring to blame Paris because of anti-French prejudice.[101]

Despite Victoria's sympathies for Prussia, Britain had adopted a strictly neutral position in the Franco-Prussian War. Accurate intelligence remained important for all sides as Britain's refusal to intervene caused tension. The king of Prussia complained to Victoria about secret reports that Britain was supplying France with coal and artillery. This intelligence likely came from Bismarck, who was driving an anti-English campaign and, as Vicky told her mother, no one had the time to properly investigate or validate such claims.[102] Queen Victoria found it incredibly frustrating, especially because the claims directly contradicted her true sympathies.[103] She loved intrigue but hated being outmanoeuvred.

Meanwhile, suspicious eyes watched Vicky constantly. Bismarck accused her of passing secrets to Queen Victoria, but Vicky insisted to her mother that she was only passing on information that 'may be agreeable and useful' as a personal act. This distinction would not have appeased Bismarck, especially because he thought these secrets were making their way to the French. Vicky knew she was taking a huge risk. 'England,' she told Victoria, 'is supposed to be on the other side.'[104]

In early September 1870, the French emperor surrendered after defeat at the Battle of Sedan in northwest France. Turmoil and confusion broke out on the streets of Paris: the emperor fell, but war carried on under a new republican government. The queen quickly learnt of an improvised, amateurish, but successful exfiltration of the French empress to England.

As word spread of Emperor Napoleon III's defeat and imperial guards abandoned their positions, a mob broke into the Tuileries palace on the bank of the Seine. The empress, grabbing only a hat and a coat, slipped out onto the street and, as the crowd surged towards her, escaped in a horse-drawn carriage to the house of her American dentist, Thomas Evans. A famous pioneer of pain-free dentistry, Evans served the French royal court, but also treated royal patients across the Continent, including Victoria's children the prince of Wales and Princess Vicky. In the process, he became an unofficial diplomat delivering sensitive messages literally between the mouths of royals.[105] When the French empress arrived at his door, Evans packed all the gold he had into a bag and rode with her out of Paris. Disguised as an English doctor and an 'eccentric nervous English lady', they dodged violent mobs and Prussian spies en route to the coast.[106]

Two days later they arrived at a harbour in Normandy where Evans met an English aristocrat, John Montagu Burgoyne, who reluctantly agreed to carry the empress across the Channel on his yacht. Under cover of darkness, she arrived just after midnight. The weather was appalling, but, with the French authorities closing in, the empress could not wait any longer; Burgoyne had already seen off one Parisian spy just half an hour before the empress boarded. The boat hurriedly set sail, landing on the Isle of Wight early the next morning.[107]

News quickly reached the palace where Victoria thought the dramatic tale of the empress's escape from mobs and spies 'too sad and shocking'.[108] Underlining the ad hoc approach to intelligence, Burgoyne was at pains to point out that his involvement was pure chance.[109] It clearly made an impression on the queen. Vicky introduced the mild, elderly dentist to her mother some fifteen years later; neither had forgotten 'that dreadful day' in Paris.[110] Another five years after that, in 1890, Burgoyne dined with the queen at Osborne House. She remembered him fondly as the 'man who saved the Empress'.[111]

The Franco-Prussian War formally ended in January 1871. Germany unified; the king became German emperor and Bismarck the first chancellor of the German Empire. Fritz warned Victoria shortly afterwards that Bismarck might try to provoke a war against England someday.[112] After unification, Bismarck stepped up his campaign against Vicky and her husband, increasing surveillance, further isolating them and reducing the flow of useful information to Queen Victoria.[113]

THE MID-NINETEENTH CENTURY pitted traditional royal intelligence channels – indeed even royal policies – against those of the nation state. In a period of great political upheaval, it formed part of a broader clash between dynastic and state interests. Royals with split loyalties like Vicky, and Albert before her, were a dying breed. Suspicious of Britain's liberal influence, Bismarck saw Vicky as an English agent. In the battle between royal and state intelligence, Bismarck was victorious.

Under constant surveillance from Bismarck's spies, Vicky, Fritz and Queen Victoria increasingly communicated by cypher. Victoria had once dodged spies simply by sealing her letters with silver paper to make tampering obvious.[114] This would no longer do. Now, only she and Vicky knew the codes, personally decrypting each message. Vicky insisted on keeping them even from the Foreign Office, lest they fall into the wrong hands.[115] Despite the increased security, the letters contained ever less sensitive information. Bismarck had frozen Fritz and Vicky out: whenever Fritz asked delicate questions, ministers gave a deliberately evasive answer. Vicky simply became withdrawn.[116]

Fritz died of cancer in 1888 at just fifty-six years old. He had finally managed to become emperor but for only ninety-nine days, a tragically short length of time. With him died Victoria's hopes of a liberal Germany, and any influence Vicky may have had as empress. Instead, Fritz was succeeded by the pompous Kaiser Wilhelm II, whose ambitions for German power were even greater than those of Bismarck.

On the eve of Fritz's death, Vicky tried to send a stash of confidential papers, hidden in her doctor's suitcase and hat box, to Queen Victoria at Balmoral. She had already taken three crates back to Windsor during the jubilee celebrations the previous year.[117] Now, Bismarck's spies in the British embassy found out. The new German emperor sealed Vicky's palace, threatened to open the luggage, and demanded all state papers. After a tense diplomatic stand-off, he backed down, but the incident underlined that Vicky was in grave danger. The Germans could have easily interpreted her letters as evidence of a treacherous conspiracy. Fortunately, the prince of Wales used Fritz's funeral as an opportunity to remove the last of Vicky's papers out of the country.[118]

Or so he thought. Decades later, after the Second World War, Anthony Blunt, working for British intelligence, and later exposed as a Soviet spy, warned the royal family that some of Vicky's papers still existed and had become 'exposed to the eyes of the inquisitive and the fingers of the acquisitive'. They contained not only secrets of state but also secrets of love. Blunt discreetly visited Vicky's ancestral home, then under American control, smuggling documents back to Windsor.[119]

By the end of the 1880s, Princess Vicky warned Queen Victoria that Bismarck's 'creatures' had infiltrated her entourage. The system of rapportage and espionage 'is so great at Berlin that they would not venture to open their lips'.[120] Bismarck had begun sending his spies into her residence at Potsdam, the Neues Palais. He chose his agents carefully, then persuaded them to apply for low grade jobs and to stay in them for a long time. His most useful spies were two menials in the accounts department, who saw much of the inner workings of the palace. Vicky and Fritz knew they were surrounded by an army of spies. When they returned from one trip abroad, they noticed the locks had been forced and desks and filing cabinets searched. These blatant intrusions were clearly designed to intimidate, and they succeeded.[121] The British ambassador in Berlin, Sir Robert Morier, warned Vicky to write down nothing incriminating in her diary or in her letters unless it was in cypher.[122] She clearly took this to heart. The best spy in Britain's royal intelligence network had been neutralized. Victoria's ability to outmanoeuvre her governments dramatically declined with it.

5

QUEEN VICTORIA'S GREAT GAME: EMPIRE AND INTRIGUE

'It is to me inconceivable that a handful of men sitting in a room in London, the greater part knowing little about Egypt, should pretend to say when there is danger or not!'

Queen Victoria, 1893[1]

QUEEN VICTORIA DEVELOPED impressive private intelligence networks in western Europe, but when it came to imperial intrigues, she reigned in the dark – a place she did not like to be. Instead of a system of royal relatives feeding back sensitive information to London, the queen had to rely on haphazard reporting from brave adventurers travelling to distant, rugged and poorly mapped frontiers.[2] More frustratingly, she was dependent on ministers to keep her updated on eastern matters. No longer could she use her own private sources to influence – and even outmanoeuvre – the government. For a demanding queen who liked to know everything first, this was quite unacceptable.

Worse still, information was patchy and took a long time to travel vast distances from the frontier. The empire quadrupled in size during Victoria's long reign and, as a result, never-ending small wars became a constant feature.[3] A serious intelligence failure before the 1857 Indian Mutiny, an ultimately unsuccessful uprising against

British rule, made it clear just how little officials in London knew about local conditions and feelings.[4] Victoria was characteristically angry at the lack of warning beforehand and grew more and more frustrated by the long wait for updates. Complaining of being kept in 'cruel suspense', it took almost six weeks for the first reports to reach her.[5]

Victoria was particularly keen for intelligence on Russia. Imperial rivalries in central Asia brought Russia and Britain into a protracted battle of intrigue and influence known as 'The Great Game'. India's northwest frontier became the key battleground for espionage, bribery and political warfare. Here, underhand activity triggered fewer moral concerns compared to debates about subverting the modern states of western Europe where Victoria's friends and relatives ruled.[6] It was a dangerous business, though: early in Victoria's reign, William Macnaghten, who was leading her Afghan policy, was violently assassinated in Kabul.

Macnaghten was a rather unlikely covert operator. More professor than plotter, he had spent his early years as commander of the bodyguard of the governor of Madras learning local languages, which he adored. One of his female friends recalled that he 'speaks Persian rather more fluently than English; Arabic better than Persian; but, for familiar conversation, rather prefers Sanscrit'. His main expertise was Islamic law in India, on which he wrote the definitive volumes. Rapidly promoted because of his obvious abilities, he pursued an adventurous policy in Afghanistan, while at the same time editing the Arabic text of *A Thousand and One Nights*. He took control of Kabul in July 1839 and installed Shah Shuja as a puppet ruler under a treaty that secretly made him the power behind the throne. Initially this seemed successful, but he needed endless soldiers and money for bribes to prop up the shah.[7]

Macnaghten's fans were so impressed by his covert rulership that they advocated the complete annexation of the country as a buffer against Russia. He would have been happy to bribe Afghan leaders forever in order to maintain his fiefdom, but London demanded retrenchment. The practice eventually backfired when the scale of bribes began to be cut back and an Afghan chief murdered him to prove that he was not secretly on the British payroll. His body parts were carried in triumph around the streets of Kabul.[8] Victoria recorded in grisly detail how the assassin had 'seized him by the hands and shot him through the breast. He seemed to think it right to do this, as a follower of the Prophet! Afterwards poor Sir William's head was cut off and his body cut in pieces.'[9] The Kabul garrison then fled, losing some four thousand soldiers as they retreated through the snow to India, signalling at an early stage that this country was the 'graveyard of empires'.

Useful intelligence on Russian intrigues was hard to come by. When Victoria's second son, Alfred, married the tsar's daughter in 1874, ministers hoped for political benefits, including insight into the Russian court. In reality, their union was never likely to recreate the sort of access Vicky had in Prussia. For a start it was a less happy marriage than Vicky's, while the queen's relationship with her new daughter-in-law was prickly. She irritated the queen's household too; Victoria's sardonic private secretary, Henry Ponsonby, thought the young Russian 'the spoilt daughter of a semi-Eastern despot'. Besides, the couple spent little time in Russia and, shortly after the wedding, the tsar dismissed a member of Alfred's entourage for being indiscreet. Although this inauspicious start left Victoria frustrated, Alfred did succeed in providing the occasional update about developments in Russia.[10]

The queen characteristically rebuked her ministers for this lack of intelligence on Russia. Before approving the appointment of a new chargé d'affaires to St Petersburg in 1877, she bluntly asked whether the candidate actually had any knowledge of Russia. Too many people, she moaned, left for important posts without any knowledge of either the country or the language. The foreign secretary assured her that no one available knew more about Russia than his man, Francis Plunkett.[11] Such knowledge was especially vital because, during this era, ambassadors doubled up as spies. Two years later,

Victoria instructed the new ambassador in Romania to 'make it your business to discover' Russian and Ottoman activity, the private views of other ambassadors and fortifications in the region, reporting everything back to the Foreign Office in cypher.[12] She later asked the British ambassador in Russia to send back 'anything of a personal nature regarding their imperial majesties the Emperor and the Empress which may come under his observation'.[13]

British intelligence did become better organized in the second half of Victoria's reign. In 1873, the War Office finally created a long-overdue Intelligence Branch following a string of reviews into the poor intelligence performance during the Crimean War. Focusing mainly on India and Africa, it collected and collated military intelligence to help plan for war.[14] Over a decade later, in 1887, the navy followed suit to create its own Naval Intelligence Department. Queen Victoria kept a close eye on these developments, dining at Windsor with new intelligence chiefs. If Britain was to have an organized intelligence service, Victoria wanted to be involved.[15]

In the nineteenth century, rather as in the time of Elizabeth I, apparatus for intelligence gathering and analysis was often set up in response to particular problems and in specific circumstances; once the problem went away or the circumstances changed for the better it was dismantled. A true sustainable British intelligence community would have to await the early twentieth century.[16]

FORTUNATELY, BRITAIN HAD its own James Bond in Moscow. Lieutenant Colonel Frederick Wellesley, a relative of Wellington, owed his position to patronage from the duke of Cambridge, the queen's cousin. He was a 'classic Victorian scoundrel'.[17] Famous for his extravagance, for six years, and especially during the crisis of 1877–8, he produced some of the best intelligence ever obtained from the closed world of Tsarist Moscow. In Bondian fashion, when it was circulated to the Cabinet in London it was often marked 'for your eyes only'. Unfortunately for Wellesley, ministers often disregarded these exhortations.[18]

Russian policy was hard to follow. The Ministry of Foreign Affairs and the Ministry of War were pursing contradictory policies, as were other individuals, often disregarding the tsar's view but claiming his authority.[19] Wellesley flourished his meagre royal connections to allow him to mingle with top Russian military leaders. His agents borrowed papers from Russian ministries, taking them just long enough for Wellesley to make copies by hand or even photograph them. He had agents in the War Office, the Russian navy and eventually the Ministry of Foreign Affairs. Most importantly, he saw the minutes of discussion across departments and even some comments written by the prime minister and the tsar.[20]

Wellesley was not typical of the Victorian spies of empire. The majority were more like Frederick Burnaby, a traveller cum adventurer cum soldier who provided intelligence from the imperial frontier and claimed to be descended from Edward I. As a slovenly young officer Burnaby was famed for his strength and, although later suffering ill-health, his bravery never deserted him. In the autumn of 1875, he travelled across Russia and central Asia on horseback accompanied by a single servant, evading Russian officers and enduring frostbite.[21] On his return, Victoria summoned him to Windsor to be regaled with tales of his adventures and hear his assessment of the Russian threat. He warned about Russian aggression and the serious threat posed to India. The queen listened avidly, agreeing with his characterization of Russia as duplicitous and dangerous. The Foreign Office was less enamoured: nervous diplomats feared his subsequent memoir, *A Ride to Khiva*, a bestseller that turned him into a spy celebrity, was so anti-Russian that it would spark a diplomatic incident.[22]

The following year, Burnaby travelled to Asia Minor. He was entering dangerous territory at a tumultuous time. In April 1877, while he rode through what is now eastern Turkey, news reached London that Russia had declared war on the Ottoman Empire.

Fighting quickly broke out in the Balkans, but the real question was whether Russia would advance to Constantinople. Burnaby survived an attempt to poison him by Bulgarian agents and then quickly wrote another book on the subject, which the queen read with interest.[23] She was vehemently anti-Russian and, according to Henry Ponsonby, persistently saw foreign affairs as a 'struggle for supremacy against Russia'. Sometimes resorting to writing in illegible blue chalk because, according to Ponsonby's son, 'ink might cramp the first ebullition of her fury', she would selectively quote any report that mentioned Russia's nefarious ambitions when pressuring ministers to take a tougher stance.[24]

Victoria, it has to be said, liked Burnaby's intelligence reports because of their anti-Russian fervour rather than their accuracy. She broadly agreed with his outlook that Turkish rule in Asia Minor, despite its faults, was better than the Russians. Later, he joined the 'Prince of Wales set', even if Bertie found his claims of royal descent rather annoying. Burnaby was more than just a poser cum royal protégé and instead was something of an intelligence visionary. Promoted to lieutenant colonel in the Blues and Royals, he became a pioneer balloonist, advocating their use for battlefield surveillance, but adding that the future of aviation lay with heavier-than-air machines.[25]

Victoria blamed Russia throughout the crisis. Turkey had brutally quashed an uprising in Bulgaria a year earlier, which sparked the war with Russia. The failed uprising had resulted in the massacre of tens of thousands of people. The queen demanded intelligence but received prevarication in response. The prime minister, Benjamin Disraeli, who cared little for oppressed minorities overseas, dismissed it as coffee house babble.[26] After consulting his 'trusty agents', the Turkophile ambassador in the region agreed, warning her not to believe exaggerations of 'alleged "Bulgarian atrocities"'.[27] This suited Victoria, herself desperate to blame the Russians. She accused them of instigating the insurrection in the first place and of then somehow preventing the Turks from sending regular troops to quell it, thereby paving the way for ill-disciplined bands of wild men, as she put it, to commit atrocities. It was all Russia's fault.[28]

Victoria lambasted politicians, especially William Gladstone, who publicly criticized the Turkish atrocities. Gladstone had been leader of the Liberal Party and alternated with Disraeli as prime minister, but Victoria detested him. He was, according to the queen, 'half-madman', a 'mischief maker and firebrand'.[29] She argued that blaming Turkey for the mass killings, as Gladstone kept doing, simply emboldened Russia. Gladstone, now in opposition, published an inflammatory pamphlet denouncing Turkish oppression and criticizing Disraeli's indifference towards the dead.

The queen was absolutely livid. Lashing out, she accused him of 'consorting with a Russian female spy'. Olga Novikov lost her brother in the Balkans and had since campaigned strongly about Turkish abuses in Bulgaria. In doing so, she regularly shared the stage at public rallies with Gladstone, who saw her as a source of authentic information about Russian affairs.[30] The queen, like much of the hostile press, thought she was an agent of the tsar, sent to influence and beguile the gullible politician – and Novikov certainly requested more information from Gladstone than he was prepared to supply.[31]

Russia moved troops into the Balkans in spring 1877, leaving Victoria convinced that they had Constantinople firmly in their sights. Disraeli was more trusting of the tsar, initially taking the Russians at their word that they would stop short of the Ottoman capital. As was so often the case, Victoria, armed with private intelligence, thought she knew better. This time her secret source was Arthur Balfour Haig, the equerry to her son Alfred who had married into the Russian royal family. Haig had secretly told her that the Russians knew it would take Britain six weeks to send troops to the theatre and so intended to get a head start on Constantinople – the real prize. Victoria passed his warning onto the prime minister but promised to keep her source secret.[32] She melodramatically warned Disraeli that if the Russians reached

Constantinople, she 'would be so humiliated that she thinks she would have to abdicate at once'.[33]

Throughout the Turko-Russian conflict, the queen was as belli-cose in her Russophobia as she was unrestrained. She scoured her intelligence to cherry-pick information, which she then used to manipulate her government into remonstrating. On one occasion she quoted a vague report indicating that some source had suppos-edly heard that Russian artillery had fired on ambulances. Neither the prime minister nor the foreign secretary had noticed this report and, in the words of her private secretary, their subsequent remon-stration was 'entirely the Queen's doing'.[34]

She urged Disraeli to 'be bold', but the Cabinet was split.[35] They agreed that Russian occupation of Constantinople would justify a military response, but the isolationist foreign secretary, Lord Derby, remained reluctant to take action, much to the queen's annoyance.[36] With more than a hint of bitterness, the prince of Wales told his mother: 'I suppose we shall now sit with our hands folded and let the Russians do their worst, and I see nothing to prevent their taking Constantinople.'[37]

Victoria was not one for sitting on her hands. On the throne for nearly half a century, her discreet meddling had grown with her confidence. She now turned to covert diplomacy. In the summer, she and Disraeli delivered an unofficial message to the tsar: Britain would intervene militarily if Russia attacked Constantinople. The messenger was Frederick Wellesley, the Bondian military attaché to the embassy in St Petersburg and a rare source of intelligence. He knew his mission was delicate. He told the tsar that 'he was in possession of information with regard to the policy of England, which could not fail to be of the deepest interest, but that he could only communicate it on the condition of secrecy'. The tsar agreed, and Wellesley delivered his message, adding that 'he knew for a fact that the decision had actually been come to'.[38] The extreme secrecy was necessary because Victoria had not consulted the passive Lord Derby about any of this. She and Disraeli bypassed the Foreign

Office entirely.[39] Wellesley had therefore deliberately exaggerated Britain's position, in a bluff of deterrence.

In return, Victoria hoped for some intelligence that she could use. Wellesley dutifully reported Russian attitudes towards war, but offered little insight into more tactical matters.[40] Meanwhile, the pro-Turkish ambassador in Constantinople, Henry Layard, warned that it 'would be impossible to obtain the intelligence' requested by the queen regarding the amount and location of heavy weaponry on the European side of the Dardanelles – and how they could be disabled if necessary. Victoria was becoming a frustrated spymaster with high expectations. She thought this inability to get intelligence on weaponry 'unsatisfactory'.[41]

The queen kept up the constant pressure on Disraeli to convince her reluctant Cabinet to intervene against Russia.[42] For much of the autumn, he had managed to rebuff her so long as Turkish forces continued to hold up the Russian advance in what is now northern Bulgaria. In December, Turkish resistance finally collapsed, opening the way for Russia to march to Constantinople. Disraeli now felt the queen's breath on his collar more strongly than ever.[43] Lady Salisbury, wife of the India secretary, complained that Victoria had 'lost control of herself, badgers her ministers and pushes them towards war'.[44]

In her anger, the queen suspected the foreign secretary's wife, Lady Derby, of leaking secrets to the Russians. Mary Derby had grown close to the dashing Russian ambassador, who mysteriously knew all about certain sensitive matters discussed in Cabinet.[45] The queen's lack of trust in Lady Derby explains the secrecy surrounding her covert diplomacy with the tsar. With Wellesley deeply uncomfortable delivering his secret message to the tsar behind Lord Derby's back, Victoria responded that if Derby knew then so too would his wife, closely followed by the Russian ambassador and the tsar. The entire chain would know it was a bluff and that, in reality, Cabinet was divided.[46]

Lady Derby does seem to have received secret material from her husband's private secretary, and she did meet the Russian ambassador at crucial moments during the crisis. Beyond that, it is difficult to say whether the queen was right. When questioned by Victoria's chaplain, Lady Derby angrily and resolutely denied any wrongdoing.[47] Either way, the queen did not trust the foreign secretary to make the strength of her feelings known to Russia, so she wrote to the tsar directly. When Ponsonby warned her that doing so was unconstitutional, she responded unrepentantly: it was a 'miserable thing to be a constitutional Queen, and to be unable to do what is right'.[48]

Wellesley had multiple security issues. He may have been peeking at Russian documents through his spies, but Tsarist codebreakers could decrypt British telegrams, something London had given up in 1844. All this worried Wellesley, who knew the Russians were reading his mail. The Russians certainly read his telegrams while he was attached to the Russian army on campaign in 1877 – not that this mattered given the fact that the Russians were intercepting both his and Lord Derby's telegrams anyway.[49] He was also aware that someone in London, probably Lord Derby or his wife, was speaking too freely to the Russian ambassador. Wellesley urged London that it was of 'the utmost importance that a Military Attaché should have no misgivings as to such information being considered secret at home'. In other words, he feared that secrets he sent back to London would not remain secret for long.[50]

In 1877, as the Russian army mobilized, Wellesley was able to report that instead of having 400,000 troops as the Russians boasted, in fact they only had just over 118,000. They were in a state of chaos and railways could not move them. A Cabinet minister showed his secret report to the French ambassador. Eventually, news made its way to the French ambassador in Moscow and in no time at all Wellesley was – quite rightly – regarded as a spy by the tsar and was socially snubbed.[51]

Wellesley perceived Russia as a paper tiger. Because he had a low opinion of Russian military capability, he was a constant advocate of strong actions against her all the way through the 1870s. He was also an advocate of operations to stir up rebellion among Russia's subjects on the fringes of her empire. By 1877 he was hugely influential.

However, by the following year, because of multiple scandals, he had been moved to the post of military attaché in Vienna, and then ran off with an actress who had been another gentleman's mistress, effectively ending his credibility and usefulness.[52]

The conflict – and undercurrent of intrigue – continued into 1878. Britain sent a fleet of battleships to the Dardanelles to deter Russia from entering Constantinople, but the situation remained deeply confused. In February, the queen learnt that Lord Loftus, the ambassador to Russia, had 'heard, from a secret source, that orders had been sent to the Russian Commander, to occupy Constantinople <u>with</u> the consent of the Sultan!'[53] Although Loftus was little respected in London, his report alarmed the queen, who was always willing to believe in Russian scheming.

Three days later, she agreed to a covert operation to buy four of the best Turkish warships and sail them on 'special service with secret orders' out into the Mediterranean.[54] The idea perhaps was to feign a Turkish manoeuvre to lure Russia away from Constantinople. Whatever the intention, it quickly failed when the ambassador in Constantinople warned that the Russians knew all about it. He wondered if they had broken British diplomatic codes.[55] Russia, he added the next day, 'had secret agents everywhere', including the German ambassador to Constantinople.[56] After the leak, one Russian mole inside the Ottoman diplomatic corps was quickly identified and dismissed.

With war between Britain and Russia looking likely, the tsar despatched spies armed with gold to Afghanistan. Their aim was to bribe local leaders and pave the way for a 30,000-strong invasion force to strike at India. With Britain distracted by the seemingly inevitable war in the Mediterranean, Russian intelligence assumed that India was ripe for revolt. The queen, like her government, had no idea of these secret plans.[57]

The tsar ultimately backed down and, with his armies just days from Constantinople, imposed a peace treaty on the Turks in early March. It gave Russia new territory and made Bulgaria independent from the Ottoman Empire, bringing it squarely under Russian influence. Britain, alongside the other great powers, strongly objected and, after tense negotiations, reached a revised deal at the Congress of Berlin in July, giving Britain Cyprus as a naval base.[58]

Although the queen continued to be perturbed by Russian 'intrigues' in Turkey, trouble was still brewing below the surface in Afghanistan.[59] The Indian government warned London about secret communications between the Russians and the Afghans, before accusing the Russians of sending a mission to Kabul in direct contravention of their pledge not to interfere in the area.[60] The Russians initially denied all knowledge, leaving the India Office back in London sceptical of their incoming intelligence. According to one official: 'I should like to know through what medium the Cabul news is received. The Intelligence I have seen for the last two years is the utmost rubbish.' It was, he continued dismissively, 'manufactured from bazaar gossip'.[61] Ever suspicious of the Russians, the queen was inclined to believe the warnings. She and Disraeli agreed to send a firm letter to St Petersburg demanding an explanation.[62] The Russians were now forced to admit the mission, but insisted it was peaceful. Unsurprisingly, the queen did not believe them.[63]

Angry that the Afghans had secretly flirted with the Russians while refusing Britain's own advances, war broke out between Britain and Afghanistan in November 1878. After a string of quick military defeats, the Afghans agreed to a lengthy list of British demands, including ceding control over foreign policy, in return for peace in spring of the following year. Victoria monitored developments as closely as she could and was thrilled at outmanoeuvring Tsar Nicholas, proudly knighting the officer who had led the negotiations.[64]

It proved short-lived. As Victoria herself put it, there was 'always something afresh' in the region. Later in the year, Afghan rebels stormed the British embassy killing the very same distinguished officer. Victoria was 'dreadfully shocked and startled'.[65] '*How* could it happen?' she demanded of the prime minister, before launching into a questionable lecture on methods of source validation: word of mouth, she thundered, was so much more reliable than written sources which 'depend on the talent of the writer'.[66] The Afghan rebellion did not end for another year.

SMALL WARS ON the frontiers of empire became a way of life during Queen Victoria's long reign. Another broke out in 1882, this time with Egypt; it kicked off the scramble for Africa. In the latter half of the nineteenth century, Egypt was a vassal of the decaying Ottoman Empire and had simultaneously fallen under strong Anglo-French influence following the construction of the Suez Canal in 1869. After years of nationalist agitation, a revolutionary colonel, Ahmed Arabi Pasha, seized control of the government early in 1882. Riots broke out in Alexandria, leaving around fifty Europeans dead.

From London, Queen Victoria watched with alarm. She knew that Egypt, through which the Suez Canal linked Europe with imperial Asia, was 'VITAL'. As turmoil spread, she impatiently insisted that any important news be ciphered directly to her.[67] She soon received intelligence outlining how Arabi was fortifying the harbour to deter the fleet of British and French warships anchored there.[68] Early on the morning of 11 July, British forces launched a ten-hour bombardment of Alexandria. War followed.[69]

The queen followed developments closely. Intelligence suggested that the Ottomans were covertly encouraging Arabi's rebellion and Victoria heard that, in her words, 'the Sultan had bribed a Tobacconist to poison' the previous ruler. 'Monstrous!' was her verdict.[70] She quickly warned her foreign secretary to be mindful of Turkish 'secret intrigues', adding that their troops could turn against British forces at any moment.[71]

Victoria was particularly concerned about the military campaign to come – and the role her third son, Prince Arthur, would play in battle. Arthur, his mother's favourite son, had been destined for a career in the army from an early age. He had already served in Ireland and Canada, and now commanded troops in Egypt. He would soon come under heavy fire from Arabi's larger and powerfully gunned army. With the worried queen's maternal instincts kicking in, the commander-in-chief of the expeditionary force, Garnet Wolseley, kept her personally updated throughout the war and made sure to praise Arthur's performance.[72]

Wolseley was a politically awkward appointment. He was an officer but not a gentleman. As his family was too poor to buy him a commission, he had only achieved his appointment through his mother's intercession with the duke of Wellington, but he proved to be a star officer and rose through the ranks by virtue of, at first his bravery, but later his intellectual mettle. Preferring the company of artists and intellectuals, he was considered a dangerous modernizer and, once having achieved senior rank, battled it out with the queen's cousin, the duke of Cambridge, over reforms, including the expansion of the intelligence department.[73]

But now, with a crisis in Egypt, a talented upstart was what was required. Despite sending regular updates to Buckingham Palace, Wolseley did not tell the queen about his great deception operation. Nor did he tell the duke of Cambridge, who headed the British army. Wolseley developed complicated plans to attack the Egyptians at Aboukir Bay, not far from Alexandria, and, after a deliberately extravagant reconnaissance mission performed with pantomime secrecy, these soon became common knowledge among the enemy. British forces deliberately kept Arabi on high alert to convince him that the advance on Cairo would come from Alexandria.[74] Prince Arthur himself was stationed in Aboukir Bay, perhaps as an elaborate – if unwitting – royal decoy.[75]

Unbeknown to the Egyptians, the real attack would come from Port Said, almost one hundred and fifty miles to the east. Wolseley's deception worked masterfully, even the local war correspondents were fooled. The queen, inevitably, did know in advance. The secretary of state for war told her, in strict secrecy, that the plan was to 'occupy Arabi Pasha' at Alexandria and 'divert his attention from the Canal'.[76] She was delighted with the success of the deception.

Her private secretary praised Wolseley's boldness in using war correspondents to spread misinformation. Doing so, Ponsonby told Wolseley, had created 'some misgivings in the press and an inclination to abuse you – but nothing is so successful as success and the ill-humour vanished when you appeared suddenly at Ismailia instead of Aboukir as they had announced'.[77]

The army then marched inland and the queen received a cypher marked 'very secret' informing her of an imminent large offensive against a village not far from the Suez Canal. Two days later, Wolseley told her of victory.[78] British troops occupied Egypt thereafter. Following the defeat of Egyptian forces, the queen demanded retribution. She wanted Arabi 'severely punished' to prevent a resurrection of revolution and rebellion.[79]

The great deception and subsequent victory would not have been possible without the brave work of Bruce Tulloch, an officer in the War Office's nascent Intelligence Bureau. Tulloch had examined coastal defences at Alexandria prior to the bombardment and, disguised intermittently as a pen-pusher and a hunter, ventured into enemy-controlled territory to gather intelligence on Egyptian positions at Port Said, the Suez Canal, and the village east of Cairo where the decisive battle would eventually be fought. He assessed the potential for sabotage and special operations, noting in particular that bribery through the payment of baksheesh would be rather effective.[80] He also pretended to be a journalist to maintain the deception, telegraphing the *Standard* that rumours of an attack on Suez were untrue. He was on a dangerous mission: the Egyptians kidnapped and slit the throat of one man accused of being a British spy.[81] Such perilous work did not go unrecognized. On his return, Tulloch dined with Queen Victoria at Windsor, regaling her with tales of derring-do and espionage.[82] In some ways, she liked the romance of it all. Throughout her reign, she loved hearing about the adventures and invited many an imperial spy to the castle.

Victoria continued to pay close attention to imperial intrigues during the latter years of her reign. She enjoyed meeting those who

had spent time in central Asia, listening intently to their assessments,[83] and continued to bemoan the lack of intelligence coming
from the frontier. 'All I know is from Reuter and the newspapers,'
she would complain to her India secretary.[84]

She also continued to scheme and make life difficult for the
Russians. On one occasion, the queen lobbied for covert sponsor-
ship of a new railway through the Euphrates valley from Aleppo to
the Persian Gulf. Construction would appear to be a private endeavour, but would secretly be backed by the government so as to 'baffle
Russian progress in the East'.[85] The foreign secretary dampened the
queen's enthusiastic plotting, pointing out how expensive it would
be to guarantee against loss and risk.[86]

Bribery was much simpler as a way of controlling local politics
and the emerging Arab press. Eventually most embassies in the
region had a special fund for this purpose. The British minister in
Tehran knew that there were few Persian clerics 'whose religious
zeal is proof against bribes'. Bribes included cigars, lightbulbs, clocks
and even an artificial limb given to one particular brigand who had
lost an arm. The foreign secretary admitted that he had 'not hesitated to use secret service money' in Persia.[87]

But neither bribery nor deception could prevent the most
visibly disastrous defeat of Victoria's reign. This was the siege
of Khartoum by local religious fighters that began in March
1884 – and ended with the beheading of Major-General Charles
Gordon, who had been sent out to oversee the evacuation of the
city but instead stayed on to defend it, in January of the following
year. This uprising determined the fortunes of two of Victoria's
spies. Frederick Burnaby, now ill and tired of ballooning, wanted
one last adventure. He died fighting in the Sudan, brandishing a
new naval twelve-gauge shotgun which his colleagues regarded
as 'unsporting' but which he thought an excellent technical inno-
vation. Wolseley was luckier, leaving Egypt just before the tide
turned and, after much intrigue, received a peerage and became
commander of the army. His main competitors for the post had

been the queen's cousin, the duke of Cambridge, and her son
Arthur, the duke of Connaught.[88]

THE BULGARIAN COUP of 1886 inflamed Queen Victoria's suspicions of Russian intrigue once more. Alexander of Battenberg had
been prince of Bulgaria for almost a decade when he was overthrown by rebels acting with Russian support. Alexander was part
of Victoria's network of royals: one of his brothers had married
her youngest daughter, Princess Beatrice, and another married her
granddaughter, Princess Victoria of Hesse and the Rhine. The
children from this latter marriage included Earl Mountbatten of
Burma and Princess Alice of Battenberg, the mother of Prince
Philip, duke of Edinburgh. Queen Victoria knew him affectionately as Sandro.

She noted with shock in August 1886 that 'Sandro has been
deposed and taken prisoner'. As ever Victoria heard the news first and,
as more sources confirmed it, she quietly told Beatrice before trying
to comfort Sandro's brother. Next, she characteristically demanded
the prime minister find out more details. What happened? Who was
behind it?[89] For Victoria, this, as was so often the case, was personal
as well as political. It was indeed a royal plot, actually the work of
Tsar Alexander III, who, in contrast to his father, disliked Sandro.
The plan was aided and abetted by Bismarck.

From Balmoral, she fired off telegrams in every direction but received
little response. Britain had few agents on the ground. Eventually, after
an anxious wait, one of her sources confirmed that Sandro was 'safe
and thought to be in Roumania'. The next day, she learnt from Sofia
that the revolutionary leaders had notoriously 'intimate relations' with
Russian agents and that Russia had spread disinformation about a
fake threat coming from Serbia. This had caused Bulgaria to send
troops to the border leaving Sofia vulnerable to a coup.

The queen continued to receive conflicting reports about Sandro's safety. Some thought him in Romania, others spotted what might have been his yacht sailing down the Danube. A few days after the coup, the queen received intelligence from St Petersburg that Sandro had been delivered, on board his yacht, as a 'prisoner' to Russian territory. According to Victoria, this was 'really, monstrous behaviour, clearly admitting, that the Russians had known and planned the whole thing'.[90]

The queen anxiously demanded more intelligence on Sandro's whereabouts. Confusion reigned once again. The longer Sandro was missing, she felt, the more the situation played into Russian hands as they shored up their position in Sofia. She wanted him back in Bulgaria. Victoria's son, Alfred, who had married into the Russian royal family, was no help. Rather than providing insight into what the Russians were up to, he had to ask his mother what was going on as 'wild rumours were afloat'. In fairness, the Russians allowed Sandro to proceed to Ukraine from where he returned to Bulgaria following a successful counter-revolution. The queen was delighted, taking particular pleasure in the Russian newspapers being 'very angry at the failure of their plot!'[91]

This was not the end of it. The ambassador in St Petersburg warned that Russia would not openly intervene but would covertly manoeuvre to 'get rid of Sandro'.[92] Not helping matters, Sandro misread the situation and offered an olive branch to the tsar, but succeeded only in antagonizing him. The tsar fired back an angry response.[93] Reuters passed a copy of both to Queen Victoria, who thought the tsar's response 'most offensive and really brutal'. She asked the foreign secretary to confirm their authenticity.[94]

By now, though, Sandro's authority had been fatally undermined. The queen received a 'very secret' message from the British diplomatic agent in Sofia that Sandro, facing widespread disaffection and continuing conspiracy, was determined to leave the country. She implored him not to.[95] Victoria's counter-schemes came to nothing. Sandro left Bulgaria, and the throne, on 8 September 1886. Three years later he married an Austrian actress, settled in Graz and became a patron of the Viennese Symphony Orchestra – privately, he declared himself to be rather happier.[96]

DESPITE CONTINUED DEMANDS for intelligence from across the empire, Queen Victoria's final years were marred by accusations of naïvety in handling sensitive material. She had long developed a stubborn tendency to go rogue when it came to intelligence overseas, but now this culminated in a security scare inside the royal household. In 1877, she had declared herself empress of India and began to learn Hindustani shortly afterwards, but her fondness for empire brought trouble. In particular, her trust of an Indian servant, Mohammed Abdul Karim, who became her secretary, caused ministers to worry about the security of state secrets and his ability to discreetly influence her thinking in favour of her Muslim subjects.

To mark her golden jubilee in the summer of 1887, Victoria appointed her first Indian servants. One of them, Karim, handsome and ingratiating, soon captured the queen's attention. She quickly elevated him to the role of 'Munshi', or teacher, before making him her secretary for India – much to the irritation of her household who jealously viewed him as a pretentious interloper. This was partly racial prejudice but also indignation at his humble origins: he was a jail clerk and the son of a hospital assistant who served a cavalry regiment, the Central Indian Horse.[97]

Karim's influence quickly grew. At Balmoral Castle, Karim was allocated the room previously occupied by John Brown, a favourite servant of the queen who had died in 1883. As with Brown, the queen simply longed for human companionship, but unlike Brown, who was unassuming, Karim was keen to secure elevation, and even requested a knighthood, one of the few things Victoria turned down. This elevation gained him regular access to the queen as she read and signed confidential documents relating to

India and the sensitive intrigues of the Great Game. Ministers did not trust Karim and feared that he might leak secrets into the hands of adversaries. In response, the queen sought to reassure the prime minister that 'no political papers of any kind are in the Munshi's hands' even in the queen's presence. His role, she continued, was limited to helping her read words she could not understand; besides, his English was not good enough to pose a security risk anyway.[98]

This may have been true in the short term, but ministers still worried that Karim, despite having no access to papers, could learn about confidential matters. He became part of Victoria's inner circle, enjoying gossip with her and other European royalty. Critics worried he had too much influence and, owing to the queen's blind affection, was untouchable.[99]

To make matters worse, Karim became close friends with a young lawyer, Rafiuddin Ahmed. With a reputation as a Muslim political activist and known to Indian police as an untrustworthy 'intriguer', Ahmed had helped found the Muslim Patriotic League and was linked to other, more radical, groups. Through his friend Karim, he now had access to Queen Victoria herself. Nervous courtiers and twitchy ministers suspected him of sending state secrets, supplied by Karim, to the emir of Afghanistan, a key figure in the Great Game between Britain and Russia. Victoria understood how intelligent and able Ahmed was, using him in diplomacy with the Ottoman sultan and even trying to have him appointed to the British embassy in Constantinople.[100]

But ministers fretted about the counter-intelligence risk. The secretary of state for India even warned against sending confidential papers to the queen if Karim would learn of their contents. Neither he nor Salisbury, the prime minister, thought Karim was deliberately dangerous, rather a bit 'stupid'. He might, they cautioned, 'become a tool in the hands of other abler men'.[101] He might leak intelligence or act as a covert agent of influence. One of the queen's secretaries agreed, warning the viceroy of India that Karim had access to his letters and was regaling their contents back to contacts in India. He told the viceroy how the stubborn old queen could not see the danger of letting Karim view confidential material and how Ahmed, the real brains of the operation, had been trying to exploit his artless friend. The police had apparently supplied details on Ahmed, but Victoria would simply not listen. The India Office repeated the warning and urged the viceroy to be careful about what he put in writing to the queen. More dramatically, the queen's physician, Dr John Reid, demanded Karim return any of Victoria's papers that he had in his possession. 'If the Queen were to die and any letters of hers were found in your possession,' he threatened, 'no mercy will be shown you.'[102]

The queen's secretary, Ponsonby, joined with Reid in a prolonged and nasty campaign against Karim. They complained to Victoria about everything they could find, ranging from Karim's multiple wives, designated 'aunts', who spat on carpets, to his sexual promiscuity and venereal disease – he suffered from repeated bouts of gonorrhoea. They complained mostly about his race and also his social status. Victoria was having none of it, pointing out that two of her archbishops had been the sons of a butcher and grocer. She was especially hot on racial prejudice, forbidding the use of the term 'black men' and even lecturing Lord Salisbury on the matter. Alas, Karim, as a dedicated social climber, greatly enjoyed discriminating against his fellow countrymen.[103]

Nevertheless, Karim – and Ahmed – were discreetly watched. When Karim returned on a visit to India in 1896, the viceroy put him under surveillance, asking the police to closely monitor his movements and contacts. Spying on a member of the queen's inner circle was inevitably a particularly delicate operation. The secretary of state for India approved 'unobtrusive supervision' but warned any amount of surveillance would backfire if the queen ever found out. Little was written down.[104]

Despite attempts at discretion, a deep rift developed between the queen and her household. Victoria continued to treat Karim with a level of respect her courtiers felt was undeserved. Karim responded with an infuriating sense of entitlement: when accompanying the queen overseas he complained about his lack of local newspaper coverage. In spring 1897, he travelled with the queen to the French Riviera against the explicit wishes of the royal household who threatened to go on strike. The courtiers were even more incensed when his friend Rafiuddin Ahmed turned up at the hotel uninvited. Fearing that Ahmed was on the hunt for sensitive diplomatic material, the queen's private secretary brusquely dismissed him.[105]

Far from thanking her advisers for protecting her from a potential security risk, the queen was furious. She invited Ahmed to a court ball by way of apology. More significantly, she suggested that her ministers recruit him to gather intelligence on Muslims, and used him in diplomacy with the Ottoman Empire. This was a quite staggering divergence from the attitude of her civil servants. The India Office thought that Ahmed's relationship with the queen – through Karim – was a breach of security.[106] Salisbury warned her that, if he were to be appointed as a diplomat, Ahmed would require 'access to most important secrets'. This was too much and Salisbury tactfully rebuffed her meddling: reports on Ahmed's character were 'too divergent' to make a judgement as to his fitness. 'The danger of misplaced confidence,' Salisbury warned, 'would be very serious.'[107]

In April 1897, Ponsonby complained to a friend about the ongoing Karim saga, admitting defeat in the face of an implacable queen:

We been [sic] having a good deal of trouble lately about the Munshi here, and although we have tried our best, we cannot get the Queen to realize how very dangerous it is for her to allow this man to see every confidential paper relating to India. The Queen insists on bringing the Munshi forward as much as she can, & if it were not for our protest, I don't know where She would stop. Fortunately, he happens to be a thoroughly stupid and uneducated man., & his one idea in life seems to be to do nothing and eat as much as he can.

Despite his obvious prejudice, Ponsonby was in a sense correct: Karim represented no threat at all and even his friends were harmless.[108]

Nevertheless, nervous ministers, high on the intrigue and paranoia of the Great Game, thought Ahmed a 'ruffian' agitator, a 'Mahomedan intriguer', perhaps even a spy. They placed him under surveillance again in 1898 but still found no conclusive proof of wrongdoing. Victoria saw him as a useful informant, providing information on the attitudes of Muslims in India. Just as she had done with European royals and the Foreign Office, she used his intelligence and insights to challenge the India Office and pursue her own instincts. She was right about Ahmed's abilities and, decades later, having served as the minister for education in Bombay, he was eventually knighted.[109]

On the prickly matter of Karim, the queen remained even more intransigent. She angrily accused her household of spying on him. 'I am terribly annoyed... I feel continually aggrieved at my Gentlemen wishing to spy to and interfere with one of my people whom I have no personal reason of proof of doubting and I am greatly distressed about what has happened.'[110] And she had a point: successive private secretaries had tried to dig up as much dirt as possible to discredit him, but the queen was ever unmoved, dismissing all their protestations as prejudice and jealousy.[111] Reid complained that 'the Queen seems off her head'.[112] She had become an increasingly emotional consumer of intelligence, relying more on instincts than objective analysis. Her blind hatred of Russia caused her to jump on any information that implied wrongdoing and ignore the rest. Her love of Karim blinded her to the security worries of the royal household. This time, though, she was right.

Eventually, the secretary of state for India tried to draw a line under the affair and told the viceroy that, after being placed under surveillance, Karim had done nothing wrong and that the royal household was overreacting to his friendship with Ahmed.[113] There remains no evidence that he passed on state secrets or that he influenced her thoughts on India.[114] It made little difference. Sadly, after Victoria's death in 1901, the new king, Edward VII, sent Karim back to India and burned his correspondence with the queen. He lived quietly on the estate at Agra that the queen had given him. Following Karim's death eight years later, Edward sent detectives to confiscate any remaining documents held at his house in India, leaving his family with few records of his loyal service. They successfully hid and preserved his diary, which only surfaced in 2011.[115] This was not the last time that the royal machine would fail to airbrush things it did not like from the historical record.

QUEEN VICTORIA'S SECURITY: FENIANS AND ANARCHISTS

'Your Majesty is as safe as any person in your dominions'

Lord Salisbury, 1898[1]

IN EARLY 1881, some revolutionaries were digging beneath a cheese shop in St Petersburg. Part of a dedicated and violent group called 'The People's Will', their purpose was to mine the road above with explosives and assassinate Tsar Alexander II of Russia. As a back-up plan, they would use four different bomb-throwing assassins, together with further groups armed with guns, knives and other exotic weapons stationed in the street above. It was the route that the tsar often took when returning to the Winter Palace from inspecting the troops. He travelled in a bulletproof carriage and had survived several previous assassination attempts, including dynamiting the imperial train and a bombing of the Winter Palace only a year before. The People's Will had been working on these preparations zealously for over a year.

The leader of the actual attack was Sophia Perovskaya, stepping in for her husband who was arrested two days before. On Sunday 13 March 1881, the tsar travelled home after inspecting his troops. He was heavily guarded by Cossacks. His carriage was followed by three sleighs transporting his chief of security, two senior police officers and yet more troops. The security-conscious retinue altered the route and avoided the laboriously constructed cheese-shop tunnel that had been packed with tons of dynamite. But the four bomb teams were waiting and Perovskaya gave the signal by ostentatiously pulling out a handkerchief and blowing her nose. At 2.15 the first bomb was thrown and exploded under the tsar's carriage.[2]

There was a tremendous roar. One of the Cossacks was killed and many civilians nearby were wounded. The coach was heavily protected with steel, leaving the tsar shocked but not injured. The bomber, Nikolai Rysakov, was captured almost immediately. Despite exhortations to leave the scene, the tsar wanted to see his would-be assassin and offer sympathy to the victims. 'Thank God, I'm untouched,' he told those around him.

A second bomber now struck, reportedly shouting gleefully: 'You spoke too soon!' There was another mighty roar. This time, the tsar was mortally injured, together with some of the assassins and many bystanders. His stomach torn open and his legs in tatters, he lay bleeding on the snow alongside his killers. Other bombers and pistoleers moved forward, but realized they were not needed. The tsar asked to be taken to the Winter Palace to die. He perished within an hour.[3]

Back in Windsor, Queen Victoria's private secretary, Henry Ponsonby, received the news via a locked despatch box that arrived as he ate dinner with his wife and children. He would usually skim its contents casually before spiriting them away from prying eyes. On this Sunday evening, he unlocked the box, glanced at the telegram inside, handed it to his wife and immediately left the room. He hurried to tell the queen personally, leaving his startled wife waving the dramatic piece of paper and explaining the news to her family.[4]

Victoria was getting older and approaching her golden jubilee. She was as straight-talking as ever and took a characteristically hard line: 'No punishment is bad enough for the murderers,' she wrote, 'hanging is too good.'[5]

The assassination formed an early high point of anarchist political violence, the first wave of modern terrorism. Victoria's sources, including her son Alfred, who had married the tsar's daughter, provided her with speedy updates about the killing and the unfolding security situation.[6] Her network of continental royals visiting Russia for the funeral supplied her with regular bulletins on the political repercussions.[7]

Victoria was no fan of Russia, but she read the incoming reports with great interest and feared for the safety of the new emperor. For obvious reasons, assassination of sovereigns – however unfriendly – was an issue close to her heart. She wondered whether anarchists had infiltrated the tsar's servants, or, heaven forbid, 'even higher classes'. No one, she continued, now 'trusted his neighbour' in St Petersburg. She read with growing dismay about excavations around the Winter Palace as security forces hunted for unexploded bombs.[8]

Even though the conspirators had no connection to Britain, the assassination resurrected the thorny issue of London's refugee policy and disinclination to spy on political discontents. Britain's apparent softness remained a sore point for European leaders, just as it had been back in the 1850s. Russian royalty, flailing angrily after the assassination, accused Britain of protecting international criminals. Victoria's position had not changed over three decades.

Under pressure from the queen, Ponsonby sheepishly explained to Victoria that Britain had no extradition treaty with Russia. She was not impressed: 'Should there not be one?' she fired at the foreign secretary.[9] Sympathizing with beleaguered sovereigns, Victoria wanted to evict all refugees from Britain, leaving the home secretary to tell her that doing so was 'politically impossible'. The prime minister agreed: it would go against British traditions.[10] It formed yet another issue over which Victoria, stubborn as ever, was at odds with her government.

Victoria was disappointed that Britain refused to work with European partners to determine, as she put it, 'the best mode of international defence against the revolutionary attempts'. For now, the country still prided itself on a liberal asylum policy and a strong tradition of civil liberties. Ahead of her time, Victoria insisted that at the very least she should express sympathy and desire 'to tolerate no murderous plots here against foreign sovereigns'.[11]

Unwilling to ramp up political espionage, the British looked to other methods to counter political violence, including clamping down on public support for terrorism. Although the matter was largely unspoken – and indeed could not be spoken of – those around her knew the anarchist threat to Victoria personally was limited because of her decision to virtually withdraw from public life following the death of Prince Albert in 1861. Secluded at Windsor, she rarely used Buckingham Palace. Appearances were few and so she presented only a fleeting target for even the most ambitious terrorist. Anyone digging beneath a cheese shop in London was probably wasting their time.

Some anarchists and trouble-makers were present, however. The Foreign Office hoped that they would remain quiet and fade into the background, but some were annoyingly vocal. Johann Most was a German anarchist who had settled in London having been exiled first from his homeland and then from France. From here, he advocated terrorism to bring about revolution, popularizing the anarchist idea of propaganda of the deed. Shortly after the assassination of the tsar, Most wrote an incendiary article glorifying the attack and was arrested after repeating his remarks at a socialist meeting. The queen thought *Freiheit*, the 'shocking paper' that published Most's article, should be prosecuted.[12] Ponsonby passed on the queen's deep concerns to William Harcourt, the home secretary, who, in turn, forwarded them on to the commissioner of the Metropolitan Police with the note: 'Tell the police to look after this.'[13] Most was imprisoned for eighteen months before emigrating to America.

Victoria went further still, asking the foreign secretary to consider 'the necessity of combining with other nations against the nihilists'.[14] This was a step too far for politicians bent on upholding Britain's liberal traditions and the foreign secretary was suitably dismissive: 'No application has yet been made to us to combine with other nations against the nihilists. Our police give all the information they obtain to the continental governments.'[15]

Most's outburst and imprisonment had coincided with the last attempt to kill Victoria. On 2 March 1882, the queen had just crossed the platform of Windsor station to say goodbye to Princess Beatrice. Roderick Maclean, standing at the entrance to the station among the crowd, fired a revolver at her. A number of nearby Eton schoolboys beat him with their umbrellas before he was seized by the police. Some tried to connect him with Most and foreign anarchism, but this, the eighth and final assassination attempt on Victoria, in fact followed a rather familiar pattern. The weapon proved to be outdated and ineffective. Some reports even claimed it was a toy gun. At his trial, Maclean complained that he had sent some of his poems to the queen at Windsor Castle and had received rude replies. Once it was revealed that he had already spent time at Somerset Lunatic Asylum, he was soon despatched to Broadmoor where he spent the rest of his days.[16]

The authorities did not know that this amateur and bewildered effort would be the last attack. Meanwhile, Irish terrorism now posed a growing problem. Despite a volatile atmosphere in Ireland, the British mainland had been reasonably quiet since 1867 when Fenian rebels spectacularly failed to break an inmate out of a London jail. The bomb, intended to blow up a prison wall, killed twelve innocent bystanders and injured many more. It caused widespread outrage, seriously undermining the Fenians' efforts to secure Home Rule for Ireland. A few intelligence scares followed, although Victoria remained aloof. When warned of a plot to kidnap her, the queen quipped that if the Fenians were 'so silly' as to seize her, they would find her a 'very inconvenient charge'. When faulty intelligence suggested eighty Fenians were travelling from Canada to murder her, she complained that the resulting security precautions made her feel like a prisoner.[17] Slightly ominously, the home secretary did tell Victoria that his detectives were 'inefficient' and their 'informers constantly false'. Intelligence was weak.[18]

The Fenian terrorist threat became much more real in the early 1880s. The queen, now in her sixties, had become stoically accustomed to threats on her life. This time it was different; and she did not feel safe. Although in some ways more dangerous, the aspiring assassins of the 1840s were hapless lone gunmen, some of whom were certifiably insane. Fast forward forty years and terrorism was part of an international conspiracy. Violent Fenians, motivated by decades of famine and oppression, emboldened by Home Rule being debated in parliament, found support and funding among Irish émigrés in America. In dynamite, they now had modern weaponry as lethal as it was portable. And with the assassination of the Russian tsar, Victoria had already seen the damage it could do.[19] She took the threat seriously, enquiring about what was being done to protect Buckingham Palace. Her home secretary, William Harcourt, dismissed it as 'a Fenian scare of the old clumsy kind'.[20]

Harcourt was wrong. Between 1881 and 1885, Fenians carried out a series of attacks across England. Early targets included police forces in Liverpool and military barracks in Chester. In 1883, bombs exploded in Whitehall, at the *Times* offices and on the London Underground. Victoria's son Alfred was inside the House of Commons when the Whitehall bomb detonated in March and heard the explosion clearly. The queen was twenty-five miles away at Windsor, but Ponsonby, who visited the scene, quickly informed her of the 'wild appearance of shattered stone, glass, wood and plaster'. He told her that 'there is no clue and can be no clue to the actual individuals who committed the deed'.[21] The next day, Harcourt confirmed that he had no intelligence, other than the obvious assumption that the same gang was behind the string of attacks.[22]

The following year, Fenians successfully targeted London rail stations and police headquarters at Scotland Yard. In 1885, explosions rocked the Houses of Parliament and the Tower of London. The sustained terrorism campaign led to the creation of Special Branch, to which Queen Victoria quickly offered royal patronage. She feared the royal family would be a target and urged for every security precaution to be taken.[23] In particular, she was scared that the royal train would be bombed as it travelled through remote countryside to Balmoral, so detectives scoured the route for explosives, inspecting every inch of track, bridge and tunnel. Undercover detectives inside Balmoral kept a discreet eye on all strangers.

The prince of Wales personally recommended one secret agent to Special Branch.[24] The queen knew that 'detectives are all over the country'.[25] Some unobtrusively followed Victoria, occasionally without her knowledge. Others followed her family. When, in 1885, detectives received intelligence about an assassination threat against one of Victoria's sons, they did not tell the prince on the grounds that he would rather not know 'that anything of this unpleasant nature was in the air'. Instead, detectives put him under secret surveillance. As one later recalled: 'When he drove anywhere in his carriage I followed at a discreet distance in a hansom; when he came out of any house he had been visiting of an evening, I was on the kerb hard by, carefully keeping in shadow.'[26]

By 1895, Harcourt had toughened security measures but he seldom pleased the queen. She now thought him boring, overly sensitive to criticism, and annoyingly overprotective regarding her security. He accused her of constant nagging, especially about his taking too many police precautions. On one occasion, Harcourt defended himself by saying 'if anything had occurred I should have been justly censured for want of care'. Summing up the classic counter-terrorism paradox, which still frustrates heads of domestic intelligence today, he added: 'It is a little embarrassing to be constantly worried, first of all to do a great deal that is unnecessary and then to be blamed for doing what is prudent... I must endure the reproach of having protected the Queen too much, but I shall not face the blame of having protected her too little.'[27]

The terrorists enjoyed support from Fenian societies across the Atlantic in Chicago, Boston and New York, where newspapers openly advocated the assassination of Queen Victoria. Ponsonby was shocked and concerned. 'Her Majesty,' he wrote to the foreign secretary on reading one particular account, 'asks if this is true?'[28] Her government complained to its US counterparts about their harbouring of dissidents and even their incitement to regicide, but received no response.[29] This was rather ironic given similar European criticisms of Britain during recent decades. The nervous queen persistently summoned the home secretary for updates and reassurance.[30] He put his faith in the stretched intelligence system, telling her that 'many suspected men are under observation and have been so for a long time'.[31]

Despite the frequency of the bombings, British intelligence did enjoy some successes. Scotland Yard and the Home Office had developed a network of informants and agents, not just in Britain, but in Ireland and the United States too. This was an international intelligence operation, but one which, on the surface at least, was still rather squeamish about espionage. When Ponsonby congratulated the police on the arrest of a particular terrorist in 1883, he made sure to note that the success was all the more impressive given the police's distaste for espionage. 'I doubt,' he wrote, 'if Englishmen could ever take up the business as the French do.'[32] The queen's circle were seemingly unaware of some of the more distasteful methods, including agents provocateurs, which the government employed unofficially.

Victoria took a close interest in those arrested. She had learnt a harsh lesson the previous year when Michael Davitt, an Irish republican politician, was released from prison. 'Is it *possible* that Michael Davitt, known as one of the worst of the treasonable agitators, is also to be released?' she asked the prime minister. 'I cannot believe it!'[33] Just two days later, republicans murdered the new chief secretary for Ireland, Frederick Cavendish, in Dublin. The queen was furious and rebuked her government: 'this horrible event' was 'the *direct result*' of releasing Davitt and other Irish prisoners. She lobbied for 'such strong measures as may give her and the country security, or at least as much security as is possible'.[34]

In June 1883, Harcourt told Victoria that 'we have the enemy by the throat'. The arrest of five members of a Fenian gang had bolstered his confidence, and he hurried straight to Windsor to tell the queen the good news.[35] The arrested Fenians – bar one, who betrayed his friends in return for deportation – were sentenced to life imprisonment for conspiracy to 'depose the queen; to levy war upon the queen; to intimidate and overawe the Houses of Parliament'.[36] Nonetheless, the dynamite campaign continued until 1885.

Two years later, the Fenians planned one more spectacular: bombing Queen Victoria's golden jubilee celebrations at Westminster Abbey. In one of the most dramatic twists of Victoria's long, intrigue-filled reign, the mastermind of the plot was General Francis Millen, an Irish mercenary – but also a secret agent working for the British, albeit intermittently and unreliably.

Millen was born in Tyrone and shaped by the conflicts of the mid-nineteenth century. With red hair, a beard and a ruddy complexion, he cultivated the image of a senior commander. He served in the Crimea and leveraged this experience to secure a commission in the Mexican liberal army, rising to the rank of brigadier-general while allegedly also working for the Americans as a spy. By 1865, he had travelled to Ireland to help organize Fenian military activity, but the locals described him as a theatrical, 'banana-republic'-style officer. His first offer to work for the British, made the following year, was the result of this bitter factional fighting among the Irish militants, together with a desire for money.[37]

Millen thereafter had worked intermittently for the enemy. The British, keen for intelligence on his erstwhile colleagues, were receptive to his advances, and the prime minister himself, Lord Salisbury, personally sanctioned the recruitment of Millen as a British agent. Salisbury took deep interest in the material he provided, his red-inked monogram 'S' appearing on some of Millen's most sensitive intelligence. Salisbury then approved using Millen as an agent provocateur to spearhead an assassination plot during the jubilee so as to smash the Fenian dynamite gangs once and for all and to destroy the Irish leader Charles Parnell by implicating him in the attempted murder of the queen.[38]

Edward Jenkinson was a key figure behind the plot, and seemingly in correspondence with Millen himself during the planning phase. He acted as an unofficial spymaster working in the Home Office, building a network of Irish agents who reported to him personally and engaged in extra-legal activities – much to the frustration of the police. Jenkinson used agents to provoke potential conspirators to take action. One of his agents provocateurs had even used secret service money to fund bombing campaigns. Differing from Salisbury in motive, Jenkinson hoped to use the plot to frighten his own government into appeasing Irish demands.[39] The queen, whose own private secretary scorned espionage, had earlier praised the efforts of Jenkinson. 'His courage and determination', she told the home secretary in 1883, 'have been of the *utmost use*'. He deserved, '*the very highest praise*'.[40] Had she known what he was up to in 1887, her opinion may well have changed.

Victoria's jubilee took place on 20 June 1887. She was a reluctant participant: naturally disliking showy occasions and for so long a recluse following Albert's untimely death. Ministers had to persuade her, stubborn and grumpy as ever, to take part in the pageantry at all. She marked the occasion with a splendid royal banquet at Buckingham Palace at which her distinguished relatives sat around a grand horseshoe table and dined off the finest golden plates. They included her private intelligence sources from across Europe who had provided such useful insights over the past five decades. Vicky was there; so too were royals from Schleswig-Holstein and most other parts of Germany, the king of Denmark, father of the princess of Wales, and many others.

The following day, Victoria processed in an open-topped carriage from Buckingham Palace to Westminster Abbey for the ceremony, accompanied by her son-in-law, Crown Prince Fritz of Prussia, dazzling in a white and silver uniform. Even the notoriously dowdy queen had reluctantly dressed up for the occasion.[41] Cheering crowds lined the route; the abbey was packed with British nobility and politicians. Plain clothes detectives watched anxiously for trouble.

The upper echelons of Scotland Yard had bigger worries. They knew that Fenians directed by Millen had set sail from New York ten days earlier. Their mission: to detonate a bomb at Westminster Abbey. Three men, led by a tough civil war veteran, were carrying Smith & Wesson revolvers, plenty of ammunition and more importantly a large amount of high-quality Atlas dynamite together with detonators.[42] Informants in America had quickly tipped off their handlers in Scotland Yard, although the intelligence would not have come as a surprise to Jenkinson in the Home Office. Special Branch stumbled upon the conspiracy quite independently and kept the Fenians under close surveillance. But no one was sure just how many attackers were converging on London.[43]

In the abbey, James Monro, assistant commissioner of the Metropolitan Police and head of its secret section, sat nervously through the jubilee ceremony. Fearing that an agent provocateur could well trigger a terrorist attack, let alone corrupt Britain's moral fibre, he had vehemently opposed Jenkinson's unorthodox espionage methods, and even arrested some of his agents. Monro won the bureaucratic battle; Jenkinson was fired earlier in the year, his networks wound up.[44] Scotland Yard quickly confronted Millen with details of the plot, causing him to back off. In truth, no one in Britain's rather fragmented security apparatus knew exactly what was going on.

Accordingly, Monro remained concerned enough about the event not to let his own children take up their reserved seats. Just in case. There still remained a possibility that the conspirators had managed to smuggle some dynamite into the vaults. Monro received a message to that effect, but it was too late to make enquiries without causing panic among the great and the good who had entered the abbey. All he could do was pray.[45]

The ceremony left the queen, in her own words, 'half dead'.[46] She was exhausted by the end, but it passed peacefully. There was no bomb. The terrorists docked late in Liverpool and missed the big day, but while plotting further attacks in the following months they inadvertently led the police to many of the Fenians operating in the mainland. They were given remarkable licence. One of them twice visited Windsor Castle, carefully timing his possible escape by train after planting a bomb. Another managed to get inside the House of Commons.[47] When they had gathered enough evidence, the police rounded them up – all but one. Millen unsurprisingly evaded arrest and managed to escape to New York. From across the Atlantic, he even offered to resume his role as an informant the following year. Strikingly, Prime Minister Salisbury was keen to accept, but the police and Home Office talked him out of it – since it would have signalled a return to Jenkinson's more dangerous agent provocateur methods.[48]

The Fenians did not realize that Millen was a British agent, but a decade later, politicians in parliament alleged that the affair had been a 'put-up job' devised by the secret service. Robert Anderson, the handler who received the intelligence about the gang's departure for Liverpool, later admitted as much: 'Millen arrived in Britain to carry out his two-fold mission on behalf of Clan na Gael and the British Government.'[49] In reality, no one was quite sure how the day would go.

Did Victoria know she was being used as bait in a dangerous agent provocateur operation authorized by the prime minister? The day before the jubilee, Salisbury told her that his only anxiety was 'the enormous number of people, half a million being expected to come into London'.[50] There is no evidence that she was given precise details, but she was certainly aware of such tradecraft. Five years earlier, in 1882, the police had told her about how they had held off arresting one particular Fenian terrorist in order, as she put it, 'to be able to get at his accomplices'.[51]

A WAVE OF anarchist assassinations on the Continent the following decade once more focused the attention of Special Branch on terrorism. In the space of a few short years, anarchists killed the French president and the empress of Austria-Hungary. The ideas also gained an alarming intellectual respectability: the painters Gustave Courbet, Camille Pissarro and Georges Seurat declared themselves to be 'anarchists', as did the dramatist Oscar Wilde, even though they were more likely to be found sipping herbal tea than throwing bombs. Fearing for her own safety, Queen Victoria was horrified. Wild rumours of worldwide conspiracies to wipe out every monarch swirled across the Channel.[52]

Luckily for her, British anarchists were a lot less successful than their continental counterparts. The nascent security establishment had gained experience from the Fenian violence, the world's first modern terrorist campaign. The government had already passed anti-explosives laws in 1883, while Special Branch acquired valuable expertise countering terrorism and protecting the monarch which now enabled them to prevent numerous anarchist bombings. The police even developed new means of disposing of recovered bombs. Neither the queen nor any visiting monarch suffered a terrorist attack on British soil; this achievement became the envy of Europe.[53]

In February 1894, a French anarchist terrorist, Martial Bourdin, attempted to detonate a bomb outside the Royal Observatory in Greenwich Park. Although he cackhandedly succeeded only in blowing himself up, the incident showed Britain could not be complacent. A week later, the home secretary, Herbert Asquith, updated the queen: the bomb, made from a gas pipe containing dynamite, exploded prematurely in Bourdin's hand after he charged it with sulphuric acid too early. Detectives, he told her, thought the intended target was only a trial before a bigger attack and were still frantically trying to trace the source of a large sum of money found on Bourdin's mutilated corpse.[54] Victoria noted the discovery of 'a shocking anarchist Club in London, almost entirely composed of foreigners'.[55]

Shortly afterwards, Lord Salisbury, now leader of the opposition, put forward an Aliens Bill designed to counter the entangled issues of anarchism and immigration. In 1894, as parliament debated the bill over the summer, an Italian anarchist fatally stabbed the

French president in Lyon. 'How dreadful!' wrote the queen, the young assassin 'glories in the deed'.[56] She quickly lobbied the prime minister, Lord Rosebery, to pass the sections on anarchism. Britain's willingness to allow 'these monstrous anarchists and assassins to live here and hatch their horrible plots in our country', she thundered, was doing the government 'incalculable harm abroad'.[57]

Although professing sympathy, Rosebery pointed out that the bill ran contrary to Britain's proud tradition of asylum. He politely reminded her that 'not a single conspiracy against any foreign power or potentate has been hatched in this country' and, firing back at the queen's perceived enthusiasm for political surveillance, added that 'our system of police supervision here is much more efficacious than that pursued on the continent'. Despite the queen's protestations, the bill failed.[58]

Four years later, another Italian anarchist assassinated the Austrian empress on the shore of Lake Geneva, fatally stabbing her as she boarded a steamboat. Queen Victoria was horrified, again receiving gory details of the weapon – a shoemaker's awl – and the blood stain on the dress of the empress.[59] She noted shortly afterwards that Italy intended to 'take stern measures to prevent these horrible murderers and anarchists from remaining in neutral Countries, and to be sent back to their own'.[60]

The queen was correct. Italy proposed an international confer-ence to counter anarchist terrorism, but her own government, having earlier helped defeat a similar initiative, was reluctant to respond to the invitation. This time, Victoria, shocked by the death of the empress, pressed the prime minister for action.[61] She was an impressively early advocate of international counter-terrorism co-operation. The head of the Metropolitan Police was not – and strongly opposed the idea. Quite simply, he found it almost impos-sible to define what an anarchist was in the first place, to be able to declare who was an anarchist and who was not. He added that 'no English anarchist had ever been found; and that even foreign anarchists made no criminal attempts here' because popular opinion was so against anarchism. For similar reasons, he insisted Victoria was perfectly safe.[62]

Influenced by the queen's persistent lobbying, Salisbury, now prime minister again, was more sympathetic to the Italian efforts and sent a delegation to the conference that took place late in 1898.[63] Despite pressure from Windsor, the British team abstained from many of the votes and worked behind the scenes to tone down what they saw as a more extreme continental approach. The British were the only country – of twenty-one represented at the conference – to dissent from the final agreement that encouraged governments to create surveillance agencies to monitor anarchists, share intelligence on anarchism, and introduce legislation to prohibit membership of anarchist organizations and distribution of anarchist propaganda.[64]

The Rome Conference of 1889 did see some progress, although, too sensitive to be committed to paper, it stayed off the record. The colourful British delegate, Howard Vincent, one of the founders of Special Branch who had since become a Conservative politician, initiated quiet meetings in the wings of the conference in which he agreed to increase intelligence sharing across borders and develop better communication between police forces. He later claimed that doing so resulted in the prevention of 'anarchist outrages' for a year and a half. Vincent, also a vociferous imperialist, was knighted that year for his services.[65] Victoria saw this as a vindication of her views and was pleased.

QUEEN VICTORIA DIED on 22 January 1901 after sixty-three years on the throne. Just like Elizabeth I, she had been the top 'customer' for intelligence, and had also directed particular operations. Not always the most objective of analysts when it came to interpreting the information, she preferred her instincts. On anarchism, her fears were correct and she knew the threat was growing. Six months before her death, King Umberto of Italy was shot four times and killed in Monza. President McKinley of the United States suffered a similar fate only a year later. Both the perpetrators were anarchists.

Partly at the exhortation of Victoria, intelligence had expanded. Special Branch had been created in direct response to the threat of assassination from the Fenians. Its commander also presided over a force of over six hundred specialist detectives, which had numbered just eight men at the start of her reign. Alongside them was a secretive political surveillance division called Section D, just the sort of thing that the queen had pressed for – and which figures like Palmerston had long resisted.[66] Victoria was straight-talking and persistently berated her ministers. She had pressed them to be tougher on surveillance, going against popular opinion in the process; she had demanded access to intelligence received by her ministers, while developing her own private networks which she used to outmanoeuvre her governments; she had opposed covert action in support of liberal uprisings, while thoroughly enjoying tales of deception and subversion elsewhere. She had even been used as bait in intelligence operations to lure out assassins. Twice.

As her reign progressed, Victoria increasingly saw security policy, like foreign policy more broadly, as her own fiefdom. This was illustrated by a remarkable conversation the queen held with the incoming foreign secretary, Lord Rosebery, in 1886. As he nervously received his seals from the queen, she impressed upon him the importance of the eastern question and, warning him that Russia was watching the new government closely, told him in no uncertain terms that there would be no change in foreign policy. Extraordinarily, she then 'urged Lord Rosebery not to bring too many matters before the Cabinet, as nothing was decided there'. It would, she continued, 'be far better to discuss everything with me and Mr Gladstone'. She told him that she 'frequently had intelligence of a secret nature, which it would be useful and interesting for him to hear, and which came from a reliable source'.[67]

Victoria used intelligence to pursue her own interests and beliefs. She was perhaps the last to do this quite so directly. Her activities created tension between crown and ministers about the limits of the constitution. Throughout her reign, Victoria constantly and stubbornly demanded the latest intelligence. Her private sources ebbed and flowed depending on the country involved and which of her relatives were on the throne. On Germany, for example, she really did have the best sources, but on imperial matters she was more reliant on her government. Victoria exploited the dearth of government sources to impose her own will. Knowledge, after all, is power. The problem for Victoria was that as intelligence started to become more professionalized towards the end of her reign, scope to use her own private sources to influence or outmanoeuvre the government narrowed.

Her son, who succeeded her as Edward VII, was less interested in statecraft. Such was his reputation as a playboy prince, she deliberately withheld sensitive information from him for as long as possible. When he finally inherited the throne, the inexperienced king hoped to use royal sources to influence foreign policy just as his mother had done. But secret service became more of a state activity in the early twentieth century, and ministers felt less reliant on royal networks. How Edward responded to these changes would help shape relations between crown and government for the next hundred years.

EDWARD VII AND THE
MODERNIZATION OF INTELLIGENCE

*'I cannot be indifferent to the assassination of a member of
my profession, or if you like, a member of my guild.'*

Edward VII[1]

IN 1863, A young and rather minor princess, Alexandra of
Denmark, crossed the English Channel. Her family had been
relatively unknown until 1852, when her father, Prince Christian,
was selected with the consent of the major European powers to
succeed his second cousin as king of Denmark. She was about to
become the wife of Albert Edward, prince of Wales, the heir apparent of Queen Victoria, largely at the behest of her daughter Vicky.
The subsequent wedding at Windsor was low key – albeit cheered
loudly by local Eton schoolboys. In the space of just a few years, her
life had transformed. Not only had she married Prince Albert and
her father become king of Denmark but her brother became king
of Greece as George I. Alexandra, or 'Alix', further complicated the
already labyrinthine connections of the British royal family, since
her sister married the heir of the Russian throne and her nephew was
the future Kaiser Wilhelm of Germany: her least favourite country.
Something was bound to go wrong, and it soon did.

☗

EDWARD, PRINCE OF Wales, and his young wife, Alix, waited nervously as Prussian forces marched across the snowy border into Denmark in February 1864. Given that the couple had recently married and Alix was the daughter of the Danish king, they had a keen interest in how the war over Schleswig-Holstein would play out. The prince, who would one day become King Edward VII, politely asked his mother for access to secret Foreign Office documents.

Queen Victoria firmly refused. A supporter of German unification, she was busily opposing ministerial plans to support the beleaguered Danes against the advancing Prussians. Bringing Edward, then in his early twenties, into the secret affairs of state would not have helped her cause. More importantly, though, she simply did not trust her own son. She admitted that he was not always 'as discreet as he should be'. Consequently, she agreed, as a rather poor compromise, to send him summaries of certain documents – which she herself had selected.[2]

The queen was not alone in her distrust. After the Franco-Prussian War in 1870, the foreign secretary also worried about Edward's indiscretion. He asked one of Victoria's advisers whether 'really confidential matters' would remain secret if divulged to him. The prince, he explained, 'asked me to keep him informed during the war. One evening I got four messages from different friends telling me to be careful. One of my first notes to him had been handed round a dinner party.'[3]

Edward served the bulk of his long apprenticeship without access to secret intelligence – or even the more mundane matters of state. Worse than being indiscreet, Edward was vulnerable to blackmail. He was a playboy prince, indulging in illegal card games and extramarital relations with glamorous actresses, wealthy socialites and high-class prostitutes. Rumour has it that a future chief of MI6, Stewart Menzies, was an illegitimate son: they certainly shared physical attributes and Menzies' mother climbed suspiciously quickly into the highest reaches of society. Either way, Menzies repeatedly used his supposed royal connection, and associated mystique, during his intelligence career.[4]

Edward tried to keep his affairs under the radar, regularly travelling semi-incognito to the Continent. He tried to shake off the undercover French detectives who tailed him on frequent visits to lovers and brothels in the hopes of discovering whether any of his mistresses were in fact royalist agents of influence operating against the French republic.[5] Another French detective served as his personal protection officer largely because of his knowledge of the Parisian underworld.[6] Meanwhile, German spies watched his movements similarly closely. They were intrigued by his dealings with French aristocrats, including the president himself.[7] Perhaps inevitably, Edward's lifestyle – so at odds with Victorian propriety – left him wide open to blackmail. On one occasion he despatched a trusted courier, disguised as an autograph hunter, to acquire incriminating letters he had written to a lover, the self-proclaimed 'greatest whore in the world', whose brother was using them to blackmail him.[8]

In addition to Edward being indiscreet and a potential security risk, he had a reputation for idleness. It is of little surprise that Victoria continued to block his access to state secrets. Instead, she allowed his younger brother, Prince Leopold, to advise her on confidential matters. Edward was well aware of the arrangement, and of the humiliating fact that his mother thought Leopold more fit to be king than he.[9] Indeed, she seemed to prefer any of his siblings, and when she learnt that Edward would be dragged into court as the result of a gambling scandal, she looked at Prince Arthur, another of her sons, and burst out: 'If only you were the eldest!'[10]

Edward watched the red boxes coming and going from his mother's rooms, piling up on her desk where they remained tantalizingly out of reach. It was not so much that he was desperate for secret material; more that he objected to being ignorant of important affairs which people discussed in his hearing. The prince decided to take matters into his own hands by befriending Charles Dilke, the radical under-secretary of state for foreign affairs whom the queen hated because his private life was even racier than that of her son. Upon meeting Dilke for the first time in March 1880, Edward quickly turned on the famed charm. They were like minds and recognized each other instantly; Dilke agreed to feed the prince information discreetly, but only after he had put his own spin on it.[11]

Towards the end of the nineteenth century, anticipating eventual succession, other ministers, including Gladstone and Disraeli, began to trust the prince with more confidential matters. Disraeli even sent him secret material behind the queen's back. More properly, Gladstone asked the queen for formal permission to, as his private secretary put it, give the prince 'closer insight into State secrets'. Again, she stubbornly refused.[12] When a senior diplomat in the Foreign Office insisted that the prince should see 'what cards are in the hands of the players in the great European game which is going on, and how they are being played', Buckingham Palace quickly rebuffed him: 'The direction of affairs is not in his hands.'[13]

Edward, now portly and middle-aged, finally received a breakthrough of sorts in the early 1890s, when Gladstone returned to Number 10. The foreign secretary gave him a special golden key, once belonging to Prince Albert, for Foreign Office boxes containing secret material. Still Edward was unsatisfied, for despite now being authorized to see secret papers, he angrily accused successive ministers of just sending him 'rubbish' and, in 1895, complained that their 'game is not to let me see any interesting or important despatches!'[14]

As prince, Edward lacked access to official state secrets, but that did not mean he was ill-informed. Like Victoria, he developed his own private system of surveillance. His frequent continental travels made him particularly cosmopolitan – fluent in French and German – and his strengths lay in cultivating relationships and drawing influential contacts into conversation. He maintained a network of international friends and relatives who provided him with sensitive information and he took great pride whenever entrusted with important confidences. As a result, Edward, as prince and king, possessed the best address book in Europe and had his own – often superior – sources of intelligence. Like his mother, Edward, the 'Uncle of Europe', had access to a continental network of royal intelligence.[15]

THE FIRST ISSUE that dominated Edward's agenda when he finally became king in 1901 had little to do with Europe at all. The second South African War, pitting Boer republics against British imperialism, had broken out in 1899 and Edward, long engrossed by military affairs, was watching developments as closely as he could. For all of Britain's superior might and resources, the unpopular war was dragging on and proving increasingly costly.

Edward wanted it over. He knew from friends across Europe that the war was seriously damaging Britain's reputation. Not that this was any great secret: he had already been shot at by an anarchist protestor in Brussels – he carried the bullet as a souvenir for the rest of his life – and continued to be heckled by defiant renditions of the Boer national anthem whenever he travelled on the Continent.

Edward took great interest in intelligence coming from the battlefield. Yet, just like Queen Victoria, he frequently complained about its inadequacy and chastised ministers accordingly. His private contacts at home and abroad therefore occasionally furnished him with more information than the government. In late 1901, Francis Knollys, his private secretary, wrote to the prime minister about something Edward had heard. 'The King hears rumours', Knollys stated, that the Cabinet had received warning of an impending insurrection in South Africa and were duly worried. 'Can you tell me for his information whether there is any foundation in these rumours?' Although Prime Minister Salisbury dismissed the rumours as exaggerated, the exchange pointedly reminded him of the new king's right to know. Meanwhile, Edward summoned the war secretary to the palace so often that his critics accused him of acting unconstitutionally.[16]

It was no secret that British forces committed terrible atrocities during the conflict. Facing insurgent tactics, including guerrillas hiding among civilians, they rounded up swathes of the population – including women and children – into overcrowded concentration camps. Food was scarce and disease spread; tens of thousands died in squalid conditions. Much to the horror of Whitehall, newspapers began to report on massacres, rape and looting. The government scrambled to prosecute the most prominent journalists using the Official Secrets Act but failed on the grounds that they had simply received stolen information and therefore had not committed an offence.[17]

Frustrated ministers turned to unattributable propaganda – and used the king himself. They needed someone serious who could discredit the negative reporting and so turned to Arthur Conan Doyle. A prolific writer and spiritualist most famous for his Sherlock Holmes detective stories, Conan Doyle was also a staunch imperialist. He was perfect for the task. The government gave him intelligence briefings, while Edward discreetly provided £500 to cover the costs of publication and marketing. The outcome – an essay called *The War in South Africa: Its Cause and Conduct* – appeared in early 1902. Translated into many languages, it was a huge success and refuted many of the charges laid against the British forces. Conan Doyle claimed to be writing from an 'independent standpoint' without any 'official authority'. This was simply not true: it was covert propaganda funded by the king. Conan Doyle unsurprisingly received a knighthood shortly afterwards.[18]

In early May 1902, Edward received surprising news from his nephew, Kaiser Wilhelm of Germany, who had heard, 'through a private channel', that Britain was offering a generous peace deal to the Boers. This was news to Edward, who demanded an explanation from the prime minister. Salisbury, although aware of preliminary talks, denied knowledge of the precise terms and despatched his ambassador in Berlin on a 'most secret' mission to find out what

Wilhelm knew. It turned out that the kaiser had an excellent – but anonymous – source inside South Africa and that his intelligence was broadly accurate. Edward was furious that his German nephew knew more than he did and, once again, demanded to be kept better informed. From then on, Salisbury reluctantly submitted the twists and turns of each proposal to the king before the final agreement was signed at the end of the month.[19]

Britain's early humiliations and then defeat in the Boer War necessitated a thorough review. Edward was especially livid about the intelligence performance, describing the War Office's Intelligence Branch as 'one of those scandals which ought to hang Lords Lansdowne and Wolseley', the secretaries of state who were responsible for it. The king quickly suggested that his friend and adviser Lord Esher should be involved in what became a Royal Commission. Esher would become a key figure in defence planning throughout Edward's reign. After every meeting, he informed the king about exactly what had been said and by whom.[20]

Esher was a dark figure who promoted the monarchy's role in politics. Edward provided him with rooms at Windsor Castle and a critically important position – superintendence of the archives, which were full of secrets. Esher artfully employed this, and his friendship with the king's private secretary Francis Knollys, to inform and advise the king. He offered evidence from Queen Victoria's papers to show that the sovereign had been better informed in previous years and so suggested that ministers submit more secret business to the king. Esher was intelligent, able and arrogant, with a gift for friendship. He possessed all the attributes for manipulation. He was a curiosity to contemporaries and has puzzled historians. A controversial *éminence grise* operating very much behind the scenes, his own work is difficult to assess. But what is clear is that Edward admired Esher. As a result, Esher provoked the suspicion tradition-ally felt for royal favourites. Many distrusted him as an intriguer who plotted, leaked confidential information and interfered uncon-stitutionally in affairs of state.[21]

The hearings vindicated the intelligence effort. Esher told Edward that military intelligence had in fact provided 'full warning' of the Boer threat as early as 1896. Frustratingly, however, requests to strengthen the Intelligence Branch had been 'scoffed at by the financial authorities' inside the War Office and were never even referred to the Treasury.[22] Esher added that the blame also lay with the commander-in-chief, who, 'for some unexplainable reason', did not show the intelligence to the secretary of state.[23] Although, as Esher reassured Edward, the Royal Commission caused a further strengthening of the Intelligence Branch, it had no great impact on the production of actual intelligence.[24]

Esher believed more reforms were needed and, with the king's support, chaired another inquiry from November 1903. In doing so, he worked closely with another favourite of the king: John Fisher, Edward's naval aide-de-camp and a root and branch reformist. Their proposals, which were laid before Edward in good time so that he could comment,[25] were designed to bridge the gap between intelligence and policymaking, ensuring that it was properly distributed to the military and Cabinet in a timely and co-ordinated manner.

Esher created a new position, inspector-general of the forces, which was filled by Edward's brother, Prince Arthur, giving the royals greater power. More importantly, Esher was using Edward and his brother to bring about cultural change. Throughout the nineteenth century, the army had scoffed at strategic intelligence and proper staff work, while glorifying tactical intelligence gathered by the plucky amateur. In contrast, France, Austria and Germany, even Russia, boasted elaborate intelligence sections within their General Staffs. Britain was now catching up.[26]

Esher's reforms also led to the creation of a special duties section in the War Office that, in 1905, worked up contingency plans for an extensive offensive intelligence system in the event of a European war. It eventually became the Secret Service Bureau, the forerunner to MI5 and MI6, in 1909.[27]

ALONGSIDE MILITARY REFORM and war, King Edward was most interested in foreign affairs. Over almost half a century, he had acquired great experience and knowledge of Europe, leaving politicians, at least in his mind, parochial by comparison. He had developed strong opinions on foreign policy and was keen to advise ministers as he saw fit. He read foreign despatches carefully, highlighting any inaccuracies or inconsistencies, and remained sensitive about being kept in the dark. The shadow of his mother loomed over him as he complained time and again that ministers neither showed him as much secret material nor consulted him as often as they had Queen Victoria. He would become deeply offended at the slightest neglect, sharply rebuking ministers in protest.[28]

Frustrated at not being treated with the same courtesy or respect, he turned to the networks he had cultivated as prince of Wales and insisted that ambassadors abroad wrote private letters to him alongside their official despatches. Outside of royalty and officialdom, the Rothschilds and other bankers provided particularly useful foreign intelligence. He even established an informal Cabinet of his own. It included Francis Knollys, his private secretary; the courtiers Lord Esher and John Fisher; Francis Bertie and Cecil Spring-Rice, both diplomats who enjoyed royal patronage; and Charles Hardinge, a diplomat who would go on to be head of the Foreign Office, and the king's inside man. Edward had breakfast with Hardinge at Buckingham Palace once a week to discuss foreign affairs. The king was not as reliant on official intelligence as ministers would have liked.[29]

Edward used his impressive black book to conduct discreet diplomacy. In spring 1903, he visited Paris at the culmination of a European tour. He planned it in absolute secrecy, without even telling his wife Alix, and, when it came to depart, left the foreign secretary at home. He travelled instead with his friend Hardinge.[30]

Predictably, Edward's planning bypassed the British ambassador to France. Instead, he worked through the military attaché, Edward

Stuart-Wortley, a friend of the French president. Edward sent secret letters directly to Stuart-Wortley's house, so as not to arouse suspicion in the embassy.[31] The channel was identical to that used by Queen Victoria when sending secret messages to Russia behind the back of her foreign secretary.

Edward had received private intelligence, including through various royal sources, on French attitudes towards Britain the previous year. He had learnt that the president wanted closer relations with London, and, through Stuart-Wortley, he now knew that the president would welcome his visit.[32] Despite Edward's affection towards France, this was no foregone conclusion. Anti-British sentiment was high in France in the aftermath of the Boer War and a series of disputes over colonial possessions. When ministers belatedly found out about the trip, they cautioned about negative political reactions in Germany and Russia, alongside the security risks to Edward personally. The foreign secretary warned of hostile crowds and bomb-throwing anarchists. Edward relied on private threat assessments and predicted he would be perfectly safe.[33]

In reality, Portugal rather than Paris posed the greater security threat. As the royal yacht sailed from the south coast to Lisbon, the first stop on the tour, the royal party received intelligence from British and French agents warning that a known Dutch anarchist was also en route to the Portuguese capital. The Iberian Peninsula had a poor reputation for security – especially when it came to protecting visiting dignitaries. Taking no chances, Edward stayed aboard the secure yacht while French authorities tracked down and detained the anarchist under the pretence of problems with his papers.[34]

The visit was ultimately successful. Edward travelled on to Paris unscathed and helped to lay the foundations for the famous Entente Cordiale between Britain and France. He was not involved in the negotiations, but his very public, if secretly planned, endorsement of better relations proved symbolically potent and helped to transform French attitudes towards Britain. This was a success for British and French diplomacy, for both countries had been rather isolated and focused on minor colonial disputes. The kaiser was especially frustrated by Edward's success, which pleased the king very much, since he hated the Germans almost as much as his wife did.[35]

Edward's intelligence sources remained useful for the government. Eighteen months after his visit to Paris, he received warning that Germany intended to attack France. The king of Spain had told the French who, in turn, had told Edward. Taking the intelligence seriously, Edward asked if the foreign secretary knew. He did not: Edward's sources insisted that the 'communication was not intended for the British Government'. 'Royal confidences,' they insisted, 'are not to be noised abroad and we cannot give the King of Spain away.'[36] Sympathetic to the privacy of royal networks, Edward instructed the French to tell the British foreign secretary – but not to divulge the royal source.[37]

To solidify the agreement with France, Edward turned to Russia. Drawing on his royal intelligence networks once again, he engaged in yet more discreet diplomacy. Suspicion between the two countries was high, having never recovered from the Crimean War in the 1850s and the competition for central Asia that had spanned much of the nineteenth century. Like Queen Victoria before him, Edward had been an advocate of the Great Game and, towards the start of his reign, was the only one to approve of the belligerent activities of Francis Younghusband, an imperial army officer turned explorer, in Tibet. At the end of 1903, Younghusband departed on a mission to uncover Russian espionage and to settle various border disputes. Unfortunately, he exceeded his instructions and, the following year, ended up invading Tibet, killing bands of poorly armed monks, and humiliating the Chinese. When Younghusband reached his goal – the holy city of Lhasa – he found no evidence of Russian intrigue. The government swiftly dismissed him as an imperial agent, but Edward ensured he received royal recognition for his efforts.[38]

In 1904, amid distrust and rumours that both sides were in secret negotiations with China,[39] Edward sent Prince Louis of Battenberg to St Petersburg as his representative at the christening of the son of Tsar Nicholas II. It was a canny move designed to bolster relations. Demonstrating the blurring of public and private boundaries, Battenberg was personally close to the tsar while also being Britain's director of naval intelligence. He had used this position, alongside his royal connections, to gather information on the naval forces of various European countries.[40] On his return from the christening, Battenberg briefed the king on Russian intentions, telling him that the Russians had no aggressive plans towards India and were in generally conciliatory mood.[41]

Rapprochement did not last. Less than a year later the tsar was again referring to Edward, his cousin, as 'the greatest "mischief-maker" and the most deceitful and dangerous intriguer in the world'.[42] The king asked the new ambassador in Russia, his old friend Charles Hardinge, on whose appointment he had insisted, to improve relations.[43]

Late the following year, revolution swept Russia. Spurred on by a recent defeat in war against Japan, strikes and military mutinies threatened the tsar's regime. Back in London, Edward demanded to know what was going on. The answer to his request came from Donald Mackenzie Wallace, a chain-smoking journalist and well-connected Russia expert. After studying at four different universities and taking a PhD in law at Heidelberg in 1867, he had become fascinated with Russia. He published a bestselling book on the subject and became a foreign correspondent for *The Times*, but also took on secret work, typically smuggling treaties sewn into the lining of his greatcoat. Having also once accompanied a young Tsar Nicholas on a tour of India, he now served as the king's private source of intelligence throughout the uprising, sending a string of long and confidential telegrams about the severity of the strikes and the prospects for the ill-fated revolution.[44] As a friend of Hardinge, he operated from the embassy in St Petersburg.[45] According to one royal biographer, 'His Majesty's Information Service was of an exceptionally high order.'[46]

There was one gap in the royal intelligence, though: a secret defence pact made between Russia and Germany earlier in the year.

Much to Kaiser Wilhelm's delight, Edward failed to make any sense of the scraps of intelligence that had come his way. 'I can't find out what has been going on,' he ranted in frustration, bemoaning how his usual sources had all dried up. The tsar's mother (Edward's sister-in-law); the Russian ambassador, with whom he regularly played bridge; and the Danish royal family were all saying nothing. Even the Russian foreign minister who, according to Edward, was *such a nice man and lets me know all I want to hear*', knew 'nothing or at least won't tell! It is very disagreeable!'[47]

The man on the other end of the rant, listening intently as the loose-lipped king reeled off his list of sources, was a German aristocrat. Unfortunately for Edward, he had been sent by the kaiser to observe Anglo-French relations and swiftly reported the conversation back to Berlin. Kaiser Wilhelm then took great delight in telling Tsar Nicholas that Edward's outburst demonstrated just 'how very wide is the net of secret information he has cast over Europe and you'.[48]

On this occasion, Edward's net of sources simply did not know about the secret deal. When the Russian government did eventually find out what the tsar and kaiser had cooked up, they refused to ratify it on the grounds that it undermined a pre-existing deal with the French.[49]

With diplomacy stalling, the British foreign secretary, Edward Grey, turned to the king asking him to visit Russia and reprise the role he had played in 1903 in creating an atmosphere conducive to the agreement with France.[50] Politicians had been worried about his safety in France, but, in the aftermath of the failed revolution and amid a number of high-profile assassinations, the security situation in Russia was far more acute. When, in 1908, a royal trip looked likely, planning took place in the strictest secrecy. Charles Hardinge, now back in London as the most senior diplomat in the Foreign Office, explained to Arthur Nicolson, his replacement in Russia, and another rising diplomat who owed his position to royal patronage,[51] that the prospect of the visit had to be kept as secret as possible to prevent terrorists from plotting Edward's assassination. He even threatened to call off the visit entirely if it became common knowledge.[52]

As a security compromise, Edward eventually made the visit on board the royal yacht, meeting Tsar Nicholas off the Baltic coast. Security was tight. As Ponsonby put it, 'uniform was no criterion' in spotting people who may want to harm the king.[53] Little of political or diplomatic importance occurred during the meeting, but once again direct contact between the charming king and the tsar helped solidify Anglo-Russian rapprochement.[54] This paved the way for a full state visit to Britain by Nicholas the following summer. He arrived at Cowes in the Russian royal yacht, ostentatiously flanked by naval cruisers. Less flamboyantly, he brought with him the top Russian codebreaker, who prepared the Tsar for meetings with Edward by providing him with decrypted British despatches.[55]

BRITISH DIPLOMATIC MANOEUVRING throughout Edward's reign was a response to the German question. The king and his nephew, Kaiser Wilhelm, had long endured a tempestuous relationship and, in a world where the political and the personal mixed, family baggage impacted just as much as national security.

Intelligence was paramount throughout. With both men trying to outdo each other, the battle for the latest information formed a constant backdrop to their meetings. Each accused the other of espionage, intrigue and deception from the very start of Edward's reign. The kaiser even brought the head of his admiralty's new intelligence service with him to Queen Victoria's funeral.[56] Each sought to extract secret intelligence from their network of contacts across the Continent, although Wilhelm was often less tactful than his uncle. On one occasion, he simply instructed his admirals to get British navy personnel visiting German ports 'as drunk as possible'.[57] He had successes, though, including the recruitment of Edward's doctor, Sir James Reid, to report on activities in the English court.[58]

In return, Wilhelm claimed that Edward ran a private intelligence network which he used to plot against Germany. When the Norwegian throne became vacant in 1905, Edward's royal sources allowed him to warn his favoured candidate about German scheming and ultimately help him claim the throne. All the while, British ministers tried to rein in Edward's meddling.[59]

Edward's access to intelligence put the kaiser on the back foot – and vice versa. In 1901, Wilhelm revelled in telling Edward about the tsar's forthcoming trip to France, deliberately allowing his uncle to interpret the news as a move against England.[60] Five years later, Wilhelm sent a warship to Zanzibar, telling Edward that local disturbances necessitated the generous German gesture. Outmanoeuvred again, Edward frantically scrambled for local intelligence, only to be told that nothing serious had occurred and that the Germans were lying.[61]

Nowhere was intelligence more important in the growing tension between Britain and Germany than when assessing the size and intentions of each other's navies. Empress Victoria, the kaiser's mother and Edward's older sister, had warned about the 'pure madness and folly' of German naval growth as early as 1894.[62] When he became king, Edward, guided by his close friend and first sea lord John Fisher, remained deeply concerned as German naval growth not only continued but intensified. Fisher believed that Germany was 'our only probable enemy' and, with Edward's personal backing, was responsible for the revolutionary Dreadnought battleship launched by the king himself in early 1906.[63]

Two years later, Fisher accurately predicted that war would break out with Germany in the summer of 1914. He held a long and secret meeting with the king to suggest launching a surprise attack on the German navy now so as to stave off the future war. Edward thought the idea preposterous, insisting that he would not approve such an aggressive act without formerly declaring war.[64] Fisher continued to keep Edward updated on the latest intelligence but, in an attempt to keep him onside, did so slightly misleadingly. He took technical reports from the naval attaché in Berlin and dishonestly upgraded their classification, as secret or confidential, before passing them on to the king. He knew that the sensitive king, so quick to take offence, would be seduced by apparent access to secret material. The ruse worked: Edward forcefully backed Fisher in his increasingly bitter battles to build more Dreadnoughts.[65]

Throughout the summer of 1908, Edward grew more and more concerned about German intentions. Fears spread that German spies had already sketched British harbours and studied coasts ready for an invasion. An anonymous article appeared in the respected *Quarterly Review* warning of 50,000 Germans disguised as waiters already hiding in place in Britain.[66] Novelists, such as William Le Queux, were churning out pulp fiction – supposedly based on insider accounts – about German spies and saboteurs overrunning the country. Perhaps influenced by his wife's library of Le Queux novels, Edward now spoke of the kaiser's plan to 'throw a *corps d'armée* or two into England, making proclamation that he has come, not as an enemy to the king, but as the grandson of Queen Victoria, to deliver him from the Socialistic gang which is ruining the country'.[67]

Meanwhile, Edward also grew wary of Austria. Wickham Steed, Vienna correspondent for *The Times*, warned him that Emperor Franz Josef intended to annex Bosnia and Herzegovina. Edward initially refused to believe the warning. He had very recently met the emperor in person and spoken widely about European politics, yet nothing had been said about Bosnia. Steed, who had served in Vienna for over half a decade, assured Edward that his intelligence came from sources who had always proved reliable in the past. Edward remained dismissive. 'I still think you are wrong,' he insisted. 'Surely the Emperor would have said something to me.'[68]

Steed's intelligence was accurate, but the king, arrogant and touchy, placed too much confidence in his own ability to elicit information. He simply did not want to hear. The Austrian emperor had taken his decision in August, said nothing to Edward, and then announced it in early October. One of Edward's advisers dismissed the Austrian foreign minister as 'a foxy type' who 'preferred to work underground',[69] but the king was furious at being deceived. To him, the political was personal. Deception – even a lie of omission – became a personal slight.[70]

Amid this febrile, paranoid atmosphere, Edward allowed the manipulative Esher to engage in some more clandestine diplomacy. In November, he secretly met the French military attaché outside Windsor and divulged that Cabinet was divided between those in favour of supporting France in a war with Germany, including Prime Minister Herbert Asquith, and those who opposed. He added, in extreme confidence, that King Edward strongly backed the former.[71]

When Asquith told Edward shortly afterwards that the German naval programme might be slowing, the king was having none of it. It was third-hand news: Asquith had heard it from the foreign secretary who in turn had heard it hinted at by the German ambassador. The king became an intelligence analyst: increasingly wary of official German sources, he assessed any such information as worthless. He then became a royal spymaster, tasking the British naval attaché in Berlin with the task of personally ascertaining the exact number of ships the government was building.[72] In the meantime, Edward insisted that 'as long as Germany persists in her present programme of shipbuilding, we have no alternative but to build double'.[73]

In early 1909, the king learnt that far from tempering the shipbuilding programme, Germany had in fact accelerated it. He was furious with the kaiser for not informing him, but, perhaps more tellingly, was angry with his own government for not keeping him updated. Edward was, in his own words, 'very much disturbed' by the latest intelligence on German shipbuilding.

He demanded to know what type of intelligence failure had happened. Did the government lack the information in the first place or had Cabinet wilfully ignored valuable intelligence provided by the navy? If the latter, Edward believed that 'it should come out'. It would be unfair to those involved if an intelligence success remained hidden. He also wondered whether naval intelligence had failed to impress the facts strongly enough upon Cabinet. In response, Fisher reassured the king that the government was building eight Dreadnoughts and blamed any intelligence failure on a combination of German lies and an inability of the naval attaché to gain access to German ports and facilities.[74]

Edward was all the more angry given that he had just visited Berlin and would have found the intelligence useful in his discussions with the kaiser.[75] It had ultimately proved an unsuccessful – if eventful – trip. Queen Alix, sitting next to the kaiser at dinner, had accused him of being 'stupid' and 'making all this commotion about nothing'. When she offered him a lozenge, he showed it to his doctor thinking that she was trying to poison him. 'I should,' Alix later recalled, 'like to have!'[76]

Esher provided Edward with intelligence and an embarrassing line of questioning. Suitably armed, he could now press Asquith for the latest information on naval preparedness. Was it a fact, the king asked the prime minister, that 'the Germans will have in March 1911: 17 Dreadnoughts ready for the seas, and we shall have 12 plus whatever we lay down this year?'[77]

Acquiring accurate intelligence on the future size of the German navy and its quality as a fighting force was proving difficult. The military attachés in Berlin offered little beyond generalities, not least because the Germans increasingly saw them as enemy spies and restricted their access.[78] Meanwhile, tight security around shipyards hampered early attempts by military intelligence to use commercial cover to investigate naval construction. The king knew well one of the key figures behind these operations, William Melville. He had previously overseen royal security, but Melville now focused on German espionage and warned of spies reconnoitring potential invasion routes across England. Anything of interest that he did succeed in uncovering was poorly co-ordinated between military intelligence, naval intelligence and the Foreign Office. It proved ineffective.[79]

Amid war scares and spy paranoia, Asquith ordered an inquiry into foreign espionage in Britain. Richard Haldane, secretary of state for war and an old friend of the king, chaired the first meeting in March 1909. Although initially bemused by the accounts of German espionage, Haldane was ready to believe the remarkable tales coming his way. Esher sat alongside Haldane on the committee and also began sceptically. He dismissed the head of counter-intelligence work in the War Office as 'a silly witness'. 'Spy catchers,' he quipped, 'get espionage on the brain. Rats are everywhere – behind every arras.'[80] But his initial scepticism gradually waned, especially as Haldane grew convinced.[81]

It is highly likely that Esher briefed the king on the ins and outs of the espionage hearings, just as he had done on previous occasions. Indeed, his very presence at the heart of government frustrated the Foreign Office precisely because he had a habit of repeating confidential discussions to the king.[82] He also had a strong influence over Edward on military policy.[83] At around the same time, Esher formed a secret organization called the Society of Islanders. Operating discreetly outside of parliament, Esher sought to shape defence policy by lobbying in favour of naval expansion at a rate of two to one compared to Germany. He was delighted when Edward repeated exactly his mantra that the next major war was building and argued that the British Empire floated on the strength of the navy and that '"two keels to one" is the only right and safe thing'.[84]

A month later, in April, Haldane and Esher asked whether Britain could create a small secret service bureau. A further team, this time chaired by Charles Hardinge, examined the matter. Hardinge, of course, was head of the Foreign Office, highly suspicious of Germany, and a long-time friend of the king.[85] On 28 April, he submitted a report that was so secret it was never printed. Only one copy existed. Hardinge created a secret service bureau and set out what the authorized MI6 historian calls 'the founding charter of the modern British intelligence community'.[86] What is striking is that three of the key individuals involved – Haldane, Esher and Hardinge – were all favourites of King Edward.

THE CREATION OF the Secret Service Bureau by Edward's protégés was entirely fitting. The king enjoyed subterfuge and secret missions; indeed, he had used this persistently to push back against a decline in the political importance of the crown. He did maintain influence, largely through the veneration in which the monarchy was still held,[87] but never as much as he hoped. As one of his assistant private secretaries recalled, 'the King always prided himself on being entirely a constitutional monarch, but at heart he was a born autocrat'.[88] Royal prerogative in appointments was one of the last formal powers of the crown, and the king was obsessive about them.[89]

Courtiers, such as Esher and Knollys, tried to bolster his direct input into decision-making but failed. After all, he was never as experienced, respected – or discreet – as Queen Victoria. His greatest skills lay in cultivating strong relationships with people and helping to create an atmosphere conducive to political agreement, so often he worked indirectly.[90]

His achievements were considerable. Historians have praised his diplomatic efforts in establishing the necessary conditions for alliances with France and Russia. To be an effective diplomat, the king needed intelligence. He had excellent private sources but was a flawed intelligence consumer. For all his experience and travelling, he remained naïve and was quick to be hurt when his contacts lied to him. Rather arrogant, he often either thought he knew best or thought his charm was sufficient to elicit intelligence from his friends and relatives. To make matters worse, his networks were not omniscient. Sometimes, as with the stillborn Russo-German treaty of 1905, they simply did not know.

Diplomacy and dynastic politics were often the same thing. When an uprising erupted in Athens during the summer of 1909, Edward's updates came via his wife's family. He then used his own 'purely private' channels to offer support for King George I, his wife's brother, and strongly urge him not to abdicate. Many of these messages were not shown to the foreign secretary, who, upon learning of Edward's activities, had to remind the king not to interfere in Greek affairs. Edward sent a prickly reply: 'I never for a moment dreamt of my government in any way interfering in the internal affairs of Greece. I only wished to point out the importance of the safety of King George, my brother-in-law, and therefore thought that the fleet should not be too far off.'[91]

Edward died on 6 May 1910. His funeral was the largest gathering of European royalty in history. It offered the kaiser, who turned up with a dozen armed bodyguards,[92] the perfect opportunity for a final intelligence mission against his uncle. His large entourage included a German officer believed to be the acting head of naval intelligence. While in Britain, the German discreetly visited an anonymous barbershop on Caledonian Road, north London. He was followed by a Special Branch officer who soon realized that the barbershop was actually a secret post office distributing communications across a major German spy ring. By intercepting and opening the mail, the British were able to track down most German agents and monitor their activity before eventually rounding them up at the outbreak of war in 1914, depriving Germany of its undercover network.[93] King Edward's death therefore marked a significant counter-espionage victory, but the intelligence battle was only just beginning.

Part II

ROYAL RELATIONS
AND INTRIGUES

KING GEORGE V AND
THE GREAT WAR

'our spies are the worst and clumsiest in the world'

King George V, 2 September 1910[1]

I N LATE MAY 1906, Edward VII's eldest surviving son and heir, George, duke of York, visited Spain. Aged forty, and accompanied by his wife Mary, he was there to represent his family at the marriage of his cousin to the king of Spain. Immediately after the wedding ceremony, they rode in a regal procession of carriages from the cathedral to the reception. As they approached the palace, a loud explosion rang out. George assumed it was an artillery gun firing the first salute.

He was wrong. An anarchist had thrown a bomb, disguised as a bouquet of flowers, at the newlyweds from an upper window as the procession passed beneath. It killed about twenty people, including their driver, and injured another fifty. Miraculously, the royal bride and groom were not badly hurt, but the bride's wedding dress was drenched in blood.[2] George recorded in his diary that the couple were 'covered with glass from the broken windows' and 'broke down' as soon as they escaped the public gaze. Stoically, the wedding feast continued inside the palace, but George's toast wishing them a long and happy life rang rather hollow.[3]

These were dangerous times for royals. The king of Spain had already been injured in an almost identical attack a year before. The king of Portugal and his son were shot and killed by republican assassins less than two years later. As we have seen, the king of Italy and America's president, William McKinley, had been despatched by the revolvers of deadly assassins earlier in the decade. The Russian royals had suffered numerous attacks, one of which had just killed Grand Duke Sergei Romanov, the tsar's uncle.

These deadly events were symptoms of social turbulence. King George V's reign would go on to witness the rise of anarchism, socialism, communism, fascism, Irish republicanism and the Indian independence movement, many of which would challenge the established order and threaten the monarchies of Europe. As George's perilous visit to Spain had also illustrated, these royals were remarkably inter-related because of an obsession with lineage and royal pedigree. Therefore, as the First World War approached, royal relations, and indeed royal intrigue, especially between George and his two cousins, the tsar and the kaiser, took on great importance.

GEORGE WAS THE second son of Edward VII and had not expected to be king, until his elder brother Albert died of pneumonia in 1892. George had been seriously ill himself with typhoid, and, sharing family grief, he married his brother's fiancée, Mary of Teck, shortly afterwards. The two brothers had been close, and because their father had decided that time in the navy provided ideal training for princes, they both served on the cadet training ship HMS *Britannia* at Dartmouth when George was just twelve years old. Later, George commanded ships and travelled extensively, visiting many countries in the Mediterranean and the Caribbean, together with South Africa, Australia and the United States. In 1881, the two brothers had visited the emperor of Japan, presenting him with two wallabies from Australia. But Albert's death ended what

George had expected to be a long naval career. He acceded to the throne in 1910.[4]

History has rather underrated George. Famously, he has been dismissed as someone obsessed with collecting stamps and shooting animals, preferring the quiet life of a country squire to public service.[5] His first prime minister, Herbert Asquith, held a fairly condescending view of the king's mental capabilities, likening his knowledge of current affairs to 'the average opinion of the man on the tube'.[6]

He worked dutifully to follow the mounting complexities of European foreign policy but found lengthy Foreign Office telegrams a bit of a bore. To spice them up, his officials would mix in secret service reports. The ones he loved best contained gossip about misbehaviour by the royal families in Europe, who were often his relatives.[7]

Most importantly, the king was anxious to avoid war. He was unimpressed by the rampant Germanophobia of his parents, which had contributed to the spy fever of the previous decade, and indeed to the creation of a modern British secret service. He instinctively realized that war might reverberate badly on his own family, with its German ancestry advertised by a baroque collection of German titles.

When George ascended the throne, his old classmate from the Royal Naval College at Greenwich back in 1884, Mansfield Cumming, was into his first hectic year as head of the overseas intelligence branch, which would eventually become MI6.[8] Diary entries record their familiarity: they played billiards and Cumming told the future king some 'interesting things' – but what these were exactly is not recorded.[9]

Partly because of such close personal contacts, George had a good assessment of the elementary state of Britain's secret activities and of the general spy mania that had seized Europe. In 1910, he told a friend that the 'Germans suspect that there are English spies everywhere'. 'Yet,' he admitted, 'we have no secret service funds, or at least they are much smaller than any other State, and our spies are the worst and clumsiest in the world.'

By contrast, George thought that 'German espionage' was 'magnificently organised and lavishly financed'. He believed there to be a 'certain number of German spies' constantly stationed in Portsmouth and Southampton. 'We have no protection against them, and so far as I am concerned German officers can examine all our ships.'[10]

Perhaps for this reason, his early use of secret service was rather peripheral. In May 1911, he decided to send a lion to Dublin zoo that had been presented to him by the king of Abyssinia. A specialist lion keeper travelled with the animal on its long journey from Africa. All the complex arrangements and indeed the costs of transportation of this tribute were taken care of by the British secret service.[11] This continued the royal tradition of using secret service for eccentric personal missions and would not be the last manifestation.

AS WAR LOOMED over Europe, George's opinion of the British secret service did not improve. On one occasion, because of repeated failed missions, he found himself having to intervene personally to rescue three spies from imprisonment.

The Agadir crisis of July 1911, a minor confrontation involving a German gunboat off the coast of French Morocco, had caused a major panic which left Mansfield Cumming under pressure for intelligence about the German fleet. Prompted by the wave of jingoism that accompanied the crisis, he received an offer from Bertrand Stewart, a junior officer and 'intelligence enthusiast', to find out more. Cumming agreed reluctantly, warning Stewart that he was running his head into a noose. But the happy-go-lucky Stewart headed for the Netherlands and then Germany to scout out the ports.

Seven days later, Stewart was arrested in a public lavatory in Bremen. German authorities had caught him red-handed trying to flush away an incriminating codebook passed to him by an agent. Unfortunately for Stewart, he had been double crossed: his agent had secretly defected to the Germans, insisting that they paid better. By February 1912, he was locked up in Glatz, a fortress prison used mainly to house Germans who had been convicted of duelling. There he joined two other luckless spies, Captain Bernard Frederick Trench and Lieutenant Vivian R. Brandon, arrested for similarly amateurish activities.

The following May, George used his royal connections to secure their release. He appealed to his cousin, Kaiser Wilhelm, who agreed to set them free in honour of George's visit to Germany to attend the wedding of the kaiser's daughter.[12] The failed British spies were thrilled to receive their royal release and skipped home to freedom, although Cumming wisely decided to keep none of them on in MI6.

Meanwhile, the wedding was a huge affair. As a diplomatic gesture, Kaiser Wilhelm invited almost his entire extended family, including Tsar Nicholas II of Russia. The wedding was one of the last great social events of European royalty before the First World War began fourteen months later. Alongside this magnanimous gesture, the Germans had hoped – and British officials feared – that George might be coaxed into discussions on naval arms control. But he deftly avoided foreign policy issues, and instead asked endless questions about shooting and the management of the Prussian royal stables.[13]

Eccentric and status-conscious, Wilhelm was delighted to have both George and Nicholas present at the wedding, the heads of two of the most important royal families in Europe. Yet he also worried about being the odd one out, since George and Nicholas enjoyed each other's company, but found Wilhelm annoying and neurotic. He therefore did everything possible to ensure his two cousins were never alone together, convinced that if they met, they would soon be plotting against Germany. George later recalled that when they did finally manage to converse privately, he was sure that the kaiser's ear 'was glued to the keyhole'.[14]

Wilhelm was right to be suspicious. George and Nicholas were not only close but also looked like twin brothers. George addressed his cousin as 'my dear Nicky, your ever devoted cousin and friend'. They corresponded frequently, sometimes touching on dynastic problems across Europe, including the future of the Greek monarchy.[15] George had assured his cousin that 'there may be difficulties with Germany, but I think they can be overcome. If only England, Russia and France stick together the peace of Europe is assured.'[16] On the intriguing subject of German plots, he added, 'I like to tell you everything.'[17]

IN NOVEMBER 1913, Archduke Franz Ferdinand of Austria and his wife visited Britain. They were obsessed with hunting and enjoyed a spectacular shoot on the edge of Windsor led by the king and the prince of Wales. Thereafter they spent their time in Britain happily moving from county to county, blasting at everything that moved. Franz's wife, Sophie, duchess of Hohenberg, was the better shot. Days later, shooting with the duke of Portland on the outskirts of Sherwood Forest, the archduke had a narrow escape. Portland recounted that 'One of the loaders fell down. This caused both barrels of the gun he was carrying to be discharged, the shot passing within a few feet of the archduke and myself.' Portland subsequently pondered 'whether the Great War might not have been averted, or at least postponed, had the archduke met his death then and not at Sarajevo the following year'.[18]

The next June, Franz and Sophie were not so lucky. They were killed on a visit to Sarajevo, the capital of Bosnia-Herzegovina, which was occupied by Austria-Hungary.

It is hard to understand why such an intelligent man as Ferdinand would have embarked on such a foolhardy visit. The moment he had chosen to visit Sarajevo, Serbian national day, 28 June, was itself provocative. Terrorism there was notorious and they had faced an earlier bomb scare themselves; yet they still climbed into an open vehicle and drove down a street known as 'Assassins' Alley' before being shot by associates of the Black Hand, a Serbian terrorist group. His death was personally distressing for George, who was almost exactly the same age and knew him well after repeated visits to Britain. George now instructed the court to wear mourning for a week.

History had already shouted its warnings. Only a few years before, King Alexander of Serbia and his queen had been horribly murdered by a gang of army officers, again including members of the Black Hand. Infiltrating the palace, they hid in a cupboard inside the queen's bedroom before leaping out and shooting the young royal couple. Afterwards, their bodies, mutilated and disembowelled, were reportedly thrown from a second-floor window of the palace onto piles of manure.[19]

The death of the archduke was a double tragedy, for Franz Ferdinand was a man of peace. He understood that war between Austria and Russia would mean the end of one of their royal houses – perhaps even both – and had urged a 'concord of the emperors' to avoid confrontation.[20] Now, Austria demanded recompense from Serbia for the assassination and, when this was not fully met, it invaded. Europe's complex web of interlocking treaties, designed to ensure peace, now dragged each country into war. Russia had already mobilized to help its Serbian ally and Germany warned Britain that it would have to respond with serious counter-measures. The kaiser, pompous, posturing, an ardent lover of exotic military uniforms and above all thin-skinned, did not want to be seen to back down. The slide towards war began.

Realization dawned in Downing Street that only monarchical diplomacy could now offer a slim chance of peace. George himself would have to persuade the tsar to suspend mobilization. On the evening of 31 July, the prime minister, Herbert Asquith, and his private secretary sat down to draft a personal appeal from the king to the tsar, 'from Georgie to Nicky'. With the ink barely dry, they then ran out of Number 10 and, with some difficulty in the gathering darkness, located a taxi and sped round to Buckingham

Palace. It was 12.45 a.m. and the king had already gone to bed. Asquith deemed the matter so urgent that he sent an equerry to wake George, who surfaced in his dressing gown to approve the message.[21] It warned about the dangers of misunderstanding as a cause of war, the classic intelligence failure of being unable to read an adversary's true intentions.

Royal diplomacy failed. George's royal connections and informal intelligence networks offered nothing but negativity. Across Europe, princes and prime ministers alike felt propelled along by uncontrolled events. Gloomily, by 1 August, the king concluded that there was practically 'no chance of peace' – and he was right.[22]

The next day, Tsar Nicholas wrote to him expressing shock at the German declaration of war. He had expected a period of talks instead.[23] Everyone knew that Russia was like a ponderous dinosaur and would take weeks to mobilize, and so the kaiser's claim to have to rush was transparent rubbish: George and Nicholas knew that he simply wished to avoid any conciliation.[24]

Two days later, German troops crossed into Belgium. Their forlorn king, Albert, appealed personally to George for help. Again, royal diplomacy and inter-dynastic intelligence amounted to little; the British ambassador in Berlin fled for the Channel ports with his staff in a fleet of cars and buses. He brought with him a message from Wilhelm to George renouncing his appointments as a British admiral and a field marshal.[25] For the crowned heads of Europe, the declaration of war was both personal and a prelude to disaster.

August 1914 also marked an upturn in espionage. Gustav Steinhauer was the man in charge of the German spy ring in Britain. As George had lamented, since the operation following his father's funeral German spies had been left free to roam about in peacetime. Just a week before the declaration of war, Steinhauer had toured Britain to refresh his remaining networks. MI5 now finally swooped to arrest those left on their 'watch list'. The kaiser was furious at the apparent obliteration of German surveillance. He screamed: 'Am I surrounded by dolts? Who is responsible? Why was I not told!?'[26]

Still, Wilhelm could always turn to royal intelligence networks of his own. A month earlier, in July, Prince Henry, Wilhelm's younger brother, was enjoying the sailing races of Cowes Week on the Isle of Wight, when he heard about the Austrian ultimatum delivered to Serbia in the wake of Ferdinand's assassination. He decided to undertake a bit of amateur reconnaissance to discover what George thought about all this.

On 26 July, on the way home to Germany, he dropped in on Buckingham Palace for a private conversation, cousin to cousin. He asked the king exactly how Britain would respond. The Royal Archives suggest that George was robust and said that if Germany went to war against Russia and France it would be impossible for Britain not to be dragged into it.

Curiously, this is the opposite of what Henry reported. He told Wilhelm that George was determined to remain neutral and would try to stay out of war. This may have been George's personal sentiment, but it was not the policy of his government. Either way, the news delighted Wilhelm, who now assumed that George was neutral and used this royal intelligence to reassure his generals as they marched to war. Henry's report was doubly odd, since having told the kaiser that Britain was neutral, he nonetheless scooted back to Germany quickly, advising his sisters to do the same, suggesting that privately he expected war soon. This puzzling mission by a minor royal at a critical moment was clearly important to German decision-making.[27]

As the realities of war sunk in, George found himself in a difficult position. He had family on both sides and, while this could have provided useful intelligence channels, it put him on the defensive. Suddenly, critics accused his German relatives fighting on the British side of being hostile undercover agents. In particular, Prince Louis of Battenberg, the first sea lord, was denounced as 'a damned German spy'.[28] Much to George's mortification, the prince resigned his position in short order, but the press simply turned its fire on other minor royals with British connections who by accident of family found themselves fighting for the enemy.

In private, George spent much time with Asquith justifying the roles of his many relatives fighting on the other side.[29] Perhaps the most problematic was the duke of Albany, the king's cousin, who also bore the title duke of Saxe-Coburg and Gotha, the same name as the British royal family. Although educated at Eton, he had joined a German infantry regiment in 1914.[30] Even the Chancellor of the Exchequer, David Lloyd George, joined in, referring to the king as 'my little German friend'.[31] The feeling was mutual. The king would be remarkably indiscreet, making little secret of his dislike of Lloyd George, whom he referred to as 'that man!'[32]

GEORGE WAS A military enthusiast who enjoyed military company. When he became king, he replaced many of his father's advisers with his own circle of military and naval officers whom he trusted. Once war broke out, this transformed into his own informal intelligence network, providing him with the latest material from the front line.

Rather like Queen Victoria's own royal intelligence network, George's personal channels of military intelligence often bypassed the government's own official machinery. Much of this sensitive material came through his close adviser, Clive Wigram. Technically, he was only assistant to Lord Stamfordham, the king's private secretary. In reality, he played a role not dissimilar to that fulfilled by Lord Esher for his father – a secret fixer and quiet modernizer. Sensing the growing tide of social unease, he secured the appointment of the first permanent palace press secretary to conduct 'propaganda' and also worked with intelligence to monitor the rise of republicanism and communism. He deemed his opponents the 'Palace Troglodytes'.[33]

Wigram was also incredibly well connected in military circles. His network included myriad officers and generals, as well as the likes of Lord Kitchener, the war secretary, and even Maurice Hankey. A former naval intelligence officer and now the influential secretary to the committee of imperial defence, Hankey operated as a tactful go-between among the military and civilians. He managed the Whitehall machine, had access to top-secret planning material and, perhaps most importantly, co-ordinated the record keeping at the heart of government. Hankey, at the palace's requests, had sent the king summaries of papers on the German invasion threat and continued to be a great source of defence information. George's network provided unfiltered intelligence on the conduct of the war, including some material that the government might have wanted to keep secret, directly to him.[34]

George received a steady flow of detailed and uncensored information from the front line. It came from relatives, Cabinet ministers, generals, newspaper magnates, businessmen, bishops, and consular officials worldwide. Wigram wrote at least weekly, if not daily, to all the main generals – and received private letters in return.[35] The king's military intelligence was, according to some historians, 'as good as, maybe better than, that on which the Cabinet had to base its conduct of military affairs'.[36] His own son, the future Edward VIII, was stationed with the Intelligence Branch of general headquarters in France and would report back to his father – although he was not the greatest of sources, being constantly bored and, as heir to the throne, frustrated by not being allowed 'out of my f***** glass case'.[37]

Importantly, George's network also allowed generals on the front line to circumvent formal channels and complain about things such as a shortage of munitions straight to the king himself. He even asked one field commander to go deliberately behind the back of his superior, the commander-in-chief of British forces in France, Sir John French, to feed back information on his superiors. Wigram asked another commander, Douglas Haig, to send his diaries direct to the palace. The king would read them and then return them to his wife.[38]

All of this activity inevitably frustrated the politicians but, like Victoria before him, it put George in a stronger position when dealing with his prime minister, service ministries and military leaders.[39] Secret letters from his sources and the king's subsequent machinations contributed to the removal of John French as commander-in-chief in late 1915.[40]

George had a broad awareness of classified material, and not just through his own intelligence network. After complaining about the lack of warning procedures, he visited the general headquarters of the home forces to be briefed on air defence operations, including the signals intelligence underpinning warnings of Zeppelin raids. Inside what one intelligence officer called 'the plotting room', he learnt about 'the mystery of the zeps', including how they were identified and tracked, in a 'straightforward clear manner'. The intelligence officers noted that the king was 'very intelligent' and grasped 'things with quickness', even though 'his appearance is against him and his accent is German'. A few weeks earlier, the same intelligence officer had visited Buckingham Palace to show Wigram and George an oil pressure pump that had been dropped by a Zeppelin during a raid. Wigram, he recalled, seemed 'very nice' and was particularly interested in the new intelligence officers' uniforms, which included a green patch and hat band.[41]

Royal residences, especially Sandringham on the east coast, quickly became targets of Zeppelin raids. An aerial defence detachment, armed with searchlights and guns, moved nearby to protect the king and queen whenever they were in residence – although both thought it a noisy overreaction. When Zeppelins attacked London, George and Mary would rush onto the palace balcony for a look. His mother, Queen Alexandra, refused to be frightened. She asked the Admiralty: 'please let me have a lot of rockets with spikes or hooks on to defend our Norfolk coast'.[42]

The king also visited the Western Front, the focus of much of the fighting. His first visit, in 1914, was surrounded by strict secrecy and press censorship. Three plain clothes Special Branch officers provided personal security. In France, George attended a meeting between the commander-in-chief and his intelligence officers, hearing the latest secret material. He came away satisfied enough.[43]

Drawing on his own networks, George concluded that the war would be won or lost on the Western Front. Others, notably Winston Churchill, disagreed and wanted to open up new campaigns, including using the Dardanelles to target Constantinople. The king unsuccessfully opposed this, but monitored events very carefully, recording them in his diary. He also objected to opening yet another front in the Balkans, seeing it as an unnecessary risk and fearing its impact on some of the royal families there. Informed by his various sources, he asked a series of pointed questions of the government – to which he already knew the answers – in an attempt to dissuade them.[44]

FOR ALL OF George's narrow focus on the Western Front, British intelligence now operated on a global scale. Indeed, the First World War is increasingly recognized as foundational for Western intelligence culture and was perhaps the moment when the secret services of states began to overtake the dynastic networks of royal spies.[45]

To the west, human spies and codebreakers anxiously watched America's search for a compromise. It seems highly unlikely that the king would not have seen some of the secret material underpinning the Zimmerman telegram that later brought the US into the war. This was a secret German offer to Mexico to recover its lost territories, including California, if it sided with Germany. Decrypting this message was perhaps the greatest British codebreaking achievement of the war.

Across the Middle East, spies secretly battled the remnants of the Turkish Empire. Around the globe, they confronted a vast conspiracy, supported by Germany, that sought to promote imperial insurrection as far afield as Canada and the northwest frontier. It was a huge relief for the overstretched spy agencies that Russia, now an ally, had ceased competing with Britain in the Great Game in central Asia.

Imperial Russia remained a focus of both intrigue and royal worries. The king's obsession with the Western Front made Russia particularly important, since Germany was currently fighting in two directions, stretching its resources. Thousands of German troops were deployed beyond Kiev and even reached the Don River. But George knew that the tsar was weak and suggestible; moreover his regime was unstable and unlikely to survive the supreme test of total war. This presented a major dynastic problem for George and a strategic problem for the Cabinet, since Russia formed an essential part of the grand alliance. Without its ally in the east, Britain might lose the war.

One of the biggest questions for intelligence networks – both formal and royal – was whether Russia would switch sides and join the Germans. George and his government knew that inside the imperial palace pro-Allied politicians battled with an inner circle who sought a separate peace with Germany. This prospect horrified London. Desperate for manpower to feed the bloody battles at Ypres and the Somme, the Cabinet had fought over the introduction of conscription and even considered improbable schemes like conscription in rebellious southern Ireland. The success of the so-called Russian peace party would have freed over a million Germans to fight on the Western Front.

By mid-1915, the Russian army was suffering defeat after defeat, and it was clear that the Romanovs were in trouble. George wrote frequently to his cousin assuring him of assistance and pleading with him to stay and fight alongside his allies. 'My dear Nicky,' he wrote on 8 August, 'I feel most deeply for you in the very anxious day through which you are now passing, when your army has been compelled to retire on account of lack of ammunition and rifles'. He insisted that Britain would 'fight out this awful war to the end' and noted that he was pleased Nicky's most recent letter showed that 'Russia also means to fight to the end'.[46]

Privately, George feared this was not the case. In September, encouraged by his wife, Nicholas fired his uncle as commander of the armed forces and took over command himself. George, who knew his kindly but ineffectual cousin better than anyone else, appreciated how disastrous this step was. He drew on all his intelligence sources to follow developments in the tsar's inner circle with increasing anxiety.[47]

By 1916, the British ambassador in Moscow, George Buchanan, repeatedly asked for permission to warn Nicholas about his deteriorating position. His superiors refused, on the grounds that it might be seen as meddling by the king. The situation was delicate, and Buchanan was unaware that some in the inner circles of the court believed that he too 'was personally aiding the Grand Dukes to overthrow Nicholas II and replace him by his cousin'. The tsarina even pressed her husband to banish Buchanan, but Nicholas decided against it.[48] Although Buchanan finally secured permission to speak to Nicholas privately, it was hopeless since he blindly refused to entertain the idea that his rule might be in jeopardy. Buchanan warned London of impending disaster, a warning that reached the king.[49]

In the late summer, with Russian armies retreating in disarray, George feared that his dearest relative might sell out to the Germans. On 23 August, he shared some intelligence with his cousin. 'Information,' he wrote, 'has reached me from more than one source, including one undoubtedly well-placed neutral source, that German agents in Russia have recently been making great efforts to sow division between your country and mine by exciting distrust and spreading false reports of the intentions of my government.' He urged: 'do not allow your people to be misled by the evil workings of our enemies'.[50]

George did not explicitly refer to the circle around the tsarina or to 'dark forces', but the language was blunt and there could be no doubt what was on his mind. He wrote again in October, returning to his worries about Germany making 'a separate peace with Russia'.[51]

The king's information derived not only from Buchanan's embassy. There was also a growing group of MI6 personnel, mostly hidden inside the large military mission, whose reports reached him directly. The king was anxious about what MI6 was telling him.

On 15 November 1916, Grand Duke Michael Michailovich, a grandson of Nicholas I who had long resided in London, visited Buckingham Palace. There he had found that 'Georgy' was 'very much upset over the political situation in Russia'. This was because 'the usually well-informed agents of the British Secret Service predict a revolution in the very near future'. Michael asked for the MI6 warning to be passed to the tsar by his brother Alex, who was the tsar's brother-in-law. This was a tricky mission and for his pains the tsarina urged he be banished into exile in Siberia immediately.[52]

The same MI6 reports clearly reached Lloyd George, the king's new prime minister. Although they disagreed on most things, they shared a view of what was going on in Russia. Lloyd George told his secretary that 'the pro-Germans in the Russian government' were manipulating the leadership of the army, adding that: 'They are one by one getting rid of all the good men in Russia and are putting in rotters or Pro-Germans.'[53] Anxiety was turning to panic and there was a gathering mood for action.

The most eminent MI6 officer on the spot was Sam Hoare, a brilliant but mercurial figure who went on to become foreign secretary and then home secretary in the 1930s. Already a rising star, he now served as the MI6 liaison officer with the Russian secret service in St Petersburg.[54] Hoare eventually left the scene in March 1917, a month after the tsar's abdication. Posted to Rome, he recruited a former socialist leader called Benito Mussolini and helped to finance his first escapades as a right-wing politician. Much later, as ambassador to Spain, Hoare presided over the bribery of Franco and his generals to keep them out of the Second World War. In other words, he enjoyed a lifetime of racy covert actions and was not just a mere gatherer of intelligence.[55]

In late 1916, Hoare assessed the situation astutely. He estimated that the growing food crisis alone in St Petersburg was likely to lead to a revolution. He added that the war effort was badly mismanaged and that, unless something was done to change things radically, 'Russia will never fight through another winter'. Although he understood Russia's problems to be complex, he noted that the parliament had focused its criticism on two particular figures, the tsarina and her adviser Rasputin, whom many believed nurtured pacifist, if not pro-German, sympathies.[56] The British, likely including the king, knew that something urgently needed to be done to prevent Russia from siding with the Germans; a move that would have devastated the war effort. By the end of the year, Hoare learnt of a plot to 'liquidate' Rasputin; indeed he might even have presided over it.[57]

GRIGORI RASPUTIN WAS a bearded mystic who gained considerable influence over the royal family. The tsarina believed he was able to use his holy powers to abate the effects of haemophilia on her son and so regarded him as simply indispensable. He also had innumerable enemies. The Russian secret service, the Okhrana, began surveillance of him as early as 1908 at the suggestion of the commandant of the imperial court. Reports about his unsavoury behaviour quickly reached the Russian prime minister, Peter Stolypin. A year later, Stolypin, thoroughly alarmed, attempted to persuade Nicholas to banish him from court, but found it impossible. Nicholas said he broadly agreed with his prime minister, but he preferred a quiet life and said that Rasputin's calming influence on the tsarina was invaluable. 'It is better to have ten Rasputins,' he quipped, 'than one hysterical Empress.' Stolypin then planned a secret operation to remove Rasputin from St Petersburg, but Rasputin found out and vanished for a while. Stolypin was assassinated the following year.[58] The tsar's sister, Xenia, an intelligent and careful observer, noted in her diary that newspapers 'are forbidden to write about him' but everyone in the inner circles was talking about him, adding 'it's terrible the things they say about him'.[59]

As early as May 1914, even before the outbreak of war, British diplomats were anxious about Rasputin. George Buchanan officially confirmed some of the wildest rumours, including the 'fact' that Rasputin was indeed a member of the Khlysty, an orgiastic cult, and was also a genuine priest. (Neither of these facts were true.) Rumours that the tsarina kept Nicholas in a drug-induced stupor also enjoyed common currency.[60] Again there was no evidence, but historians have noted that this did not really matter: the ubiquitous gossip that Rasputin slept with both the tsarina and her closest friends, and had defiled the tsar's daughters, 'was kind of a metaphor for the degradation of the regime itself'.[61]

When the Germans declared war on Russia, Nicholas had ordered the Okhrana to keep a protective watch on Rasputin. Allocating him a codename, 'The Dark One', the Okhrana co-opted the servants in Rasputin's house to spy on him and recruited an agent to stake out his hometown. They gathered ample evidence of his misdeeds, but further efforts to remove him simply resulted in the tsarina switching the chief of the secret police to make the problem go away.[62]

When Nicholas assumed personal control of the armed forces, he spent long periods away from the capital, creating a dangerous political vacuum. This void was filled, with the encouragement of her husband, by the tsarina – and her close adviser. Britain, and presumably George himself, grew increasingly worried. Although the accusations of pro-German sympathies were misdirected, both the tsarina and Rasputin favoured peace with Germany. This made them a direct threat to the British Empire.

Having already survived numerous assassination attempts, Rasputin's luck finally ran out on 30 December 1916. He was finally killed at the home of Prince Yusupov, one of the richest men in Russia. Nearly a century after his death, the dramatic circumstances of his murder – the poisoned cakes, the gunshots, the icy grave and rumours of British connivance in his fate – continue to fascinate. Astonishingly, persuasive evidence of British involvement, designed to save the Russian war effort, now exists, patiently unearthed by determined historians.[63]

One of the conspirators, Prince Felix Yusupov, was a Romanov but had always been a wild child. Tutors came and left with rapidity; one ended up in a mental asylum. 'I still remember my music teacher,' he recalled, 'whose finger I bit so savagely that the poor woman was unable to play the piano for a year.'[64] He had been a student in Oxford where he made many English friends. Returning to Russia in 1909, he was initially fascinated by Rasputin, but by 1916 became convinced that the monarchy had to be saved from Rasputin and the tsarina because of the chaos they created. His co-conspirator was another relative of the tsar, Grand Duke Dmitri Pavlovich. Their team also included a medical doctor, Stanislaus Lazovert, and a member of the parliament, Vladmir Purishkevich.[65]

Predictably, they lured Rasputin to the Yusupov palace with the promise of women. Although there is no evidence to support the widespread assertions that Rasputin belonged to a sadomasochistic religious cult that used momentary debauchery as a way of suppressing desire, police reports do show that he frequently consorted with prostitutes, sometimes many in a single evening.[66] His strongest preference was for women of a higher social order. On this particular evening, he had hoped to meet Prince Yusupov's wife, Irina, a woman of fabled beauty. His ambitions were not altogether unrealistic given that marital infidelity was not unusual in Yusupov's aristocratic social circle. However, while Yusupov asserted that his wife would be present, she was in fact safely ensconced 2,000 miles away in the Crimea.[67] The tsarina herself later confirmed that the prince had indeed 'asked him to come over at night' and that 'he would see Irina'.[68]

Prince Yusupov's own widely publicized account involves failed poison and fatal gunshots. Yusupov insists he had laced cakes with enough potassium cyanide 'to kill several men instantly', but despite Rasputin eating two of them, the poison had no effect. Yusupov was forced to watch 'horror-stricken' as he partied on into the night unaffected. At three in the morning, Rasputin was drowsy with drink. Yusupov claims he rushed upstairs, borrowed a friend's revolver and tried to despatch Rasputin with a volley of shots. Rasputin nevertheless rose up and only a second volley of shots from his friend, Vladimir Purishkevich, finally killed him. Purishkevich claims that he fired at Rasputin from behind at a range of about twenty yards, hitting him in the back of the head.

This torrid story has been repeated a thousand times. There's just one problem: Rasputin did not ingest a drop of poison that night. An eagle-eyed policeman spotted the corpse, wrapped in a fur coat beneath a sheet of thick ice, two days later. A detailed autopsy conducted at a nearby hospital found no trace of poison but did find bullet wounds from multiple revolvers, including a close quarter shot to the forehead (unmentioned in the royal Russian accounts).[69] Something did not add up. Fascinatingly, shortly before his departure from Russia, Sam Hoare, the lead MI6 man on the ground, was the only foreigner to be offered sight of Rasputin's decomposing body.[70]

The notorious poison narrative was an artistic fiction; more than that, it was an information deception operation executed by another MI6 man. Perhaps the most remarkable intelligence officer serving under Hoare was Oswald Rayner. He hailed from humble origins, being born in the Smethwick district of Birmingham to Thomas Rayner, a draper, and his wife Florence. He was highly intelligent and won scholarships to study modern languages at Oriel College, Oxford. Here he made influential friends including Prince Felix Yusupov, who was already living an exotic existence and styled himself after his literary hero Oscar Wilde. Rayner later translated and copy-edited Yusupov's famous memoirs. In late 1915, because of his fantastic language ability, Rayner began espionage work and was soon sent out to work under Hoare in Russia.

One of the reasons that this was the perfect assassination was because it was followed up by a discreet and diligent MI6 information operation. Rayner could not have picked more perfect partners, since Purishkevich and Yusupov wished to take full credit and quickly became regarded as national heroes for what they had done.[71]

More remarkable still, many now believe that Yusupov did not fire the deadly shot – that it was in fact none other than Oswald Rayner, using his Webley revolver. Rayner was serving in the MI6 station in St Petersburg and had visited the nearby Yusupov palace half a dozen times in the month prior to the assassination. He then visited several times on the day of the murder itself. Recounting these visits, his driver, William Compton, later cryptically added that 'it is a little-known fact that Rasputin was shot not by a Russian but by an Englishman'. He dropped a final clue: the culprit was from the same part of the country as Compton himself. Compton and Rayner both came from the Birmingham area.[72]

Two other MI6 officers in Russia, Stephen Alley and John Scale, were also friendly with Yusupov. Alley wrote to Scale afterwards triumphantly talking of the 'demise of dark forces'.

'Although matters here have not proceeded entirely to plan,' he conceded, 'our objective has clearly been achieved.' He warned that 'a few awkward questions have already been asked about wider involvement', but reassured Scale that 'Rayner is attending to loose ends'.[73] The sizeable MI6 station was determined to keep Russia in the war against Germany and had assessed the Rasputin–tsarina nexus as its biggest impediment.

The tsar's brother-in-law suspected 'encouragement given to the plotters by the British ambassador'. He fully understood the wartime context and British motive, accusing ambassador Buchanan of 'protecting the interests of the Allies' in trying to nudge Russia towards a more liberal, effective and anti-German government.[74] Even Tsar Nicholas, not exactly the brightest monarch in Europe, pointed to Rayner, telling the British ambassador that he suspected 'a young Englishman who had been a college friend of Prince Felix Yusupof, of having been concerned in Rasputin's murder'. Buchanan predictably assumed the pretence of British propriety, assuring the tsar that his suspicions were 'absolutely groundless'. In fact, even the ambassador, who did not enjoy the best of relations with either the MI6 station or his masters in London, had known about the assassination in advance. Buchanan also knew of the impending March revolution some three months ahead.[75]

Sceptics have made much of the fact that MI6's authorized historian Keith Jeffery found nothing about Rasputin in the archives of the service. Indeed, he insisted that the archives do not hold a single document linking Rayner, Hoare or any other British officer, agent or diplomat to the murder.[76]

But this is to misunderstand the nature of different types of secret service archives. MI6 did most of its work abroad, and very little documentary material came home from its overseas stations. In any case, MI6 had little operational rationale for curating it well. What remains in the MI6 archives is sometimes quite simply misleading. Alan Judd, the leading expert on Mansfield Cumming, notes that a 1924 internal MI6 report claims that little was happening by way of operations in Russia before the Bolshevik revolution, but observes that other evidence now contradicts this.[77] Indeed, the material in Hoare's private papers shows a great deal of MI6 activity in Russia. In short, historians are much more dependent on family archives and papers in private hands to reconstruct the operations of MI6. By contrast, the files of Britain's domestic security service MI5 are voluminous and well kept, partly because most of its work was done at home and also because finding spies often requires combing through the files of past cases to which they are connected.

Scores of historians have examined the Rasputin case. The recent work of Richard Cullen, former commander in the Metropolitan Police and for a while director of forensic training, has provided the breakthrough. After reviewing the documentary and forensic evidence, including the distinctive marks left by a British .455 service-issue revolver, his conclusion is compelling. While many preferred to cling to the romantic heroics of Purishkevich and Yusupov, the truth was different. He concludes: 'Rasputin's death was calculated, brutal, violent and slow and it was orchestrated by John Scale, Stephen Alley and Oswald Rayner through the close personal relationship that existed between Rayner and Yusopov.'[78]

Among the British community in Russia, the death of Rasputin triggered an exhalation of relief. Buchanan had believed that Rasputin was not only planning a separate peace with Germany but was also plotting against him personally. Francis Lindley, one of the senior diplomats at the embassy, explained that 'No one is shocked by it.' For the Russians, the scandalous stories about Rasputin and the tsarina were 'an intolerable humiliation' to their national pride. Moreover, he added, both the tsar and tsarina were unpopular 'and their assassination is quite openly discussed'. Buchanan expected more assassinations to follow and noted that a list had been drawn up of intended targets, including members of 'the empress's so-called clique'.[79]

KING GEORGE HAD worried about the direction of Russia; about the influence of 'dark forces' close to the tsar. Seventy-two hours after the assassination, Hoare sent a ten-page report to MI6 headquarters and suggested that Cumming show it to the king himself. He apologized for its sensational nature, wondering if it was more in the style of the *Daily Mail* than MI6, but presciently added that it was an event that 'might well change the history of a generation'. It was a colourful, if far from accurate, account of Rasputin's death, dwelling on his 'unquenchable appetite' for debauchery, and insisting that 'it was at an orgie that he met his death'.[80] Hoare was rewarded with multiple royal decorations and ended the war appointed Commander of the Order of St Michael and St George (CMG). He received the Orders of St Anne and St Stanislas of Russia, and of St Maurice and St Lazarus.

Another local officer, assuming that the king had received 'verbal news of the "removal" of Rasputin', happily told George's private secretary that many Russians thought the assassination had checked German influence. He told the palace that Rasputin's 'disappearance from the scene has given much relief to those who knew what a mischievous game he played here'.[81] The whole royal family breathed a sigh of relief, thinking the Romanovs were now rescued. Queen Alexandra, the king's mother, told George that she was delighted by 'the death of that wretched monk', adding that he 'might have ruined the whole future of Russia through his influence'. She remained anxious about the tsarina, whom she compared to Catherine the Great.[82]

Queen Alexandra was right to remain anxious. The assassins had hoped Rasputin's death would be a warning shot across the bows of the tsar. They also hoped that Nicholas would send the tsarina away, perhaps to a convent, and assume a more rational course. But in fact, Nicholas and Alex retreated into isolation. Buchanan, who simultaneously welcomed the covert action but worried about its unintended consequences, reported that if 'it was thought that Rasputin was dead: this was a mistake, Rasputin was killed and even buried after a funeral service attended by the imperial family but he is not dead'. He was now 'daily invoked in the secret councils' at the palace, and the tsar and tsarina 'are isolated and appear like a besieged fortress'.[83]

Meanwhile, rumours continued to spread about the pro-German tsarina. The pulp fiction writer William Le Queux wove stories about Rasputin and the tsarina doing German bidding into his best-selling books, claiming to have inside information.[84] In Moscow, Buchanan's daughter reported that the tsarina was widely considered to be communicating with the kaiser by radio from her palace rooftop.[84] These stories were clearly false. She probably favoured a separate peace, but even Yusupov, who had arranged Rasputin's assassination, was clear that 'neither the Tsar nor the Tsarina like the Kaiser'.[85] Facts barely mattered any more. Despite Britain's best efforts, the tsar was sleepwalking towards disaster.

KING GEORGE V AND
THE BOLSHEVIKS

'Heard from Lockhart (our Agent in Moscow)
that dear Nicky was shot.'

George V, diary, 28 July 1918[1]

'BAD NEWS FROM Russia,' noted George in his diary on 28 February 1917. Mass protests had erupted in St Petersburg. Large demonstrations and strikes culminated in violent clashes on the streets. Many soldiers switched sides and joined the workers. The tsar's days were numbered.

George struggled to recognize this. He added hopefully that although the 'rising' was 'practically a revolution', it was against the government not the tsar and, most importantly of all, was 'not against the war'.[2] Nevertheless, the first Russian revolution in the spring of 1917 soon forced the tsar's abdication and a moderate Russian government came to power. Would Russia stay in the war? And what would become of the tsar's family? George's diary also revealed that he understood the problems, noting pithily: 'I fear Alicky is the cause of it all and Nicky has been weak.'[3]

Although Nicholas was soon under house arrest in the Alexander Palace south of St Petersburg, the provisional government was keen for the whole imperial family to leave Russia altogether. The new minister of foreign affairs repeatedly asked the British to send a naval vessel to carry them off into exile. Indeed, they were not only willing but *anxious* that the tsar depart for Britain, warning that extremists were 'exciting opinion against His Majesty'. Britain's ambassador, George Buchanan, also took it for granted that a British ship would appear on the horizon at any moment.[4] Unfortunately for Nicholas, the newly renamed 'Windsors' secretly wished him to go anywhere else.

George wrote a fulsome letter of support to his cousin quickly after the abdication. Privately, he blamed the peculiar dynamic between the Russian royal couple for their misfortune, pointing to Alexandra's eccentricities and obstinacy, together with Nicholas's stupidity and weakness. The new British wartime government, led by David Lloyd George, and dominated by the Liberals and Labour, was divided over the provisional government in Russia but, with Britain being bled by a war of attrition on the Western Front, Lloyd George simply wanted Russia to stay in the war. Also hoping for a new trade treaty, he did not want to damage relations with the new regime.

The new Russian government feared, even expected, violence. As early as 2 March, it concluded that while the wider royal family could stay, indeed many minor royals had been complicit in the revolution, hoping it would deliver a constitutional government and improve the war effort, it was 'absolutely essential and urgent' that the tsar and his immediate family leave Russia.[5] On 19 March, the British ambassador warned the provisional government that 'any violence done to the emperor or his family would have a mostly deplorable effect'; they responded by repeating their desire that they leave quickly, even speaking of their 'deportation'.[6]

On the same day, Major General Hanbury-Williams, one of the Allied commanders in Russia, met the tsar's mother, who was also King George's aunt. They both agreed that Nicholas should leave Russia immediately, while accepting that he would not leave for anywhere without his family. She worried about German U-boats and so preferred Denmark as a destination, but Hanbury-Williams was happy to take full responsibility for their safety. On balance, after a long discussion, an exit to Britain seemed the most sensible option, even though the tsar still fantasized about living out his days as a figurehead constitutional monarch, secluded in the Crimea.[7]

Shortly afterwards, the provisional government agreed that the whole family could travel up to Murmansk on Russia's icy Arctic coast. This was the golden moment. Hanbury-Williams, as the self-styled 'doyen of the Allied mission', rightly urged that time was 'of the essence' and offered to escort Nicholas personally to the port.[8] All that was required was approval from London, but there was only silence. Hanbury-Williams and Buchanan sent urgent telegrams to London. No reply came.[9]

Anxious discussions had broken out in Downing Street. On 22 March, Lloyd George met the king's private secretary, Lord Stamfordham, along with senior ministers. They pondered many possibilities, even including 'a plot to reinstate the emperor'. Lloyd George thought that while Nicholas might not be interested, the feisty tsarina could well be enthusiastic. Money was a major stumbling block in any potential exile to Britain. The war had depleted the Treasury terribly and Lloyd George wanted to know how the deposed family would be supported.[10] Remarkably, Buchanan was asked: 'can you possibly ascertain what are the private resources of the emperor?' The extravagance of the Russian royal family was notorious – Lloyd George did not want to foot the bill.[11]

The question of where they would live posed another problem. Windsor, Buckingham Palace and Sandringham were already in use by George's royal family. Osborne House on the Isle of Wight had become a wartime hospital; Balmoral was supposedly too chilly. These were preposterous reasons for procrastinating and actually Balmoral, far from the public eye, would have been ideal.[12]

They turned to possible alternatives. Lloyd George strongly opposed letting the tsar go to Denmark. It was 'too near Germany, and there would be a serious danger of His Imperial Majesty becoming a focus of intrigue of Germany'. Despite the emotional family connections, the hard realities of war dominated the debate. Desperate to keep the Russians onside, Lloyd George had just sent a letter to the new government stating that 'the revolution is the greatest service which the Russian people have yet made to the cause for which the allies are fighting'. The king thought this was 'a little strong', and Stamfordham explained that the word 'revolution' 'had a disagreeable sound coming from an old monarchical government'. Lloyd George smiled and countered: 'no, an old constitutional government', adding, 'our present monarchy was founded on a revolution'. Stamfordham admitted that he stood corrected.[13]

Lloyd George and his colleagues confronted the classic problem of hosting eminent exiles. They feared that the Romanovs would become the centre of plots for restoration, or even simply rumours of plots. The Romanov presence would reverberate on future relations with a more constitutional Russia. Down the years, the same problem presented with other refugee royals, typically when the shah left Iran in 1979 and he too was denied refuge for similar reasons.[14] At the same time, they needed to keep the provisional government on side for the sake of the war.

Tensions were high. Ultimately, the politicians agreed that, given their pledge to support the new Russian government, they could hardly refuse the request to take the tsar. Stamfordham insisted that George be consulted before the government reached any final decision.

The tsar certainly thought Britain was a likely option. In late March, he noted in his personal diary: 'I looked through my books and things, and started to put aside everything that I want to take with me, if we have to go to England.'[15] But back in Buckingham Palace, George grew more concerned.

Having endured the slings and arrows of public distrust at the start of the war on account of his German relatives, he now feared public reactions to receiving a fellow monarch, who was a decadent and failed ally, and his German-born wife. In the third year of a gruelling war, long-standing concerns about pacifism in Britain now bled into fear of a social revolution.

The king began to receive more and more warnings against hosting the Russians. Stamfordham showed him an alarming file – called 'Unrest in the country' – of newspaper clippings and letters.[16] Lloyd George was lax in formally showing intelligence to the king, and so Stamfordham's skills and networks, drawing on sources from outside mainstream politics, became crucial. In return, Stamfordham rated George as an open-minded consumer of intelligence, being receptive even to material that was highly critical of him. In truth, the king was sensitive to criticism, but Stamfordham, rather impressively, insisted on presenting the world 'unvarnished'.[17]

When the War Cabinet eventually made its hesitant offer to Nicholas, George was 'panic stricken'. He feared that bringing his cousin to Windsor, together with the reportedly pro-German tsarina, would be unpatriotic – even dangerous.[18] Stamfordham reminded the foreign secretary, Arthur Balfour, that while the king had 'a strong personal friendship for the emperor, and therefore would be glad to do anything to help him in this crisis', he had growing concerns. 'His Majesty,' he continued, 'cannot help doubting, not only on account of the dangers of the voyage, but on general grounds of expediency, whether it is advisable that the Imperial Family should take up their residence in this country.' George hoped that Balfour would talk again to Lloyd George on the misassumption that 'no definite decision has yet been come to on the subject by the Russian government'.[19]

As George waited anxiously for a reply, he received more intelligence. Republicans had held a meeting at the Royal Albert Hall to celebrate recent events in Russia. A friend of a palace official wrote up an eye-witness report for the king himself; it reassured him only slightly on the grounds that no one had specifically expressed hostility to the crown. Another source, consulted by George and Stamfordham, was a London bishop. Well connected with the working classes, he warned that the public suspected royal backing of the disgraced tsar. Another contact, a colonel who worked with the poor in Essex, reported something similar the very same day.

Stamfordham also showed George private intelligence, received via the editor of the *Spectator*, suggesting people assumed that some sort of 'Trade Union' existed among kings.[20] Earlier, a member of parliament had warned George that 'If the emperor and empress and their family come here now or during the war they will be surrounded by a vast system of intrigue and espionage.'[21]

When Balfour insisted that the government could hardly withdraw the offer now it had been made,[22] the king's panic intensified. Stamfordham sternly warned that 'every day the King is becoming more and more concerned about the question of the Emperor and Empress of Russia coming to this country'. He received piles of information, from his own network as well as letters from random subjects, 'saying how much the matter is being discussed, not only in Clubs but by working men, and that Labour Members in the House of Commons are expressing adverse opinions to the proposal'. 'As you know,' Stamfordham continued, hardening the palace line, 'from the first the King has thought the presence of the Imperial Family (especially of the Empress) in this country would raise all sorts of difficulties, and I feel sure that you appreciate how awkward it will be for our Royal Family who are closely connected both with the Emperor and Empress.'[23]

George was so agitated that he instructed Stamfordham to send a second missive to Balfour later on the same day. 'He must beg you to represent to the Prime Minister that from all he hears and reads in the press, the residence in this country of the ex-Emperor and Empress would be strongly resented by the public, and would undoubtedly compromise the position of the King and Queen from whom it is already generally supposed the invitation has emanated.'[24]

George had assessed the open-source intelligence in the press and heeded warnings from his own networks. He came to believe that there were more Bolsheviks – or at least sympathizers – in the country than he could tolerate. Alarmed, he clearly linked the invitation to his own position. He was genuinely worried, having long thought that, with aristocracy in retreat and the proletariat on the march, the crown was now less secure than it had been under Queen Victoria.[25] George loved his cousin, but not enough to sacrifice his own throne.

Four days later, the palace again lobbied the prime minister to revoke the invitation. Lloyd George now admitted that 'evidently the matter was more serious than he was aware'.[26] A strange alliance emerged, since neither Lloyd George nor the king liked each other's company. The king regarded his prime minister as dangerously radical and too sympathetic to Russia, while the prime minister regarded the king, unfairly perhaps, as someone with a small brain. There were also social tensions: Lloyd George was uncomfortable in the royal presence and did his very best to avoid royal functions, while George abhorred the leader's 'rude and uncultivated manners'.[27] Yet, on this single issue, they eventually agreed.

The Foreign Office warned Buchanan, Britain's man on the spot, that receiving the tsar risked bolstering the domestic anti-monarchical movement. Buchanan found himself in an awkward position because the new Russian government was still under the impression that the tsar would leave. However, he accepted that 'were we to do so extreme Left Parties, which are not at all well-disposed to us, as well as German agents, would be sure to make capital of his presence in England to stir up public opinion against us'.[28] And so, 'with tears in his eyes', Buchanan withdrew the offer of asylum.[29] Balfour further warned him that even minor members of the family, including mere dukes, of which there were many, would not be welcome.[30]

George remained resolute in his opposition. The following month, Charles Hardinge, the senior official in the Foreign Office, confirmed that, regarding the tsar, the king 'was most anxious he should not come here'.[31] In Moscow, Buchanan was still upset, and the Foreign Office offered comfort that they were 'sounding out the French'.[32] Senior diplomats knew this was a non-starter. The British ambassador in Paris had already warned Downing Street that the tsarina was publicly reviled in France: 'The Empress is not only a

Boche by birth, but in sentiment. She did all she could to bring about an understanding with Germany. She is regarded as a criminal or a criminal lunatic and the ex-Emperor as a criminal for his weakness and submission to her promptings.'[33] The tsarina herself was a major stumbling block. She insisted that the tsar 'would be a scoundrel' if he was to leave Russia, adding for good measure, 'They can do what they like with us… but we will not leave Russia in any circumstances.'[34]

For five months following his abdication, through the spring and early summer of 1917, Nicholas lived under house arrest with his family on the edge of St Petersburg. He passed his days teaching his children Russian history, reading popular novels and planting a vegetable garden. Secretly, he still hoped to live out his days quietly in the sun at his holiday home in the Crimea. George has been repeatedly blamed for this saga, but Tsar Nicholas was the architect of his own fate. He failed to appreciate the severe danger that surrounded him. A weak and indecisive leader believing in absolute monarchy as a divine right and willing to accept 'God's wishes' does not make for a sophisticated consumer of intelligence. No warnings could have impressed him.[35] Nicholas was beyond the efforts of George and indeed other relatives to help him.

UNBEKNOWN TO LONDON, amateur British agents still hoped to rescue the tsar. MI6, with its influential network on the ground, did not receive any instructions to exfiltrate the royal family – but that did not stop others.

The best plot was concocted by Oliver Locker-Lampson, an eccentric figure who commanded an armoured car squadron in Russia while simultaneously serving as member of parliament for Huntingdonshire. Locker-Lampson was a superb linguist, having achieved a first in modern languages at Cambridge, and soon became embroiled in Russian politics. He claimed that he had been asked to participate in the rather crowded British plot to assassinate Rasputin. He also corresponded privately with King George periodically.

Perhaps unaware of the king's wishes and worries, Locker-Lampson came up with the best – and simplest – rescue plot. He had recruited a servant at the Alexander Palace who would arrive to cut the tsar's hair. Once there, he would shave off Nicholas's beard, don a false one himself, and then quickly swap clothes. The tsar would simply walk out unchallenged. Outside he would meet Locker-Lampson in a lorry and, joining up with the British military, move out to Archangel on the north coast and back to Britain by sea.

Tellingly, Locker-Lampson received no green light from Britain. In any case, most of these ideas focused on getting the tsar out alone – and he was unwilling to leave without his family.[36] Locker-Lampson would have been a good bet for an attempt to rescue the tsar. He later rescued the physicist Albert Einstein from the Nazis in Europe, and then helped Ethiopia's Emperor Haile Selassie find sanctuary in Sussex to evade the clutches of Mussolini. He also assisted scores of ordinary Jewish families fleeing Germany.

There were reasons for hesitation. In the spring and summer of 1917 some optimism was in the air. Although Nicholas had abdicated, Russia was still in the war and the provisional government might yet prove more effective than the pantomime presided over by the Romanovs. Moreover, America had finally joined the war effort on 21 March.

MI6 attention now switched from trying to save the failing Tsarist government to supporting the new provisional government in the struggle against Germany. But, as with so many British interventions, even the killing of Rasputin, action was cumbersome and tardy. MI6 sent the famous writer Somerset Maugham, an experienced operative with substantial funds, but remarkably this mission did not depart until June, taking an inexplicably tortuous route via Japan and Vladivostok. Meanwhile, the moderate government was losing influence to the hard-line Bolsheviks. All Maugham was able to do was return to London and convey a secret message that the

Russians had no faith in the ambassador George Buchanan and wanted him replaced. This was told privately to Lloyd George, but even now, events overtook him.[37]

Maugham improbably claims the message was so secret that it could not be written down. More likely it was part of a turf war between Buchanan and MI6, for the ambassador had been hostile to the mission from the outset and was offended that an MI6 emissary had turned up carrying a huge bag of money on a secret operation about which he knew nothing. Buchanan had arrogantly demanded that Mansfield Cumming's MI6 network in Russia be placed under his direct command, a request that received a rapid rejection from the War Office. All this time, Cumming was also fighting off rival bids for control from the War Office and the director of military intelligence.[38]

Meanwhile, in London, the summer of 1917 marked the sum of all fears for the British royal family. Against the background of a Bolshevik ascendancy in Russia, the bestselling author H.G. Wells encouraged an active discussion of the possibility of republicanism in London. Pacifism, strikes, resistance to conscription and general anti-institutionalist feeling unsettled the monarchy and contributed to a sense of an impending end to the old order. Some two hundred thousand workers were on strike in Lancashire alone. The security apparatus began to turn inwards, examining defeatism, working-class organizations and suspicious persons. Even Lloyd George urged the king to visit industrial centres in an attempt to bolster his flagging popularity with the people.[39]

IN AUGUST 1917, possibilities for rescuing the Romanovs closed down dramatically. The tsar and his family were suddenly relocated, with a reduced retinue of forty staff, to the Siberian town of Tobolsk, a thousand miles to the east. Ironically, Russian authorities moved them for their own safety, fearing that a revolutionary crowd might try to seize and kill them in St Petersburg. Now, east of the Urals, they lived behind a high fence in the ramshackle governor's mansion guarded by respectful soldiers. The local population were also deferential, and the family were able to see the villagers bowing and crossing themselves as they passed by. Even here in August 1917 something might have been done; even a deal struck for their release.

Instead, disaster followed. In the absence of organized rescue activity by MI6, more enterprising amateurs filled the vacuum and made the situation worse. Rita Khitrovo, a young friend of the Russian royal family, travelled to Tobolsk on her own initiative with a supply of personal letters and small presents, hoping simply to improve the morale of the incarcerated Romanovs. Suspicious local authorities viewed it as a royalist rescue mission and quickly apprehended her. The letters she carried were innocent and she went free, but the ill-advised visit triggered an urgent review of security procedures. A new hard-line commissar arrived from Moscow to guard the royal family. Escape from this remote location was always difficult due to distance, but this innocent blunder only served to lengthen the odds.[40]

The clock was winding down. Various adventurers and fantasists continued to hatch plots, but once the Bolsheviks took power in October 1917, the family became more likely to face revolutionary justice. Vladimir Lenin considered a public show trial, but had other things to worry about, and so put the problem off, leaving them incarcerated for almost a year. Eventually, Allied plots and a loose army of anti-communist rebels and Czech prisoners of war advancing on the Romanovs' place of imprisonment would force the hand of the Bolsheviks.

Lenin and the Bolsheviks quickly proved tough customers. The British Cabinet were divided over how to deal with them. The hawks, including Winston Churchill, feared the spread of Bolshevik ideas in London, noting that two of Leon Trotsky's comrades, Georgy Chicherin and Peter Petrov, were arrested there for spreading propaganda. Trotsky, in charge of Russian foreign affairs, immediately threatened to take Buchanan and other British diplomats in Russia hostage unless they were released. The king successfully urged the Cabinet to accede to his demands.[41]

Shortly afterwards, Britain began the evacuation of many of its embassy staff including Buchanan, leaving a few diplomats but mostly military personnel and intelligence officers on the ground. Trotsky strung along the remaining representatives, but in March 1918, Chicherin and Petrov, recently released from London, negotiated a long-feared peace treaty with Germany known as Brest-Litovsk. Some fifty German divisions were released for the Western Front.[42]

After Brest-Litovsk there was little to lose, so, Mansfield Cumming, an old friend from the king's days at the Naval College, finally considered a rescue plot. In the spring of 1918, new plans to rescue the Romanovs from their remote location focused on the Norwegians. A Norwegian businessman called Jonas Lied arrived in London from Norway for discussions with MI6. Lied had been Norwegian consul in Siberia and held timber and mining interests in the area. Working alongside Fridtjof Nansen, Norway's greatest explorer, Lied had developed new routes into Russia's interior via the Yenisei River.[43] The MI6 plan seems to have been to use these routes to extricate the tsar. There followed dinners at which he met Reginald Blinker Hall, head of Naval Intelligence, and even the prince of Wales. But although Nansen later worked with Hoare to rescue others from Russia, for now Cumming turned elsewhere.[44]

In April 1918, just as the tsar and his family were moved to the town of Ekaterinburg, some four hundred miles further west, MI6 drafted in the dashing Major Stephen Alley, a fluent Russian speaker whose family had worked in Russia since the 1870s. He had worked for MI6 since the start of the war and, as we have seen, was implicated alongside Oswald Rayner and his boss, Sam Hoare, in the assassination of Rasputin. Viewing him as valuable but 'too hot', or perhaps because of an argument with Cumming, MI6 had withdrawn Alley when the Bolsheviks took over, but his local knowledge was irresistibly excellent. Because he was able to pass as a native Russian, he returned to Murmansk in the spring of 1918 and remained there as a secret service officer under naval cover until August. Remarkably, in 2006, Alley's personal notebook surfaced. Contained within it was a sketch map of Ekaterinburg, showing details of the house where the family were being held. Most likely a reconnaissance by one of his extensive networks of agents, the map indicated a review of the potential for rescue.

On 24 May 1918, all this was confirmed in the most coded language. Alley informed MI6 headquarters of a possible mission in which seven 'valuables' would be secured and delivered to Murmansk. To pull this off, he required £1,000 and four top intelligence officers who, like him, were native speakers and could pass as local Russians.

There is no evidence MI6 ever implemented the plan, and depressingly little detail as to how it might have worked has since emerged. Even if the Romanovs could be spirited past 400 fervent revolutionary guards, possibly against their own will, it is unclear how they would have made it to Murmansk.[45] Indeed, even now, the tsar still insisted on being rescued under two improbable conditions: 'he will not hear of the family being separated or leaving Russian territory'. Nicholas had effectively signed their death warrants.[46]

The early summer formed the last possible moment for MI6 to move the Romanovs, perhaps along the Yenisei River, given the hideous travel problems that existed due to the underdeveloped roads and terrible weather that persisted for nine months of the year,[47] but they aborted the rescue most likely because the house seemed impregnable – and because of the reluctant tsar.[48]

MI6's eleventh-hour reconnaissance of a very hard target is puzzling. It is highly unlikely that Mansfield Cumming would have acted without royal approval. Perhaps it reflected a dawning anxiety on the part of the king that the worst was now possible. Equally likely, it was perhaps a response to fears of a German plot to rescue the tsar by forcible kidnap, overcoming the main problem of his stubborn reluctance to leave Russia. The route to Ekaterinburg through

German-occupied Russia was more navigable. Karina Urbach, the distinguished historian of European royal families, confirms there was a German plan to rescue the tsar in 1918, and British diplomats across Europe were certainly aware of it.[49] Although he had been something of an outcast during royal gatherings before the war, the kaiser was godfather to the tsar's son and heir, the weak and ailing Alexei, and genuinely wanted them to be rescued. Realistically, once the Bolsheviks had taken power in October 1917 and then imprisoned the Romanovs securely at Ekaterinburg, the kaiser had the best chance to free them. Germany had already enforced a difficult treaty upon Russia from a position of strength and had the leverage to extricate them. In other words, there were rival plots to secure the seven 'valuables' at this last critical moment.

On 28 May 1918, cautious British diplomats considered whether to approach Trotsky to at least save the tsar's children. Even if he agreed, they faced a difficult dilemma. A Bolshevik escort would be 'unsafe', yet a British escort would be 'suspected of some Czarist conspiracy'. The logical conclusion was that any attempt to rescue them would most likely endanger the lives of the very people it was designed to save.[50]

ON THE GROUND, British operatives displayed much less caution – resulting in dangerous unintended consequences. The torch now passed to Sidney Reilly, a legendary figure in MI6. An adventurous secret agent, he was busy in Moscow organizing nothing less than a counter-revolution. Working with colleagues in the French secret service, he did his best to covertly unify and fund the fragmented opposition groups. Lenin, as he well knew, had been receiving subsidies from the Germans; a veritable secret service war was now under way.

On 6 July 1918, two men claiming to be from the Cheka, Lenin's secret police, turned up at the German embassy demanding to see the ambassador, Count Wilhelm von Mirbach. When he eventually appeared, they produced revolvers, fired repeatedly and then threw a bomb. Mirbach survived for a few hours but died of his wounds.[51]

In the chaotic hours following the assassination, the Socialist Revolutionary opposition group seized the Cheka headquarters, and held its head hostage. They failed to press their advantage, and the Bolsheviks counter-attacked the following day, retook the Cheka headquarters and arrested many opposition leaders. The following month, the head of the St Petersburg Cheka was assassinated, and a young Socialist Revolutionary member attempted to kill Lenin by firing at point blank range. One bullet penetrated Lenin's lung, and another entered his body above the heart. He was not expected to live.[52]

It remains unclear whether MI6 had a hand in these intrigues. The British had motive: the assassination of the German ambassador would have damaged relations between Russia and Berlin. Meanwhile, Reilly was trying to kill Lenin at this very moment, but there were many plots and any MI6 effort seems to have been aborted at the last minute.[53] Keith Jeffery, the official MI6 historian, insists that the shooting of Lenin was not directed by MI6 in London.[54] But perhaps Reilly, the so-called Ace of Spies, was acting off his own bat. Robert Bruce Lockhart, one of the last remaining diplomats in Russia, certainly recalls his Napoleonic addiction to 'playing a lone hand'.[55]

The Bolsheviks responded with ferocity. They killed alleged conspirators in their thousands – and one of the suspects they wanted particularly badly was Sidney Reilly. Only dimly aware that something had gone wrong with his own plot, Reilly waited in the street for his friend Captain Francis Crombie from the British embassy, but he did not come. 'Not like Crombie to be unpunctual,' he noted. Uneasily, at midday, he decided to risk a visit to the embassy himself. Even before he arrived, it was clear that the Cheka were sweeping the streets and he 'met some men and women running'. A line of bodies – 'the dead bodies of Bolshevik soldiers' – greeted him outside.[56]

Suspicious of British involvement in a coup, the Cheka had raided the embassy hoping to catch Reilly. Some staff had dashed upstairs to the chancellery to destroy sensitive papers as fast as they could. 'Meanwhile the gallant Crombie, a Browning automatic in each hand, had held the stairs against the red guards, and had emptied both magazines into them before he had fallen, literally riddled with bullets.'[57]

The high drama continued. Most British diplomats had evacuated months ago but the remaining British representative, Bruce Lockhart, was arrested and marked for execution. The Cheka demanded to know where Reilly was – and whether Bruce Lockhart knew the terrorist who had tried to assassinate Lenin.[58] He was only saved by the counter-arrest of Maxim Litvinov, the Russian diplomat in London, on yet more charges of spreading propaganda. It had become an extraordinary battle of body politics. Reilly and others working for MI6 fled to Sweden.

It was during this purge, triggered by the wake of the attempt on Lenin's life, that the Romanovs were executed.[59] This, together with the fact that the strongest allies of the anti-communist White Russians, the Czech Legions, supported by the British, were gradually advancing towards the royal captives at Ekaterinburg, almost certainly sealed their fate.[60]

So often, the eventual execution of the Romanov royal family is reported in isolation. The focus is on their final days and hours, with documents mined for every last grisly detail. But the lack of context clouds our understanding. The Romanovs died in a wave of panic retribution in response to a failed coup, a veritable secret service war in St Petersburg pursued by MI6 and the secret services of several allied countries. It is important to remember that in the wake of these assassination attempts – there was yet another attack on Lenin in August 1918 – paranoia and spy mania had broken out. During this brief period of madness, nobles, aristocrats and White officers were rounded up and 'shot like dogs' all over Russia.[61]

The executions of the Romanovs were ghastly. Around midnight on 17 July, the sleeping family was woken and asked to put on their clothes, under the pretext that they would be moved to a safer location due to the advancing Czech forces. The Romanovs were then taken to a small semi-basement room no more than twenty feet across. Pandemonium broke out, leading to waves of shooting with revolvers and then the use of bayonets.[62] The Czech Legion arrived a week later and sifted through the ghostly remains of the house, but there were no bodies to be found. The only survivor was the young Alexei's spaniel, who was adopted by a British officer and, ironically, lived out his last days in the shadow of Windsor Castle.[63]

For over a month, MI6 could tell the king little about the fate of the imperial family. Most assumed that the tsarina and children remained alive. In a gesture that was perhaps more show than substance, George now asked Spain for help to 'rescue the family from their pitiable position'. The Spanish king and queen were related to the tsarina and George still hoped that, in the unlikely event of a rescue, she would be better off in neutral Spain than in Britain where she had been vilified in the press for years as a pro-German traitor. On 28 August 1918, news arrived that she and all her children had most probably died with the tsar.[64]

In September 1918, George received confirmation. The intelligence officer at Murmansk had learnt 'from a source that he has no reason to doubt' that the whole family had been murdered.[65] According to Stamfordham, George was 'deeply grieved at the ghastly fate which has befallen his relatives'. He found it 'almost incredible that the innocent children should not have been spared'.[66] George wrote to his mother, Queen Alexandra, a few days later that he feared that 'these disgusting brutes in Russia' had killed everyone.[67]

But the so-called intelligence was patchy and filled with rumour. The king forwarded a disturbing report to his younger sister, Princess Victoria, that suggested the family might all have been burned alive. Lord Mountbatten recalled that some months afterwards 'King George V showed me secret service reports that they had all been raped', but then asked him not to tell other family members. Thankfully, neither of these things were true, but they must have strongly framed the king's outlook on the new Bolshevik regime.[68] Eventually, Sir Basil Thomson, director of intelligence, conducted an extensive and more accurate inquiry on the last days of the Romanovs that was given to the king.[69]

With the British Army still fighting on the Western Front, George commanded his court to wear mourning clothes for a whole month. He did so not out of respect for the millions who had died on the battlefields of Europe, but for Nicholas and his family, whose execution had now been confirmed. George and his wife Mary quietly attended a memorial service at London's only Russian Orthodox chapel.[70] Afterwards, the king noted in his diary: 'I was devoted to Nicky, who was the kindest of men.'[71] As the war drew to a close, the final years of this dramatic decade seemed to promise social turbulence threatening the future of royal families everywhere. A real sense of fear pervaded the secret emissaries that continued to move backwards and forwards between London, St Petersburg and Moscow, battling against the rise of Bolshevism.

DESPITE THE OVERTHROW of the monarchy, the tsar's mother initially refused to leave Russia. In 1918, there was a rescue attempt by a distinguished British intelligence officer, George Hill, recently awarded the Military Cross, together with Reilly. The queen of Romania, who was Queen Victoria's granddaughter and who had been brought up in Britain, offered support. Taking a Romanian ship and an escort of 200 soldiers, and even the Romanian prime minister's limousine as a getaway car, they finally reached her. But the stubborn dowager refused to leave and even denied that her son was dead.

Only in 1919, at the urging of her sister in Britain, did the mother of King George V begrudgingly depart, fleeing Crimea over the Black Sea to London. George sent the warship HMS *Marlborough* to retrieve his aunt. The party of seventeen Romanovs included her daughter, the Grand Duchess Xenia, and five of Xenia's sons, plus six dogs and a canary. After a brief stop in the British base in Malta, they travelled to England where she stayed with her sister. Queen Alexandra treated her well enough and they spent time together at Marlborough House in London and at Sandringham, but Maria Feodorovna, as a deposed empress dowager, always felt that she was now 'number two' in contrast to her popular sister. She eventually elected to return to her native Denmark. Here, rather as the British had feared, she lived at the huge expense of the Danish royal family and ran up 'mountains of unpaid bills'.[72]

The wily dowager had persuaded George to grant her a pension of £10,000, something he could ill-afford.[73] Yet secretly, she brought with her the pride of the Romanovs' jewel collections that had been concealed in her St Petersburg home. She then hid this fantastic hoard of treasure for a decade. In October 1928, the box was finally opened to everyone's astonishment. Some of the prize items made their way into the collections of George's wife, Queen Mary, their total value being about £10 million at current prices.[74]

In Britain, the royals went to inordinate lengths to suppress the story of George and the Romanovs. Buchanan, Britain's embattled ambassador in St Petersburg, wrote his memoir, but was threatened with prosecution under the Official Secrets Act and the stoppage of his pension if he revealed the truth. Even more remarkably, Lloyd George was required to drop an entire chapter of his memoirs. The main purpose was to quash any reference to the anti-monarchical movements in the country that had so terrified George and his private secretary into inaction in 1917.[75] Maurice Hankey, the Cabinet secretary, 'thought that the chapter on the Tsar's future residence should be suppressed altogether'.[76] Indeed, the king had urged the former prime minister to drop his memoirs entirely, but Lloyd George characteristically replied, 'He can go to hell.'[77]

By late 1918, tension between Lloyd George and the king increased. The prime minister made the idea of putting the kaiser on trial a key part of his election campaign, employing the slogan 'Hang the Kaiser'. This issue had bubbled along all the way through the war. The German execution of the British spy Edith Cavell had caused widespread anger, as had the sinking of the *Lusitania*. Both Lloyd George and his foreign secretary pressed the War Cabinet to charge the kaiser with crimes against humanity.[78] King George did not have the same affection for the kaiser as he felt for Nicholas, but he did not wish to see further relatives face an execution squad.

Bizarrely, at this very moment, and quite unknown to the king, his own uncle, Prince Arthur, duke of Connaught, had triggered a renegade effort to bring the kaiser to justice. On 11 June 1918, Arthur was in France inspecting a unique American regiment, the 114th Field Artillery, the only volunteer American regiment in the war. As such, it had been singled out for a royal visit. The commander was Colonel Luke Lea, in civilian life the publisher of the *Nashville Tennessean* and, as a former senator, someone of firm opinions. In his view, victory was rendered incomplete by the knowledge that 'the number one war criminal, Kaiser Wilhelm, had escaped to Holland and was living there in relative luxury'.[79]

After the inspection was over, Lea sat politely taking tea and making small talk with Arthur. He asked about the war settlement and soon Arthur was holding forth and 'boasted of his close blood relationship to the Kaiser of Germany'. He added that he was uncle to the kings of both England and Germany. Lea was soon convinced that the British were engaged in successful efforts 'to protect the Kaiser'. He was also annoyed by the fact that Arthur was covered in medals but 'had probably never been near enough the front line… to hear a shell shriek'.[80]

Arthur had convinced Lea that the European establishment would secretly protect the kaiser and intended for him to live out his days in luxury. Lea had other ideas. In January 1919, he and a group of three officers and three sergeants commandeered a military vehicle and headed out along snow-covered roads and attempted to seize the kaiser and bring him to the Paris Peace Conference for a war crimes trial.[81]

At first the secret party were refused entry to the Netherlands. Later they flourished documents that they claimed had been signed by the Dutch queen and so on their second attempt were saluted on their way past the border. Using false civilian passports and carrying concealed weapons, they arrived at the castle where the kaiser was in exile. Lea bluffed his way in by claiming to be local nobility. Soon they were inside, but wisely the kaiser refused to see them. After a long stand-off, and with a hostile crowd gathering outside, they finally retreated to their cars and fled back to France.[82]

General John J. 'Black Jack' Pershing, commander of the American Expeditionary Forces, ordered his inspector general to investigate the escapade quickly. But fearing an embarrassing diplomatic incident, he decided against a court martial and opted for a private disciplinary warning. Ironically, Lea was unaware that it was in fact American diplomats, led by the tough-minded secretary of state, Robert Lansing, and supported by President Wilson, who were the keenest to avoid the prosecution of the kaiser and probably saved his neck.

The amateur kidnap plot had repercussions. Further rumours of missions to capture the kaiser were now taken very seriously. There were even reports that a unit of the Belgian air force had decided to bomb the castle. During winter, the ice on the moat of the castle was broken up regularly to keep people away. In autumn 1920, the guard was reinforced because of rumours that a band of British ex-servicemen were heading across the Channel in an airship to kidnap the kaiser.[83]

PERHAPS TO OFFSET private shame at the fate of his Russian cousin, George now showered MI6 with awards and medals for its officers' exploits in Russia. Sidney Reilly was awarded the Military Cross,

George Hill received a Distinguished Service Order, while Paul Dukes, MI6 chief in Moscow, received a knighthood, and is still the only MI6 officer to be knighted for his services as a spy. Bruce Lockhart was invited to come and describe his dangerous mission to the king. Moreover, George knighted Mansfield Cumming, chief of MI6, at Buckingham Palace on 26 July 1919. He wore full dress uniform and his previous decorations, which notably included the Orders of St Stanislas and St Vladimir awarded to him by the tsar three years before.[84] The most remarkable recipient was Augustus Agar, who was awarded the Victoria Cross for agent-running in the Baltic with motor torpedo boats under the directions of Cumming.[85]

Compton Mackenzie, the MI6 chief in Athens, was also awarded the OBE for similar activities in Greece. Just like Sidney Reilly, he had worked with the French in another undercover war, this time against the pro-German king Constantine and his wife, whose sister was married to the kaiser.[86] Mackenzie often went too far, roaring around Athens with armed gangs in fast cars – his escapades had even included stealing sealed Greek mailbags that held correspondence between the Greek royal family and their relatives in Germany.[87] After much violence, Constantine was eventually forced to abdicate in favour of his son, Alexander. Prince Arthur, George's uncle, was sent out by sea on a 'mission' to settle Alexander on the throne, narrowly dodging death at the hands of a German U-boat. Greece remained pro-Allied for the rest of the war, but sadly Alexander died of an infected monkey bite in 1920.[88]

After the war, George nurtured a life-long hatred of Bolsheviks. Impressively, and intelligently, this did not transfer into visible anxiety about British socialists. After updating him about domestic republicanism, his private network of correspondents persuaded him to undertake a more open reign, engaging regularly with working people and even cultivating trade unionists and Labour Party members of parliament.[89] As Labour gained ground, George pragmatically thought it a matter of survival. His son and heir, the future

Edward VIII, praised his 'propaganda' – although George preferred to see it as 'duty'.[90]

Perhaps because of the king's intense hatred of Lloyd George, Ramsay MacDonald shone by comparison and the king developed a warm and supportive relationship with Britain's first socialist prime minister. It certainly helped that, by this time, republicanism was not Labour Party policy. In January 1924, on his first meeting with MacDonald, the big issue was a treaty with Russia and he told his new prime minister that he did not even want to shake hands with 'the murderers of his relatives'.[91] Anxious diplomats in the Foreign Office were nervous about showing MacDonald Soviet decrypts and so procrastinated. For this period, the king might have seen more sensitive intelligence material than the head of his government.[92]

MacDonald lost the general election later that year, an event overshadowed by the 'Zinoviev letter' – a document published by the *Daily Mail* four days before the election. The letter purported to be a directive from Grigory Zinoviev, the head of the Communist International in Moscow, urging subversion and welcoming the opening of diplomatic relations as a gateway to revolution in Britain. Perhaps misinformed by his right-wing contacts, the king wrongly noted: 'I suppose there is no doubt that Z's letter is genuine? I see the Communists say it is a forgery.'[93] It was almost certainly a forgery.[94]

This did not prevent the king from creating both informal and formal organizations to keep Buckingham Palace better informed of communism and republicanism within Britain. Stamfordham continued to solicit information from his network of religious and military figures whom he thought had fingers on the pulse of working-class opinion.[95]

Neither did it prevent him from launching a covert campaign to counter Soviet propaganda against the royal family during the interwar years. At around the same time, George made contact with the legendary MI5 spymaster Maxwell Knight by offering him a highly secretive and personal mission. The greatest secret of Knight's career was embodied by his most treasured possession, a gold cigarette case with the royal cypher of King George V and the inscription 'Maxwell Knight, 1931'. He had performed some secret service for which the royal family was extremely grateful – but what it was remains a mystery.[96]

By the 1930s, the king's hatred of Moscow had somewhat subsided. On the evening of 27 November 1934, Buckingham Palace threw one of the grandest receptions for some years. The event honoured the forthcoming marriage of George's young-est son, the rather dissolute duke of Kent, to Princess Marina of Greece. Almost a thousand people attended, including many of Europe's royal families and even Kirill Vladimirovich Romanov, the deposed tsar's cousin and head of the exiled imperial family. One of his daughters, Kira, was a bridesmaid. Princess Marina's mother, Elena, was also a Russian princess. The event was attended by all the ambassadors in London.

It created a degree of awkwardness, since the Soviet ambassador, Ivan Maisky, was present and, for some, the murderous events of 1918 were still fresh in the memory. Most royals, led by the elderly King George, joined the line and shook hands with Maisky politely, but Marina's mother demonstratively walked past him and his wife without greeting them. 'Two or three wizened old witches ugly as sins, came out of the corner room and hesitated, whispering secre-tively and glancing in our direction,' Maisky recorded in his diary, and skipped the line-up altogether. The Russian emperor's retinue, decorated with ribbons and diadems, 'stumbled at the sight of me and immediately backed off every which way'. Maisky noted with quiet satisfaction that 'the Soviet ambassador had given them a fright!'[97]

Even in 1934, the very mention of the Romanovs conjured up multiple horrors for the king. Their violent deaths formed a potential focal point of a world revolution that now threatened to sweep away empires and monarchies – indeed the Bolsheviks had avowed to do just that. To make matters worse, Nicholas had 'let the side down' and was now seen for what he was, a kindly but incompetent idiot who had managed the war against Germany badly. Far worse was Alicky, his wife, who had been German by birth and formed the centre of lurid accusations of German plots, with scurrilous pamphlets and books circulating not only in Russia but in Britain too.

The German problem had plagued the last years of Victoria, had obsessed Edward VII and had underpinned the secretive efforts of George V to save the Romanovs. The British royal family understandably feared similar accusations of being 'pro-Boche' and had done their best to escape this by rebranding themselves 'The Windsors' in the summer of 1917. But now, by shaking hands with the amiable Russian ambassador Ivan Maisky in 1934, George gave a clear signal: Britain's future problems lay not with Moscow – but with Berlin.

10

ABDICATION: SPYING ON
EDWARD VIII AND WALLIS SIMPSON

'under surveillance'

Edward VIII, *A King's Story*[1]

IN MAY 1935, a secret message from Adolf Hitler made its
way circuitously to King George V. It set out nothing less
than Hitler's vision for a future world peace. Framed in predictably racist terms, it called for co-operation between Britain and
Germany, 'the two Germanic nations'. Hitler offered a crude deal:
if Britain gave Germany a free hand to pursue *Lebensraum* on the
Continent, he would leave Britain free to pursue its imperial ambitions elsewhere.[2]

George was horrified. Confirming all his worst fears, he interpreted it as Hitler warmongering and conspiring against the French.
The palace sent an icy reply through the same backstairs channels,
and rebuked Lord Rothermere, the pro-Nazi newspaper proprietor,
for serving as its conduit. George urged the prime minister and the
foreign secretary to take note.[3] The secretive exchange was important, for it not only illuminated Hitler's overarching world view, but
underlined his outdated obsession with the British royal family as a
means to realize it. This would not be, by any means, Hitler's last
attempt to reach out to British royals.

George had followed the rise of Hitler and Mussolini with alarm. He diligently read the daily top-secret material sent from Whitehall with 'exact attention'. Ever higher piles of red boxes arrived and, despite his declining health, he read them all and was keen to demonstrate his command of their detail. He saw the prime minister each week, as was the custom, but topped this up with more frequent meetings with the foreign secretary and intelligence chiefs.[4]

The slaughter of the First World War had appalled George, but he squarely blamed the Germans and, not wanting to give an inch to Hitler, he monitored developments carefully. In 1933, the British ambassador in Berlin wrote directly to him warning that the 'atmosphere and mentality' in Germany was alarmingly similar to the moments before the previous war. The king responded that 'we must not be blinded by the apparent sweet reasonableness of the Germans'. The following year he spoke sternly and in person to the German ambassador, telling him that 'at the present moment Germany was the peril of the World'.[5]

The king enjoyed access to the latest intelligence. In February 1935, he read secret service reports on rapid German rearmament, which left him 'gloomy'.[6] But even he was not told everything. Around this time, he dined with Stewart Menzies, deputy chief of MI6. Mindful of the previous escapades of Sidney Reilly in Moscow, which he had followed closely, the king mischievously asked the name of the most senior British intelligence officer in Berlin. Menzies smiled and refused to answer. George asked whether the famous threat, 'Off with your head', would change his mind. Menzies was adamant: 'My head would roll with my lips still sealed.'[7]

By December, rumours circulated that George was dangerously ill. He managed to broadcast a flawless Christmas message to the empire, alleviating concerns, but then faded fast on Sunday 19 January 1936. He died the following night just two months before Hitler's adventure in the Rhineland. His eldest son, David, taking the formal title of Edward VIII, now ascended the throne at the age of forty-two. Edward VIII, always ambivalent about his formal role, would reign for just less than a year. Presciently, George had predicted some ten years before that his son would abdicate.

The king's funeral took place on 28 January. Such events, bringing together world leaders, offered the opportunity for discreet diplomacy in their shadows. The next day, Maxim Litvinov, Moscow's foreign minister, headed for Buckingham Palace to spend an obligatory fifteen minutes with the new king, but at Edward's request he stayed rather longer. Edward was courteous and amiable, but bombarded Litvinov with questions, some of which were of 'a very delicate nature'. He asked 'why and under what circumstances was Nicholas II killed. Was it not because the revolutionaries feared his reinstatement?' Bounding from one hot subject to another, he then fired off questions about Trotsky. Edward agreed with Litvinov on the importance of peace: 'no one wants war'.

The king added a curious qualification. 'Germany and Italy have nothing at all. They are dissatisfied. Something should be done to improve their condition…' The Russians seem to have overlooked this ominous interjection and came away 'impressed' with Edward as someone who was 'a lively and spirited man, with a keen interest in world affairs'. In the evening, Ivan Maisky, the Soviet ambassador, took his boss to the cinema to see *Top Hat*, the iconic Fred Astaire and Ginger Rogers film, which he dismissed as 'a very silly comedy' that Litvinov 'did not enjoy'. Edward would doubtless have been in his element.[8]

EDWARD VIII WAS born in 1894 and spent his childhood with his great-grandmother Queen Victoria still on the throne. Yet he was the very antithesis of Victorian values and instead embraced a modern spirit. Like his father, he spent time in the Royal Navy as a boy, but then went to Oxford before serving in the First World War.

Much to his frustration, Edward was not allowed to serve on the front line for fear of his capture. His lowest point was being awarded a Military Cross that he did not deserve, but which preserved the fiction that he was fighting. However, Edward, like his father, was assiduous in visiting military hospitals and worrying about the privations of the troops. Although his French was modest, his German was good and this opened the door to some useful work, including taking part in the interrogation of German prisoners. After a while he moved on to matters concerning the supply of ammunition, which he rated as 'so much better' than 'the Intelligence branch where I was before'.[9] In truth, Edward enjoyed neither. He wanted to be closer to the front.

German intelligence was, meanwhile, watching France for royal visitors. In July 1917, Edward had discreetly joined King George and Queen Mary at Vimy Ridge and Messines. Despite strict secrecy, German spies spotted them. Within hours of the royals leaving Messines, the town suffered its heaviest air raid of the entire war.[10]

Edward enjoyed the support of clever and thoughtful organizers, including Alan 'Tommy' Lascelles, who would serve as secretary to four monarchs between 1920 and 1953. He was joined by Godfrey Thomas, who had previously run the Foreign Office cypher department and who had a special talent for secrecy. Edward failed to appreciate their skills – even though he often deployed them to get him out of scrapes. He preferred the company of his fun-loving favourite equerry, Captain Edward 'Fruity' Metcalfe, an Irish officer initially employed to look after the horses. Although professing to hate formal duties, Edward loved travel and the relative freedom it brought, undertaking sixteen overseas tours before ascending the throne, often in the company of 'Fruity'.[11]

Edward was considered to be remarkably good-looking as a young man and flaunted a sense of style. Embracing the jazz age, fun and 'flappers', he loved everything American and would have been perfectly comfortable inside the Jeeves and Wooster novels of P.G. Wodehouse. He dressed flamboyantly and the camera loved him; every photo looked like it had come from the latest pages of *Vogue* magazine.[12]

From the outset, he preferred elder married women with a domineering personality, perhaps, as one historian has observed, because he was 'neurotic, self-pitying', even 'neo-masochistic'.[13] As a young officer in France he enjoyed a long liaison with Marguerite Alibert, a high-class Parisian prostitute. Infatuated, Edward wrote to her constantly. She carefully preserved the letters, creating a blackmail opportunity in the process. Not long after the end of the war, she visited London with her husband with whom she had a stormy relationship. Returning to the hotel after seeing the operetta *The Merry Widow*, they had one of their frequent arguments. Early in the morning, Alibert shot her husband repeatedly from behind with a .32 calibre Browning automatic. He was taken to Charing Cross Hospital but died within hours.[14]

The royal family were desperate to hide her connection to the prince. The next day, his entourage acted fast. They cancelled a summer schedule and packed him off on a three-month tour of Canada. While she awaited trial in Holloway prison, Special Branch opened all of her correspondence. The best lawyer was hired to portray her wealthy Egyptian husband as a sexual monster and sadist. With strings pulled behind the scenes, she went free in a trial that lasted only days. Most importantly, Edward was not mentioned – but the episode pointed to future trouble.[15]

Although Edward's minders tried to keep him out of further scrapes, he did not like 'protection'. In the words of his official biographer, the presence of plain clothes policemen was irksome and 'affronted his passionate desire for privacy'. This attitude had serious consequences for his safety. In August 1922, a panic erupted over an IRA murder plot in London. The primary target was Winston Churchill, who was then secretary of state of the colonies. 'Winston is first on the list to be murdered,' Edward wrote to his mistress of the moment, Freda Dudley Ward, adding 'your poor little parpee is the second'. The home secretary ordered extra security for him, but Edward would not have it and ordered them to back off: 'I will not stand for having a car following me.' He added: 'So please don't worry any more. If anyone wanted to kill me all the CID in the world won't stop him.'[16]

But Edward badly needed protection. By the mid-1920s, he was conceivably the first global celebrity, pursued by hordes of photographers. Perhaps the most eligible bachelor in the world, he did not hesitate to have fun, flirting his way through royal tours, even with the wives of local officials. He struggled to keep to a time schedule because he was not especially committed to his royal duties. They bored him.[17]

George V found the playboy prince increasingly infuriating, and worried about his suitability as the future king. He worked closely with Edward's endlessly patient private secretary, Clive Wigram, to try to manage his worst habits.[18] Edward received his own private residence, Fort Belvedere, on the edge of the Windsor estate, in the hope of keeping his more esoteric activities out of the public eye. He decorated it in the latest art deco style and added a swimming pool, where he could entertain his friends.[19] Nor was he the only one straining at the royal leash; his youngest brother, Prince George, later the duke of Kent, travelled an even more dissolute path, including drug use, something from which his elder brother eventually rescued him. All this was a stark contrast to his father's twin passions for shooting and stamp collecting.

In January 1935, George's concern turned to panic. Courtiers secretly told the king that Edward had given a mysterious new woman £110,000 worth of jewels, close to £8 million at current prices, together with a substantial allowance. The prince was known to be rather strange about money, spending freely on luxuries yet rarely paying his bills and showing a notable reluctance to tip waiters, but this was peculiar behaviour even for him. George suspected foul play – perhaps even blackmail. The awkward episode with the many letters he had written to the dangerous and wily Marguerite Alibert in Paris was still a painful memory.

George took the remarkable step of putting his son and heir under Special Branch surveillance. This was facilitated by the fact that he got on rather well with his later prime ministers, especially the confident Stanley Baldwin, who had recently replaced the ailing Ramsay MacDonald. Together they met the head of the Metropolitan Police, Philip Game. Game needed a top officer whom he could trust and who would treat the incredibly sensitive operation with the utmost discretion. He turned to a rising star, Albert Canning.

Canning was an outstanding policeman. The son of a prosperous Essex businessman, he had joined the police in 1906 where his superior abilities quickly became apparent, and transferred to Special Branch after only six months on the beat. Politically sensitive and astute, he spoke fluent French and was a capable surveillance manager able to run a substantial team. He also knew the Edward of old, as he had travelled with him as his personal detective to Le Touquet in the summer of 1924. By all accounts, on this visit, Edward was delighted by him.[20]

During George's last months, at his special request, Special Branch began to probe the life of a certain 'Mrs Simpson'. Born Wallis Warfield in Pennsylvania in 1896, she had travelled extensively, including a period in Shanghai, making details hard to collect. They established that she had been divorced and was now married to Ernest Aldrich Simpson.

Police attention centred on Wallis Simpson's address at 5 Bryanston Court, a block of high-class flats just north of Hyde Park, where she lived alone. Surveillance teams noted that the prince 'visits frequently', but, they added, so too did other men. In addition to tracing her movements, Special Branch gathered intelligence on her personal relationship with Edward. Anxious about blackmail, they analysed the power relationship and even the most minute details of their everyday lives. They watched the couple as they visited an antiques shop in Pelham Street, South Kensington, making purchases for 'The Fort'. Afterwards they interrogated the poor antiques dealer who explained 'that they were on very affectionate terms and addressed each other as "darling"'. Most importantly, the dealer, who was good at sizing up his customers, suggested that the lady 'seemed to have The Prince of Wales completely under her thumb'.[21]

As Canning and his team dug deeper, they concluded that Wallis and Ernest Simpson were simply a pair of professional hustlers, preying on the prince for money. The police reported that Simpson, whom they described as 'of the bounder type', made no secret of his wife's association with Edward and seemed to enjoy some reflected glory, clearly hoping that it would lead to some sort of sinecure or well-paid promotion. One source reported that Simpson expected to become a baron at the very least when Edward took the crown.[22] These intelligence reports confirmed the worst fears of both the king and Baldwin.[23]

The Special Branch watchers must have been considerable in number to be able to chart her movements in such detail. Some of their reports even suggest telephone monitoring and letter opening. The operation was becoming intrusive. The watchers – and listeners – soon discovered tensions between Wallis and her husband:

Mrs Simpson has said that her husband is now suspicious of her association with other men as he thinks this will eventually cause trouble with the Prince of Wales. Mrs Simpson has also alleged that her husband is having her watched for this reason and in consequence she is very careful for the double purpose of keeping both the Prince of Wales and her husband in ignorance of her surreptitious love affairs.[24]

Wallis was right about being followed, but wrong about the culprits. She thought it might be private eyes working for her husband or even for Edward. In fact, it was Canning's teams of detectives, keen to discover who else she was seeing. There was one especially alarming candidate: Hitler's ambassador to London, Count Joachim von Ribbentrop. He was a regular guest at Bryanston Court – sometimes visiting Wallis on his own. This created a dangerous security risk, with the foreign secretary anxious that Britain's secret diplomatic cyphers could be 'compromised' because 'Mrs S is said to be in the pocket of the German ambassador'.[25] Indeed, in London, Ribbentrop was referred to by some as the 'arch-Hitler spy of Europe'.[26] The idea that the heir to the British throne's lover was also having intimate relations with a leading Nazi was too ghastly to contemplate. So, it was a considerable relief when Canning discovered more.[27]

SPECIAL BRANCH LEARNT that Wallis Simpson's secret lover was currently Guy Marcus Trundle. A successful Ford car salesman, he was clearly a charmer. The police reported that he was 'very good looking, well-bred and an excellent dancer. He is said to boast that every woman falls for him.' The report continued, 'he meets Mrs Simpson quite openly at informal social gatherings as a personal friend but secret meetings are made by appointment when intimate relations take place. He receives money from Mrs Simpson as well as expensive presents.' Wallis was using her considerable allowance from Edward to fund this exotic lifestyle.[28] Meanwhile, she feared that Edward might be transferring his affections to a new woman he had met in Austria. To describe this as a love triangle would have been something of an oversimplification.

In early 1936, after the death of King George V, this espionage and intrigue took on a more serious tone. Special Branch were no longer watching the prince of Wales and Wallis Simpson on behalf of the king and the prime minister, they were watching the new monarch and the person he wished to marry. The intelligence dossiers they compiled have been the subject of endless speculation down the years but the poet Osbert Sitwell got in early and asked Baldwin what they contained. Baldwin dismissed the idea that Wallis was a Nazi spy but did concede that her MI5 file showed that 'she was a paid agent of the Hearst press'.[29]

Albert Canning now presided over all Special Branch activity, including its surveillance of Britain's burgeoning fascist movements, and must have found this rather confusing. Was he watching the new king to protect the monarch from a pair of hustlers? Or was he watching both Edward and Wallis because they were mixing with some of Britain's extreme right? After all, Oswald Mosley, Britain's most prominent fascist, had recently become the brother-in-law to Edward's favourite equerry, 'Fruity' Metcalfe, leading to open speculation about Edward's politics. Although Mosley deliberately cut down his meetings with Edward once he became king to avoid embarrassing him, they were firm friends and remained so into old age.[30] When Edward did meet Mosley during his brief reign, oddly he was accompanied not only by Wallis but also her husband, Ernest. Years later, Edward told Mosley that he 'should have been prime minister' and insisted that 'it was the Jews that brought us into the war'. Even Mosley was shocked.[31]

Edward's political views have long been a subject of speculation. He has been the victim of gossip, exaggeration and innuendo, not least because so many of Britain's upper classes feared communism and saw the rise of the far right as an antidote, so loose talk on this subject was common. Despite this, we cannot escape the fact that Edward expressed profound admiration for the Nazis in Germany and for fascism more generally, especially as a social system. As early as July 1933, he told former Kaiser Wilhelm II's grandson, Prince Louis Ferdinand, that it was 'no business of ours to interfere in Germany's internal affairs either re Jews or re anything else'. 'Dictators are very popular these days,' Edward had added. 'We might want one in England before long.'[32]

SPECIAL BRANCH OFFICERS, as Canning knew from his own experience, specialized in personal protection. They spied on Edward but also had to keep him safe. This seemed easy, for he was one of the most popular personalities in the world and had a natural gift for connecting with the crowd. He was mostly hounded by harmless lovesick women and nuisance paparazzi rather than anarchist assassins or dangerous lunatics. Nonetheless, the biggest threat to royals in the early twentieth century remained assassination and, with politics increasingly febrile, the king needed protection.

At midday on 16 July 1936, only a few months into his reign, Edward, resplendent in full-dress scarlet tunic and bearskin, rode back towards Buckingham Palace. He had been attending a military ceremony in Hyde Park and the crowds were lining Constitution Hill for a glimpse of their glitzy monarch. Suddenly, a mysterious figure in a brown suit stepped forward from the front of the crowd. He dropped a newspaper to reveal a revolver which he aimed squarely at the king.

A woman standing next to him, a Mrs Alice Lawrence, cried out in alarm and immediately grabbed his arm. Noticing the commotion, a special constable punched the man's arm, sending the gun flying into the parade. Other policemen scooped it up and muscled the assailant away.

The mysterious figure was George Andrew McMahon. Arrested and bundled into a car, he was immediately escorted to Hyde Park police station, where he was cautioned. McMahon insisted that it was merely 'a protest' and he had no intention of harming anyone. However, when searched, he was found to have a picture of the king and two rounds of live ammunition. Closer inspection revealed that the newspaper he had used to hide the gun had the words 'May, I Love You' written on the back page.[33]

When brought to trial at the Old Bailey, McMahon insisted that a foreign power had paid him to shoot the king, but he had merely pocketed the money and then deliberately bungled the mission. The court did not believe him and instead chose to regard him as an unhinged solo eccentric perhaps with an Irish republican connection.[34] The episode had strong echoes of the many attempts against Edward's great-grandmother and McMahon was lucky not to be placed in Broadmoor. Instead, he merely received twelve months for possession of firearms, which was distinctly odd. Even at the time, leads suggested this was part of a wider plot. Before the attack, Alice Lawrence had seen McMahon talking intently to a tall, well-dressed man with a moustache and hat. Perhaps he was not acting alone.[35]

McMahon was a hard drinker and a petty criminal, but most importantly a gunrunner during the Italian invasion of Abyssinia in early 1935. The efficient Italian military intelligence service paid him for information about weapons and clearly regarded him as an agent. Recently, McMahon's memoir has been discovered by the historian Alex Larman. It claims that the Italians had paid him to assassinate Edward, but that he was in fact a double agent working for MI5 – and MI5 had ignored his warnings. Strikingly, declassified MI5 documents corroborate the memoir, including records of MI5 conversations with him before the attack.[36] McMahon was a long-term paid MI5 informant whose job was to convince the Italians that he was a willing recruit, but secretly to spy for the British. He was also seen selling copies of the fascist *Blackshirt* newspaper and may have had connections with the German or Austrian embassies. All of this was covered up at the trial where McMahon came across as a lone fanatic.[37]

This has presented historians with more questions than answers. Some have even wondered if MI5 and Special Branch were aware of McMahon's planned attempt and allowed him to go ahead. It would have removed a monarch whom some thought had Nazi sympathies.[38] Confusion is more likely than conspiracy. MI5 probably just wanted to cover up the fact that they had previous contact with McMahon, but had no idea about his intentions. The most intriguing part of the story is that McMahon's lost memoir finally turned up in the papers of Walter Monckton, Edward's close confidant and legal adviser. Monckton most likely informed Edward of its contents and even perhaps allowed him to read it. Historians will never know what Edward made of the story himself, or who he thought was lurking behind 'The Man in the Brown Suit'.[39]

WITH FASCISM BOOMING and royal protection requiring ever more resources, the Special Branch swelled to a strength of 180.[40] There was no shortage of work for Canning, who was now head of all these activities, and would keep this position all the way through until the end of the Second World War, working closely with MI5.[41]

Oswald Mosley had a great deal of working-class support. He was also popular among the nobility; so too were a miasma of other right-wing and pro-German organizations that operated alongside him. Edward and Wallis moved in some of these circles, but also mingled with a new rising class of the global super-rich whose pacifism seemed well intentioned but was in fact designed to protect their business interests. These included a number of Swedish, French and American industrialists.[42]

Security and society overlapped. Clive Wigram, the king's private secretary, became especially disturbed by his social habits: his subservience to Mrs Simpson's wishes, his extravagance, and his bad treatment of the staff at Buckingham Palace. Wigram believed that Edward was mentally unbalanced and once, after a particularly trying encounter, announced that 'we shall have to lock him up'.[43] But Wigram's greatest anxiety was official security, and Edward's cavalier treatment of classified documents. Top-secret Cabinet papers were carried in red boxes from Downing Street to Buckingham Palace for the king's eyes only, and that is where they were meant to stay.

Edward, who still spent much of his time relaxing at his unofficial residence, Fort Belvedere, had other ideas. The famous red boxes lay open there – a cocktail of Cabinet papers, intelligence reports and telegrams from top diplomatic posts. Wigram worried about who might be reading their sensitive contents. They were often not returned for weeks and some of these red boxes were actually lost. This was more than Wigram could take, so in August 1936, horrified by proceedings, he resigned and was replaced by Alec Hardinge.

Baldwin, for the first time in British history, urged that the monarch should only be sent material requiring his signature.[44]

Odd things happened with the sensitive papers. One of the periodic guests at Fort Belvedere was Mike Scanlon, the air attaché at the American embassy. As he left after a night of revelry, he was rather surprised to be passed some official red boxes with a request to drop them off at Buckingham Palace on his way back into London. He noted: 'I had a feeling that Hardinge did not approve of the practice of confiding state papers to the care of an American intelligence officer.'[45]

Clive Wigram did not disappear; instead he remained in the shadows of Windsor Castle, and continued to exert influence. Passionate about the security of documents, he retained a role as keeper of the Royal Archives, Britain's most exclusive and secret repository. More importantly, the following month, he joined a secret meeting in Scotland to discuss 'up and down the problem of His Majesty'. The gathering consisted of Wigram, together with his successor as private secretary, Alec Hardinge, and the archbishop of Canterbury, Cosmo Lang, a man of outspoken views on the crown, constitution and royal consorts. This was prelude to an even more important meeting a month later.[46]

In September, Lang met Baldwin at the historic Hatfield House, the Cecil family home for more than four hundred years. In the presence of Elizabeth I's Rainbow Portrait, they held a rather private conversation. Baldwin's views were already firm. He told his closest advisers: 'I have grown to hate that woman', adding that he considered Wallis a 'hard-hearted bitch'. Having consulted government lawyers, he set out his options. 'If he marries her,' they warned, 'she is automatically Queen of England.' Lang was of even firmer opinions. Over the next few weeks, he and Baldwin met in secret seven times, spoke on the telephone, exchanged letters and shared their correspondence about the king. Lang provided Baldwin with theological arguments to use in his audiences with Edward as they moved him towards a shared objective: either dropping Mrs Simpson or abdication, preferably the latter.[47]

On 16 November, Edward summoned Baldwin to Buckingham Palace. The king announced he would marry Mrs Simpson despite the prime minister's opposition. He already knew the Cabinet was against him, since Sam Hoare, first lord of the Admiralty and one-time MI6 officer, had been secretly briefing him on their ruminations.[48] Two weeks later the British press, which, unlike the world's media, had been gagged, finally broke the story. Wallis received credible death threats and had already fled to France where she laid low, under siege, at the Villa Lou Viei, near Cannes, home of her close friends Herman and Katherine Rogers. Two Special Branch men accompanied her – they were now both her protectors and her watchers, reporting direct to Scotland Yard's chief, Philip Game, in London.

Baldwin and Lang wanted to force Edward to abdicate. They believed the British public and the commonwealth would never accept an American divorcee as the king-emperor's wife. Edward's affection for German and Italian fascism lurked in the background, quietly shaping debate. Some even feared that he might dismiss the government, triggering a right-wing coup by what some called the 'King's Party'. This was no mere fiction and Britain's most senior civil servants weighed up the possibility in their private journals, talking of Winston Churchill, Lloyd George and Max Beaverbrook, the press baron, as conspirators.[49]

If a 'King's Party' existed, then Beaverbrook was probably the most active conspirator. His main reason for supporting Edward was, as he admitted in his own words, to 'bugger Baldwin' and keep the king on the throne.[50] Acting as one of Edward's closest advisers, he hoped to persuade Edward to drop Wallis, or at least abandon his intention to marry her, and thus remain on the throne. Although Churchill was coy about his own role in the affair, even when discussing it with friends, he later admitted that Beaverbrook was behind some of the threats made to Wallis Simpson in late 1936 that persuaded her to leave the country. This even included bricks 'thrown through her windows' and letters threatening acid attacks.[51] Beaverbrook hoped that once she had departed for France, the king would be more malleable and might even give her up.[52] Meanwhile, Baldwin, who wanted abdication, described himself as being 'like a dog in a sheep-dog trial who has to induce a single sheep into a narrow gate'. He needed every shred of intelligence possible to outmanoeuvre the king. For this reason, he cranked up the surveillance operation yet again.[53]

Downing Street now turned to MI5. Horace Wilson, a key adviser to Baldwin, asked its director, Vernon Kell, to tap the phones of Edward, of his younger brother and the future King George VI, and of Wallis Simpson in France. Kell, a rather proper civil servant, was horrified. He did not see Edward and Wallis as a national security issue and so thought it entirely inappropriate to rummage through the knicker drawers of the aristocracy. To Kell, it was clearly a political, even social, issue more about hedonistic lifestyles and transgressions of social norms.[54]

Wilson was particularly influential during the abdication crisis, stoking up fears of mob riots and violence. He and Baldwin's private secretary, Tommy Dugdale, 'did much delving into the gangster side of this affair; the seamy side not politic for the Prime Minister to know about'. Dugdale's wife thought Baldwin was 'very suspicious' of their activity.[55] Baldwin was more worried about a constitutional revolution – the first since 1688 – which itself would have caused much upheaval during these febrile years.[56]

Remarkably, the top-secret MI5 internal history, written by one of its senior officers, John Curry, reveals that Kell's objections were overridden. The MI5 board agreed with Number 10's arguments that this was not just about politics, it was also about national security. Eventually, they advised Kell to do what the prime minister requested. As the abdication crisis accelerated in November, MI5 went ahead with telephone tapping. The final authority was given by Horace Wilson, conveying the authority of the home secretary, John Simon.

> Most Secret. The Home Secretary asked me to confirm the information conveyed to you orally with his authority by Sir Horace Wilson that you will arrange for the interception of telephone communications between Fort Belvedere and Buckingham Palace on the one hand and the continent of Europe and various addresses in London on the other.

A normal telephone tap was too prone to leaks, and MI5 could not count on the loyalty of those who staffed the royal exchange at Windsor. MI5 therefore required an especially secret alternative plan.[57]

Kell turned to one of MI5's most distinguished officers, Thomas Argyll Robertson, known as 'TAR' Robertson. A very efficient intelligence officer, Robertson was also a personal friend of Kell and had served in the same elite Highland regiment as his son. Robertson would later rise to prominence as the strategic mastermind behind Britain's brilliant wartime 'Double Cross' deception operations, but for now he had a more tactical mission.

In early December, Robertson entered Green Park in the dead of night. By placing a wiretap inside the telephone junction box, he and his colleagues could eavesdrop on phone calls between Wallis Simpson, the king and his brother, circumventing the royal exchange at Windsor. Listening in on a conversation between Edward and the future George VI, Robertson apparently picked up some earth-shattering news. The king now intended to abdicate and hand over his reign to his brother George.[58]

WALLIS SIMPSON HAD hoped to be queen of England. Edward, on the other hand, could not take the pressure and finally threw in the towel. On 10 December, Baldwin announced this to a packed chamber in parliament. After Baldwin's parliamentary statement, Leo Amery, the Conservative politician, found Churchill in the smoking room of the House of Commons 'completely in a rampage', insisting that he was totally for the king and was 'not going to have him strangled in the dark by ministers'. Privately, Amery, who knew Churchill very well, reflected that 'Winston' only got this worked up when he had a secret scheme under way 'for his own private ends'. [59]

Baldwin feared conspirators of the 'King's Party', such as Churchill, with good reason, but he did not fear the king. He thought Edward quite nice on a personal basis, but possibly insane, and entirely unsuitable to be king.[60]

It also turned out that Edward had secretly installed 'five private telephone lines, one direct to Lord Beaverbrook'. The rest of the royal family did not know this until after the abdication; eventually Queen Mary discovered this rather surprising fact while 'poking about upstairs'. Given Beaverbrook's understandable caution on the phone it is unlikely that MI5 managed to capture the full story.[61]

Others watched the manoeuvrings of Lloyd George. One of his associates concluded that 'like Winston', in this matter, Lloyd George was only concerned with his personal advancement and 'had no thought but for himself'. But, by announcing the abdication, Baldwin had thwarted the 'Kings Party'.[62]

ON THE SAME morning as Baldwin made the dramatic announcement, Edward signed his abdication papers at Fort Belvedere.[63] That night, Scotland Yard moved all available policemen into central London. Five hundred fascists joined the crowd outside Buckingham Palace shouting, 'One two three four five! We want Baldwin dead or alive!', before making their way to Downing Street.[64]

The next day, Edward made his fateful speech to the nation: 'I have found it impossible to carry the heavy burden of responsibility and to discharge my duties as King as I would wish to do, without the help and support of the woman I love.'[65] Rather typically, he then retired to his bedroom and sat drinking whisky and sodas while having his toenails trimmed by a servant.[66] The very next day he headed for the Continent, perhaps not knowing that hereafter his return visits to his home country would be short and infrequent.

How much difference did the bugging make? Edward and Wallis clearly knew that they were bugged. During the days leading up to the abdication, Wallis insisted that she had known less than anybody because 'It had been impossible to talk freely' with Edward on the telephone 'as the wires were constantly tapped'.[67] But like all those who know they are bugged, it is still hard to resist the medium of immediate communication and much later she confessed that 'I spent a long time over a very bad telephone line from France begging him not to abdicate. I went so far as to say if he abdicated I would not marry him!'[68] Did these unguarded moments impact the last minute negotiations? Edward had tried to persuade Baldwin to 'let the matter of his marriage hang fire' until after the coronation, but the prime minister clearly scented future trouble and wanted them both gone.[69]

It was not just MI5. In fact, a world of spies was listening in, including the French police. A Paris detective later confirmed that his job had been to 'review the recorded telephone conversations between King Edward and Wally Simpson'. When the king had called to tell her that he had definitely decided to abdicate and was about to announce this on the radio, her prompt response had been a curt 'You God-damned fool!'[70] Lord Brownlow, Edward's loyal equerry who had escorted Wallis to France, was especially sensitive to surveillance, and whenever he had left written messages for Beaverbrook from Edward they were in code.[71] Months later he confronted Kell and complained vehemently about the tapping of the king's phone by MI5, who 'couldn't deny it'. But the strange clicks and hissings on the line that he had heard most recently may well have been the work of the French.[72]

The surveillance had been helpful to Baldwin, but even more important was the effect of the mere idea of surveillance. Those who were intent on working against him, especially Beaverbrook, with whom he had a long-running feud, were frightened by the idea that they might be overheard. Beaverbrook had already figured out this possibility and recalled a disturbing conversation with Edward on the phone at 2 a.m. at the height of the crisis. Beaverbrook had been 'embarrassed' and 'alarmed' because Edward had been speaking with 'such freedom' while Beaverbrook was painfully conscious that there were others lurking on the line. Edward, he noted, was increasingly impatient, because of the 'guarded nature of my replies'.[73]

The government has always maintained that it does not intercept or tap royal communications. But this episode turns history on its head. Moreover, in late December 1936, as Edward departed for his new life on the Continent, with the prospect of marriage and exile ahead, he probably thought he was now free from surveillance. Nothing could have been further from the truth. Incredibly, the surveillance became part of a far greater operation involving hundreds of spies across four continents, which would continue for at least a decade.

ON 11 DECEMBER 1936, an uncertain King George VI, with no idea that MI5 had eavesdropped on him, stepped up to replace his brother. Alarmingly, he was the third British king in just over a year. A series of official meetings and state occasions lay ahead before the coronation at Westminster Abbey in May 1937. One of his pressing duties was to meet all the ambassadors of the Court of St James's, in other words all the top foreign diplomats in London. On the morning of 4 March, they lined up together once more in order of seniority to present their credentials in the Bow Room of Buckingham Palace. Although this was something they had done recently for George's brother, things were slightly different this time. The Russian ambassador, Ivan Maisky, noted that Anthony Eden was there to help George with the conversation as the king was 'taciturn and easily embarrassed', adding 'he also stammers'.[74]

The ceremony seemed to be passing off relatively smoothly. Then suddenly, Ribbentrop, Hitler's ambassador, greeted the king not with the customary bow, but with a Nazi salute, something that 'offended the English deeply'. Maisky was secretly delighted, since the two ambassadors were compared widely in the press and people observed that, by contrast, the nice Russian revolutionary had managed to greet the king properly, without 'raising a clenched fist above his head'. To Maisky's disbelief, things only got better, for at five o'clock the same afternoon, the king and queen hosted a tea party for the ambassadors and their wives. Even in this more relaxed setting, among the canapés and cucumber sandwiches, Ribbentrop repeated his gaffe and gave another Nazi salute. The two young princesses, Elizabeth and Margaret, began to giggle, and then misbehave, much to the 'considerable embarrassment' of the queen.[75]

The press and public enjoyed mocking Ribbentrop's multiple faux pas. In private, though, it is unclear whether the royal family knew that he was a friend of Wallis Simpson and had enjoyed private meetings with Edward. Even if they did not, their anxieties could hardly have been higher. Across the Channel, at Château de Candé in the Loire valley, preparations were under way for a rather unusual royal wedding. Once again, Special Branch kept a close eye on the comings and goings.

Meanwhile, Edward, now duke of Windsor, had headed for Austria to stay with his friends the Rothschilds at Schloss Enzesfeldt. The visit was arranged by the security-conscious Lord Brownlow, in the greatest secrecy since half the newspapers in Europe were on his trail. Having accompanied Wallis on her flight to southern France the previous year, Brownlow now used coded language to prevent phone calls from being leaked to the press. He asked Baroness Rothschild if he might come to stay and also bring his 'brother David' who was recovering from a cold. Rothschild hoped that this would 'hoodwink the telephone tappers and journalists who were tracking the exiled King'.[76]

The most important watcher was already there. London had arranged for Edward to be protected by a Special Branch officer called David Storrier. Just before the First World War, Storrier had left Angus, north of Dundee, with his brother, to join the police. The elder brother rose to be assistant chief constable of Glasgow; the younger brother, David, had an even more fascinating career. For eighteen years he served as one of the few direct links between Edward and the government.[77]

As early as 1932, Storrier had served as King George V's bodyguard, earning the trust of the royal family.[78] Amid mounting concern about Edward's activities, Storrier's duties changed and he was assigned to the prince of Wales.[79] Working with Edward would be difficult. Knowing that any protection officer would have to keep up with irregular hours and esoteric behaviour, the prince's equerry asked for a man of 'about thirty' who was single. Sensitive to Edward's feelings about his diminutive size, they also wanted an officer who was 'not a very big man'.[80]

Storrier had quickly become a hit with his new master. In September 1934, Edward's equerry reported the prince's 'great satisfaction' with Storrier. At home and abroad, the dedicated royal detective had to be a discreet fixer and, as one observer put it delicately, 'Storrier had on many occasions difficult tasks to perform, all of which he accomplished with great success and no fuss'.[81]

The police usually filled these posts with 'good, keen ambitious detectives' and expected them to last about four years, or 'else the appointment will be regarded by men of this type as a dead end'.[82] Curiously, Storrier stayed for rather longer: almost two decades. He was delighted to find that he was treated in an extremely courteous and friendly way by the duchess and was told privately that she described him to others as 'one of the family'. He repaid the compliment by describing her in his reports to London as 'HRH', a title that the Windsors worked tirelessly to deny her.[83]

Storrier's role was to protect his royal charge, but also to watch him closely. An honest policeman from rural Scotland, he clearly struggled with being asked to spy on his master. During early 1937, Storrier nurtured growing anxieties about his dual role. Writing from Schloss Enzesfeldt near Vienna, he told his superiors in London: 'I shall communicate with you again, Sir… I trust, Sir, you will not regard the foregoing as a breach of confidence on my part so far as HRH is concerned as I know you understand the already difficult position and I feel it my duty to report to you.'[84]

Edward and Wallis borrowed their beautiful wedding venue from Charles Bedaux, one of the wealthiest men in France. Bedaux had purchased the sixteenth-century château in 1927, and lived there with his American second wife, the former Fern Lombard from Michigan. Bedaux had made his fortune pioneering efficiency studies for major manufacturers around Europe and his companies were some of the first management consultancies. His work had the added benefit of creating high-level contacts across Europe, including in Germany and Sweden.

On 3 June 1937, Storrier was among a select group of guests gathering for the royal wedding. Even some of the couple's closest friends had boycotted the nuptials, for fear of censure by Buckingham Palace, and, despite the conspicuous displays of flowers, the château felt curiously empty. No royals were present, not even Edward's closest brother, and all royal staff were warned that if they attended, they would be dismissed. The guests did include significant figures including Walter Monckton, Baron and Baroness Rothschild and Winston Churchill's son Randolph.[85] 'Fruity' Metcalfe was best man. The guests were almost outnumbered by the world's press, for the Windsors were more famous than ever, already achieving a cult status. Back in Britain, on the outskirts of Windsor Castle, the caretaker of Fort Belvedere, Walter Willis, cashed in on their prolonged absence. For a hefty fee, he took hardcore Windsor fanatics on private tours of the 'closed' house and gardens. The crown estates office eventually caught him in the act and he was fired.[86]

AFTER THE WEDDING, the couple headed off on honeymoon to the mountain resort of Schloss Wasserleonburg in Austria. His ever-present shadow, David Storrier, reported to London: 'I must confess Sir, that never before have I seen HRH so obviously touched as at the conclusion... and HRH seems so far extremely happy with his bride and surroundings.'[87] He found the south Austrian police efficient, comparing them favourably to the indolent French gendarmerie. 'Apart from shopping expeditions to the neighbouring towns HRH and The Duchess seldom leave the Castle...'[88]

Storrier also noted boredom was slowly setting in. Edward, who had often complained about his official duties both as prince of Wales, and then briefly as king, now rather missed them. His friend and attentive law officer, Walter Monckton, came and went at weekends dealing with 'business', but Edward longed for the buzz of London society. The astute Storrier noticed this, and as August turned to September, reported: 'I personally feel that he is now experiencing greater difficulty in agreeably occupying his time and I notice also that HRH is now more easily irritated by minor details such as the non-arrival on time of things he may have ordered or a temporary breakdown of the weather.'[89] Edward's friend Duff Cooper had warned him about possible tedium the previous year, but the duke had replied breezily: 'Oh you know me, Duff, I'm always busy. I shall find plenty to do.' He was now restless.[90]

Boredom offered opportunities for dubious characters; one already waited in the wings in the form of Charles Bedaux. He and the Windsors shared the same political world outlook, believing that western European democracies had grown weak and vulnerable to the Bolshevik threat. They saw fascism as an attractive alternative, an expression of modernism allowing society to move forward and perhaps offer full employment. Although philosophically Bedaux's ideas might have been closer to Italian syndicalism, British diplomats record that he 'held pro-fascist views'. The American authorities reached the same conclusion, but neither country yet had all the details. More spies and surveillance were required.[91]

Above all, Bedaux was an entrepreneur and opportunist. Exploiting Edward's ennui, he decided to arrange some more vigorous activity for the duke. Reporting on the last day of August from the Schloss Wasserleonburg near the Italian border, Storrier explained to London that they would leave on 7 September 1937 'for Hungary for a few days shooting with Mr Bedaux', then to Paris, arriving about 28 September, then onwards to Germany in mid-October. Shock and horror reverberated across London. Storrier's report was the first that the British knew about Edward's intention to visit Nazi Germany.[92]

The political establishment had blundered badly. Having cut Edward off, and shunned his wife, they now had a royal who was out of control – a veritable loose cannon. The downside of cutting an ex-king loose was that you could not manage him. The British government could do nothing to stop Edward being friendly with the Nazi enemy. Neville Chamberlain, who had replaced Baldwin as prime minister the previous spring, took the view that it was 'not possible to stop the Duke of Windsor going to Germany'.[93] Britain's embassy in Berlin was ordered to have nothing to do with the duke, but to watch his every move closely.

Bedaux was clearly a key orchestrator. He came to Germany about a fortnight before Edward, staying at the Adlon Hotel, to help arrange everything.[94] He planned the visit with Dr Robert Ley, head of the German labour organization, who would later hang himself at Nuremberg before he was tried for war crimes. While the details are murky, there are strong suggestions that Bedaux's own business dealings in the Reich benefited from arranging this special visit.[95]

Days later, drawing on local sources, London heard that the duchess herself admitted 'that when in Germany they would be entertained by Herr Hitler'.[96] Ribbentrop, until recently Germany's flat-footed ambassador in London, arrived and played a leading part in entertaining the Windsors. Having then met Hermann Göring, commander of the Luftwaffe, and Joseph Goebbels, minister of propaganda, by 27 September, they were on their way to meet Hitler in Munich.[97]

Oddly, while Storrier continued to be managed by Special Branch during this period, there is no indication of whether he travelled to Germany with them. It appears not.[98] The duke was accompanied by his loyal equerry, Dudley Forwood, but it is not clear who was watching them while they were there, nor whether any record of their meeting with Hitler survived. For some unknown reason, Churchill's son Randolph also accompanied the tour.[99]

During 1937, Edward and Wallis were lavishly funded by the shadowy Bedaux couple, their French-American millionaire hosts. After the successful visit to Nazi Germany, they suggested that the Windsors visit the United States the following year. Bedaux had clearly been 'running' Edward and Wallis and paying many expenses. Bedaux also told Edward that after the United States they should visit Italy and Sweden, where he would be put in contact with a Swedish millionaire, Axel Wenner-Gren, who was also interested in 'world peace'. Bedaux advised him to take this world peace line in public too, and even went so far as to express the opinion that by taking this line he might in due course be the 'saviour' of the British monarchy. Edward took this to heart and publicly emphasized his pacifist desire to avoid the horrors of the Western Front, rather than his admiration for the Third Reich, two views that he found entirely compatible within his somewhat elastic conceptual universe.[100]

AT THE END of 1937, the Windsors headed down to Cannes once more. They spent Christmas in the same villa where Wallis had taken refuge a year earlier. Others came to join them, including Winston Churchill and Lloyd George. Billed as a light-hearted festive gathering, it was nothing less than a reassembling of the 'King's Party' and it is hard to resist the conclusion that the duke briefed them on his recent talks in Germany. Once again, Storrier noticed that the duke had 'great difficulty' in 'filling in' the hours there, adding that 'time hangs heavy'.[101]

The 'King's Party' had not been inactive. The avid supporters of the Windsors were a curious amalgam of public figures. One of their more colourful individuals was Compton Mackenzie, the energetic MI6 officer who had run the Athens station during the First World War and helped to push the pro-German king towards abdication. In the early 1930s, he had published several volumes of memoirs, recounting his intelligence exploits in Greece, and was prosecuted under the Official Secrets Act for his pains. Because of the royal aspect, Mackenzie believed that George V had 'encouraged' the decision to take legal action against him.[102] He first responded with a comic novel about MI6, called *Water on the Brain*.[103] But the abdication offered him a bigger opportunity to fire back at the authorities. Already an established royal biographer, he quickly researched *The Windsor Tapestry*, a study of the 'life, heritage and abdication of HRH The Duke of Windsor'. He wrote so fast that at one point he collapsed. Nursed back to health, he finished the book, which was serialized in the *Sunday Dispatch*.

'What the European secret services were doing about King Edward's friendship with Mrs Simpson – that is what Mr. Compton Mackenzie tells us in the next instalment of the *Windsor Tapestry*,' boasted the paper on 17 July 1938.[104] There were in fact six episodes and the *Dispatch* had paid £5,000 for the serialization, almost half a million pounds at current prices, and it was worth it – the paper's circulation grew by 100,000 overnight.[105] The book attacked Stanley Baldwin and Geoffrey Dawson, editor of *The Times*. It made assertions of multiple instances of 'conspiracy'.[106]

There followed a vicious spat between the various newspapers, who even resorted to putting pamphlets about the abdication through letter boxes in the more expensive parts of London. MI5 gathered examples of the pamphlets for its files.[107] Indeed, Mackenzie's suspicions would surely have been confirmed had he known how closely he was being watched by the authorities and that a large MI5 dossier was compiled, noting his associations with figures like Oswald Mosley. Mackenzie was a fervent Scottish nationalist and

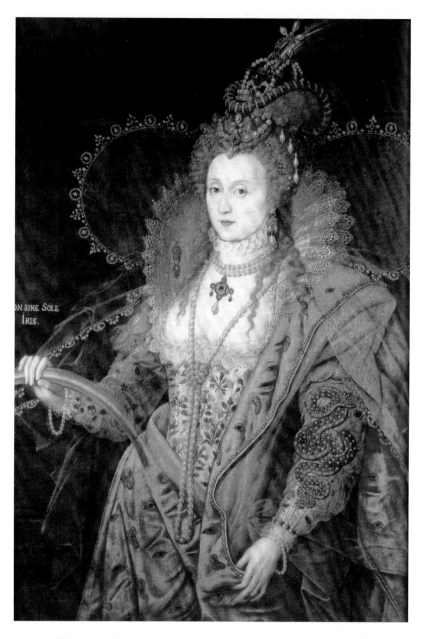

Elizabeth I's 'Rainbow Portrait' which glorifies the place of surveillance in royal statecraft.

Victoria with her eldest daughter and 'informant' Vicky.

Tsar Nicholas II and George V with their heirs, Edward and Alexei.

Rasputin was killed in an effort to save the Russian royal family.

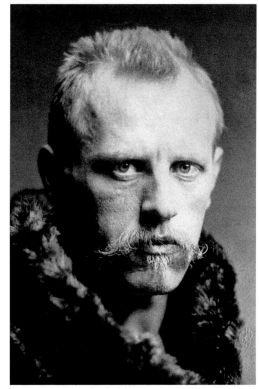

MI6 turned to Norwegian explorers like Fridtjof Nansen, hoping to rescue the Tsar in 1918.

The police arrest George McMahon in 1936 after his
attack on Edward VIII.

Preparing for the new order – Edward and Wallis with
Charles and Fern Bedaux.

The Windsors on the loose in Florida in 1941.

Gray Phillips, a friend of MI6 officer H. Montgomery Hyde,
followed Edward (*left*) with care in the 1940s.

'Mouse' Fielden who ran both RAF 'Special Duties' and the Royal Flight.

The royal family inspect the 6th Airborne Division to assist with deception.

George VI inspects a special forces raiding jeep.

Churchill and George VI competed to be the first to hit the D-Day beaches.

MI5 agents had seen the two 'in close and friendly conversation' after speaking together at London events.[108] One of the last secret servants to contribute material to his bulging files was a figure called Anthony Blunt.[109]

Mackenzie's book caused a sensation and went through many editions. But the literary enemies of the Windsors were also busy. Osbert Sitwell, another well-known author and former Guards officer, had privately circulated a racy poem about the abdication, called 'Rat Week'. Sitwell was a close friend of Edward's brother George, now the king, and the poem criticized not only the Windsors, but also their friends who had deserted them so quickly after the abdication. This poem was leaked to the press, leading to court actions over copyright and discussions of libel.[110] There was much debate about who exactly was a 'rat'. The newspapers loved it, but all this discomforted the authorities and kept the story in the public eye.

Edward had been in correspondence with Mackenzie about his book, and his mail was being opened by MI5.[111] Mackenzie also worked with Walter Monckton, Edward's solicitor. In the end, Edward decided not to officially endorse *The Windsor Tapestry*, because of its 'violent' language, although he clearly enjoyed it.[112] Alongside all this propaganda and public bickering, the Windsors spent 1938 house-hunting in Paris and Storrier found himself promoted for his diligent surveillance efforts.[113] Back in London, various government departments were still arguing over who should pay eye-watering bills from Harvey Nichols for furniture removal from Fort Belvedere a year before.[114]

As for Bedaux, his attempt to cultivate Edward and Wallis ended in disaster. His plan for the promised royal visit to the United States ran up against serious opposition, not least from the British embassy. The British ambassador, Ronald Lindsay, was 'staggered' by the strict instructions to cold-shoulder the Windsors, but when he visited Balmoral in 1938, the matter became clear: the royal family stated plainly that they feared Edward might be 'trying to stage a come-back'.[115] This was little short of paranoia, but it explains the continued close surveillance. The trip was cancelled. Bedaux found that raising his American profile led to serious tax demands on his subsidiaries that he could not pay and, by late 1938, he concluded that the Windsors were a losing proposition.

Meanwhile, Edward's shy and stammering brother George, a rather improbable publicist, scooped the pool with an enormously popular royal visit to North America the following year. In 1939, as the Windsors sat out in Paris, the ever-patient Inspector Storrier watched and waited.[116] Walter Monckton, who knew more than almost anyone about Edward, and was a true friend, nevertheless confided to the head of the Metropolitan Police that staying close to the exasperating Windsors was hard work – and so Storrier was remarkable. 'It would really take a saint to hold that job indefinitely without some deterioration.'[117] Little did they know that international events were about to offer all of them a change of scene.

Part III

ROYALS AND
SPIES AT WAR

OUTBREAK OF THE
SECOND WORLD WAR

'The Duke expressed himself very freely…
He was surrounded by agents.'

German ambassador to Spain, July 1940[1]

ALONGSIDE MUNICH AND Chamberlain, 'appeasement' has long become a dirty word. This was not always the case and, in the 1930s, many people, kings included, gave it far more positive connotations. Some advocated appeasement as a means of addressing genuine German grievances in order to deliver long-term peace. Others promoted it as the only rational response to a situation in which Germany had strong allies, in the form of Italy and Japan, while Britain only had the friendship of a fractured and internally divided France. Even those distrustful of Germany viewed it as a necessary way of buying time while Britain tried to catch up in a race for rearmament. Only in the wake of Germany's invasion of Czechoslovakia in the spring of 1939 did appeasement start to become a by-word for a policy of craven submission.

Neville Chamberlain, who became prime minister in 1937, is the British leader most infamously intertwined with appeasement. But he was not alone. Although now remembered as a victorious wartime king, George VI was an equal – if not more ardent – fan of appeasement. In 1938, he actually vied with Chamberlain to establish closer relations with Hitler, even drafting his own personal letter to the German leader. Trying to find common ground, he wrote: 'This is a letter to Hitler, not as one statesman to another, but one ex-serviceman to another', exhorting him to spare the youth of Europe another disastrous conflict.[2] George was desperate to send it and had to be restrained not only by Lord Halifax, the foreign secretary, but also by Chamberlain himself. The prime minister explained that he feared Hitler might send 'an insulting reply', but perhaps also privately wished to retain the plaudits of any peace deal for himself.[3] Restless for appeasement, George then wanted to send similar missives to the Japanese. Most members of the royal family took a similar line, especially the king's youngest brother, the duke of Kent.[4]

George was effusive when Chamberlain returned from meeting Hitler at his Berchtesgaden retreat in mid-September 1938. 'How I admire your courage and wisdom,' he told the prime minister, 'in going to see Hitler in person.'[5] He then sent him a haunch of venison from Balmoral as a gift, although, in a perhaps fitting metaphor, by the time the meat arrived in London it was so bad that Chamberlain had to destroy it.[6]

On 27 September, Chamberlain took to the airwaves, lamenting the fact that Britain might go to war for Czechoslovakia: 'a people of whom we know nothing'. He even seemed to be evincing sympathy for Germany's position. Immediately afterwards, the king sent him a message of praise.[7] A couple of weeks later, when Chamberlain returned from Munich loftily waving his agreement with Hitler, the king's aides had to stop him from rushing to the airport like an adoring fan. Instead, he sent a congratulatory letter, delivered as soon as Chamberlain landed, inviting him to 'come straight to Buckingham Palace, so that I can express to you personally my heartfelt congratulations on the success of your visit to Munich'.[8] George then engineered a photoshoot on the palace balcony where he publicly and visibly aligned himself with appeasement, a move that some thought imprudent and perhaps bordering on the unconstitutional.[9]

Just before Christmas 1938, the king started to change his mind. On 18 December, he complained at length to the Czech ambassador, Jan Masaryk, about the difficulties of implementing appeasement when faced with 'people such as Hitler and Mussolini'. He had once seen them as inspiring their troubled nations with courage and confidence, perhaps seeking to address genuine grievances. 'But,' he added, 'the useful mission of Hitler and Mussolini is over. Everything they do now is directed against us and against civilization.'[10]

The king had not yet abandoned hopes of an agreement, though. In January 1939, he praised Chamberlain for developing 'personal contact' with Mussolini in Rome. He then blamed Spain for being 'the bugbear to any kind of appeasement in Europe'.[11] Two months later, George acknowledged that Hitler's invasion of Czechoslovakia was a 'blow', but comforted Chamberlain: 'your labours have been anything but wasted, for they have left no doubt in the minds of ordinary people all over the world of our love of peace and of our readiness to discuss with any nation whatever grievances they think they have'.[12]

By the summer of 1939, even Chamberlain had accepted the need to threaten Hitler with force. On 3 July, George offered to talk to Philipp of Hesse, a German great-grandson of Queen Victoria and son-in-law of the Italian king. Hesse had been a member of the Nazi party for a decade and enjoyed easy access to both Hitler and Mussolini. The go-between would be George's youngest brother, the duke of Kent, who was often in Italy.[13] George wanted to use this royal channel to 'convey to Hitler that we really are in earnest'. Chamberlain turned him down, saying that Hitler already knew 'we mean business this time'.[14]

Chamberlain was wrong yet again. Hitler did not believe Britain would go to war for Poland and pushed ahead with his invasion. Britain declared war on Germany on 3 September 1939 and when Hitler received the news he turned to Ribbentrop with a look of

complete puzzlement and asked: 'What do we do now?' Soon afterwards, George's wife, Queen Elizabeth, thought she needed to learn
a little more about what they were facing and decided to read *Mein
Kampf*. On 15 October she sent a copy to Halifax warning him: 'I
don't advise you to read it through, or you might go mad, and that
would be a great pity.' She suggested 'a skip through' would reveal
much about Hitler's extreme mentality.[15] Chamberlain resigned the
following year in May 1940.

PERHAPS BECAUSE OF the king's multiple contacts with Germany
and his earlier enthusiasm for appeasement, the intelligence services remained wary of the royals even after war began. Officials
agreed to special arrangements to supply confidential information
to George on a daily basis. Scarred by the experience with his elder
brother, these came with a big caveat. Because the palace had lost a
few red boxes recently, a duty officer from the Cabinet Office would
now deliver the papers, stand outside as the king read them, and
then return them to the government. The intelligence services, or
perhaps his private secretary, Alec Hardinge, did not trust George
enough to leave them unattended. Other sensitive documents went
to Hardinge, but had to be returned to the secretary to the committee of imperial defence personally and by name.[16]

Britain's wartime intelligence and security agencies were now
expanding fast. Many of the codebreakers moved to bigger premises
at Bletchley Park in the countryside north of London. MI6 found
its sabotage department taken away and developed into a whole new
organization called the Special Operations Executive (SOE). MI5
moved to new premises at Wormwood Scrubs prison. A fortnight
after the outbreak of war, Vernon Kell, the director of MI5, sent
two of his officers to the duke of Windsor's former residence, Fort
Belvedere, to consider whether he could requisition it as the headquarters for an MI5 section. It now looked rather different. Having

stood empty for a year, the flagpoles were rusting in the miniature golf course, dead leaves clogged the surface of the swimming pool and weeds had sprouted everywhere. Kell doubtless enjoyed the idea of a section of MI5 being based at 'The Fort', but he eventually rejected it as 'too small' for his purposes.[17]

Buckingham Palace began to develop its own security organization. George soon boasted his own private army called the 'Coats Mission', named after its commander, Major James Coats from the Coldstream Guards. This was a handpicked body of five officers and 124 men from the Brigade of Guards and Household Cavalry, equipped with armoured cars, on twenty-four-hour call to take the king, queen and young princesses to a safe house in the country should the German threat of invasion materialize.

In an emergency, Rolls-Royce armoured cars would pull out of the Royal Mews; military police with special racing motorbikes would control traffic as Coats escorted the royal family to one of four country houses in remote locations, and, if necessary, on to Liverpool and eventually Canada. On Vancouver Island, Hatley Castle, a forty-room mansion built at the turn of the century in the Tudor revival style, was purchased in 1940 as part of the plan.[18] Margaret Rhodes, Princess Elizabeth's cousin who lived at Buckingham Palace for part of the war, was initially comforted by this arrangement until she realized that while the royal corgis were on the list of evacuees, 'it did not include me'.[19]

The threat felt real enough. Lord Hailsham, the lord chancellor, warned the new prime minister, Winston Churchill, that the Nazis were obsessed with royal families. 'I observe that the Nazis both in Norway and in Holland made a desperate attempt to capture the Royal Family; no doubt they will do the same in this country if they can.' He advised Churchill that the two princesses should be sent away to safety but thought that the king was determined to stay and fight.[20]

Hailsham was right. The Germans had successfully captured the king of Belgium. In the Netherlands, Otto Begus, a former military police officer, had led the effort to capture Queen Wilhelmina.

She escaped his clutches by only half an hour and eventually arrived in London on a train at Liverpool Street station. The king rushed to greet her on the platform and found her wearing a tin hat and clutching nothing more than a shopping bag. Wilhelmina stayed in London to help organize the Dutch resistance, but the rest of her family soon fled to Canada.[21] Hailsham, Churchill and the king wondered whether Begus would now lead a plot to kidnap the British royal family, perhaps twenty-four hours before the invasion.

Begus and his unit moved to a villa in Boulogne, just across the Channel from Dover, where a scrambler phone connected them to the Abwehr, the German secret service. He later claimed, perhaps somewhat extravagantly, that from here, he had presided over a Nazi plan to capture the royals. A crack 'Royal Unit' of several hundred Nazi commandos would parachute into the palace grounds, kidnapping the family within just ten minutes.[22] Although Begus was a real figure and did belong to an elite unit – indeed both MI5 and US counter-intelligence had files on him – it appears he may have exaggerated his role, the stage of preparations, and the dramatic speed with which he could 'take' the royal family.[23]

Regardless of the reality, George exploited the perceived threat for propaganda purposes. He defiantly and publicly insisted that the family would stay and fight – even as the converted armoured cars of the Coats Mission stood secretly by. Far from being evacuated to Canada, Princess Elizabeth soon donned service uniform and joined the war effort with the Auxiliary Territorial Service (ATS).

Fears of invasion accelerated in late May 1940 with the Dunkirk evacuation. George summoned Hugh Dalton, who would become the politician responsible for SOE, to Buckingham Palace to talk about covert warfare and propaganda. Conversation then turned to Dunkirk where a flotilla of hastily assembled small ships was dramatically rescuing stranded British soldiers from French beaches. The king asserted firmly that Hitler 'wants to come here', suggesting the invasion date had been fixed by the Germans for 1 August. He became increasingly excited, insisting that Hitler planned 'to exterminate us and plant Germans in the island. What will he do next? He will stop at nothing, neither raining gas from the sky nor poisoning our water.' Dalton was a little unnerved by the royal outburst and tried to reassure the king that Britain had scientists working behind the scenes on preventative measures.[24]

In August 1940, with the invasion seemingly on the horizon, the king resolutely declared that he wanted to kill at least one of the invaders. Churchill responded that he needed to be able to kill more than one German. Shortly afterwards, out of the blue, a specially gift-wrapped package arrived at Buckingham Palace. Churchill had sent the king a Tommy Gun. George, his family and equerries eagerly began shooting practice with pistols, rifles and his new Tommy Gun.[25] This was a whole family activity.[26] Queen Elizabeth enjoyed firing in the palace garden where huge numbers of rats ran free because of the bombing raids. They formed moving targets to practise on.[27] The queen took instruction on her revolver every day, insisting, 'Yes, I shall not go down like the others.'[28]

Gift-wrapped Tommy Guns aside, George's relationship with Churchill was complex. Once an avid supporter of Chamberlain and appeasing Hitler, now George was king of a nation at war and partnered with the most outspoken opponent of appeasement. There is no doubt that the king would have much preferred Halifax as Chamberlain's successor and bent constitutional precedent to try to secure this outcome.[29] Temperamentally, the king and his new prime minister were very different: Churchill charismatic and bullish; George shy and reticent. More importantly, for the last four years they had been on opposite sides over Edward VIII. George could hardly forget that Churchill had joined Beaverbrook, Lloyd George and other renegade figures in forming the 'King's Party' and had been one of the few prominent figures to visit the Windsors in 1937 on the French Riviera. Nor had he forgotten that his brother was still in France, a problem that he and Churchill would soon have to confront.

IN MAY 1940, the Germans had attacked France. The Phoney War was over. By the end of the month, they had reached the gates of Paris. The speed with which one of Europe's great powers collapsed astonished the world and led to much talk of a covert Nazi 'Fifth Column' that had undermined the Allied war effort. Fears quickly spread about a similar fifth column lurking in Britain. Taking no chances, Churchill ordered the security agencies to 'collar the lot' and so large numbers of 'enemy aliens' and expatriates, especially those of German descent, even Jewish refugees, were rounded up and sent off to detention camps in places like the Isle of Man.[30] The new home secretary personally briefed George on the security swoop which rounded up some of Churchill's relatives.[31]

There was one notable British expatriate still living in France who was of special concern: the duke of Windsor. Edward and Wallis had been at their luxury villa in Antibes, in the South of France, when war was declared. George offered to put his plane at their disposal to rush them back to London, but instead they opted to return at a more leisurely pace, taking a naval destroyer from Cherbourg accompanied by Admiral Mountbatten.[32] A week after the outbreak of war, Edward and George had met; what words passed between them remain unknown, but it was reportedly a frosty exchange. Beneath the surface was the queen's lingering distaste for Wallis, whom she refused to see at this tense moment. Shortly afterwards, she told Queen Mary: 'I haven't heard a word about Mrs Simpson – I trust she will soon return to France and STAY THERE. I am sure she hates this dear country, & therefore she should not be here in war time.' Her views on Edward were no more charitable, now characterizing him as 'exactly like Hitler' in thinking that anyone who disagreed with him was wrong.[33]

George changed his mind about what his brother might do in terms of the war effort. A special post was created for him with the Military Mission in Paris as a liaison officer to the French high command, but this did not keep him very busy, since everyone had been told he was a security risk and ordered to show him as few documents as possible. Indeed, he was even forbidden from entering the British sector. Chamberlain had remarked that 'France can never keep a secret for more than half an hour' and so this seemed the perfect job for him since here neither he nor Wallis could do much harm, so they were left to bumble around Paris.[34]

Edward's liaison work during the Phoney War has often been dismissed as pointless. In fact, he proved rather useful to his new commander, General Howard-Vyse, whose mission was based close to the French headquarters at Vincennes. Their task was to report on the robustness of the French war effort, but their allies were suspicious and secretive, refusing to allow anyone near the Maginot Line. Edward had a background in intelligence work from the previous war and the mission now saw his arrival as 'a heaven-sent opportunity' to take a close look at the French front. Edward was restricted in terms of visiting British troops, but the French gave him a free pass. He was soon sending perceptive and critical reports back to London, suggesting that the French officers were obsessed with the 'excellence' and 'impregnability' of the Maginot Line. Edward was sceptical and thought that, once breached, there would be nothing to 'stop an advance on Paris'. However, his intelligence reports do not seem to have permeated the thinking in London; indeed, letting Edward and Wallis loose on the Continent in wartime eventually proved to be a major security miscalculation.[35]

As France fell in May 1940, the Windsors were still renting a gorgeous and impeccably stylish house at 24 Boulevard Souchet on the outskirts of Paris. Edward had been naïvely contemplating another holiday, but in London, the palace and Philip Game, head of the Metropolitan Police, began to panic about how to keep a Special Branch officer with him as the situation in Europe deteriorated.[36] With bombs falling on Paris, the duke's staff stopped thinking about holidays and suddenly pleaded for better protection. On 27 May, with the evacuation towards Dunkirk in full swing, Game wrote to the duke's equerry, Gray Phillips, about the tricky business of providing continuing police protection. Because British forces had been depleted, some six hundred police who were military reservists had now been called up, leaving Game stretched to the limit.[37] The duke promised to write personally, but, with all eyes on the beaches at Dunkirk, communications were interrupted.[38]

Suddenly, the Windsors fled Paris, perhaps tipped off by officers from the local MI6 station.[39] The party abandoned the flamboyant 'Fruity' Metcalfe, Edward's long-serving unofficial assistant and best man. Poor Metcalfe rang in the morning to ask for his daily instructions from the duke only to be told by a servant that they had fled at 6.30 a.m.[40] Edward's close friend was much aggrieved and later reflected that 'His plans must have been made twenty-four hours before' yet he left without saying a word, he took all the cars and, with the Germans closing on Paris, he ungallantly left Metcalfe and his wife with 'not so much as a bicycle'.[41]

Instead of escaping to Britain, Edward escorted Wallis south along crowded roads to Biarritz near the border with Spain. The town was choked with Rolls-Royces carrying their elegant owners and expensive luggage south towards safety.[42] MI6 seems to have played a role in keeping them away from their German friends. Noting the extreme secrecy involved, the American Federal Bureau of Investigation (FBI) later reported that 'British Secret Servicemen covered the move'.[43] MI6 not only travelled with them to Biarritz but watched their every move and communication. 'The British Secret Service,' according to the FBI, 'ascertained that the Duchess of Windsor had informed Ribbentrop of her itinerary, schedule etc. prior to her departure.'[44] Although the FBI was probably wrong to conclude that 'the Duchess of Windsor had an affair with Ribbentrop' during his time as ambassador in England in 1936, she and Ribbentrop were clearly friends and do seem to have been in contact during this difficult period.[45]

By 5 June 1940, the remnants of British forces had completed their week-long evacuation from Dunkirk, rescuing most of their troops. A fortnight later, the battle for France was effectively over. Many felt Britain would be the next European country to fall. In some confusion, the royal couple moved backwards and forwards around France and then sped over the border into Spain where inexplicably London lost track of them. Urgent telegrams arrived at the British consulates in Nice, Marseilles and Bordeaux: 'Please send me any information you have or can get from consular offices under your supervision regarding the Duke of Windsor's whereabouts and do anything you can to facilitate his return to this country.'[46]

The Windsors finally surfaced in Barcelona, then moved to the luxurious Ritz Hotel in Madrid. Although Spain was neutral, it had close ties to Nazi Germany, which now dominated the European continent. Edward arrived just in time to meet up with the new British ambassador, his old friend and former MI6 officer Sam Hoare, also known in Whitehall as 'Slippery Sam', whose main mission would be bribing the Franco government, paying millions to secure their continued neutrality.[47] Hoare had previously been the first British operative to report the death of Rasputin in 1916 and had held a string of Cabinet posts through the 1930s.

Hoare was regarded as an arch-appeaser and a defeatist by many in Whitehall. Therefore Alexander Cadogan, the senior official at the Foreign Office, worried about what he would get up to with Edward. Walking through the gardens of Buckingham Palace with Halifax and his wife, Cadogan exclaimed hopefully that with any luck an Axis agent might assassinate him. He said 'there was one bright spot – there were lots of Germans and Italians in Madrid and therefore a good chance of S.H. [Sam Hoare] being murdered'. Halifax looked pained, but Dorothy Halifax 'agreed heartily'.[48] The next day Halifax asked why Hoare was in such a hurry to get to Spain. Cadogan replied 'because he's frightened', adding 'he's the first rat to leave the ship'.[49]

In Spain, Hoare outwardly showed no fear and welcomed his old friend with gusto. There now followed a wave of lavish entertainment to win over the Windsors. Hoare put on the biggest Madrid cocktail party in living memory to influence which way they would jump.[50] He wanted them to board a flying boat for England, while the Spanish press, bribed by the Germans, warned loudly that they would be arrested as soon as they set foot in Britain.[51]

In their tempestuous flight south, the Windsors had not only abandoned 'Fruity' Metcalfe; they also left behind their closest French collaborator, Charles Bedaux. During the Battle of France, he had 'personally welcomed the German General Staff to his house near Tours'. Bedaux then spent most of this time in a Parisian office controlling a large German staff organizing Jewish industries which the Nazis had taken over and ensuring maximum production.[52] Later he worked with the sabotage branch of the Abwehr to command a covert mission to Persia to capture the British refinery at Abadan from his former client, the Anglo-Persian Oil Company.[53] A few years later he would commit suicide in a Miami jail while charged with being a Nazi collaborator.[54]

Despite the blatant pro-Nazi behaviour of their closest friends, the Windsors felt ideologically vindicated. In Spain, and encouraged by Hoare, the royal couple now professed their admiration of fascism more explicitly than ever. They clearly respected Hitler and believed in the modernity of fascism, which would herald economic progress and a new order. More than that, they now gloated that they had accurately predicted the future. Speaking to a US diplomat, Edward elucidated the dramatic military events they had just witnessed by asserting that: 'In the past ten years Germany has totally reorganized the order of its society in preparation for this war.' He added: 'countries that were unwilling to accept such a reorganization and concomitant sacrifices should direct their policies accordingly and thereby avoid dangerous adventures'. The duchess said much the same thing, but in darkly Darwinist language, observing: 'France had lost because it was internally diseased and that a country that was not in a condition to fight a war should never have declared war.'[55]

These provocative statements had personal consequences. They placed the Windsors at loggerheads with one of their friends and most powerful supporters, Winston Churchill. The tricky Windsor problem now landed on his desk at Number 10. He had gone out of his way to support them during the abdication crisis and had remained closer to them than any other leading British politician during the late 1930s. Despite the awkwardness, Churchill now sternly ordered Edward to return home, reminding him that he held military rank and with that came inescapable duties. The language was unambiguous, and, as the historian Deborah Cadbury has observed, perhaps even threatening: 'Your Royal Highness has taken active military rank and refusal to obey direct orders of competent military authority would create a serious situation.'[56]

Edward stood his ground, perhaps believing that defeat for Britain was only weeks away. He then bargained, demanding a suitable official post in Britain before pursuing his dearest ambition, securing 'HRH' status for Wallis. The latter proved the deal breaker – King George would not hear of it. Moreover, politicians and the palace disagreed about where the Windsors should go. Churchill wanted to bring them home, but George and Elizabeth, who watched them closely, wanted to keep them as far away from England as possible. On 3 July, the king exhorted Churchill about this, exclaiming: 'I did not see what job he could have in this country and that she would not be safe here.'[57]

While London weighed options, the Windsors were on the move again. They followed the advice of their friend Sam Hoare to travel to Lisbon, a more neutral but nonetheless dangerously spy-infested capital. They had to pause before departing, since Edward's youngest brother, the duke of Kent, was visiting Portugal and nobody wanted two royals in the country at the same time.

The duke of Kent's visit in July 1940 is mysterious. Cadogan noted in his diary that there was now a 'Funny pause' in the war. 'Hitler doesn't like the look of invasion and is trying to tempt us to parley.' Indeed, Hitler had said publicly that he saw no reason 'why this war should go on' and appealed 'once more to reason and common sense in Britain'. Cadogan noted cryptically that approaches had been made through countries such as Sweden, the Vatican and the USA. Was this another of the many feelers? Three weeks after Dunkirk, and with the skies thick with German fighters, it is unlikely that the duke of Kent was in Portugal simply to celebrate a national anniversary or play a round of golf. [58]

Edward's youngest brother had been enlisted as a source of valuable information by British intelligence as early as July 1939. The king had suggested that he act as an emissary to Hitler via his cousin, Prince Philipp of Hesse, who was then the go-between for Hitler and Mussolini. Halifax and Chamberlain were lukewarm and the project was eventually shelved. But in June 1940, the duke of Kent stepped up to carry out a 'series of delicate and important missions'. Some high-level German secret service agents were trying to pressure the neutral Portuguese dictator António de Oliveira Salazar into openly committing to Hitler. The duke was sent to find out what Salazar was really thinking and also to gain his confidence. A 'perfect cover was found' in that he was selected to lead a delegation to attend the seven-day celebrations of Portugal's 800 years of independence. The duke spoke good Portuguese and his presence was symbolic of the long-standing alliance between the two countries. He flew home on 2 July 1940, the same day that Wallis and Edward set out by car from Madrid to Lisbon. [59]

The duke of Kent's visit also underlined that air travel was still possible from Lisbon, even if it was hazardous with the Battle of Britain raging. Britain was not sure that it wanted Edward, and, for his part, Edward hesitated to fly to what he regarded as an almost defeated nation. He held out for a better offer from elsewhere. Perhaps he knew that, even before the invasion of France, German diplomats had sought an opportunity to reach out. As early as 27 January 1940, Julius Count von Zech-Burkesroda, German ambassador to Netherlands, confided to his superiors: 'Through personal relationships I might have the opportunity to establish certain lines leading to the Duke of Windsor.'[60]

Hitler misunderstood many things in world politics, including the role of the royal family in Britain. Assuming the king played a role more like the kaiser in 1914, he saw monarchical politics as central to manipulating Britain. When Edward had abdicated, Ribbentrop had pandered to this bizarre view, reporting that it was all an anti-German plot. He suggested that 'The abdication of King Edward is the result of the machinations of dark Bolshevist powers against the Führer-will of the young King.' He promised that even more sensitive details about the royals would soon be reported to Hitler by word of mouth.[61] Hitler interpreted the abdication as driven by Edward's desire for Anglo-German rapprochement. There was now, he believed, 'No other person in England who is ready to play with us'. A depressed Hitler lamented that if only Edward had remained on the throne, 'There would have been no differences – and no war – between England and Germany'.[62]

Anglo-German friendship was fundamental to Hitler's world vision. In the summer of 1940, as he personally toured Paris, he appeared to be at the pinnacle of his success. But fundamentally, he was troubled by his evolving pattern of alliances. Hitler regarded Axis countries like Italy and, particularly, Japan as racially inferior. He had also concluded an opportunistic pact with Russia to carve up central Europe. All this had delivered well for him, but what he really desired was to be allied with Anglo-Saxon countries such as Britain against the likes of Bolshevik Russia. In 1940, he still thought this might be possible – and hoped the Windsors could help.[63]

EDWARD AND WALLIS arrived in Lisbon in early July. Looking out across the Atlantic Ocean they still faced a moment of decision – whether to follow Churchill's order and return or stay in Lisbon hoping for a better offer from the Nazis. Meanwhile, MI6 gathered intelligence on the assiduous way in which the Germans were courting them.

The duke and duchess were addicted to luxury and conspicuous consumption. They worried about their property in France and especially the fate of their very expensive bed linen. Exploiting this, the Nazis back in Paris attended to their every whim. Gray Phillips, one of Edward's closest aides, told the chief of MI6, Stewart Menzies, about the 'exceptional care' with which the Germans had fulfilled all of Edward's desires regarding their personal effects in France. 'Special camions were sent to and fro, and a detailed inventory list was made of all the furniture and personal property of Duke and Duchess of Windsor, which was shown to the Duchess for approval...'[64]

The top British secret service man on the ground in Lisbon was David Eccles. Rather than belonging to MI6, he was a member of Churchill's new sabotage service, the Special Operations Executive. A future Tory MP and later a viscount, he had royal connections, being married to the daughter of the royal physician. Comfortable moving in the upper echelons of society, Eccles met Edward frequently in Lisbon. He told his masters that he was determined 'to watch him at breakfast, lunch and dinner with a critical eye'.[65]

Eccles soon reported back to London. Once again, Edward and Wallis were spouting their defeatist views. 'I had some conversation today with Duke and Duchess... They are very clearly 5th column; at least they reckon we pushed France into a war she didn't want...' Asked by Eccles if he thought the Germans would keep the terms of their deal with France, the duke simply replied: 'Why Not?'[66] This intelligence quickly found its way to the eyes of Britain's most senior diplomat, Alexander Cadogan, and the foreign secretary.[67]

Eccles oversaw a team of willing assistants. They included Tommy Burns from Spain and a number of key figures involved in the dark arts of propaganda and economic warfare. Their best intelligence came from the garrulous Nicolás Franco, the Spanish dictator's brother and ambassador to Portugal. He revealed to Eccles that a secret mission to get the Windsors back to Spain and hold them there was gathering pace. Spain, he explained, had sent Ángel Alcázar de Velasco, a bullfighter turned assassin, to assist the Germans. The border would be key to the plan's success: Germany had paid off the Spanish secret police, but Britain had paid off the Portuguese secret police. Everyone was warning the Windsors of the possibility of their assassination.[68]

Always professional spongers, Edward and Wallis had now found another new host with deep pockets: Ricardo Espírito Santo Silva. A banker and one of Lisbon's most respected residents, Silva had hosted members of the royal family before the war, but his allegiances were suspect. MI6 reported: 'It appears that the Duke of Windsor is now occupying the house of a certain... Santo Silva... and is seeing a good deal of his landlord. We have learned from a reliable and well-placed source in Lisbon that Silva and his wife are in close touch with the German Embassy and that Silva had a three-hour interview with the German Minister.' Again, Cadogan and Halifax, the foreign secretary, read the intelligence closely.[69]

Desmond Morton, a veteran MI6 officer who had been Churchill's most trusted aide for the last decade, was now the go-between for Downing Street and the intelligence agencies. His latest mission was to gather more intelligence on the Windsors' new host. MI6 reported: 'Senor Espirito Santo is very pro-German and a centre of peace propaganda... Politically he is a crook... He is handling very large sums in bank notes and securities from Germany... These monies are almost certainly German loot from captive countries.'[70]

MI5 confirmed this shortly afterwards. His bank was 'an agency for the transmission of funds to German agents' in both Spain and Portugal.[71] For years Churchill had defended the duke publicly and privately, but his patience now wore thin. Multiple intelligence sources showed that Edward was effectively consorting with the enemy. It was time for action.

On 4 July, British newspapers announced that Edward would be taking up a new post as governor of the Bahamas, a small collection of islands close to Florida, separated from the European war by thousands of miles of ocean. A few hours after the press was told, Edward also received the news of his new posting – a fait accompli. As a military officer he was being given his marching orders. 'I have done my best in a grievous situation,' Churchill told him, putting it politely but firmly.[72]

Six days later Churchill arrived at Buckingham Palace for his weekly meeting with the king and found they were in full agreement. They knew they had both sent Edward into exile on a desert island and were understandably anxious about it. George recorded in his diary: 'It was better that he should not come here', adding: 'What I had done, had had to be done for the country's sake.'[73] Given the increasing volume of alarming intelligence, this was quite an understatement.

More warnings arrived on the desk of Stewart Menzies, the chief of MI6. Edward had not yet left for the Bahamas. The Germans thought that Britain was losing the war and that Edward and Wallis had switched sides. They were determined to seize what they saw as a fantastic opportunity. 'A new source... has reported as follows: – Germans expect assistance from Duke and Duchess of Windsor, latter desiring at any price to become Queen... Germans have been negotiating with her since June 27th. Germans propose to form opposition government under Duke of Windsor...' Halifax urged that this intelligence be shown to Churchill at once.[74] But by the middle of the month, Churchill did not need to depend on MI6 for this sort of information; it was being reported openly in the world press.[75]

Edward may not, at this point, have settled on the Germans, but the Germans had settled on him. They now began one of the most bizarre plots of the entire war. Codenamed Operation Willi, the SS placed their top agent, Walter Schellenberg, in charge. Schellenberg's plan was for a Spanish friend of the duke to lure him to Spain on the pretext of a hunting trip. He could then either be kept in Spain, perhaps as the head of a rival British government in exile, or even taken to Germany.[76]

Above all Edward wanted to be perceived as a peacemaker, and so was reportedly delighted and flattered by what he saw as a German peace initiative. According to German accounts, 'the Duke paid tribute to the Führer's desire for peace', admitting it was, 'in complete agreement with his own', because he 'was firmly convinced that if he had been King it would never have come to war'. He now asked Santo Silva to relay 'an expression of admiration and sympathy for the Führer'.[77]

Remarkably, with the Battle of Britain raging but tempted by a Spanish offer of asylum, Edward even considered a public declaration disassociating himself from Churchill's policy of carrying on the war. He told Berlin that he would 'postpone his journey to the Bahamas for as long as possible', hoping for an 'early change in his favour'. The German ambassador relayed Santo Silva's assessment that Edward was 'a firm supporter of peaceful compromise with Germany'. He added that Edward believed 'with certainty that continued heavy bombing will make England ready for peace'.[78]

British flying boats tasked with bringing Edward back to Britain came and went without their royal passengers. A sense of crisis developed in London. All telegrams dealing with his arrangements were marked for immediate action.[79] The critical turning point had arrived. Alcázar de Velasco, Spanish agent of the Abwehr, was pressing them to come to Spain for 'a hunting trip'. Edward hesitated, realizing the historical magnitude of his decision.[80]

Churchill now played his trump card. He sent out one of Edward's most trusted friends, Walter Monckton, one of the few to break the 1937 social embargo on his wedding. Edward countered with a trump card of his own by responding to fears of a German plot with accusations of a British plot. Monckton told Churchill that Edward claimed to have 'received from various sources, which he was not at liberty to disclose, though he regarded them as reliable, a report that he would be in danger if he went to Bahamas'. Edward dramatically added 'that there was a plot afoot against his security and that British influences, including probably some members of the Government, were implicated'.[81]

Monckton was one of the few men Edward trusted and managed to persuade him that any assassination plot was a German fabrication to keep him in Lisbon. 'I said that... what was wanted was some concrete evidence of the existence of such a plot...'[82] Either way, the deliberations again delayed their departure.[83] With orders to move Edward and Wallis out of Lisbon as soon as possible, officials finally booked them onto the American liner *Excalibur*, bound for the Caribbean on 1 August. The Windsors reluctantly agreed to go.

Willing to do anything to prevent Edward's final departure, Schellenberg sabotaged the car carrying his luggage to the ship. He knew how important expensive clothes and personal effects were to the couple.[84] He also sent 'bouquets of flowers to the Duchess warning her that the offer of an appointment in the Bahamas was merely a plot by the British to do away with him'.[85] In the meantime he 'was empowered to offer to deposit fifty million Swiss francs in a Spanish bank account' if Edward was to co-operate and make statements distancing himself from London.[86] Schellenberg's charm offensive, warnings and sabotage all failed. He watched among the crowds as the ship sailed off.

The Windsors had hesitated and then departed mostly for reasons of their personal safety. They had not finished scheming, though, and so, even as they departed, still contrived to keep their options open. MI5's deputy director, Guy Liddell, recorded that even as Edward left, he fixed up 'some kind of code with Espirito Santo Silva in order that he might fly back to Portugal from Florida if his intervention was required'. Shockingly, as early as mid-August, at the height of the Battle of Britain, when Hitler hoped to overwhelm his adversary, the duke despatched a coded telegram asking his pro-Nazi friend if that moment had now arrived. Liddell's diary, kept secret for so many years, now clearly reveals which way Edward was leaning.[87] Santo Silva alerted the German ambassador in Lisbon, who asked Berlin: 'Should anything be sent in reply?'[88]

THE NAZIS NOW tried other – more ambitious – royal avenues. Just before the Windsors sailed for the Bahamas, King Gustav V of Sweden approached George offering to act as a back channel for peace with Germany. Churchill helped the king draft a stern rejection, detailing Hitler's crimes and pointing to Swedish complicity. Churchill's language was so strong that diplomats had to tone it down before it reached the palace.[89]

Hitler's Scandinavian overtures gave Britain further insight into the racial nature of his thinking – and the odd role of British royalty within it. Hitler believed that 'the white race' now consisted of two economic units: Germany on the Continent and the British Empire together with America as an ocean-based economy. Their mission was to work together to resist Russia as 'a potential enemy' and above all to 'resist the encroachment of the yellow race'.[90] Once again there was a sense that Hitler found the realities of world politics out of step with his bizarre racial vision, and he wished to use discreet royal diplomacy – whether from Edward or even George – as a means to correct this. The palace, government and secret intelligence had to work closely together to counter it. In a curious way, royal peace feelers contributed to Hitler's hesitation on Operation Sealion – the invasion of Britain – and perhaps worked to Churchill's advantage.[91]

There is no doubt that the summer of 1940 still contains Britain's greatest secrets and mysteries. Some relate to the royal family, and members of their household were as keen to unravel them as anyone. Perhaps best placed to do this was Tommy Lascelles, the king's private secretary who had relatives in MI5. Late at night over dinner at the Travellers Club, his cousin, Cecil Liddell, revealed a successful intelligence operation that involved bugging senior German officers who were held as prisoners of war in a country house on the northern edge of London called Trent Park – harvesting what the Germans thought were private conversations. They repeatedly referred to Hitler as 'the carpet-biter', confirming his tempestuous moments of intoxicating rage, and expressed frustration about his interference in the final day of Dunkirk when he ordered the Wehrmacht to hold back. Lascelles learnt that they complained that 'but for Hitler's contrary orders, they could have concentrated enough artillery to make our embarkation impossible'. Instead of destruction, Hitler wanted peace with Britain, ideally facilitated through emissaries to figures like Edward in Portugal, and clearly thought it possible.[92]

In this respect, Edward's temporizing in Lisbon perhaps makes him an accidental hero. The tantalizing possibilities he offered Hitler provided a moment of fascinating distraction at a critical point in the war and may have saved many British lives at Dunkirk. Hitler had obsessed about Edward for years, scheming to marry him to a minor German royal as early as 1934. Hitler had always displayed a habit of hesitation and Edward's own behaviour in June and July exacerbated it. As Michael Bloch has persuasively argued, it is no coincidence that, on 1 August, the very day the Windsors sailed westward from Lisbon, Hitler, after weeks keeping his generals waiting, finally issued his Directive No.17, accelerating the air war against England.[93]

Whatever the Windsors' collective inner thoughts or allegiances, the German plots to use them for the purposes of the Third Reich were real. What would Churchill have done if they had not embarked on the *Excalibur* and set sail in early August? What if they had headed back into Spain, or even to Berlin? Against the backdrop of the Battle of Britain, these were desperate times.

12

WAR IN THE AMERICAS

'might be kidnapped'

Duke of Windsor, 1941[1]

IN THE SUMMER and autumn of 1940, Britain was fighting for its life. France, the Netherlands and Belgium had already fallen, leaving the southeast coastline vulnerable to invasion. The German Luftwaffe filled the skies overhead, designed to force Churchill's surrender or, failing that, soften Britain up for an invasion across the Channel. Bombs hit Buckingham Palace, narrowly missing King George VI and Queen Elizabeth. The Royal Air Force famously won the battle but, for the next year, the empire and commonwealth fought on alone against the odds, holding out only because of a vital but vulnerable chain of supply crossing the Atlantic.

Support from President Franklin D. Roosevelt, often in the face of domestic criticism, was essential. The United States was not yet in the war and American public opinion tilted towards isolationism; many did not want to get dragged into a bloody conflict on the other side of a vast ocean. Churchill was therefore fighting on two fronts: a military campaign in Europe to hold off a Nazi invasion, and a deeper political struggle, often conducted by covert means, to keep the American material support onside.

The first shot in this clandestine political struggle was fired back in the early summer of 1939, before war was even declared.

George and Elizabeth set out on a long tour of Canada, initi-
ated by Governor General Lord Tweedsmuir, better known as
John Buchan, the spy-novelist and author of *The 39 Steps* who
had worked on British propaganda during the First World
War.[2] The royal couple spent the final week in the United States
hoping to generate support for the coming war.[3] They visited
Mount Vernon, once George Washington's estate, on 9 June and
New York's World's Fair the following day. They then dined at
Roosevelt's estate at Hyde Park in New York state, during which
a smiling and relaxed Roosevelt served hotdogs, smoked turkey
and strawberry shortcake.[4]

The British worried the royal couple would be poorly received.
Accompanied everywhere by their two detectives as well as the US
secret service, George and Elizabeth potentially faced 'unfriendly
demonstrations' caused by 'suspicions that Britain is continually
scheming to involve the United States in its European troubles'.[5]

Such protests failed to materialize. The visit was instead a massive
triumph and had huge psychological significance for a king and
queen who were new to large-scale public engagements. For the first
time they far outshone their glitzier celebrity rivals, the duke and
duchess of Windsor. Queen Elizabeth later observed emphatically,
'that tour made us'.[6]

In May 1940, the British covert psychological campaign in North
America stepped up a gear. In New York, a Canadian MI6 officer
called William Stephenson established a secret organization called
British Security Coordination (BSC). A secret service department
store providing a home for the burgeoning undercover organizations
inside the United States, BSC operated from the thirty-fifth and
thirty-sixth floors of the Rockefeller Center throughout the Second
World War. This prime real estate was only the tip of the iceberg
since some three thousand people were engaged in its operations
across the Continent. Notable secret operatives and collaborators
included Noël Coward, Roald Dahl, Ian Fleming, and the philoso-
phers Freddie Ayer and Isaiah Berlin.[7]

Ernest Cuneo, a newspaper editor and enthusiastic Anglophile, summed up BSC activities perfectly. 'Throughout the neutral Americas, and especially in the U.S.,' he admitted, 'it ran espionage agents, tampered with the mails, tapped telephones, smuggled propaganda into the country, disrupted public gatherings, covertly subsidized newspapers, radios and organizations, perpetrated forgeries – even palming one off on the President of the United States – violated the aliens registration act, shanghaied sailors numerous times, and possibly murdered one or two persons in this country.'[8]

On top of all this, BSC helped to create the forerunner of the Central Intelligence Agency (CIA). In 1940, America had no centralized foreign intelligence service. Stephenson worked closely with Roosevelt's friend, Colonel William J. Donovan, to create the Office of Strategic Services, which undertook both human espionage and sabotage, modelling itself closely on British activities.[9] The diminutive Stephenson was dubbed 'Little Bill' while the larger Donovan was 'Big Bill', and they became firm friends. Donovan, like Stephenson, was staunchly anti-Nazi and his conviction that Britain would hold out against Germany, underpinned by repeat visits to London to tour secret service headquarters and meet the king, strongly influenced Roosevelt's thinking.[10]

Within hours of his first arrival in the summer of 1940, Donovan went to Buckingham Palace. After a hearty welcome from George, the conversation quickly turned to secret intelligence. The king showed Donovan a single flimsy sheet – a deciphered message from Hitler to his field commanders about the invasion of Britain – explaining it had come from 'most secret sources'. George knew not to share the precise secret of Bletchley Park with Donovan, but the American quickly worked out that Britain had so much inside information on the German high command that they must have had some success intercepting its communications. Although the source was left unspoken, Hitler's message revealed both his disappointment at the failure of his many peace overtures and his intention to invade and 'eliminate England as a base for the prosecution of war against Germany'.[11]

Discussing the intelligence, George assured Donovan that Britain would hold out in the air, making Hitler hesitate, adding that Buckingham Palace was now a target for bomber raids. Equally importantly, Donovan concluded that the royal family had no plans to run away.[12] He reported all this back to President Roosevelt, countering the more defeatist assessments of US isolationists.

BRITISH INTELLIGENCE WORK in America was dangerous, complicated and awkward. On the one hand, BSC used disinformation and covert political warfare against American isolationists.[13] On the other hand, MI6 had to work closely with the FBI to battle Nazi agents in Latin America and the Caribbean.[14]

A vast mail-opening operation located in New York and Bermuda proved particularly valuable. The American authorities grumbled about it at first, but eagerly co-operated once they saw the fantastic haul of intelligence it generated.[15] Bermuda and neighbouring islands in the Caribbean were a vast communications nexus, with real intelligence opportunities. From 1940, some twelve hundred staff operated the main censorship centre from a sprawling pink building, the Hamilton Princess Hotel, on the Bermudan shoreline.[16] The Pan-American Clipper Service ran from New York via Bermuda to Lisbon, carrying most air mail passing from the United States to Germany. Other islands carried German mail to South America. Secretly opening it uncovered Axis spies operating in the western hemisphere and also allowed MI6 to keep its finger on the pulse of public opinion in neutral America.[17]

The BSC representative in the region was the formidable Harford Montgomery Hyde. He had begun his intelligence career as a mail opener, learning the trade from his boss, 'Steam Kettle Bill', in the censor's office in Liverpool during the First World War. Now he presided over an enormous operation. His censors processed a hundred mailbags a day containing some 200,000 letters, of which they checked

15,000 daily for microdots or secret ink. In late July 1940, MI6 transferred a crack unit from Gibraltar commanded by Hyde's friend,
Humphrey Cotton Minchin, which used special equipment to open
and reseal mail without a trace.[18] The immense operation did not always
work perfectly. On one occasion, the team opened a letter sent from a
German woman to her lover in Argentina enclosing a lock of pubic
hair. They lost the hair and replaced it with bristles from a broom![19]

As the effort gathered pace, the colonial secretary told governors to expect an influx of intelligence officers to the region. They
included Lieutenant Commander J.C.D. Harington who, based in
Jamaica, also covered British Honduras and the Bahamas.[20] Years
later, he told his family over dinner that his most important wartime
task was covering two particular new arrivals in the Bahamas: the
duke and duchess of Windsor.[21]

Edward and Wallis set out across the Atlantic in early August
1940 on the American liner *Excalibur*. They were now out of sight,
but not out of mind. They had expected to call in on New York en
route, the ship's normal destination, and do some shopping, but the
Foreign Office had other ideas. London offered to pay the shipping
company the full costs of diverting to the Caribbean, estimated at
somewhere over $15,000. The Windsors did not go straight to the
Bahamas, but first visited the island of Bermuda, which was fast
becoming Britain's regional intelligence centre. They stayed with
the governor, Denis Bernard, and soon became 'something of an
embarrassment at Government House'. [22] According to Hyde, they
brought with them fifty-eight pieces of luggage (and three dogs),
but still Wallis moaned that she did not have enough clothes. Hyde
later met them in Nassau, where their baggage had been reinforced
by fourteen additional pieces, including a trailer. 'Every refugee has
a trailer' was Wallis's sage comment.[23]

Habitual big spenders, they quickly made trouble from their
far-flung outpost.[24] With the British population at home plunged
into wartime rationing and austerity, the Windsors demanded huge
sums to refurbish their own Government House in the Bahamas,

which they considered distinctly unfashionable.[25] British officials were shocked at the extravagance.[26] But back in London, Churchill arranged for Hugh Dalton, minister for economic warfare, to suspend wartime currency regulations so that Wallis could send 10,000 francs back to German-occupied France to settle their affairs. Dalton noted that Churchill 'always had a soft spot for the Duke'.[27]

Within days of their arrival, Lord Lothian, Britain's ambassador in Washington, sounded a warning note. Support from the United States was on a knife edge and, he argued, it was 'most important' to avoid the view that Edward was 'not taking his duties in the Bahamas entirely seriously'. The Americans rightly associated Edward and Wallis with 'frivolity and extravagance', something which was likely to provoke 'sharp criticism and disillusionment' with the British cause. Unfortunately, no one in London had much traction with the bitter and arrogant Windsors; not the foreign secretary, not Churchill, not even Edward's old friend Walter Monckton.[28] Any warning would go unheeded.

The Caribbean was far from the idyllic and trouble-free destination some had hoped. The whole region became a playground for agents, gunrunners and neutralist millionaires on the make.[29] Indeed, the Windsors' ship the *Excalibur* was at the centre of just such a scandal on its very next run through Bermuda and the Bahamas. In October, it was found to be carrying a haul of 500 contraband French impressionist paintings, including 270 by Renoir, thirty by Cezanne and twelve by Gauguin. Hyde took a keen interest, since the cargo was intended to raise much-needed dollar currency for the Nazis. When the captain refused to open the ship's strong room, Hyde and a British naval team burned through the bulkhead with blow-torches and recovered the treasures. MI6 later turned the whole lot over to the National Gallery in Canada.[30]

Hyde now faced multiple kinds of Windsor trouble. Although countries like Brazil and Mexico swarmed with smugglers and Nazi spies, his main problem lay in the United States. Only fifty miles away, the Florida coast was a magnet for the rich and famous, just the sort of people with whom the loose-lipped Windsors loved to mingle. MI6 worried about who they would meet, what they would say, and whether they would encourage American isolationism.

As long as Britain appeared to be doggedly resisting the Nazis, Roosevelt would support them with money and supplies. If Britain wavered, or looked like it would fall, Roosevelt, under strong pressure from isolationists, might withdraw his support. This is precisely why the king had met Colonel Donovan, Roosevelt's factfinder, only months before, to bolster the idea of stalwart British resistance. The secret battle for the president's mind was intensifying. Needless to say, the Germans were keen for Edward to speak defeatism to Roosevelt. Alarmingly, Roosevelt was also keen to speak to Edward.

In September 1940, Churchill was incensed to learn that his chief diplomat in Washington, Lord Lothian, had raised the possibility of Edward meeting Roosevelt. He feared that Edward would indulge the president – and anyone else who would listen – in neutralist and pacifist talk, with potentially disastrous consequences. Sternly, the foreign secretary, Lord Halifax, told Lothian that any meeting 'should be avoided for as long as possible'.[31] Lothian insisted that Roosevelt was keen to meet Edward, and that it was a mere social call.[32] The American press, however, knew it was far more than that. One report put it bluntly: 'President Roosevelt will try to bring about peace negotiations between great British and the axis powers… the duke of Windsor may also play a part in this attempt.' It ominously added that 'the government sent him to the Bahamas to get him out of the way, but he accepted the appointment so that he could be within easy reach of the USA'.[33]

Things went from bad to worse. In November, Downing Street was disconcerted to discover that Roosevelt was planning a tour of the Caribbean the next month and positively yearned for a royal audience. British officials plotted to keep the two men apart, asking Lothian to tell Roosevelt that we 'discourage' any meeting and ensuring that Edward was deliberately 'left in ignorance of the suggestion'.[34]

Working with figures inside Edward's household, they contrived to fill the duke's diary by packing him off to Miami. Edward was told that it was supremely important that the governor of the Bahamas go there to present a cup at the local horse races.[35] Only after the trip was arranged, they hoped, would he realize that he would miss Roosevelt. The British ruse failed, since Roosevelt managed to catch up with the Windsors by using a ruse of his own.[36] He fooled the British by telling them their schedules now seemed out of line. 'I am very sorry,' Roosevelt added, 'that I shall probably miss him.'[37] In fact, he was so keen to meet Edward that he secretly sent a US naval aircraft to fly him out to join him.[38]

Roosevelt viewed appeasers as his political enemies. After winning a historic third term in the White House, he told King George that 'there is absolutely no question that the appeasement element, the pro-Germans, the communists and the total isolationists did their very best for my defeat'. He promised that he would now send every bit of spare military equipment to Britain, adding that 'I have what we call a "hunch" – not necessarily based on cold figures, that you have turned the corner' and that 'luck will be more and more with you'.[39] Despite this, he remained keen to hear the alternative point of view from George's older brother.

Roosevelt and Edward exchanged more than social pleasantries. What the president did not tell the duke was that, at that very moment, he was pondering the possibility of another deposed king, his brother George, arriving in the western hemisphere in the event of a successful cross-Channel invasion. Roosevelt knew about the plan to evacuate the royal family to Canada. He did not like it at all and instead wanted George to be made governor of Bermuda, an even more remote outpost than the Bahamas. Roosevelt perhaps thought the idea of two former British kings – each with their own little Atlantic island – rather amusing.[40]

PREDICTABLY, EDWARD AND Wallis were soon spending time with the wealthiest resident on the Bahamas. This was the Swedish multimillionaire Axel Wenner-Gren, the owner of Electrolux, then the leading brand in both vacuum cleaner and refrigerator technology. They had camped out with him for two months during the expensive refurbishment of Government House.[41] In December, he had ferried them to Miami on his magnificent yacht.

Wenner-Gren was an appeaser; a self-styled peacemaker. He was friendly with Hermann Göring, whose first wife was a Swede, and had acted as an intermediary between Göring and the British and American governments. Edward's predecessor as governor had told MI5 that Wenner-Gren had held 'extremely confidential' conversations with Neville Chamberlain and was a friend of Roosevelt. He was also closely connected to the Windsors' previous sponsor, Charles Bedaux, and, like him, was soon added to the 'Trading with the Enemy' blacklist. Yet his peace efforts had proved unsuccessful, with all parties regarding him as a self-promoting nuisance.[42]

By late 1940, Wenner-Gren's recent visits to Rome and Berlin convinced Guy Liddell, deputy director of MI5, that he 'may be playing the German game'.[43] Liddell was alarmed but knew that Edward and Wallis would ignore any warning about their wealthy new friend if it came from London. Instead, he approached the American ambassador to Sweden and arranged for a warning to reach Edward from the Americans.[44] MI6 was also suspicious. William Stephenson reported that Wenner-Gren was 'friendly to Nazis, and associated with appeasement circles'. What bothered London most was that it simply looked bad in the American press and risked undermining the British cause. On 11 December, the colonial secretary warned Edward that the press was saying that he had travelled to Miami in the yacht of 'Goering's pal'.[45] If anything, American suspicions of Wenner-Gren were even more intense, though exactly what he had done to make the whiskers of the FBI twitch so vigorously is still not clear.[46]

Edward simply did not care. In London, this triggered an anxious debate over whether to show him classified intelligence to back up warnings about his new friend. On 14 December, Alec Hardinge, George's private secretary, received the security file on Wenner-Gren and duly showed it to the king. They were so alarmed that Hardinge thought the government should warn Edward formally 'against this man'. Revealing his view of Edward as a slippery customer, he added that if there was ever any scandal in the future, the duke might claim he knew nothing about Wenner-Gren, 'whether it was true or not'.[47]

Edward needed proof. Remarkably, given the duke's past record, Stewart Menzies, the chief of MI6, finally agreed to send him this classified material. Alexander Cadogan, the head of the Foreign Office, noted 'he may not be impressed by it, but he will at least have been warned'.[48] Churchill repeatedly ordered the duke to stay away from Wenner-Gren who was 'in communication with the enemy'.[49]

Bizarrely, the Windsors were now both targets of surveillance and also customers of the same sort of intelligence material. They read intercepted material on Wenner-Gren, while British intelligence intercepted material on their own conversations. American guests who visited the Windsors loved to brag to their friends about having met royalty and so reported every detail – every conversation – to them in letters. The massive MI6 mail censorship operation ensured that these details fell straight into the hands of British intelligence.[50] The Windsors also knew this, since hundreds of people were employed in the operation. Indeed, with the near cessation of tourism, the arrival of a veritable army of stealthy letter openers in the region, complete with their steam kettles, had boosted the economy. But once again Edward and Wallis did not seem to care.[51]

Perhaps the Windsors thought the only way to preserve their sanity was to see surveillance as a huge joke. The FBI had now begun to monitor the Windsors as well, and one FBI source emphasized that Edward was well aware that his staff were reporting back to London.

He said that on one occasion when they were at a dinner party the Duke had joined in singing 'There'll Always be an England' and then in an aside had asked if there would always be a Scotland

Yard... He also stated that at a dinner at Government House where the Duke and Duchess were piped in, after being seated the Duchess made some remark to a dinner guest and then turned to the piper and made the statement, 'You can also report that to Downing Street,' which indicated to everyone present that they thought the piper was some kind of spy for England.[52]

Strangely, this did not cause them to moderate what they said to their dinner guests, indeed rather the reverse. One of their more powerful visitors was the wealthy American Frazier Jelke, who seems to have known Edward quite well, and met him repeatedly. In March 1941, at dinner, Edward said it would be 'very ill-advised of America to enter the war against Germany as Europe was finished anyway'. Several nights later, Wallis told Jelke that if the US entered the war this country would go down in history as 'the greatest sucker of all time'. Jelke came away with the impression that they both admired Hitler. MI6 read it all.[53]

BETWEEN 18 AND 23 April 1941, Edward and Wallis spent five days in Palm Beach, a wealthy town on the east coast of Florida known for its glitzy estates and white sandy beaches. Roosevelt seems to have ordered a veritable orgy of surveillance on the Windsors as they mingled with the ultra-rich over chic cocktails.

Roosevelt chose Adolf Berle, a close confidant and assistant secretary at the state department, to manage the surveillance.[54] He, like the FBI head J. Edgar Hoover, had been a staunch opponent of British intelligence activities against US isolationism, fearing that BSC had tried to smear him. Now, in a strange turn of events, Berle found himself overseeing an intelligence operation targeting a key advocate of defeatism and isolationism. He confirmed that an FBI agent was to 'exercise discreet observation' when Edward visited Miami, and that 'a Special Agent to the Department of State' was acting 'as personal guard'. It was not enough, for Berle added that 'a wider and less obvious coverage is desirable'.[55]

The FBI took the operation seriously. It recorded that it had 'issued instructions for an agent to be assigned to assist in the watch of Duke of Windsor on his visit to Palm beach... Mr Tamm was handling the matter personally'.[56] Tamm was one of two deputies to J. Edgar Hoover.

The FBI was keen to secure more intelligence on the Windsors, but ironically its biggest impediment was British Special Branch. On the ground, the operation was run by the special agent in charge, Percy Wyly, a crack shot who had been personal assistant to Hoover. He explained that the Special Branch bodyguards were proving a problem. They made 'it impossible to get within 100 yards of the Duke for surveillance purposes'. Perhaps because of lingering tensions with BSC, the FBI was under strict instructions not to notify Scotland Yard 'of our activities'.[57]

Unable to get physically close enough to the duke, Wyly ensured that he had 'all communications covered'. This particular phrase, part of professional espionage parlance, suggests the use of microphones as well as telephone taps.[58] This is doubly interesting since Congress had recently restricted the FBI's use of such intrusive surveillance. Clearly the Windsors were a special case. The FBI also interviewed their known friends and associates.[59]

The FBI's extensive intelligence operation proved unnecessary. The views of the Windsors, which British intelligence had gone to great lengths to keep quiet, were soon in plain sight. In early May, on returning from Miami, Edward gave a remarkable interview to *Liberty*, a popular American weekly magazine, on the world situation in which he advocated a peace deal with Germany. He suggested that there was no real substance to the Anglo-American friendship and that the haughty British looked down on Americans as 'colonial and provincials'. He added that Britain would probably never repay its American loans and that the US would be better abstaining from the conflict and instead stepping in to mediate at some later point.[60]

Reaction in London was incandescent. In staggeringly undiplomatic tones, Foreign Office officials ranted to their new secretary of state, Anthony Eden, that 'the Duke of Windsor is a notoriously pro-Nazi. He is also a heavy drinker, and what few wits he had have wilted.' 'He should,' one diplomat continued without pausing for breath, 'of course never have received a post like this, where, despite his intellectual insignificance, he is capable of much harm as is now clear.' Eden agreed that the interview could hardly have been worse.[61] More minders were clearly needed.[62]

MI6 KNEW THAT while the Windsors had eluded the Nazis' clutches in Spain and Portugal, German agents remained active in Latin America. British intelligence teams in the Caribbean were doubled and redoubled to ensure that there could be no further plots to 'liberate' Edward and Wallis from the island. It was for this reason that Hyde, the MI6 regional chief, made his way to the Bahamas in May 1941 where he intriguingly managed to solicit information from Edward's private secretary, Major Gray Phillips, 'whom I have known personally for some years'.[63] On his arrival, Hyde discovered that the Windsors were conducting much government business from their private residence. Secret files on Axel Wenner-Gren, Göring's friend, and other 'individuals of security interest' were lying about in their accommodation for all to see. So much for London's decision to share MI6 intelligence with Edward.[64]

Hyde also spotted suspicious signs of Edward taking personal counter-surveillance a bit too seriously. He learnt that 'certain files', including on Wenner-Gren, were not to be shown to anyone without the duke's permission, and that Edward kept all the code and cypher books in his personal residence.[65] He was extremely concerned that his own correspondence should not be opened, and local officials insisted they had received 'a direct order from HRH that his mail and that of his staff must not be censored'.

But the net was tightening. Hyde decided to crank up the surveillance further and ordered his friend, Humphrey Cotton Minchin, the crack specialist in secret mail opening, away from Bermuda to take up the post of censor at Nassau.[66]

Hyde's main concern was not the files but personal security. He warned the duke that a German U-boat could 'carry off Your Royal Highness and the Duchess and the rest of the occupants of Government House, before the Bahamians realized the island was being attacked'. He followed this up with a warning to London about the severe danger of Edward being captured and used 'as a puppet sovereign'. He recommended more troops on the island and even 'an electrified fence around government house'. The dramatic request made its way through MI6 headquarters in New York and eventually ended up on Churchill's desk.[67] Edward was not keen on the suggestions and protested that 'local drunks would undoubtedly blunder into the fence and electrocute themselves'.[68]

Meanwhile, Hyde had discovered that Wenner-Gren's yacht was secretly 'heavily armed with bofors machine guns'. He also received reports that the Swede was building an aerodrome and submarine base on his private island. In the mind of MI6, Wenner-Gren was taking on the character of a future Bond villain with corporate interests in the globalized nebulae of the Caribbean and organized crime.[69] Hyde was concerned enough to send out two more operatives in quick succession. One began an 'under cover' investigation into the millionaire's new crayfish canning plant at the west end of the island. The other overflew the island to look for signs of submarine base construction and then probed Wenner-Gren's staff, although they found nothing.[70]

Playing the victim, Edward dramatically told Hyde that he was 'apprehensive that he might be kidnapped' from the Bahamas.[71] Apparently, his main fear was not being used as a puppet but instead 'being traded for the release of Rudolf Hess', Hitler's deputy who was being held following an ill-fated solo flight to Scotland.[72] MI6 was perhaps more worried that Edward would have been a willing target, voluntarily stepping onto a U-boat, maybe even from

Wenner-Gren's mythical submarine base, after sending a coded message to his friends in Portugal.

IN THE EARLY morning of Sunday 7 December 1941, Japanese aircraft launched a surprise attack on Pearl Harbor, the US naval base in Hawaii. At a stroke, the subsequent US entry into the war ended the hopes of those on both sides of the Atlantic who had sought a compromise with Hitler. Dreams of appeasement became a distant shadow as rhetoric everywhere, even in America, turned to fighting on until total victory. That night, Churchill recalled how he 'slept the sleep of the saved and thankful'.[73]

Back in London, one-time appeaser King George VI was busily winning back the trust of the intelligence services. In a curious way, though, he did not always need access. George now had his own secret service, allowing the monarch, like Queen Victoria and Kings Edward VII and George V before him, to resort to a DIY approach. Through the royal families of Europe to whom he was related, he boasted a remarkable intelligence network of his own. Many of them were now refugees in London and were at the heart of governments in exile that powered the growing European network. These ersatz nations, most visibly the Dutch, the Norwegians, the Poles and the French, were often run from slightly shabby hotels in Bayswater and Kensington, but their contacts were extraordinary.

George's use of his private network could cause momentary surprises. One intelligence officer recorded that the king received a couple of bottles of 1941 burgundy, one of which he served to Churchill at one of their regular Tuesday luncheons 'à deux'. Churchill asked sharply how he had got hold of it and was much put out to be told 'Kings have their secrets too'. Churchill had no idea that George was able to secure the wartime vintage from occupied France because his royal pilot, Edward 'Mouse' Fielden, also happened to fly missions for the Special Operations Executive, which Churchill had created – in his own words – 'to set Europe ablaze'. Fielden was dropping off secret agents in France but was wise enough not to return to the palace with an entirely empty aircraft.[74]

The royal family were now flashing their military credentials. The young Princess Elizabeth would eventually be allowed to join the Auxiliary Territorial Service, spending time servicing military vehicles. Her cousin, Margaret Rhodes, chose a rather more exotic career. Initially joining the Women's Royal Naval Service, she quickly found herself mysteriously transferred to MI6. Each day she was, in her own words, 'a small cog in the shadowy world of espionage' and by night she returned to sleep in the palace. Initially, she worked in the department controlling all MI6 personnel in the Middle East before moving to a more central role. 'One of my daily tasks,' she recalled, 'was to read every single message transmitted by our spies all over the world.' Aged just eighteen, she enjoyed a ringside seat on the 'above top secret' war; for example, she knew 'all about Germany's wartime race for nuclear weapons and the planned raid on the heavy water plant in Norway'.[75]

Rhodes was also aware of MI6 intelligence supplied by brave agents from plants on the Baltic coast where the Germans developed their long-range missiles. Later in the war one such rocket would miss MI6 headquarters by only a hundred yards. Margaret dived to the floor as it whizzed past, killing 121 people in the nearby Guards chapel in Wellington Barracks. Although living at Buckingham Palace was very convenient for MI6 headquarters, being 'just a short walk across the park', it was a more dangerous place than MI6 – the palace was bombed nine times during the war.[76]

Increasingly, George summoned Hugh Dalton, ministerial chief of covert action, to Buckingham Palace to brief him on SOE escapades.[77] One of his favourites was Operation Rubble. In 1940, the Nazis hoped to cripple the British war effort by blockading Swedish cargo ships containing ball bearings, steel and tools vital for making arms and equipment. Dalton's newly formed SOE was asked to rescue these badly needed supplies and so set about creating a secret team to steal the ships. This was a dangerous mission and George followed it in real time, knowing that the operatives might not return. The aged transport ships outran the Luftwaffe and German navy; George gloried in its success.[78] Hugh Dalton, a Labour minister in Churchill's coalition government, loved his trips to the palace and confessed himself a republican and anti-monarchist 'in every country but my own'.[79]

The king was increasingly fascinated by the secret war. It offered glimpses of success at a dark time during the war and so he demanded increasingly frequent updates, even when away from London. Accordingly, engineers installed the latest scrambler phones at Balmoral and Sandringham so that his staff could provide updates – they noted that this was 'a remarkable invention, and is said to be perfectly secure'. [80]

George did not always need to turn to ministers for stories of secret success against the Axis. One member of the royal family closest to the secret world worked at the cutting edge of covert warfare: David Bowes-Lyon. He was the queen's brother and a member of the Political Warfare Executive (PWE), an organization so new that he had actually named it. Based at Woburn Abbey and known colloquially as 'Pee-Wee', the PWE engaged in black propaganda, psychological warfare and political subversion under the control of Dalton.

In late 1941, Bowes-Lyon invited his sister, the queen, and George to visit him and inspect the work of the new department for themselves. On 19 November, they arrived at Woburn Abbey, a large country house in Bedfordshire. They listened to a remarkable presentation that was recorded and can still be heard today. The Political Warfare Executive humbly presents, the king and queen were told, 'The free voices of Europe, a picture in sound of the use of a new force in your majesties' service'. Bowes-Lyon then recounted the latest secret service ideas to his royal relatives:

I am here to introduce one of Britain's secret armies. An army which strikes from within the enemy's lines. You are going to hear the voices of this army – the voices of the black radio stations of Europe. At all hours of the day and all hours of the night they are transmitting messages of defiance, encouragement and hope to the victims of Hitler. The first of these voices was heard a year ago in Germany. A patriotic German calling on true Germans to defy Hitler. This was followed immediately by a group of German socialists who were calling other German socialists to join with them in their fight for the socialist revolution. Today there are nineteen different stations.[81]

To their delight, the king and queen were then treated to recordings of German subversives denouncing Hitler by radio.

David Bowes-Lyon worked closely with Dalton and was heavily involved in the political struggles over the control of sabotage and political warfare. Dalton had his own royal connections since his father had been a chaplain to Queen Victoria and tutor to King George V. In 1941, he had noted that while the king knew a little about economic warfare, he knew next to nothing about sabotage and secret agents. By the following year, George had found out about these more exciting activities – and wanted to know more, especially 'what sort of people they are whom we use'. He had also just discovered that Bowes-Lyon was being sent to Washington to work with Donovan's embryonic Office of Strategic Services.[82]

ON TUESDAY 3 November 1942, Churchill was late for lunch at Buckingham Palace. The prime minister visited the monarch every Tuesday lunchtime, but on this particular day Churchill did not appear, and as the minutes turned into hours, eventually his limousine arrived and he scurried in, carrying a battered red despatch box. Confronting the king and queen together he blurted out the words: 'I bring you victory.' The queen recalled that they looked at each other and thought: 'Is he going mad?' as they had not heard those words since the war began – everything had been retrenchment, retreat, or complete disaster.[83]

Churchill was quite correct. His authority was Bletchley Park and he produced two top-secret decrypts of messages from Rommel to Hitler. These were especially doleful and told of Rommel's defeat in the battle for Egypt and forecast the German retreat from North Africa. He had run out of petrol, supplies, transport, tanks, everything, and disaster loomed. The king was radiant and all of them sat basking in glory. They realized that the Battle of el Alamein, fought to prevent the Axis from venturing into Egypt, was not just the turning of the tide in the desert war but the beginning of the end for Hitler. The king noted in his diary: 'What rejoicing there will be.'[84]

Having once been arch-appeasers, the king and the queen now shared the innermost secrets of the war – even Bletchley Park. They also shared the inevitable paranoia that they brought. The king worried about becoming ill and accidentally blurting out secrets that might jeopardize the war. The queen was later asked if she was allowed to know the king's secrets. She replied that 'he told me everything'. This was partly about the loneliness of command. 'There was only us there.' The burden of secrecy they shared together was heavy and years later she recalled how 'even now I feel nervous sometimes, about talking about such things'. One of the effects of being on the inside track and receiving a constant newsfeed from Bletchley Park was knowing what was really going on. People around the palace were 'talking nonsense' but you 'couldn't say a word about it'.[85]

King George was gradually learning about new aspects of his secret service: black radios, deception, even the beginnings of electronic warfare. Now, with members of the royal household and even his family involved in the secret fight, he wanted to know more – and perhaps even join in a little of the action himself. His family connections provided the perfect opportunity and now, with the tide of war beginning to turn, he headed for the battlefront.

13

THE END OF THE
SECOND WORLD WAR

'thank the boys in the backroom'

King George VI, 1943[1]

O N 7 JUNE 1943, a month before the invasion of Sicily, General Lion stepped down from an RAF York transport aircraft onto dusty tarmac in Algiers, a busy hub in the accelerating war against the Axis. His flights, first from Britain to Gibraltar and then onwards to the Mediterranean, had been shrouded in secrecy and necessitated extremely elaborate protection plans. Indeed, the visit even warranted its own deception scheme, called Operation Loader, with British authorities spreading false stories that a secretary of state was en route to visit General Eisenhower in order to mask the real identity of this shadowy yet high-value passenger.

Even the aircraft was special. It was Churchill's personal, and specially adapted, aeroplane. Named *Ascalon*, after the sword St George used to slay the dragon, it boasted extra cabin space, a telephone for talking to the flight crew, a table with an ashtray, the latest newspapers and a bar. Designers even added an electrically heated toilet seat, although Churchill found it too hot and so it was eventually disconnected.[2]

The mysterious General Lion was none other than King George VI. And even Buckingham Palace had taken part in the deception by making a false announcement that the king had gone away to visit the fleet at Portsmouth.[3] His trip was so secret that the real secretaries of state had no idea about it until he safely arrived in North Africa.[4]

And with good reason. Churchill had made the same journey shortly before George. Ever the showman, his own secrecy was quickly blown, and German pilots swarmed over the Bay of Biscay waiting for his return leg. Taking no chances, they shot down everything in the area while Churchill was in the vicinity, including a passenger plane operating a regular service from neutral Lisbon.[5] All on board this aircraft were killed, including Leslie Howard, perhaps Britain's most famous wartime actor, and his accountant, Alfred Chenhalls, who, bald, rotund and rather fond of cigars, bore more than a passing resemblance to Churchill.[6]

Churchill knew his own visit had stirred up a hornet's nest and the king's trip, only five days later, using the same precarious route, was highly risky. The most senior civil servants in the land insisted that all necessary precautions were taken 'to avoid identification of the principal passenger'.[7] Privately, Churchill feared the worst and even discussed what the pilot should do if enemy fighters successfully hit the king's plane: whether it was better for him to ditch in the sea, or for the plane to crash-land in neutral Spain or Portugal.[8] As the war climaxed, the prime minister and king played a ludicrous game of competitive battlefield tourism, all the while rebuking the other for being too important to engage in such foolhardy ventures. Churchill would even write to George in dramatic prose about what to do 'in case of my death in this journey I am about to undertake'.[9]

THE DECEPTION WORKED, and King George landed safely. He was met personally by General Eisenhower, commanding Allied operations in North Africa, with whom he had already established a strong friendship. They drove from the airport at Maison Blanche, southeast of the city, to Eisenhower's beautiful villa that his forces had requisitioned from the Vichy French after a major Allied victory the previous year. For all the intense secrecy and worry about George's personal safety, the visit was a great success.

Once there, the biggest frustrations came from within his own party. George's private secretary, Alec Hardinge, whom he had inherited from his brother after the abdication, continually fussed and fretted. He offered George ridiculous advice not to visit the Americans and plunged into detailed discussions with Harold Macmillan, the British minister in Algiers, about the politics of the French resistance and the possibilities of deals with Italian 'quislings' – whom George visibly despised. Macmillan dismissed Hardinge as 'idle and supercilious', and George, growing in confidence by the day, ignored his advice and visited all Allied troops.[10]

Although it was Hardinge who had first tipped off George about the possibility of the abdication back in 1936, tensions between the king and his private secretary had been growing for years. Hardinge had thought him ignorant about public affairs and had not forgiven him for his love of appeasement. Meanwhile, George was now more assertive and, to Hardinge's shock, he fired him shortly after they returned home. His replacement was his deputy, Alan 'Tommy' Lascelles.[11]

One of the king's top priorities was to visit Massingham, the headquarters of SOE in North Africa. Created at a former French luxury pleasure resort called 'Club des Pins' some fifteen miles outside Algiers, Massingham was one of the first and most successful forward bases for dirty warfare. It served as a command centre and training base for most clandestine operations across the western Mediterranean and southwest Europe, including in France and Italy. It played a major role in the liberation of Corsica and facilitated the secret armistice negotiations that led to the Italian surrender in September 1943. Later, officers based there instigated several large uprisings deep behind enemy lines during the Allied invasion of southern France. Over the course of the war, Massingham despatched 400 agents and 14,000 crates of arms to the French resistance.[12]

Given the secrecy and deception surrounding the trip, George arrived at short notice. Douglas Dodds-Parker, a senior SOE officer at Massingham, assigned him the only spare room available in his own villa which also served as the officers' mess; it was a remarkable structure set on a remote beach and projected out into the sea on a series of piles.[13] Affable, yet highly astute, Dodds-Parker was enjoying a distinguished – if secret – career with SOE. He had found himself involved in the planning to assassinate Reinhard Heydrich, acting Reich Protector of Bohemia and Moravia, and later issued a pistol to one of SOE's French instructors who would kill Admiral Darlan, a senior Vichy figure and the highest-ranking officer in Algeria before the Allies arrived, on Christmas Eve in 1942.[14]

Now Dodds-Parker found himself in the company of the king. After a refreshing swim, during which they were guarded by some of SOE's toughest operatives, they sat alone together for a while as George opened up about the strains of the last few years and how much he had valued the support of his family. This risky trip to Algeria was his first solo mission overseas since 1940. Over four sunny afternoons at Massingham, George toured the station and its extensive training grounds, meeting Britain's experts in sabotage and irregular warfare. He watched fighting with daggers, parachute training and even the detonation of improvised bombs. SOE staff received strict instructions to carry out all their duties as normal when in the presence of the king so that he could get a detailed sense of ordinary life in a most unordinary field station – he loved every minute of it.[15]

As much as he was enjoying himself, George had business to do. His main purpose for being there was to present a medal to Paulin Colonna d'Istria honouring his daring missions launched from a British submarine, HMS *Trident*, into enemy-occupied Corsica to reorganize the resistance.[16] A former police chief on Corsica and son of a leading noble family, he had single-handedly transformed the local government into a secret underground network, paving the way for further successful networks in southern France and Italy.[17]

Among the motley ranks of the resistance fighters were Poles, Italians, elderly Spanish communists and plenty of American special operatives, including the film star Douglas Fairbanks Jr. On the last day of George's visit, this curious international underground army turned out to cheer his departure.[18]

A WEEK AFTER arriving in Massingham, King George personally insisted on visiting Malta.[19] He knew that the civilian population on the small Mediterranean island had suffered horribly during a brutal siege that had lasted some two years. He also understood that their bravery had proven critical in putting the squeeze on Field Marshal Rommel's Nazi supply lines, enabling only a few ships to reach Tripoli during the last months of 1942.

Here the work of Bletchley Park was especially crucial. With decrypts of German communications revealing that the Axis was running out of supplies in North Africa, Axis forces became trapped in a pincer movement during the spring of 1943, between British advances from Egypt and the Americans who had landed further west.[20] German forces were already in a 'dire condition' by early April and, as the Allies closed in, Rommel fled leaving 250,000 troops to surrender in Tunisia on 12 May. Church bells rang out across Britain. Together with the Battle of Stalingrad, which had ended two months earlier, this marked the shift of power in the Second World War. George personally wanted to thank the Maltese people for playing a valiant part in this victory.[21]

Still subject to air attacks and occasional commando raids, Malta was a dangerous place to visit. Nevertheless, on 20 June, George sailed under the cover of darkness aboard HMS *Aurora*, accompanied by Harold Macmillan and the chief of the naval staff, Admiral Andrew Cunningham. Arriving in Malta the following morning, the *Aurora* had to weave its way into the harbour through a graveyard of sunken ships. Wildly cheering crowds greeted George as he waved from a special platform constructed on the ship's bridge. 'You have made the people of Malta very happy today, Sir,' observed the governor gratefully as the day drew to a close. The king replied, 'But I have been the happiest man in Malta today!'[22]

At the end of June, with George safely back in Britain, MI5 deliberately leaked to the Germans news of his successful morale-raising tour. They used Agent Cheese as the channel. An Italian of Jewish parentage, Cheese was a double agent who served as one of Britain's top deception operatives in wartime Cairo. He, and his fictional sub-agent created by MI5, had been cleverly feeding a mixture of false information and so-called chicken feed, information that is true but not damaging, to the Nazis since 1941.[23] Cheese's 'intelligence' about the king's secret visit was classic chicken feed. It bolstered his credibility with the Nazis while doing no damage itself; but it also tormented them with the knowledge that two of their most prized assassination targets had visited the region and escaped unscathed.[24] The Mediterranean was no longer an Axis sea; it now belonged to the Allies.

GEORGE'S SOJOURN IN an SOE headquarters was not the only secret aspect of his Mediterranean tour. His meetings with planners covered the forthcoming invasion of Sicily and the elaborate deception schemes, which included the famous Operation Mincemeat, later portrayed by Hollywood as *The Man Who Never Was*. This imaginatively involved dropping a dead body carrying false plans off the shores of Spain, in the hope that it would wash up on a beach, reach the Germans, and disinform them that the main Allied thrust would come through Greece. Remarkably, it worked. Following the successful invasion of Sicily in July 1943, the king wasted little time in thanking the 'boys in the backroom' for the elaborate schemes to which he attributed such little loss of life on the Allied side.[25]

More than anything, it was his four days with Dodds-Parker and SOE at Massingham that had fired the king's imagination, so much so that he wanted his whole family to see something of their extraordinary activities. Accordingly, the following autumn, the king and queen, accompanied by the two young princesses, took a short train ride north of London into the Bedfordshire countryside. Alighting at a quiet station in the quaint market town of Sandy, the royal family transferred into an unmarked saloon car to take them the last few miles to a small RAF station at nearby Tempsford. Unbeknown to the locals, the aerodrome here housed the special duties squadrons that flew MI6 and SOE agents into Europe and was superintended by 'Mouse' Fielden, who also doubled as head of the King's Flight and so was a member of the king's household. The royal family enjoyed a full appreciation of the equipment the agents used, including their distinctive 'striptease' camouflage jumpsuits with large zips for easy exit, together with a complete rundown of the arms, rations and methods of jumping.[26]

Nearby Gaynes Hall, a handsome Georgian mansion, served as the holding station of these agents. It was a secret service hotel of sorts, where foreign nationals waited nervously for weather conditions suitable for 'Mouse' and his team to drop them into occupied Europe. One of those working there recalled how much the queen loved the gadgets and agent toys. She was fascinated by the camouflaged exploding devices disguised to look like wine bottles, rocks and logs – even stuffed rats and mice – that the resistance used to ambush the enemy. Her favourite gizmo was the exploding horse droppings that could be left innocently on a road but were powerful enough to destroy a vehicle; she was so excited by this that she rushed over to George, persuading him to come and have a look. The details of agent clothing were no less fascinating; they were shown lipsticks, buttons, corks and shaving brushes all made with hidden compartments for pills or microfilm. Shoelaces contained 'giglis', or flexible saws, so agents could cut their way through wood or metal if imprisoned, while heels and soles contained compasses and silk maps. Most sinister were the tiny drills for implanting a cyanide capsule inside the back tooth of an agent if required.[27]

With Sicily secured, the Italian campaign now lay ahead. This had been a highly contested matter, with Churchill wanting to invade Italy, which he saw as the soft underbelly of Europe, but the Americans had prioritized France. Italy eventually won out and, shortly after the invasion in autumn 1943, the king spotted an opportunity. Far from being a passive observer of grand strategy, he wrote to Churchill expressing his desire to now see Greece and Yugoslavia liberated quickly. He had his own wartime priorities focused around the preservation of European royal houses in countries as far apart as Greece and Sweden. The possibility that Russia might sweep across the Continent, eliminating the crowned heads of Europe, was already causing anxiety, a worry that Churchill as an ardent monarchist also shared.[28]

THE TURNING POINT for the king's secret war occurred in July 1943 and was something of an accident. When he replaced his long-serving and rather stuffy private secretary Hardinge with Tommy Lascelles, little did he know that he was taking on a former secret service officer. Lascelles had spent the early part of the war working part-time for MI(R), a sabotage organization that was eventually incorporated in SOE, along with elements of MI6.[29] More importantly, Lascelles was close to two of his cousins, Guy and Cecil Liddell. The former was deputy head of MI5 while the latter was head of MI5's Irish section. Cecil was an excellent cello player and all three got together for musical sessions where they exchanged the latest secret service gossip. Lascelles was a massive intelligence fan. When the queen asked for his recommendations for evening reading to while away the Blitz, he sent her one of Eric Ambler's thrillers, *Epitaph for a Spy*.[30]

By 1943, every secret establishment and wonder weapon was on the royal tourist trail. The king and queen visited the 'Dambusters'.

RAF 617 squadron was in training at Scampton in Lincolnshire preparing for their famous mission, since immortalized in film, to attack German dams. They were briefed by none other than Guy Gibson and Barnes Wallis, who designed the purpose-built bouncing bomb and explained how it could skip across water and bounce into dams. After the raid, the king presented Gibson with the Victoria Cross, before he was killed in action in September 1944 during a raid on Germany.[31] Another royal favourite was the facilities for the secret X-craft submarines used against the Tirpitz.

Even more secret things were to come. In October 1943, King George was briefed on one of the biggest secrets of them all: the emerging plans for D-Day, known as Operation Overlord, and the liberation of France. The presentation did not go as expected, for George reacted uneasily and feared disaster. His opinions clearly mattered and, early the following year, Eisenhower discussed Overlord with him personally in an attempt to reassure the nervous monarch about possible casualties.[32]

Perhaps because of these concerns, the authorities now chose to give George an operational role in the highly sensitive deception plans that would screen the D-Day landings and reduce risk. On 2 March 1944, two MI5 men turned up at Buckingham Palace. Sitting in the office of his private secretary, Tommy Lascelles, they quietly explained 'how the King's visits in the next few months could assist in the elaborate cover scheme whereby we are endeavouring to bamboozle the German Intelligence regarding the time and place for "Overlord"'.[33] As king, George had clearly come a long way from his early days as an appeasement sympathizer and, over the course of the war, had won the trust of the security establishment.

George was already broadly aware that Britain was running something called the Double Cross, or XX, System. This was a deception operation led by MI5 in which German agents in Britain were captured and turned, then fed dummy information to their Abwehr controllers. The brains behind the operation were provided by John Masterman, ably assisted by people like Johnny Bevan and TAR Robertson, who had earlier spied on King Edward VIII. Under their command, scores of people worked on this deception and were effectively the conductors of a vast orchestra.[34] Another was Dennis Wheatley, one of the go-betweens who linked the palace and the Cabinet Office. Wheatley was also the king's favourite thriller writer and George insisted on reading all his planning papers. Indeed, George was surprised by how often writers and entertainers he admired suddenly appeared in a secret wartime role. Noël Coward, the king and queen's favourite entertainer, had also enjoyed a secret wartime role in Paris.[35]

MI5 now deployed this vast deception mechanism to cover D-Day. As Churchill said, sometimes the truth is so precious that it must be covered 'by a bodyguard of lies'. The bodyguard was provided by Operation Fortitude, designed to deceive the Germans about the location of the Normandy landings in France. The idea was to reinforce German assumptions that the attack would occur at Calais. Simply using double agents to hand over false plans would have created suspicion. Instead, the Germans had to be allowed to piece the puzzle together themselves, fragment by fragment. Agents gave the Germans minutiae, such as inspections, unit numbers and details of exercises. In the east of Britain, George Patton, a well-known US general, was involved in the building up of an entire fake army all pointing to Pas de Calais. Deception planners even used inflatable tanks to trick German aerial surveillance.[36]

The king provided puzzle pieces of his own after MI5 began to work with Buckingham Palace from May 1944. George visited numerous fake installations to bolster the fictitious narrative that the Allies would invade Calais. With the press reporting it near and far, deception planners co-ordinated further royal visits, including to inspect troops in carefully selected locations, in order to maintain the ruse.[37] MI5 planners painstakingly co-ordinated George's movements with the material being fed back to the Germans via double agents. When he visited troops on the south coast, a double agent fed disinformation back to the Germans that traffic in the Isle of Wight had been stopped to clear the roads for troop movements.

This was a team effort and, for the first time, the queen and heir apparent Princess Elizabeth were enlisted in the ruse. The royal family went north on the royal train to visit airborne and glider formations in Lincolnshire and Yorkshire. They were very obviously and visibly attack formations. It was the seventh such inspection by the king in recent weeks, but it was the first time the princess had made a full-length tour with her parents and so garnered wide publicity.

Double Cross agents again sent corresponding material back to the Germans to increase credibility of assumptions drawn from the king's movements. When George visited troops in Hampshire, one agent sent a well-timed report warning of an imminent invasion from the region; another warned of military activity in the Channel which may or may not be a rehearsal or a diversionary attack. The most famous was Agent Garbo who was awarded the Iron Cross by the Germans for his excellent intelligence work and then decorated by King George himself for his Double Cross activities.[38]

George was a wonderful tool with which the Double Cross team could highlight certain troops and locations to which they wanted to draw German attention.[39] As a small cog in the elaborate deception, he naturally wondered if his role was having an effect. Using incredibly sensitive intercepts of German communications processed at Bletchley Park, the intelligence services kept him informed about how far the Germans had bought it. On 18 April, Johnny Bevan, one of the leading strategic deception specialists, briefed Lascelles and explained that 'the elaborate "cover scheme", intended to bamboozle the Germans… seems to have succeeded'. Lascelles was satisfied the plans were going well.[40]

The royal deception operation was elaborate, complex and not limited to the British mainland. In May 1944, George embarked on his most dangerous mission – to the sheltered waters of Scapa Flow in the Orkney Islands, home of a large UK naval base. The newspapers omitted George's destination, but one clue made it very clear to the Nazis where the monarch was. The front page of the *Daily Mail*, from 15 May, reported the king in cold and lonely northern waters under the headline, 'The King Takes Leave of His Fleet'. It stated: 'The King has taken leave of his captains in the Home Fleet, and has bidden them, their ships' companies and their ships God Speed before battle.'[41]

Here the king was playing his part in a further deception plan, Fortitude North, suggesting that the Allies were preparing a full-scale invasion of Nazi-occupied Norway. George's visit to the Orkneys was hazardous. The islands are further away from London than they are from Norway and the area was fiercely patrolled by aggressive German U-boats. He took quite a significant risk to give credence to Fortitude North. A few days after the visit, double agent Garbo warned Berlin that an Allied invasion of Norway was imminent and that it might be the first attack in the invasion of Europe.[42]

Aware of Operation Mincemeat and involved in Operation Fortitude, George clearly developed a keen interest in deception. MI5 kept the palace up to date on other deceptions, including the 'bogus Monty' ruse. Sergeant Clifton James had been an actor before the war and bore a remarkable resemblance to Field Marshal Bernard Montgomery, in command of Allied ground forces for the invasion of Normandy. MI5 flew with James to Gibraltar where the governor arranged for a Spaniard, who was a known German agent, to get a good look at him. In the palace, Lascelles listened intently. He noted: 'It all worked, and within a few hours a telegram to Berlin was intercepted by our people reporting that General M[ontgomery] and an unknown French general... were in Gib. on their way to Algiers.' All this bolstered the idea that the Allies might land on the French Riviera.[43]

The following month, George joined Eisenhower and Churchill at a mammoth final five-hour briefing on Overlord held in St Paul's School, Kensington.[44] On 6 June everyone held their breath as thousands of troops crossed the Channel heading for the Normandy beaches. Two days later, George and Churchill lunched together at Buckingham Palace before travelling to Eisenhower's headquarters at Bushey to be shown progress of the battle. From George's side, Lascelles could sense the relief that the invasion was finally under way. 'All those who have been entrusted with the secret', he remarked, now 'look 10 years younger'.[45]

As the battle progressed, George and Churchill dined together and had Stewart Menzies, chief of MI6, read them a sheaf of intelligence telegrams about D-Day. All seemed 'decidedly encouraging'. Armed with the latest intelligence, the two men stayed up late talking with the chief of the general staff. At one o'clock in the morning the king asked the prime minister: 'well aren't you going to bed tonight?' 'No sir,' Churchill responded before carrying on the discussion into the small hours.[46]

D-DAY REIGNITED KING George and Churchill's competitive battlefield tourism. Both wanted to be on board HMS *Belfast* to watch it unfold close to the action. Unsure of exactly who was in charge of whom, each gave the other strict orders explaining that they were not expendable and, in the event, successfully persuaded each other not to take the risk.

Churchill did not impede the king for long. In late July, under the new cover name of 'General Collingwood', George set off to Italy to visit Allied Force Headquarters.[47] Churchill acquiesced and again lent the king his own customized aircraft for the trip.[48] Known as Operation Trigger, this was no less hazardous than his earlier Mediterranean escapade and he was soon moving forward to visit troops on the front line and inspect the mountainous monastery of Monte Cassino, eighty miles southeast of Rome, which had provided the Germans with a natural fortress.[49]

Anthony Eden, the foreign secretary, was alarmed. He thought Rome a political snake-pit and, in no uncertain terms, instructed the king to stay away from any meetings with the king of Italy, which he deemed would be 'highly embarrassing', or with the pope, in view of his war record and letters 'sympathizing' with Germans. Ever the worrier, Eden was also extremely anxious about the king's personal security in a country replete with guerrillas and which, he reminded Churchill, was only recently an enemy state.[50] Churchill had concerns of his own: that the visit of a king would prejudice the delicate discussion of whether post-war Italy should be a monarchy or a republic.[51]

For all his fretting and micro-management, Eden was a perceptive politician. He was right to suspect that George's visit would prove to be rather more than ceremonial. The king wanted to know about the progress of the war and to boost morale, but he was also deeply interested in the subterranean world of royal politics across the Mediterranean. Much of this involved SOE, another of the king's passions, since they often took the lead on policy towards the resistance in occupied countries. The enthusiasm for minor princes seemed to be reciprocated; SOE's first wartime chief was baffled by the fact that his officials displayed what he called 'a Servants' Hall' mentality and so 'always seem to be glamoured and bamboozled by local Kings'.[52]

A month before D-Day, Fitzroy Maclean, a redoubtable adventurer and Britain's special representative to Josip Tito's partisans in Yugoslavia, had briefed the king. He told George about SOE assistance to the resistance there and the implications of this irregular warfare for the royal families in the Balkans. Leading a motley band of SOE fighters that included the author Evelyn Waugh and Churchill's own hard-drinking, aggressive and courageous son Randolph, Maclean had first-hand knowledge of the vicious politics of Balkan resistance.[53]

George had taken a rather paternal approach to the young King Peter of Yugoslavia since the assassination of his father during a visit to Marseilles back in 1934. In April 1941, while still prince regent, he had co-operated with a British coup organized by SOE, but his regime was soon swept aside by the German invasion of the Balkans a few weeks later. Peter joined the many exiled in London and no one knew quite what to do with him. He drifted and eventually British officials were 'shocked' to find him at a cottage owned by the Queen Mother in Bedfordshire playing darts alone in a shed at the back of the house. Eventually he joined the RAF and inevitably became involved in resistance politics.[54] Dalton saw him periodically in connection with SOE business and thought him 'a funny little creature'.[55]

However, Maclean now told the king frankly that Peter was not playing his hand well. He had lost any chance of holding his throne by not serving with the guerrillas and instead aligning with pro-German factions. Peter was to be cut adrift; Britain now supported Tito's partisans. George seems to have taken it well, for, after the meeting, Lascelles noted that Maclean was 'a most impressive young man, of whom we shall hear more'.[56] Britain's decision to back the communists in Yugoslavia proved controversial and, as we shall see, Tito presented one of the first diplomatic challenges with which George's successor, Elizabeth II, had to deal.

The successful invasion of Europe presented George with other problems of royal politics. One of the most urgent was deciding what to do about Leopold III, king of the Belgians. His country, which had declared itself neutral in 1936, was invaded without warning by Hitler in May 1940 and had desperately appealed for help. Anglo-French forces took up defensive positions but were soon pushed back by the Nazi advance. Although urged to flee to Britain and join the other governments in exile, Leopold unwisely opted to stay under German rule despite his entire civil government decamping to London. He met Hitler but failed to persuade him to restore Belgian neutrality and instead remained a prisoner in his own country.

In June 1944, following the Allied invasion, Heinrich Himmler ordered Leopold's transfer to Germany and then Austria under armed guard. Meanwhile, in London, secret plans to replace him with his brother Charles were afoot. SOE even prepared to exfil-trate him out of the country. Although the ambitious attempt to rescue him failed, Charles did manage to escape to the country-side where, living under a fake name, he hid until the liberation of Belgium.[57] On 27 September, George sent a personal message to Charles telling him to prepare to act as regent in co-operation with advancing Allied forces.[58] The king's intervention was too late and unnecessary; Charles had taken the oath a week earlier and Leopold, who never recovered from his decision to stay in Belgium, eventually abdicated following a period of exile.

Similar issues arose in Denmark. Since 1943, Flemming Muus, head of the Danish resistance, had been visiting London to deliver messages from King Christian of Denmark to George, often returning to his home country by parachute drop from a special duties flight. In September 1944, worried that the Germans knew about the Danish royal family's pro-resistance activities and fearing that they were planning on kidnapping the king and taking him to Germany, SOE considered a mission 'of high secrecy' to smuggle him out to neutral Sweden.[59] Eden, long wary of SOE shenanigans, unsurprisingly had reservations. He did not think it was in King Christian's long-term interest for him to 'make a bolt to a neutral country' but conceded that if he decided to flee then SOE should help him.[60]

In the event, the Danish king was unmoved by the risk of kidnap and opted to stay on and work with the resistance as the Allies gained more and more ground. In January 1945, George received Muus once again, this time decorating him with a Distinguished Service Order. Under his command sabotage operations against the Germans had increased dramatically, and he had played a central role in co-ordinating Danish resistance and organizing receipt of arms and ammunition. He regaled Lascelles with tales of espionage and parachute drops, including detail about how a four-page letter could be reduced photographically to the size of a pinhead.[61] Muus had undergone plastic surgery to disguise himself but, by 1945, as Buckingham Palace put it, 'the Gestapo had identified him, circulated his photograph and placed a price of 500,000 Kroner on his head'.[62] Shortly afterwards, Muus's colleague, Ole Lippmann, was sent back to Denmark to replace him as head of the resistance forces. He carried a message from George in a tube in his rectum.[63]

The story of the Greek royal family was another SOE success for Buckingham Palace. Churchill and George were united in supporting the monarchists and SOE provided them with the perfect secret conduit to do so. King George II of Greece, who had fled into exile after the German invasion in 1941, eventually settled in London. However, by 1944 the concerns of Buckingham Palace were less about combating the Nazis and more about which entity would replace them in Athens as the Germans retreated, since King George II and the Greek government in exile were not especially popular back home. This was hardly surprising since George II was ineffectual and his younger brother, Prince Paul, even worse. Churchill lamented that the latter, who worked with PWE in Cairo, was completely incapable of any public role and was 'fit only for a life of luxurious seclusion'.[64]

Meanwhile, the highly fragmented Greek resistance initiated a civil war between royalist and communist factions. British support for the royalists reflected fears that a Soviet dictatorship might be forced on Greece with the demise of yet another royal family.

Remarkably, in January 1945, as these events reached their dramatic height, George and Lascelles poured over intercepts from Bletchley Park that gave them the inside track on negotiations between King George II and the Greek Cabinet about British policy and the future of Greece.[65] From the US, President Roosevelt was horrified by British efforts to restore the monarchists. George II was a poorly regarded extreme conservative who converged with Edward VIII in his affection for Adolf Hitler. Nonetheless, he returned to the throne after a referendum marred by allegations of electoral fraud. Roosevelt was privately incensed. 'How the British can dare such a thing!' he ranted. 'The lengths to which they will go to hang on to the past!' The Greek monarchy survived, with George II being succeeded by his unpopular brother Paul in 1947.[66]

KING GEORGE CONTINUED to visit field commanders and the front line. October 1944 saw Operation Partridge, a carefully managed royal expedition in which he, disguised as a General Chester, travelled to meet Montgomery in France and inspect his forces.[67] Churchill, worrying as ever about the king's proclivity for battlefield tourism, asked Montgomery if George would really be safe from enemy action. Montgomery was not concerned about the threat from the Luftwaffe, which had almost been eliminated by then, but worried about the king's constitution, knowing this could be fragile. 'The only real danger might be to the visitor's health. I live in a caravan… it is very cold. I seldom wear less than 4 woolies and a fur flying jacket. The change from a house to this is great and the visitor will need to be careful about chills and so on.'[68] Prior to meeting him, the king asked Field Marshal Alan Brooke what sort of man the blunt, arrogant and ambitious Montgomery was. Brooke said: 'He is a very good soldier, but I think he is after my job.' George replied: 'What relief! I thought he was after mine!'[69]

On 16 June, George crossed the Channel and made his way to the beach. Monty showed off his famous caravan, but it was now parked on the lawn of a luxurious château at Creullet where the commander mostly resided. They enjoyed a lunch with Camembert cheese, which had not been seen in London since 1940. George was keen to visit soldiers on the front line about six miles away, but Monty would not hear of it because the intervening countryside was 'still full of stray snipers'. He revealed that, in the garden of his château, they had just discovered a German soldier who had been hiding there for four or five days, who could easily have shot Monty or indeed anyone else. The sniper was just a teenage boy, typical of the last desperate conscripts thrown into the German army, and when he was found he had simply burst into tears. Press coverage of the royal visit accidentally revealed the location of Monty's bucolic headquarters, and he was 'greatly upset' by the hurried evacuation to a less attractive alternative.[70]

Threats from German planes and snipers – or the French weather – were not uppermost in the king's mind. As the end of the war slowly came into view, his main worry was relations with Stalin and the Soviet Union. Knowing that Churchill had developed a rapport with the Soviet leader, bonding in particular over one 'savage' late-night drinking session in 1942 when a senior Foreign Office official found them 'merry as a marriage bell' at three in the morning,[71] George personally urged Churchill to use all of his famous powers of persuasion to secure a favourable settlement in Europe.[72] He and Churchill consulted again in considerable detail before Yalta in February 1945, perhaps the formative conference of the post-war era and still the most controversial.

As the war moved into its final chapter, King George grew progressively more optimistic about the prospects of the west in its developing war of nerves with Stalin. Although Britain was numeri-cally the weaker of the Big Three, George was increasingly aware of the importance of science and technology to the future of warfare – an area in which he knew Britain was well ahead. He was aware of Churchill's enthusiasm for 'radio-location' and other 'black magical war-winning devices'.[73] The previous summer he had visited the Telecommunications Research Establishment housed at Malvern College in Worcestershire to see the latest developments in radar technology. He and Lascelles were enthralled by the 'astonishing' inventions without which, they learnt, 'we should never have over-come the U-boats, nor the German bombers' and would probably have lost the war.[74] In fact, George was so taken with these inven-tions that he was still talking fluently about radar long after the war had ended.[75]

George loved visiting all sorts of 'hush-hush' places – but his favourite subject was still SOE.[76] Towards the end of the war, he and the queen were thrilled to tour a curious private museum exhibit: a startling display of SOE's secret gadgets and gizmos hidden deep inside the Natural History Museum in South Kensington.[77] Taking advantage of the museum's wartime closure, SOE's section XV took over six rooms and put on a display of weapons for VIPs only. XV equated most closely to James Bond's famous 'Q' branch, the fictional research and development wing of MI6 responsible for a range of improbable gadgets from invisible cars to bagpipe flamethrowers.

In reality, XV was based at an unlikely headquarters on the Barnet bypass at Borehamwood, a former hotel called the Thatched Barn.[78] Constructed as accommodation for film stars working at the emerging Elstree studios, it was requisitioned at the start of the war and was soon producing silent guns and exploding briefcases destined for real life. Other parts of the exhibition were put together by SOE's camouflage and makeup section based more locally at 2–3 Trevor Square in more fashionable Kensington, west London.[79] The king and queen adored the exhibition. Scheduled to last only forty-five minutes, they stayed for one and a half hours and viewed 'a great diversity of death dealing devices' together with some very ingenious methods of communications.[80]

The most important secret science project was the atomic bomb. The first to brief Buckingham Palace about this deadly secret was the chief of MI6, Sir Stewart Menzies. On 4 May 1944, he related 'hair-raising stories about the effects of bombs of the future', adding that their realization was not far away.[81]

On 7 February the following year, Sir Edward Appleton, who ran the government's scientific research department, arrived at the palace. He updated Lascelles on the 'rapid development' of the bomb and explained how the whole project had moved to America because of the Blitz. He briefed on the latest MI6 intelligence which indicated that the Germans did not have an atomic bomb but told how the Allies might have one in time to use against Japan. This pricked Lascelles' interest and he asked what the result would be. 'Oh,' Appleton answered matter-of-factly, 'a couple of them would end the war overnight – there is no doubt about that.'[82]

Both George and Churchill were elated upon learning that this new and devastating weapon would soon be tested and again turned their attention to the post-war Soviet threat. By April, George demanded increasingly regular bulletins about relations with Stalin. He began to feel out of the loop, causing Lascelles to convey a mild rebuke to the prime minister. Lascelles assured Hastings Ismay, a key adviser to Churchill, that the king 'reads carefully (under lock and key of course) all the weekly summaries you send him'. So, he was a 'little disturbed' not to have been informed of the increasing military tensions between Churchill and Stalin. George had hoped that Churchill would have 'come over to Windsor on Easter Sunday' to brief him, and was disappointed that he had not done so.[83] The king had become accustomed to his excellent access to secrets and now felt it sharply whenever his government was less than forthcoming. Inducting a monarch into the subterranean world brings certain expectations; once the black box is opened it is difficult to close.

On 25 July 1945, Churchill, at almost his last meeting with the king as prime minister, casually mentioned that the US would drop atomic bombs on Japan 'next week'.[84] The king was fascinated by the emerging landscape of nuclear war. Almost a year after Hiroshima and Nagasaki he was one of very few outside the Cabinet Office to be allowed to see the mythical 'Revised Tizard Report'. Prepared by Sir Henry Tizard, the government's senior defence scientist, it brought together all that Britain had learnt from recent events and from the plundering of Nazi secret science in Germany, including V weapons, jet fighters and nerve gas. Presciently, it predicted an age of mutually assured destruction and the emergence of nuclear deterrence as the major dynamic of the Cold War era. Much more sinisterly, it recognized that it might be ten years before Britain acquired its own nuclear weapons and urged the production of nerve gas and biological weapons to fill the gap.[85] Tizard was right on the timescales at least; Britain did not acquire its own bomb until the reign of Elizabeth II. As we shall see, she also took a close interest in the development and implications of such devastating capabilities.

For now, though, the monarchy faced more pressing and personal problems. The fall of the Nazis risked exposing all sorts of royal secrets about collaboration between the Windsors and the Germans. A further clandestine operation would be necessary to tie up loose ends.

RAIDING MISSIONS:
FIGHTING FOR THE SECRET FILES

*'It was always a relief to me to lay before my
Sovereign all the dread secrets'*

Churchill, August 1945[1]

O N 8 MAY 1945, King George VI and Queen Elizabeth appeared
on the balcony of Buckingham Palace to greet ecstatic crowds
on VE Day. With Winston Churchill between them, and the two
princesses either side, Princess Elizabeth wearing her ATS uniform,
they waved to the thousands of people who had amassed outside
to revel in a cathartic release of joy and relief. Such was the fervour
that George and Elizabeth even allowed the young princesses, only
nineteen and fourteen years old, to venture into town, 'swept along',
Elizabeth remembers, 'by tides of happiness and relief'.[2] The scenes
were repeated in early August, with the defeat of Japan.

At the end of the war, Churchill, accompanied by Stewart
Menzies, the chief of MI6, reaffirmed to the king the importance
of intelligence from codebreaking. Bletchley Park was one of the
few secret places George had not visited during the last five years.
'It is thanks to the secret weapon of General Menzies, put into use
on all the fronts, that we won the war!'[3] Menzies happily basked in
the praise lavished on Bletchley Park, his reputation never higher,

but perhaps the most important figure in the codebreaking effort was the shy and reclusive Alan Turing, the early leader of Hut 8, who, at the start of the war, was one of the few who believed that the Enigma code used by the Germans could actually be broken. George awarded Turing an OBE the following year, although the reason was kept carefully obscure from the public. With the Ultra secret highly classified for almost thirty years, Turing, much to the amusement of his friends, kept his award in a tin box filled with screws, nails, nuts and bolts.[4]

Although he did not visit Bletchley Park, George enjoyed a detailed and strategic understanding of the unravelling of Enigma, including the dramatic capture of codebooks from a U-boat off Iceland in October 1942, which had altered the course of the entire war. The recovery of secret German coding material from U-110, at the cost of the lives of two of HMS *Petard*'s crew, enabled Bletchley Park's codebreakers to crack a new Enigma system introduced to cover a U-boat offensive. After ten critical months with no U-boat signals intelligence available, this breakthrough was the crucial factor in defeating Hitler's Atlantic wolf packs. Awarding Captain Baker-Cresswell his Distinguished Service Order, the king told him that this engagement was one of the most significant events of the war at sea – he was probably right.[5]

Public celebration and private congratulations were accompanied by a more serious business: the scramble for secret wonder-weapons. Since D-Day, in a race against the Russians, special teams had been hunting down everything they could find, including rockets, jet fighters, the latest U-boats and nerve gas samples – all the eye-wateringly secret things that the king read about in the 'Revised Tizard Report'.[6] Teams also scrambled for treasure and booty, recovering Hermann Göring's vast stolen art collections, looted from all over Europe. Nazi files formed another sort of treasure. Germany's own equivalent of Bletchley Park, which had been listening in to Russia with some success, was carefully dismantled and driven in a convoy of trucks back to Britain. SS and Gestapo archives with files on every communist in Europe were spirited away into the hands of MI5. Even more secret and sought-after were Hitler's files on the royals.[7]

THE STRUGGLE TO hide embarrassing history had begun as early as the summer of 1943. One of the worrying things that MI6 had learnt when on the trail of the Windsors was the existence of a hidden stash of classified papers at their villa, the Château de la Croë, a spectacular house in twenty acres of grounds near Nice. MI6 discovered that 'all the papers taken from Fort Belvedere were there' and, although they were concealed, the staff at the house knew of their existence.[8] Churchill, always working energetically to cover the trail of someone whom he still considered a personal friend, sprang into action. He approved, at great expense, secret missions to France, Switzerland and Italy to buy back the contents of Edward's safe. The sum MI6 handed over to secure this transaction is still thought to be one of the British Treasury's most closely guarded secrets.[9] On 12 June 1943, the duke asked London that the 'Swiss Government be thanked for rescuing his archives from Antibes'.[10]

But there was much more to find. Every royal family in Europe was interconnected through an intricate spider's web of marriages. George had many such connections in Germany and, as early as 15 May 1945, just a week after victory in Europe, he began to probe these delicately. He first sought news of the duchess of Kent's sister, Countess Törring, now stranded in occupied Germany.[11] Freddy Morgan, the most senior British officer in Eisenhower's Supreme Allied Headquarters, tracked her down to a house thirty miles north of Munich. The countess had recently separated from her husband who was apparently sympathetic to the Nazis, a subject that had to be handled rather delicately.[12]

Before the war, she had been part of a royal network developed by George to promote appeasement, using his youngest brother, the duke of Kent, as a discreet emissary. As late as July 1939, as we have seen, he quietly offered to use a pro-Nazi German prince, Philipp of Hesse, as a secret messenger.[13] At the outbreak of war shortly afterwards, George made a remarkable admission: of having used his relations in Germany to 'try and spy and to get particulars from other members of the family'.[14] By 1945, he must have been relieved when Morgan assured him that the occupying forces would now 'politely ignore' the countess and her family.[15]

The king's elder brother, the duke of Windsor, posed a more pressing – and potentially disastrous – problem. Over the last five years, George had moved from supporter of appeasement to stalwart opponent of Nazi Germany. He was a king who had applied himself dutifully to the war effort, while the queen had taken decisive and measured steps to make sure the public saw his hard work. As a result, they were both extremely popular, but knew that all this good work could be jeopardized if correspondence between his brother and the Nazis, now scattered through the ruins of the Reich, ever came to light. Much was known about Hitler's many overtures to Edward, but no one was quite sure how he had responded, or whether any record had survived.

Buckingham Palace had some of its worries confirmed on 12 August 1945 when it learnt about 'top-secret telegrams between Ribbentrop and Stohrer', the German ambassador in Madrid, found lying in the German foreign office archives at Marburg. The files recounted overtures made by German agents while the Windsors were marooned in Spain in 1940. Two royal servants who had worked with Edward as early as 1918, Tommy Lascelles, the king's private secretary, and Godfrey Thomas, put their heads together and concluded that if the Windsors' reactions 'were as implied in the correspondence' then they were 'highly damaging'. Remarkably, Lascelles at first considered keeping them hidden from the king entirely, knowing that they would upset him. In the end, he waited until George had got two major speeches marking the end of the war out of the way before breaking the news to him.[16]

Edward had briefly returned to Britain at the end of the war, but seemed typically oblivious to the emerging Marburg problem. Others around him were more anxious and knew his telephone calls needed to be carefully protected from eavesdroppers. Lascelles installed a scrambler at Marlborough House, home of the duke's mother, Queen Mary, to allow Edward to talk to George in Sandringham. The very next day Edward called the king 'for forty minutes on the scrambler' and was in a friendly mood prior to his 'departure for Paris'.[17] Lascelles thought Paris was too close to home and still hoped that some semi-ambassadorial role could be found for him in America, but Edward's insistence on immunity from taxation continued to be a sticking point. He added that the duke has 'certain disagreeable personal skeletons in his cupboard' including Axel Wenner-Gren, Charles Bedaux and Ricardo Espírito Santo Silva, 'all proven German agents'. In November, the king and Lascelles had a further conversation 'on the scrambler' about overtures to President Truman 'on the Duke's behalf' about a post in America but nothing came of it, and the resumption of exile in Paris loomed ahead.[18] After the war, Lascelles remained Edward's most strident critic within royal circles. Edward detected this and denounced him as 'an evil snake'.[19]

THE PALACE MADE energetic efforts to lock down errant German files relating to royals of many generations. On 25 July 1945, Lascelles picked two men for this special mission. One was Owen Morshead, the trusted librarian who presided over the archives at Windsor Castle and had commanded the castle's home guard unit. An old stager, he had already been engaged on previous escapades against bothersome manuscripts. Earlier that year, he had sought out letters written by Prince Arthur, Queen Victoria's favourite son, to his married 'friend' Lady Leonie Leslie (who also happened to be Churchill's aunt). Lascelles had hoped the correspondence would

be 'destroyed' and so 'set royal minds at rest'.[20] By all accounts
Morshead was successful.[21]

The other member of the team was a new arrival, Anthony
Blunt. Recently appointed as surveyor of the king's pictures, he
had met Lascelles for the first time only on 14 May 1945. A
talented art historian, Blunt had spent the war in MI5, working
alongside other academics, in a highly secret unit that exploited
material from Bletchley Park and MI6 to counter the spies of the
German Abwehr. In 1944, he moved on to work on deception,
partnering the king in fooling Hitler about D-Day. Like so many
top academics he combined wartime work with academia and,
as the world's expert on Poussin, he was often consulting with
Morshead at Windsor about art catalogues and royal art purchases.
He also became a close friend of the artist Sir Gerald Kelly who
spent much of the war years at Windsor painting state portraits of
the king and queen.[22]

Blunt lived a double life: by day a brilliant art historian and by
night a thief. One of his main jobs for MI5 was to preside over the
robberies of neutral diplomatic mail bags, including those of Turkey,
Spain and France, something the British government still does not
wish to admit. This was racy stuff and involved outwitting security
staff and forging seals on secret correspondence, combining artistry
and criminality all while working at lightning speed. He loved the
sense of danger.[23]

Indeed, Blunt was in fact living nothing less than a triple life.
Along with Kim Philby, Guy Burgess, Donald Maclean and John
Cairncross, he was one of Russia's top spies in Britain. Although he
left MI5 at the end of the war and no longer had access to top-secret
material, he did continue to pass on gossip about his old colleagues
as well as documents from Burgess to his Russian controllers until
at least 1951. Moving in well-informed royal circles and rubbing
shoulders with the likes of Lascelles, he was also well placed to
gather other sorts of exotic information. The Russians optimistically
hoped that he would even gain access to the king's secrets.[24]

Although exhausted by the war, he was used to living several lives, and so was the ideal man for this secret mission to Germany. Moreover, for someone who was a Soviet spy, conducting secret missions for the king formed the perfect cover.[25]

Undoubtedly, Blunt's trips to Germany were in part about seeking royal art, jewels and rare coins, some of which the king had little claim over. In March 1946, Blunt set off on a second mission to the palace of the duke of Brunswick, in central Germany, to gather more items. The Foreign Office tried to block this, thinking it legally wrong and altogether a 'pretty tricky business' and fearing the palace might be accused of 'looting' by the American press.[26] There had already been rumblings and the Treasury also warned that it would be easy for a paper like the *Chicago Tribune* to work up 'a fearful story, making it sound too like the art-dealing activities of the Nazi bosses in occupied territories'.[27] To the horror of officials, in the midst of all this, Field Marshal Montgomery decided to give the king a white Arab stallion that had belonged to Rommel. Lascelles breezily declared that George was 'agreeable' to the gift and that this was not 'loot' but simply 'military equipment captured in battle'.[28] The justification sat uneasily with the diplomats, who grew increasingly worried by Blunt's activities and urged: 'No more raiding expeditions'.[29]

But these raiding expeditions were about more than art or horses. Before Blunt's departure, Lascelles asked Edward Playfair, the senior official in charge of the occupation of Germany, to call him at Sandringham on the 'scrambler'. The subject was clearly not art but 'another matter that Blunt has been discussing with us'.[30] What they discussed is not clear but the forthcoming visit was then facilitated by General Gerald Templer, who had been in charge of SOE's German section and was now deputy chief of staff in Germany.[31] On 4 March 1946, Blunt noted happily that 'we can now go ahead'.[32] Playfair told Templer: 'I have now heard that the King agrees with all our arrangements... I agree that it is unnecessary to put anything on paper.' He added that 'Blunt of course, will be as silent as the tomb'.[33]

Exactly what Blunt and Morshead were looking for on their trips to Germany remains mysterious. They were probably on a general fishing trip for both archives and objects, hence the combination of academic skills. One impressive find we can be sure about was the remaining letters of Vicky, the eldest child of Queen Victoria and Prince Albert. She had married the future German emperor, Frederick III, in 1858, thus becoming empress of Germany and queen of Prussia. Her eldest child was Kaiser Wilhelm II, the last emperor of Germany and cousin of King George V, reigning until 1918. Vicky died in 1901, just seven months after her mother, at Schloss Friedrichshof, an impressive neo-gothic castle outside Frankfurt. As we have seen, they had written to each other regularly, providing the queen with impressive foreign intelligence, but also touching on affairs of the heart.

King George VI knew that a number of papers and diaries belonging to the empress were 'of considerable historical importance' and 'of great interest to the Royal Family'. He felt it was 'essential that these papers should not fall into the wrong hands'. The castle was in an area controlled by the Americans and its importance became clear when George asked for Eisenhower, the military governor, to be personally appraised of the mission. Churchill's chief military assistant, Hastings Ismay, astute and experienced having spent the whole war, as he put it, in the 'middle of the web',[34] clearly understood the subtext and contacted Eisenhower the very same day.[35] Blunt and Morshead then charmed Landgravine Margarethe, granddaughter of Queen Victoria, into handing over the papers for safekeeping.[36] Two weeks later, George conveyed his thanks to the Americans for the 'care taken in the accomplishment of their mission which was in every respect successful'.[37]

Superficially, George had gratefully secured his grandmother's secret love letters. Long before her successful marriage to Prince Albert, the fifteen-year-old Princess Victoria had had an embryonic affair with the dashing Scottish 13th Lord Elphinstone. After the liaison was exposed, Elphinstone was banished to India and appointed governor of Madras. With him out of the way, Victoria's mother managed to engineer a royal union with Prince Albert of Saxe-Coburg and Gotha. After five years of pining for her exiled lover, Victoria finally gave in and married Albert. Many attempts were made to bury the memory of Lord Elphinstone, but Victoria recorded it in letters to her confidante, Vicky.[38] Intriguingly, however, and belying the supposed significance of the mission, the letters only remained in Windsor Castle temporarily. Queen Mary, George's mother, returned them to Germany in a specially constructed crate in December 1951.[39] So what had all the fuss been about?

George was actually angling for a more contemporary catch. According to Alexander Cadogan, the most senior official in the Foreign Office, the king was possibly seeking several files of Nazi documents on either the duke of Windsor or Philipp of Hesse, who was Landgravine Margarethe's son. Hesse, now in Allied detention, had held secret talks with George's brother before the war, and George himself had offered to use him as a messenger between Chamberlain and Hitler.[40] Hesse had possibly come out to visit Edward or his youngest brother, the duke of Kent, in Lisbon in 1940. Towards the end of the war, he had fallen out of favour, suspected of links to those who prepared the 1944 bomb plot against Hitler, and ended up in a concentration camp. His wife, daughter of the king of Italy, was held in another camp. No one knew what files the Nazis had kept on the myriad interactions of minor British and German royals.[41] Either way, the castle was high on the list of places to look for incriminating correspondence from Edward.

Blunt also travelled to Schloss Marienburg, near Hanover, where officials feared other incriminating documents existed, revealing the pro-German attitudes of the British royal family, including letters from Queen Mary to the father of another Nazi-affiliated prince. Ostensibly, Blunt was there to prevent valuable cultural artefacts from falling into Soviet hands, rather ironically given his secret life as a Soviet mole. He successfully brought back various treasures for the crown, causing more consternation in the Foreign Office that the palace might be discovered removing art from Germany at a time when Britain publicly took the moral high ground on the issue of war looting.[42]

Blunt made four visits to Europe between 1945 and 1947 for the royal family. The royal biographer Sarah Bradford notes that his last trip was to the late kaiser's residence in the Netherlands. George possibly sent him to follow up a lead about discussions between the exiled kaiser, who did not die until 1941, and the Windsors.[43] What did he find? Famously tight-lipped, all we know for sure is that Blunt was knighted for his service in 1956.

Remarkably, at the moment he received his knighthood, Buckingham Palace had known he was a Soviet agent for eight years. In 1948, Lascelles escorted the duchess of Kent's new private secretary down the corridors of the palace, passing Anthony Blunt on the way. A few moments later Lascelles whispered: 'That's our Russian Spy.' And Lascelles was not the only one who knew of Blunt's misdeeds.[44]

But what mattered most to the royal family at the end of the war was not the Russian connection but the successful raiding expeditions. To the amusement of British officials, their own multiple missions bumped into the Belgians who were trying to locate equally embarrassing material about the Nazis and their exiled King Leopold III. Paul-Henri Spaak, the Belgian premier, raised this issue personally with Stewart Menzies, the chief of MI6.[45]

Meanwhile, Edward remained restless. To the king's dismay, even as his emissaries were trying to cover Edward's potentially treasonous past, the duke was attempting to return to his beloved Germany. Officials could hardly believe their ears. The authorities had to forbid him from going there 'on grounds of security', instead encouraging him to stay away by talking up the threat from die-hard Nazi 'werewolf' resistance fighters.[46] Although wheedling for a pseudo-diplomatic appointment somewhere else, the offers were never quite what he wanted. It is thought Edward was offered the governorship of Australia but turned it down.

They eventually settled in forlorn post-war Paris, to the dismay of the French government who feared they would renew contact with 'collaborators', creating a 'most embarrassing situation'. The Windsors were also unhappy in the austerity of post-war France, and feared a sudden Soviet invasion or a communist take-over. So much so that Edward made arrangements with the local British army barracks for three lorries to be on stand-by to take thirty-two crates of his most precious possessions from the vaults of the Bank of France to England in an emergency.[47] The Windsors interspersed their time in Paris with sojourns in London and New York.

These interludes triggered one more raid that remains especially mysterious. Wallis brought a large part of her jewellery collection on one of their periodic trips to England in the autumn of 1946. On 16 October, her personal maid moved a locked trunk into the duchess's bedroom. She later returned to find that someone had forced the trunk open. The jewellery inside was gone. Scotland Yard established that the thief had shinned up a drainpipe, crossed a flat roof and entered the open bedroom window. They found some of the jewellery scattered across the neighbouring golf course the next morning, including a string of pearls that had belonged to the duke's grandmother, Queen Alexandra.[48] For many years some suspected that it was an inside job to recover family property for George VI and his daughters, Elizabeth and Margaret. The police suspected Leslie Arthur Charles Holmes, a known cat-burglar, as the thief who had escaped with up to £13 million at current prices – most of the haul was never recovered.[49]

THE SECOND WORLD War brought with it an orgy of archival destruction. Much of this was simply routine procedure for preserving security. King George VI had received summaries of the most secret papers for much of the war and into the period of uneasy post-war peace. When travelling, he received special copies typed on thin paper. Lascelles explained that his job was to 'burn them as soon as the King has read them'.[50] But towards the end of the war, this destruction increased. Retreating enemy forces often burned their headquarters' papers. Many key archives vanished in the bombing of cities such as Berlin and Tokyo. Even the victorious Allies burned their secret files in vast bonfires rather than bother to bring them home from far-flung outposts.[51]

Miraculously, the special archives of the German foreign office survived. When Germany was defeated in the late spring of 1945, some four hundred tons of diplomatic documents, seized in the last days of the war, were brought to the American zone and deposited safely in the majestic Marburg Castle. Karl von Loesch, one of Hitler's interpreters, explained to British intelligence that while orders had been given to burn the most important material, the security orderlies carrying out this duty had been tricked into burning empty boxes. The real files were actually buried in the forests of Thuringia.[52]

There was a growing public appetite for a reliable history of recent events. Perhaps reassured by the Blunt missions, the British joined the French and American governments in agreeing upon a huge historical programme to select the most interesting documents and prepare them for publication, beginning with the years 1937–1943. They appointed top historians and, promising complete freedom of action, asked them to determine what merited publication. With the Cold War accelerating, officials rubbed their hands with glee about being able to publish some of the secret protocols of the 1939 Nazi–Soviet Pact that carved up eastern Europe and the Baltic states.[53]

Something was wrong. The British quickly realized that a neatly bound volume belonging to State Secretary Ernst von Weizsäcker, Ribbentrop's closest assistant, had escaped their attention and lay in the middle of the historians' pile of juicy material. This soon became known as the 'Marburg Files' and contained, among other things, copies of the top-secret telegrams between Ribbentrop and the German ambassador in Madrid about the overtures of German agents to the Windsors during their time in Portugal. As we have seen, it was this material that had reached Tommy Lascelles in August 1945; it now triggered one of the most energetic and prolonged cover-ups witnessed during the twentieth century.[54]

Lascelles consulted his cousin, Guy Liddell, deputy director of MI5, to obtain an expert counter-espionage opinion. They met in the Travellers Club, a famous spy haunt in Pall Mall. Liddell thought that some of the documents 'might suggest that Charles Bedaux was behind the whole thing' but was particularly concerned about the involvement of Ricardo Espírito Santo Silva, whom both MI5 and MI6 knew had provided 'an agency for the transmission of funds to German agents'. He agreed that various statements 'attributed to the duke by these agents are not of a very savoury kind' and told Lascelles that, for him, the smoking gun was the revelation that Edward had 'fixed up', before he left Portugal, 'some kind of code' so that he might fly back from Florida if the opportunity arose for his 'intervention'. MI5 were interrogating Walter Schellenberg, the agent who had tried to stop Edward's departure from Portugal, now in British custody, and Liddell offered to press him on the Windsor angle.[55]

Alexander Cadogan, the long-serving senior diplomat, noticed that George 'fussed about the Duke of Windsor's file and captured German documents'.[56] The new prime minister, Clement Attlee, like Lascelles, rightly noted that most of the material was about German plans, rather than the duke's actions, yet he still thought they might do 'the greatest possible harm' when they finally emerged. Winston Churchill, now consigned to leader of the opposition, was the most anxious and asked for Attlee's assurance that 'all traces' of them 'would be destroyed'.[57]

Yet doing this was already remarkably difficult. The Americans owned the originals but each national team of historians had copies. The State Department happily handed over the original file, which the British diplomats quickly consigned to the flames, but refused to return the microfilm copy, claiming they would need to debate it in Congress. Privately, American officials worried about how to explain all this to their independent historians who had already noticed the intriguing file.[58]

By March 1947, Ernest Bevin, the Labour foreign secretary, was on his way to Moscow for the most frigid inter-allied conference of foreign ministers dealing with early Cold War issues. There was a growing war of words between east and west and so no one wanted this embarrassing tale of Nazi intrigue to emerge. In the shadows of the conference, Bevin had a secret word about the file with the new US secretary of state, George Marshall, who promptly sent a highly secure 'eyes-only' message to Dean Acheson, one of his most senior officials, asking for its destruction. But Acheson refused, since awkwardly the material was already in the hands of independent historians.[59] The American historians made it clear that they wanted to publish the material and would resign otherwise. It was now a ticking bomb.[60]

As late as 1948, many other original files from the wartime German foreign office were still in Berlin. The Soviet blockade of the city now raised the temperature of the Cold War and risked the files falling into Russian hands. To prevent this, the British flew them to a secret location in north Buckinghamshire: Whaddon Hall. An outstation of Bletchley Park, Whaddon Hall was where MI6 had developed its wartime wireless network and tested its secret weapons. Now it was a centre for MI6 technical development and one of the most secure places in the country. This seemed a suitable place for the continuation of the tripartite history project and for several years it progressed in the countryside north of London.[61] Perhaps Downing Street was reassured by the fact that the 'historian' heading the British team was General Sir James Marshall-Cornwall, whose previous job had been vice chief of MI6. He was an old friend of Stewart Menzies, with whom he had served in France during the First World War.[62]

Indeed, there was now a veritable secret service team engaged on the mission. John Wheeler-Bennett, who had worked alongside

David Bowes-Lyon in the PWE Washington office, was busy writing an official biography of George VI. He was sure that the German archives contained much that needed to be covered up, including, as he put it, the fact that 'Ribbentrop had used Mrs Simpson'. Presumably he meant as an agent gathering intelligence or covertly influencing events.[63]

Churchill returned to power in the early 1950s. Fascinatingly, amid all the pressure of the accelerating Cold War, including a 'hot' war in Korea, he had not forgotten about the Windsor file and contacted the White House about the issue. His friend President Eisenhower was keen to help and sent out an experienced enforcer.

On 3 July 1953, General Walter Bedell Smith turned up in the history section of the state department. Bedell Smith, known as 'the Beetle', had a notably direct style and had just completed a three-year term as director of the CIA. He bluntly ordered the 'elimination' of the offending Windsor documents. He told the historians that the 'British government is going to communicate a list of the documents on the Duke of Windsor which it wishes to have left out'. Unfortunately for the British, the independently minded historians dragged their feet, rightly surmising this was Churchill protecting his old friend, and assuming that the octogenarian British premier might not be in office for long.[64]

In August, the issue had top billing in Cabinet discussions. Churchill's friends and colleagues argued that 'suppression' would only serve to spotlight the issue, but the stubborn prime minister eventually got his way.[65] Meanwhile, Edward's other fixer, Walter Monckton, now also a minister in Churchill's last government, was sent off to Paris, since the French were the other party in this three-country historical project and also had copies. George Bidault, the foreign minister, would not co-operate on suppression. Then suddenly the West Germans, now re-emerging as a nation from three occupied zones, asked the Allies for their documents back.[66]

A desperate Churchill now tried every trick in the book. By day he argued, rather sentimentally, that the appearance of these papers about the Windsors in an official publication would cause too much pain to Queen Elizabeth, the queen mother.[67] This was hardly a plausible argument given her visceral hatred of both the duke and duchess. By night, Churchill repeatedly phoned Margaret Lambert, one of the 'independent' Foreign Office historians, to apply forceful pressure.[68] One can only assume that Churchill, on his frequent painting trips to France, had seen Edward and rashly given his word that this material would be hunted down and exterminated.

Unbeknown to Churchill, he had already failed in his mission. There were many other documents about the duke of Windsor and his dealings with Nazi Germany, and the historians had mischievously managed to slip some of these into a scholarly volume of diplomatic papers that was published in 1954. Amid much laughter in the House of Commons, Churchill had to explain himself. He admitted that he had even taken the offending documents to Paris to 'show them to the Duke of Windsor'. Churchill urged the house that the documents ought to be 'treated with contempt' and insisted that the claims in them were quite untrue. But the fact that he had fought three teams of eminent historians for a decade to prevent their publication suggests otherwise.[69]

Nor could the American historians be dissuaded and so the publication of the dreaded Windsor file finally appeared in 1957. Edward insisted on adding a statement written by Walter Monckton, which inadvertently turned a mere embarrassment into a media sensation. The royal family were given a full briefing by the Cabinet Office beforehand.[70] The documents remain astonishing. The most incriminating piece of information was that Joachim von Ribbentrop, the German foreign minister, had sent a secret message via Madrid underlining that Berlin was 'prepared to accommodate any desire expressed by the Duke', including any ambition he nurtured to assume the British throne after a Nazi victory.[71] Whatever Edward's failings, he had loyal friends, and no one served him better than Walter Monckton who somehow coaxed him onto a boat for the Bahamas on 1 August 1940. Probably only this saved him from meeting his fate at Nuremberg, rather than living out his post-war days with Wallis and her pugs in Paris.

THE ACTIVITIES OF the Windsors were not the only wartime secrets that the government tried to cover up. There were two deep secrets that King George had known about in detail that Whitehall officials were especially anxious to hide: the achievements of Bletchley Park in breaking Axis codes and the elaborate deception effort that had shielded so many strategic operations, most famously D-Day. They not only wanted to hide these secrets for use in a future conflict, but rather oddly feared that if the Germans found out they would claim they were 'not well and fairly beaten'.[72] Now the war was over, the chiefs of staff mounted a further secret operation to hide these matters, in effect a deception to conceal the fact that such deceptions had ever existed. 'It is imperative,' they noted, 'that the fact that such intelligence was available should NEVER be disclosed.'[73]

Although more than ten thousand people had worked on these secret schemes, they were all very security conscious. Trusting in wartime discipline, at first the Joint Intelligence Committee, Britain's highest intelligence authority, thought it would be simple to keep all this under wraps. Its chair, Victor Cavendish-Bentinck, asserted confidently: 'I expect all we will need to do will be to send half a dozen people out to see the right archives are being sealed and placed under guard and that the proper security measures are being taken.'[74]

'Bill Bentinck', as he was known, was one of those fascinating figures who connects royals and secrets down the years. Eventually succeeding as the 9th duke of Portland, his relatives had shot with the gun-mad Archduke Franz Ferdinand of Austria on the fringes of Sherwood Forest in 1913. Later in his career he would work with the Bilderberg Group, a secretive institution that tried to draw Prince Philip, Lord Mountbatten and Prince Bernhard of the Netherlands into its discussions.[75]

But for now, Bentinck's most pressing duty was to protect Britain's twin top secrets: codebreaking and deception. By the end of the war, it gradually dawned on the horrified guardians of secrecy that they were more vulnerable than they thought. Simply by comparing detailed accounts of Allied and Axis decisions, historians would soon figure out that Enigma had been broken. Moreover, the public was already demanding detailed historical accounts of the war, while enterprising former leaders, including Churchill and Montgomery, had accepted staggering sums to write their memoirs.

Whitehall therefore had to embark on an ambitious plan to airbrush Bletchley Park and strategic deception from history. First, an army of civil servants kept watch for people writing their autobiographies. One of Eisenhower's assistants caused a scare by mentioning deception in an early draft of a memoir.[76] Churchill was especially petulant, and in the end, Stewart Menzies had to persuade him to remove offending passages that threatened the security of British cyphers.[77] Civil servants doubtless remembered that Churchill had form here, since his writing in the 1920s had blown the secret of reading German communications in the First World War. Indeed, there is a case to suggest that the very creation of Germany's Enigma system owed something to Churchill's loose-lipped behaviour about previous British codebreaking triumphs against the 'Hun'. Over the next twenty years, historians independently uncovered stories about Ultra and had to be persuaded to remove any reference from their books.[78]

Whitehall created a smoke screen. It commissioned a large number of official histories of particular aspects of the Second World War, including detailed histories of various campaigns, for public consumption. These were popular with those who had fought in the war and also with families who had lost loved ones and required a detailed narrative. These official historians, allowed sight of classified material, were told at an early stage that they should never breathe a word about Ultra or deception.

This was tricky, for in some campaigns, typically the Battle of the Atlantic and D-Day, these secret techniques were at the very heart of the story.[79]

Alongside these public histories, the secret services began writing their own private histories to preserve the clandestine ideas and techniques that had helped to deliver victory. Produced by insiders in very small numbers, often only in typescript, they were given limited circulation. MI5 produced a history of organizational change.[80] MI6 wrote a history of William Stephenson's BSC, with which Bowes-Lyon had served.[81] GCHQ managed a number of histories of particular codebreaking efforts, but its general history of Bletchley Park was so huge it was never finished. Officials viewed deception on the scale witnessed during the Second World War as a relatively new secret art and saw it as so precious that a special unit, with the wonderfully innocuous name Directorate of Forward Plans, was set up under an MI5 officer to keep it alive.[82] One of the most remarkably secret books describing these techniques was a history of the Double Cross or 'XX' deception operations, which were designed to manage the flow of information to Germany via a network of double agents.[83]

No one was more interested in this sort of secret history than King George. As we have seen, once the war effort got going, George discovered that almost everyone around him had either served in the secret service, was moonlighting for the secret service, or had a relative in the secret service. Buckingham Palace was a curious crossroads where these came together and by 1942, he was inducted into almost every wartime secret, from agent drops to the electronic 'wizard war'.

But the secret operations George liked best were those in which he played a part: the secrets of deception. He fully understood just what these elaborate operations had achieved and the vast numbers of lives saved during D-Day, but he wanted to know more about what he called the 'backroom boys' and how they had successfully masterminded the whole effort. Accordingly, in 1951, increasingly plagued by ill-health, he particularly enjoyed reading MI5's highly secret history about deception. This had been penned by John Masterman, Oxford don, first-class amateur cricketer and creator of the Double Cross system.

Masterman had, quite improperly, lent this book to George. Originally only three copies had been prepared, but the book was so secret that the first two were destroyed almost immediately. This final surviving copy was loaned to Buckingham Palace; only the king and Lascelles were allowed to read it.[84] In formal terms, this breached MI5 regulations, but given that the king had viewed virtually every secret of the war and had participated in the D-Day deception himself, it would have been difficult for anyone to object. Nevertheless, Lascelles was grateful to Masterman for lending him such a precious item.

Dear Masterman,

Thank you so much for trusting me with the book. I'm most grateful. It looks thrilling. I know that my master will read it with as much interest and admiration as I shall myself.

Yours sincerely,
Alan Lascelles

Lascelles read it first and told Masterman: 'I recognize quite a few of the episodes', but now understood the immense and intricate machinery that had 'made them possible'.[85] George clearly enjoyed reading it, and re-reading it, and was slow to return the book. It was not returned, and by the summer of 1951 Masterman was concerned for its safety.

By autumn, the secret book had been out of his hands for ten months. He was 'beginning to be worried' and asked Lascelles to tell him exactly where it was – and return it urgently.[86] On 6 October, Lascelles tried to reassure him:

My dear Masterman,

I cannot answer your question definitely, and the only person who can is, as you know, ill in bed. But I can tell you, with complete assurance, that the book was safely locked up in his most personal despatch box, and from what I know of his extremely methodical habits, I would stake my life that it is still there.

When we are in smoother water, I will do my best to recover it and send it back to you. In the meantime, please do not worry.

Yours very sincerely
Alan Lascelles

Masterman was now extremely worried.[87] When George died in February 1952, it had still not materialized. The MI5 official history suggests that it was the last thing the king was reading before his death.[88]

Days later, no one could find the secret book. Palace officials, with bigger things on their mind, were sure that the report was somewhere safe and reassured Masterman that it was probably still locked up in the late king's most personal despatch box. This did little to soothe Masterman, whose anxiety turned into panic as time ticked by.

Masterman knew that the MI5 registry would eventually notice that the book was missing and an inquiry would follow. He also knew that there were changes at the top in MI5. Dick White replaced Guy Liddell as deputy director in 1952 and then became director general the following year, sweeping away his informal connections and making severe punishment more likely. 'I am nervous,' he confessed. 'I can't very well say I haven't got it – or where it is!' The palace staff hunted increasingly frantically – but to no avail.[89]

In early April 1952, George had been dead for two months, but the book was still missing and Masterman was rather desperate. Salvation came from an unlikely source. Lascelles explained, as straight as ever, 'my trouble has been that all the personal despatch boxes (where I knew your book was) have been out of my control. However, this very day I got the Queen Mother to look at them and, sure enough, there it was.' Anxious about its safety, Lascelles delivered it to its owner personally on a visit to Oxford to attend a dinner at Trinity College.[90]

The secret book remained secret. Masterman spent the next twenty years arguing with people like Martin Furnival-Jones, a later director general of MI5, and Dick White, now the chief of MI6, trying to get permission to publish. In the late 1960s, White accepted that with the story of Kim Philby dominating the headlines, and the public focus on what he called 'the traitors in our entrails', his service did need 'a shot in the arm' in terms of favourable publicity, but still nothing happened.[91] Finally, in 1972, Masterman published his 'secret book' without permission, choosing an American publisher to avoid an injunction.[92] As an Oxford history don who had taught at least two former prime ministers, he thought prosecution was unlikely.

Only in the 1970s, with the unveiling of wartime secrets like deception and Bletchley Park, was King George's bedtime reading made available to the eyes of ordinary mortals. But even then, three decades after D-Day, Masterman still chose to hide the participation of the king in the wonderful deception that was Operation Fortitude.[93]

Part IV

ROYAL SECRETS

15

PRINCESS ELIZABETH: CODENAME 2519

'why can't I meet the Queen?'

Oleg Penkovsky[1]

JUST AFTER MIDNIGHT on Friday 13 October 1950, Police Constable McVitty was on guard duty in the gardens behind Buckingham Palace. In the darkness, he heard 'rustling in the bushes' and, after investigating for a while, saw a dark figure balanced on top of a wall near the palace kitchens. Not aware that he was being watched, the man jumped down, almost landing in McVitty's arms.[2]

The intruder, named Douglas Munro, was arrested and marched off to Canon Row police station. About an hour later, a sergeant from the Irish Guards patrolled Victoria Street around the corner from the palace. He was approached by a tramp who led him to a rubbish bin. Rummaging in the gloom, he produced a secure despatch box with the initials 'G.R.' that had been prised open and was full of official papers. Munro had successfully broken into the office of Major General Salisbury-Jones, the marshal of the diplomatic corps, located in the entrance to the Ambassadors' courtyard in Buckingham Palace and made off with reams of Foreign Office material sent to the king.

This proved to be the second successful attempt by Munro to break into the palace and, later, he showed the police just how easy it was.[3] Another burglary took place the following year. The palace had previously resisted the idea of installing barbed wire around the garden perimeter, arguing that it would give the area a 'prison like appearance'. The police now warned that the only other way of making security effective at night was 'to have a P.C. at about 5-yard intervals around the entire perimeter!'[4]

Buckingham Palace contained piles of top-secret documents. In 1950, these were mostly provided to George VI, but some were also for the eyes of the young Princess Elizabeth, then aged twenty-three. The king was already training his daughter in affairs of state.

She had not initially expected to be queen. Growing up more interested in ponies than politics, she certainly never considered that she might eventually know more British secrets than any person in history. When she was aged ten, her uncle David, Edward VIII, decided to abdicate, and things changed. In December 1936, his dependence on the American divorcee Wallis Simpson, and refusal to give her up, catapulted Elizabeth's stammering, tearful father, Bertie, to the throne as a reluctant and thoroughly accidental King George VI. As crowds outside chanted 'God Save the King', Elizabeth heard the life-changing news, that she was now heir to the throne, from a footman. 'Poor you,' her little sister Margaret consoled.[5]

PRINCESS ELIZABETH'S HOME-SCHOOLED childhood education was decidedly informal, but it intensified after her uncle abdicated. She began learning about the constitution from the age of twelve and was still able to recite the ideas of Walter Bagehot, the venerable Victorian essayist and constitutional scholar, decades later. The monarch, as Elizabeth well knew, had the right – indeed the duty – to counsel, encourage and warn.[6] As she grew older her private secretaries, including Jock Colville, who had worked closely with Churchill during the war, helped her prepare for her role as queen.

From her early twenties, she received bundles of Cabinet minutes and papers from Clement Attlee, the first post-war prime minister, to help familiarize her with matters of state.[7] This formed a break from the past. Her father had lamented that he had never seen a single state paper until he was thrust upon the throne. Attlee's predecessors had been especially protective of Cabinet committee minutes and deemed them too sensitive and secret, not least because some gave away ministers' personal opinions.[8]

Pursuing a charm offensive, and perhaps in the knowledge that King George VI was no fan of his socialist Labour government, Attlee hosted a dinner party to allow Princess Elizabeth, young, attractive and naïve, to meet members of his Cabinet. At around the same time, she began to receive Foreign Office telegrams; the princess had access to an increasing range of sensitive documents.[9]

Some inside Downing Street maintained lingering doubts about the wisdom of sending classified material to such an inexperienced princess. Attlee was therefore relieved that her new assistant Private Secretary, Martin Charteris, was an old hand. Serving as an officer in the desert war, he had only narrowly survived when his transport ship was torpedoed in the Bay of Biscay. After the war, he had been head of military intelligence in Palestine and worked closely with Maurice Oldfield, later chief of MI6.[10] 'Choosing me was an act of pure nepotism,' he later recalled. 'I knew Jock Colville, her previous secretary, who wanted to return to the Foreign Office, and his wife was friends with Tommy Lascelles, who was the King's private secretary.' He added that there 'was no vetting, no security clearance, no board interviews, nothing like that. In fact, years afterwards when it was too late it was realized that I had never signed an Official Secrets document.'[11]

Despite his irreverent snuff-taking facade, Charteris was fully accustomed to handling secret papers. Unstuffy and cheery, he guided the princess through daily documents with quiet efficiency and good humour. By his own admission, he had been in 'no revolting hurry' to take the job, but Charteris became a firm favourite of Elizabeth and stayed at her side until retiring in 1977. Despite appreciating the experience and discipline that Charteris brought to the role, Attlee stopped short of sending over confidential annexes to the Cabinet papers, which often contained the most prized secrets.[12] Routine minutes and memoranda that were merely 'top secret' would have to suffice.

Princess Elizabeth had crossed paths with spies from an early age. We have already seen how she shared her childhood home with her cousin, Margaret Rhodes, who worked for MI6; how her father had close links with the intelligence services; and how her uncle worked for wartime intelligence conducting covert actions. During the war, she also witnessed the frustrating side of secrecy and security. Early in the conflict, technicians had installed a scrambler telephone inside the palace to prevent hostile intelligence services from intercepting the king's calls. Elizabeth would watch her father become more and more frustrated with it, later recalling that 'he used to get so cross when it didn't scramble'. George was not known for his patience, and the equipment, according to Elizabeth, 'took some time to heat up'.[13] Meanwhile, top-secret codes were used to protect messages exchanged between the royal family and the government. Princess Elizabeth's codename was 2519; her little sister Margaret was 6101.[14]

By 1947, secret intelligence helped ensure her wedding to Prince Philip ran smoothly amid fears of a communist plot. Prince Philip, born into both the Danish and Greek royal families, suffered a famously turbulent and lonely childhood. Like the family into which he would marry, he too was no stranger to intrigue. Legend has it he was smuggled out of Corfu in an orange crate to escape the political turmoil of the early 1920s. Tall and dashing, he first met Elizabeth when she was just eight years old and, five years later, after meeting at the Royal Naval College in Dartmouth, Elizabeth reportedly fell in love. As their romance became more serious after the war, so too did the king and queen's worries about their future son-in-law.[15]

Moving in the shadows was Philip's dynastically ambitious uncle Admiral Lord Louis Mountbatten. During the latter part of the war, he was supreme allied commander in South East Asia, superintending Britain's war against Japan. But on 23 August 1944, he suddenly flew into Egypt on a special mission. He had come to ask Philip's Greek relatives about him adopting British nationality. His explanation to local British diplomats was preposterous: Philip might help George VI in carrying out 'royal functions'. The real purpose, of course, was to clear the way for Philip as a suitor to Elizabeth. He secured the approval of the king of Greece, and then returned east to resume his command a satisfied man.[16] This episode perhaps explains a curious message from Tommy Lascelles to Mountbatten a few days earlier marked 'most immediate' that had been sent through senior MI6 channels in view of the 'private matter it concerned'.[17] Over the next three years, Mountbatten was focused and determined on his nephew's behalf, so much so that Philip had to warn him to curb his enthusiasm.

There were still obstacles. High up on the list was concern about Philip's background and pro-Nazi elements in his family. Simultaneous anxiety about the Marburg Files did not help his case. All three of Philip's sisters had married German princes. One sister had joined the Nazi women's auxiliary and her husband, Philip's brother-in-law, had taken up a post in the Nazi government, even becoming head of Hermann Göring's 'Research Office' in Berlin. The inter-war aristocracy was a small world, and the assignments of this German prince included tapping the phone calls of none other than the duke and duchess of Windsor when they visited Salzburg in 1937.[18]

What followed was remarkable. A decade earlier, George's father had used Special Branch to spy on Wallis Simpson. As we have seen, the operation expanded and, after his death, involved MI5 officers listening in to Edward VIII's personal communications, including with his brother. Now the king followed suit and sought intelligence on Philip. Like his father, he turned to Special Branch for a secret dossier on Philip's background, loyalty and politics.[19]

Discreet surveillance provided George with insight into Philip's habits and personal life: his messy rooms, coarse language and late-night drinking.[20] This probe probably also revealed that his first girlfriend was Osla Benning, a Canadian debutante, who worked in the naval section of Hut 4 at Bletchley Park.[21] Jock Colville, Elizabeth's outgoing private secretary, apparently warned George that Philip was 'unlikely to be faithful'.[22] Lascelles agreed, adding that Philip was 'rough' and 'uneducated'.[23]

A more serious impediment was the detail on Philip's three sisters, Sophie, Cecile and Margarita, and their Nazi connections. There was even photographic evidence of Philip, at sixteen years old, walking alongside Nazi officials back in 1937.[24] Given the lingering worries surrounding the duke of Windsor's loyalties and the repellent revelations about the Third Reich that continued to emerge in the months after the Second World War, Philip looked like a scandal in waiting that the king could well do without. The queen referred to Philip as 'the Hun' and tried to set Elizabeth up with other eligible bachelors.[25] Her brother, David Bowes-Lyon, who had served in the wartime Political Warfare Executive, was strongly opposed to the relationship, detecting a certain un-Britishness in Philip.[26]

Although on the surface his German ties looked alarming, the material was mere innuendo. Philip was, like so many royals, a citizen of the world, but he thought of himself as primarily Danish. More importantly, he enjoyed a splendid war record and eventually received royal – and government – approval to marry Elizabeth. Ironically, it was his youthful socialist leanings that frustrated his future in-laws more than any supposed Nazi sympathies. On more than one occasion, he had to apologize to the queen for starting heated discussions and begged her not to think him 'violently argumentative and an exponent of socialism'.[27]

With Philip suitably vetted, the royal wedding was set for November 1947. His sisters did not receive an invitation, but intelligence officers in MI5 had bigger things to worry about as the burgeoning Cold War threatened to provide the wedding party with a taste of ideological struggle. Elizabeth and Philip's marriage ceremony, held in the pomp and splendour of Westminster Abbey, was to be a glorious occasion, momentarily distracting the nation from the drudgery of austerity, rationing and shortages. Clement Attlee worried that the Communist Party of Great Britain had other ideas.

Just three days before the ceremony, as wedding fever began to grip the nation, Attlee paid a worried visit to Percy Sillitoe, the director general of MI5. He expressed 'deep anxiety' about the communists, fearing that they were 'deliberately promoting strikes to sabotage the Royal Wedding'.[28] In particular, the luxury Savoy hotel group had been mired in an industrial dispute for much of the year – a dispute that could easily be exploited.

Trouble had flared at the Savoy again ten days earlier and the home secretary, James Chuter Ede, warned that workers hoped to drag out the strike precisely to disrupt the royal festivities.[29] As tensions grew, drivers delivering oil supplies refused to cross the picket line. Without a solution, the vast hotel group, which employed over a thousand people, would have to close its doors.

This was a serious problem given the huge influx of kings, queens, princes, princesses and grand dukes arriving for the royal wedding. Sillitoe, the burly former policeman who got on better with Attlee than with many in his own service, responded to the prime minister's fears by asking him if he had heard of an Italian waiter called Pietro Piazza, known as Francis or Frank.[30] The prime minister looked blankly. He had not.

Frank Piazza, with his distinctive gait caused by curvature of the spine, was twenty-seven years old and well known to MI5. He had been interned during the war and was now, as MI5's secret file on him recorded, 'an active Communist in the catering industry'. Intelligence officers deemed him a particular troublemaker and, as a key instigator of the strike, he had begun stirring animosity between workers and management only five days after starting his job at the Savoy back in March. Managers at the hotel were horrified at who they might have employed and quickly pressed MI5 for intelligence on Piazza. At this point the royal engagement had not yet been announced and Dick White, a senior MI5 officer who went on to be director general, refused point blank to hand over any material. Doing so would have been tantamount to intervening in a private trade dispute.[31]

By November 1947, on the eve of the royal wedding, the situation had become more serious. Royal relations from Norway to Iraq began to arrive and, aside from Philip's mother who stayed in Buckingham Palace, many were put up at Claridge's, which was part of the Savoy Group. The largest collection of royalty anywhere in the entire century slowly amassed, and, one evening had dinner around a single enormous table in Claridge's stylish dining room.[32]

Meanwhile, in the Cabinet room, George Isaacs, the minister of labour and national service, accused the British communists of deliberately planting Piazza at the Savoy. As disruption spread to a nearby shipyard and meat market, Ernest Bevin, the foreign secretary, smelled a communist plot. More alarmingly, Nye Bevan, the health secretary, feared dangerous consequences if the communists took control of London's most exclusive hotels. He warned that they could become hotbeds of espionage targeting royals and world leaders alike, and that hotel managers could be blackmailed to obtain compromising material on high-profile guests.[33]

Amid the panic, Sillitoe reassured Attlee that the strike was a purely industrial dispute. It had nothing, as far as he knew, to do with subverting or disrupting the royal wedding. Frustrated, Attlee asked why Piazza had simply not been deported. Sillitoe patiently reminded him that his government's policy did not regard communism as a bar against naturalization.[34] Attlee just had to hold his breath and hope that Piazza would not disrupt the wedding.

At the very same moment across London, the police cracked down on the strikers who had begun lying in the road. With one girl in hospital, MPs demanded an investigation into the unnecessary levels of force used by police, but Chuter Ede, desperately hoping to end the disruption before the wedding, held unapologetically firm.

He was not alone; in the House of Commons, long-standing MP and former Nazi sympathizer Thomas Moore asked: 'How does one remove a recumbent body except by force? Is it by speech?'[35]

As the wedding drew nearer, the police stepped up their patrols and inspections, checking manhole covers for explosives and eavesdropping on 'student types'.[36] Fortunately, the wedding passed off remarkably smoothly. The biggest threat of disruption came from the thronging mass of people who risked being crushed, but police handled the crowds effectively. Officers were left most frustrated about the slow-moving queues at their mobile canteen erected in Green Park.[37]

King George VI appreciated the 'immense amount of work' put in by the police, and Princess Elizabeth sent her own special message of 'sincere thanks'.[38] The Savoy dispute was formally settled in December when Piazza accepted a new and better-paid job elsewhere and the hotel agreed to work with the union on a new complaints procedure, but in fact most staff had gone back to work during the wedding.[39] Monarchy and money had trumped ideology. For now.

THE COMMUNISTS MAY have been trying to infiltrate agents into London's top hotels, but another – friendly – intelligence service had the juiciest material on the young royal couple. Unknown to the British, the CIA was reporting on Princess Elizabeth. The agency opened a London station in 1947, and its first chief was Winston Scott. Handsome, brash, and still only in his late thirties, Scott had an impressive intelligence pedigree having previously run the final elements of Colonel Donovan's Office of Strategic Services in London as the war ended. He opened new premises at Grosvenor Street in Mayfair, in which a mattress shop on the ground floor provided cover for people coming and going. MI5 watchers used the top floor. Scott's closest British friend was an MI6 officer called

Kim Philby, who eagerly pressed the American for details of their new organization.[40] In 1948, the CIA acquired intelligence that Elizabeth was pregnant with her first child. The agency was the first to break the news to Washington.[41]

It is not clear how Scott, who presided over all American intelligence operations in Britain, achieved this scoop, but it probably came through the MI5 and MI6 contacts with whom he rubbed shoulders. Most likely the news came from Guy Liddell, deputy chief of MI5, who regularly saw his courtier cousin Tommy Lascelles. Scott went on to oversee all CIA special operations in western Europe in the early 1950s before becoming a long-serving chief of station in Mexico City, where, among other things, he presided over surveillance of Lee Harvey Oswald shortly before the assassination of President Kennedy in 1963.

There may have been more about Princess Elizabeth in the memoir Scott was writing after his retirement. Determined to publish, he sadly died just a few days before meeting the CIA director, Richard Helms, about its exciting content. Shortly afterwards, James Angleton, the powerful CIA head of counter-intelligence, flew to Mexico City to secure the explosive memoirs. After a tense, unpleasant meeting with Scott's grieving widow, Angleton succeeded. When the memoirs finally surfaced again twenty years later, all references to the CIA – including Scott's time in London and the royal family – had vanished.[42] When Princess Elizabeth and Prince Philip visited Washington in 1951, CIA officers downed tools and lined the street to cheer the royal couple. The CIA rent-a-crowd came at the command of President Truman himself.[43]

It did not take long for the newly married couple to have another brush with international espionage. Almost a year to the day after the royal wedding, and three days after the birth of Prince Charles, senior diplomats discreetly gathered in the Foreign Office to discuss the burgeoning Cold War. Worries about subversion in London's elite hotels paled in comparison to what was happening on the Continent. The Soviets had taken power via a coup in

Czechoslovakia in February 1948 and the Berlin blockade, another flashpoint in the early Cold War, was well under way. As the resolve of Ernest Bevin slowly stiffened, British planners pondered how best to counter Soviet aggression. After much acrimonious deliberation, they settled on a secret scheme to detach Albania from the Soviet bloc.

In one of its first major Cold War covert operations, MI6 began to identify and train a team of rebels ready to infiltrate Albania. They were ordered to gather intelligence on the ripeness of revolution, and eventually launch an insurrection if conditions were right. Discussing the operation just prior to its launch date with his American opposite number, Dean Acheson, Bevin pondered 'what government would replace Hoxha' as the Albanian leader. He added what was needed was 'a person they could handle' and asked: 'Are there any kings that could be put in?'[44] Bevin liked pliant overseas royalty, so much so that King Abdullah of Jordan was affectionately known in the Foreign Office as 'Mr Bevin's little king'.[45]

In Albania, the task fell to David Smiley. Son of a fearless sportsman and military adventurer who lived by the adage that 'where there is a daring deed to be done in any part of the world, an Englishman should leap to the front to accomplish it', Smiley was no stranger to special operations. A veritable James Bond, at an early stage in the Second World War he had sought detachment from the cavalry to join first the Somaliland Camel Corps, then the commandos, before settling on SOE. Here he served bravely behind enemy lines in Albania supporting partisans against fascist rule. Bearing the scars to prove it, he boasted impressive credentials when it came to blowing up bridges, training guerrillas and ambushing convoys. Now, MI6 sent him to Malta to train a new generation of fiery exiles.

Smiley was blue-blooded to the core. The youngest son of a baronet, he led a privileged life and was no stranger to the upper echelons of the British establishment. After 1945, he alternated between the Royal Horse Guards and blowing things up for MI6.

Indeed, he would later ride alongside Elizabeth as commander of her escort at the coronation in 1953.[46] For now, Smiley relied on his aristocratic connections to maintain his cover. Although working undercover from a top-secret MI6 camp based inside a Napoleonic fort accessible only by rough tracks, Smiley was supposedly living an ordinary military life with his wife Moy. Only a few senior officers and the local MI5 man knew Smiley's real purpose; any absence from the social life of Malta would therefore raise eyebrows.

Malta was the headquarters for the British Mediterranean fleet, a prestigious command for much of its history. It is no surprise, therefore, that Lord Mountbatten, Philip's mentor, was a senior naval officer on the island and that Philip himself, thoroughly enjoying time back in the navy, served there too. On 20 November 1949, their second wedding anniversary, Princess Elizabeth flew out to see her husband and spend a few happy months as a navy wife. She whiled away the sunny days watching her husband, Mountbatten and David Smiley – keen to reduce suspicion about his secret role – play polo.[47]

Smiley's mind was elsewhere as Princess Elizabeth arrived. He nervously awaited news from the first batch of MI6 recruits infiltrated into Albania. They had earlier sailed from Malta to Albania in a discreetly armed fishing boat before switching to light rowing boats as they neared the rocky shore. One group was ambushed; others had to flee for their lives. It soon became clear not only that Albanian security was better than MI6 expected but that the mission had been betrayed. In London, MI6 planned to push on regardless. Back on Malta, Smiley tried to put on a brave face and in a remarkable move introduced at least two of his Albanian secret agents to none other than Princess Elizabeth herself.

Jani Dilo was in charge of the trainees. He had escaped from communist Albania at the end of the Second World War before being recruited to the MI6 operation. Fortunately for him, neither he, nor his colleague, Ishan Toptani, were part of the infiltration teams and so had stayed in the safety of Malta. Toptani, another

Albanian, was a wartime guerrilla leader who had close contacts with Britain's special operations adventurers. He provided specialist propaganda training and went on to become a leading member of the Free Albania front committee, even liaising with the CIA-sponsored European Movement in London.[48] Here, quite by coincidence, Elizabeth's cousin, Margaret Rhodes, was working, having previously worked for the MI6 Near East section.[49] The future prime minister Harold Macmillan was also deeply involved in these MI6/CIA schemes.[50]

Dilo and Toptani met Elizabeth as she watched her husband play polo. Like Smiley, Dilo was undercover. He wore a British colonel's uniform, allowing him to blend easily into Maltese high society – except for the slightly awkward problem that he could not speak English. Smiley therefore provided him with fake documents suggesting he was a French commanding officer from Quebec. Introduced as such to Elizabeth, the two spoke only in French.[51]

Another curious MI6 character on the Maltese scene was Robin 'Doc' Zaehner,[52] an opium-smoking bon vivant who, like Dilo, served as translator. An Oxford don by profession, Zaehner found himself on the island between periods in Iran where his chief functions successively involved bribing the press and trying to overthrow the prime minister, Mohammad Mossadeq. It is striking that, leading her own double life as a naval wife, Princess Elizabeth mixed with such a motley bunch of spies, saboteurs and eccentric adventurers, which, it should be remembered, also included Smiley's wife Moy. Under cover herself as a military wife and bringing up a baby son, she served inconspicuously as a cypher clerk ensuring communications back to MI6 were secure.

Despite being all smiles at the polo club, Dilo, Toptani, Zaehner and the Smileys became increasingly worried as autumn turned to winter. They desperately waited for news but heard only disappointment. The princess had, wittingly or otherwise, helped maintain their covers; but a combination of ill-discipline, moles and Kim Philby's treachery had well and truly blown the covers of their fateful agents inside Albania. Elizabeth remained a regular visitor to Malta over the following years, celebrating carefree Christmases and her twenty-fourth birthday with Philip on the island.

PRINCESS ELIZABETH ENJOYED travel. In 1952, she and Philip departed on a royal tour of Africa, New Zealand and Australia. Because of his growing frailty, King George was unable to join them, but he was determined to see them off at Heathrow. Elizabeth was very fond of her father and sadly she had no inkling that this was the last time she would see him. Soon she was in the famous Treetops hostel and game lookout deep inside the Kenyan forest watching elephants, leopards and baboons. The view was remarkable: Mount Kenya rose a few miles to the east and the Aberdares a few hundred yards to the west.[53]

Meanwhile, a violent rebellion was beginning across the White Highlands; arson attacks against European settlers intensified. Security at the royal lodge was superintended by a tough Special Branch officer called Ian Henderson, who had considered cancelling the African leg of the tour altogether because he could not guarantee the princess's safety. On the night she acceded to the throne, Elizabeth and Philip were under the protection of game wardens, but they were also alert to the threat from the Mau Mau rebels as they moved into the area. Privately, Henderson was perhaps relieved that the tour was curtailed and the princess quickly headed back to the safety of London.[54]

Shortly afterwards somebody went inside Treetops and stole a souvenir: a royal toilet seat. They painted 'GUESS WHO SAT ON HERE' around the rim and then placed it over their neck before parading around a drunken party in Nairobi. Although a hit at the party, colonial officials were horrified. Orders had come down from on high that there was to be no repetition.[55]

Two years later, when Elizabeth returned to Africa, insurgents had burned down the Treetops viewing platform in a giant fig tree, and kidnapped five members of domestic staff who had looked after her and Philip. Only one, a handyman, was ever seen again, albeit with a bullet wound to his arm.[56] Because this area had the densest forest in Kenya it would become the heartland of the insurgency.

Henderson now ran many of the intelligence and special forces operations against the Mau Mau. His secret plan was to create 'pseudo-gangs' from surrendered guerrillas held in interrogation camps. These were led by young European security officers, most of whom had been born in Kenya. Dressed in rags, with faces blackened by burnt cork and boot polish, they roamed through the forest with their recently turned guerrillas and hunted the enemy.[57]

One of Henderson's greatest successes came towards the end of the insurgency in 1956. They managed to track down the elusive Dedan Kimathi, the last important Mau Mau leader still at large. As they approached his forest hideout, Henderson was dismayed to be called away. Right in the middle of the operation, he had to leave the jungle hunt to be presented to Princess Margaret at a tea party at Government House in Nairobi, an incongruous interlude, after which he quickly flew back to interrogate the captured Mau Mau leader.[58]

Although this supposedly marked the end of the Mau Mau uprising, insurgencies tend to fizzle out rather than simply stop. So, there was still some ongoing Mau Mau activity even in the late 1950s, with the last remnants of guerrilla forces focused around the dense forest where Elizabeth had once visited. Local authorities therefore greeted news that yet another royal visitor was heading their way with some trepidation. In February 1959, the queen mother decided to follow in the footsteps of her two daughters.

Once again, the task of protecting the latest royal party was overseen by Henderson. He deployed special forces under the command of Captain Peter Franklin, who looked after one of the deadly 'pseudo-gang' units. Franklin declared that he found his new role to be both 'interesting' and 'just that little bit different'.

The plan was for the queen mother to picnic alongside a waterfall, but the neighbouring forest still harboured a few die-hard Mau Mau guerrillas and, so under the watchful eye of Henderson, Franklin positioned his crack force, codenamed the Blue Doctor Pseudos. Franklin was also assigned as 'Royal Taster' to guard against poisons and so he briefly had to abandon his well-hidden 'pseudos' to 'test various "open" samples of food'. He was sad to learn that the champagne that had been lowered into the waterfall to keep it ice cold was considered safe and did not need tasting.

The visit passed off without incident, but Franklin's duties were not quite over. His final and most important task was to gather up all the toilets and wash basins used by the royals and to 'destroy them'. He then even had to 'submit a destruction certificate to prove this had been done'. For some reason unknown to him the lavatory seats were seen as especially important. The colonial government were adamant that this should be carried out with ruthless efficiency. Franklin thought this at best a rather mysterious task for a crack special forces unit.[59]

Royal lavatory seats in Africa were a serious business. The queen mother's lady in waiting, Lady Patricia Hambleden, recalled that 'special loos' were constructed for their exclusive use in the most remote locations. The queen mother's had a crown on it, while her attendants sat on facilities that were not quite so regal. At one point she announced mischievously to her attendant: 'This time I am going to use yours – just to see how inferior it is to mine!'[60] Sometimes huge sums were spent on elaborate bathroom facilities in anticipation of a royal visit and there was distinct disappointment if they were not used.[61] Embarrassment from Princess Elizabeth's 1952 visit perhaps loomed large.

INTRIGUE AND DANGER followed Elizabeth when, later that year, she became engulfed in Cold War politics. Back in 1948, Moscow had expelled Yugoslavia from the communist bloc. The resulting rift between Stalin and the Yugoslav leader, Josip Tito, provided an opportunity for the west to present Tito as a national alternative to Stalinism and the imperialist aggression associated with the Soviet leader. Tito was that rare thing, an anti-Soviet communist. He could be exploited.

Diplomats called their new approach 'national deviationism': a combination of diplomatic manoeuvres to challenge Moscow and efforts to expose its satellites to liberal democracy; covert intelligence operations, including blackmail, bribery or planting evidence, to undermine Soviet rule outside of Russia; and unattributable propaganda to build up national leaders, like Tito, as alternatives to Soviet communism. The key was to provoke trouble in the Kremlin's backyard. In 1952, against this Cold War backdrop, Anthony Eden, the foreign secretary, invited Tito to Britain.[62]

Tito had an enormous ego and happily accepted. His visit, the first of a communist head of state, created constitutional difficulties and mild panic in London. By this time, Elizabeth was queen but had not yet been crowned and the palace faced a queue of world leaders – much friendlier than Tito – wishing to visit. In a classic Whitehall fudge, civil servants portrayed Tito's visit as private but official, rather than a full-blown state visit, despite it boasting many trappings suggesting otherwise.[63]

Tito arrived in London by boat amid thick fog. Disembarking at Westminster Pier, the first hand he shook belonged to Prince Philip. Enjoying the opportunity to take centre stage while, in a rare role reversal, his wife was constitutionally required to lurk in the wings, Philip was delighted to be there. According to Tommy Lascelles, the queen's private secretary, he was personally 'interested in Marshal Tito'.[64]

Suddenly Philip's constitutionally anomalous position, which had caused him such deep frustration, became an asset. He found himself part of the Foreign Office's national deviationism, offering a visible complement to MI6's simultaneous subterranean efforts to undermine Soviet authority in the Balkans. He hosted a reception at Buckingham Palace, at which Tito enjoyed a fifteen-minute audience and photo opportunity with the queen, before dining with the great and the good. It is all rather ironic that, while lapping up the attention, Tito had recently overthrown his own monarchy.

This was a sore point given the ever-tangled web of European royalty. In 1944, King George VI had been best man at the wedding of King Peter II of Yugoslavia, later ousted by Tito.[65] Peter had married Princess Alexandra of Greece who had spent the war in Mayfair with her relative the duchess of Kent. Prince Philip was the cousin of Queen Alexandra and was even rumoured to have been engaged to her at one point. Now Philip became part of the public propaganda for Tito's visit. Diplomats hoped that friendly relations would embarrass Stalin, visibly demonstrating an alternative to Stalinism, and encouraging more liberal policies in Yugoslavia and elsewhere.[66] Meanwhile, British propaganda in Belgrade portrayed Tito as 'a small Marshal in a big pond', with plenty of shots of him surrounded by royalty and famous London landmarks.[67]

Unfortunately for the Foreign Office, all of this came with risk attached. The visit was the first time Tito had left Yugoslavia since his acrimonious split with Stalin. Away from home soil, he became a vulnerable target and insisted on changing the dates at the last minute so as to disrupt potential assassination plans. US intelligence warned of at least one threat to Tito's life, while MI5 and MI6 pointed to groups in Germany, France and Argentina who wanted to 'do something' to Tito when he arrived in London.[68] Meanwhile, Winston Churchill, back as prime minister, caused a 'frightful flap' when he personally received faulty intelligence that fourteen Yugoslav monarchists were en route from Rome by motor boat to assassinate Tito. MI5 rebuked whoever had sent this fantastic file to the prime minister, who, when it came to secret intelligence, was apt to get carried away.[69]

David Maxwell Fyfe, the home secretary, gloomily warned that 'I cannot rule out the possibility that an attempt will be made on Marshal Tito's life'. 'I cannot,' he continued, 'give a guarantee that an attempt, if made, will be frustrated.' With Philip scheduled to be at the dictator's side, this flurry of intelligence had ramifications for his personal security. According to one MI5 officer, Churchill was 'very sensitive' and 'took every possible precaution'.[70] He had already barred Philip from sharing a car with Tito in case it got attacked, and the security services now cleared the river, bridges and piers of the public. Thousands of policemen lined the route. 'The public were nowhere to be seen,' quipped one passenger in the entourage.[71]

Tito's visit triggered the formation of a whole new protective echelon, the Special Escort Group, an elite group of police motorcyclists, whose first duty was to escort Tito and who then went on to protect the British monarch for the next fifty years. Tito was moved from place to place in an armoured limousine, a precaution never hitherto used either for the royal family or for visiting heads of state.[72] The Home Office, drawing on MI5 material, warned that myriad groups 'had it in for' the marshal and there might be 'shooting'.[73]

Intelligence agencies feared foul play by the KGB – and these worries were not misplaced. The KGB had been trying to liquidate Tito for a decade and the London visit to meet the new queen offered the perfect opportunity. The chosen operative was Iosip Grigulevich, alias 'Max', a KGB illegal operating under deep cover, who had already been involved in operations against Trotsky. Preparations had already begun in late 1952; 'Max' had visited Yugoslavia twice, gradually making contact with 'circles close to Tito's clique'. He masqueraded as a Costa Rican diplomat and, with the moment now arriving, wrote a farewell letter to his wife in case he died in the course of the operation.

The plan was so secret that the only copy was sent to Stalin: 'In connection with Tito's expected visit to London, to send "Max" there to use his official position and good personal relations with the Yugoslav ambassador in England, [Vladimir] Velebit, to obtain an invitation to the expected Yugoslav embassy reception in Tito's honour.'[74]

The KGB explored three rather baroque options for the 'Max Mission' to London. The first involved releasing a lethal plague bacterium at the diplomatic reception. The second was shooting him with a silent gun disguised as a personal article such as a pen or a lighter. The most elaborate plan was to present Tito with a beautiful jewel box that would emit a deadly gas when opened. Max was an enthusiastic killer who enjoyed his work and the KGB noted darkly that '"Max's" personal qualities and intelligence experience make him suitable for such an assignment'.[75]

By the time of his visit to London, Tito was so fed up with endless KGB kill missions that he had recently written a personal letter to Stalin: 'Stop sending people to kill me. We've already captured five of them, one of them with a bomb and another with a rifle... If you don't stop sending killers, I'll send one to Moscow, and I won't have to send a second.' Fortunately, Stalin had died ten days before Tito's visit to London – indeed, this threatening letter was reportedly found on his desk and was perhaps the last piece of correspondence he opened.[76] It is widely thought that only Stalin's death impeded the final approval of the 'Max Mission'. It is easy to understand why MI5 was nervous about Tito – a mobile target – rubbing shoulders with the British royal family.

No attack ultimately happened. Even so, the security services failed to prevent a far-right group from setting off a magnesium flare, wrapped in newspaper, shortly after Philip shook Tito's hand.[77] The flare singed a bystander's hair, but the security breach did not disrupt proceedings and the visit passed reasonably successfully, albeit with two hiccups.

The first came as Tito held talks with Churchill and Eden at the Ministry of Defence's Map Room. Both Britons excitedly fought past and future wars with a long stick against large maps adorning the walls. Eden, trying to illustrate a point, dramatically pulled aside a curtain. The military officials in the room howled in horror as he inadvertently revealed a top-secret map to Tito.[78] Tito also visited Windsor Castle, the Tower of London and the Royal Opera House. The second hiccup arose when he witnessed a tragic crash at an air show in Duxford. Two pilots died while showing off some of the

RAF's fastest and most sophisticated jet aircraft, including some still designated secret.

Elizabeth had kept a low profile during the visit but maintained a close interest in Yugoslavia and the Cold War. Early the following year, she asked diplomats for updates about secret talks between the UK, US and Yugoslavia over the future of Trieste, to which both Yugoslavia and Italy, a NATO ally, laid claim. The topic had come up during discussions with Tito the previous year and, no matter how secret British intrigues and negotiations, the young monarch liked to be briefed in order to exact her constitutional duties. With officials fearing that Tito might go to war over the issue, Elizabeth knew all the details as an agreement was signed in London later in the year. Some details came from briefings and papers; others came, more informally but equally importantly, as a result of cocktail evenings involving her staff and Foreign Office officials.[79]

ELIZABETH'S INNOCENCE WAS short-lived. She moved quickly from princess, to heir, to monarch and, in the years following the end of the Second World War, she experienced covert action, insurgency and assassination plots. By her mid-twenties, Queen Elizabeth had access to highly sensitive intelligence and relied on spies to keep her safe. But she was also spied on and faced a steep learning curve as the Cold War intensified.

Never again would she have to hear about world affairs and international crises from footmen – although no doubt they continued to provide a uniquely valuable brand of personal intelligence. Instead, she would impress a procession of prime ministers with her knowledge of the constitution, her penetrating questions, and her mastery of the information locked inside her red despatch box.[80] She would catch out the intimidating figure of Winston Churchill by asking him for thoughts on Foreign Office telegrams he had not read. Perhaps Churchill was an easy target: the old man, her first prime minister, was ill and increasingly lazy. Harold Wilson, her fifth prime minister and previously an Oxford research fellow, was also caught out at his first ever audience with the queen, proving a more impressive scalp.[81]

She soon found herself mired in superpower intrigue, worried about potential Soviet blackmail, discussing assassinating foreign leaders, and as a confidante to a prime minister unburdening himself of secrets he could not tell anyone else. Elizabeth was now firmly part of the secret world; she never looked back.

QUEEN ELIZABETH II:
CORONATION AND COLD WAR

*'I find that I can often put things out of my
mind which are disagreeable.'*

The Queen on Anthony Blunt[1]

ON THE MORNING of 6 February 1952, Tommy Lascelles, private
secretary to the king, was at Sandringham. He called his deputy
in London, Edward Ford, and said: 'Edward, Hyde Park Corner. Go
and tell the Prime Minister and Queen Mary'; he then abruptly hung
up. King George VI's closest advisers had a series of secret codewords
to signal special eventualities. 'Hyde Park Corner' was Buckingham
Palace speak for 'the King has died'. The use of these codewords
belied the increasing use of scrambler phones at royal residences –
there were some things that were just too secret to be spoken.[2]

George had died peacefully in his sleep just four months after
an operation on his right lung. The sombre news quickly reverberated around government. Parliament suspended debate. The weekly
meeting of the Joint Intelligence Committee was in full swing when
the announcement came through at 11.30 a.m. The most senior
intelligence body in the land halted its discussion of the Cold War,
Egyptian riots and the expansion of NATO; its chairman solemnly
asked all present to stand silently and adjourned the meeting.[3] Flags

across London were at half-mast by noon – with one exception. Queen Mary refused to lower hers. The octogenarian wife of George V made it staunchly clear that, for her, the crown never dies.

With the crown still very much alive, government attention soon turned to welcoming the new monarch, twenty-five-year-old Elizabeth, back from a visit to Kenya and then how best to ensure a smooth succession.

Seemingly, there was little threat to the queen or the crown. Mass observation surveys, used to track popular opinion, revealed scant appetite for republicanism among a population still suffering the effects of the war. For many, King George VI had been a superb symbol of national unity and resilience: he left the monarchy in good health. As for his daughter, the young queen was particularly popular, epitomizing what many hoped would be a new era of optimism and peace.

The only shadowy manoeuvrings came from inside the upper classes themselves. Kenneth de Courcy, a right-wing politician, pre-war go-between for Germany and one-time head of a private intelligence network, tried to stir controversy. Alongside Winston Churchill and Walter Monckton, de Courcy was one of the Windsors' oldest friends and had stayed close to them throughout the late 1940s, often visiting or writing to them in France and facilitating their visits to New York.[4] Back in 1949 he had suggested to Churchill that Elizabeth form closer relations with his friend and confidant, the duke of Windsor.[5]

With the king's health failing, de Courcy had conspired for the exiled duke to return to England as regent to the inexperienced Elizabeth. Desperate for any formal position and adulation he once enjoyed, Edward was inevitably keen to return, and he found support among those fearing the influence of the ambitious Mountbatten on the impressionable young princess.

Intriguingly, de Courcy chose to make his pitch to the more ambitious Wallis. Rather well informed, he explained that the king was in fact 'gravely ill' and effectively already 'out of circulation'.

He warned that the royal family now faced a crisis in which the influence of the Mountbattens 'might be fatal' and urged Edward and Wallis to head this off. 'All these dangers could be averted... if the duke were to return to live in England' where he would be a discreet but 'decisive influence... upon the Regency'. De Courcy chose his words carefully, but added that with 'extremely careful and painstaking work' Edward might succeed in 'laying entirely fresh foundation stones upon which the monarchy in the latter part of the 20th and 21st century might be built'.[6] Edward decided to stay in Paris, but these conversations with Churchill and others triggered an ugly reaction.

In 1951, the crown launched a propaganda counter-offensive against the Duke and Duchess of Windsor. It was precisely at this point, de Courcy recalls, that 'the authorities repeatedly and widely asserted that the Secret Services had prepared a dossier about Mrs Simpson'. This was the infamous 'China Dossier' and was said to contain details of her private life in China while married to her first husband, Earl Winfield Spencer. 'The alleged details were wholly sexual and the authorities said she became expert at deviationist sexual activity which she learned in China and that was one reason why she had a hold over Edward VIII.' The individual chosen to brief about this was Jack Coke, Queen Mary's equerry, later gentleman usher to King George VI and finally extra gentleman usher to Queen Elizabeth II. Both Churchill and de Courcy were told that this dossier was the main issue that 'was held against the duchess'. De Courcy was probably right in asserting that the dossier was 'totally false' but was nevertheless a 'winning story'.[7]

The royals were firing their propaganda in the wrong direction. By the time George died, Edward was drifting among the overfed and idle rich in France and Florida, resigned to life as a mere café society royal. But suspicions about the intentions of Prince Philip's power-hungry uncle had more substance. A sense of intrigue now swept the palace again. Many saw 'Uncle Dickie', as Louis Mountbatten was affectionately known, as an arch-manipulator who, over a decade, had engineered his nephew's improbable rise to the heart of the British royal family. When Edward briefly returned home for his brother's funeral, he noted of Mountbatten that 'one can't pin much on him but he's very bossy and never stops talking. All are suspicious and watching his influence on Philip.' Rumours even circulated that Mountbatten plotted to make Philip the king consort.[8]

An article warning of Mountbatten's leftist influence was the source of much of the gossip. It appeared in the freelance 'Bulletin of the International Services of Information', run by a former American intelligence officer, Ulius Amoss. Specifically, it warned that Peter Murphy, a long-time confidant of Mountbatten, was a member of the Communist Party. Although the FBI rated Amoss an eccentric, MI5 conducted its own investigation and sent the deputy director of naval intelligence to raise its concerns with Mountbatten personally.[9]

Mountbatten was furious at being accused of wielding subversive leftist influence inside palace circles, but he accepted that suggestions about his sway with the queen were inevitable. He reeled off a long list of his staff for MI5, emphasizing that each was beyond reproach. Unfortunately, the intelligence services forgot to make a note of their names.[10] A few days later, MI5 received information that Mountbatten and his entourage were 'looking at' not only Murphy, but also a known communist called Pavitt.[11]

Less than three weeks after George had died, Elizabeth's grandmother, Queen Mary, highly attuned to politics where they affected the crown, angrily summoned Jock Colville from Number 10. She trusted Colville, who had once been Elizabeth's private secretary and had provided discreet advice on Philip before he married into the family. Still an influential member of the establishment, he now performed the same role for Winston Churchill. Mary had been keeping a close eye on Mountbatten and, as perennial matriarch of the House of Windsor, had long enjoyed an unofficial surveillance network across British aristocracy.

News quickly reached her from Prince Ernst of Hanover that Dickie was boasting of victory. At a dinner party of royal guests held at his house at Broadlands he had announced: 'the House of Mountbatten now reigned'. She 'spent a sleepless night' and passed on the reports to Colville, who, in turn, informed the prime minister. Philip had even written a document protesting against the royals remaining as the House of Windsor. This had 'annoyed' Churchill and indeed the whole Cabinet.[12] To the anger of Mountbatten and Philip, and to the resigned frustration of Elizabeth, Churchill insisted on the queen taking the name Windsor – rather than Mountbatten. The ageing prime minister, perhaps influenced by the gossip, saw Mountbatten as a subversive rival.[13] Despite the intrigue and meddling, the succession passed smoothly and the House of Windsor still reigned.

THE CORONATION ITSELF, taking place in June 1953, proved a vast undertaking. It was the first to be broadcast on television – and an utter headache for security. Westminster Abbey was closed for an entire year as additional seating was added to expand the capacity from 2,000 to 8,000 guests, allowing minor royals and dignitaries from around the world to attend. Behind the scenes, courtiers and government officials tussled over the guest list. The Maltese prime minister struggled to secure an invitation despite Elizabeth's long associations with the island and then complained about being 'lumped in' with the Africans. Some African leaders were not welcome at all and officials went to considerable lengths to deter the leftist Kwame Nkrumah, prime minister of the Gold Coast, from turning up. There was also the problem of pretenders. Guests included the 'Princess of the Pitcairn Islands', a self-styled title adopted by a resident of Tahiti who had never set foot on Pitcairn.[14]

Physical security was important. A successful attack on the coronation might have rendered upper-class spats about Elizabeth's surname utterly immaterial. By this time, three months after Stalin's death, MI5 did not expect the communists to pose much danger. Instead, the threat came from a more unexpected quarter. Scottish nationalists had earlier stolen the Stone of Scone, an ancient symbol of Scottish monarchy, from Westminster Abbey. Ever since the death of George VI, they had made what Colville described as 'an absurd fuss about the Queen being Elizabeth II rather than Elizabeth I', on the grounds that Elizabeth I had never ruled Scotland.[15]

This culminated in a so-called pillar box war. Angry young Scots sabotaged – and even blew up – Scottish post boxes marked with the new 'EIIR' ensign just six weeks before the coronation.[16] Quietly, the decision was taken to replace them with a new design that carried the crown of Scotland. Guy Liddell, of MI5, noted that this was causing 'some concern', especially given that police thought republicans – 'equivalent to the IRA in Ireland' – were to blame.[17] A couple of weeks before the coronation, Liddell warned of 'extreme irresponsible splinter groups within the Scottish Nationalist Party, who are quite capable of student pranks or something worse'.[18]

On coronation day itself, the Metropolitan Police, reinforced by units from across the country, battled the abnormally miserable weather to maintain close watch over the crowds. They paid particular attention to unoccupied premises, foreigners and, as the police put it, 'suspected mental cases'.[19]

Pavements were packed with people braving the rain; thousands more watched for the first time on brand-new television sets. Celebrations rang out, and the coronation passed smoothly. A string of formal dinners followed, with the banquet thrown by the Foreign Office serving the most potential hazards. Nehru, the Indian prime minister, went out of his way to talk about his imprisonment by the British. Meanwhile, the young queen struggled with minor royals, finding them 'impatient and difficult to deal with'.[20]

With the coronation out of the way, Queen Elizabeth was able to devote more time to her constitutional duties. She enjoyed access to top-secret intelligence and, like her fastidious father, took her reading seriously. Every evening at around seven o'clock, except for Easter and Christmas, she received a red leather despatch box stuffed full of important matters of state. Its contents included Foreign Office cables, budget documents, Cabinet papers and highly classified secret intelligence, including MI6 reporting on international crises.[21] Copy number one of the government's weekly summary of current intelligence went to the queen.[22] If war broke out, she would have had access to highly classified daily situation reports alongside all intelligence, no matter how secret, on future operations. This was on one condition: she burn them after reading.[23]

In stark contrast to King Edward VIII's sloppy practice, which risked secrets falling into Nazi hands, tight security surrounded the box. Elizabeth was orderly and well drilled perhaps, as Clement Attlee had earlier hoped, by the likes of Martin Charteris who had served with military intelligence in Palestine before joining the queen's staff. Only four keys existed: Elizabeth held one, and her private secretaries kept the others.[24] By eight o'clock the next morning, she had returned her box, having ticked off each document and underlined interesting bits in red pencil. Rarely did she write comment.[25]

Elizabeth was not the only member of her family reading classified material. In July 1954, the queen mother began receiving her own daily box of Foreign Office telegrams and practically all the material sent to the Cabinet. She deliberately stopped short of asking for 'anything of a very secret nature',[26] but appreciated access to classified state papers. Moreover, mother and daughter spoke to each other on the telephone every day, providing the monarch with a sounding board for difficult issues.

Strikingly, the queen mother wanted them in a personal capacity – out of nosiness rather than duty. She had been used to knowing everything during the war, when George would confide the most sensitive business – from secret intelligence to military deception – to his wife. Frustrated with now being out of the loop, she told Churchill that 'one can read the newspapers with much greater interest and less suspicion, if one knows a little of the true back-ground of the news'.[27]

Anthony Eden, the foreign secretary, was hesitant. He insisted that, regardless of her previous access and influence, nothing top secret should now reach her.[28] This was hardly a 'need to know' scenario, yet, perhaps influenced by their close relationship during the war, Churchill quickly agreed to her request. He justified it on the grounds that when Elizabeth was away, her mother became the senior member of the council of state.[29]

Not wanting to freeze Philip out, for the prince could be touchy about such things, Churchill extended the offer to him as well. Palace staff assumed that the queen privately showed her husband papers of interest anyway,[30] but Philip, ever desperate for recognition in his own right, jumped at the offer.[31] This was partly because the queen never shared the contents of her own red boxes with him – but now he had his own green boxes.

Private audiences formed another useful source of material on the secret state for the young queen. They took place in a sitting room on the ground floor of Buckingham Palace, lasted around ninety minutes each morning, and gave her a chance to meet ambassadors, civil servants, military officers and the occasional spy chief. She would press a buzzer, the doors would open, and her guest would step inside, bow or curtsey, take another three steps and then repeat the gesture. Such archaic tradition and formality belied the freedom of discussion. These audiences formed the queen's 'way of meeting people without anyone else listening'. They gave, she later explained, 'a very broad picture of what is actually going on, either in govern-ment or in the civil service'.[32]

Her Tuesday afternoon audiences with prime ministers, themselves deeply interested in intelligence after the war, were particularly fruitful. For Elizabeth, this was a time when her prime ministers could 'unburden themselves or they tell me what's going on if they have got any problems'. 'Sometimes,' she added, 'one can help.'[33]

Sitting across from the prime minister, she would put forward her own point of view. 'Perhaps,' she later noted, 'they hadn't seen it from that angle.' More often, she asked questions in a Socratic manner, subtly arching an eyebrow, to indicate her concerns. Although initially sceptical of the inexperienced monarch, Winston Churchill, a veteran of many an audience with her father, soon found her conscientious, well informed and serious minded. Their meetings grew in length and the queen was one of the very few whom he informed about his strokes, a secret he kept even from his Cabinet colleagues.[34]

When Churchill finally retired in 1955, she thanked him for his leadership during the Cold War. Its 'threats and dangers', she told him, were 'more awe inspiring than any which you have had to contend with before, in war or peace'.[35]

BY NOW THE Cold War had been under way for a decade. Amid growing tensions between east and west, the queen adopted a quasi-political role. According to one royal biographer, she 'was deployed as a lure to defuse the Cold War between Britain and Russia'.[36] Soviet leaders Nikita Khrushchev and Nikolai Bulganin arrived for a historic high-profile state visit to Britain in April 1956. It included a controversial meeting with Queen Elizabeth and Prince Philip.

Intrigue and espionage were endemic. The Soviet delegation included Ivan Serov, officially serving as chief of their security. In fact, he was head of the KGB and later became head of Soviet military intelligence, the GRU. Famously oppressive of Russian minorities in areas like the Ukraine, he was hated by exiles from the 'captive nations' inside the USSR and became a walking target for terrorists. Prime Minister Anthony Eden had banned offensive intelligence operations for the duration of the visit. He feared that a potential spy scandal would undo his pre-summit hard work, but Britain's propagandists could not resist a small operation of their own. They discreetly tipped off journalists about Serov's real job and the brutality it involved. As a result, reporters hounded him up and down the country, giving him unflattering nicknames including Ivan the Terrible and Ivan the Butcher.[37]

Predictably, Special Branch, who were guarding the Soviet party, were unhappy about the propaganda effort. Partly because of Serov's presence, officers worried about assassination attempts by dissident nationalists. These concerns were redoubled when the Foreign Office accidentally released a detailed programme of the visit complete with places and times a week beforehand. 'These were supposed to be secret for security purposes.' There were many receptions with much vodka, but at each event, guests had to enter single file to be scrutinized by 'obvious Special Branch men'.[38] Most events went well, other than a dinner for the Soviets held by the Labour Party. The shadow foreign secretary, George Brown, heckled Khrushchev during his speech and attacked him over the Nazi–Soviet pact of 1939. Khrushchev was in 'a furious temper' and replied tartly that if he lived in Britain he would vote Conservative.[39]

Like Eden, Khrushchev and Bulganin also hoped intelligence activities would not mar the occasion.[40] Guy Burgess and Donald Maclean, two Soviet agents inside the Foreign Office, had defected to Moscow five years earlier as British intelligence closed in on their double lives. A couple of months before the state visit, the Kremlin had permitted them to hold a press conference from Moscow. It was the first proof of life since their defection and inevitably caused a furore back home.

For all the drama, the Soviets intended to put their one-time prize agents to good use and instructed Burgess to share political intelligence in advance of the visit. He provided insight into the places Khrushchev and Bulganin would visit, and the people they would meet. This included Queen Elizabeth herself. Burgess assessed that 'in line with the family tradition, to say nothing of political considerations, the Royal Family harboured hostile feelings for Soviet leaders, because they have not forgotten what happened to the last

Tsar and his family'. He recommended that when visiting Windsor, they ask to see portraits of great statesmen, including Alexander I, to remind both sides of when Britain and Russia had been allies against a European tyrant.[41]

Shortly after their arrival, Khrushchev and Bulganin were escorted to Buckingham Palace, accompanied by William Hayter, the ambassador to Moscow, and Thomas Barker, a specialist from the Foreign Office who would later become head of its propaganda unit.[42] A few days later, armed with Burgess's intelligence, 'B&K', as the press dubbed them, arrived at Windsor Castle.

Elizabeth, dressed in a plain white outfit, with Philip and their children at her side, met the Russians at the door. Eden had told Khrushchev that the queen was a simple, pleasant person and Khrushchev thought her 'the sort of young woman you'd be likely to meet walking along Gorky Street on a balmy summer afternoon'.[43] She offered them a tour of the castle, perhaps taking in the portraits recommended by Burgess, and now curated by his friend Anthony Blunt, before sitting down to tea. Philip had thought the idea of tea with the Russians 'bloody silly', but soon warmed to his guests.[44]

An encrypted Russian telegram sent back to Moscow recorded that Philip praised the hospitality received by British naval officers during a visit to Leningrad in 1955. He joked that he would like to visit the city incognito.[45] Elizabeth asked polite questions about the plane that delivered the Russians' mail to them while in England. Khrushchev, desperate to show it off as one of the first passenger jets in the world, was delighted.[46]

He was less keen to receive questions about his other mode of transport, the Soviet cruiser on which he had arrived, currently docked in Portsmouth's large natural harbour. Three days earlier, an MI6 diver, Buster Crabb, had embarked upon an unauthorized mission to inspect its hull – but never returned. As MI6 scrambled, Khrushchev made a cryptic reference over dinner to the ship and lost property.

It is unlikely that the queen had advance knowledge of the Crabb dive, but if she did it would have come via Mountbatten. Despite his denials, Uncle Dickie seems to have known all about the controversial operation – and tried to hush the story up. He had known Crabb in Gibraltar during the war and afterwards when Crabb was supposedly doing 'some type of secret work' at a research lab in Bushey Park. There are even accounts of Mountbatten meeting Crabb shortly before the fateful dive.[47]

Either way, Khrushchev left the castle 'very impressed' by the queen. 'She had,' he recalled, 'such a gentle, calm voice. She was completely unpretentious, completely without the haughtiness that you'd expect of royalty.' He downplayed her role, portraying her more as a mother and wife than as the queen.[48]

But the royals maintained discreet influence. The queen mother later had a quiet talk with President Eisenhower, whom she had known since the war. 'We must be firm' in dealing with the Soviets, she stressed, before catching herself and adding that this was her own private opinion, rather than the government line. Either way, it had an impact. During talks with the British Cabinet the very next day, Eisenhower repeated what the queen mother had told him after ministers complained of the weak hand they held. The foreign secretary tempered the queen mother's line: 'we have to be firm on essentials'.[49]

The Americans exploited royal influence in other ways too. The CIA watched Bulganin and Khrushchev's visit to Britain closely, using it as part of a large psychological warfare operation targeting East Germany. Codenamed LCCASSOCK, the CIA was disseminating 20,000 copies at a time of material made to closely resemble official East German publications. The operation aimed to 'exploit special events' in order to 'promote the spirit of resistance.' One CIA publication mimicking an East German weekly newspaper criticized the state visit to Britain, reporting 'statements of Khrushchev which aroused the indignation of the British'. Another article told readers that Queen Elizabeth would not wear a fur coat presented to her by the Soviets on the grounds that British officials feared that Moscow 'would make propaganda of this matter if she appeared in the coat'.

Ironically, in doing so, the CIA was secretly making its own propaganda of the queen.[50]

Khrushchev's compatriots were not so dismissive of the monarchy. Six months after the state visit, a spontaneous uprising erupted in Hungary taking MI6 by surprise. Rebels, some of whom were armed only with kitchen knives, scored a string of improbable successes before Soviet tanks rolled in. Over two thousand Hungarians died as the Russians put a brutal end to the revolution; hundreds of thousands fled. It was one of the darkest episodes of the Cold War.

Shortly afterwards, in the face of mounting pressure, the Soviets tried to use the queen as a pawn in the propaganda war. Buckingham Palace received an odd telegram from Marshal Voroshilov, the Soviet head of state. He asked that the queen 'correctly' understand Soviet action in Hungary. Diplomats in the Foreign Office thought it an outrageously hypocritical and sanctimonious move.[51]

More cynically still, the Russian embassy in London quickly telephoned the Foreign Office to ask if they could publish the letter alongside the queen's reply. This really ruffled the mandarins because Elizabeth had not sent any letter to the Soviets, and the Foreign Office had no intention of allowing her to send one now. They worried that the Soviets were fishing for anything they could publish to give the impression that the queen tacitly accepted the Soviet version of events. Criticizing the ploy as 'cynical hypocrisy', senior diplomats refused even to allow Elizabeth to have anything to do with the letter at all.

They were particularly nervous because just ten days earlier, Moscow had released a letter from Bulganin to Eisenhower to the local press before Eisenhower had even received it.[52] Voroshilov's letter to the queen was, according to one diplomat, a 'serious and most displeasing incident' that warranted summons of the Soviet ambassador to the Foreign Office.[53]

Diplomats called the Soviets' bluff. The next day, a Russian official admitted that there was in fact no message from the queen. Moscow recognized their letter was a 'serious mistake', apologized profusely, and agreed to withdraw it.[54] The humiliating climb-down took senior diplomats by surprise. Patrick Reilly, soon to become ambassador in Moscow, was surprised that the Russians had behaved 'almost humanely' over the withdrawal. It was, he thought, a 'very queer affair'.[55]

Oleg Penkovsky was another Russian who did not doubt the queen's importance. He was a dynamic and aggressive colonel in Soviet military intelligence. Penkovsky was also an MI6/CIA agent, passing much secret material, mostly on missiles, but also delicious Kremlin political gossip, to the west. He was undoubtedly one of the top agents of the Cold War. When offering to defect, he wrote a letter addressed to Queen Elizabeth among others. It read: 'I ask you to consider me as your soldier. Henceforth the ranks of your armed forces are increased by one man.' Instead of defecting, he was kept as a spy in place, both more valuable, but also more dangerous. Therefore, meetings with Penkovsky were infrequent to protect his security.

An opportunity arose in the autumn of 1961. He was sent to London on official business and was able to meet secretly with both MI6 and CIA, including Harry Shergold, one of MI6's most experienced agent handlers. Penkovsky had an intriguing request. He pointed out that when the Soviet cosmonaut, Yuri Gagarin, visited London recently, he met the queen, so Penkovsky asked: 'why can't I meet the Queen?'

The CIA recalls that this was where Shergold really 'sweated crocodile drops'. Penkovsky hoped to swear his loyalty to the queen personally. He was a star agent, providing bundles of useful intelligence to MI6 and the CIA, including, as we shall see, on the Cuban missile crisis. All the while, he wondered why he had not yet met the queen.[56] In the event he had to settle for a message from Mountbatten delivered by Dick White, the chief of MI6. White assured him that the queen's cousin would tell her all about his important work. White sensed his disappointment and later recalled: 'He wanted to be praised personally by the Queen for his monumental contribution and to have a medal pinned on his chest. There was no possibility of this.'[57]

PENKOVSKY WAS A fantastic asset for MI6, but the Russians had recruited spies of their own. They were buried surprisingly deep in the heart of the British establishment. Both the KGB and their military counterparts, the GRU, were keen to gather intelligence not just on the government, but also on the upper echelons of society for blackmail and subversive purposes. A series of spy scandals punctuated the first decade of the queen's reign.[58]

Some inside government and the palace worried about Prince Philip's behaviour. At one point in 1956, the palace was forced to put out an unprecedented denial that the royal marriage was on the rocks following Philip's lengthy solo tour to Melbourne where he had opened the Olympic Games. Behind the scenes, officials grew concerned as, according to one royal biographer, they knew from intelligence reports that Philip and his equerry, Mike Parker, gallivanted flirtatiously around London's clubs and risked causing embarrassment to the queen.[59]

This was more than about marriage. Philip risked opening himself up to Soviet blackmail. He was a member of the notorious Thursday Club, which met in Soho every week for boozy lunches, sometimes stretching long into the night. Members included controversial spy-turned-writer Compton Mackenzie, the witty actor David Niven, and Stephen Ward, the infamous society osteopath at the heart of the Profumo affair.[60]

Even Kim Philby, the MI6 officer and Soviet spy, once attended Philip's club and yet, for all his famed charm and charisma, he was apparently deemed too boring to be invited back.[61] 'The dullest man in the place', as Mike Parker counterintuitively recalled.[62] Philby was already under intense suspicion at the time for being a Soviet agent. Perhaps someone received a quiet warning about the guest list.

Prince Philip has always denied rumours that he was unfaithful to Elizabeth during these early years of marriage, pointing out that his protection officers would have prevented him from indulging in clandestine assignations. Whatever the reality, this is a fairly weak defence: protection officers protect their charges. They do not cast moral judgement or prevent them from doing something which would not otherwise imperil their safety.[63]

Protection officers can – and did – report behaviour which compromised security and made their charges vulnerable to blackmail. King Edward VIII's policemen, as we have seen, had him under surveillance during and after the abdication crisis. Whatever the truth and source, Philip's behaviour was enough to concern the prime minister, Winston Churchill. He summoned the prince, deliberately kept him waiting, and then growled: 'Is your objective the destruction of the whole royal family?'[64]

When Philip was invited to tour the US, Whitehall officials conspired to keep him away from public or social engagements. The British ambassador in Washington suggested keeping his time in the capital and New York as short as possible, with the prince instead touring Ohio, Omaha and Colorado Springs. Even Churchill insisted that the visit be 'as military as possible'. Philip, it seemed, had to be kept away from temptation and trouble.[65]

The Thursday Club brought the royal family dangerously close to the toxic Profumo scandal in 1963. John Profumo, the secretary of state for war, denied having sexual relations with a nineteen-year-old model, Christine Keeler. In March 1963, as rumours swirled, he defiantly stood up in the House of Commons to threaten writs for libel and slander against anyone making scandalous allegations of impropriety. That very afternoon, he attended the horse racing in Surrey with the queen mother. Labour politicians angrily derided what they saw as a public show of support from the royals.[66]

Prime Minister Harold Macmillan privately worried that 'the tide of gossip might even lap around the Royal Family'.[67] As well as having plenty of mutual friends, Philip had known Ward personally for quite some time. He had attended parties thrown by Ward back in the late 1940s and had stayed in touch through the 1950s. Ward was also an accomplished portrait painter, and Philip sat for him in spring 1961, followed by Princess Margaret. In June 1963, the FBI reported that Philip was involved in the Profumo affair but did not say exactly how.[68]

Ward was a complex character. He mixed with the highest in society and revealed to Christine Keeler that he, Prince Philip and his cousin the Marquess of Milford Haven had visited 'all the night-clubs together' in the period before the prince was married. 'They were quite wild times and it was thought a little delicate for Prince Philip when Elizabeth became Queen.'[69]

Publicly, Ward was a determined social climber. His mostly female friends were amazed that his patients included Winston Churchill, Frank Sinatra and a significant section of the nobil-ity: 'His main weapon was his connections.' But privately he disdained them. Christine Keeler recalled that he had 'no time for Prince Philip and was always putting him down in conversation' because he hated the establishment. Becoming quite animated, Ward ranted: 'they marry their cousins and land up retarded and deformed with the interbreeding'.[70]

At this time, within Soviet intelligence, the GRU took the lead on targeting the royal family, rather than the KGB.[71] Captain Eugene Ivanov was a GRU military intelligence officer under cover as an assistant naval attaché at the embassy in London. He was friends with Ward, but also enjoyed sexual relations with Christine Keeler. Ivanov's involvement turned a society sex scandal into a security affair. Keeler explained the chain of events precisely:

If I hadn't gone to bed with Yevgeny Ivanov that night it is very likely that none of it would ever have happened. My love affair with John Profumo, the Minister of War, would never have developed overtones of treason. Harold Macmillan's

government might not have been rocked to its socks. Stephen
Ward would never have killed himself.[72]

Given the security paranoia that the Profumo affair eventually triggered, it is truly remarkable how smoothly Ivanov swam in the higher
echelons of society in early sixties Britain. Whizzing round London,
sometimes at the wheel of a Rolls-Royce owned by his friend Paul
Richey, the famous fighter pilot, or weekending at Cliveden with the
Astors, his rise was irresistible – yet intensely puzzling.

Ivanov's entrance into British society came via a chance meeting
at an embassy party with Sir Colin Coote, managing director of the
Telegraph and close friend of Churchill. They bonded over their
mutual suspicions of West German re-armament and later Coote
introduced Ivanov to Stephen Ward at the Garrick Club. Ward was
trying to get a visa for Russia to sketch members of the Politburo
and Coote thought Ivanov could help – the friendship between the
two quickly took off. Ivanov was being watched and so Ward was
approached by MI5.[73] Some have suggested that this was all arranged
by MI5 as an entrapment, but whether this was true or not, Ward
provided Ivanov with some royal opportunities. On 21 July 1960,
Ivanov attended his first garden party at Buckingham Palace.[74]

Ivanov was deeply interested in the royals, especially Philip, and
believed that the connection between Ward and the royal family
was valuable. He first contrived to meet Philip by acting as an
interpreter to a famous Soviet polar explorer, Mikhail Somov, who
was visiting London. The location was a reception at the Royal
Geographical Society. Ivanov engaged the prince in conversation
and 'the subject of physical geography soon gave way to political
geography'. He tried to engage Philip on topics such as the German
question, the nuclear arms race and the Common Market but 'he
cautiously evaded my bait'.[75]

Ivanov concluded that his 'head-on attack' had failed, so he
resolved to try 'more subtle means'. He returned to his trusted
friend Ward and plied him for more background information on

Philip. 'Remember that photo album?' Ward helpfully responded. Ivanov had forgotten about it. 'Look at the photographs again and you'll understand,' he added significantly. Ivanov looked again and saw Philip and his cousin David at a club together with Antony Beauchamp, son-in-law of Churchill, Arthur Christiansen, editor of the *Daily Express*, and a number of girls – 'Nicole' and 'Maggie'. Ward drifted away towards the kitchen to make coffee and Ivanov momentarily thought about stealing the photos, but, thinking better of it, he produced his Minox camera and 'photographed five or six of the snapshots'. Ward returned and talked about Philip's life in parties and clubs. Ivanov reciprocated with gossip about high life in Moscow. Later he recalled: 'I sent the photographs and my report to Moscow Centre.'[76]

All this was part of a wider Russian operation targeting the whole royal family called Operation House.[77] MI5 knew that the Russians were spying on the royals and that Ivanov had sent various society titbits, supposedly including photographs, back to his headquarters in Russia. Neither Ivanov nor his colleagues ever used the compromising information to try to blackmail the royal family, however. This, according to one senior MI5 officer, was because the GRU thought it was fake.[78] Either way, it caused enough consternation to be taken seriously by the inquiry into the Profumo affair – and for the relevant files to remain locked away from historians' eyes.

How did MI5 know all this? It appears that the security service had an agent at the very centre of Ward's flamboyant social circle. This was Mariella Novotny, aka 'Miss Kinky'; Keeler confidently believed she was 'an informant' for both the police and MI5.[79] Lord Denning interviewed her at length but completely airbrushed her from his report into the scandal.[80] The other reason that Novotny vanished is that she most likely had a relationship with John F. Kennedy. The Kennedy connection set the nerves of the White House jangling and waves of FBI officers were despatched to London and New York to uncover any stories of espionage or scandal.[81] They were ordered to keep it close to their chests and only 'personally advise the president' of anything they found.[82] Novotny continued to work for the authorities for two decades and died in curious circumstances in 1983, shortly before the scheduled publishing of a personal memoir. The book has never been published.[83]

Profumo was obviously Ivanov's top target. Second were the Astors, who opened amazing doors for him into the establishment. 'Third on my list were Princess Margaret and Antony Armstrong Jones.' Again, he recalled that he was introduced to them by Ward, 'who also equipped me with certain details about their life' which were available to him because 'he loved gossip and had known the royal family for years'. This connection, he added darkly, 'held out the possibility of getting information through provocation and blackmail'.[84]

Ivanov targeted Princess Margaret, the queen's sister, quite successfully. He met her on numerous occasions, hoping to elicit some scandalous information. He even attended the reception that followed her wedding to Antony Armstrong-Jones and then spent time with them at Ascot and at the Henley Regatta. They never missed a regatta and afterwards 'they usually invited me into their boat'. After chatting to Margaret on a voyage along the Thames, he then returned to Ward and traded royal gossip.[85]

Unfortunately for Ivanov, blackmail was hardly possible, since he soon found himself in hopeless competition with the newspapers; rumours detailing Margaret's personal life were rarely out of the press.[86] Ivanov was apparently not the only one targeting Margaret: an unnamed senior officer from Soviet military intelligence later claimed that one of her butlers, Thomas Cronin, was actually a Russian agent – codenamed Rab. He apparently fed maps of state rooms and royal gossip back to Moscow.[87]

In April 1963, the Profumo scandal broke. Ivanov fled back to Moscow, escaping what was possibly a honey-trap operation that was about to envelop him.[88] Meanwhile, investigative reporters from the *Sunday Times* stumbled upon the royal dimension. They were interviewing an expressionist painter, Felix Topolski, who hosted

Ward's circle in his studios, when Philip's name came up. Four years earlier, Philip had commissioned Topolski to paint a huge ninety-five-foot-long mural commemorating Elizabeth's coronation. It was to be hung in the state apartments at Buckingham Palace. Now, after mentioning Philip's name in relation to the Profumo affair, Topolski quickly dried up.

Soon afterwards, a certain 'Mr Shaw', from MI5, telephoned one of the reporters and asked if he, along with two colleagues, could meet him in a hotel near St James's Park tube station. Shaw, in his mid-fifties, appeared with two younger men. They had known about pretty much every person the journalists had interviewed, but specifically wanted to know what Topolski had said about Prince Philip. The journalists explained that they were investigating political cover-ups and the consequences for Macmillan's faltering government. The Philip angle, tantalizing as it may be, was irrelevant. Shaw and his colleagues seemed relieved, leaving the journalists suspicious that MI5 had a special team to protect the royal family's interests.[89]

And maybe it did. Three years earlier, Princess Margaret had privately alluded to MI5 making special arrangements for her partner Antony Armstrong-Jones to meet the queen and ask permission to marry. Officers had escorted him across muddy fields of the Sandringham estate to avoid any watching photographers. Margaret told a friend shortly after the engagement that 'it's wonderful no one guessed the reason of his visit and I only wish you had been in on the MI5 arrangements by which he was whisked into the Queen's room to ask the vital permission'.[90]

Profumo resigned in disgrace in early June 1963; he begged to be excused the customary valedictory audience with the queen.[91] Labour politicians were disappointed. They hoped that any such meeting would highlight the closeness between the royals and Profumo, doing immense damage to the establishment and helping to create the conditions for a Labour government.[92]

Meanwhile, Macmillan, ill and fading from office, wrote personally to the queen to apologize after this latest sorry episode in the series of spy scandals that had dogged his administration. He apologized for mishandling the crisis which, with its mixture of sex, spies and the establishment, had damaged the fabric of society. Macmillan explained that he had had no idea 'of the strange underworld in which other people, alas beside Mr Profumo have allowed themselves to become entrapped'.[93] This was all the more humiliating for Macmillan because his wife, Dorothy, was having a decades-long affair with Robert Boothsby, the bisexual politician – and the royal family knew all about it.[94] The queen consoled Macmillan, saying how difficult it was for people with high standards to suspect others of lacking them.[95]

Elizabeth, via her red boxes, the press and her connections, knew about the Profumo affair as it unfolded. She refused to blame the beleaguered minister and remained on good terms with him as he publicly devoted his later life to charity work. However, it appears his private life remained unreformed and he rather enjoyed his notoriety. At a dinner party thrown in his honour by the queen mother, he took the opportunity to proposition a teenage girl, using the most direct language.[96] The queen mother still lunched with Profumo as late as 2000.[97]

THE QUEEN KNEW all about Anthony Blunt as well. As we have seen, Blunt, a close friend of Queen Mary, had worked illustriously for MI5 during the war, and accepted the position of surveyor of the king's pictures, effectively the royal art historian, when it ended in 1945. If spy and art historian were not enough, Blunt had a third life as a talent spotter for Soviet intelligence since 1937.

In 1945, the KGB was delighted with Blunt's position in the palace, hoping that his royal connections would give him access to the king – and the king's secrets. Sadly for Moscow, this turned out not to be the case.[98] He avoided royal social events and, from the early 1950s, when Queen Elizabeth inherited him, he delegated much of this work to his deputy, Oliver Millar.[99] Before the war Blunt was a charismatic socialite, but his secret life took its toll. Outwardly appearing the composed and elegant academic, Blunt suffered from exhaustion and turned to drink in the 1950s. He gradually became more introverted and colder, concentrating on his academic work.[100] Nonetheless, MI5 intercepted mail from Guy Burgess in which the Soviet spy, now living in Moscow, played upon 'his knowledge of the association between BLUNT and the British Royal Family'.[101]

What is now clear is that the royal family knew that Blunt was a KGB agent as early as 1948. As we have seen, Tommy Lascelles referred to him as 'our Russian spy'. Blunt's treachery was tightly held in MI5 but became the subject of common or garden tea-time gossip in the palace. The following year, Mark Milbank, master of the royal household, made exactly the same quip to Oliver Millar when he arrived as Blunt's deputy.[102]

Blunt had undertaken discreet business on behalf of the royals in the past. As we have seen, he visited Europe twice in 1945 and twice again in 1946. Nearly two decades later, as the Profumo scandal broke, Blunt had apparently conducted another discreet mission, purchasing an embarrassing portrait of Prince Philip drawn by Stephen Ward.[103] A teenage assistant to Ward, who later became a Labour MP, recalls only that 'a member of the royal household' bought the picture for cash, 'no questions asked'.[104]

Although he no longer had direct access to classified material, Blunt did keep in touch with Soviet intelligence while working at the palace passing on gossip or titbits that came his way. And he certainly came into enough contact with royal life for the palace to raise concerns about him as early as 1951. The dramatic defection of Guy Burgess and Donald Maclean in May of that year provoked questions about Blunt, who was a known friend of Burgess. King George VI pressed Lascelles for details on the case soon after the pair went missing. Guy Liddell, Lascelles cousin and deputy director of MI5, replied that he had no more news beyond what the papers had reported.

This was not the whole truth. After the Foreign Office put out a bland statement that two diplomats, one of whom had suffered a mental breakdown a year before, were missing from their homes, the press revelled in wild speculation. Journalists asked embarrassing questions about widespread sexual perversion in the Foreign Office. Behind the scenes, the government launched an urgent inquiry into security and the net began to close in on the most famous traitor of all, Kim Philby.[105]

Liddell held back on the truth about the treachery of Burgess and Maclean, but the king was more concerned about Blunt. The art historian had barricaded himself in his flat, away from the legions of hungry journalists outside on the street. Blunt and Burgess had shared a flat during the war; the two were close. Liddell reassured him that 'no mention was made of Anthony and his association with Burgess, which had been referred to by at least one paper'.[106]

A month later, Lascelles was on the phone again. The palace was still concerned about Blunt. Liddell again reassured him that he was 'convinced' Blunt, whom he knew well, had 'never been a communist in the full political sense, even during his days at Cambridge'. Lascelles was 'very glad to hear this, since it was quite possible that the story might get around to the royal family'. He worried that the king or queen would raise the topic with him and was glad to be able to reassure them.[107]

Lascelles then told Liddell how 'Blunt had on one occasion intimated to the Queen that he was an atheist... and that the Queen had been a little shaken by his remarks. He was certain that if he now went up and told her that Anthony was a Communist, her immediate reaction would be "I always told you so".'[108]

Liddell was wrong; the king was right to be worried. While working at the palace, Blunt had acted as a courier for Burgess between 1945 and 1947 and had occasional meetings with Russian intelligence. He later confessed that Burgess had warned him about the net closing in on Maclean and that, using his Russian contacts, he had facilitated their arrangements to defect.[109] Afterwards, still working at the palace, he also assisted Philby's contact with the KGB on one occasion. Later he insisted that he had had no contact with Russian intelligence after 1956.[110]

Yuri Modin, the key KGB handler for the Cambridge Five, recalled just how important Blunt was at this time:

> Blunt, in effect, served as Burgess's permanent liaison with me. I would also seek him out whenever I needed information about MI5, where he still had plenty of friends. Sometimes I even asked him to procure up-to-date data on individual agents in the British counterespionage service... I was to continue seeing Blunt until 1951.[111]

Blunt was a Soviet spy in the palace. He maintained his position in the royal household after the Burgess and Maclean scandal, and even after the writer Goronwy Rees made what turned out to be accurate allegations about him to MI5 shortly afterwards. Rees offered no evidence, but the allegation generated eleven interviews between MI5 and Blunt. He remained composed and appeared in control. As part of the royal household, he received a knighthood in 1956.

In April 1964, armed with new intelligence, MI5 was ready to try interview number twelve. On 13 April, its director general, Roger Hollis, informed the most senior official in the Home Office, Charles Cunningham, that MI5 intended to interrogate Blunt the following week. Given their previous failures in getting anything to stick, intelligence officers now wanted to offer Blunt immunity from prosecution in return for a confession. Three days later, the attorney general agreed.

The deal – if Blunt accepted – had clear implications for the royal family, given that he still worked for the palace. Hollis and Cunningham briefed Michael Adeane, Queen Elizabeth's private secretary, immediately afterwards.[112] They told him that Blunt was suspected of having been a Russian agent, but that, provided he confessed and co-operated in MI5's inquiries, he would be granted immunity.[113]

Adeane listened intently, before asking what action the queen should take if Blunt did indeed confess. None, Hollis responded, because any action, such as firing him, would alert Russian intelligence and any other potential moles under investigation.[114]

On 23 April, Blunt confessed. 'Give me five minutes while I wrestle with my conscience,' he responded, before admitting to MI5 of having been a Russian intelligence agent during the 1930s and that he had been privy to the defection of Burgess and Maclean in 1951.[115]

Shortly afterwards, Adeane apparently called Peter Wright, a senior MI5 officer investigating Soviet moles, to the palace. Adeane was 'punctilious and correct', assuring Wright that 'the Palace was willing to co-operate in any inquiries the Service thought fit'. He spoke, Wright recalled, 'in the detached manner of someone who wishes not to know very much more about the matter'. The queen, Adeane continued measuredly, 'has been fully informed about Sir Anthony, and is quite content for him to be dealt with in any way which gets at the truth'. He did insist on one stipulation, though: 'you may find Blunt referring to an assignment he undertook on behalf of the Palace – a visit to Germany at the end of the war. Please do not pursue this matter. Strictly speaking, it is not relevant to considerations of national security.'[116] The palace duly followed the MI5 advice and allowed Blunt to remain in post.[117]

Wright's account is not the most reliable, but other evidence corroborates that the queen did know. Prime Minister Edward Heath offered the queen a detailed report about Blunt's spying in the early 1970s.[118] It was the first time the government had formally told her, although successive prime ministers and Cabinet secretaries professed not to know how much Adeane had informally passed on back in 1964. Such conversations were sacrosanct.[119] Heath was surprised to learn that she had already been told in general terms a decade earlier.[120]

Historians will likely never know her reaction. Perhaps a remark made by her mother could act as a guide. When talking about Burgess and Maclean, the queen mother once declared, in a comment relayed back to Blunt: 'The one person I cannot stand is a traitor.'[121]

Importantly, Queen Elizabeth knew far more about the case than the prime minister of the time, Alec Douglas-Home. Indeed, even Michael Adeane knew more about it than the prime minister.[122] Douglas-Home was not told about Blunt's activities, in his words, 'before the knowledge was public property' in November 1979. This was surprising given the seriousness of the matter and involvement of the queen, but Douglas-Home insisted he would have remembered being told – even only orally.[123]

Perhaps it was precisely because it affected the queen that Douglas-Home was frozen out. Hollis apparently advised against briefing him. The aristocratic prime minister got on well with the queen. When he visited Balmoral, he did so as a friend as much as a prime minister. Hollis feared that Douglas-Home might refuse to compromise the queen by allowing Blunt to stay in the role. Doing so would have fatally undermined Blunt's co-operation.[124]

This seems unlikely. The secret was bound to come out at some point, embarrassing both Douglas-Home and the queen. When later digging into the affair, Margaret Thatcher's government deemed it far more likely that 'in order to avoid the risk of compromising Blunt's co-operation, knowledge of his confession should be strictly confined to those who really needed to know, and that did not include Ministers'. Failure to tell Douglas-Home was more misjudgement or negligence rather than conspiracy.[125]

Either way, the secret created a constitutional quandary. If the queen did know – and the prime minister did not – then it is striking that she did not raise the issue with him during their weekly audience. The unmasking of a Soviet spy was, after all, an extraordinary development.[126] Perhaps she was warned against it. The queen would have been unable to conduct her constitutional duties of advising and warning – this time for the unusual reason of knowing more secret information than a prime minister.

If Blunt now thought he could quietly stick to his scholarly day job and put his murky past behind him, he was sorely mistaken. The immunity deal did not spell the end of his association with intelligence – even as he continued his career at the palace.

From 1964, he agreed to collaborate with MI5. He provided information about Russian intelligence activities and his association with Burgess, Maclean and Philby. On top of this, and more intriguingly, he 'collaborated with the Security Service in counterespionage operations, some of which are continuing'.[127]

It is not clear how extensive these operations were. Hypothetically, they could have been rather active and involved him passing information, carefully curated by MI5, back to the Russians in order to mislead them. MI5 certainly wanted Russian intelligence to be 'left in uncertainty about the extent of his disclosures to us'.[128]

More likely, Blunt provided information to the British security services. MI5 acknowledged that, for years after his confession, he 'provided information about his own activity in the service of the Russians during wartime, when he passed a great deal of material to them, and about others whom he knew or believed to have worked for the KGB or GRU before or during the war'.[129] He also provided information about his role as a talent spotter in the 1930s. MI5 used Blunt's information to establish a 'research team' to investigate the alleged ring of moles inside British intelligence. He helped it to achieve 'considerable success' in uncovering both individuals and activities, including the removal of a senior Admiralty scientist from a sensitive post.[130]

An MI5 'special unit' also spent six years investigating communist involvement in student politics between 1929 and 1945, covering not just Cambridge University, but also Oxford, London, Bristol, Leeds, Liverpool, Southampton, Sheffield and others. Blunt would have been a key source, and the investigation ultimately examined some eight thousand cases.[131] One thing is certain: Blunt's confession was not a one-off. He continued to discreetly collaborate with MI5 for a decade – all while working for the queen.

At the same time, MI5 did not trust him. Intelligence officers assumed he was still holding information back: 'he may still be protecting friends'. Over a decade after his confession, they wondered whether he still had some loyalty to the Russians or was even under a degree of Russian control – but after twenty years of investigation, they could not prove it.[132]

MI5 therefore put Blunt under surveillance. Every home secretary, from 1964 onwards, signed 'interception warrants on Blunt'.[133] They clearly watched him – and listened to him – closely, wondering whether he was still double crossing them. This raises the intriguing possibility that his communications with the royal household were tapped as part of the broader surveillance operation.

All the while, Elizabeth continued to see her royal art historian at various official events, including at the opening of the new Courtauld galleries in 1968. In general, though, he avoided the queen in daily court life. When he had to go to the palace, for example when offering tours to distinguished guests from the art world, he would creep around desperately trying to avoid bumping into her.[134] On another occasion, he stood silently next to Prince Philip as the duke and Hugh Casson, the architect and designer, picked out paintings for the guest wing at Windsor Castle. Blunt, disdainful of their modernist choices, said nothing.[135] He did, however, maintain a good relationship with the queen mother. She thoroughly appreciated her own tour of the Courtauld galleries, and the two very occasionally shared a box at the opera.[136] It is highly unlikely she knew about his treachery.

Queen Elizabeth personally congratulated him on his eventual retirement in 1972. Finally, Blunt would leave the royal household and the government could draw a line under his complex and sensitive career. Unfortunately, the retirement degenerated into classic Whitehall farce. Martin Charteris remembers how he nearly fell off his chair when the lord chancellor, who did not know about Blunt's treachery, offered Blunt the honorary post of adviser on the queen's pictures, thereby continuing his association with the palace for a further six years.[137]

Blunt had few qualms about remaining in the royal household. He had no idea that MI5 had told Adeane back in 1964 and did not accept any suggestion that he should have resigned. 'I was there to do a job, and I still thought it was important to do and I was still doing it. I don't see why a confession in 1964 made any difference.'[138]

By mid-1977, a super-sleuth was on his trail. This was Peter Hennessy, Whitehall correspondent for *The Times*, adored but also feared by civil servants. He had just written a KGB 'fourth man' story about Donald Beves, a don at King's College Cambridge and other suspected communist trainers at the university in the 1930s. In September, over a quiet dinner at Odin's restaurant, he confided in Callaghan's senior policy adviser, Bernard Donoughue, that he had other suspects: 'One possible line had led to Sir Anthony Blunt, keeper of the Queen's pictures. Another pointed towards a former head of MI5.' Donoughue concluded that there was 'a time bomb in there somewhere', adding 'as usual a lot of public school homosexuality… All very messy.'[139]

But for some strange reason his editor, William Rees-Mogg, was trying to 'put him off the story'.[140] Donoughue began watching the situation for Downing Street. Two months later, he discovered that Hennessy's source for the story about Donald Beves was none other than Dick White, former head of MI6. He concluded that 'this was clearly a delicate plant, to mislead Peter' and keep him away from a bigger story. The blameless Beves had been dead for years and so was ideal distraction material. The security agencies were worried about something with a royal aspect emerging. Donoughue noted in his diary: 'Blunt?'[141]

Still under surveillance,[142] Blunt resigned his final honorary consultancy in November 1978, after learning that his identity was about to be revealed. He was overseeing a Holbein exhibition when, nervous and depressed, he asked to see an MI5 officer. They talked about Blunt's 'residual connection' to the palace; a connection that was severed almost immediately afterwards.[143] Remarkably, Blunt's association with the palace lasted until the very end.

The scandal started to emerge at the start of 1979 when it became clear that a revelatory book would indicate that the so-called fourth man was Anthony Blunt. Prime Minister James Callaghan was troubled by the developments, even though he knew the story well and, as home secretary, had signed warrants for the intelligence services to intercept Blunt's communications long after his confession.[144] As prime minister, he now asked why Blunt should retain his knighthood, why the problem was not dealt with earlier, and why it took the publication of a history book to prompt government disclosure.[145]

When the secret was about to be spilled, the Cabinet secretary, Robert Armstrong, warned him that he 'would have to consider very carefully how he had acquiesced in the continuing secrecy'. Armstrong helpfully suggested that Callaghan might simply state that he did not want to embarrass the queen. This provided Callaghan, and others, with a pre-made get out of jail free card.[146] Sometimes the royals – and the secrecy surrounding them – provided a useful excuse for governmental obfuscation.[147]

With Blunt's identity about to be revealed, Callaghan needed a line to take on Blunt's palace connection. John Hunt, Armstrong's predecessor, had come up with the following: the prime minister was not responsible for appointments in the royal household; 'by 1964 he had his appointment for nearly 20 years during which time he had no access to classified information'; and 'although he had confessed he had been given immunity from prosecution'. Blunt was also, the government thought it prescient to point out, 'undoubtedly a most distinguished art historian'.[148] Hunt followed up with a detailed briefing on the royal dimension to the scandal, much of which remains classified.[149]

This was a fair defence. However, the relationship was more complex than the government wanted to admit. There are rumours that while working for the royal family, Blunt travelled to Beirut to tip off Kim Philby about his impending interrogation in the early 1960s. Blunt may well have had access to the inside story through his friendships with Dick White and Victor Rothschild, and he lied about supposedly visiting Lebanon in search of the frog orchid – a flower that did not grow there. The ambassador there was an old friend and, upon finding out about Blunt's guilt, was furious at the thought that Blunt might have used him as an excuse to make two trips to see Philby.[150]

Even if those rumours are false, documents show that he continued to collaborate in counter-espionage operations and remained under MI5 surveillance: a reality far removed from the anodyne government line that Blunt had no association with the secret world while a member of the royal household.

By the time the scandal finally broke in November 1979, Margaret Thatcher had just replaced James Callaghan in Downing Street. With the heady mix of royals, security and spies, Robert Armstrong knew this was a 'minefield'. He warned Thatcher's team that 'if you are not thoroughly familiar with it, it is both easy and dangerous inadvertently to put a foot wrong'.[151]

So delicate was the question of the queen that successive private secretaries had to give their express permission for Thatcher to reveal publicly that Adeane 'had been kept fully in the picture throughout the episode'.[152] There was no question of revealing whether he had told the queen.

We are unlikely ever to know the full truth about Blunt and the royals. In November 1979, as the Blunt bombshell burst in public, Thatcher privately gave Armstrong the mission of exploring the affair on her behalf and finding out just what deals had actually been struck down the decades. First, he carefully read all the top-secret material and then contacted the key participants. He later recalled: 'I wrote to Michael Adeane, who had been Private Secretary to the Queen, and to Sir Charles Cunningham, who had been Permanent Secretary at the Home Office. Cunningham and Adeane both had totally different recollections from the account that was in our official files.'[153]

Meanwhile, others scrambled over lurid stories emerging in the press. The *Sunday Times* reported a garbled story that accused Jock Colville of having lunch with John Cairncross while the former was Princess Elizabeth's private secretary. Colville panicked and quickly telephoned the prime minister's office to set the record straight. They had actually lunched in 1939 – long before Cairncross was a Soviet spy and long before Colville worked at the palace.[154] Anything mixing the queen and Soviet espionage, however wrongly or tangentially, was dynamite.

Thatcher barely commented on the palace dimension, merely pointing out that Blunt's knighthood, conferred in 1956, was 'the queen's personal gift' and that he forfeited it not on the government's recommendation, but that of the palace.[155] Blunt, trying to save face, claimed that when he found out the queen was going to strip him of his knighthood, he immediately wrote 'to the proper authority offering to resign it, but presumably the letter did not arrive before the announcement was made'.[156] Shortly afterwards, friends asked the queen mother for her opinion. 'Lovely day, isn't it,' she replied, remaining smiling and inscrutable.[157] It was not for nothing that Tommy Lascelles dubbed her 'the imperial ostrich'.[158]

Blunt divided opinion among the establishment. In some ways this mirrored his own schizophrenia as both a professional snob and long-time secret servant of the Soviet Union. He offered a self-serving and dishonest account at a press conference stage managed by *The Times*, where he was served with white wine and smoked trout.[159] Roy Strong, director of the Victoria & Albert Museum and intimate of the royal family, challenged William Rees-Mogg, the paper's editor, about this – who then rather sheepishly conceded that Blunt was indeed vile. In Strong's opinion, Blunt had emerged into the spotlight with 'suave condescending deviousness', expressing not a word of regret for the embarrassment he had caused the queen; everything was 'blurred by deceit and deviousness'.[160]

Thereafter, as Strong probed his friends among the history of art world, he was 'amazed by how many people seem to have known about it'. While many shared his 'revulsion' for Blunt, this did not extend to the royals.[161] In November 1981, Strong attended a private dinner given by Princess Margaret for about twenty people at Kensington Palace, which he noted was now rather 'grubby and run down'. The princess was 'straight onto the whisky and cigarettes'. Strong did not enjoy himself and 'escaped' early, noting that 'it was awful to hear HRH droning on about how wonderful Anthony Blunt was'.[162]

ELIZABETH WAS A young queen at the height of the Cold War. She soon found herself dragged into international intrigue and spy scandals. Through it all, she was, as Harold Macmillan put it, 'incredibly well informed'.[163] She knew all about Profumo and Blunt. She once abruptly shut down the Labour politician Richard Crossman when he tried to ask her about Kim Philby.[164]

She also knew about some of the most sensitive aspects of international politics. Macmillan briefed her, for example, on the CIA's secret army in Laos.[165] He took full advantage of her total discretion, and found her a great support.[166] He once confessed to the queen that he had fallen asleep as the West German chancellor, Konrad Adenauer, delivered a post-lunch speech about how to counter communism.[167] Macmillan was enthusiastic about royalty and a loyal defender of the establishment, but perhaps the royals did not enjoy his company as much as they pretended. Behind his back they enjoyed calling him 'The Horse' and were inclined to laugh at him. In fact, they rather preferred his less stuffy Labour opponent.[168]

Harold Wilson, who came to power in 1964, also treated the queen as a confidante. He attached great importance to his weekly audiences, which became longer and longer. One lasted for two hours; another finished with an invitation to stay for drinks. He never divulged what was said in those meetings, but returned to Number 10 in a euphoric mood and sometimes seemed to have modified his opinions as a consequence of talking to the queen.[169]

The feelings were reciprocated and Wilson was probably the queen's all-time favourite prime minister. Shortly before, the Americans had expressed worries about Wilson's loyalty amid swirling rumours about his relations with Soviet intelligence. Did his Conservative predecessors brief the queen about these worries? The CIA had indeed asked Macmillan directly about Wilson, but he considered this quite 'absurd', adding, 'I don't suppose in the history of this country – at least in modern history – a P.M. has had such an extraordinary question asked by an ally about the Leader of the Opposition'.[170] MI5 had taken an interest in him for some time because of his frequent trips to Russia while in opposition during the 1950s. Like many other politicians, the KGB had assigned him a codename, 'Olding', but they did not recruit him.[171]

For all the intrigue, espionage and discreet diplomacy of the Cold War, Britain was also facing a more existential threat, the possibility of 'hot war'. Having already witnessed one major conflict, this was a subject about which the queen cared deeply. All the royal family found themselves, for the second time in a generation, on notice for panic evacuation and scarily close to the nuclear button.

17

NUCLEAR SECRETS

*'Commanders are to carry out any instruction
received from the royal household.'*

Plan Synchronise, 1968[1]

A T THE START of August 1945, days before the momentous bombings of Hiroshima and Nagasaki, President Truman stopped off in Plymouth Sound on his way back from talks in Germany to meet King George VI. Accompanied by his new secretary of state, James Byrnes, the president met George for lunch in the harbour. George's private secretary, Tommy Lascelles, who recorded the meeting in his diary, was distinctly unimpressed by Byrnes: 'clever as a wagonload of monkeys', he recalled, 'a tremendous chatterbox who rarely paused for breath'. George was supported at the meeting by Edward Halifax, Britain's ambassador in Washington.

The king, Lascelles and Halifax were all totally stunned when Byrnes began wittering on – within earshot of the waiters – about the impending bombing of Japan. Byrnes made them 'gasp by talking freely about the "T.A.", or heavy water, atomic bombs', with Lascelles adding, 'as this is so secret a matter in this country only about six people have ever heard of it'. Byrnes was being 'somewhat indiscreet, even for an American'. George, who already knew about the impending attack, was equally mortified. He intervened politely yet decisively: 'I think, Mr Byrnes, that we should discuss this interesting subject over our coffee.'[2]

Four days later, the US, with British consent, detonated the first atomic bomb over Hiroshima. Around eighty thousand people died instantly. Lascelles was happy that the war was over but on the matter of the atomic bomb he mused, 'I would rather it have never been invented at all.'[3]

The gloomy reflections of Lascelles beg a rather bigger question: whether the king should have been consulted. America had taken the lead and paid for most of the costs of developing the bomb – indeed, Byrnes revealed to the king an 'astronomical figure' – but 'Tube Alloys' was nevertheless an Allied project.[4] Key parts of the bomb, especially the problematic trigger mechanism, had been the work of British scientists at Los Alamos, and also a German communist scientist, Klaus Fuchs, provided by the British.[5]

Not everyone was keen on immediate use; Halifax wanted an ultimatum to Japan first. Churchill was clearly in favour, but it was to Attlee, his successor, to whom Truman wrote informing him that America was about to use the bombs. Attlee deliberated for only a few minutes before replying that he was happy for Truman to take this momentous decision. It is highly unlikely that the king was consulted.[6] However, Attlee's Cabinet encouraged George to reference the future implications of atomic weapons in his public speeches to mark the end of the war, since the public were presently talking 'of little else'.[7]

Where were the royal family as the first bomb detonated over Hiroshima? Princess Elizabeth, aged just nineteen, was enjoying herself at Ascot. She watched the celebrated jockey Gordon Richards win five races, including carrying the royal colours to success. Over lunch at nearby Windsor, her father received the news of a different sort of victory.[8] The war would soon be over. Lord Louis Mountbatten was another royal who had known about atomic bombs in advance. As supreme allied commander in South East Asia, he had endured the frustrating experience of watching all his subordinates work on plans for a vast amphibious invasion of

Malaya later in 1945, 'Plan Zipper'; an operation he secretly knew would never take place.[9]

It was not long before Elizabeth was entrusted with the nuclear secret herself. Prime Minister Winston Churchill, returning to office in late 1951, discussed Britain's nuclear ambitions with the new queen, still only in her twenties, at a very early stage of her reign. These ambitions were soon fulfilled.

Churchill happened to be at Balmoral in early October 1952 when Britain tested its first atomic bomb off the coast of north-western Australia. A deep flash lit the antipodean sky, followed by an unusual double bang and a blast of wind. Eight and a half thousand miles away in Scotland, Churchill and the queen were asleep when the bomb exploded. Not wanting to wake the prime minister at four in the morning, his staff in Number 10 waited until breakfast to inform him. The old man proudly, if patronizingly, briefed the queen shortly afterwards.[10]

Journalists immediately speculated about whether the unusual-shaped cloud – larger and flatter than the familiar mushroom – indicated a new technique or even an entirely new, more devastating, weapon. The government had planned the tests with the utmost secrecy. Military officials were desperate to prevent the Soviets from sabotaging the operation or from gaining advance knowledge of the timing which would have allowed them to monitor the site and gather intelligence on Britain's closely guarded capabilities. This crucial counter-intelligence dimension provided Whitehall's moribund deception specialists, largely dismissed as a hangover from the war, with an excellent opportunity to revive their unique skills for peacetime.[11]

The deception specialists, a bunch of oddballs, lateral thinkers and empire builders, had already linked nuclear deterrence to deception. Their early ideas involved exaggerating both Britain's nuclear capabilities and its willingness to strike the Soviets if war broke out. In April 1951, eighteen months before the atomic tests took place, they turned their attention to misleading the Soviets about the nature, timing and location of the activity – and even whether the British were responsible at all.[12]

After a great deal of creative scheming, the most sensible plan involved planting false information to convince Soviet intelligence that a technical fault had delayed the test. This included fake travel plans for the key individuals expected to be present and using secret channels inside Europe to ensure disinformation got back to Moscow. If the Soviets could be convinced that the test would take place at a later date, they would be surprised when the bomb did go off, thus leaving them unable to reach the site quickly enough to gather useful intelligence or radioactive samples. The top-secret plan was named Operation TIGRESS.

In spring 1952, months before the tests, Britain's leading deception planner, John Drew, suggested a royal connection to bolster the plan's credibility. Specifically, he wondered whether Prince Philip might act as a human decoy to deceive the Soviets about the timing. Philip, still finding his feet as the queen's husband and itching for a role in his own right, was famously interested in science and technology. He had already visited a series of factories and laboratories as part of his public duties, including, just a few weeks earlier, the atomic research station at Harwell in Oxfordshire.[13] Perhaps it was this visit that planted the idea in Drew's head.

Bringing Philip into a top-secret deception operation, which ultimately involved not only deceiving the Soviets but also the British press, was a remarkable suggestion. It was not, however, unprecedented. The plan afforded Philip a similar role to that played by his father-in-law, King George VI, in the run-up to D-Day in 1944 when, as we have seen, the palace secretly co-ordinated his movements with MI5 so as to mislead the Germans about the location of the invasion. This time Britain was not at war; and Philip was young and inexperienced. He did not even have access to confidential state documents let alone nuclear secrets.

Drew, who had been involved in the D-Day deception, envisaged Philip's role playing out in two acts. First, he would visit the ships assigned to transport the test components to Australia, HMS *Plym* and HMS *Campania*, before they set sail. It was to be HMS *Plym*'s last ever voyage: in order to simulate the effects of a nuclear weapon being smuggled into a British harbour, the bomb was to be detonated on board, instantly obliterating the ill-fated ship. Philip visiting both the *Plym* and the *Campania*, which was to be the command ship, would provide the watching Soviets with a crucial link between the prince and the atomic tests.

This would lay the foundation for the second part of Drew's plan: Philip would cancel his engagements – giving no reason – for three weeks from 10 November. The Soviets would assume that he was attending the atomic tests in Australia in the latter part of the month, which were actually planned for early October.[14] Albeit a simplified version, the similarities to King George VI's D-Day deception role are striking.

Involving Philip was risky. The deception would become obvious to the Soviets immediately after a successful test, quickly implicating Philip himself. Drew knew that this would have been controversial: dragging the royal family into the murky world of intelligence and deception during peacetime would have undermined their supposed global brand of honesty, integrity and a reputation for remaining above politics. He therefore suggested that Philip take a three-week unadvertised holiday anyway. This, he hoped, would prevent critics from accusing the prince of manipulation and deceit.[15]

It is unclear whether the government approved Drew's suggestion. Churchill certainly had qualms about peacetime deception, wondering how far 'this weapon should actually be used in time of peace – at any rate for peacetime purposes'. The ageing prime minister forgot that he had approved the operation in the first place – and then expressed ambivalence upon being reminded.[16] Philip's involvement might well have been too much.

Indeed, there is no evidence that Philip visited either ship. There was little time before they set sail for Australia, and Philip spent much of it in Scotland. He did, however, lunch with the prime minister of

Australia, Robert Menzies, during a visit to London in late May when the latter received a detailed briefing on the deception.[17] Neither is there evidence that he took an unadvertised holiday in November, although he did begin flying lessons around this time. On 7 November he inspected other classified weaponry at Woolwich Arsenal.[18]

With or without Philip, Operation TIGRESS went through various iterations before being executed in stages from the summer of 1952. As well as creating fake travel plans, officials planted misleading stories in the domestic and international press. The *Sunday Express* published a dramatic front-page article in August which conveyed the deception planners' line perfectly. They forwarded an advance copy to Downing Street the day before publication, and Drew approvingly described it as 'an inextricable mixture of the true and the doubtful the idea being that the true facts – all of which are harmless – should give weight in the minds of the other side to the points we are trying to put across to them'. Churchill remained unenthusiastic about manipulating the British press in peacetime, but it was too late.[19]

The *Sunday Express* article was a coup for the deception planners. According to the historian who unearthed the TIGRESS documents, Huw Dylan, the broader operation was 'skilfully coordinated' and 'skilfully executed'. Drew and his colleagues celebrated some success in misleading the Soviets, although their impact is difficult to judge. Rather damningly, Stalin was certainly far better briefed about the British bomb than most British ministers.[20]

WEEKS LATER, AT an isolated atoll surrounded by the vast Pacific Ocean, the Americans unveiled their far more destructive hydrogen bomb. A thousand times more powerful than the British attempt, it unequivocally demonstrated, in a single explosion, British inferiority. The ferocity of the bomb astounded Churchill, who learnt that a quarter of Britain's population would perish if a dozen ten-megaton hydrogen bombs hit the country. Eighteen months later, in

May 1954, he and his senior ministerial colleagues agreed to pursue their own hydrogen bomb. Without one, the country would be left behind on the world stage.[21]

The following month, he informed the queen. She had recently returned from the longest royal tour in history, taking in the West Indies, Australia, Asia and Africa. When Churchill called on the palace after her protracted absence, the queen perhaps expected to receive – at long last – his resignation. Approaching eighty years of age, the ailing prime minister had been dragging out the issue since his stroke a year earlier. Elizabeth was no stranger to the petty soap opera playing out between Churchill and his foreign secretary, Anthony Eden, who was impatiently waiting in the wings for the old man to retire. On one occasion, she sent Eden into a dramatic spin after privately declaring that the longer it dragged on the more likely she was to ask someone other than Eden to form a government after Churchill's demise. On another occasion, Buckingham Palace had to intervene in a dispute between Eden and Churchill about which of them should receive the distinguished Order of the Garter, the highest honour bestowed by the sovereign. Only one could have it, but both men had been individually offered it, turned it down, and then changed their minds.[22]

Eden refused to meet the queen on her return. He and his wife, Clarissa, had worked themselves up into a terrible state after some confusion about whether or not he should be part of the delegation to welcome her home. Throwing a customary tantrum, Eden now refused on the grounds that Elizabeth had somehow 'treated him very strangely'. 'Anyhow', he spluttered, he 'did not like the Royal Family'. Taken aback, his long-suffering advisers wondered whether Eden, narcissistic and neurotic in equal measure, was jealous of the queen. They emphasized – in vain – the importance of keeping good relations with Buckingham Palace.[23]

Arriving back in Britain, instead of a resignation, Elizabeth faced the realities of the Cold War and found Churchill – if not Eden – on spirited form. The Cabinet met in early July to listen to a

Churchillian *tour de force* in favour of the new bomb, but his cavalier approach to such an important issue apparently led to a mass walk-out of ministers.[24] Glossing over the acrimony, he told Elizabeth shortly afterwards that the Cabinet were 'considering whether it would be right and advantageous for this country to produce the hydrogen bomb, and have meanwhile agreed to the continuation of the preparatory work which has been going on for the last few months… There is very little doubt in my mind,' Churchill defiantly added, 'what the outcome will be.'[25]

He ambitiously told Elizabeth that a bomb would be ready in two years.[26] The inexperienced monarch could hardly object to Churchill's newfound obsession, even if she wanted to, and she duly expressed her gratitude to the prime minister. A few months later, Churchill raised the subject again, this time during an audience at the palace. With royal approval, he left her a top-secret document about nuclear warfare and, ever fretting about protocol and standards, sent her another version 'on better paper' after returning to Downing Street.[27]

Churchill emphasized the importance of nuclear deterrence as Britain's 'only hope' against a potential Soviet attack and the unprecedented devastation it would cause. Drawing on the latest intelligence, just before Christmas 1954, he warned Elizabeth that the Soviets were 'certainly catching up' with the Americans, 'both in nuclear weapons and their delivery, with every month that passes'. He told her that it was a shame the west had not come to terms with Russia immediately after the war when America still enjoyed over-whelming nuclear dominance. He ended on a positive note: Russia would not try to achieve world domination until it had at least gained nuclear parity with the west. Therefore, 'the next two or three years may well be the safest the world will see for a long time'.[28]

On 1 March 1955, Churchill devoted his last parliamentary speech to progress on Britain's first hydrogen bomb, which was tested two years later. Meanwhile, at just twenty-eight years old, the queen endured lessons on nuclear strategy at a time when these new and devastating weapons could annihilate her realm in a way her forebears could have scarcely imagined. Sitting alone in the palace, she surely felt the gravity of the situation weighing on her shoulders.

As for Philip, he continued to take an interest in nuclear weapons. In the same year as Churchill publicly announced pursuit of the hydrogen bomb, Philip sought permission to fly over Aldermaston, the headquarters of the United Kingdom's Atomic Weapons Research Establishment in Berkshire. Showing his knowledge of what went on inside – if not the scientific details involved – he jokingly worried about getting a 'hot seat' as he flew over.[29]

In 1959, just months after Britain had finished successfully testing the new H-bomb in the Indian Ocean, Philip visited the highly radioactive site for himself. Showing little appreciation of the dangerous residual effects, he took an unpublicized helicopter ride over Christmas Island to see 'ground zero'.[30] His personal views on nuclear weapons are unclear but, three decades later, he was reported to have said that 'nuclear weapons are not going to go off by themselves. Some idiot has to order it to happen.' Even the biggest idiots, he assumed, must know the dangers.[31]

Philip's uncle, Lord Mountbatten, was particularly concerned about nuclear weapons. Serving as first sea lord during the late 1950s, he enjoyed remarkable insights into western plans for Armageddon and was disturbed by what he saw – and fed much of this disquiet back to Buckingham Palace. Around the same time as Philip's nuclear tourism, he was visiting Washington and went to the US Navy's Atomic Top-Secret Room to meet Admiral Rickover, who was head of their nuclear programme. Rickover's reputation ran before him and Mountbatten noted that he was indeed a brilliant and 'cantankerous genius'. 'He loves being rude to people and enjoys it even more being answered back.'[32]

Rickover warned Mountbatten that the British nuclear programme was falling behind because it did not have a tough man at the top. 'What you want to run a show like this is a real son of a bitch!' Mountbatten smiled and conceded that this was where the Americans had the edge over the British: 'you have the only real son of a bitch in the business!'

Rickover loved the repartee and expanded Mountbatten's tour, to make sure he saw all of America's latest secrets, adding, 'You are the first Britisher to be allowed to see this!'[33]

By August 1959, Mountbatten had been promoted to be chief of the defence staff and this, together with his impeccable royal credentials, opened all of America's nuclear secrets. Rather like Edward inspecting France's Maginot Line during the Phoney War, nothing was held back. After briefly visiting 'Aunt Olga', the sister of Tsar Nicholas II, who now lived in a small bungalow near Toronto, he met the chief of Strategic Air Command; a man who 'can never be more than ten seconds away from a telephone'. He inspected British crews being trained on the Thor nuclear missile soon to be based in Britain. He then went on to examine vast and newly constructed Titan missile silos. The size of the American nuclear arsenals was a 'staggering shock' to him and he did not like it. 'The whole thing has a gruesome and horrific effect, which makes one really fear for the sanity of mankind.' It is highly likely that he passed this all back to Elizabeth and Philip. Either way, his worries about nuclear safety were soon to be confirmed.[34]

LIKE HIS PREDECESSORS, Prime Minister Harold Macmillan happily shared top-secret material with Queen Elizabeth. Aside from his romantic reverence for the monarchy, he valued her as a perennially discreet confidante. It was lonely as prime minister, and he very much looked forward to his weekly audience on Tuesday afternoons. He recognized the queen's 'absolute right to know' and was deeply impressed by her ability to absorb reams of information and to express her views, as is customary, in the form of polite questions. He insisted on strengthening royal prerogative, encouraging her to exercise her constitutional duties of advising and warning. In return, she sent him a surprisingly large number of handwritten letters.[35]

By this time, Britain, the US and the Soviets possessed devastating quantities of nuclear weapons. France had just joined the nuclear club, detonating a bomb four times the size of that dropped on Hiroshima in the Algerian desert in 1960. Macmillan was worried. He explained to the queen how more nuclear testing risked undermining the west's moral standing. He therefore proposed to her that a 'secret reconnaissance' take place of the facilities at Christmas Island, recently visited by Prince Philip, to determine whether the benefits of any further tests 'outweighed the moral loss to the West'.[36] Britain did continue to test nuclear weapons, although not in the Pacific, but, now equipped with warheads, the bigger issue was how to deliver them to their intended Russian targets if war broke out.

In spring 1960, Macmillan cancelled the leading missile programme that Britain had been quietly developing over the last few years. Blue Streak, as it was known, was beset with technical problems, including, rather seriously, taking far too long to fire. He turned to American technology instead, specifically the Skybolt missile still under development. Both systems were rather like modern-day cruise missiles, but designed to be launched from aircraft when they were about five hundred miles from their target. Using Skybolt missiles, he explained to Elizabeth, would allow Britain to use its own warheads and, as was always a priority, maintain its own independent nuclear weapon. A few days later, the queen read in the Cabinet minutes that there was 'no absolute certainty' the Skybolt system would even work.[37]

The Cuban Missile Crisis made transatlantic negotiations about deterrence and delivery systems much more immediate. Suddenly the two superpowers came devastatingly close to nuclear conflict. In the middle of October 1962, US intelligence discovered Soviet attempts to place offensive nuclear missiles in Cuba, only ninety miles from the American mainland. Just over a week later, on Monday 22 October, President Kennedy ordered a so-called quarantine, preventing further shipments reaching the island, and told Khrushchev that the US would not allow offensive missiles on Cuba. Macmillan described it as 'the first day of the World Crisis!'[38]

At one o'clock the following morning, Macmillan telephoned the American ambassador to offer British support for a decision that Kennedy had already taken. The ambassador was David Bruce, an intelligence officer turned diplomat who had overseen special operations in western Europe during the war and was an old friend of the royal family, having known the queen since she was a girl.[39] He was a man who had danced the twist with the queen mother and confessed to 'a fancy' for her daughter, Queen Elizabeth. 'She blends openness with dignity,' he confided to his diary, 'has a dazzling complexion, and cordial, sympathetic, unaffected manners.' He claimed that foreign ambassadors 'considered her the best briefed person in the United Kingdom'.[40]

By lunchtime that day, Bruce was enjoying lunch at Buckingham Palace. He tucked into 'the usual excellent palace food' accompanied by French wine and sat next to Elizabeth herself. They discussed the latest developments, and, according to Bruce, the queen 'displayed a lively interest in the Cuban imbroglio'.[41] If she had not yet seen photographs of the missile sites taken by American intelligence, and shared by Macmillan, then she would have seen them in the press a couple of days later after Macmillan insisted they be published to satisfy a sceptical public.

Panic about war was now widespread. On his way back to the US embassy at Grosvenor Square, David Bruce had to dodge anti-American protestors, and, by the evening, hundreds of policemen were guarding the building. The chief of the Metropolitan Police even appeared in person, having been called away from dinner at Claridge's. 'Had the demonstrators succeeded in breaking in,' Bruce noted, 'we might have had a nasty time.'[42]

The following day, Wednesday 24 October, Khrushchev responded that Kennedy's quarantine was an act of aggression and insisted that Soviet ships heading for Cuba would proceed. The best western source on the progress of these missile delivery ships was GCHQ monitoring sites in Britain. As the weekend approached, US intelligence reported that the missile sites were nearing operational readiness.[43]

Macmillan and his patrician foreign secretary, Alec Douglas-Home, met the queen frequently during the crisis. According to her private secretary, Michael Adeane, Elizabeth was 'fully and continuously informed of what was going on'.[44] They shared the latest developments, including the contents of Macmillan's late-night telephone calls with Kennedy and, most probably, any incoming US intelligence.

On Sunday 28 October, as the world watched with bated breath, Khrushchev publicly stated that the Soviet missiles would be dismantled and removed from Cuba. The crisis was over. Adeane told Macmillan after the dust had settled that Elizabeth knew 'very well what a heavy strain both you, the foreign secretary and your staff were working under during these days'. She wanted him to know 'just how much she appreciates the trouble which was taken in your office and the Foreign Office to see that she was kept up to date with rapidly changing news'.[45]

Macmillan kept the queen fully informed throughout the crisis, but she quite rightly had no active role beyond this. Even Macmillan had little input, acting more as a confidant to Kennedy, listening attentively and offering affirmations as the president unburdened himself. Perhaps the queen played a similar role for Macmillan.

Oddly, Philip's eyes were trained further north and closer to home on Scotland. The Cuban Missile Crisis had overshadowed a rather bizarre expedition, led by Conservative MP David James, to find the Loch Ness Monster. After uncovering what he called 'somewhat striking phenomena' on 22 October, the day Kennedy made his dramatic announcement, James discussed his plans with Philip. The prince was well known for his interest in the paranormal, especially flying saucers, and the Balmoral estate was not too far from the loch.[46]

Even Elizabeth maintained a childlike fascination with the mystery – although she stopped short of allowing the monster to be named after her, without irrefutable evidence of its existence. Her private secretary was worried that it might turn out to be a hoax.[47]

Philip encouragingly advised James to pass his dossier of findings on to Solly Zuckerman, the government's chief scientific adviser and a close friend of Mountbatten. In turn, Zuckerman declared that the question of the monster's existence was still open, but the navy blocked his suggestions for further investigation using expensive sonar equipment.[48]

Shortly afterwards, and back in the real world, Britain's impotence in the so-called special relationship was exposed to the queen. Kenneth Strong, head of the Joint Intelligence Bureau that oversaw scientific and atomic matters, had coincidentally been in Washington at the outbreak of the Cuban Missile Crisis. He was well connected in the American capital, having previously served as Eisenhower's intelligence chief at the time of D-Day, and received briefings from his friend John McCone, director of the CIA.[49]

When he returned to London, Strong offered a stark and deeply troubling assessment. The Americans had been prepared to 'go it alone', irrespective of the British position, if the Russians moved against Berlin during the crisis. He believed that the Pentagon was prepared to 'escalate into the nuclear' and that the US planned to launch a pre-emptive strike against Soviet missiles based on what he thought was an overly optimistic assumption that their intelligence had accurately pinpointed the location of each one. In short, Strong warned that the US had been prepared to launch a third world war without formally consulting Britain. Macmillan was horrified; he immediately sent a copy of Strong's report to the queen.[50]

That said, Kennedy did appreciate British support during the crisis and, as a token of his gratitude, invited Elizabeth and Philip to stop off in Washington on their way to, or returning home from, their upcoming trip to Australia. Macmillan declined on the grounds that the invitation had come at too short notice.[51]

By the end of the year, attention had returned to the delicate issue of Britain's own nuclear weapons, specifically access to American Skybolt missiles. British policy was thrown into disarray in December, just weeks after the crisis, when the Pentagon cancelled development of the weapon. It was, according to the US secretary of defence, 'an absolute pile of junk' for which the 'British hadn't put in a dime'.[52] A week later, Macmillan flew to Nassau in the Bahamas for highly charged talks with Kennedy about what to do next.

Macmillan kept the palace updated about his progress and, at a particularly difficult point in the negotiations, Elizabeth sent him a special message of encouragement.[53] The key issue was how Britain could gain access to the American submarine-based Polaris missile instead, and maintain the appearance of an independent British nuclear weapon.[54] During the negotiations, Macmillan insisted that 'the Queen had the ultimate power and right to draw back in the case of a dire emergency similar to that in 1940'.[55] He was delighted by her encouragement, and proudly told her of the agreement that was reached. Britain had secured, he wrote, at least $800 million worth of 'research and development on Polaris free of charge as well as a weapon which has passed out of the stage of development into production'. Most importantly, he told her that it was an independent nuclear weapon, thereby 'maintaining Your Majesty's Sovereign rights'.[56] It was indeed perhaps the greatest triumph of Macmillan's government.

NUCLEAR WAR CONTINUED to play on Prince Philip's mind. He concluded that propaganda had 'won' the Cuban missile crisis and, recognizing the apocalyptic dangers of nuclear weapons, he suggested that 'by its very efficiency and destructive ability, the military has virtually put itself out of business'. Propaganda would therefore become 'the main weapon of nations in the settlement of disputes' in the Cold War. Propaganda, according to Philip, was an 'effective' means of achieving political goals 'without the direct risk of starting a nuclear war'. He gave a bizarrely freewheeling lecture on propaganda to the NATO Defense College in Rome in late 1964 – much to the horror of civil servants back home.[57]

Philip enthusiastically called for more propaganda. He acknowledged that propaganda had a 'sinister ring' to it but urged NATO not to condemn the activity just because 'we did not like the way' the Nazis used it. 'After all,' he quipped, Goebbels 'presumably drove in a Mercedes car, but that does not really condemn the motor car.' He emphasized the importance of propaganda during the Second World War, claiming that 'No lie, no terminological inexactitude, no twist of the phrasemaker's talent was missed in the endless attempts to confuse, to mislead or to misrepresent the facts.' But he criticized it as amateurish.[58]

Philip admitted to being the 'sole unaided author' of the speech – and it showed. It was littered with errors; alarmed civil servants huffily scribbled 'not true' in the margins. The lead deception planner in the Ministry of Defence lamented it 'a great pity that such lectures given by H.R.H. are not perused before being delivered'. In a withering critique, he added: 'Not only is a great deal of what was said inaccurate but H.R.H. mixes propaganda with information thereby displaying fundamental ignorance of his subject.'[59] To be fair to Philip, though, he did admit to being rather ignorant and sought to provoke rather than instruct.

Philip offered an unusually broad approach, conflating propaganda with 'war dance', satire and 'brave speeches of the "once more into the breach" variety by gallant leaders before action to rouse the spirits of the less belligerent'. Officials greeted this with horror; his interpretation more akin to critical scholars than government planners. Propaganda could win friends as well as mislead enemies, Philip argued. Oddly, he suggested 'the art of making love, which at any rate in the preliminary stages is the art of persuasion, has reached a very advanced state indeed. The creation of international friendship by deliberate propaganda might be equally effective in achieving the desired result.'[60]

He called for more and better propaganda in places like Yemen, where the British were covertly engaged in a proxy war with Egypt. And he called for more in Indonesia, seemingly unaware of the vast secret effort already under way as part of Britain's role in the confrontation between Indonesia and Malaysia.

Despite the civil servants' derision, he did make some important observations. First, he suggested the 'future propaganda cockpit of the world is going to be in Africa'. This was on the money: British diplomats at that very moment were posting forgeries and creating fake dissident groups across the African continent as part of a growing battle with the Soviets for post-colonial influence. Second, he had a rather modern, almost postmodern, depiction of the purpose of propaganda: 'it does not really matter what is going on inside the Yemen; what matters is what the world thinks is going on inside the Yemen'. Perception of such conflicts were – and remain – everything. Third, and most important, he recognized the battle of ideas as central to the Cold War.[61]

THE BLUNT REALITIES of nuclear confrontation exposed during the Cuban Missile Crisis raised difficult questions about Britain's arrangements for transitioning from peace to war – and what would become of the queen as Soviet missiles sped towards her realm. Macmillan did not instigate a war cabinet during those tense days in October 1962; nor did he instigate any of the carefully planned protocols developed in top secret by meticulous planners. Treating Cuba as a diplomatic crisis, he gambled that the tension would not escalate to warfare and so adopted a more improvised response instead. He got lucky. Had the crisis lasted just another day or so, it would likely have become a transition-to-war matter forcing him down the more structured route of codewords and operation rooms. As it was, the queen and her family stayed put above ground. Contingency plans were not activated.[62]

Relieved at his gamble paying off, and perhaps aware of the risk he had taken, Macmillan ordered a review of war protocols shortly afterwards. Cuba had exposed deep flaws in Britain's ability to respond to a military confrontation in which it was not directly involved. Strategic planners had assumed Berlin would be a flashpoint, but the government needed to be able to respond flexibly to any sudden international emergency that could escalate to military conflict.[63] They dutifully revised the Government War Book, the government's meticulous and top-secret manual outlining what measures to take if the worst happened.

By the spring of 1965, ninety-six copies of the War Book, terrifying and mundanely bureaucratic by equal turns, sat under lock and key in various safes across Whitehall. Planners suddenly realized that they had overlooked the queen: Buckingham Palace did not have a copy. This meant that, while the queen was excellently briefed on Britain's nuclear capabilities, she did not know what would happen if those weapons were ever used. As the historian Peter Hennessy put it, Elizabeth was 'very largely in the dark about an important area of state'. She had little idea of what would become of her smouldering realm in the event of nuclear exchange, and how the government – if it survived – would continue. After a mad dash around Whitehall, officials agreed that the queen must be told.[64]

Telling the queen raised a second problem. Many of the baroque protocols which now needed to be communicated to the palace were hidden behind so many codewords that they were utterly unintelligible to anyone outside of the inner circle. This, of course, was the point. They included MACMORRIS and FLUELLEN to indicate different states of warning; the manning of TURNSTILE, which was the underground government bunker in Wiltshire; and Operation VISITATION, which would whisk the prime minister out of Downing Street if diplomacy failed. Officials decided that Elizabeth clearly belonged in the inner circle and accordingly prepared a guide to help her and Michael Adeane decipher the baffling array of codewords.[65]

Operation VISITATION, the evacuation plan for the core executive, was hair-raising. Realizing that the tunnels under Whitehall now offered only 'limited protection' against massive hydrogen bombs, the scheme was to airlift the prime minister, the foreign secretary and some two-dozen official and security advisers from the vicinity of Downing Street using RAF helicopters. These helicopters would head direct to the TURNSTILE bunker in the old limestone quarry under Box Hill near Corsham in Wiltshire. Rather bravely, the plan was for the prime minister and his inner group to remain in Whitehall for as long as possible to pursue negotiations, leaving London only at the very last minute when Armageddon seemed inevitable.[66]

Macmillan was adamant that in a nuclear crisis 'control should remain in Whitehall for as long as possible'. Nevertheless, in 1962 he allowed an exercise to go ahead that included the transition from Whitehall to the alternate seat of government. The exercise, held at Wilton Park in Buckinghamshire, included a team of senior officials playing the Cabinet who would mimic 'the sort of decisions which would face the Cabinet in reality at a time when war was imminent'. Wilton Park was itself the designated wartime joint headquarters for the commanders-in-chief and UK Land Forces.[67]

Elizabeth did already know her own evacuation plans. Preparations had been under way for as long as she had been queen. Tommy Lascelles, her first private secretary, ensured some continuity with the reign of her father who had been the subject of detailed plans during the Second World War, including what he called a private army, known as the 'Coats Mission'.[68] That said, there seems to have been no comprehensive plan for a similar royal protection force for the queen until after the Cuban Missile Crisis.[69]

Early plans saw the royal family taking refuge in citadels and tunnels beneath central London. Planners, working shortly before the death of George VI, expected to complete 7,000 places in these bunkers by 1957, which would provide 'first-class protected accommodation' not just for the royals, but also the Cabinet and vital operational staff. Tunnel accommodation under Abingdon Street, running from Parliament Square to Millbank, would provide an underground commons chamber for around 187 members of parliament and a lords' chamber for fifty peers. Three parallel tunnels underneath Horse Guards Parade, codenamed PIRATE, would contain a Cabinet room and beds for the prime minister and his colleagues, as well as accommodation for up to a thousand staff. The exact location of the royal tunnel remains a closely guarded secret, but, given the proximity of the other tunnels to their occupants, it would likely not have been far from the palace.[70] In the end, the advent of the H-bomb – and its massive destructive power – meant that the parliamentary tunnels and PIRATE facility were never constructed.[71]

Mysteriously, in the mid-1950s, all the trees were cut down alongside Broad Walk in Kensington Gardens, just behind Kensington Palace. This was visibly dramatic, since the trees were full height and mature, prompting speculation that aircraft could now land to whisk the royal family away. Prince Michael of Kent later confirmed that this was in fact the case.[72] Indeed, the location is one of the few places that an executive aircraft carrying around thirty people might be landed in central London. This probably reflected the shift from atomic to hydrogen weapons, with a blast that no bunker under central London was likely to withstand.[73]

Another option, according to Peter Hennessy, involved Elizabeth escaping on the new royal yacht *Britannia*, which came into service in spring 1953 and boasted impressive communications equipment able to reach anywhere on the globe. It could have sailed off to the safety of international waters or served as a floating bunker around the sea lochs of northwest Scotland. If war came too quickly for her to reach the yacht, she would have found a safe place on *terra firma*, probably at a country house in western Scotland.[74]

By summer 1964, the government issued a new highly classified protocol known as Plan CANDID. During the precautionary stage when war was looking likely, the queen would move from Windsor to London to be with her government. As war became inevitable and central government moved out of London, she would 'probably move to her wartime place of residence', wherever this was, either by rail, road or air. Her family, including the young heir, Prince Charles, would travel under special protection to other undisclosed destinations to prevent the monarchy from being wiped out in one blast.[75] The home secretary would accompany her, enabling Elizabeth to form a privy council alongside Prince Philip and Michael Adeane, so that she could appoint any surviving politicians to ministerial posts.[76]

The details of these plans still remain highly secret, but by the 1960s, a massive 'special duties' force, including an air portable armoured reconnaissance squadron from the Household Cavalry, was designated for this role. It was not dissimilar to the wartime Coats Mission that had been designed to rush the royal family to a chain of hidden country houses if German parachutists had arrived in 1940. By 1968, an entire infantry battalion had been assigned to these 'special duties' with the royal household. A further battalion would move people from Downing Street and the Cabinet Office, while yet another would save Britain's gold reserve and art treasures.[77]

The secret plans stated that the queen would move to her mystery wartime place of residence when the central government moved from London. She would not have waited for the prime minister, who bravely – or suicidally – planned to stay in London until the last possible minute before evacuating to Corsham from Horse Guards Parade. As soon as the signal to man TURNSTILE went out, the queen would leave.

Warning times were uncertain. As tension mounted, these steps had to be taken quickly. If the Soviets launched an attack out of the blue, British intelligence would have been able to provide very little warning, leaving the queen precious time to escape. Radar could provide about an hour and a half of notice if the Soviets used manned bombers to attack, but the newly opened Ballistic Missile Early Warning Centre could only offer a few minutes of chillingly futile warning if the Soviets used missiles.[78] Philip heard this for himself when he visited the warning station at Fylingdales on the North Yorkshire moors in 1965.

Competition and confusion, exacerbated by the excruciatingly high secrecy, hampered plans – pitting the royals against the prime minister. Those planning the protection of the queen urgently requested transport to help spirit her away, and would have been surprised when military planners turned it down. Little did the royals' team know that they had accidentally stumbled upon vehicles designated to the Cabinet Office's own TURNSTILE plans. 'All 60 vehicles are required to carry out a top priority task on behalf of the Cabinet Office.' Access denied: on this occasion the prime minister trumped the queen.[79]

Within a few years the protocol for royal evacuation had changed again. At the end of 1968, the Cabinet Office approved another top-secret plan, this time called SYNCHRONISE, setting out arrangements to protect the royal family in an emergency. The main difference was that this time they would stay together, rather than being separated, and would leave London by air to another undisclosed location.[80]

Wherever the queen was destined to take refuge from the flames, it would not have been *Britannia*. By this time, the royal yacht was earmarked to host limited government functions. Soviet intelligence had been sniffing around the vicinity of the massive underground bunker in Wiltshire and, as the amount of time available to man the sprawlingly cavernous bunker when war approached dwindled, planners decided to disperse the functions of central government across numerous locations instead, one of which was *Britannia*.

The royal yacht would host a highly classified PYTHON group, where survivors would make contact with other groups dotted around what was left of the country supposedly within a week of the attack. The locations – and even total numbers – of these groups were a tightly held secret, only recently revealed. There were four based on land: in Cornwall, Portland off the Dorset coast, Tonfanau Camp, on the mid-Wales coast (before moving to the University of Aberystwyth as quickly as possible after the attack), and Perthshire.[81]

The PYTHON groups would control the military and nuclear forces, conduct foreign affairs, and direct policy relating to air transport and supplies.[82] *Britannia*, or its designated reserve, had to be 'continuously available' as far as possible 'at seven days' notice in normal times and at not more than twenty four hours' notice in time of severe international tension'. About sixty officers and ministers would embark at Loch Torridon or Oban in northwest Soctland.[83]

District commanders based across the country would then be informed if the queen, or any member of the royal family, ended up in their jurisdiction – or whatever was left of it after nuclear exchange. This suggests that the royals could still split up after being evacuated from London. Ominously, Plan SYNCHRONISE closed as follows: 'Commanders are to carry out any instruction received from the royal household.'[84]

THE QUEEN, LIKE her father, was one of a tiny group of individuals who knew Britain's nuclear secrets. While Prince Philip expressed interest in the scientific and technological side of things, creating intriguing potential for a reprisal of his father-in-law's deception role, Elizabeth had to get her head around the devastating consequences of a nuclear exchange – consequences that only became more devastating as the weapons became ever-more powerful. She was a confidante, providing prime ministers, especially Harold Macmillan, with a sounding board to think through the implications of their decisions. She provided encouragement at crucial moments in delicate transatlantic negotiations and personified the political desire for an independent nuclear weapon. It is therefore staggering that planners forgot to provide the palace with the War Book, although they quickly scrambled to rectify the embarrassing oversight, ensuring that the queen remained at the very heart of the inner – and most secret – circle.

Part V

ROYAL DIPLOMACY

18

QUEEN ELIZABETH'S EMPIRE:
INTRIGUE IN THE MIDDLE EAST

'Queen Elizabeth was "surprised nobody had found means of putting something in his coffee".'

Evelyn Shuckburgh diary[1]

DURING QUEEN VICTORIA's reign, the British Empire ruled the world. It had expanded to become the biggest in human history, covering a quarter of the world's land surface. It stretched from the white sands of the Caribbean in the west to the dense jungles of Malaya in the east. Although its economic power was declining even in the nineteenth century, its geographical vastness peaked shortly after King Edward VII's death in 1910; after the two world wars that followed, the British Empire was visibly faltering. George VI was the last king-emperor of India, for so long the jewel in the imperial crown. It achieved independence in 1947. Burma, Palestine and Ceylon followed suit soon afterwards. Many of the transitions from empire to commonwealth were presided over by Lord Mountbatten in grand and colourful ceremonies; the royal undertaker of empire 'who never wore black'.[2]

By the time Queen Elizabeth ascended the throne, the empire had dwindled to parts of southern and eastern Africa, British Guiana and some small Caribbean islands, Malaya and Singapore. Fervent nationalism, emboldened by success after success, swept from one moribund colony to the next. The young Elizabeth inherited a communist insurrection in Malaya that had broken out in 1948. One of the very first documents which bore the now-familiar line 'Her Majesty's Government' was a blueprint for winning it. As we have seen, another insurgency was beginning in Kenya even as she became queen in 1952.

Elizabeth's reign oversaw colossal change: the decline of Britain and the death of its empire. The commonwealth, of which she was head, was to be the future. Supporters have lauded her role in steadfastly guiding this transition as the defining achievement of her reign. In truth, the commonwealth was little more than a myth; for while it played a significant development and education role, its global significance was ever decreasing.[3] The Middle East underwent an especially messy transition; by 1952 much of the formal empire had gone in that region, but the British presence remained provocatively strong, taking the form of military bases, businesses, co-dominions and close advisory relationships with pliant sultans.[4]

Accordingly, the Middle East became a flashpoint of rising nationalism and declining imperialism in the early years of Elizabeth's reign. It was a region of vital strategic importance. Aden, one of the few remaining real colonies, allowed Britain to project force into the Far East, essential given that Conservative Party leaders intended the country to remain a global power; the Suez Canal, running through Egypt, formed the core artery for transporting goods and oil between east and west; and oil fields in the region, especially in Iran and Iraq, were of immense importance for Britain's faltering post-war economy. British influence was such that historians often describe the region as an 'informal empire'. Managing this was a ticklish business: Britain had to balance the security of oil and imperial communications with the retention of Arab and Iranian tolerance by showing some recognition of nationalist aspirations.[5]

By the 1950s, the scales tilted in the nationalists' favour. As the British desperately tried to cling on to their influence, the communists

– and the Americans – sought their own foothold and emboldened nationalists pressed for more autonomy. The Middle East became a hotbed of subversion and intrigue, coups and counter-coups. Given the importance – and constant turbulence – of the region, it is unsurprising that Elizabeth took a keen interest in intelligence and shadowy goings-on. Harold Macmillan, as foreign secretary in the mid-1950s, repeatedly praised her 'uncanny knowledge' of Middle Eastern politics and its leaders.[6]

IRAN WAS PARTICULARLY rife with intrigue and espionage. It had been a theatre of Anglo-Russian competition during the Great Game and, more recently, Britain had quietly supported an Iranian coup in 1921 to counter Soviet designs on the country, something that had brought the shah to power. But in September 1940, during the Second World War, German intrigue began to bubble up in the region and so the British and Soviets invaded Iran, removed the suspect shah and replaced him with his son, Mohammad Reza Pahlavi. The new shah never forgot that British intrigue had been responsible for both the rise and fall of his father, who died a British prisoner in South Africa in 1944.[7]

In late July 1948, the young shah, still only in his late twenties, visited Buckingham Palace. The focus of the visit was military power, and the shah, himself a qualified Spitfire pilot, was taken to RAF and naval flying displays.[8] Later, he asked King George VI, constitutional monarch to constitutional monarch, for an alliance between their two countries. George snubbed him with an 'extremely noncommittal' response. Diplomats sitting across St James's Park in the Foreign Office breathed a collective sigh of relief. They worried that any such alliance would create unnecessary trouble by upsetting the Soviets for little material benefit. After George dismissed the request, the young shah had better sense than to raise it again.[9]

In 1951, Iran's popular and nationalist prime minister, Mohammad Mossadeq, nationalized Iranian oil. At a stroke, he wiped out around £170 million – around £3 billion in today's terms – of British revenue each year. In London, Cabinet ministers described the move as 'dynamite'.[10] Through the Anglo-Iranian Oil Company, Britain had come to enjoy the lion's share of Iranian oil profits upon which politicians heavily depended as they struggled with the brutal financial consequences of the Second World War. America's war loans now had to be repaid and so Iran's oil nationalization was financially disastrous for Britain.

By early 1953, the situation had deteriorated even further. For Britain, with Queen Elizabeth now on the throne, Iran was a priority, indeed a crisis. The shah was still in power, but endured a tempestuous relationship with his prime minister. Meanwhile, Mossadeq's dramatic move rang alarm bells about the spread of nationalism elsewhere, notably in Iraq, where the UK managed the Iraq Petroleum Company, and Egypt, where it controlled the Suez Canal. The government quickly instigated a campaign of subversion, propaganda and bribery, hoping to remove Mossadeq as prime minister. Plans centred on discrediting the prime minister and ultimately convincing the wavering shah to replace him with a more amenable candidate.[11]

In February 1953, it looked like the shah, whom the lead MI6 officer described as 'a kind of Hamlet',[12] was on the verge of leaving Iran – potentially forever. His departure would have fatally undermined plans for a coup. Without him, the Iranian opposition would have had no rallying point; Mossadeq would be the uncontested leader of Iran.

On 14 February, Mossadeq lashed out at British subversion. He had already expelled Britain's diplomats and intelligence officers from the country. Now he told the US ambassador, Loy Henderson, that the 'British whilst pretending that they desired settlement were using their numerous Iranian contacts to overthrow him through alliances of forces'.[13] He had a point: in the very same week, the chief of MI6 was in Washington trying to persuade the CIA to join them in engineering a coup.[14]

Meanwhile, diplomats in the Foreign Office got cold feet and, a week later, decided to gradually 'taper off' the monthly sum of £10,000 that they had been giving local agents to buy politicians and column inches for the past year and a half. This reflected the sentiments of Britain's foreign secretary, Anthony Eden, who had doubts about covert action.[15]

Against the background of all this uncertainty, rumours began to circulate about the shah's imminent departure. Alarmed, American and British officials knew that the shah was their main asset and his absence would provide a golden opportunity for communists and other domestic opponents to smear him. The shah would have no means to defend himself once in hiding.[16]

On 27 February, Queen Elizabeth, on the throne for almost exactly a year, appeared to discreetly meddle in Iranian affairs herself. Naturally sympathetic to the plight of another constitutional monarch, she shared the growing concerns that the shah's departure would have had a disastrous impact on Iran. With the shah due to leave the following day, Elizabeth seemingly urged Eden to find 'some means of dissuading him from leaving'.[17]

Back in Iran, Henderson, the US ambassador, was himself desperately trying to dissuade the shah from departing. With the British embassy closed he was the main conduit for messages not only from Washington but also from London. Suddenly, he received an encoded telegram 'from Anthony Eden from Queen Elizabeth' exhorting the shah to stay in place. At once, he leapt on the message, ensuring it reached the shah personally. It indicated, Henderson told one of the shah's aides, that a 'very important personage' for whom the shah 'had most friendly feelings had also expressed sincere hope that Shah could be dissuaded from leaving country'.[18]

The shah was about to flee. But ever the prevaricator, the message piqued his interest enough for him to speak to Henderson directly. The stakes were high and the risks were real. Henderson knew full well that Mossadeq might have tapped the telephone line between the embassy and the palace, but, given the circumstances, thought it a risk worth taking. He implored the shah not to leave and, worrying about eavesdroppers, told him as indirectly as possible that Queen Elizabeth wanted him to stay. The shah expressed appreciation, but insisted that he must go anyway.[19]

Elizabeth's supposed message was particularly sensitive because Mossadeq still accused 'British agents' of 'trying to stir up dissension' in the country. Any hint that the queen herself was personally involved in interfering in the internal affairs of Iran would have been explosive.[20]

Remarkably, there had been a colossal misunderstanding. The message had come from a different Queen Elizabeth: the boat, not the monarch. Anthony Eden had been on board the SS *Queen Elizabeth* en route to a conference in Canada when he had urged the shah to stay.[21]

The US embassy in London hastily sent an embarrassed follow-up and correction: 'Queen Elizabeth refers of course to vessel and not – repeat not – to monarch.' The garbled original message was badly drafted and open to misinterpretation. By this time, though, the damage had been done. Henderson had alluded to the queen's intervention in error. He was aghast and confessed that he would never have dared do all the things he had done in the last twenty-four hours unless he had thought he was under direction from Buckingham Palace.

And so began an American cover-up. Knowing that Britain – and the monarch – would have been furious, the US diplomats quietly agreed among each other not to inform their British counterparts. They also kept it from the shah. He had listened to the message 'from the queen' in good faith. If the US told the truth now, he would have felt misinformed – or even intentionally duped. This could have had terrible implications for the already fragile relationship between the shah, Britain and the United States. He had been persuaded to take a big risk in staying; and had thought that – monarch to monarch – the queen had provided advice. It was a false premise.[22]

News of the shah's impending departure leaked to two of Mossadeq's most implacable enemies: Ahmad Qavam and the family of Fazlollah Zahedi (who had been arrested shortly before). Qavam, with the secret encouragement of Britain, had briefly served as prime minister in 1952 before protests forced him out.[23] Zahedi, a general and former police chief, would become the MI6/CIA choice to head the eventual coup.

Qavam quickly called Ayatollah Behbahani, a friend of the beleaguered shah and widely believed to be under British influence. Foreign Office diplomats had rated him as 'quite unscrupulous and corrupt, ready to sell his influence on the bazaars to the highest bidder'.[24] Meanwhile, Zahedi's family called Ayatollah Kashani, a one-time ally of Mossadeq who now derided him as a communist puppet. Both Behbahani and Kashani successfully rallied a crowd of a few thousand to protest against Mossadeq. Other pro-British political organizations, military personnel and paid thugs soon joined in. The mob besieged the prime minister's house a few hundred yards from the palace. At 3 p.m., the shah informed his supporters that he would not, after all, leave the country.[25]

Just over a fortnight later, in mid-March, the CIA delivered the news for which MI6 had long been hoping: the US was finally ready to discuss tactics for a coup against Mossadeq. Under pressure from Prime Minister Winston Churchill and reassured by the offer of a joint covert operation, the Foreign Office finally approved it a month later.[26] Conveniently, the ever-anxious Eden was in hospital awaiting an operation, leaving the bullish Churchill in full control of foreign affairs.

The shah remained nervous of the British as he had a notably exaggerated view of the capabilities of the British Empire and its secret service. In mid-May, he confided in Henderson that they could 'keep him in power or remove him as they saw fit'. Despite believing he had received a message from the queen asking him to stay, he was very anxious to know what London was thinking and was full of wild fears. He asked: 'Did the British wish to substitute another Shah for himself or abolish the monarchy? Were the British behind the present efforts to deprive him of his power and prestige?'[27] On 22 May 1953, Churchill sent him a message again asking him to stay, adding that he would 'be very sorry to see the Shah leave his current post or be driven out', and asked Henderson to assure the shah that 'it comes personally from me'.[28]

In August, amid a blizzard of protests and propaganda, the shah replaced Mossadeq as prime minister with Zahedi. The move almost unravelled when Mossadeq evaded arrest and his supporters took to the streets. The shah hid, never quite trusting the British. Back in London, Churchill was furious with the lack of updates.[29] In the end, as mob violence eventually turned the tables against Mossadeq, the plan succeeded.

Norman Darbyshire, the MI6 officer who worked most closely with the CIA, recalled: 'My brief was very simple… use the intelligence service for any money you might need to secure the overthrow of Mossadegh by legal or quasi-legal means.' In creating rent-a-mobs and buying newspapers he spent 'vast sums of money, well over a million-and-a-half pounds'. Together with CIA officers he was personally 'directing the street uprising'.[30]

The similarities between the August coup and the events of late February when the queen 'intervened' are striking. It formed a prelude for the eventual overthrow of Mossadeq; the shah demanded a secret message from London proving that Britain was on board before launching the crucial order, while the CIA and MI6 resurrected many of the propaganda lines used back in February, especially those accusing Mossadeq of forcing the shah to abdicate and instigating a regime change of his own.[31]

In the aftermath of the coup, Loy Henderson, the US ambassador in Tehran, was in celebratory mood. He suggested that 'it might be useful for Queen Elizabeth II or Prime Minister Churchill to send an oral message of congratulations to the Shah through American channels'.[32] Eisenhower had already sent a missive praising the shah and, with no evident sense of irony, he urged strong leadership to 'eliminate foreign-inspired subversion'.[33] With words like 'subversion' in the air, officials in London mused: 'I don't think there can be any question of the Queen sending a message.'[34] They did not need to worry, for the very next day, Churchill, enamoured by the covert operation, insisted on sending the message himself: 'I salute and congratulate Your Majesty on your safe return to your country.'[35]

Privately, animosity and suspicion remained. In January 1954, Eden, now returned from hospital, warned his officials that 'the shah is a miserable and despicable character'.[36] Much of the tension surrounded the fact that the oil nationalization issue remained unresolved and difficult.

With the British embassy in Tehran now reopened, opportunities presented themselves for more secret work. One British diplomat there, Charles Wiggin, was at a function when he found himself in the company of Eva Karl, the mother of the Iranian queen, whom he described uncharitably as 'a pretty hefty German blonde'. Explaining that she had married the Iranian ambassador to West Germany in the 1950s, she was now stuck in Tehran where she was kept short of money by her new family. Wishing to escape and retire to Switzerland, she made the British an unusual offer: 'She would fix the oil dispute for us for cash; there need be no formalities about it; she had influence and, if we gave her the money, she would soon get the government to sign; was I influential enough to see that our side played their part in the deal?'

Wiggin was less worried about 'the Queen's mother soliciting a bribe' and more worried about the fact that, having been drinking, she had spoken rather too loudly. He reflected that top society in Tehran held 'dangers' for the inexperienced. In London, officials found the report rather amusing and noted: 'Strongly recommended reading. Ought we to send... to the Palace?'[37]

In February the following year, with the vexed oil issue finally settled, the shah himself visited Buckingham Palace to meet the queen.[38] He was a demanding guest, but Churchill was especially keen that it go well.[39] He was very clear that he owed his position to British intelligence and, when back at home, now insisted on meeting with the MI6 station chief weekly.[40] Even in the 1960s, he continued to meet both the MI6 and CIA station chief once a fortnight.[41] What exactly he said to the queen in Buckingham Palace is lost to history, but the lessons of the uncertain dynasties around her must have been clear; nothing could be taken for granted.

On a personal level, she thought him 'rather a bore' and 'very heavy'. She was most comfortable conversing about horse racing, but all he ever wanted to do was talk shop. As we shall see, Elizabeth went on to recognize the importance of personal obligations between sovereigns and appreciated the loyalty the shah, who now ruled as an autocrat, would show Britain during the Cold War.[42]

Because of oil, the shah and his dynasty remained a key intelligence target. A month after his visit, Britain received royal medical intelligence from the CIA. Medical intelligence on leaders was a new field and, in some cases, it even involved competition by field agents to collect urine samples from foreign leaders in the hope of gauging their health and longevity.[43] In this case, in 1955, Kermit Roosevelt of the CIA informed Britain that the shah and his wife had undergone medical tests to explore why they were having difficulty producing children. Sadly, and partly for these reasons, the shah and his wife, Queen Soraya, whom he loved deeply, eventually divorced.[44]

This provided a remarkable intelligence opportunity. The shah was now in search of his third wife, and particularly desired a European princess. He was rejected by Princess Maria Gabriella of Savoy, a daughter of the deposed Italian king, and then turned his attention to Princess Alexandra, daughter of the duke of Kent and Princess Marina – and cousin of Queen Elizabeth. Belatedly, he realized that marriage to a Christian princess would raise too many difficulties at home and was now 'resigned' to marrying an Iranian girl. Very privately, he told Geoffrey Harrison, the British ambassador, that 'there are three girls in the running' and he was likely to choose quickly. He badly wanted a 'British court official of advanced years and proven discretion to coach the bride-to be in Court etiquette'. The shah felt the British court 'was far more experienced and wise in court procedure than any other'. London could not believe their luck.[45]

Securing intelligence from within Iranian inner court circles was hard. Now they had an extraordinary opportunity to insert a secret listener, plucked from British royal circles and placed into the heart of the Iranian court. But they worried that an elderly courtier, a Hardinge or even a Lascelles, would arouse 'hostility'. Better to go for a discreet ex-lady in waiting to Princess Margaret who 'could be represented in Teheran as a private secretary or English tutor... and would be less likely to give offence or arouse suspicion'.[46] The British court remained quietly useful on these most sensitive of missions.

The subterranean court battle for intelligence on the shah was constant. Some years later, with a heavy heart, MI6 had to warn the head of the shah's entourage that the palace housekeeper, a British woman called 'Florence', again engaged for her expertise in royal protocol and procedure, was in fact 'having an affair with the chief of the KGB at the Soviet embassy'. The minister of the court was horrified but the shah seemed unsurprised and simply sent her on her way.[47]

THREE MONTHS AFTER the Iranian coup, Elizabeth and Philip embarked on a marathon tour of the commonwealth. It provided an opportunity to highlight the strength of the growing multinational organization, with a young and dynamic queen at its head, but also to demonstrate the resilience of the faltering empire.[48] The royal couple left in November 1953 and sailed back up the Thames on the royal yacht *Britannia* six months later. They travelled over forty thousand miles and took in Aden, Australia, Bermuda, Ceylon, the Cocos Islands, Fiji, Gibraltar, Jamaica, Malta, New Zealand (from where Elizabeth broadcast her 1953 Christmas message), Tonga and Uganda.

The tour was a huge success. Three quarters of the entire population of Australia turned out to see the royal couple, foiling attempts by the local communist party to sabotage enthusiasm for the monarchy. The communists were particularly active there and the Australian Security Intelligence Organisation (ASIO), Australia's equivalent of MI5, compiled a special booklet listing the names of all those deemed a potential source of trouble and printed 400 copies to be circulated to state police.[49] At the time, ASIO was handling the defection of KGB man Victor Petrov, one of the biggest spy cases of the 1950s. Rather deviously, ASIO allegedly delayed the defection both to fit in with a forthcoming election and to avoid any embarrassment during the royal tour. So, on 3 April 1954, just two days after Elizabeth and Philip had sailed from Freemantle, Petrov, who was in some peril, was finally allowed to defect.[50]

Fears of communist agitation failed to prevent the royal couple from visiting Ceylon either – a visit which proved to be a highlight of the entire tour. Nevertheless, Elizabeth and Philip could not fully escape the shadows of mounting nationalist unrest. They had to avoid British Guiana and Cyprus altogether, while the Mau Mau insurgency in Kenya constrained their visit to neighbouring Uganda.[51]

The queen's layover in Aden, in late April 1954, posed a particular intelligence headache. Sitting on the south coast of the Arabian Peninsula, the colony overlooked a bustling natural harbour resting beneath the crater of a dormant volcano. Aden was a strategic port, vital in the flow of oil between the Mediterranean and the Gulf, and an important base from which to defend Britain's client states elsewhere in the Persian Gulf. It was crucial in projecting power into the Indian Ocean and beyond towards Hong Kong.

Like many other colonies, nationalist unrest picked away at British authority at the time of the queen's visit – and would explode into a vicious urban insurgency within a decade. Nearby Yemen, separated from Aden by the mountainous buffer zone of South Arabia, opposed the British position and was intent on causing trouble. At the same time as MI6/CIA covert operations peaked in Iran, Churchill secretly sponsored tribal raids into Yemen to destabilize the ruling imam and deter incursions into British-protected South Arabia. The aim was to protect Aden from subversion and maintain the British position.[52]

Colonial security authorities were desperate to prevent this simmering trouble from marring the long-awaited visit of Elizabeth and Philip. Local police took the legally dubious decision to arrest – without cause – twenty-four people whom they deemed subversive. The plan was to take them off the streets on the morning of the visit and, when the queen had safely returned to her yacht that evening, to release them apologetically, pretending it had been an error. As one colonial officer remembers, the police 'would then say "Oh! I'm frightfully sorry – this is all a ghastly mistake – you can go now."'[53]

Overenthusiasm fatally derailed the plan. The police, wanting to make sure the targets were behind bars, ended up arresting them a day early. Within two hours, local politicians demanded their release and, under intense pressure, the commissioner of police reluctantly released twenty-two of them back onto the streets. Had the authorities held their nerve and waited for the day of the visit to make the arrests, the plan would have worked: the local politicians would have been too busy shaking hands and lining the streets to make a fuss about the unlawful arrests.[54]

The failure left the police nervous. But the crowds were wildly enthusiastic. They watched intently as locals ran alongside the queen's car as it navigated narrow streets, delaying her arrival to a garden party. The queen was already learning to engage with her global fan base and would not be hurried. 'Where on earth have you been?' Philip asked when she pulled up twenty minutes late.[55]

SAFELY BACK IN the UK, Elizabeth still could not escape the intrigue of the Middle East. In 1955, she grew concerned about developments in Jordan. The country had been a close ally since the First World War and its rulers allowed Britain to retain air bases and a military force inside their territory. In return, Britain provided support to the Arab Legion, headed by British officers, which had become the nucleus of the Jordanian army. Communist influence was negligible, but Egyptian and Saudi subversion was rife. The Egyptians tarred King Hussein of Jordan as an imperialist puppet; the Saudis bribed Jordanians, including members of the royal family, to weaken the king's influence.[56]

British intelligence soon warned of nefarious influences on young Hussein. Groomed for power by his grandfather, King Abdullah, from an early age, he had studied at Harrow School in northwest London where, incidentally, he befriended Faisal, the future king of Iraq. Hussein was at his grandfather's side when an assassin murdered him. Just thirteen months later, in 1953, Hussein took the throne himself after his schizophrenic father abdicated. He was woefully inexperienced and only seventeen years old.

Hussein looked to his uncle, Sharif Nasser bin Jamil, for support and guidance. Britain feared that Nasser was turning the impressionable king against the British officers running the Arab Legion, including its British commander, Lieutenant General John Bagot Glubb. Small and courageous, 'Glubb Pasha', as he was known, had led the legion for over twenty years, building it into one of the most formidable forces in the region. Out-surviving the British Empire, he still enjoyed unparalleled influence and respect in the country. Some saw him as a second Lawrence of Arabia or an uncrowned king of Jordan. He became a symbol of British influence and a target for anti-colonial sentiment. Nasser's hostility towards Glubb stemmed partly from understandable nationalist rancour, but also from the more pragmatic fact that he saw Glubb as an obstacle to his hashish and arms smuggling business.

When diplomats in the Foreign Office found out that he sought to remove Glubb and his British colleagues from Jordan, they decided to 'get rid of Nasser'. They planned covert political action to discredit and smear him. They had to do so discreetly: if an operation was too obvious, it would simply have turned Nasser into a martyr and consolidated the king's anti-British stance. Therefore, they subtly tried to implant doubts in Hussein's mind about Nasser's loyalty, thereby engineering his removal.[57]

Queen Elizabeth discussed the situation with Evelyn Shuckburgh, the diplomat in charge of Middle Eastern affairs, in a bright room sporting orange and gold pillars inside Buckingham Palace. Shuckburgh briefed her on the 'machinations of the wicked uncle, Nasser'. She responded by criticizing the impressionable young king: 'she didn't really think it a good idea to send Arabs to English public schools. She had seen poor little Hussein fresh from Harrow a year or two ago, and all he could do was stand stiffly to attention, saying "Your Majesty" and not another word.'[58]

'As for Uncle Nasser,' Shuckburgh remembered Elizabeth as saying, 'she was surprised nobody had found means of putting something in his coffee.' This may have been a light-hearted comment, but it was not too far off the mark. MI6 would begin various plots to assassinate the other Nasser – the president of Egypt – the following year, and British covert operations were spreading like wildfire across the region. In the middle of the 1950s, MI6 officers were plotting regime change in Yemen, Saudi Arabia, Syria and Egypt. Wittingly or not, Elizabeth was helping to legitimize covert action from inside Buckingham Palace.

Distracted by a cigarette steadily burning his fingertips behind his back, Shuckburgh replied that assassinating him 'was a good idea which ought to be applied to a number of people in the Middle East'. He 'promised to send her the gossip we have heard about Hussein'.[59]

Elizabeth's quip played on Shuckburgh's mind. 'It was not until afterwards that I thought of what I ought to have said to this – that it was dangerously like a remark made on a famous occasion by her predecessor King Henry II.'[60] Here, he was alluding to Henry's exhortation: 'Will no one rid me of this troublesome priest', leading to the death of Thomas Becket, archbishop of Canterbury, in 1170. The analogy points to the expression of a royal wish which may be interpreted as a command by subordinates.

British covert operations to discredit – rather than assassinate – the Jordanian Nasser failed. King Hussein expelled General Glubb less than a year later in March 1956. He felt the need to publicly distance himself from the British as, throughout the region, political opponents commonly accused each other of being agents of a foreign power.[61] Hussein, equally keen to shake off his playboy prince reputation and prove himself as a serious king, was therefore susceptible to his uncle's whispers.[62]

Glubb was given just two hours to leave the country. The stunned general refused: 'I have lived here for twenty-six years. Almost all my worldly possessions are here, to say nothing of my wife and children.' As a compromise, he agreed to leave the following morning. It was a personal tragedy for Glubb and another blow to Britain's position in the region.[63] The United States replaced Britain as the main country training Jordan's officers and supplying arms, while King Hussein soon became a paid agent of the CIA.[64]

This underlined the curious relationship between the CIA and MI6 in the region, simultaneously co-operating against Russia, but also competing for influence, especially with the various royal dynasties. A couple of weeks later, the queen learnt of a new British covert action planned for neighbouring Syria. Communism posed a far greater threat in this unreliable and unstable country than it did to the south in Jordan; so too did pan-Arab nationalism. With echoes of Iran, Britain had been trying to bring the reluctant CIA on board for a joint operation to overthrow the Syrian government for months. Together, a CIA–MI6 working group eventually drew up a plan complete with the names of those they would assassinate.[65]

In March 1956, Anthony Eden approved regime change in Syria. His Cabinet instructed the Foreign Office and MI6 to 'establish in Syria a Government more friendly to the West'.[66] This striking line – an incredibly rare allusion to covert action in a Cabinet document

– would surely have come up during his weekly audience with the queen. Shortly afterwards, officials assured the foreign secretary that 'covert action to diminish' Egyptian influence across the region was 'being actively prepared'.[67] Unfortunately for Eden, Britain's secret attempts to overthrow the Syrian regime collapsed in October 1956, not least because of concurrent events in Egypt – the infamous Suez Crisis was now unfolding.

A DIFFERENT NASSER now caused Britain a far greater headache than Hussein's 'wicked' uncle. Gamal Abdel Nasser, president of Egypt and bête noire of Prime Minister Anthony Eden, spearheaded a wave of Arab nationalism in the middle of the 1950s. It was this Nasser whose influence from Jordan to Syria and elsewhere really alarmed the British. MI6 officers, spurred on by Eden, really did consider slipping something in *his* coffee.

In July 1956, Nasser nationalized the Suez Canal following months of growing tension with Britain and France. Eden, suffering from ill-health and increasingly unstable, reacted violently. Secretly colluding with Israel and France, he launched an ill-fated invasion. This precipitated a crisis which destroyed Eden's reputation, damaged relations with President Eisenhower and offered a visible symbol of British imperial decline. Behind the scenes it ignited decades of speculation about how much Queen Elizabeth knew – and whether she approved.

Nasser dramatically announced his decision about the canal on Thursday 26 July 1956. The following weekend Elizabeth and Philip were staying with Mountbatten at Broadlands, his country estate in Hampshire. An urgent phone call from Jean Chauvel, the French ambassador in London, interrupted Mountbatten's entertainment of the royal couple. On the phone, Mountbatten learnt that his French counterpart, the chief of the naval staff, had just arrived in London to convey the sense of urgency in Paris about the Suez Crisis. He wanted to make it abundantly clear that France would use military force to remove Nasser once and for all.[68]

Mountbatten apologized to his nephew and the queen before rushing up to London on the Sunday morning. The French offered Mountbatten and the defence secretary the full support of their armed forces to defeat Nasser.[69]

Elizabeth knew what was unfolding during the tense summer of 1956. She received intelligence reports, including the Joint Intelligence Committee's highly sensitive weekly summary of current intelligence, which gave a clear impression of growing Soviet influence in Egypt and across the region more broadly. She received intelligence warnings that the threat of force alone would not reverse Nasser's position and that any military intervention had to be quick and decisive. Anything less would risk extreme international embarrassment. This turned out to be rather prescient; and international embarrassment was something about which the queen cared deeply.[70]

She also received papers from the Cabinet's unwieldy Egypt Committee, established to undertake both the military preparations and the diplomatic efforts to resolve the crisis.[71] Although Eden increasingly side-lined the committee as the planning became more secret, even cutting out the Joint Intelligence Committee, the queen remained informed through personal contacts, including Mountbatten. In August, he spent four days with her at Balmoral and, by the autumn, was a regular visitor at Windsor and Buckingham Palace.[72]

Uncle Dickie was critical of plans for an invasion and, as first sea lord, exercised much influence during the crisis. With the chair of the chiefs of staff committee away ill, Eden treated him as the key figure when asking for service advice. Mountbatten, never lacking in self-confidence, was often willing to stray into political territory – much to the irritation of the Foreign Office. At the same time, Eden was sensitive to concerns that Mountbatten, whether directly or through his nephew Philip, had an unhealthy influence on the queen.[73]

From early August, Mountbatten urged restraint and even considered resigning. It is inconceivable that he, never known for discretion, did not share his reservations with the queen. According to Martin Charteris, her assistant private secretary, Mountbatten told Elizabeth that Eden's plans were 'absolutely lunatic', hoping that she would then pass this message on to Eden, but representing it as her own warning. Charteris even claimed that the queen shared Mountbatten's concerns – much to Eden's anger.[74]

Elizabeth, of course, had more sources than just Mountbatten. She knew from Foreign Office papers that diplomats were becoming increasingly uncertain about Eden's policy.[75] On 24 October, following three days of intensely secret negotiations outside of Paris, Eden agreed to collude with Israel and France. The plan involved Israel invading Egypt, paving the way for Britain and France, feigning surprise, to intervene and separate the combatants. Foolishly, Eden hoped that this would provide a pretext to justify British military action.

That night, Patrick Dean, a senior diplomat, returned from the secret meeting in France to brief Eden and the inner circle. The only chief of staff present was none other than Mountbatten. Uncle Dickie was almost certainly one of the very few people to see a copy of the notorious 'collusion' agreement before it was burnt.[76]

The next day, with collusion in place, Eden told the Cabinet – and the queen – that the Israelis were 'after all, advancing their military preparations with a view to making an attack on Egypt'. He continued that, if British forces went in, 'we must face the risk that we should be accused of collusion with Israel'. Cabinet 'agreed in principle that, in the event of an Israeli attack on Egypt, the Government should join with the French Government in calling on the two belligerents to stop hostilities'. If they failed to do so, 'British and French forces would intervene to enforce compliance.' Eden gave a clear – and deceitful – impression that all this was a mere contingency plan to be executed if, rather than when, Israel invaded.[77]

The eminent historian Peter Hennessy thinks that Cabinet ministers, in claiming not to know about the collusion plot, were deluding themselves: 'they did not need a background at GCHQ to decode the import of those messages given in the Cabinet Room'. They should have subjected the prime minister to 'the heat of questioning'.[78]

Unlike the Cabinet, the queen had probably cracked the code. After all, Mountbatten did and it would have been outrageous for a constitutional monarch to be kept in the dark about such an important development, preventing her from exercising her duty to advise, encourage and consult the prime minister. An anonymous source told the respected biographer Ben Pimlott that 'she knew the inside story'. Elizabeth 'knew about the secret deals beforehand'.[79] Eden, furious about any suggestions that he had misled the queen, later insisted that she 'understood what we were doing very well'.[80]

It is telling that, after the invasion, Norman Brook, the Cabinet secretary, anxiously asked the palace to return papers from those crucial Cabinet meetings held in the run-up to Suez. He reminded Michael Adeane, the queen's private secretary, that 'some of the points' discussed were 'of a particularly sensitive nature'. This is an understatement given the hints of collusion they contained. More surprising, and demonstrating the enormous significance of those papers, is Brook's nervousness that they would not have been safe locked away inside Windsor Castle.[81]

It is likely that Eden or Brook kept the queen broadly – if informally – aware of the crucial developments unfolding outside Paris, but given the lengths Eden went to keep it secret, it is highly unlikely that any of the documents sent to the palace explicitly mentioned the collusion. Given Eden's growing desperation and mental instability, it is difficult to know exactly how much he told her in terms of specific details and timings.[82]

Even if she did not know, Elizabeth would still have been in a position to submit Eden to her own 'heat of questioning' during her two audiences with the prime minister in the run-up to Suez.

According to Charteris, she 'in some ways was better informed in advance of the operation than many members in the cabinet'.[83] After all, she received a range of sensitive intelligence and papers, had Mountbatten whispering in her ear, and two of her assistant private secretaries, both experienced in Middle Eastern politics, opposed Eden's approach to Egypt. Courtiers remember tense conversations and Eden fidgeting edgily around the palace.[84] He was extremely agitated at his weekly audience with the queen and, according to Charteris, she thought 'Eden was mad'.[85]

However, she was a young and inexperienced monarch. By contrast, Eden was a man whom she had recently knighted precisely for his mastery of foreign affairs.[86] Almost as much as Churchill, he retained the reputation of having resisted wartime fascism. Therefore, he represented this episode as a further effort to resist a dictator. Michael Adeane, her most senior adviser, unlike his assistants, supported the invasion of Suez.[87]

It seems that Adeane and Eden failed to persuade her. Anecdotal evidence strongly suggests that Elizabeth did not support the Suez invasion, and may well have had strong reservations about it. Charteris later recalled that 'the basic dishonesty of the whole thing' left her worried, as did the effect it would have on the commonwealth where Australia was broadly supportive, but India opposed the invasion. This put Elizabeth, as head of the commonwealth, in a difficult position. She was torn between leaking secrets to commonwealth prime ministers or withholding information and deceiving them about British plans.[88]

The queen had influence but not power. Perhaps she arched an eyebrow and asked Eden her trademark question: 'are you sure you are being wise?'[89] Not doing so, with all the information at her disposal, would have been as self-deluding as the Cabinet; a dereliction of her duties as a constitutional monarch.

On 29 October, as planned, Israeli troops invaded the Sinai Peninsula and made their way towards the canal. Feigning surprise, Britain and France issued their ultimatum, which, also as planned,

Israel promptly ignored. Two days later, Britain and France began bombing Egyptian positions to force the reopening of the canal. In response, Nasser sank forty ships, blocking the waterway. The next day, the queen received the first of her daily bulletins, many of which contained top-secret intelligence. It informed her about the progress of the Israeli attack and where forces had met Egyptian resistance.[90]

On 5 November, British and French paratroopers landed at Port Said, near the entrance of the canal. Intelligence kept Elizabeth personally updated on the Soviet response. Alarmingly, she learnt how a source warned that the Soviet military attaché in Beirut was 'reported to have told a Joint Arab Command that Russia has decided to help Egypt and was examining the most efficient and least dangerous way of doing this'.[91]

Eisenhower was angry about Suez. He was cross that American intelligence received warning of the conspiracy but did not act on it, and furious that Eden had not kept him informed. He felt that Anglo-French aggression in the Middle East undermined his own criticisms of simultaneous Russian aggression against the rising in Hungary. These twin crises, Hungary and Suez, had both hit him during an election campaign, so the timing was especially unwelcome. He rang Downing Street to protest and an official picked up the phone. Thinking he was speaking directly to Eden, Eisenhower barked: 'I can only presume that you have gone out of your mind.'[92]

The president responded by putting economic pressure on the British pound. Facing overwhelming American opposition, Britain and France agreed to a ceasefire two days later. The following evening, Buckingham Palace hosted a reception. In the margins of the palace, Rab Butler, the lord privy seal, took the American ambassador to one side and 'deplored the existence of what he termed mutual misunderstandings of policy' between the two governments. He was clearly 'greatly disturbed' by the actions of the Cabinet – although stopped short of actually saying so.[93] As for the queen, she told Churchill that she hoped 'the present feeling that this country and America are not seeing eye-to-eye will soon be speedily replaced by even stronger ties between us'.[94] The language was different to that of Eisenhower but the meaning was clear. This was a classic understated rebuke.

Elizabeth's bulletins continued during the final two days of fighting. They covered photographic intelligence from British planes on Egyptian and Israeli positions,[95] as well as intelligence on Egyptian subversion: 'underground resistance is... increasing and the populace is being incited to take up arms against the British'. She had access to even the most sensitive intelligence acquired by GCHQ – codenamed EIDER – which officials candidly told her came from 'signals intelligence sources'.[96] It monitored possible Soviet preparations for war and whether any other states were preparing to intervene in the conflict. Despite ominous reports of Russian aircraft flying towards the theatre, this intelligence was generally reassuring throughout the crisis.[97]

On 22 November, the day after the first United Nations troops landed in Egypt, Elizabeth received her final bulletin: 'Port Said remains quiet and there has been less curfew breaking.'[98] She thanked all those who had been involved in preparing them and recognized the trouble taken to keep her 'supplied with the latest information'.[99]

America had applied immense economic might and began to sell the pound heavily, and so the outcome was inevitable. Towards the end of the month, Britain reluctantly started withdrawing troops from the theatre. Eden, ill and under immense stress but determined to continue as prime minister, left for Ian Fleming's Goldeneye estate in Jamaica to recover. Back in London, the Cabinet agreed a common line to take. The spin was nothing short of outrageous: 'we have stopped a small war and prevented a larger one'; the UK had 'unmasked Soviet plots in the Middle East and have done something to awaken the United Nations to the dangers there'; the Cabinet was 'united and firm'. The queen read and returned it without comment to the Foreign Office.[100]

The pressure was too much; the outcome too humiliating. Eden resigned in early January the following year. Elizabeth wrote to him: 'You know how very deeply I felt your resignation last week and how much I sympathize in the tragic turn of fate which laid you low at the moment when our country is beginning to see the possibility of some brightening in the international sky.'[101]

She consoled him that 'there is no doubt that you took the only possible course, after the doctors had given you their verdict but one can only guess at what it must have cost you to do it'. And she thanked him not only, 'for the loyal and distinguished service you have given to me, first as Foreign Secretary and then as Prime Minister, but for the many years work, both in and out of office, which you have devoted to the greatness and prosperity of our country'.[102] Eden promptly lost the letter.

Many in the palace were quietly relieved by Eden's resignation. The royals had never liked Eden and the personal relationship between monarch and prime minister had been much more forced than during Churchill's day. One former courtier recalled that Eden 'didn't give you the feeling he trusted you with sensitive information'.[103] Despite this, the queen seemed to bear Eden no ill will over the collusion at Suez. Eden later recalled that she had never indicated 'anger or humiliation' towards him. 'On the contrary.' The two stayed in touch and she even took the rare step of accepting private hospitality from him.[104]

Privately, Elizabeth had thought invasion of Egypt, inadequately hidden by the hopeless 'collusion' with Israel, was stupid. Now she was confronted with consequences for her own empire, a dramatic decline in British prestige and grotesque embarrassment at the hand of Nasser. Why had Eden not followed the simpler approach of just slipping something in his coffee? Prince Bernhard of the Netherlands, who followed the invasion closely, told British insiders 'that you should not have mounted a military operation at all, instead you should have offered £5,000 for Nasser's head'. British ministers pretended to be 'very shocked', but many were doubtless thinking the same thing.[105]

BIZARRELY, JUST AT the very moment when assassination was in the air, the real worlds of 007 and the queen actually crossed. In 1956, Martin Charteris sought to recruit Ian Fleming, the creator of James Bond, as a speech writer for the queen. Fleming had written a speech for Elizabeth back in 1949, although in the end Charteris did not use it.[106] As so often in the upper echelons of British society, connections existed between the Charteris and Fleming families. Charteris was the cousin of Ann Fleming, Ian's wife, so they saw each other socially. Although Fleming had published his first Bond novel, *Casino Royale*, a few years before and was a rising celebrity, he still had a day job working for the *Sunday Times*, managing its network of foreign correspondents. Charteris wondered if a little '007' magic would not help to lift the queen's oratory. There were other connections, since both Fleming and Charteris enjoyed a background in intelligence work in the 1940s.

But there was also a problem. Fleming did not like the idea of regular dealings with one Commander Richard Colville, the queen's press secretary. Colville was a famously negative figure, described as 'stiff, irascible and something of a snob'. For years, the royal press office had been under the command of this notorious figure, an old Harrovian of fabulously gloomy temperament. He was entirely unsuitable and had only secured the post through his cousin, Jock Colville, who had been a predecessor to Charteris.[107] Some have called him an 'anti-press secretary' and his approach to press management was simple: allow as little access as possible and avoid all excitement. Because his demeanour was so dour and miserable, his nickname within the royal household was 'Sunshine'.[108]

Famous for refusing every reasonable request, Colville had a different nickname among the press of Fleet Street: 'the Abominable No Man'. In 1957, after some hesitation, Fleming 'found the prospect of dealing with Colville hard to take, and retired gracefully to Goldeneye', his holiday retreat in Jamaica where Eden had recently convalesced. There, under the Caribbean sun, 'the talent that might have worked wonders for the royal word' was instead poured into writing *Dr No*.

This new Bond book was a rather more salacious work than his previous adventures.[109] The character of Dr No was loosely based on Fu Manchu, the fictional villain created by Sax Rohmer, but where did the name come from? It is well known that Fleming was something of a naval magpie when choosing names for his characters. Typically, the name of 'Drax', the villain in *Moonraker*, was borrowed from an admiral.[110] Perhaps Commander Colville, the queen's press secretary and Abominable No Man, was the inspiration. Either way, when his novel hit the silver screen a few years later as the first '007' film it was a runaway success.[111]

IN THE WAKE of the political and economic humiliation that was Suez, the monarchy arguably became yet more important. The queen, working through the vehicle of the commonwealth, tried to rescue the remnants of great power, offering the narrative of a liberal democracy engaged in a willing retreat from empire and seeking a new partnership with the global south. But this was a hard sell set against the awkward aftermath of the Suez misadventure which rendered British decline more apparent than ever. Nationalism continued to spread across the Middle East, threatening Britain's position elsewhere. Behind the scenes the secret services worked frantically to stop the rot.

Iraq, another state with a young constitutional monarch, was Britain's closest ally in the region. Britain was a leading member of the Baghdad Pact, a military alliance founded in 1955 to contain Soviet ambitions in the Middle East. The following year, Iraq worked closely with MI6 in the ill-fated covert operation to overthrow the Syrian government – and shouldered the blame when it unravelled. King Faisal II paid a state visit to London that summer; Queen Elizabeth, dressed in a summer floral frock and straw hat, greeted him in all his green and gold military finery on the platform at Victoria station. Accompanying him to the palace, she described Iraq as 'the model of a modern state, built on ancient and famous foundations and confidently facing towards the future'.[112]

The confidence was misplaced. Many Iraqis resented the Baghdad Pact as a means of western meddling. Egyptian propaganda was quick to whip up discontent further, especially in the aftermath of the Suez debacle when Iraqi association with Britain became particularly toxic.

More and more Iraqis, including military officers, found themselves sympathetic to Nasser's nationalist line. In February 1958, the joining of Egypt and Syria to form the United Arab Republic bolstered pan-Arab nationalism further still. A group of Iraqi officers now vowed to put the ruling regime on trial as collaborators with the British imperialists.[113] Faisal's uncle, the crown prince of Iraq, became worried about growing anti-British feelings among the Iraq establishment. Faisal's beautiful fiancée, Princess Fadhila, was a particular concern. She was descended from Ottoman and Egyptian royalty but, with wedding plans and a palace refurbishment under way in Baghdad, she made some unfortunate remarks about Britain.

In April, with nationalist disturbances on the rise, the crown prince had a private word with the British ambassador to Iraq, Michael Wright. He explained 'how anxious' he was 'that Princess Fadhila should come to feel the same affection for Britain as the King and himself'. He wondered whether Queen Elizabeth might discreetly intervene to win her over. Fadhila was currently a pupil at Heathfield School, near Ascot. Might Elizabeth 'feel able to pay her some attention, and enable her to make the acquaintance of the younger members of the Royal Family?'[114]

Wright thought this a good idea: 'when Princess Fadhila becomes Queen she will be in a position to exercise great influence in the background. Whatever can be done while she is in England to befriend her may be of considerable importance for the future.'[115]

Britain's most senior diplomat, Frederick Hoyer Millar, passed the message on to Michael Adeane at Buckingham Palace. 'Princess Fadhila's family background,' he explained, emphasizing the necessity of the queen's task, 'has on the whole been anti-British. It is therefore all the more important that her stay here should be a success and she should take away a happy memory of this country. She is only 16 ½ and at an impressionable age. I am sure that any attention paid her would be worthwhile.' Hoyer Millar, whose own daughter went to the same school and spoke well of the princess, added some briefing notes to help the queen influence her: the princess was 'very keen on music and the ballet'.[116]

Queen Elizabeth agreed. She thought it a 'good plan' to invite her to Windsor Castle during the forthcoming race meeting at Ascot in the middle of June.[117] As Elizabeth and the Foreign Office planned to cultivate Fadhila as a long-term person of influence, other plans were afoot back in Iraq. British intelligence was oblivious to plotting by a secret military group, the Free Officers, to emulate Nasser's achievements in Egypt and overthrow the Iraqi monarchy.

MI6 had excellent sources among pro-British and royal factions but had been unable to penetrate the nationalists. The Iraqi prime minister maintained that the military were apolitical and, despite four foiled plots so far in 1958 alone, would remain loyal to the monarchy. One of the problems was that MI5's attempts to liaise with the Iraqi security authorities severely impeded the scope for covert intelligence operations run by MI6.[118] As a result, with coup plotting at an advanced stage, the Foreign Office received skewed intelligence and the queen continued to plan a charm offensive to win over Fadhila.

The revolutionary Iraqi officers struck in the early hours of 14 July 1958; just ten weeks after the Foreign Office request to the palace and four weeks after Ascot. At 5.30 a.m. the palace was attacked with machine guns. The queen, the crown prince and his sisters were killed outright. The king died later of his wounds. The house of the prime minister, Nuri el-Said, was also attacked and although he escaped, a price of 10,000 dinars was put on his head and he was soon hunted down. The body of the crown prince was given to the mob, mutilated, publicly hanged and 'dragged by the crowd through the streets'. A body alleged to be that of Nuri was either handed to the crowd on 16 or 17 July or dug up by them after burial, then 'dismembered'. A howling mob then lynched some visiting Jordanian ministers, three American citizens and a German.[119]

British intelligence maintained close liaison with the ill-fated regime until the end – one former intelligence officer lamented how British agents were hanged in the square after the coup – but were unable to predict or prevent the revolution.[120] Princess Fadhila was not in Baghdad on the night of the attack as she was preparing for her wedding to Faisal the next day, and so escaped with her life. However, her long-term utility to the British died amid the gunfire.

Even so, the British remained loyal to the exiled minor royals of Iraq. Diplomats used the secret intelligence fund to pay off one prince on the grounds that he had been deprived of his inheritance. After a while though, a senior diplomat met him in an upmarket Washington hotel to deliver the unwelcome news that he would no longer receive any more payments. The prince later turned up at the Foreign Office with his family and threatened to camp on the premises until he was paid. Britain's soft spot for royalty – and use of intelligence to support them – only stretched so far.[121]

Arab regimes gradually turned to America, and in particular the CIA, to escape the taint of British imperialism. Unbeknown to them the CIA was heading in an opposite direction. The 1958 coup in Iraq represented a turning point in Anglo-American relations and secretly the CIA and MI6 began to work together, not only against Soviet influence but to contain Arab nationalism and bolster the last pro-western monarchs in the region. Despite the reverse in Iraq, the CIA was increasingly a fan of the queen, commonwealth, constitutionalism and corgis.[122]

THE EGYPTIAN AND Iraqi monarchies had fallen in the space of a few years, while the Jordanian monarchy had publicly distanced itself from the British, turning to America. Saudi Arabia also looked to Washington and only the minor sultans of the Gulf remained resolutely loyal to Britain. Each of these events was a considerable blow for Britain's position in the Middle East, but also for Queen Elizabeth, the commonwealth – which had little traction in the region – and the brand of constitutional monarchy. She had maintained a close interest in the intrigue and turbulence of the Middle East in the years following her coronation, and had even been prepared to intervene personally to influence events discreetly. Yet as British power collapsed alongside friendly potentates, she must have wondered whether it had all been in vain.

DISCREET DIPLOMACY:
THE ROYALS AND AFRICA

*'you may easily wish to return them at once with
a strong hint that they should be burnt!'*

Prince Philip delivering his own diplomatic intelligence
reports to Harold Wilson, 1964[1]

THE BRITISH EMPIRE continued to crumble. Elizabeth and Philip responded by sailing on through the rubble, stoically promoting what they hoped would be the strength of the commonwealth and the valuable global role Britain could play in leading it. But the wind of change had bewildered Britain's ruling classes. The Suez debacle eviscerated any renewed sense of optimism following the royal couple's hugely successful – and onerously lengthy – commonwealth tour shortly after the coronation. Meanwhile, criticism of the monarchy increased. The *Daily Mirror*, Britain's bestselling tabloid, pointedly asked if the New Elizabethan Age was destined to be a flop. One journalist, after conducting a business efficiency analysis of the queen's public engagements, concluded it was 'hardly a back-breaking programme'.[2] International travel was one area where the queen could – quite literally – put in the miles. Royal diplomacy projected continuity on behalf of a disoriented nation. Doing so was not as easy as it seemed. It required delicate political discussions and close co-operation with the intelligence services.

GHANA ACHIEVED INDEPENDENCE in 1957 under the influential
nationalist leader Kwame Nkrumah. His contribution to Pan-
Africanism made him doubly important across the whole continent.
Two years later, Elizabeth prepared to make her first visit to the
former colony. Much to Nkrumah's disappointment, her third pregnancy, with Prince Andrew, delayed the trip until autumn 1961.
By this time, Ghanaian politics had become a lot more turbulent
– putting the queen at political and even physical risk.

In December 1960, Michael Adeane, Elizabeth's private secretary, suggested that Harold Macmillan, the prime minister, consider
postponing or even cancelling the trip altogether.[3] The queen, he
explained, had agreed to visit Ghana before its population had
approved a dramatic new constitution declaring it a republic. Elizabeth
was no longer the sovereign. To make matters worse, rumours swirled
that Nkrumah was flirting with the Soviets – he visited Moscow in
autumn 1961 – and threatened to pull Ghana out of the commonwealth altogether. Leaving the commonwealth so shortly after a state
visit from the queen would have humiliated Elizabeth.

Nkrumah, once outrageously popular among his people as the
first man to lead an African colony to independence, began to
act in a more and more dictatorial manner. At one of his private
Tuesday audiences in the palace, Macmillan agreed with the queen
that Nkrumah 'would probably sacrifice anything, including the
commonwealth connection, for the sake of his African ambitions'.[4]
Secret despatches from British civil servants at home and in Accra
left Adeane with neither enthusiasm nor confidence about the
upcoming trip.[5]

Security worries compounded the political risk. Macmillan did
not think the queen would be a target of violence herself but patronizingly feared that inept local planning would put her at risk from a
crush of overenthusiastic well-wishers as she attended social events.[6]
The security liaison officer in Ghana, an MI5 man who revealed

his true identity to Nkrumah shortly before independence and stayed on to work closely – and discreetly – with the new domestic counter-subversion authorities, became a reassuring source as officials in London fretted about the queen's physical safety. His intelligence, acquired through excellent communication channels with Nkrumah's government, reassured Macmillan and Martin Charteris, the queen's assistant private secretary, that no security reason existed to cancel the tour.[7]

As the date of departure neared, Macmillan received further advice from MI5 and Special Branch, both of which had sent senior officers to Ghana to assess the situation.[8] Charteris, an old military intelligence hand, had earlier conducted his own reconnaissance as well.[9] The latest intelligence indicated 'no significant security threat from any agency outside Ghana'. On the internal front: 'there is no foreseen risk of any violence to Her Majesty or any expression of hostility being directed against the Queen at any time during the visit'.[10]

This was not enough for Whitehall's worriers. Threats against Nkrumah rather than Elizabeth could still pose a risk to the queen. Intelligence warned of 'widespread resentment against Dr Nkrumah personally', noting that any attempt to assassinate the president when in the company of the queen would indirectly threaten her own life. Likewise, demonstrations against Nkrumah could cause embarrassment to the queen – or worse.[11]

MI5 offered reassurance on both counts. The scale of protection would be 'massive', while Ghanaians held great 'respect and affection' for the queen and would not target Nkrumah in her presence. If dissidence did break out, there was 'no doubt' that it would be 'suppressed by the police with great firmness'. Sometimes authoritarianism overseas had its advantages. MI5 added that opponents to Nkrumah wanted to postpone the queen's trip in order to stir tension between the UK and Ghana, but once she actually arrived, they would be very unlikely to engineer further demonstrations.[12]

Macmillan and Adeane breathed a collective sigh of relief as they read the MI5 reports. Then, all of a sudden, with arrangements finally proceeding satisfactorily, another thorny issue came from nowhere to draw the queen's ire in the form of an ex-spy and British traitor.

Alan Nunn May was a gifted physicist specializing in several fields ranging from pioneering radar work, measuring sub-atomic activity, to developing nuclear reactors. From Cambridge, he went on to work on the top-secret Manhattan Project – the US–UK attempt to build a nuclear bomb – during the Second World War. Nunn May was also a spy and had passed secret intelligence about nuclear weapons to the Soviets.

British intelligence learnt of his betrayal through a defector in 1945 and Nunn May eventually confessed after intense questioning and round the clock surveillance. He was sentenced to ten years of hard labour, of which he served six, and became the first person convicted for supplying atomic secrets to the Soviets. The case shocked the British public and had wider political ramifications: Washington was furious at the revelations and dramatically slashed nuclear co-operation with the UK.

In 1961, Kwame Nkrumah offered Nunn May a professorship in physics at the University of Ghana. The disgraced physicist was one of a number of leftist academics and anti-apartheid activists invited by Nkrumah as part of his attempts to steer a course between the two Cold War superpowers, so-called positive neutralism.

The queen, due to visit that very university, was in Balmoral when she heard the news. Michael Adeane quickly fired off an unusually strongly worded letter to Downing Street. He made it abundantly clear that Elizabeth 'would not in any circumstances be prepared to meet Dr Nunn May either at the University or anywhere else'. There could be no room for misunderstanding: she would not be prepared to make any concessions on this – and should not be pressed into doing so by the Ghanaians.[13]

Alexander Clutterbuck, the most senior official in the commonwealth relations office, shared the queen's concerns. Although Nunn May was not due to start his tenure until after the queen's visit, he might make a preliminary trip to the university to coincide with

Elizabeth's arrival. Officials grew paranoid about the possibility of a plot by left-wing academics to present him to the queen.[14]

Clutterbuck instructed British representatives in Accra to 'take early opportunity of making it absolutely clear to Nkrumah himself without any possibility of misunderstanding that the Queen would under no circumstances agree to meet May'. Nkrumah might also be reminded of British disappointment at his decision to employ Nunn May in the first place. With the palace breathing down his neck, Clutterbuck sent a copy to Adeane.[15]

Nkrumah was furious. He demanded to know where Britain had got the idea that Nunn May was even coming to Ghana, let alone that he might be presented to the queen. This degenerated into a rant about the British press: 'do they take me for a fool? Do they not realize that Ghana is now independent?' He did, however, recognize the potential for humiliation and promised that Nunn May would not be presented to Elizabeth. Given Nkrumah's bad mood, the high commissioner did not think it wise to remind him of Britain's regret at the appointment more broadly.[16]

This was the last day of October; the queen was due to travel on 9 November. Still, another bullet had been dodged. Planning continued. A few days later, less than a week before Elizabeth and Philip were due to depart, political and security problems again threatened to call off the problematic trip altogether.

On 2 November, Macmillan received 'very bad' news from Ghana: 'it is now thought that Nkrumah will <u>leave</u> the Commonwealth immediately after the Queen's visit. This,' he recorded in his diary, 'will put us in a ludicrous position.'[17]

Two days later, the sound of exploding bombs pierced the early morning quiet in Accra. The target, a statue of Nkrumah outside Parliament House, suffered serious damage to its legs and plinth. Another explosion occurred afterwards, fanning rumours that dissidents were plotting to assassinate Nkrumah. Macmillan promptly sent the commonwealth relations secretary, Duncan Sandys, to Ghana to assess the situation for himself and to steady growing worries at home.[18] Across St James's Park, a grateful Elizabeth felt reassured by the Sandys mission.[19]

Macmillan and Adeane turned to the security arrangements. They wondered whether Elizabeth should travel in a car with Philip – rather than Nkrumah – for fear of attacks against the president's vehicle. Growing nervous, the queen had been thinking the same thing and spoke to Nkrumah personally about the possibility of doing so. Continuing the theme, Macmillan suggested placing a British policeman in the queen's car, avoiding any unscheduled detours, and, once the queen was in the car, she would ask the driver to travel as quickly as possible. Adeane conceded that if things did not go well the queen could always shorten her programme under the guise of feeling tired.[20]

Both Macmillan and Adeane were fairly confident that the recent bombings would fizzle out. Drawing on the latest intelligence, they assumed that if the dissidents hoped to prevent or postpone the queen's tour then, by virtue of her successfully making the trip, their cause would dissolve. The following evening, two days before the scheduled departure, Macmillan discussed all this with the queen directly.[21]

He told her that there was 'no real evidence of such security risks as to justify me in asking Dr. Nkrumah' to rescind the invitation. He also warned that if Ghana were to leave the commonwealth, there 'can be no doubt that the Russians would move in'. Perhaps the queen's visit would persuade Nkrumah against leaving. And, in a candid moment, he told the queen that Britain should not overly criticize the 'younger Commonwealth countries for their follies', after all, 'we have not been entirely blameless in our own history'. Therefore, on political, as well as security, grounds, the visit should go ahead.[22]

This came as a relief to the queen. She wanted to go, but had grown irritated by the to-ing and fro-ing. As Macmillan put it, 'she loves her duty and means to be a Queen and not a puppet'.[23]

Meanwhile, Sandys hurriedly met security authorities in Accra. They advised him that if the dissidents really aimed to assassinate

Nkrumah during the tour, then surely they would not have blown up a statue as a dress rehearsal just a few days before the queen arrived. All this had achieved was a dramatic increase in police surveillance.[24]

MI5 was more cautious. Intelligence officers warned Sandys that the explosions added to the risk facing the queen. The group behind the attacks were an unknown quantity – and therefore dangerously unpredictable. Besides, the violence might 'encourage others to have a bash'. MI5 only dropped their objection after Special Branch gave the green light.[25]

Sandys wanted to test the theory that President Nkrumah was living in fear of assassination. He bravely persuaded Nkrumah to travel alongside him in an open-topped car, with little police protection, over the route which the queen would follow in Accra a few days later. As word of the president's whereabouts spread, cheering crowds assembled at street corners. The enthusiastic welcome convinced Sandys that the risk to Nkrumah's life was indeed minimal. He recommended that the visit go ahead as planned.[26]

A local intelligence operation carried out with 'utmost secrecy' the night Sandys left provided further confidence. An unnamed source lay what British officials called 'a police trap' by enticing plotters with plastic explosives and luring them into the arms of Special Branch. The British high commission in Accra swiftly told Number 10 that 'these developments represent a diminution of risk to the Queen'. It was a local operation and the British were not yet supposed to know about the arrests. With the queen due to travel the next day, officials simply could not wait to be informed through proper channels and, for source protection reasons, had to feign surprise when the proud Ghanaians eventually told them.[27]

With the House of Commons growing increasingly restless, Macmillan convened a Cabinet meeting the next morning, Wednesday 8 November. He needed final approval before he could provide Elizabeth with a decision as to whether the trip would definitely go ahead. She and Philip were now due to travel in less than twenty-four hours.

Sandys dashed from the airport to brief his colleagues on the latest intelligence. Macmillan closed the discussion with a homily to the queen's stoicism. The risk to the queen was no greater than usual, but the public and politicians alike failed to appreciate the size of the usual risk.

He then turned to a more political justification. Given the widespread anxiety about this particular visit, the greatest risk was now actually to his government, which, many people felt, was sending the queen into a dangerous situation. Macmillan faced a backbench revolt on the issue, which he feared the Labour Party would be more than happy to exploit.

After months of planning and prevarication, the Cabinet finally agreed that Elizabeth should go. Macmillan informed the palace immediately afterwards.[28]

Despite the mounting risks, the queen wanted to go. The stakes were high for both her and Nkrumah. The world was watching. The trip was important for the future of the commonwealth; Elizabeth accepted the inevitability of decolonization but she dreaded Ghana leaving an organization about which she cared deeply. She also recognized its symbolic importance in the context of the Cold War, supposedly telling Macmillan 'how silly I should look if I was scared to visit Ghana and then Khrushchev went and had a good reception'.[29]

Elizabeth and Philip toured Ghana for eleven days. The itinerary included – without embarrassment – a visit to the university. Security was excellent throughout; the crowds enthusiastic. Despite Adeane's worries, she even managed to travel in an open-topped car with Nkrumah. Adeane sent Macmillan reassuring updates about the security situation as the tour unfolded, especially after the local police made some arrests. In his typically grandiloquent manner, the prime minister told Elizabeth that 'my anxieties will remain until Your Majesty and His Royal Highness are safely returned to these shores'.[30] Indeed, he found the week of the visit particularly trying, talking of little else.[31]

On the last night, photographers famously captured Elizabeth and Nkrumah dancing across a ballroom floor, smiling and intimate. British officials thought the trip was 'an outstanding personal triumph for The Queen and Prince Philip'.[32] Ghana did not leave the commonwealth, but the queen's visit had failed to alter its leftist path. Elizabeth had found Nkrumah 'muddled' in his world views and 'naïve and vainglorious' in his ambitions. The very next year, the Soviet Union awarded him the Lenin Peace Prize.[33] Neither did the queen's visit bolster Nkrumah's own position; he faced at least one assassination attempt every year afterwards. Nkrumah mostly blamed the CIA and eventually wrote a remarkably polite letter to President Lyndon Johnson asking him to order the CIA to stop 'fomenting ill will' and to cease its 'clandestine and subversive activities'.[34]

A few years later, the British high commissioner to Ghana spoke with those who had schemed to overthrow Nkrumah. When they discussed the queen's visit they said some of them had considered whether to make a demonstration, or, as they politely put it, 'do something even worse', against Nkrumah. Ultimately, however, they had decided that it would be absolutely wrong to do anything that might harm or embarrass Elizabeth whom 'they greatly loved'. In the end they did not do anything.[35]

The queen's staff faced one final security concern on returning from Ghana. Her private secretary recalls: 'I had to have a bucket full of baby alligators in the plane with me.' Since then, palace advisers have stuck to a simple rule for royal gifts: 'nothing wot eats'.[36]

HISTORY THREATENED TO repeat itself three and a half years later as the queen prepared to visit Sudan in February 1965.

The vast state spanning much of northeastern Africa might now seem a strange destination, but it was strategically important at the time. The UK possessed a chain of military bases stretching from the British mainland to the Far East. The best way to travel between them involved flying via Libya, which was still a monarchy and under British influence, Sudan and Kenya. Doing so required overflight rights from the Sudanese government.[37]

Sending Elizabeth and Philip to Sudan was risky. In October the previous year, mass strikes and protests against the military government had culminated in a revolution and widespread unrest. As one senior diplomat remembered, fighting between traditionalists and communists had left the streets 'full of bodies'.[38]

In classic British understatement, the revolution and its bloody aftermath made the queen's invitation 'awkward'. Trying to stay calm, diplomats simply hoped not to provoke a renewed invitation from the new government and that the problem would go away. Unfortunately, the queen's assistant private secretary, Edward Ford, was already on his way out to Khartoum on a reconnaissance trip. This, in another example of British 'diplomatese', formed an 'additional complication'. Asking the new Sudanese government whether Ford would still be welcome risked provoking the very re-invitation that diplomats were so keen to avoid.[39]

Despite the violence, Edward Ford was allowed in.[40] The visit was still on. British officials tried to see the positives and noted that accepting an invitation from a military government, only to reject it when civilians came to power, would have sent entirely the wrong message.[41] Besides, those overflight rights still needed shoring up.

The following month, diplomats back in London grew nervous. Strikes, riots and even the murder of a Briton by a local gang had inflamed the British press. To make matters worse, the new government, according to the *Daily Express*, had received rebel leaders from Congo who had threatened the lives of British hostages. The press bellowed against the queen's trip.[42]

The foreign secretary, Patrick Gordon Walker, worried he could not in all good conscience advise the queen to go ahead. He also pointed out that Sudanese elections were due shortly afterwards and that it might look like the queen was trying to influence them.[43]

Special Branch sent an officer to assess the security risks.[44] Under pressure, and demonstrating striking parallels with Ghana, the Foreign Office held off making a final recommendation to the queen until just a few weeks before she was due to leave.[45] When the ambassador, Ian Scott, interjected in defence of Sudan, diplomats refused to send his telegram to the palace fearing it would give a 'misleading impression'.[46] They thought he had gone native.

With forty-eight hours to go before the queen was due to arrive, Scott visited the revolutionary council. He told them, in no uncertain terms, that 'shooting was still going on in the streets' despite the imminent arrival of Elizabeth and Philip. 'We can't have this.' He threatened to cancel the whole trip unless 'each of you will order your political parties to stop fighting and make the visit a huge success'. Scott's tour de four successfully convinced each faction to announce a ceasefire publicly on the radio; his Arabic-speaking colleague, Anthony Parsons, would be listening.[47]

'One by one, Communists, National Democrats whatever they were, all said: down tools, boys; let's give the Queen of England a first class visit; and it was a first class visit.'[48] The revolutionary council agreed and, with a green light from Special Branch, the queen received a warm welcome when she landed in early February. She and Philip were able to stand in an open-topped Land Rover for a leisurely drive from the airport – a stark contrast, Scott proudly pointed out, to an eastern European leader who had recently been escorted in a bulletproof car at remarkably high speed.[49]

Indeed, throughout the 1960s and 1970s, the outstanding quality of royal visits was their bravery, even sheer effrontery in the face of danger. Visiting Turkey in 1971, their hosts noted that previous visitors, including the shah of Iran and President de Gaulle, were cowards – both of them saw very little of the public because of security fears. A key issue was the speed at which the queen's car should travel. The Turks said that, as with the shah, they should travel at fifty miles an hour. British diplomats scoffed that 'the Queen prefers to travel at more like fifteen miles an hour'.

The chief of police of Ankara 'looked a bit shocked'. In the end, a million Turks turned out to wave as the queen cantered by: 'a rather novel experience'.[50]

And so it was in Sudan. A couple of inevitable security incidents raised heartrates, though. One came when the car slowly carrying the queen and the president of the revolutionary council, Dr Tajani, drove past an Egyptian secondary school. Suddenly a student stepped out from the crowd and hurled a tomato at them. Scott asked the queen if she was all right. 'Yes,' she replied. 'I got two pips and Dr Tajani one.' Scott asked whether it had been a red or a green tomato. 'A red,' she replied, unsure why the colour mattered. A green tomato would have been a missile, Scott explained, but a red one was just a protest. Elizabeth laughed and repeated the story to the head of the Foreign Office.[51]

Elizabeth thanked the Sudanese people for their warm welcome. 'It is often the case,' she said, 'and it is certainly so where Sudan and Britain are concerned, that where two peoples have come to respect each other's courage in time of war… their friendship in peace is so much stronger.'[52]

On the last night of the visit, the revolutionary council held a party for the queen on a nineteenth-century river boat. What some recalled as 'General Gordon stuff'. The head of the local Communist Party, 'who enjoyed parties very much', drunkenly approached her and, swaying slightly, lifted his glass. 'Your majesty, I would like to drink a toast to you; Your very good health; and I speak as the Head of Her Majesty's loyal Communist Party in the Sudan.'[53]

Watching carefully, the CIA predicted another coup in Sudan. For now, though, American intelligence noted that the 'political parties seem to be honouring their promises to avoid trouble during Queen Elizabeth's visit'.[54] The Americans were half right: the parties did honour their promises, and in fact there was no further coup – at least for another four years. 'The interesting thing was,' Anthony Parsons, Scott's Arabic-speaking colleague, later recalled, 'we all wondered when she left whether the fighting would resume;

but it didn't.' The various factions 'had downed tools and it was really too much of an effort to pick them up again and get down to business, as it were'. In a sense, 'her visit actually stopped the civil war going on in Sudan'.[55]

BY 1964, THE repeated success of these royal visits seems to have encouraged an effort to create a new conference organization for the commonwealth, led jointly by Prince Philip and Lord Mountbatten. They would model it on the secretive Euro-American Bilderberg group, an elite transatlantic meeting of politicians and financiers that had already been in operation for a decade. Bilderberg had its own royal dimension given that it was chaired by Prince Bernhard of the Netherlands. Bernhard's position as the consort of Queen Juliana had been an asset and he had carved out a place for himself as an impressive powerbroker on the global stage. Both Philip and his uncle, who was retiring as chief of the defence staff, eyed this with interest.[56]

As the historian Philip Murphy has observed, Bilderberg's strong links with the western intelligence community have been the cause of much comment, even a degree of paranoia. There can be no doubt that an informal club of senior intelligence officers helped to bring it into existence. The concept was created by Dr Joseph Retinger, who had served in the Polish government in exile during the Second World War, and worked with the British Special Operations Executive, later becoming the *éminence grise* of the early European Movement. Other early British enthusiasts of Bilderberg included Victor Cavendish Bentinck, wartime chairman of the Joint Intelligence Committee, and former MI6 officer H. Montgomery Hyde. Although the initial meeting of the group in 1954 was funded by the CIA, it was a confidential talking shop rather than an instrument of the intelligence agencies.[57]

Intriguingly, the initial suggestion for a commonwealth version seems to have come from Harold Wilson and his defence secretary,

Denis Healey. The latter was an enthusiastic member of Bilderberg and a keen Atlanticist.[58] Moreover, he had been working closely with Mountbatten on defence reviews and the centralization of defence intelligence.[59] Mountbatten and Healey agreed on intelligence, but not much else.[60] Healey found both Mountbatten and his close friend Solly Zuckerman, the defence scientist, to be devious. Perhaps he thought this an ideal project to distract Mountbatten from further meddling in defence issues.[61]

Both Philip and especially Mountbatten were known to hold moderate left of centre views. Both got on well with Wilson. Moreover, it is hard to imagine that Wilson would have suggested this royal-led initiative without raising it first at his Tuesday afternoon meeting with the queen. By April 1965, Mountbatten and Philip had jointly drawn up a set of proposals, but Downing Street officials dismissed them as 'woolly'. Deputy Cabinet secretary Philip Rogers observed that the idea that commonwealth high commissioners might be let loose with this scheme 'fills me with horror'.[62]

Others feared the scheme was too transatlantic and out of step with a new commonwealth; it looked too much like an exclusive 'club'. Healey and Wilson continued to pursue it, but events simply overtook them. Prince Philip never got to chair a secretive club of his own. A crisis developed in Rhodesia that shook the entire commonwealth and, together with apartheid in South Africa, beset the organization for more than two decades.[63]

In November 1965, the obdurate Rhodesian prime minister, Ian Smith, read out, in his distinctive nasal tone, an illegal unilateral declaration of independence. In doing so, he ensured white minority rule over the country and became a resistance hero to some and an unrepentant racist to others. Rhodesia, or Southern Rhodesia as it had been known, was a self-governing British colony in which European settlers had become spooked by the pace of decolonization and the march towards black majority rule. Unilateral independence offered a way out.

Ian Smith, or 'Smithy' as he was affectionately known to certain members of the royal family, wanted to keep Queen Elizabeth as head of the newly independent state, insisting that his problem was with the government not the crown. Indeed, Rhodesia's armed forces and intelligence services still professed great loyalty to, and affection for, the monarchy. Its secret service kept in close contact with their counterparts in London.[64]

The royal family inevitably took a personal interest as negotiations stalled and the situation deteriorated into a mess of constitutional difficulties. In July 1965, as a sense of crisis built, Prince Philip decided to speak out. He advised in favour of 'spinning out' the process to resolve the Rhodesia problem, emphasizing the need to 'get a peaceful result' rather than risk a 'blood bath'.[65]

The backlash was quick and severe. Newspaper coverage, especially from the *Daily Mirror*, was highly critical of his 'astonishing' intervention, apparent support for Smith's racist regime and desire to delay black majority rule.[66]

All was not as it seemed. Cecil King, proprietor of the *Daily Mirror*, quietly admitted to Prime Minister Harold Wilson that 'our attack' was not in fact caused by Philip's 'pretty innocuous remarks'. Instead, over lunch a few days earlier, Philip had stressed the 'urgent importance of the re-unification of Germany'. King's editor was present and had taken umbrage: 'we cannot have Prince Philip saying in public anything like what he had said in private at this lunch'. Therefore, as King told Wilson, the newspaper seized 'on his remarks about Rhodesia as an opportunity to fire a shot across his bows. We are informed from the Palace that the point has been taken.'[67] The brief row highlighted the perils of royal diplomacy.

In his war against racist Rhodesia, Wilson turned to economic sanctions and secret intelligence. A covert campaign sought to 'bring about the downfall of the Smith regime and a return to constitutional government and the rule of law in Rhodesia, with a view to the resumption of progress toward majority rule as quickly as possible'. Secret operations, including fake rebel groups created by the Foreign Office solely to spread propaganda, explicitly targeted the white community.[68]

Wilson complemented this by using white Rhodesian affection for the crown to undermine Smith's government. One plan involved sending Mountbatten to Rhodesia to deliver a personal message from the queen indicating her indignation at the racist regime. Mountbatten would fly out to the capital, Salisbury, in a plane specially painted as part of the Queen's Flight, thereby drawing attention to the queen's personal investment in the crisis and her displeasure.[69]

When Wilson raised this at the palace, Elizabeth was broadly supportive. Mountbatten himself, a veteran of sticky end-of-empire situations and a lover of special tasks, was highly enthusiastic about the plan. However, she soon got cold feet, not least because of the risk to Mountbatten, and refused to allow any of her personal household to accompany him. Although Mountbatten himself, enticed by the prospect of adventure, remained keen – and offered to work on the queen – Wilson also grew cool. He recognized that the queen could only act on advice provided by the government, thereby undermining any attempt to present her as personally opposed to the Smith regime.[70]

A more dramatic and outlandish option involved the queen mother. The wife of the beleaguered governor of Rhodesia, Lady Gibbs, was staying with the prime minister of Northern Ireland, Terence O'Neill, in October 1966. One night O'Neill suggested, 'how about smuggling the Queen Mother out to Government House', in other words, the governor's residence in Salisbury. Lady Gibbs slept on it and the following morning replied: 'do you know I believe your idea about the Queen Mother might work! Do please suggest it to the PM.'[71]

Clearly enjoying the intrigue, O'Neill outlined a most peculiar plan to Wilson in a handwritten note, itself hand-delivered by a trusted emissary. 'A plane could leave England after dark carrying officials. It would be known that Lady Gibbs was on board – perhaps even a female Gibbs relative could be said to be in the party. At

Salisbury airport the secret would emerge,' and the queen mother's 'fantastic natural charm would win the day. Vast crowds would gather outside Government House to express their loyalty. Smithy would be "on the spot". If he tried to expel the Queen Mother the Regime would risk offending the strong latent pro-British sentiment, which I gather still exists in Rhodesia today.' The queen mother, O'Neill concluded, is a 'strange amalgam'. 'She might just bring this off.'[72]

Wilson politely declined.[73] O'Neill clearly saw something in it, though, and tried to revive a similar plan four months later.[74] Wilson now had to personally 'kill the idea'.[75] Even had he approved it, the queen mother might have opposed the unusual mission anyway. She reputedly urged ministers 'not to be nasty to Smithy' and was critical of Wilson's approach to the Rhodesia crisis. Indeed, she was rather a supporter of the Smith regime.[76]

The queen mother was at the centre of these considerations for another reason. She was the colonel-in-chief of the British South Africa Police, the semi-militarized force that provided not only law and order functions, but also intelligence in Rhodesia. They had largely been trained on the lessons of Britain's brutal campaign against the Mau Mau rebels in Kenya.[77] Ken Flower, who became head of Rhodesia's intelligence, took the salute for this force when the queen mother visited in 1960. Roger Hollis of MI5 was also a regular visitor and Flower, in return, was a regular at MI5 and MI6 in London.[78] Flower perceived the queen mother as especially sympathetic to the Smith regime. Meanwhile, the queen herself had a higher-level engagement with law and order in Rhodesia, since the privy council in London was still the illegal state's last court of legal appeal.

In August 1967, all this took on a new importance when the Rhodesian government announced that it would go ahead with the execution of three condemned guerrillas. Elizabeth quickly issued a royal reprieve and the British government warned of the 'gravest personal responsibility' to anyone involved in the proposed hanging. Indeed, the government warned that if the executions were carried out it would be 'murder'. Waving the royal card, those carrying out the death sentence, including the Rhodesian Cabinet, the prison officials and the executioner, would all be liable to capital punishment for treason.[79]

On 10 March 1968, things came to a dreadful culmination. Smith called in Ken Flower to brief him before an emergency Cabinet meeting with the hangings imminent. Flower was seen as close to MI5 and especially MI6, so 'the PM greeted me as if I was an intruder'. Flower told Smith 'that the Queen's reprieve should be upheld'. He added that the executions would have a negative impact on the overall intelligence and security situation. However, Smith ignored his advice. 'The Queen's reprieve was rejected and the "terrorists" were hanged at dawn.'[80]

Two years after the executions, Ian Smith's rebel government declared itself to be a republic. The crown was eventually removed from the badge of the British South Africa Police, and the appointment of the queen mother as honorary commissioner was suspended.[81] But this was done with reluctance, Queen Elizabeth advised the Foreign Office: 'Suspend but not Sever! It could be cunningly written in.'[82] There was a lingering hope that the racist regime in Rhodesia would be removed and the country might eventually be restored to partnership in the commonwealth.

Restoration and renewal had been the story of the governments of Germany, Italy and Japan in Elizabeth's own lifetime. Even now she was working for their rehabilitation through an energetic programme of global diplomacy. Her biggest challenge would be the Soviet Union. Diplomats hoped to use her in cooling tensions, but the queen had other ideas.

20

DISCREET DIPLOMACY:
THE GLOBAL QUEEN

'The Queen is personally interested'

January 1980[1]

LIKE HER GREAT-GRANDFATHER, King Edward VII, Queen Elizabeth recognized the value of royal diplomacy. She recognized it so much that after thirteen years on the throne, it dawned on her that she was running out of friendly countries to visit. This became a worry: travelling outside of her commonwealth comfort zone would create difficulties for the intelligence services and diplomats alike.

Some places remained off-limits. Despite hosting the Soviet leaders Khrushchev and Bulganin back in 1956, Elizabeth made it known to the Foreign Office a decade later that she still had no intention of visiting Russia. Michael Adeane, her private secretary, warned the UK's most senior diplomat that the assassination of her relatives after the 1917 revolution was not yet consigned to the glass case of history.[2]

Adeane offered a more guarded assessment to Tony Benn, the Labour politician, during a state banquet at Hampton Court Palace. 'The memory of the massacres at Ekaterinburg would certainly have prevented George V or VI from going' and a state visit to the

Soviet Union 'still might be difficult'. Benn, always happy to needle the monarchy, asked why there had been no embarrassment about Elizabeth's German relatives who had fought against Britain in two world wars. Adeane replied, 'Oh but the German royalty are all very decent chaps.'[3]

When the queen visited Germany in May 1965, Anthony Eden wrote to her from his retirement. Still in touch with her almost a decade after the humiliating Suez collusion, he now drew comparison with Edward VII's personal diplomacy in the run-up to the First World War. Eden told the queen that the Germans lacked political sense and, as a result, were too easily led and lacked standards. 'Their fervour and loyalty can be misplaced.' The impact of Elizabeth's visit would be similar to how Edward's 'diplomacy and personality thawed the more sophisticated French', leading to the Entente Cordiale.[4]

Prince Philip made a private visit to Germany the following year and raised eyebrows in the British embassy. On the guest list for lunch at a yacht club was one Alfred Krupp von Bohlen. He was a keen yachtsman, but he was also a prominent industrialist who had supplied weapons to the Nazis. After the war he was convicted of crimes against humanity for using slave labour in his factories and served three years in prison.[5] Now, the duke of Edinburgh was inviting him – effectively a convicted Nazi war criminal – for lunch.

British diplomats in Bonn did not know what to do. Frank Roberts, the ambassador, worried that 'it would clearly be very difficult and could cause serious misunderstandings if we were to try to get Krupp "disinvited" or even to use such behind-the-scenes influence as we have to suggest that Krupp should not come'. Unable, or unwilling, to meddle in private royal affairs, he simply hoped that the press would not be looking too closely and that no one would notice Philip's dodgy company.

Watching from the side-lines, he suggested that 'we should take no action and let matters take their course, which I hope will not be an embarrassing one'. The diplomats essentially crossed their fingers and hoped. Von Bohlen was certainly less toxic than he used to be, but Roberts feared public 'prejudices, however irrational, where the Royal Family are concerned'. There was clearly a sensitivity to the connection, however distant or unfair, between the Windsors and Nazi Germany. The Foreign Office duly told Philip about the predicament – but did not actively intervene.[6] When a revised guest list reached Bonn two weeks later, von Bohlen's name had mysteriously disappeared.[7] Perhaps Philip had got the hint.

The Foreign Office raised the prospect of Japan, another wartime enemy, as a 'difficult' country for the queen to visit. She was more amenable, professing to 'be prepared to contemplate a visit one day'. She suggested that if the Japanese emperor visited the UK, then he might arrive in Windsor rather than in the capital. Feelings about Japan's treatment of prisoners of war still ran high in Britain.[8] Conscious of security, she thought this would 'avoid the possibility of any untoward happening during a carriage drive in London'.[9]

QUEEN ELIZABETH WAS reluctant to visit Latin America. This was not because of any historical animosity, personal conflicts of interest, or even the distances involved; she simply feared being upstaged by Charles de Gaulle's extensive trip undertaken in autumn 1964. The French president had taken in ten countries, from Guadeloupe to Venezuela, regaling cheering crowds with an impressive message of non-interventionism, respect for the developing world, and self-determination. Watching from London, Elizabeth worried that she could not compete.[10] She only acquiesced four years later, once local memories had faded, to a Foreign Office request to visit Chile and Brazil.

British diplomats had paid close attention to Latin America since the start of the decade. Regional growth combined with the perceived decline of the US after the CIA's disastrous attempt to overthrow Fidel Castro in 1961 created a golden opportunity to capture a new economic market.[11] British policy cynically centred on 'making the Latin Americans feel that they are being taken seriously'.[12] A royal visit was one way of doing this; another, as officials recognized, was a massive increase in covert action and propaganda in the region.[13] Royal diplomacy and covert operations were not mutually exclusive.

As early as 1961, the Foreign Office supported a visit by Philip to the region. Diplomats hoped a trip might deter 'further defections on the Cuban model'.[14] Royal diplomacy was one tool in the state arsenal complementing a wide variety of others – overt and otherwise. An information campaign, including distributing 9,500 booklets on the British monarchy, accompanied the queen's visit in autumn 1968.[15] On top of this, the Foreign Office commissioned specially written feature articles on 'royal themes' to be used by the local press.[16]

Meanwhile, more covert attempts were under way to ensure the queen's visit was a success. Nigel Clive was a specialist in the dark arts of statecraft. He had earlier headed MI6's special political action unit, tasked with covert influence operations. He now ran the Foreign Office's propaganda arm, the Information Research Department (IRD).

Ahead of the queen's trip, Clive visited the embassy in Chile to discuss 'ways and means of getting the maximum advantage from the State Visit'. The bulk of these were open and obvious, such as exhibiting replicas of the crown jewels,[17] but the IRD had recently bolstered its covert effort in Chile and its local representative in Santiago found himself very busy during the state visit. He was so preoccupied that he had been unable to visit any other cities and had fallen behind in his efforts to interfere in forthcoming Chilean elections. Both British intelligence and the CIA were keen to retard the efforts of the hard left.[18]

Since the 1964 US-backed coup in Brazil, the IRD had sought to covertly manipulate *Ultima Hora*, a leftist newspaper which had opposed the coup and the ensuing dictatorship. By the time of the queen's visit, British officials boasted of having 'assiduously cultivated' its founder and editor, Samuel Wainer.[19] The influence proved successful: *Ultima Hora* published remarkably positive coverage of the royal visit. In fact, it was so positive that the US assumed Britain had simply paid off the newspaper. 'Not a penny,' came the IRD's proud response.[20] Over the period 1964 to 1974, the CIA had, by comparison, spent a total of $10 million on covert action in Chile, mostly on propaganda projects to support President Frei.[21]

Meanwhile, in Chile, British propagandists had busily tried to provoke a split among the socialists between the 'hot-heads' who believed in violence and others who were 'at heart "drawing-room revolutionaries"'. They did so by disseminating pamphlets to the Chilean security services, trade unions and student leaders, and by placing IRD articles in local newspapers using pseudonyms.[22]

Shortly after arriving in Chile, Elizabeth and Philip met one of the main propaganda targets: Salvador Allende, the socialist politician who later became president. He used the opportunity of a royal visit to criticize western treatment of underdeveloped countries, accusing the rich of getting richer by sucking raw materials from poorer nations. He boldly turned up to meet the royal couple in improper attire of 'street clothes' rather than formal dinner wear. According to US diplomats present, Allende 'stuck out like a sore thumb amongst the tails, trains and tiaras'.[23]

Philip, not one, according to the US diplomats, to be 'intimidated by such plebeian airs of superiority', could not resist a swipe at his dress sense. Their exchange heated up when Philip mocked him for failing to win three presidential elections. Allende told Philip that the people were dissatisfied with Chilean politics and that he, as the representative of those people, would change things for the better. Philip retorted that he quite understood Allende's dissatisfaction as a representative of the people given that he had been rejected by them three times in a row.[24]

The dig was particularly acerbic because, four years earlier, British propagandists and MI6 had attempted to influence the Chilean presidential election – precisely to keep Allende out of power. 'Once in power,' the local ambassador had warned, 'the chances are that Allende would be manoeuvred by the communists, either willingly or otherwise, and that the end-product might well be a Government on the Cuban pattern.'[25] Although British operations were dwarfed by those of the CIA, covert action continued and, by the year of the state visit, IRD expressed its secret goal with unusual directness: 'because there is a very real danger that the Communists might gain control of this country by constitutional means, we are concentrating on covert operations which we think could influence the result of the next election'.[26]

The palace's briefing pack included the line that Chile was a 'Parliamentary Democracy and there is a very strong tradition of democratic government and respect for the rule of law. President Frei was elected in September 1964 (for a term of six years) as the head of the first Christian Democrat Government in Latin America.'[27] No mention, of course, of the covert action to put him there.

After Elizabeth and Philip had left, the British ambassador rated the visit a triumphant success. He predicted an increase in trade, but also noted the political impact. The tour had 'probably brought a welcome boost to President Frei's Government' at a 'time when he badly needed it'. Frei had also told him with satisfaction that 'the fractious Opposition leader, Allende, so closely and warmly associated himself with the visit that the entire Chilean people seemed for one week to be united in agreement at least on one subject'.[28] This was short-lived, but it aligned with the simultaneous intelligence operations designed to split Allende from the 'hot-heads'. The royal trip to Chile and Brazil demonstrates the different arms of British influence – royal, diplomatic and secret – working together in harmony.

WITH DÉTENTE IN the air, Downing Street now resurrected discussions about a potential royal visit to the Soviet Union. As early as July 1965, Prime Minister Harold Wilson had suggested an exchange of visits between the two heads of state, Queen Elizabeth and the Soviet president, Anastas Mikoyan. But the problem was not only the liquidation of the Romanovs in 1918; Mikoyan hated the British as he had been a prisoner of British forces during the Russian civil war.[29]

Wilson did not give up and in February 1967, just a year after the queen had ruled it out on the grounds of bloody family history, he told Alexei Kosygin, the Soviet premier, over lunch at Number 10 that the queen would now like to visit Russia after all. He added that it would be necessary to break the ice by first sending a more junior member of her family. Kosygin excitedly interjected that he knew all this already: Elizabeth had told him personally over dinner the previous evening.[30] She also told him, slightly dismissively, that Princess Margaret was 'for some reason anxious to go'.[31]

Kosygin would have been disappointed to learn that Elizabeth had not told him the whole truth. As their conversation had become more awkward, moving into personal and diplomatic territory that made the queen uncomfortable, Elizabeth flailed and had to be rescued by the prime minister. An urgent message reached Wilson as he was drinking coffee nearby; he gallantly strode over to the queen and steered the conversation away.[32] It was too late.

Personally, she liked Kosygin, so much so that she had lent him the royal train for a visit to Edinburgh on 10 February. Yet in private, she was actually rather anxious to avoid Russia – at least for the time being. According to senior diplomats, she and Philip both wanted to 'avoid identification with the 50th anniversary of the Communist Revolution and its attendant family tragedy'.[33]

A year later, the Soviets raised the question more formally. This time Wilson rebuffed them with the standard line that the queen was unavailable due to unspecified 'other commitments'; but he did say that she might be willing to send Princess Margaret in her place.[34] In truth, there was no prospect of Elizabeth visiting Russia 'for some time to come'.[35] Aside from the queen's lingering familial animosity, another sticking point involving Cold War espionage made any visit politically problematic. But it also provided an opportunity.

In April 1965, the KGB had arrested a young British lecturer, Gerald Brooke, as he led a group of student-teachers in Moscow. The Soviets found him guilty of passing propaganda leaflets to dissidents and jailed him for subversion. He was sentenced to five years' detention, and later admitted to distributing documents on behalf of an anti-Soviet organization but claimed not to know their contents. Brooke had in fact been under MI6 control and had been engaged on a fairly worthless operation which, once discovered, annoyed Downing Street.[36]

With Brooke labouring in gruelling camps and British public opinion clamouring for his release, the Kremlin tried to use him in an old-fashioned spy swap for Helen and Peter Kroger. The Krogers, a husband-and-wife duo of spies, were in prison for gathering classified intelligence on Britain's underwater warfare technologies. Wilson rejected the Soviet offer as tantamount to blackmail.[37] Instead of a spy swap, he wondered whether the dangle of a royal visit could convince the Soviets to release Brooke – or at least ease his harsh treatment.

Queen Elizabeth did not object to playing a discreet role in an unprecedented spy-royal swap, but she wanted these issues to be linked only 'very obliquely'.[38] It had to be deniable; Elizabeth, for good reason, did not want to be used too obviously as a pawn in a Cold War espionage game.[39] After consulting the palace, Wilson chose his words carefully: without any 'helpful gestures' on the Brooke case, he told Moscow that 'there might be certain difficulties about a Royal visit'. He left it at that, and Elizabeth expressed her gratitude.[40]

The royal visit did not happen, and not simply because the dangle was too oblique. The Soviet invasion of Czechoslovakia in the summer further dislocated diplomatic relations, effectively making a royal visit impossible. The Soviets unsuccessfully continued to press for an exchange with the Krogers regardless. As stalemate ensued, they blackmailed Britain even more outlandishly by threatening to increase Brooke's sentence if the government did not hand the couple over. This time Wilson reluctantly agreed and, in summer 1969, Gerald Brooke, pale and thin, stepped off a plane at Heathrow airport into a scrum of journalists.[41] Meanwhile, the Krogers headed home, having received what one British diplomat called 'a royal pardon'.[42]

Princess Margaret enjoyed fewer constraints and a greater sense of adventure than her older sister. She did get her visit behind the Iron Curtain – albeit to Yugoslavia – in June 1970. The visit, which the Foreign Office inevitably dubbed a resounding success, began with a curious security incident.

Shortly before she left, Princess Margaret's private secretary, Francis Leigh, received some worrying intelligence from the queen's detective. An Air Commodore Panton – whom Leigh did not know – had apparently warned that the Russians planned to plant a bomb on Margaret's aircraft. It would not go off but rather be 'discovered' as part of a KGB operation to 'make bad blood between the UK and Yugoslavia'. The tipoff was suitably alarming and mysterious to work Leigh up into quite a state. The Foreign Office's protocol department did not have a clue who Panton was either, but cautiously warned that 'we cannot afford to ignore any story of this nature, however fantastic'.[43]

It turned out that the enigmatic Air Commodore Panton was a credible source: the Ministry of Defence officer responsible for the security of the Royal Air Force. As this was the first time the Queen's Flight was due to venture behind the Iron Curtain, he had grown particularly anxious. Panton warned the palace not to leave Margaret's luggage unsupervised lest 'anyone who might wish to embarrass Anglo-Yugoslav relations by planting an explosive device would have an opportunity to do so'. Officials were already nervous about sending a senior member of the royal family to eastern Europe. Their paranoia transformed Panton's advice into a stark intelligence warning of KGB mendacity.[44] After investigation, the Foreign Office reassured Leigh that there was 'no specific threat of any such action'.[45]

Queen Elizabeth visited Yugoslavia herself two years later, in autumn 1972. It was her first visit to a communist country. According to an assessment by the CIA, the trip was an 'unqualified success'. At a time when the western press speculated about Tito turning to the east, it 'demonstrated dramatically that Tito is still maintaining friendly ties in the West'.[46]

IN THE SAME year, 1972, discussions about royal trips to the Soviet Union resurfaced. The Soviets remained eager; the British reluctant. Aside from the usual historical and political sticking points, the British embassy in Moscow worried that the visiting royals would simply not enjoy themselves: they would rather be taking in the beautiful tourist sites of Moscow and St Petersburg than required to show an 'appropriate amount of interest' in the staid achievements of communism.[47]

Despite the reluctance, Britain's propagandists covertly used the royal family to shape eastern European understanding of Britain. The Information Research Department busily planted articles about the royals in Soviet magazines. They published two about Princess Anne's equestrian activities between 1972 and spring 1973. When the European three-day event championship was due to be hosted in Kiev, the IRD included, with palace approval, a line about the princess 'perhaps defending her title in Kiev'.[48] Meanwhile, her father and chairman of the International Federation for Equestrian Sports, Prince Philip, was keen to take advantage of the opportunity to 'see something of their home-world'.[49] A royal visit was finally becoming possible.

The Soviets attempted some propaganda of their own. Victor Louis, a journalist with close links to the KGB and politburo, publicly hinted about a royal visit to the Soviet Union in an article for the *Evening News*.[50] Louis had a track record of spreading stories which the leadership would not want to acknowledge openly and this time they hoped unattributable press coverage would put pressure on the palace to send Philip to Kiev.[51]

British diplomats were well aware of Louis's connections and quickly realized that the Kremlin was discreetly trying to sound out British public opinion. This, they assumed, 'would be greeted with incredulity by the British press in general' as a result of the poor state of Anglo-Soviet relations.[52]

Incredulity would not have rendered the operation a failure. It was a clever move by the Soviets because, whatever the reaction, 'it would almost certainly prompt press enquiries which would oblige the Palace to confirm that the Duke of Edinburgh has received an invitation'.[53] When later challenged by a Soviet specialist from the Foreign Office over another story written by Louis, this time intimating the queen herself would visit, Russian diplomats denied all knowledge of having briefed Louis. These denials, however, were 'belied' by a 'knowing grin'.[54]

British diplomats did not oppose Philip visiting Kiev, but they did warn of Russia trying to make political capital out of it. This was less than two years after Britain had dramatically expelled 105 Soviet intelligence officers in Operation Foot. The unprecedented mass expulsion left the Soviets reluctant to do business with the Conservative government. They instead sought to use Philip to bypass 'reactionary Conservative ruling circles' and improve their image with the British people by dealing with Philip directly. Diplomats warned that he could not be used as a pawn in a Russian Cold War public relations campaign.[55]

That said, the Foreign Office knew that a visit by Philip could improve Anglo-Soviet relations in the longer term and could provide a way out of the impasse post-Operation Foot.[56] The royals were a valuable tool: 'We should not underestimate the impact of the Royal mystique on the Russian mind.'[57]

Philip told Denis Greenhill, the most senior official at the Foreign Office, that both he and Anne 'very much' wanted to go to Kiev.[58] As the prince pestered diplomats for a response,[59] his private

secretary, William Willett, worried about security aspects. He imagined that the duke and his party would 'have to be very cagey about
social contacts' and assumed that 'we cannot put it past the hosts to
"bug" the hotel rooms'.[60] He also wanted Philip's police officer to
have a voice in the local security arrangements.[61] The ambassador
reassured the palace that, although 'security arrangements will be
largely out of our hands', they would be 'very effective'.[62] The KGB
did not mess around.

With the palace reassured, Philip accepted the invitation.
Detailed planning could now begin. Planning for overseas trips was
always detailed, combining byzantine protocols about dress codes
and seating plans with meticulous security assessments. The legacy
of Operation Foot gave this particular trip an added complication.
The British learnt that one of the Russian officials involved on the
Kiev side was a man called A.A. Gresko. His name was familiar: one
of the 105 intelligence officers expelled from London back in 1971.
He had since supposedly taken up a post in the state committee for
sport and was due to accompany Philip throughout the visit. Over
the next ten years he would become the key interface between the
KGB and Olympic sport. The embassy in Moscow was suspicious,
assuming that the Russians 'clearly seemed to be testing the water'.[63]
In effect, they were taunting the British by putting a known intelligence officer – who had been expelled from London – alongside
Prince Philip.

Diplomats in the Foreign Office's protocol department whirred
into action. In normal circumstances the advice would have been to
'maintain a dignified silence', 'however distasteful it might be', and
avoid contact with Gresko as far as possible. But the royal dimension
upped the stakes. If journalists found out, they might interpret it as
a deliberate snub to Philip. The Foreign Office would be criticized
for allowing a KGB man to get close to the duke.[64]

What if Philip found out? The Foreign Office could hardly ask
him whether he minded being accompanied by 'one of the 105'. He
could not be involved in such a political matter and, if he did mind

but the Soviets refused to budge, then the royal family would have been 'officially snubbed'.[65]

Roderic Lyne, a young British diplomat in the Moscow embassy, received prompt instructions to 'stifle this at birth'. He caught up with Gresko and warned him off. It would not be appropriate, he insisted, for Gresko to 'appear in public with the Duke'. Instead, he should 'stay entirely behind the scenes'. Gresko listened carefully before railing against the unjustness of Operation Foot. He passively accepted what Lyne had said and then promptly disappeared. Mysteriously, he failed to turn up for a final meeting three days later.[66] Back home, the sticklers in the protocol department were relieved to learn that 'he had been moved to other duties'.[67]

It came at a price. The Foreign Office had planned to use Tony Bishop as an interpreter for Philip.[68] Bishop had been expelled from the Moscow embassy in 1965 as part of the Gerald Brooke spy case – a mutual friend had advised Brooke to pass his subversive material to Bishop if he was unable to deliver it to his contact himself. This was enough for the Kremlin to declare Bishop *persona non grata*.[69]

Diplomats had privately accepted that the trip did not require a formal interpreter, but wanted to use the opportunity to slip Bishop back inside the Soviet Union 'under the Duke's wing'. The Gresko démarche derailed the plan and there was now little chance of getting Bishop into the country without a row.[70] The Foreign Office refused to draw parallels between Gresko and Bishop. They assumed that the Russians had 'no real evidence of any illicit activities by Bishop' and that the 105 expelled in Operation Foot were an 'entirely different kettle of fish'.[71] Nonetheless, it was not worth pressing the point. The Soviets would provide their own interpreter for Philip.[72]

After the Gresko and Bishop tangles, diplomats warned Philip to avoid any conversation about Soviet spies. The gaffe-prone duke was also warned off talking about the fate of the Russian royal family – especially conspiracy theories about their survival – and internal Soviet politics. Nationalism inside the Soviet Union was also off-limits, even though Philip was briefed that nationalist feelings were 'still very much alive in non-Russian areas, especially in the Ukraine and the Baltic republics' and that the Soviets had launched propaganda to quash it. Philip, unsurprisingly, was not told that British intelligence operations sought to foster and exploit this very nationalism in order to undermine the Soviet Union. Instead, he was allowed to talk about sport, youth exchanges, environmental protection and Anglo-Soviet co-operation during the Second World War.[73]

Philip visited Kiev, via Moscow, in September 1973. The KGB assessed that it was a major political, rather than sporting, event for the British. As predicted, Russian intelligence did put the buildings where Philip and his staff were staying under surveillance; the KGB was especially suspicious of diplomats travelling down from the British embassy in Moscow, some of whom the Russians were convinced were intelligence officers. The KGB also covered the journalists, competitors, and spectators – but stopped short of active intelligence operations targeting the British and Philip.[74]

The British ambassador informed the queen that the visit, despite being unofficial, was 'of very great importance and an undoubted success'. He was particularly struck by the role of the KGB. Russian intelligence had intervened at the last minute and revised the programme 'in direct contradiction of Prince Philip's wishes, which we had been invited to express and which, we were told, would be paramount'. The KGB's eleventh-hour intervention confined Philip 'far too much in the straitjacket reserved for high-level official visitors to the USSR, from which he had great difficulty in escaping'. He did manage to give his minders the slip once, though, nipping 'smartly out of his lunch tent at the cross-country' with 'hordes of leaden-armpitted KGB' in pursuit.[75]

The KGB impressed and frustrated in equal measure. The ambassador confessed that 'it was a bizarre experience to be working in close co-operation with that part of the KGB which concerns itself legitimately and properly with security in the Soviet Union. Those of its personnel involved were indeed of a type whom I should not care to run into if I myself were on illegitimate business on a dark night. But their performance in our service on this occasion was irreproachable.'[76]

Although constrained to 'antiseptic VIP meals, with virtually identical and unbelievably boring guest lists and menus', Philip played his part stoically and scrupulously adhered to his equestrian role – much to the disappointed surprise of the Russians who hoped to politicize the visit. The journalist Victor Louis suspiciously appeared during the three-day equestrian event in Kiev 'in the highly unlikely role of equestrian correspondent'. Once again, he did the Kremlin's bidding, this time by floating the idea of a visit by the queen herself.[77]

The KGB was suspicious of British journalists ostensibly there to watch Philip. Intelligence officers noted the journalists' wide array of cameras and sound recording equipment – although this can hardly have come as a surprise. They also noted, with slightly more alarm, that the journalists paid rather too much attention to ordinary Soviet citizens, accusing some of trying to secretly record conversations. They thought one worked for MI6; others were merely rude. The KGB managed to acquire the reflections of a sympathetic *Daily Mirror* photographer. They recorded with interest his description of Princess Anne as 'capricious, arrogant and not very bright'. He seems to have told the KGB that 'I would like the princess to fall from a horse or something similar would happen to her. Then my mission would be justified, and I would be able to take great shots.' Soviet intelligence assessed Anne as 'leading a modest lifestyle' and sinisterly added that she always travelled with her personal bodyguard who would be staying in the hotel room next door.[78]

Despite all the intrigue, Philip clearly enjoyed his visit to Russia, as he returned in the winter of 1979, this time to Moscow, to plan for a future Olympics. What the embassy loved about the tour was that things had now relaxed somewhat; unusually, Philip got to meet real everyday Russians, something the KGB normally conspired to prevent. He met Russians who 'bred horses, rode horses, owned horses, raced horses, photographed horses, wrote about horses, legislated for horses; in short the equestrian society of the Soviet Union'. These people were not 'the cardboard cut-out' Soviet figures with whom British diplomats normally did business. Soviet security officials decided to borrow a British embassy Range Rover because they thought it would cope better with heavy snow than their own military vehicles. However, the KGB was rather taken aback when Prince Philip provocatively suggested that 'Soviet security arrangements for the competitors were inadequate'.[79]

IN NOVEMBER 1975, the governor-general of Australia, John Kerr, dramatically sacked the Labor prime minister, Gough Whitlam. The move came after a series of scandals and a decisive Conservative by-election victory which the opposition used to block money from reaching the government. It created a constitutional crisis and risked dragging the queen into the internal politics of a country almost ten thousand miles away.

Rumours quickly circulated about various hidden hands. The Australian press wondered whether the CIA had been involved. After all, spy fever was mounting in Washington as eager senators investigated and uncovered spiralling CIA operations, including its activities in Australia. Kerr told Queen Elizabeth herself that any such claims were 'absurdly tenuous'.[80]

The potential hidden hand of Buckingham Palace proved far more controversial – and difficult to dismiss. In July 2020, after a lengthy legal battle, the Australian archives finally declassified the secret letters between the palace and Kerr. They had initially been classified as 'personal', and so lay beyond the prying eyes of historians for the best part of half a century.

Kerr floated the idea of sacking Whitlam with Martin Charteris, the queen's private secretary. They had been discussing the possibility of dismissal and the powers of the governor-general since the summer of 1975.[81] In October, Kerr confided in Prince Charles about the possibility of Whitlam racing to the queen first and asking her to sack Kerr instead, replacing him with someone more amenable to Whitlam's cause. If he had hoped that Charles would relay this fear back to his mother, he was correct. Charteris comforted Kerr that the queen would 'take most unkindly' to such a move but ultimately conceded that, if requested to do so, she would have to agree.[82]

The secret conversations continued as the crisis reached its climax. A week before the dismissal, Charteris agreed that Kerr had 'the powers' to sack Whitlam and could use them 'in the last resort and then only for constitutional and not political reasons'.[83] This was not far short of a green light from Buckingham Palace.

On 11 November, Kerr did just that. Significantly, he did so without informing the palace in advance, telling Charteris that 'it was better for Her Majesty not to know in advance'. Charteris was delighted that the queen effectively had plausible deniability: 'if I may say with the greatest respect, I believe that in NOT informing the Queen what you intended to do before doing it, you acted not only with perfect constitutional propriety but also with admirable consideration for Her Majesty's position'.[84]

Nobody knew about the palace's role, but the sacking sparked widespread demonstrations against Kerr and his interference. On Commonwealth Day the following June, Kerr and his wife were guests of honour at a reception in Melbourne. Around four hundred demonstrators arrived and, as Kerr told Charteris, 'the scene was pretty nasty'. In a 'highly organised affair', protestors smashed the front window of his car, leaving one of his aides requiring medical attention.[85] The queen was 'extremely sorry to hear of this unfortunate business' and Charteris added that he hoped any response would be 'robust'.[86]

Kerr stayed in close touch with the palace, passing on Australian intelligence about subversive and extreme organizations on both sides of an increasingly angry debate. He shared the usual warnings about anti-governor-general demonstrations by local communists, but also passed on a report by the Australian Security Intelligence Organisation into what he called a 'very right wing' organization: the Australian League of Rights. A pro-monarchy group, it publicly supported him with pamphlets and adverts. Kerr told the palace that 'the sort of things it is saying are accurate enough'. Australian intelligence was more cautious, warning that the group was racist and anti-Semitic as well as being pro-monarchy and pro-empire. Beyond its 'respectable stated objectives', its policies were 'extreme' and its aims 'radical.' The report made its way to the palace. The queen's reaction to support from such unsavoury bedfellows remains unknown.[87]

Whitlam would doubtless have been fascinated to follow the inside story of a simultaneous and somewhat smoother transfer of power in London. During 1975, Prime Minister Harold Wilson had become increasingly tired and, in the words of one of his closest advisers, Bernard Donoughue, had 'lost the appetite for power and the will to govern'.[88] By the autumn, he had concluded that he should resign and hand over to his successor, Jim Callaghan. The queen was the first to know. In September, while they were visiting Balmoral, she drove the prime minister and his wife to a small chalet on the estate. To ensure complete secrecy they left their detectives behind. When they arrived, the queen filled the kettle while Wilson imparted his unusual announcement.[89]

Privately, the queen was 'very concerned' about the departure of her favourite prime minister. She did not want him to step down, even though she knew his mental health was not good.[90] 'She does not want him to do it and there has been discussion of trying to get him to change his mind,' noted Donoughue. Once again, Martin Charteris loomed in the shadows, and in January 1976 he told senior political figures that the palace 'was concerned about the succession'. But by March, after he held private discussions with the Cabinet secretary, John Hunt, he was 'quite properly dissuaded from taking such an approach' not only because of 'constitutional proprieties' but also because everyone knew it would be unsuccessful – Wilson was determined to go.[91] Indeed, the prime minister had become increasingly anxious about bugging and even prone to conspiracy theories.[92] There may have been 'dark forces' trying to destabilize him during his two administrations, but perhaps he was reassured to know that the most senior member of the establishment was desperate for him to stay on.

Joe Haines, Wilson's press secretary, recalls that there was 'still one moment of pure, if black, comedy to come'. In the short period before Wilson's departure was publicly revealed, the weekly meetings between the prime minister and the queen focused on another forthcoming announcement: Princess Margaret and Lord Snowdon would soon divorce. The queen was anxious about all the fuss in the press that was bound to follow. Helpfully, Wilson offered a plan to mitigate this. He suggested that the palace should reveal the divorce on the same day that he announced his resignation, adding 'my going will blanket it'. But Wilson's scheme was not a complete success, as the royal-hungry tabloids still featured Margaret on the front page and pushed Wilson's news into 'second place'.[93]

THE COMMONWEALTH CONTINUED to create problems for the government and palace. Courtiers and officials had successfully protected the queen from embarrassment over the sacking of Whitlam, but two years later the government turned to covert operations to protect her from diplomatic embarrassment closer to home.

In the early 1970s, Idi Amin, the Ugandan president, had grabbed power in a military coup orchestrated by the Israelis and swiftly become a brutal dictator. Initially, he seemed an improvement on his predecessor, Milton Obote. But soon he turned nasty, murdered political opponents, seized the property of Uganda's Asian and Jewish communities, forced swathes of people into exile, and terrorized intellectuals, destroying books and locking up journalists.

Public order evaporated, leading to widespread looting, rape and murder. Amin declared himself president for life.

British politicians – and likely the palace – reacted with horror at this prospect. They had advised the queen against travelling to Ottawa for a commonwealth meeting in 1973 simply to prevent her from having to shake his hand, but the queen insisted on going.[94] She quipped to the foreign secretary that it 'would not have been the first time' she 'had met murderers' at such a meeting.[95] But her courtiers were still anxious to curtail any incident.

Fortunately, Amin nurtured well-founded fears about overseas conferences. He had himself seized power when his predecessor had been abroad at a commonwealth conference in Singapore. Accordingly, in 1973, to 'great hilarity' at Buckingham Palace, a message arrived from Kampala. Idi Amin said he had the greatest respect for the queen and looked forward to meeting her in Ottawa but was anxious about his security. He therefore asked whether 'Her Majesty' would 'kindly send a regiment of her "Scotch" Guards to protect him'. The queen sent a notably 'deadpan reply' and Amin decided not to attend, to everyone's considerable delight.[96]

In 1975, the queen was deployed in a last-ditch attempt to control Amin. A rather esoteric British citizen living in Uganda, Denis Hills, had written a book about Amin called *The White Pumpkin*. The fearsome Ugandan security authorities had secured a copy before it was published and duly presented it to Amin. He ordered Hills to be arrested on a charge of treason, which carried the death penalty. The Foreign Office protested in vain.

Elizabeth sent out a delegation carrying her personal message asking that Hills be released. When they arrived, Amin kept them waiting for three days, eventually receiving them in a large thatched hut miles away in the countryside. The entrance was so low that they had to enter on their hands and knees. Amin had carefully arranged for photographers to take pictures of the queen's emissaries crawling on their knees as they entered. Having humiliated them, Amin sent them back empty-handed. Hills was only liberated when the foreign secretary, Jim Callaghan, turned up and pleaded for his life. This, of course, was what Amin had wanted all along. He took Callaghan for a spin around Kampala in his Maserati and then Hills was finally released.[97]

Unfortunately, in 1977 the issue of the commonwealth heads of government meeting returned. Uganda was still in the commonwealth; its leaders would therefore be invited to London for the 1977 meeting. To make matters worse, the meeting would coincide with the queen's silver jubilee. Idi Amin, the mass murderer, would meet Elizabeth.

By 1977, Amin had only become more authoritarian and more widely reviled in Britain. He had murdered thousands of people in repeated security purges. It was also now known that he had divorced and then killed one of his four wives, whom he suspected of adultery, and personally mutilated her body, cutting off her legs and arms.[98] Backbenchers lobbied the government to prevent him from coming to London. Parliament passed a motion that he would be unwelcome, and Prime Minister Callaghan secretly planned to use special forces to bundle him back out of the country if he attempted to land at a British airport. The elaborate operation was codenamed BOTTLE and served as a dramatic last resort. It would have had serious consequences not only for the impending commonwealth meeting but also for the safety of around 250 British nationals living in Uganda who would likely have suffered violent reprisals.[99]

It was a delicate situation: the UK had no veto over who could and who could not attend the meeting, while trying to dissuade Amin from attending would offend other African delegates and risk a continent-wide boycott altogether. London could not openly appear to be interfering in the affairs of what were once imperial territories. They were, after all, now equals. When British diplomats used Saudi Arabia as a discreet emissary to pass on a confidential warning not to come, Ugandan radio publicly accused Britain of inappropriately neo-colonial heavy handedness.[100]

The Foreign Office turned to covert action to deter Amin and to protect the queen from embarrassment. Officials plotted to spread disinformation inside Uganda, warning of an impending coup if Amin dared to leave the country. It was a plausible line given the circumstances in which Amin himself had assumed power – and Britain had a long track record of using black propaganda in post-imperial Africa to maintain influence, spread fear and attack adversaries. The secret capabilities were in place.

The historian Spencer Mawby discovered that, shortly before his death, Foreign Secretary Anthony Crosland recommended using what he called 'private deterrents' to convince Amin that he would lose power if he left the country or, worse, he might be assassinated on the streets of Britain. Prime Minister Callaghan was initially reluctant but, as opposition grew and it became increasingly likely that Amin would attend, he returned to the idea of spreading 'misinformation about a possible coup during his absence' and spreading 'misinformation about a possible attempt on his life in this country'. Another option, to be conducted by MI6, remains classified.[101]

British intelligence launched its covert action to prevent Idi Amin from shaking the queen's hand. Although the archival trail dries up, there is enough evidence to show that the UK did indeed successfully run operations to deter him. In June 1977, coinciding with the meeting, local newspapers suddenly reported turmoil and assassination plots. Amin went missing. One South African magazine reported that his disappearance was a consequence of a well-organized assassination attempt that had very nearly succeeded. At the same time, the foreign secretary, David Owen, discussed plots against Amin with his Kenyan counterpart.[102]

The moment of high drama – whether or not Amin would turn up – occurred at St Paul's Cathedral during a service of thanksgiving for the silver jubilee with all commonwealth leaders in attendance. Mountbatten noticed that the queen was not her normal self and asked why she looked 'cross and worried'. She laughed and replied: 'I was just thinking how awful it would be if Amin were to gatecrash the party.' Mountbatten then asked her what she would have done if he showed up. The queen responded that the lord mayor's pearl sword had been placed before her as part of the ceremony, and so she would seize it and 'hit him hard over the head' with it.[103]

Elizabeth did not have to draw her sword; Amin did not show up in London for the start of the commonwealth conference. But, being Idi Amin, he launched an influence campaign of his own: his mysterious absence stole the show as delegates and officials speculated where the mercurial leader might be. Amin deliberately confused onlookers by putting decoys onto various aeroplanes and hinting he was aboard. One false rumour suggested he was circling Dublin airport. Callaghan insisted to reporters that Amin was still in Uganda. When he did eventually reappear, he dramatically announced that imperialist agents had tried to kill him.[104]

Amid all the discreet diplomacy, subterfuge and counter-subterfuge one thing is clear. Amin was nowhere near the queen – much to the government's relief. But Idi Amin could not be evaded forever. Prince Charles found himself just a couple of seats away from the bloody dictator at the funeral of Kenyan president Jomo Kenyatta in Nairobi in August 1978. They eyed each other up rather warily.

Repeatedly discomforting multiple royals has its price. David Owen, Britain's foreign secretary, recalls that 'Amin was a menace and I got rid of him'. On his return to Uganda Amin went to war with Tanzania, and its president, Julius Nyerere, came to Britain for help. Owen privately increased Nyerere's aid budget 'to buy ammunition'. Owen mused that he might go to jail now for using aid money to buy ammunition. 'But there was nothing on paper.' Idi Amin lost the battle and was soon in exile, never to return.[105]

ONE ASPECT OF the queen's global itinerary caused constant tension: Iran and its despotic ruler the shah. The Foreign Office prioritized Iran as the second biggest export market in the Middle East 'and expanding'. It was the source of about 20 per cent of Britain's oil and it provided military stability. Arms sales were voluminous and effectively subsidized the British military. GCHQ also had hidden ground stations there for listening to the Soviets. Diplomats noted that relations were 'extremely close and friendly'. They continually begged for more royal visits, as they knew the shah and all his family loved to visit Britain.[106]

But the shah's visits to Britain were increasingly a security nightmare. His regime was blood-thirsty and repressive and in 1972, when he arrived on one trip, about a hundred students back home in Tehran were on trial; seventy were expected to be shot. Iranian students abroad therefore tended to riot when he arrived in a European city, as had happened recently in Munich and Geneva. The Swiss regarded the threat as so high that they moved him only by helicopter.[107] There were also tensions with other Arab states, especially Libya, which meant he might be shot at by any number of rebel groups. Accordingly, he brought his own security team of ten men all with their own weapons.[108] They also had plenty of machine guns in the embassy and were disappointed when Special Branch refused to allow them onto the streets.[109]

The shah was determined to ride to Ascot alongside the queen in an open-topped carriage and 'totally rejected' the idea of a bulletproof limousine.[110] Special Branch were horrified, and thought it 'extremely unwise', as did the shah's own security detail, and indeed the matter went all the way up to the prime minister, Ted Heath.[111] In his weekly meeting with the queen he implored her not to do this as it was 'high risk'.[112] But the queen said she had little choice and went ahead. As if to torment British security officials further, the shah also hoped that some of his intelligence officers might go to Northern Ireland to study MI5 techniques for dealing with 'subversives'.[113]

Security was not the only problem. The queen considered the shah a crushing bore and hated his company, as he only talked about administrative matters. When she was finally persuaded to make a return visit to Iran in October 1973, diplomats noted privately:

'the poor Queen', adding 'she didn't want to do this at all'.[114] In the Middle East, the October War between Israel and a coalition of Arab states was now in progress and security of royal flights became an extreme concern. Although perilous, she clearly thought the gamble was worth taking, not least because her contact time with the shah was now limited to just a few hours.

Remarkably, the RAF found that the best way to make the flight safe was to notify the Russians of the queen's route and then fly her to Tehran along the northern border of Iran, 'going into the Soviet Union'. Because of Philip's recent successful visit, they thought Moscow would be helpful and that the Soviet air force was less likely to shoot down the queen's plane than anyone else.[115]

Predictably, on arrival, the shah treated the queen to a dull monologue on steel production in his country.[116] She tried to lighten the mood by voicing her dislike of the Sydney Opera House.[117] Later, the October War caused the cancellation of visits by Princess Margaret and the Kents to Egypt and Jordan. MI5 were deeply worried about their security in both countries.[118]

The diplomats pressed for yet more royal visits, ideally with the shah coming to Britain again. The queen was completely horrified. The palace stalled and said she 'would be pleased to do something for the Royal children'.[119] Accordingly, in 1974, a tour of Scotland for the shah's three children was arranged. The eldest son, Crown Prince Reza, was 'fascinated by all things tartan' and was a manic Rangers fan. So, the highlight was a match at Edinburgh's Easter Road stadium between Rangers and Hibernian on 31 July 1974. The crown prince fortified himself beforehand by having two helpings of hamburgers, chips, beans and peas at the nearby Epicure Snack Bar. He then spent the match 'cheering wildly' at each of Rangers' three goals. The only moment of anxiety for the British security team was when he insisted on shaking hands with many Rangers fans after the third goal.[120]

Privately, British diplomats hated these visits as much as the queen, but they were essential to grease the wheels of the special relationship with Iran. In public they were professional, but in private they occasionally vented their feelings. In May 1975, Anthony Parsons, Britain's ambassador in Tehran, was compelled to devote much time to the details of a visit to London, via Paris, for the shah's elder sister, Princess Shams, whom he regarded as 'neurotic'. The princess would not go anywhere without her dogs and so demanded to circumvent Britain's quarantine regulations. Parsons complained bitterly to London: 'she has a large number of revolting little brutes, each about the size of an average rat: and she herself is not much bigger, but looks more like a Pekinese than a Yorkshire terrier which her dogs are, I think.' He told the Iranians that it was no good and quarantine meant she would have to leave her beloved pooches in Paris.[121]

IRANIAN MATTERS BECAME much more complicated towards the end of the decade. Serious unrest broke out in 1978. The queen was due to visit Iran in February the following year as part of another tour to generate goodwill and encourage trade.[122]

As late as mid-December, amid growing violence, Elizabeth's visit to Tehran was still scheduled to take place. Finally, David Owen, the foreign secretary, now declared it impossible due to the 'staggering numbers of demonstrators' on the streets.[123] As domestic opposition to the shah mounted, Prime Minister Callaghan cancelled the Iranian leg of the trip altogether. It was now too dangerous. He even explored the possibility of cultivating alternative leaders in case a coup became necessary.[124] Hard-line Iranian clerics had other ideas – and launched a revolution of their own.

After months of disorder, martial law finally broke down on Wednesday 27 December 1978. There was terrible violence and general anarchy. Police and army headquarters were attacked and the buildings used by the shah's feared secret police, Savak, came in for special attention. The homes of Savak officials were targeted and even their families killed. In early January 1979, one of the shah's military aides spoke to him with unusual frankness and said if he stayed, he risked meeting the fate of Nicholas II of Russia. Queen Farah said that if her husband departed, she would stay and lead the resistance, but the aide scoffed and asked if she wanted to be Marie Antoinette. They both expressed shock and sent him away, but hours later they began to pack their bags.[125]

Elizabeth and Philip were on board the royal yacht in the Gulf when the revolution broke out. George Walden, the principal private secretary at the Foreign Office, was with them as he received a flurry of telegrams. Carrying crucial updates about events in Tehran, they arrived on a silver tray in his cabin. Prince Philip jokingly asked if they were Dead Sea Scrolls.[126]

Back in Iran, the British ambassador, Anthony Parsons, deliberately kept his distance from the shah during the turmoil. With memories of 1953 looming large, he did not want to give the impression of foreign interference. After the shah had decided to leave, Parsons called on him to say goodbye and agreed that it was the right move if the monarchy was to stand a chance of surviving.[127] Meanwhile, Elizabeth and Philip's tour of the Gulf continued regardless with the revised aim of steadying the nerves of local rulers and encouraging them to respond to internal and external problems efficiently.

By February, the shah had fled to Morocco but was causing trouble for his hosts. Threats against the Moroccan embassy in Tehran had recently forced its evacuation. Complicating matters further, Palestinian and Arab leaders refused to visit the country so long as the shah was there. The embarrassed Moroccan king wanted him gone.[128]

This created a diplomatic problem – where would he end up? President Sadat repeatedly invited him to Egypt, but the shah did not want to go there. He ended up temporarily in the Bahamas; he was not the first exiled monarch to wash up there.[129]

Meanwhile, the shah made it clear that he wanted a permanent move to Britain, the country that had supported him back in 1953 and ever since. Prime Minister Callaghan had doubts. Just like

David Lloyd George after the Russian Revolution, he worried that allowing the shah into Britain would damage relations with the new Iranian regime. His foreign and home secretaries agreed, citing security and domestic public order issues. The shah's presence on British soil would also have given rise to plots and – just as bad – rumours of plots. David Owen worried that an Iranian royal court would soon assemble around him, inevitably leading to conspiracies which would taint London. To make matters worse, the shah might even be assassinated on British soil.[130]

Indeed, assassination was Owen's main worry, since, for a decade, London's streets had seen several professional 'hits' by Middle East terror groups. He warned:

> Most important of all, the security problem would be very difficult and continuing. The extremist groups – Fedayeen and mujahidin – are tough and devoted people with a long and impressive record of political assassination. They and others will never give up trying to assassinate the shah and, given the vast number of Iranians in Britain at any one time, we would have to deploy a very large security force indeed to give the shah any kind of guarantee of protection...

Owen thought they should try to give the shah an intimation, 'of an informal but fairly clear nature, that his coming would not be welcome to us'.[131]

In May 1979, Margaret Thatcher replaced Callaghan as prime minister. She initially wanted to offer the shah a home in Britain but was persuaded to change her mind. Ever sensitive to issues of export and business, it would clearly be the end of any dealing with the new regime. Moreover, Anthony Parsons warned that over a thousand Britons living in Iran would be taken prisoner or even shot.[132] With sadness she secretly sent Sir Denis Wright, a former ambassador to Iran, to explain to the shah personally why he was not allowed in.[133]

Despite all the risks, Queen Elizabeth still wanted to offer the shah asylum. She passed a message through royal networks to let him know that she would have liked 'to have the Shah come' but that her government was 'reticent'.[134] She also brought up 'the fate of the shah' when sending her new ambassador off to Washington.[135] Elizabeth was angry about letting the shah down and, unusually, let this be known. It was the beginning of a frosty relationship with her new prime minister.[136]

Meanwhile, the shah travelled to New York for cancer treatment. His stay validated many of the British government's concerns: it attracted great criticism from the revolutionary regime in Iran and necessitated intense security on the ground. President Jimmy Carter's brief and reluctant hospitality even contributed to the Iranian hostage crisis, when revolutionaries held fifty-two US diplomats and intelligence officers hostage in Tehran for over a year.[137] There was no way he could come to Britain now.

Blocked from his initial destination of choice, and despite the queen's earlier wishes, the shah travelled to Panama in December 1979. He lived under virtual house – or hospital – arrest. The following month, ambiguous intelligence reached the Foreign Office suggesting that he had been arrested and faced extradition back to Iran. In the confusion, the queen left diplomats in little doubt that she expected updates about his fate. 'The Queen,' one ominously wrote to colleagues on the spot, 'is personally interested.'[138]

Back in Tehran, the Iranian hostage crisis rumbled on, putting pressure on President Carter. Meanwhile, and adding yet more pressure on the US, the Soviets invaded neighbouring Afghanistan. The Soviet occupation sparked one of the largest western covert action campaigns of the Cold War in which the CIA and others supported local resistance fighters with money and weapons. Thatcher told Princess Margaret how Iran and the hostages 'dominated every conversation' she had had on a recent trip to the US. She lamented that 'the events in Afghanistan have cast a shadow over the whole world'. 'If only Iran had never taken those hostages, or would not release them,' she continued, 'we should be in a far better position to tackle the Russians in that part of the world.'[139] Princess Margaret complained that she found 'it quite impossible to find out <u>what</u> is happening in Afghanistan'. She asked the prime minister: 'are they about to wheel into Iran and get all the oil?'[140]

The shah, who had reluctantly moved to Egypt, finally died in July 1980. Attention turned to whether his family would be allowed to visit, or even live, in the UK. Remarkably, Prince Charles asked the Foreign Office to consider exfiltrating a minor member of the Iranian royal family out of the country. Given the state of diplomatic relations between the UK and Iran, he must have known such a request would have entailed a daring MI6 covert operation. British diplomats dutifully followed up the royal request but soon grew puzzled. They had never heard of the target, and their 'discreet enquiries' among Iranian exiles in London had 'drawn a blank'. In a bizarre twist, Charles had got the wrong name.

Diplomats told the prince that overt exfiltration – once they had worked out who he meant – would be impossible after the Iranians had seized American hostages. As for a covert exfiltration, they told Charles that several clandestine organizations did exist to get people out of Iran, but that it was dangerous, expensive and that the government was not involved. It was, however, fairly easy to access these channels through Iranian exiles in London – especially with enough money.[141]

The efforts of Charles to get people out were rather urgent. The Khomeini regime was conducting a vicious purge of those associated with the shah, many of whom were personally known to the British royal family. Almost the only royal courtier to evade the firing squad was Hossein Fardust, the shah's friend since childhood and trusted aide. He did this by quickly writing a memoir that accused the shah of corruption, torture, sexual perversion and espionage for foreign governments. He focused on the historic theme of MI6 influence in Tehran and explained that the 'secret brains behind Savak's special intelligence branch was actually the "satanic" Queen Elizabeth II'. He insisted that the shah met the MI6 head of station every day to receive his instructions like a puppet.[142] This, of course, was not true, but, almost uniquely for a foreign leader, the shah had met the MI6 and CIA heads of station regularly throughout his reign; albeit more out of fear than affection.[143]

Royal diplomacy was not over yet. In August, the queen used an audience with Thatcher to ask about the possibility of the shah's widow coming to the UK. Royal networks were in full swing, for she had received the message via ex-King Constantine of Greece who had been holidaying in Cowes. The Cowes Regatta had hosted the tsar, the kaiser and a hundred less distinguished royals down the years. The idea put the government back into a spin, fearing that allowing the former empress's entry could lead to demonstrations, domestic terrorism and diplomatic rows.[144]

Constantine continued to intrigue on behalf of the Iranians. He advised the deposed royals to 'form some sort of committee – not a government in exile – which would form a focus for the Iranian exiles', presumably for opposition and counter-revolution.[145] Meanwhile, supporters of the shah talked of quietly sounding out the UK about the possibility of a potential coup. The British ambassador in Dubai urgently warned that his counterpart in London 'was cooking up a plot of some kind'.[146]

Remarkably, in October 1980, the empress asked the British to use their influence, working alongside Arab monarchies, to restore the Iranian throne. She had assumed that Britain would be predisposed to help because of close ties between both royal families. Diplomats reacted with surprise and alarm. It was out of the question.[147]

At the same time, though, the likes of Julian Amery, a Conservative politician involved in many covert operations since the Second World War, maintained contact with the shah's supporters and unsuccessfully lobbied for a counter-coup.[148] All the while, Queen Elizabeth watched closely, asking about the empress's fate and receiving letters from her via the embassy in Cairo.[149]

A year later, Amery, who was still in contact with the exiled royal family, asked the foreign secretary if the shah's son could visit the UK. Once again, diplomats refused on security grounds. MI5 added that the risk of assassination was simply too high.[150]

ROYAL DIPLOMACY WAS a tricky business, intertwining discreet influence and security. Relations with Iran catapulted the queen – often reluctantly – into a quasi-diplomatic actor. Her influence and the importance of royal networks were clear; but Iran also showed the limitations of monarchy given that neither Elizabeth nor Charles succeeded in helping their royal counterparts.

The queen worked hard to transform empire into commonwealth and old enemies into friends. All the royals offered insights of their own from their contacts and conversations. They could even play a more active role, such as being dangled as an incentive to release an imprisoned spy, as in the Brooke case. On more than one occasion the world of royalty and espionage collided, as the aftermath of Operation Foot demonstrated.

Most importantly, royal activity was an important means of projecting British influence. In the case of Chile, it perfectly complemented Britain's covert action. Two arms of the British state – both secretive and misunderstood in their own ways – were working together in harmony. But there were limits. The queen remained reluctant to visit the Soviet Union. Right up until 1989, she continued to pointedly call Leningrad 'St Petersburg'.[151]

Intelligence also kept the royals safe as they travelled to dangerous places, and protected them from political embarrassment at home. But as the turbulent last years of the shah underlined, royals were now, more than ever, not just vulnerable to protest and political turmoil but inviting targets for terrorists everywhere.

Part VI

PROTECTING THE
REALM AND THE ROYALS

TERRORISTS AND LUNATICS,
1969–1977

'Your greatest danger is still the lone nutcase'

Princess Anne, 1980[1]

THE QUEEN'S ROYAL diplomacy placed her into some hazard-ous situations. Politicians, journalists and the broader public worried about her safety – especially when visiting countries in the midst of upheaval such as Ghana and Sudan. But the new danger in the 1960s and 1970s was the growth of international terrorism, often targeting heads of state. These fresh worries put serious pres-sure on her governments, which feared putting the queen in harm's way. Harold Wilson and then Edward Heath both endured sleepless nights fretting not just about the queen's welfare overseas but about opposition MPs exploiting it to make trouble for the government about 'royal risk' – and there were certainly a few narrow squeaks.

On other occasions, the government cynically played the security card to prevent a royal from doing something politically embarrass-ing. The prime minister even lied to the queen to spare her blushes. In 1967, Prince Philip was due to holiday in the Indian city of Jaipur, famous for its romantic dusty pink hues and historic build-ings, as a guest of the maharajah. The local political situation was in turmoil: state government had broken down and, from the Jaipur palace, the maharajah's wife led intense political agitation against Indira Gandhi's premiership. Some twenty-one people died in riots before Gandhi imposed direct rule and a twenty-four-hour curfew.

Despite the turmoil, Philip faced little personal threat. The emergency powers removed any serious risk to his personal safety and Mountbatten, who was already in Jaipur, offered a sanguine assessment from the ground. Back in London, the British government accepted this intelligence but remained deeply concerned about the trip. To have Philip staying with a prominent anti-government figure would lead to some 'pretty wild allegations' about royal meddling in Indian affairs. It would create a highly embarrassing impression – however unfair – of Philip subverting the elected government. Prime Minister Harold Wilson cancelled the visit entirely. He did not let on the real reason, preferring instead to hide behind the security explanation, telling the queen simply that 'there was a risk to life'.[2]

Queen Elizabeth sensed that the institution of royalty would wither and die if its current placeholders locked themselves away in a tower or hid behind lines of armour and shields. She was quite fatalistic about the prospect of assassination, perhaps inheriting some of Queen Victoria's divine faith in god's protection. Royal protection officers were not allowed to hurl the queen to the floor to protect her – as their US equivalent could do to presidents. Instead, they could simply advise – strongly if necessary – to change course. She did not always agree.

The royalty protection group was small. Recruitment was opaque and lacked proper vetting procedures. Like the intelligence services, it relied on tapping 'good chaps' on the shoulder. The queen typically had full-time protection, as did her immediate family so as to preserve the line of succession. Each had an allocated plain clothes police officer. The individuals were doggedly loyal, but the overall organization was fragmented, poorly co-ordinated and asking for trouble. Underpinning this was a belief that the British royal family were wonderful and no one could possibly want to attack them – this proved to be wrong.[3]

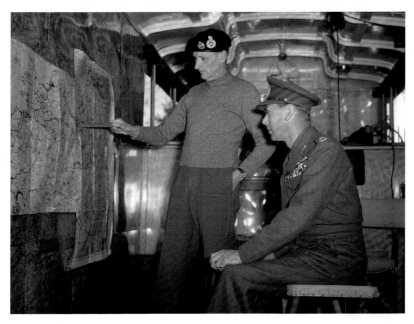

George VI in Monty's caravan in Normandy where snipers were a worry.

George VI and the young Margaret both learned to be careful about phone security and new 'scramblers' were installed in the late 1940s.

The Treetops Hotel in Kenya where royal toilet seats were stolen.

Tito's visits to the queen were of intense interest to the KGB.

John F. Kennedy, Mountbatten and Chairman of the Joint Chiefs
General Lyman Lemnizter talk nuclear weapons in 1961.

An anxious queen with President Nkrumah in Ghana, 1961.

Anthony Blunt, the Kremlin's man in the palace.

Ian Fleming preferred writing *Dr No* to royal speeches.

Prince Charles was almost kidnapped as a student at Cambridge in 1968.

Charles enjoys pistol practice in West Berlin.

The aftermath of the attempted kidnap of Princess Anne in 1974.

The queen's favourite prime minister, Harold Wilson, departs in 1976.

The queen's most dangerous moment with the Shah at Ascot.

Prince Charles eyes Idi Amin (*far right*) in 1978, just before he was toppled.

Diana effectively said goodbye to her royal security in December 1993.

In 2019, the queen unveiled a plaque in London celebrating the centenary of GCHQ. She was accompanied by the director Jeremy Fleming.

The role of intelligence became rather more crucial if the queen could not be locked away behind a ring of steel. Forewarned is forearmed, as intelligence officers say. Accurate and timely information would have to identify trouble before it arose, allowing the queen to see and be seen, as she put it. Intelligence allowed the royal family to maintain an illusion of accessibility and to make their legend – chosen by God to lead loyal subjects and affirm the authority of the state – a reality.[4]

This was easier said than done. Fears increased after the assassination of President Kennedy in 1963 and his brother in 1968. By the end of the decade, the rise of international terrorism drastically complicated royal security planning. Prince Philip had vetoed the use of armed protection – calling it unbecoming and unnecessary – and was only persuaded to alter his opposition once Prince Charles and Princess Anne entered their teens.[5] Even then, royal security remained flimsy.

IN THE 1960s, Prince Charles went to Trinity College at Cambridge University accompanied by his loyal security guard, Michael Varney. Charles was a naturally active and enthusiastic person who threw himself into university life, especially amateur dramatics, and was adored by his fellow students. He appeared in many productions including the Joe Orton play *The Erpingham Camp*.[6] Although his tutors banned him from joining a number of student societies, everything from the Buddhist Society to the Conservative Association, for fear of seeming political, university life allowed him some scope for social and philosophical exploration.[7]

His minder recalls that he also 'had a talent for getting himself into situations that were potentially embarrassing or even physically dangerous'. He enjoyed performing in plays at the Pitt Club, which, as his bodyguard noted, was rather unlike the Athenaeum and brought the prince into close proximity to a range of unconventional characters including belly dancers. But the most alarming situations occurred when he was the 'victim of other people's machinations'.[8]

Providing discreet protection for Charles at Cambridge was tricky. His Special Branch guards did not want to embarrass him by sticking close behind him 'like a police dog'. Charles preferred to cycle around Cambridge and his security followed in a rather beaten-up old Land Rover at a respectful distance. Everyone was trying to preserve the pretence that he was just any student out on his own. Their biggest worry was young women, especially during Rag Week when, in their words, 'licence became almost anarchy'.[9]

Rag Week in the famous year of 1968 'came within a hairsbreadth' of disaster. Varney learnt, through police intelligence, that a group of female Manchester University students, 'all Women's Libbers of the most strident kind', planned to raid Trinity and kidnap Charles and hold him to ransom. Worse still, 'a fifth column' existed inside Cambridge since the team from Manchester had eager and willing accomplices from the women of Girton College. Together they were keen to pull off 'their coup' without 'any male assistance whatsoever'.[10]

'It was a well-planned operation almost worthy of professional kidnappers'. The Manchester team had not only hired a getaway car but had also arranged a safe house for their victim. The snatch was assigned to what the police called a 'squad of Amazons' who were ready for a fight and who 'prepared to cart Prince Charles off bodily'. His loyal guard had a sneaking suspicion that Charles might have enjoyed the whole escapade and was perhaps politically sympathetic, but at the same time he was 'painfully aware' that if the kidnap was successful 'it would be my head that rolled in the basket'. Varney was, in his own words, 'totally unamused'.[11]

Varney engineered a face-to-face meeting with the leader of the kidnappers. He warned her that they already had all the details of the plan and that if it went ahead it would cause a great deal of legal trouble for all those involved. 1968 was not an era of political correctness and so he also offered a stark warning that 'if you do go ahead and try to pull it off, I will personally see that you won't sit down for a fortnight'. The leader of the kidnap gave as good as she got, calling him by 'all the four letter names I'd ever heard' – in a posh Cheltenham accent. Either way the Manchester kidnap was off.[12]

MORE SERIOUS DANGERS awaited him in Wales. Charles had been prince of Wales since boyhood. In July 1969, he interrupted his studies at Cambridge for the formal ceremony of investiture. During his second year he undertook a short period of study at Aberystwyth University before being formally bestowed with a bejewelled crown, ring, mantle, sword and gold rod, at Caernarfon Castle in front of a televised audience of millions. Around two hundred thousand people lined the streets to catch a glimpse as the archaic pomp and circumstance rolled through the ancient town, an antidote to the swinging sixties.

Not everyone was excited. Violent Welsh nationalism was on the rise, and Britain's intelligence services worried about the threat terrorists could pose to the ceremony. The nationalists interpreted royalty as an English institution imposed from across the border and the title of prince of Wales an insult, especially since Charles's own links with Wales were rather thin. The ceremony was a mock medieval charade, an exercise in regional tokenism which national-ists believed masked historic English oppression of the Welsh.

The location, a medieval castle in remote northwest Wales, a long way from the well-protected streets of London, caused particular concern. In the years running up to the ceremony, Welsh national-ists had attacked reservoirs and water pipelines between Liverpool and Birmingham. A bomb exploded in the non-religious Temple of Peace in Cardiff hours before the first meeting to organize the investiture took place inside. Another bomb at the Welsh Office deliberately coincided with a visit of Princess Margaret. This campaign, carried out by the shadowy Mudiad Amddiffyn Cymru (Movement for the Defence of Wales) or MAC, culminated with an attempted bombing of four different locations.[13] One of the leaders of MAC was a former British soldier, Brian Jenkins, who had seen service in Berlin and Cyprus. His time in the latter posting had offered him insights into the nationalist Cypriot movement EOKA, and he recalls how he was influenced by seeing at first-hand how a small but organized group of revolutionaries could free a country in the grip of colonialism.[14]

Burke Trend, the Cabinet secretary, told Harold Wilson that MI5 and Special Branch had increased efforts to gather intelligence against Welsh extremists and were working closely together.[15] Special Branch established a unit in Shrewsbury to focus specifically on the threat to Charles. Demonstrating a lack of confidence in the Welsh police, it co-ordinated all incoming intelligence sources before passing details on to the Welsh chief constables.[16]

MI5 tried to reassure Wilson that while extremist propaganda was increasing, the threat of violence was in decline. An explosion at the tax office in Chester and at the new police headquarters in Cardiff, both in April 1969, suggested that this intelligence was rather optimistic. MI5 wondered whether the attack was linked to the forthcoming trial of nine Welsh nationalists, a trial which would take place when Charles was due to be in Aberystwyth. More violence might well be expected.

The trial spotlighted the worst weakness of the Welsh nationalists: their addiction to publicity. One militant boasted that he had fitted a harness to his dog which he said would be used to carry sticks of explosive gelignite towards the royal family. He claimed he had dozens more dogs all trained to carry magnetic devices under security vehicles. The story about these 'kamikaze dogs' duly appeared in newspapers and prompted hundreds of angry letters from dog-lovers. It was as a result of this revulsion among Welsh opinion that the nine members had been arrested in the first place. They were charged with a number of offences including possession of firearms, explosives and public order offences. The trial, in Swansea, lasted fifty-three days, ending on the day of the investiture. Self-proclaimed leader Cayo Evans, his second-in-command Dennis Coslett and four other members were convicted. Evans and Coslett spent fifteen months in jail.[17] The arrests prevented the group from carrying out other bizarre plans, including flying a radio-controlled helicopter carrying manure over the castle and dropping its fetid cargo on the prince's head.

As the ceremony neared, intelligence still assessed that the risk to Charles was 'more a matter of personal embarrassment than of physical harm, although it is never possible to rule out the activities of a determined fanatic'.[18] The home secretary, Jim Callaghan, found it all rather 'disturbing';[19] Wilson considered cancelling the Aberystwyth prelude to the trip altogether.[20] In the end, Charles made it to Aberystwyth to study Welsh language and history for a few weeks – a sop to the principality and a red rag to nationalists – but found his student accommodation cell-like, his fellow scholars rather hostile and his existence lonely. This was a far cry from his idyllic existence in Cambridge.[21]

Harold Wilson took royal security very seriously. Keen to emphasize to the royal household that this was a priority, Wilson developed a decidedly hands-on approach.[22] Prime ministerial meddling frustrated Callaghan, the Cabinet minister actually responsible for Charles's safety. Wilson's staff warned the prime minister to back off before Callaghan found out that Wilson was receiving his own private intelligence updates outside of Callaghan's reach. Callaghan would have exploded. More cynically, Wilson was also told not to meddle too much because 'if anything were to go wrong' Callaghan 'might possibly take the line that you had in fact assumed the responsibility'. Downing Street wanted Callaghan to be the minister for disaster if the worst happened.[23]

Nevertheless, Wilson did feel a sense of personal responsibility not least because it was he, as an ardent monarchist, who had originally pressed for this expensive and constitutionally unnecessary expression of formidable pageantry. Moreover, the rise of Welsh nationalism was challenging Labour's electoral support across Wales, and Wilson's government hoped the ceremony would promote dual British and Welsh identity.[24] Egged on by the Welsh Labour Party, he pushed hard for it to go ahead despite some reluctance from the palace.[25]

Elizabeth was personally worried. With the BBC pre-recording obituary tributes in case of Charles's assassination, she told Wilson that she feared for her son's safety.[26] This unsurprisingly sent Wilson into another spin. He even suggested cancelling the entire ceremony after a live bomb was found near a pier at Holyhead, where the royal yacht *Britannia* was due to dock, just days before Charles was to be crowned.[27] Another was planted near the castle but failed to go off. It was found by a ten-year-old boy on holiday from the home counties. Believing it to be a football, he kicked it and it exploded. He was seriously injured and spent weeks in hospital and remains disabled.[28]

As the investiture approached, the actor Richard Burton, who was providing the television commentary for ITV, noticed this was a rather risky outing. He was staying with Princess Margaret and her husband, Lord Snowdon, and remarked to them that his own role on the day was all fairly straightforward, 'unless some shambling, drivel mouthed, sideways moving, sly-boots of a North Wales imitation of an Irishman might decide to blow everybody to bits'.[29]

Lord Snowdon, Princess Margaret's husband, knew the threat was serious. But as a close friend of Peter Sellers, he also felt the need to add an element of pantomime – the possibilities were irresistible. Using a walkie-talkie radio in his Aston Martin to connect him to the Buckingham Palace switchboard he insisted that he be addressed by an assigned codename. 'Call me Daffodil,' he suggested. 'Yes, me lord,' replied the young woman on the exchange obediently. But Princess Margaret was unable to handle the confusion of cover names, quickly ending her husband's attempts at discretion.[30]

Wilson was particularly worried about the security of the royal train. It was the biggest of its kind in living memory – with some fifteen coaches – and packed with dignitaries. Mountbatten was thrilled to be on board and noted happily that he had his own large bedroom and bathroom. But this mobile entourage of royals presented a dream target for terrorists.[31] Drawing on the latest intelligence, Callaghan had earlier warned Wilson that 'certain extremists are said to be considering plans to disorganise selected railway junctions on or before the day of the Investiture by derailing trains'.[32] Wilson pressed for a 'pilot train' to travel ahead of the royal party to test the tracks and prevent what he euphemistically called 'any untoward incident'.[33] The royal train was bulletproof and had two diesel engines, a specification dating back to 1937 when one had failed and the train got stuck.[34] Neither would have prevented it from derailing.

Wilson also demanded special precautions, including troops if necessary, at all vulnerable points before and during the ceremony. Officials in the Home Office had to tell him that this was impossible but reassured him MI5 had identified the most important vulnerable points throughout Wales and the border counties and had advised the local police forces about suitable precautions. 'All of the most important points,' officials insisted, 'are being watched or frequently visited by police.'[35] The army provided three surveillance helicopters to help out.[36] 'Everything possible is being done,' the prime minister was told, 'but one must not underestimate the difficulties.'[37]

Amid all the focus on Welsh extremism, nobody noticed a secret Soviet plot to disrupt the preparations, embarrass British intelligence and stir up tensions between the government and the Welsh. Operation Edding involved blowing up a small bridge on the road from Porthmadog to Caernarfon using British manufactured gelignite. On the eve of the explosion, a letter was to be sent to a Plaid Cymru MP, Gwynfor Evans, warning him that MI5 planned a 'provocation' to discredit the nationalists and provide a pretext for a major security clampdown in Wales. The Soviets hoped that when the bridge exploded, Evans would accuse the British government of a false flag attack designed to undermine the nationalist cause. The Soviet leadership eventually cancelled Operation Edding on the grounds that KGB involvement would come to light and fatally undermine the deception.[38]

Ultimately, it was the Welsh nationalists who almost got through. One extremist group tried to plant a bomb at a government office in Abergele, where, just as Wilson feared, the royal train would shortly be passing through. Their device exploded prematurely, killing two members of MAC, Alwyn Jones and George Taylor.[39]

On the evening of the investiture a vast royal party boarded the train. In an attempt to relieve the tension there was much 'joshing and horseplay'. Members of the BBC were also on board and showed a re-run of its film of the rather chaotic 1911 investiture of the future Edward VIII. Charles arrived in the middle of this showing to be told by his grandmother that, because of the worsening security situation, and his likely liquidation, they had decided to go ahead with the ceremony but to replace him using a stunt double.[40]

Despite the jokes, one member of the royal household later recalled that 'there was a fairly tense atmosphere the night before with bombs going off as we were on the Royal Train'. At one point, a bomb hoax stopped the train altogether.[41] Although it 'looked like a time bomb' it was in fact just a packet of clay with an alarm clock attached – most royals slept through the alert.[42] On the day itself, some devices failed to detonate, apart from one small explosion close to the castle which was drowned out by the twenty-one-gun salute.[43]

The investiture was a qualified success; albeit one in which the police outnumbered the crowd in places.[44] In the courtyard of the medieval castle, the queen draped her eldest son in a purple velvet robe, trimmed with ermine. With a crown on his head and sceptre in his hand, Charles delivered his speech. Lord Snowdon later recalled that the young prince was 'shit scared'.[45] As for his mother, afterwards Elizabeth retired to bed for six days with nervous exhaustion.[46]

How close had Prince Charles come to meeting his end? The answer is quite close. MAC supremo John Jenkins was arrested in November 1969. Incredibly, he had been in Caernarfon on the day of the investiture while still serving as a sergeant in the British Army. He has claimed he could have taken a rifle and shot the prince during the ceremony. Convicted of offences involving explosives, Jenkins was sentenced to ten years' imprisonment in April 1970.[47]

IN 1973, THE question of personal security for Charles returned to the prime ministerial agenda. The prince was due to visit Bermuda, but the Caribbean island was marred in violence. Black power militants known as the 'Black Beret Cadre' had recently assassinated the governor, Richard Sharples, outside Government House as he walked his dog after a dinner party. His aide-de-camp was also shot dead, ambushed from nearby shrubbery. Sharples took regular evening walks and just two weeks earlier had been accompanied around the grounds by Prince Charles, visiting as part of a naval tour on board HMS *Minerva*.[48]

The acting governor quickly declared a state of emergency and Scotland Yard sent a team of detectives out to investigate the murders. The new governor, Ted Leather, advised that Charles's next visit, when HMS *Minerva* was due to return for repairs, should go ahead as planned, but ministers back in Whitehall were nervous. They had already banned Charles from taking a flight from Bermuda to visit Mountbatten on the tiny Caribbean island of Eleuthera shortly after the assassination. Mountbatten broke the news to a disappointed Charles who had been desperate for a break from navy life. The prince refused to take no for an answer and vowed to use 'every method at my disposal (including bribery!)' to get there. He was successful.[49]

As for the return visit aboard HMS *Minerva*, Leather insisted that the police had the manpower to provide adequate security and Charles faced no direct threat so long as he avoided the centre of town after dark and refrained from nightclubbing. Keeping the prince aboard the ship, Leather warned, would do 'grave damage to public confidence and be harmful to everything we are trying to achieve'.[50] Visibility was integral to the monarchy's role.

Alec Douglas-Home, the foreign secretary, and Robert Carr, the home secretary, disagreed. Influenced by reports coming from British police officers on the island, they warned that it was not worth the risk. The visit of HMS *Minerva* should be kept as short as possible and the prince not be allowed to go on shore.[51]

Ted Heath did not like the idea of confining the prince to his ship but was due to meet the queen and needed advice on what to tell her.[52] From Bermuda, the governor made a last-ditch plea to allow Charles to come ashore. Amid a battle between governor and ministers, Duncan Watson, an experienced former head of the colonial office's intelligence and security department, suggested a compromise: rather than banning Charles entirely from going ashore, arrangements could be made with the Ministry of Defence to transfer him safely.[53] Safety fears won out: Charles was briefly transferred to the hydrographic survey ship HMS *Fox*.[54]

The anxieties about royal safety reverberated widely. The principal suspect in the killing of the governor of Bermuda, Erskine Durrant 'Buck' Burrows, was captured in October 1973, carrying two loaded guns. Ballistics apparently matched his shotgun with the one used in the murder. Burrows duly confessed and was sentenced to death. In spite of a mercy petition to the queen signed by 6,000 Bermudians he was hanged during the early hours of 1 December 1977 within the walls of Casemates Prison.

THE MOST DRAMATIC royal security breach of the Windsor era targeted Charles's younger sister on 20 March 1974. A lone gunman, Ian Ball, attempted to kidnap Princess Anne and hold her for ransom. He had been planning the kidnap for a long time, selecting Anne because she was the only young woman in the family and, in Ball's own words, 'would have been the easiest'.[55]

At about 7.45 p.m., the princess, then in her mid-twenties, and her husband, Mark Phillips, were being driven down the Mall towards Buckingham Palace. Ball's white Ford Escort, following them across town, quickly overtook the royal car and forced it to stop suddenly. Anne was thrown to the floor. Ball got out and marched towards Anne's car. From the front passenger seat, Anne's protection officer, James Beaton, assumed that Ball was approaching to argue about some imagined traffic incident. Beaton climbed out of the door ready to diffuse the situation.

Out of nowhere, Ball whipped out a pistol and shot Beaton in the shoulder. Wounded, Beaton drew his own weapon and tried to return fire but missed and hit the back of the car. Bleeding from his shoulder, he tried again, this time steadying his gun with both hands. It failed to fire, jamming at the worst possible moment.[56]

Anne's driver, Alex Callender, bravely rushed from the car to disarm Ball, grabbing his arm. 'I'll shoot you,' Ball shouted back at him before firing from point blank range at his chest.[57] On the floor, Beaton fiddled with his gun, trying to fix the jam. 'Put your gun down or I'll shoot her,' Ball instructed. Beaton obediently placed his useless gun down on the road.[58]

Ball turned his attention to the princess, trying to persuade her to get out of the car. 'I want you to come with me for a day or two, because I want £2 million,' he said politely. 'Will you get out of the car?'

Anne replied: 'Not bloody likely; and I haven't got £2 million.'

'I only want you for two days,' he responded, surprisingly courteously. 'I don't want to hurt you.' He then managed to open the door and tried to drag Anne out by the forearm. She tried to stay calm, repeating again and again that she did not want to get out of the car. 'Come out or I'll have to shoot you,' he insisted.

'I nearly lost my temper with him,' Anne later recalled, 'but I knew that if I did, I should hit him and he would shoot me.'[59] Her husband, Mark Phillips, grabbed her other arm to prevent Ball from pulling her out. Ball shot Beaton again in the melee, this time in the right hand. A glass window behind him shattered.[60] The tussle over the princess continued, splitting her dress and ripping the shoulders; this, she recalled, was 'his most dangerous moment' as 'I lost my rag at this stage'. Another police officer, Michael Hills, wandered onto the scene but did not notice that Ball was armed or that two people had already been shot and so when he tapped Ball on the shoulder, he also quickly received a bullet.[61]

As the surreal negotiations between Anne and her assailant continued, a number of pedestrians walked past. Anne recalled that the first one came quite close to get a good view of the struggle. 'He came all the way across the road, looked in through the window, and then went "Hmm, so it is", and turned and he walked all the way back, wandering off down the Mall.'

Eventually more passers-by turned up and tried to help. The first was a journalist, Brian McConnell, who was also shot for his pains. The second was Ron 'The Geezer' Russell, a former heavyweight boxer, who punched Ball twice in the back of the head. As he did this, more police arrived on the scene.[62]

Ball then fled into St James's Park but was quickly rugby-tackled to the ground. He had fired eleven shots in all, hitting four people. Anne thought he must be running out of bullets. Remarkably, she was unscathed but Beaton was shot three times.[63] Sir Robert Mark, the Met commissioner, concluded: 'It was a miracle no-one was killed.' The queen decorated both Beaton and her daughter for bravery.[64] She also awarded Ron Russell the George Medal, and as she presented it told him: 'The medal is from the Queen, but I want to thank you as Anne's mother.'[65]

Prime Minister Harold Wilson enjoyed reading a classified report of the incident. 'A very good story,' he noted in the margins. 'Pity the Palace can't let it come out.'[66] He praised Anne for behaving with 'quite extraordinary courage and presence of mind'.[67] Prince Charles, serving in the navy on HMS *Jupiter* some eight thousand miles away, echoed these sentiments and recorded in his diary: 'Imagine seeing four people shot in cold blood in front of you and still refusing to get out... My admiration for such an incredible sister knows no bounds!'[68]

Queen Elizabeth was half a world away in Indonesia. Number 10 moved to reassure the royal party, telling Charteris that it was just the work of an 'isolated nutcase'. Although it could inspire copycat attacks, 'perhaps it is less worrying than it would be if it seemed that there was something more behind it'.[69]

The police quickly recovered Ball's ransom letter, addressed to the queen. It demanded £3 – rather than £2 – million to be paid in used, unmarked, £5 notes and delivered in an 'unlocked thirty-inch suitcase'. Ball also sought immunity from prosecution, not just for the kidnapping but sinisterly for any crimes committed prior to it 'from parking offences to murder'.[70]

Ball's plan was byzantine and bizarre in equal measure. He had sought to take Anne to Heathrow airport where, under police escort, they would board a plane. The queen would arrive to offer the pardons in person. She would first be 'asked questions and required to give a sample signature to ascertain that she is in fact the queen'. Ball would then take Anne to Zurich while he deposited the money in a Swiss bank, before flying back together to London where Ball would release her. 'The above instructions are quite clear,' Ball wrote, 'and are not capable of any ambiguity. Unless they are carried out to the letter ANNE WILL BE SHOT DEAD. If the police make any attempts to find the hideout or if they try to storm the hideout ANNE WILL AUTOMATICALLY BE SHOT DEAD.'[71]

This was clearly the work of a dangerous lunatic. Ball was working alone and was not known to Special Branch.[72] Anne later stated that 'perhaps the greatest danger seems to be the lone nutter who had just enough to pull it together. That said, if anyone was seriously intent on wiping one out, it would be very easy to do.'[73] Queen Victoria would have agreed with this analysis.

The ill-fated kidnap spurred a speedy review of royal security. Special Branch and the intelligence services assessed that the royal family faced a threat from 'madmen and exhibitionists' on the one hand and 'groups of criminals or political extremists on the other'. Violence in Northern Ireland and the assassination of President Kennedy and his brother risked inspiring people who wanted to attack the queen. On the plus side, Britain lacked a tradition of assassination, allowing officials to hope that public revulsion would provide enough deterrence – at least against domestic terrorists if not madmen. Kidnapping provided a far greater threat, not least because developments in mass media, especially the growth of television, would ensure publicity for the kidnappers.[74]

The Princess Anne kidnap attempt was also a classic case of Whitehall departments not talking to each other. Over the previous four years several British diplomats and officials had been kidnapped and held for ransom. In 1971, the ambassador to Peru was captured and eventually freed after Ted Heath had approved the payment of £100,000. President Allende of Chile had chaired the negotiations personally between British officials and the kidnapper in a darkened room to hide his identity.[75] The Foreign Office had already begun to use the Special Air Service (SAS) to check on the security of overseas embassies. Kidnapping had also happened in Northern Ireland, but Whitehall thought it could not happen in London, and a royal attack was just unthinkable.

These events now had an impact on planned royal visits. Weeks before the attack on Princess Anne, British diplomats had been thrilled to receive the 'splendid news' that the queen and the duke of Edinburgh might make a royal visit to Mexico in March 1975. 'No news could be more welcome,' they gushed. Keen for the royal visit to go ahead they wanted to offer London reassurance about the 'security situation here' but perhaps offered too much detail.

They gave an enthusiastic account of the Mexican government's success in battling the rise of political kidnapping. Although admitting that there had been an increase in kidnappings, bank robberies and murders recently, they added that the government was now 'cracking one group after another'. The Mexicans had decided to get tough rather than giving in to ransom demands after the kidnapping of the British consul in Guadalajara. One official enthused: 'Lately various known ring-leaders have mysteriously been "found dead" after what the authorities described as inter-gang fights. I suspect that one of the "gangs" is frequently security forces.' Therefore, they assured London, things were totally 'within the grip' of the local authorities.[76] Predictably perhaps, the royals had seen enough of kidnapping and the visit did not go ahead.

Despite the mounting danger, as late as 1974, the royals were not subject to regular threat assessments.[77] Royal security was still surprisingly lax. The royal protection group consisted of just twelve men. Anne, along with the queen, Philip, the queen mother, Charles and Margaret, had full-time protection. Her younger siblings, Andrew and Edward, had limited protection, while minor royals such as the duke and duchess of Kent had protection only when required. Some of the wider family flapped after the kidnapping attempt. The queen's cousin, Princess Alexandra, on the 'C' list, requested further protection of her children but this was not granted.[78]

Even full-time protection for key royals was underwhelming. It simply involved a single 'protection officer' accompanying their royal charge from the moment they left their residence to the time of return. Each of the police officers had undertaken limited weapons training and carried – at their own discretion – a Walther self-loading pistol.[79] Often they chose not to carry weapons. Princess Anne had a single protection officer; Charles had two.[80]

The protection officer sat in the front passenger seat of each car. Only the queen had a second following behind – backup that Princess Anne would surely have craved during the kidnap attempt. Royal cars lacked decent radio communications, bulletproof glass and armour plating. None of the royal family had a motorcycle escort – something despised by the queen as an indicator of despots and dictatorship. The sight of police outriders, with sirens flashing, would have been too 'militaristic in appearance'.[81] James Beaton, who later became the superintendent in charge of royal protection, explained that their vehicles were still not fitted with radios as 'it was deemed on a royal car that it would spoil the look of it'.[82]

The government scrambled to bolster royal security in the days after the incident. But armour plating remained too heavy;

bulletproof glass too obtrusive. The queen did agree to increasing the size of the royal protection team and to installing radio sets and mirrors despite her concerns that radio calls would destroy the solitude of her car journeys. Beaton's jammed gun became the main scapegoat and within days protection officers switched to a better pistol and more expensive bullets.[83] Again, the main impediment was Philip, who was adamant that they should not have a 'tremendous increase in security' that would impact their lifestyle.[84]

Nevertheless, behind the scenes, certain members of the royal household were discreetly despatched to undertake training to deal with hostage situations.[85] Early the following year, the queen's protection officer, Michael Trestrail, visited the SAS's new specialist facility for training in hostage rescue.[86]

The SAS had acquired an elite counter-terrorist mandate in the early 1970s and had been practising bodyguard duties for some years. Their officers travelled the world to train the bodyguards of friendly heads of state – Britain became the defensive shield of the world's remaining sovereigns. To perform their newfound hostage rescue function, the SAS began training in a specially constructed six-room house in Hereford known colloquially as the 'Killing House'.

Designed on a single piece of graph paper and built by a local builder for £30,000, the house included a number of rooms, joined by corridors, full of furniture and other obstacles. The SAS could hone skills in entering a building, distinguishing terrorists from hostages, and deciding when – and when not – to shoot.[87] Here they shot hundreds of live rounds into 'Carlos the Jackal' targets 'almost daily'. Trestrail attended a three-day course, including the use of live ammunition, exposing him to the latest developments in hostage release operations. He was the first of many royal protection officers to tread this path.

Prince Philip's protection officer followed suit, but returned to the palace unimpressed and resistant to the Hereford commando style which was a million miles from the low-profile approach long favoured by the royal family.[88] The courses were also intended to give royal protection officers a better idea of what the SAS could do. Although the police maintained primacy, the SAS could be called on by the home secretary if a member of the royal family was kidnapped.[89]

Within eight years, the protection force had grown from twelve officers to forty-three, largely as a result of the failure to protect Anne.[90] The main issue was the imbalance between armed personal protection and static duty. Over a hundred officers were patrolling royal residences, but only fifteen persons were providing personal protection with their elegant Bond-style Walther PPK automatics.[91] The royal squad at least had better firearms, while those protecting Britain's Cabinet ministers had to put up with clunky old-fashioned Smith & Wesson revolvers until the mid-1990s.[92]

What of Ian Ball, Princess Anne's would-be kidnapper? During his interrogation after being arrested, the then twenty-six-year-old told police that he had intended to draw attention to the plight of the mentally ill, adding sadly: 'I suppose I'll be locked up for the rest of my life.' Ball was right and he remains detained in Broadmoor, despite frequent attempts to secure a review of his case and a period on hunger strike. His solicitor insists that had he done this to anyone other than a member of the royal family he would have been quietly freed long ago, so now he is effectively 'a political prisoner'.[93]

ROYAL PROTECTION WOULD face its biggest challenge yet in 1977. The queen and the duke of Edinburgh paid a tense visit to Northern Ireland that August as part of the lengthy silver jubilee celebrations that saw her criss-cross the country. But Northern Ireland was not like the rest of the country. The sectarian violence between Irish nationalist paramilitaries and those loyal to the crown ensured that the short trip became the biggest royal security operation in history. Some thirty-two thousand troops and police were deployed in Belfast alone.[94] All eleven battalions of the controversial, mostly

Protestant, Ulster Defence Regiment were called upon to contain the IRA threat in the run-up.[95]

Royal trips to Ireland were not commonplace. Shortly before the outbreak of the Troubles in 1969, the Irish government quietly blocked Princess Margaret from travelling to County Offaly in the heart of Ireland on a family holiday to visit her mother-in-law. Margaret was furious, but security authorities warned that the threat posed by extremists 'to create trouble' was too great.[96] When Princess Alexandra, the queen's younger cousin, was due to visit Northern Ireland on an icebreaking trip a few years later, Elizabeth questioned whether Belfast was safe enough.[97]

Visiting Northern Ireland in 1977, at the height of the Protestant marching season, would be politically sensitive and personally risky. The schedule was inevitably confined to Protestant areas to minimize the threat and reduce adverse publicity, but this did nothing to reassure the Catholic minority that the crown was not above politics.

The problem was the timing. The queen's silver jubilee coincided with sensitive dates including the anniversary of internment. Back in August 1971, amid much controversy, the Stormont government had introduced detention of suspects without trial under the Special Powers Act. The army swept in and quickly arrested hundreds of Catholics and nationalists. When John Hume, the moderate deputy leader of the Social Democratic Labour Party, eventually heard about the royal tour he was incredulous at the folly of the queen's advisers for planning her visit on what he called 'the most emotive days possible'.[98] Therefore, when those in charge of planning the jubilee tour started to consider just what would be possible in any Northern Ireland leg, they did not dare ask for security advice. So tense was the situation on the ground that they feared the security authorities would simply advise against any trip at all. Instead, they worked out a tentative plan with the palace first.[99]

This put the queen in a bind: any suggestion that she was unable to visit part of her own country would have granted the IRA a propaganda coup. Yet the physical risk was real and dangerous. At

Elizabeth and Philip's request, Martin Charteris, now the queen's private secretary, asked directly about the latest intelligence on the IRA threat and whether the trip could be cancelled if necessary – even at the last minute.[100]

The Whitehall response hardly filled the palace with confidence. Charteris learnt that the threat was more 'oblique than direct'; that the 'normal bubblings of discontent' would be inevitable; and that intelligence could not identify an 'individual fanatic' as a threat. The best they could do was identify a 'positive collective threat' – and even then the chances of doing so were only 'fair to good'. On the plus side, the trip could be cancelled at any time.[101]

Officials in the Home Office asked Charteris bluntly: 'does she want to go or not?' They discreetly offered to 'get her out of it' if necessary. Charteris duly put the question up to Elizabeth. Typically, she responded that since the visit had already been announced she had better follow through with it.[102] Northern Ireland could not be seen as a no-go area for the crown. And, if she was going to go, then, as ever, she had to be visible and accessible. She insisted on 'seeing and being seen'.[103] This phrase haunted the planners; everyone knew it would increase the risk further.

Military intelligence and the local police took the lead in assessing the threat. Planning was conducted on a strictly need to know basis, and palace officials were involved throughout. The list of potential threats reeled off by the army was terrifying: a mortar attack on the royal yacht; a shooting from a nearby vessel; an underwater mine on the hull of the royal yacht; and there was even a remote possibility of a personal attack on board by a terrorist carrying a concealed weapon. On land, the queen faced more threats from mortar attacks, remotely detonated bombs, hoax bombs and ultimately assassination.[104]

Overall, the actual physical risk to the queen herself was slight, especially with rigorous security precautions in place.[105] The royal yacht *Britannia* was to be moored beyond the range of land-based missiles and fitted with special sonar able to identify metal on the seabed. Naval divers would hunt for bombs planted below the water line.[106] Those in charge of security wondered how much counterterrorism and hostage release training the royal protection officers had undertaken with the SAS. 'Had they done the course?'[107] Many of them, including Trestrail, were successful alumni.

Amid all the morbid thinking, a local policeman made a throwaway remark trying to reassure Trestrail. 'We expect no serious trouble. Just, maybe a wee demonstration somewhere.' Trestrail asked what sort of a wee demonstration. 'Well now,' came the response, 'they might just blow up the oil refinery.'[108] Military intelligence told Charteris that the security forces would probably be able to contain this, but warned that 'some spectacular incident, such as the bombing of a prominent building, is possible'.[109]

The IRA certainly did demonstrate in the weeks before Elizabeth and Philip arrived. Terrorists mounted a campaign of violence, including arson attacks on Protestant shops in Belfast, hoping to force the government to cancel the trip on safety grounds. When that failed, they promised to give the queen 'a visit to remember'.[110] As tensions rose, their loyalist counterparts threatened to retaliate against any disruption of the visit.[111]

Charteris, a veteran of military intelligence and many a risky royal trip, was on board; others were less keen. Royal jitters reverberated from the palace. Ronald Allison, the queen's press secretary, went offscript and raised security fears with the man tasked by the government to ensure positive press coverage. Charteris was furious. He insisted on the culprit's correspondence being hunted down and 'abolished'. Given the sensitivities surrounding any official announcement about the visit and the constant need to steady nerves, both the government and palace piled pressure on Allison to be more positive.[112]

The visit would go ahead as planned. Outside of the security realm, the palace pondered what the queen might say publicly during her stay. Charteris offered some ideas, which were so astonishingly out of touch with the politics of Northern Ireland that they horrified civil servants and would have inflamed the security situation in their own right.

Delicate language was at a premium. He suggested the queen acknowledge that 'some of my ancestors behaved less than well in this part of the world in centuries gone by' but added the provocative qualification that their thinking was 'understandable enough'. 'Implanting a British garrison,' on the island of Ireland, 'made a certain sense.' If that was not enough of a red rag to nationalist opinion, Elizabeth would go on to say: 'What happened three, four hundred years ago is not our fault. It is our business but not our fault.' One alarmed civil servant scribbled 'phew!' after reading it.[113]

On the morning of 10 August, *Britannia* arrived in Belfast Lough. Elizabeth, alongside Trestrail, then nervously and reluctantly boarded a helicopter – something she had always steadfastly avoided.[114] The terrorist threat on the ground precluded her from travelling by car. Even hoax roadside bombs would have disrupted the carefully arranged programme. Marchers descended on the republican Falls Road in Belfast behind a black banner declaring 'ER Queen of Death'. Riots followed. The IRA even managed to set up a brief roadblock. The queen's helicopter was painted khaki instead of its usual conspicuous bright red, and the ride was 'undignified, uncomfortable and noisy',[115] but Elizabeth flew successfully if anxiously over the divided city to the relative safety of Hillsborough Castle.

The next day she opened the New University of Ulster at Coleraine, on County Londonderry's scenic north coast. Derry itself was off-limits and even though Coleraine was loyalist territory, this function was the riskiest part of the brief visit. The new university buildings could never be as secure as Hillsborough Castle or *Britannia*. The queen arrived once again by helicopter before taking a cautious two-minute drive to the campus where she and Philip spent most of the day.

Intelligence focused on the bomb threat but did not rule out the possibility of an assassination attempt.[116] Security services had kept the campus under close surveillance before the royal visit, but despite extensive electronic sweeps, they had found nothing and received no tip-offs until the end of July when a routine search uncovered a small bomb hidden in a campus toilet. The army quickly defused it, and Charteris was quietly informed.[117]

Forty-eight hours before Elizabeth and Philip arrived another bomb exploded on university grounds. Roy Mason, the Northern Ireland secretary, now thought the queen showed 'none of the excitement and interest that had been so evident the day before'. Still, calling the visit off would have given the IRA a propaganda victory over the British crown. The opening went ahead but against a level of security that, in the words of one historian, 'practically created conditions for martial law'.[118]

Soldiers and bomb disposal experts watched nervously as the queen undertook her formalities.[119] She toured the library, unveiled a plaque, and attended a function for 2,000 carefully screened guests. Merlyn Rees, the home secretary, fretted terribly and tried to prevent the queen from doing all manner of things.[120] She was, according to one British minister, 'terribly, terribly tense'.[121] Elizabeth made her speech – a greatly toned-down version of the inflammatory remarks the palace had initially suggested – in front of television cameras after lunch. 'There is no place for old fears and attitudes born of history,' she said, 'nor for the attribution of blame for the past.'[122]

She and Philip left by helicopter at 5 p.m. All had passed smoothly until five hours later when a third bomb exploded on the campus. It caused little damage. The IRA had mistimed the detonator: it was supposed to go off at 10 a.m. By now, the queen was long gone.[123] Prince Philip patted Elizabeth's hand and comforted her: 'There now, it's over. Unless they sink the *Britannia* we're safe.'[124] A relieved Charteris, who retired afterwards to become provost of Eton, recalled that it 'felt wonderful sailing away'.[125] The queen did not return until 1993.

The jubilee visit to Ireland, amid rioting and sectarianism, had particularly important consequences for the royal family. The tight security cordon and static locations prevented the crown from performing its traditional function of *affirming* the authority of the state by greeting jubilant subjects. Instead, the queen performed a rather more constitutionally dubious *assertion* of state authority – an assertion carried out with the help of armoured troops. The brief visit aimed to reassure loyalists, but inevitably associated the monarchy with the unionists. It inadvertently helped to politicize the monarchy and, in the eyes of violent republicanism, to legitimize the royals as a target for attack.[126] Although it was to have lethal consequences, this sombre thought was far from Charteris's mind as he sailed off into retirement.

THE ROYAL FAMILY faced increasing threats from violent nationalists and lone fanatics. But they simply ignored the politics and adjusted to being targets with a certain *sang froid*. As she grew more experienced, the queen remained famously stoic but reassuringly nervous. By the mid-1970s, terrorist incidents were occurring across Europe and the Middle East almost daily.

In 1976, the queen mother visited Paris to open a new British cultural centre. Her escort was the famously flamboyant British ambassador 'Nico' Henderson. She arrived at Le Bourget airport 'dressed in her usual powder blue Norman Hartnell attire' and wearing her familiar 'beaming smile'. She embodied the French word *rayonnement*, for which there is no exact English equivalent.

She boarded the ambassadorial Rolls-Royce and a footman placed a tartan rug over her knees. As they sped across Paris, Henderson explained that her visit coincided with that of King Juan Carlos of Spain, who was under dire threat from Basque terrorists, a group that was desperate to kill him. The two royal motorcades frequently crossed each other's paths, and he quipped to the queen mother: 'It would be such a pity if our car was mistaken for his and she found herself dying for Spain.' The queen mother laughed and enjoyed 'the bad taste joke' but the detective sitting in the front of the limousine failed to see the funny side.[127] It would not be long before terrorists successfully killed a senior British royal.

22

TERRORISTS AND LUNATICS, 1979–1984

'A mixture of desperate emotions swept over me – agony, disbelief, a kind of wretched numbness, closely followed by a fierce and violent determination to see something was done about the IRA'

Charles on the death of Mountbatten, 1979[1]

IN SUMMER 1979, Queen Elizabeth was due to visit yet another war zone. This time she would be catapulted into the long-running bush war on the border between Zambia and Rhodesia. Guerrilla violence had broken out after Rhodesia's unilateral declaration of independence some fifteen years earlier. Back then, the queen had resisted royal involvement as both sides tried to drag her into the political quagmire.

Now, she was supposed to travel to Zambia to undertake a nine-day tour of the region and open the commonwealth heads of government meeting. Not for the first time, fears for her personal safety threatened to derail planning of an overseas visit. Guerrilla rebels used sanctuaries inside Zambia to attack targets across the border. The Rhodesian air force responded by frequently bombing their bases, including sites near Lusaka where the queen was scheduled to arrive.

Prime Minister Margaret Thatcher worried about a missile attack on the queen's aircraft. This was not out of the question, especially after Zambian anti-aircraft guns had accidentally fired on their own helicopters in the chaotic aftermath of one Rhodesian raid on rebel intelligence headquarters in a suburb of Lusaka.[2] Indeed, Thatcher also worried she herself might be physically attacked as she stepped off the plane at night and indeed wore sunglasses for fear of an acid attack.[3]

The Joint Intelligence Committee, Britain's most senior intelligence assessment body, issued a stark warning. 'The concentration of air-defence equipment at Lusaka International Airport and the proximity of trigger-happy' guerrillas forces 'whom the Zambian authorities are unable to control will continue to make the use of the airport hazardous'. There is, the intelligence continued, 'a considerable risk of further mistaken attacks' on aircraft. The Cabinet secretary, John Hunt, warned that 'we may have to give rather careful thought to The Queen going to Lusaka'.[4]

Two Rhodesian civilian airliners had recently been destroyed in exactly this manner. One disintegrated mid-air as the missile struck, killing all on board, while the other crashed. Eighteen people survived from the second aircraft, but the majority were executed by guerrillas as they escaped the wreckage.[5]

Julian Amery, the right-wing Conservative MP with links to the intelligence world, and Britain's long-time unofficial minister for covert action, offered a more outlandish threat assessment. He told Thatcher about a Cuban-sponsored plot to murder the queen. Amery's conspiracy theory involved an assassination which would then be blamed on the Rhodesians.[6]

The risk of an accidental attack on the queen's plane seems far more plausible than an assassination plot. Thatcher was keen to exploit it for political gain. She was reluctant to attend the commonwealth meeting herself, knowing that both apartheid in South Africa and the status of Rhodesia would dominate discussions. She knew full well that other leaders would criticize her for not doing enough to end the two conflicts.

Thatcher was reluctant for Elizabeth to go either. The whole meeting undermined British policy and threatened to embroil the queen in a commonwealth row.[7] If the queen was to go, then Thatcher thought the visit might as well be used for political leverage. It offered a 'strong card' that could put pressure on the Zambian president to remove ground-to-air missiles from the rebels, whom she called terrorists, in his territory. There was no point in sending the queen without receiving anything in return.[8]

Thatcher's zealous and political use of the security card irritated the queen. Elizabeth also had access to the intelligence assessments, and, as a great supporter of the commonwealth, did not see anything inside them to put her off. The two had a frosty relationship at the best of times and now the queen objected to being used as a pawn in the government's Rhodesia policy, and the palace made it clear she intended to go. Thatcher backed down and both attended.[9]

As it happened, Elizabeth's role was a great success – it is a rare documented example of the monarch directly involving herself in international politics. Sitting alongside the Zambian president in the back of his official car, she persuaded him, after Thatcher had failed to do so, to drop offending passages from a speech likely referring to the rebels as freedom fighters. The summit paved the way for the settlement of the long-standing Rhodesia problem.[10]

Sadly, shortly after Elizabeth returned from Africa, assassination from a somewhat more predictable source struck closer to home.

ON 27 AUGUST 1979, at about 11.30 a.m., Louis Mountbatten, now an old man of seventy-nine, climbed into his fishing boat, *Shadow V*. The boat was docked, unguarded, in the small harbour at Mullaghmore on the northwest coast of Ireland near Sligo. Mountbatten had been holidaying in the area for the best part of thirty years at Classiebawn Castle, a country house built for Viscount Palmerston and inherited by Mountbatten's wife, Edwina.

A decade earlier, when terrorist violence broke out in the north, the intelligence services had advised him that the risk of holidaying in County Sligo was 'one that can reasonably be taken'.[11] But there were always precautions and as early as 1971, he reassured the queen that twelve policemen were on duty during his time at the castle. The following year he sought Cabinet Office advice before setting out; the main anxiety was him being taken hostage. By 1974, the twelve-man guard had become twenty-eight. The 'castle' was more like a small picturesque eighteenth-century folly and so this was almost one policeman for each room.[12]

All across Europe the terrorist threat was growing. In May 1978, his distant cousin, Prince Moritz of Hesse Kassel, had been kidnapped and injured in Germany. Moritz reported that his captors had also expressed a strong interest in Mountbatten, adding 'we have been going into his case very carefully'. As a result, the commissioner of the Met, Sir David McNee, had despatched one of his most senior officers and a member of MI5 to find out more. It was assumed that kidnappers were connected to the leftist Baader-Meinhof gang, but when asked about this they were indignant, insisting they were entrepreneurs and 'were only out to make money by way of ransom'. Mountbatten listened to the police advice carefully, and thereafter always went to bed with a loaded shotgun.[13]

As the bitter war against the IRA dragged on, the security advice grew dangerously outdated. A raid on an IRA safe house in Southampton, ten miles from his Broadlands estate, confirmed that Mountbatten was an IRA target and that there had been a plan to attack him in the early 1970s. The IRA had called it off due to the risk of civilian casualties. In August 1978, the IRA aborted another plot to shoot him aboard his boat only because choppy waters made it impossible for the sniper to take aim. In the same summer, someone tried to sabotage the boat by loosening a rubber bung and letting in water. All this pointed to trouble.[14]

Given these serious threats, the police advised Mountbatten against taking his annual Irish holiday in 1979.[15] Maurice Oldfield, until recently the head of MI6, personally advised him not to travel because of intelligence warning that the IRA planned to target the royal family.[16] They had the capabilities: terrorists had recently assassinated the Conservative MP Airey Neave and had come close to assassinating the head of NATO. 'But the Irish are my friends,' Mountbatten protested. 'Not all of them,' came the reply.[17]

The IRA watched him all summer. Its intelligence units reported that Mountbatten's Monday trip around the lobster pots might be the last chance to kill him that season. The only drawback was that the other passengers on the boat could also be killed. The IRA weighed it up and, on balance, ruthlessly decided that the chance to assassinate a royal target – a world-famous imperial figure whom they thought personified British arrogance – was too good to miss. IRA volunteers arrived in Mullaghmore especially for the operation.[18]

A young SAS-trained corporal involved in Mountbatten's protection was suspicious. He warned that *Shadow V*, moored in a public harbour and easily boarded unseen at night, was a soft target. He also reported that a car with a Belfast number plate kept returning to the quayside; the driver watched the boat through binoculars. The army and police recognized the car as being used for transporting IRA bombs. Remarkably, it had apparently been bugged for months by army intelligence tracking its movements. The warnings came to nothing.[19] The IRA volunteers managed to smuggle a bomb, rigged to a radio-controlled detonator, directly beneath Mountbatten's seat.[20]

The circle of people who knew there was trouble ahead was truly remarkable. The earl of Durham later recounted that, for weeks before it happened, Mountbatten had problems getting any local boatmen to take him out: 'they must have heard that something was being plotted against him'. He considered Mountbatten 'foolhardy' for refusing to take precautions.[21]

The local police prepared to follow the boat from the coastal road in case of trouble. They watched as it left the harbour walls and sped up towards the lobster pots. The bomb then exploded. It killed

Mountbatten instantly along with his teenage grandson and a young boatman. Another passenger, Dowager Lady Brabourne, was fatally injured. Mountbatten's body was found floating face downwards a few yards away.[22] On the same day a roadside bomb killed eighteen soldiers at Warrenpoint.

The IRA quickly accepted responsibility. The successful 'execution' was designed to 'bring emotionally home' the costs of imperialist occupation 'to the English ruling-class and its working class slaves'.[23]

The queen was having lunch in Balmoral when her assistant private secretary delivered the sombre news. This was a terrible blow to the royal family. Mountbatten was not only a family member whom she saw regularly but an important adviser and trouble-shooter. For all his faults, he had never been afraid of telling Elizabeth what she did not want to hear and he had long provided an important link with Whitehall, especially the military and intelligence establishment.[24] He had been first sea lord at the time of the Suez Crisis, providing valuable updates about the subterranean scheming, and chief of the defence staff in the 1960s, proving an enthusiastic supporter of covert action in places like Yemen where others in the queen's circle such as David Smiley and David Stirling were unofficially supporting royalist forces in the civil war.[25]

Prince Charles was particularly devastated. He confided in his diary that Mountbatten was 'a combination of grandfather, great-uncle, father, brother and friend', adding, 'life will *never* be the same now that he has gone'.[26] 'I fear,' he wrote angrily, 'it will take me a very long time to forgive these people.'[27]

Princess Margaret was also bitter, referring to the Irish as 'pigs' when she visited Chicago shortly afterwards. She then travelled to Los Angeles where local police received intelligence from London of an IRA plot to assassinate her. US authorities immediately doubled her secret service protection, added snipers to her entourage, and upgraded her limo to one equipped with bulletproof armour. The FBI raided a room where the gunman, known as 'the Jackal', was believed to be staying. It was empty.[28] A later visit by Margaret to

Washington was cancelled on account of security threats. 'Serves 'em right' was her typically forthright response.[29]

The royal family's anger was not soothed by concerns shared by the British ambassador in Dublin, Robin Haydon. In a state of high emotion himself, he wondered whether the murder would have happened at all had the Irish police been more 'vigilant and conscientious'. In particular, he found it 'extraordinary' that they had not bothered to search the boat before it sailed. He accepted that Mountbatten did not want intrusive surveillance, but insisted that a proper inspection of the boat would have been acceptable. More broadly, he criticized the Irish taoiseach's 'apathetic' response in initially refusing to return from holiday in Portugal and blamed the Irish media for not asking tougher questions in the aftermath of the murder. All of these failings and frustrations reached the palace.[30]

The assassination of Mountbatten and the attack at Warrenpoint prompted a rethink on personal protection and much else. Thatcher set up a new secret security directorate under Maurice Oldfield. Two days after the attack, she visited County Armagh against the advice of the Northern Ireland Office.[31]

Mountbatten's death brutally highlighted the vulnerability of the royal family. Despite this, just six months later, the queen was riding with her cousin, Margaret Rhodes, through heavy mist on the Sandringham estate. She turned and remarked: 'I've been informed that the IRA have a new sort of sniper that sees through the mist.' They rode on.[32]

FOR ALL THE famed stoicism of the royal family, something had to change. Immediately after the murder of Mountbatten, and still only five years after the attempted kidnap of Princess Anne, the commissioner of the Metropolitan Police, Sir David McNee, instigated a much-needed review of royal protection. The main difficulty, as ever, came in the management of risk. The royal family were in what they liked to call 'the happiness business' and to be popular they had to be accessible.[33]

It was a paradox that made protection difficult and placed a premium on intelligence. Timely and accurate intelligence minimized the need for visible protection. In turn, discreet security perpetuated legitimacy and a sense of popularity. This was the theory. In practice, senior civil servants were scathing of the quality of protection. Security was discreet, not because of timely and accurate intelligence but because it was practically non-existent.

They reeled off an embarrassingly long list of failures: 'many of the Royal protection officers are inadequately trained; some of them are not physically fit; and there are doubts about the techniques they use and the effectiveness of their weapons'. Royal vehicles 'were frequently left unattended and not properly checked' and 'some of the Royal residences, including Buckingham Palace, are very vulnerable to intruders'. The whole set-up was 'distinctly amateur'.[34] It was grossly inadequate in an era of rising terrorism.

For all the shocked indignation in the Home Office, Scotland Yard handled the royal family more diplomatically. Commissioner McNee glossed over the Mountbatten and Anne incidents when informing the queen's private secretary, Philip Moore, that 'over the past years the system of protection has worked, by and large, reasonably well'. By and large.

He then warned: 'we are now however in an era where terrorism is carried out nationally and internationally by intelligent and dedicated persons capable of highly effective tactics and sophisticated weapons. Faced with these developments it is essential that those responsible for the security of Her Majesty and others are better organised, equipped and trained than their adversaries.'[35]

All police officers providing royal protection would now come under one command, headed by a new supremo, and run from a permanently manned headquarters inside Scotland Yard. More efficient communications would also be necessary. Royal safety was the responsibility of more than one government department, including MI5.[36]

Those beleaguered civil servants used to dealing with palace intransigence knew all this would be controversial. 'The greatest possible tact', they advised, 'was needed in handling the Royal aspect', especially when it came to the 'new overlord post'. The royal household much preferred the existing decentralized system in which separate units, led by the queen's protection officer, Michael Trestrail, were assigned to individual family members. Sensitive to their feelings and scared to push too far, McNee was at pains to point out that the new co-ordinator would complement rather than dismantle the traditional system.[37]

Another key change created back-up units to assist the individual protection officers. Each would include a specially equipped vehicle and nine specially trained sergeants. Something similar was proposed after the attempted kidnap of Princess Anne, but it had amounted to little. Even now royal intransigence blunted the idea: individual royal preferences would still decide how active each unit would be.[38]

The government publicly initiated a programme to 'install security devices' at royal residences. In total, ministers spent around £2 million on improving royal security in the two years after Mountbatten's death.[39] It resulted in little real change.

While the monarchy and government bickered over policing levels, the IRA did not let up. In the spring of 1981, the security services managed to intercept and defuse a letter bomb addressed to Prince Charles.[40] At around the same time, Elizabeth and Philip, accompanied by King Olav of Norway, visited the Shetland Islands for the opening of a new BP oil terminal, the largest in Europe. The police had undertaken little advance preparation. Dense fog had prevented many officers from leaving the mainland in time to complete security checks and 'sterilize' the area.

As the national anthems played, a bomb exploded in a nearby BP power station just 500 yards from the queen. It was a damp squib:

few people even noticed; no injuries were inflicted; and the queen was decidedly unruffled, not least because she had no idea that a bomb had even exploded until later.[41]

The IRA were disappointed by the anti-climax. They had hoped to disrupt the ceremony at the very least, but still boasted afterwards to have successfully breached the queen's security. They added that the queen would have been assassinated had the bomb been closer.[42] This was a stretch, but the IRA did have a point.

It was yet another royal security failure, although this time MI5 deflected the blame onto BP. An intelligence officer from MI5's C branch, which oversaw security of key economic sites, had visited the remote location several times in the run-up to the queen's visit. He made specific recommendations about protecting the facilities, but BP had baulked at the seven-figure cost. Discussions were still ongoing when the IRA struck in May.[43]

There was a further narrow squeak the following month. A fame-hungry teenager fired six blanks at Elizabeth during the annual Trooping the Colour ceremony. Marcus Sarjeant stepped out of the crowd and, unable to get hold of a real gun, shot a starting pistol at close range as the queen rode side saddle from Buckingham Palace to Horse Guards Parade. It was nothing more than a fantasy assassination, but for a moment it appeared very real.

For a split second, the queen had stared down the barrel of Sarjeant's gun. The Household Cavalry immediately turned towards her, causing her horse to rear up. Elizabeth famously controlled the startled horse calmly and expertly, continuing on to Horse Guards Parade. Sarjeant, a loner obsessed with the attempted assassinations of Ronald Reagan and Pope John Paul II, was taken to Canon Row police station, the established repository for many such assailants down the years, and charged. Ian Blair, the young detective inspector looking after the case, expected to have about five weeks to take statements and prepare the necessary paperwork before the case was committed to the Crown Court. But then, he recalls, something odd happened:

A week after the events an Assistant Commissioner came unannounced into my office, a much more senior figure than anyone I had ever met or thought about meeting. He told me, not as a suggestion but as an unassailable fact, that he had just come from a meeting with the Private Secretary to the Queen, who he had assured that the committal would take place by the end of the coming week. With that and without seeking any response, he walked out.[44]

Sarjeant was indeed committed for trial within days and sentenced to jail under the Treason Act dating back to 1842 and similar attacks on Queen Victoria.[45] He became the first person since 1966 to be prosecuted under this act and spent five years in Grendon Psychiatric Prison in Buckinghamshire.

Later in the same year, while touring New Zealand, Elizabeth came closer to being assassinated. Again, it was not the IRA but, as Princess Anne had predicted, another disturbed lone gunman. As the queen stepped out of her Rolls-Royce, Christopher Lewis, another teenage would-be assassin, fired a rifle towards her from a deserted toilet cubicle five storeys above. The bullet missed.

The toilet cubicle had not been Lewis's first choice of location. A police search had forced him to delay his plans a few days earlier. His original choice of shooting position was far better – and he would likely have hit the queen.

Local authorities, embarrassed by the failure of royal protection, played down the incident. They told the British press the loud bang was caused by a traffic sign falling over, then, fumbling with the cover-up, changed their story to firecrackers. Rather than trying Lewis with treason or assassination, prosecutors downgraded the charges to discharging a firearm in a public place on the tenuous grounds that he had not been able to find a suitable vantage point to kill the queen. Although local intelligence discreetly investigated the assassination attempt, authorities never revealed Lewis's true intent, perhaps fearing the queen would not return to the country.[46]

Once more, Elizabeth was unruffled. This was more through ignorance than stoicism. She had no idea what was going on and it remains unclear when – or even whether – she was later told. British security authorities did not learn that anything had happened at all until Lewis was jailed.[47]

DESPITE THESE GROWING incidents the royal family remained fearless in the face of danger. In 1982, Princess Anne decided to visit the Lebanon, one of the most dangerous locations in the world. Initially scheduled to embark on a tour of Africa for the Save the Children charity, she suddenly announced that she wanted to finish up in Beirut. This was in the middle of the Lebanese civil war, and Oliver Miles, the diplomat superintending the Middle East and North Africa, recalls understandably there was a lot of 'sucking of teeth in the Foreign Office'.

They asked: 'was it sensible for her to go in the middle of a civil war?' But they were also impressed by her bravado and so nobody wanted to take the decision. The awkward question weaved its way up through the Whitehall hierarchy and eventually reached the prime minister. Risk-averse mandarins were confident that 'if we put a piece up to Mrs Thatcher she will blow it out of the water', and that would be the end of the matter. Hostages were already big business in Beirut and Thatcher 'had very strong views about the Royal Family not getting involved in anything which was too risky, so we thought we knew her mind'.[48]

The queen stepped in. The diplomats had forgotten that it would come up during one of the Tuesday meetings between Thatcher and the queen. Thatcher emerged from the palace with a change of heart: she saw no reason why Anne should not travel to Beirut, provided the security assessments pointed in the right direction. Diplomats confessed they would have loved to have been 'a fly on the wall' during that particular exchange between monarch and prime minister.

Unsurprisingly, David Roberts, the ambassador in Beirut, was especially keen for the princess to visit. He sent back a breezy security assessment saying everything was fine. He had personally walked down the main thoroughfare, Rue Hamra, 'where Her Royal Highness will go', and he was glad to report that the security situation was better than it had been for months. 'There is scarcely any heavy shelling to be heard and machine guns can hardly be seen, except in the side streets.' Eventually, a Special Branch reconnaissance team agreed. The visit went ahead and Roberts did walk down Rue Hamra with Princess Anne, accompanied by machine guns to left and right. Later, he gleefully reported that his French diplomatic colleague was green with envy.[49]

IN THE SPACE of eighteen months, the queen had faced assassination in her own backyard, the outermost reaches of the UK, and the other side of the world. Yet remarkably, very little had changed since Mountbatten's death.

The royal family remained deeply resistant to improvements. For the queen, protection officers were not simply responsible for discreetly keeping her safe but also for providing a screen between her family and the more militant arms of VIP protection whom she called the 'Thugs'. She had seen presidential personal protection up close on five continents and was repulsed by it. Rivalry between security authorities and protection officers also hindered progress, with the former deriding the latter as 'protocol officers'.[50] Two more security breaches the following summer, both involving the queen, jolted the ancient wheels of royal bureaucracy into action.

The first was the most dramatic, an almost unbelievable lapse. At about 6.45 in the morning of 9 July 1982, Michael Fagan, a scruffy unemployed labourer, climbed barefoot over the railing near the Ambassadors' courtyard of Buckingham Palace and entered the ground floor through an unlocked window. The doors were locked.

Undeterred, he climbed back out of the window and shimmied up a drainpipe onto a flat roof before entering the main palace building through another unlocked window. He walked, unchallenged, through palace hallways for around fifteen minutes, managing to find his way towards the queen's private apartments.

He entered an anteroom and smashed a glass ashtray, later claiming he wanted to slash his wrists in front of the queen. With a shard of glass in his hand, he entered Elizabeth's bedroom at about 7.15 a.m. and opened the curtains close to her bed. She quickly pressed the alarm.

Nothing happened. The footman was outside walking the dogs; the maid was cleaning in another room; and the policeman had clocked off over an hour earlier when the day staff arrived. She phoned for the police, but they were slow to arrive. The queen found herself alone with an unknown intruder.

'I got out of bed,' she later told a courtier, 'put on my dressing gown and slippers, drew myself up to my full regal height, pointed to the door, and said "Get Out!" and he didn't.'

Elizabeth managed to usher him into a nearby pantry on the pretext of offering him a cigarette as he talked about his personal troubles. She, and her footman who had now returned, managed to keep him there until help belatedly arrived. According to the queen, 'he just talked the usual sort of bilge that people talk to me on a walkabout, I can handle that'. She was angry, though, excoriating the police after Fagan had been led away.[51] Famously, when the palace chambermaid first saw Fagan in the queen's apartments, she uttered the words, 'Bloody hell, ma'am, what's he doing here?'[52]

The news of the Fagan break-in bounced around the world. In Washington, President Reagan told the British ambassador that he was greatly impressed by the queen's 'sang-froid', but could not help adding that it had produced a 'snide' reaction from the US security authorities. Reagan had visited the queen only a month before and British security officials had been 'dismissive' of the elaborate security precautions that their American counterparts had wanted to take against the possibility of an assassination attempt. 'Such things don't happen here' had been their attitude. Reagan knew the score, having survived a serious assassination attempt only the previous year.[53]

Days later, in an unconnected incident, the queen's long-standing and trusted police officer, Michael Trestrail, was forced to resign following a blackmail attempt. After the Fagan story broke, a man got in touch with *The Sun* hoping to make a few quid with a classic tabloid sex and royals story. He claimed to be a male prostitute employed over a period of years by Trestrail.

Editors refused to publish the story but informed the palace, sparking an immediate police investigation. The same prostitute had earlier tried to blackmail Trestrail for £2,000, claiming to have had a compromising photograph of the two of them together. Trestrail, knowing his career would be over, failed to report it. A subsequent inquiry found that 'in behaving as he did, Trestrail clearly laid himself open to blackmail'. There was 'no actual breach of security', but he had to resign because 'the risks he took and the indiscretions he committed, no matter how compulsive the urge which drove him to act as he did, must be seen as raising serious doubt as to the soundness of his judgement'.[54]

Trestrail's relationship with the male prostitute raised questions about the reliability of those close to the queen. No formal method of selecting royalty protection officers had existed at all before 1969.[55] Protection officers did not have to undertake positive vetting until early 1982 and the acknowledgement that some, like Trestrail, needed access to secret intelligence.[56] He duly received clearance in April, successfully hiding his secret double life in the process.[57]

In a kneejerk reaction after the scandal, Sir David McNee, the Met commissioner, quickly insisted that all forty-three officers involved in royal protection should be subject to positive vetting clearance, even though it had achieved little in the case of Trestrail.[58] As of late 1982, just eight members of the royal household, likely including the queen's private secretaries, had clearance.[59]

Sadly, Trestrail resigned having served the royal family for almost two decades. McNee thought that 'his record of service had been outstanding', displaying an eye-catching personality and 'an impeccable demeanour'. All those who served with him had 'extremely high regard for him' and thought it was a tragic end to a distinguished career of public service. Lord Bridge of Harwich, who was appointed to report on the affair, noted: 'I share those sentiments.'[60]

Fagan's cavalier trespassing was by far the bigger incident of the two. 'It was a disgraceful sequence of events,' observed McNee, that included a mixture of technical failures and lazy policing. The media clamour for 'heads to roll' made McNee feel vulnerable, rightly concluding that it was 'the higher the person whose head rolled the better'. It looked like either him or the home secretary, William Whitelaw, on the chopping block.[61]

On 13 July, McNee was sitting in his office at Scotland Yard. He received an unannounced visit from Sir Brian Cubbon, the permanent secretary at the Home Office, 'never a man readily at ease'. Focusing on Fagan, he suggested 'out of blue' that it should be McNee who resigned. McNee refused and pointed out that the Home Office and the stubborn royal household had resisted his efforts at security reform, dragging their feet. Cubbon then essentially admitted that the visit was his own private 'mission' to protect his boss, Whitelaw, and that he had kept it from the home secretary.[62]

In the end, William Whitelaw brassed it out. He defended the system by pinning the blame on 'human error rather than any defect in the arrangements themselves'. He insisted that the main problem was 'a failure by the police to respond efficiently and urgently' and tried to reassure colleagues that those responsible had either resigned, been transferred to other duties or faced disciplinary action.[63] Secretly, the Home Office began a review of the law of trespass which they noted was in response to 'public pressure' to give more protection to the royal family after 'the Michael Fagan incident'.[64]

Others were unconvinced. Prince Philip was predictably volatile and wanted to hand all royal protection duties to the army.[65]

Opposition politicians accused the government of squandering the £2 million pledged in the aftermath of Mountbatten's murder. Whitelaw maintained that he had doubled the number of uniformed police at the palace and installed new devices at various residences – on top of the money spent since 1979.[66] He also instigated a separate review of the risk to the royal family posed by psychiatric patients. The results remain classified.[67]

After the dust had settled, and security tightened up, a team from the SAS made five attempts to enter Buckingham Palace covertly. This had been arranged by the greatest government admirer of the SAS, Margaret Thatcher herself. Apparently, each of the five attempts succeeded and in the final raid they managed to lift a small silver 'trophy'. Efforts to return the trophy failed, since the palace 'denied all knowledge'.[68]

The shock of these various intrusions, in the most private part of the palace, necessitated deeper change. Royal reticence could no longer halt reform. Whitelaw informed Cabinet that 'The division of responsibility for the security of the Royal Family, which had existed for many years with the approval of the Palace authorities, would have to be ended.' A new royalty protection department led by a senior police officer, Deputy Assistant Commissioner Colin Smith, would take its place. Smith would oversee the security arrangements for all members of the royal family. Whitelaw also created a new permanent group, which reported to him personally, to examine the effectiveness of security arrangements. Pointedly, he told parliament that the queen's staff had now 'promised their full co-operation'.[69] This had not always been the case.

The IRA soon struck again. In the same month as the Fagan break-in and the Trestrail resignation, terrorists detonated a nail bomb in Hyde Park. It targeted the Household Cavalry, the queen's official bodyguard regiment. Four soldiers and seven horses died. Two hours later, another bomb exploded, this time targeting soldiers in Regent's Park. Six died instantly and another was fatally wounded. That night the queen lamented over and over again: 'The horses, the poor horses.'[70] She described it as 'the most ghastly day of my life'.[71]

A year later, the IRA tried to assassinate Prince Charles and Princess Diana during a royal gala to raise money for the Prince's Trust charity. Duran Duran and Dire Straits were headlining the event at the Dominion Theatre in central London. Terrorist leaders, desperate for revenge after the death of ten hunger strikers in 1981, instructed Sean O'Callaghan to plant a bomb close to the royal box. Fortunately for Charles and Diana, O'Callaghan was an informant working for the Irish police.

Echoing the plots against Queen Victoria, the Irish police were unsure about how far to let the planning develop before stepping in to make arrests. Going in too early would deprive them of evidence; going in too late would risk royal lives. To make matters worse, the Irish police feared losing control of the plot and so refused to tell their British colleagues. They hoped to make the arrests before O'Callaghan set foot in England by raiding an IRA meeting in Dublin, finding incriminating evidence, and convicting everyone present of IRA membership.

Unfortunately, the police bungled the arrests by making so much noise outside the door that the targets had ample time to burn incriminating documents. Without sufficient evidence, all bar one received bail. Remarkably, O'Callaghan still had the opportunity to travel to England to assassinate Charles and Diana.

He reached London with a false passport, fake driving licence and £2,000 cash. He even got as far as the flimsy royal box inside the old theatre. The plan was to plant a bomb in the men's toilet directly behind the box, preferably behind the wall tiles, as would happen in the successful Brighton bombing of the Conservative Party conference the following year. O'Callaghan knew that such a bomb would certainly kill the prince and princess – and many others too. He needed to find a way out without making the IRA suspicious. The explosives were due to arrive in Highgate, north London, in five days.

The Irish police had little choice but to brief Scotland Yard, which, in turn, leaked a story to the press that an IRA assassination team, headed by a man again nicknamed 'the Jackal', had arrived in England. The revelation prevented O'Callaghan from going ahead and allowed him to quietly leave England with his cover still intact.[72] Duran Duran only found out about the plot years later. Their drummer, Roger Taylor, described being told as the 'scariest moment' of his life.[73]

IN THE 1970S, many of the police who served as royal protection officers were still unarmed. Their American opposite numbers, the US Secret Service, found this laughable. But by the 1980s this had changed, and the police officers who provided royal protection were required to make their way to the SAS headquarters at Hereford for specialist training in firearms. Triggered by the Fagan incident, their numbers markedly increased and a new police station was built inside the grounds of Buckingham Palace behind the Queen's Gallery at a substantial cost. More like a military bunker, it was artfully hidden from public view and screened by a mound of earth and a row of trees. This not only had state of the art communications but a direct line to SAS headquarters including a series of codewords to indicate the seriousness of any incident when they called for help.[74]

For decades the SAS have trained for an incident that might involve a royal kidnapping or, worse, a hostage situation. After the Fagan incident they undertook a target-mapping of the whole network of royal palaces. Each and every room in every palace was photographed from multiple directions and the pictures curated carefully at SAS headquarters. This was to ensure that if the SAS ever needed to storm Sandringham, or abseil down the front of Buckingham Palace, the troopers would know the precise layout of each room and exact position of each chair or sofa.[75]

The royals also needed direct reassurance. The queen visited the SAS headquarters at Hereford and viewed the infamous 'Killing House' herself. Most members of the royal family would eventually follow suit to watch demonstrations of rescue operations. Security authorities hoped to give them the confidence that professional help would quickly be at hand if they were ever kidnapped.[76]

The queen watched and waited. All of a sudden, an explosion rang out across the room and an assault team burst inside, springing, diving and rolling across the floor, firing bullets inches from her nose. She was apparently 'absolutely unperturbed'. A second demonstration followed in pitch black where the hostage – and the queen – could see nothing but the flashes of gunfire. Using night vision goggles, SAS officers watched her look nervously towards the exits but 'her stiff upper lip never quivered'.

The final demonstration involved a helicopter rescue. This time the hostage wore a Margaret Thatcher mask. One soldier recalls: 'as we rose into the sky, dangling beneath the heli with our imitation Maggie, I thought I detected a slight change in the queen's expression. For a moment I could have sworn that there was a twinkle in her eye.'[77] Perhaps Thatcher's apathy towards the commonwealth still rankled.[78]

Elizabeth was likely unaware of how much personal attention the prime minister gave to the queen's security. In June 1983, Thatcher reviewed the arrangement for a brief military inspection by the queen in Belfast. Although the entire visit was within the safety of a military base, Thatcher was anxious about her security and wrote in her own hand: 'I note that it will be reassessed just before the visit.'[79]

Indeed, with the terror threat increasing in the early 1980s, there was an endless stream of royal visitors to the Killing House. In late 1982, Prince Charles and Princess Diana made their way to Hereford for a full demonstration. Their guide was a salty senior non-commissioned officer, Rusty Firmin, who had taken part in the Iranian embassy siege in 1980. Since then, he had been honing his skills by spending 'endless hours' on the close quarter battle target ranges. Their VIP visitors were not just there to view the capability, they were also present as 'prime kidnapping targets', and so the SAS wanted to familiarize them with exactly what would happen if they needed to be rescued. In other words, this was in part SAS training for the royals.[80]

The operation that the SAS chose to show Charles and Diana was an assault on a building containing hostages. They used three Range Rovers that carried ladders. Firmin explained that they would quickly exit the vehicles, scale the ladders and throw special stun grenades, charges that had loud bangs and flashes but no harmful blast, before freeing the hostages and killing the terrorists.

Diana, delighted and entering into the spirit of things, volunteered to drive one of the Range Rovers herself. The exercise started and Diana roared up to the building accompanied by other vehicles. Firmin recalls: 'Unfortunately, Princess Di hadn't fully closed her driver's side window, and when the flash-bangs started to go off one of the little pellets – which we called screamers – came back through the window and stuck in her hair. Now these things are hot and as I watched, I could see her hair was catching fire.'[81]

Firmin quickly brushed it away and started patting the princess's hair to stop it burning. 'Prince Charles and his entourage were laughing their head off,' not the most sympathetic response. Nevertheless, the SAS was now firmly on the royal tourist trail and Princess Anne followed her brother the year after. The only person who loved the SAS more than the royals was Margaret Thatcher, who visited them so often, Firmin recalls, that she 'practically has her own bunk at Hereford'. The founder of the SAS, Colonel David Stirling, an old shooting buddy of the royal family, was once thought to be a political embarrassment, since he was rather right wing, but he was now politically 'rehabilitated' and so was finally knighted in 1990.[82]

RESPONSIBILITIES OF THE new royalty protection group extended beyond the queen's domestic trips. Overseas travel formed a trickier proposition, given the propensity for even more turf wars. The group had to liaise with local police, British embassies and British intelligence. Concerned about the potential for fatal confusion, the Foreign Office reminded the palace to keep diplomats informed of all royal visits overseas, including private ones, so that posts abroad and the intelligence agencies could consider proper security measures.[83]

In March 1984, the queen was due to pay a state visit to Jordan. Thatcher asked Peter de la Billière, until recently the director of the SAS, to fly to Amman, the capital, and conduct a personal risk assessment.[84] It was not the first time that a former special forces solider had conducted overseas reconnaissance for the palace. A decade earlier, when Philip was due to visit Bulgaria as president of the International Federation for Equestrian Sports, the advance security reconnaissance was conducted by none other than Colonel Stirling, veteran of many a covert operation.[85]

Terrorist activity in the Middle East was high. There had been six attacks in Amman alone during the previous year, and close to 500 in the wider region.[86] On Wednesday 21 March, five days before the queen was due to arrive, de la Billière delivered his verdict to Thatcher, Philip Moore, the queen's private secretary, and Colin Smith, the new royal protection supremo. The Jordanians would be able to protect the queen despite the high level of terrorism. With the queen keen to go, the meeting lasted only an hour.[87] Thatcher promptly advised her to travel as planned and thanked King Hussein for accommodating the 'rather unusual request' of sending a former director of the SAS.[88]

Days later, on the Saturday, a small bomb exploded in an Amman hotel used by journalists ahead of the trip. Three people suffered minor wounds. Jordanian officials blamed the Black June terrorist organization for trying to force the cancellation of the trip. According to the CIA, Black June targeted the queen's visit in retaliation for British imprisonment of its members responsible for attempting to murder the Israeli ambassador in London in 1982. The CIA predicted that 'further attacks are likely during the Queen's visit in an attempt to embarrass the Jordanians'.[89] British intelligence probably concurred.

Senior figures debated the issue all Saturday at Chequers. The assembled team included Michael Heseltine, the secretary for defence, Richard Luce, minister of state, Robert Armstrong, the Cabinet secretary, Philip Moore, the queen's private secretary, Tony Duff, the chairman of the Joint Intelligence Committee, and John Leahy, one of the most senior officials in the Foreign Office. Thatcher explained that she would take it upon herself to make the final decision, but first she wanted to hear what each one of them had to say. The Cabinet ministers were worried and said that the government would never be forgiven if anything happened to the queen. Thatcher cut them off and said that if anything happened, 'she would resign within the hour'. Philip Moore quietly explained that the queen wanted to go and so if she was to be dissuaded the argument 'would have to be a very strong one'. Thatcher heard this but then spoke to King Hussein on the telephone before deciding the visit should go ahead.[90]

The debate then dragged on as more important intelligence came in. Thatcher summoned de la Billière to Downing Street for an emergency meeting of the inner Cabinet. Philip Moore returned from the palace. Discussions started at 6 p.m. and dragged on over dinner until 10.15 that night.[91]

It was a risky trip given the high terrorist threat, but it was important in terms of arms sales both to Jordan itself and as a discreet funnel of arms to Iraq. Thatcher knew as early as 1981 that military equipment supplied to Jordan quietly found its way there, in contravention of the ban on selling lethal equipment to either side in its conflict with Iran. As a moderate Arab leader, King Hussein was also important in the Middle East peace process.[92] It was vital to keep him onside. After lengthy debate, Thatcher agreed the benefits outweighed the risks; the queen could still go.[93]

She arrived amid incredibly tight security. Sharpshooters kept watch from the rooftops, police were stationed every few hundred yards, and a ring of soldiers hugged the runway. Brand-new anti-missile devices were clearly visible under the wings of her aeroplane.[94] On the same day as she arrived, Jordanian authorities discovered and defused three bombs, two of which were directed against British targets.[95]

The visit passed off peacefully, with the queen declaring it a 'lifelong ambition' to visit Jordan. She praised King Hussein as having made Jordan a 'beacon of stability' in the region.[96] Hussein interpreted the visit as 'a striking gesture of confidence in Jordan'.[97] Once the queen had safely returned, Thatcher wrote to the head of GCHQ, Peter Marychurch, to thank his staff for their success in intercepting related terrorist communications and monitoring the threat.[98]

In October, just five months after the queen's trip, Michael Heseltine visited King Hussein to clinch a deal to sell to Jordan defence equipment worth £300 million. A month later, defence intelligence warned that Hussein was diverting arms to Iraq.[99]

Elizabeth's visit was controversial for another reason. The press accused her of wading into the Arab–Israeli conflict by disapproving of Israeli occupation of the West Bank. She had told her hosts that no country had been more affected than them by 'the tragedy which has befallen the Palestinian people'; described a map showing Israeli activity on the West Bank, which was captured from Jordan in 1967, as 'depressing'; and dubbed Israeli planes flying over occupied territory 'frightening'.[100]

It was a theme President Reagan picked up during a visit to the UK a few weeks later. The Middle East, and Jordanian entry into talks with Israel, was a designated talking point for his meeting with the queen.[101] A few years earlier, US diplomats had hoped that Elizabeth, whom they thought enjoyed 'high prestige in much of the Arab world and in Israel', would personally sponsor activities which might create an environment for useful contact between the Arabs and Israelis.[102] What Reagan and the queen spoke about remains unknown, but both her own government and that of the US clearly appreciated her regal connections to King Hussein.

Sadly, there was a cost to the queen's visit. Unable to attack Elizabeth because of the incredibly tight security, terrorists decided to strike in Greece. On the third day of the queen's visit to Jordan, an unidentified Arab gunman murdered British diplomat Ken Whitty, a first secretary at the Athens embassy, in his car in downtown Athens and also killed a Greek woman riding with him. The gunman flagged down Whitty's car as it came to an intersection two blocks from the embassy and cruelly shot him three times in the head when he rolled down his window to speak.[103] The British ambassador in Athens recalls: 'It was a political murder. It was done because the Queen was in Jordan at the time and they didn't like that… They wanted a British victim.'[104] The perpetrators were the Abu Nidal group, one of the most dangerous terrorist organizations that had been especially active in Jordan.[105]

QUEEN ELIZABETH RULED by common consent and refused to hide behind armed guards. Improvements to her protection therefore moved at a glacial pace. It was not until 1986 that Thatcher finally announced palace acceptance of the various security changes. An additional £1 million would be spent on electronic surveillance at royal homes. The queen was still not happy and pushed back against a proposal to erect barriers around Buckingham Palace, including the Queen Victoria memorial which security authorities warned could be used as an excellent sniper position. She refused to be hidden from the public.[106] Elizabeth, like Queen Victoria before her, maintained a rather fatalistic attitude towards assassination. Both were unwilling to limit their interactions with the public.[107] When credible intelligence warned of an IRA mortar attack on Windsor Castle in the early 1990s, she refused to leave.[108]

For a long time, the royal family formed an impressively stubborn counterforce against trends towards more firepower and tougher security. Queen Victoria had no intention of hiding like a fugitive inside Buckingham Palace; neither did Queen Elizabeth.[109]

Elizabeth could not hold back the tide forever. Just a single personal security officer protected her at her first Trooping the Colour ceremony in 1952. By 1986, around three and a half thousand policemen were on duty, including armed detectives undercover in the crowds.[110]

Once the tide finally broke, it led to a flood of enhanced security. After the 9/11 terrorist attacks in 2001, MI5 insisted on installing an extensive new alarm and camera system outside and inside Buckingham Palace and strengthening the palace perimeter. Three years later, the new security arrangements allowed police to quickly assess the threat when protestors climbed on top of the palace roof. The Met commissioner, John Stevens, confirmed that the intruder would have been shot before entering the building if assessed as a threat.[111] A stark contrast to Fagan.

Intelligence kept the queen and her family safe. But it was more than that. The security of the monarch was political. The queen needed to appear visible and accessible for the institution to survive. She was fond of saying: 'I have to be seen to be believed.'[112] Intelligence allowed her to be seen safely. It kept the legend of the monarchy alive, perpetuating an illusion of power, popularity and divine protection.

23

GOING PUBLIC

*'on each of my visits to MI5, I have been impressed by the way
that you have adapted to the changing threats to our nation'*

Queen Elizabeth, 2020[1]

A FLURRY OF PUBLIC interactions between the monarchy and the
secret services in the early 1990s brought the royal relationship
with espionage creeping slowly out of the shadows and eventually
into the limelight. Both institutions, each shrouded in secrecy in
their own way, suffered a bit of a wobble in the years after the Cold
War, with critics questioning their purpose and value. The excru-
ciating indignity of *It's a Royal Knockout* in 1987 still loomed large
in the public consciousness, underlining the dangers of 'moderniza-
tion' for the monarchy. This outdoor gameshow, in which younger
members of the royal family captained four celebrity teams to raise
over £1 million for charity by completing inane tasks in fancy dress,
was roundly viewed as toe-curling.

Meanwhile, the queen was embroiled in a public row about tax,
there were family tensions, and the Gulf War was waged without any
royal involvement. Prince Andrew had served as a helicopter pilot
during the Falklands War in 1982, yet although still in the navy,
he was playing golf in Spain when the war against Iraq broke out.
The year of 1992 was perhaps the low point – famously described

by the queen as *annus horribilis* – three royal marriages were visibly deteriorating and Windsor Castle caught fire, triggering a row over who would pay for the damage and signalling a wider debate about the complex relationship between the private privilege of royals and the public purse.

Yet oddly, just as the queen faced unprecedented disaster at home, she had never been more useful or popular abroad.[2] In diplomatic and security terms she had hardly ever been busier. In the face of public criticism, the palace emphasized with disdain how the queen went far beyond her constitutional duties and stayed impeccably well briefed on military developments. Prince Philip even turned up in full uniform after the Gulf War to hear, among other things, about the performance of intelligence.[3] One of these royal duties was to assist the secret services as they navigated their way towards a more visible public presence and a different role in what proved to be the new world disorder of the 1990s.

The intelligence agencies were also suffering their own crisis of confidence. For almost half a century the 'spooks' had been indelibly associated in the public mind with the territory of John Le Carré and Len Deighton – a dimly lit world of shadows and half-muttered conversations in Whitehall corridors. Even in the final decade of the Cold War, the biggest triumph for British intelligence, the recruitment of the KGB officer Oleg Gordievsky, had been all about containing the Russians. If the Cold War was over, many wondered who now needed the spies?

On Capitol Hill, one of America's most distinguished senators, Pat Moynihan, called for the abolition of the CIA. In the Netherlands, the Dutch actually went so far as to wind up their equivalent spy organization and made its spies and agents redundant. The head of the British MI6 station in The Hague cheekily began to buy up some of the best ones in what he saw as a fire sale of espionage assets, but was expelled for his pains. Back home, parliamentarians called for budget cuts in the absence of the Soviet threat. John Major's government obliged, cutting their funding and leaving the intelligence services forced to justify their existence. Not for the first or the last time, MI5 and MI6 faced something they feared even more than the KGB: the possibility of merger.

Victory in the Gulf War, perhaps even more than the collapse of the Soviet bloc, seemed to signal the end of an epoch, marked by the apparent ability of America to vanquish all its former foes. In July 1991, London hosted the G-7 summit and, during the main reception held at Buckingham Palace, the queen congratulated past and present leaders on their achievements. One figure whom she singled out for praise was her former prime minister Ted Heath who had headed out to Baghdad at the start of the Gulf War on an improbable special mission. He had persuaded Saddam Hussein to release thirty-three elderly British hostages and brought them home. The job was judged to be too dangerous for a serving prime minister and Saddam had indeed given Heath 'a very rough time'.[4] Patting Heath on the arm, the queen grinned and said: 'Ah, but you are expendable now.' He chuckled with delight. Perhaps the queen privately pondered whether this applied to other figures and institutions as Britain moved into a new era.[5]

ALL THREE OF Britain's secret services certainly looked sad and careworn in the early 1990s. The MI6 headquarters positively reeked of post-imperial decline. Located at the top of Century House, a crumbling 1960s concrete tower block south of the river, it seemed to epitomize decay. When the service first moved there from its old headquarters in prestigious St James's, close to the Guards Chapel and only a few minutes' walk from Buckingham Palace, the debutantes who served as MI6 secretaries complained that they could no longer get out to Bond Street or the Burlington Arcade for their shopping and so 'C' had granted them longer lunch hours so that they might stroll north of the river. Not only shabby but also highly insecure, it now had a malodorous petrol station at its base. The days of debutantes were gone and the remaining inhabitants nicknamed their building 'Gloom Hall'. The queen had never visited MI6 or indeed any other intelligence headquarters before.

The closest she had come was perhaps her visit to the Metropolitan Police headquarters in Westminster back in 1967. Together with Philip, they toured its so-called Black Museum and enjoyed seeing espionage artefacts from the Portland Spy Ring case, during which Russian agents had successfully acquired classified material on British underwater weaponry. These included a cigarette lighter, a tin of talcum powder, a whisky flask, and a torch battery with secret compartments used by the KGB mastermind, Gordon Lonsdale, to hide micro-film. They also saw an 'escape' wallet containing passports and paper currency, as well as a belt with a zip on it to conceal money.[6]

Elizabeth and Philip viewed items relating to Roger Casement, an Irish nationalist executed for treason for his role in the 1916 Easter Rising. These included a warrant for his arrest, various items which were found buried on the Irish beach where he landed, such as a German signalling lamp, German pistol and ammunition, a German railway ticket and a packet of German tobacco.[7] In particular, the royal couple had expressed great interest in pickpocketing and were treated to a demonstration by a senior officer.[8] All this underlined a long family fascination with the secret world and so it is surprising that no royal had yet crossed the threshold of a British spy headquarters.

Back in 1980, plans were briefly afoot for the queen to visit MI5. The director general, Howard Smith, had hoped that a royal visit would bolster staff morale.[9] But visiting MI5 headquarters was an entirely different matter from Scotland Yard. MI5 did not officially exist, although it had been publicly discussed in widely read documents such as Lord Denning's report into the Profumo affair. The palace eagerly accepted MI5's invitation and the detailed planning which precedes all royal visits whirled into action.

Suddenly, diplomats in the Foreign Office found out and insisted it be cancelled. Elizabeth had been inadvertently dragged into the petty institutional rivalry of the British intelligence community. The diplomats argued that the queen was unable to visit MI6 – which was even more secret – and therefore any visit to MI5 would be unfair. Smith, himself a distinguished former diplomat who had served as ambassador in Moscow, accepted the snub from his erstwhile colleagues without a fight.[10]

Ten years later, the end of the Cold War offered new opportunities. There was a demand for 'Glasnost', a new openness, not only in Moscow but also in London and Washington. The Security Service Act of 1989 put MI5 on a legal footing (with MI6 following in 1994). From her throne in the House of Lords, Queen Elizabeth announced, with characteristic understatement, that 'a Bill will be introduced to put the Security Service on a statutory basis under the authority of the Secretary of State'. It came nestled between government pledges to better train young people and improve the protection of children.[11]

Britain's security service came blinking into the sunlight slowly and cautiously. Officials had to work out what an avowed intelligence service actually looked like and how it operated in practice. It was a confusing time and so the queen's public interactions with MI5 unsurprisingly started rather slowly. In late 1992, she invited its new director general, Stella Rimington, to lunch at the palace. Rimington was the first intelligence chief to be publicly named on appointment, and the press were desperate for photos. Now, after a career shrouded in secrecy, she suddenly found herself in eclectic company at the palace, alongside the sprinter Linford Christie and England football team manager Graham Taylor.

Characteristic of the uncertain levels of openness, the palace's archaic court circular publicly announced Rimington's attendance. Journalists and photographers rushed to the palace gates to take her photo as she left. The royal household helped her to, in her words, 'slink out ignominiously' through the Royal Mews. More adept at her tradecraft than many of the younger royals, she successfully evaded the many photographers. This did not put reporters off writing about the meeting and speculating about its content: 'Oh to be a Fly with the Spy at the Palace'.[12] The journalists failed to realize that, all the way back to George V, monarchs had lunched and dined with spy chiefs for almost a century.

Elizabeth finally visited MI5 headquarters, at 140 Gower Street near Euston station, in June 1993. Its building was only slightly less dilapidated than its sister service and boasted failing lifts. Elizabeth had a tour and received a briefing from Rimington, who reminded her that, unlike MI6 and GCHQ which responded solely to outside tasking, 'the Security Service is required under the Act to assess threats to national security and to deploy its resources accordingly'.[13] In other words, it was more its own master and was allowed to sniff about where it wished.

Her historic visit, again publicly announced via the court circular, opened the way for other members of the royal family to follow suit. By March 1995, MI5 had moved into much better premises, Thames House, a striking 1920s building at Millbank on the north bank of the river, just south of parliament. Prince Charles himself toured its newly refurbished headquarters and received his own briefing from Rimington.[14] Almost three years later, his younger brother, Prince Andrew, did the same.[15]

MI6 went one better. In the early 1990s, its chief, Colin McColl, sensed that times were changing and sequentially entertained the editor of every national newspaper over lunch. They were followed by most of the senior editors from the BBC and ITV. The only exception was Kelvin MacKenzie, editor of *The Sun*, whose secretary replied that he 'does not lunch'.[16] The charm offensive seemed to pay off. While MI5 was given a refurbished facility opened by the prime minister, MI6 wangled a new-build on the opposite bank of the river that was opened by the queen in July 1994. Nine storeys high and designed by postmodernist architect Terry Farrell, perhaps one of the quintessential bling designers of the 1980s, this was the essence of 'stepping out'.[17] John Major had only admitted the existence of MI6 to the House of Commons two years before.[18]

Its showy and expensive new headquarters at Vauxhall Cross indicated that MI6 maintained influence within Whitehall. Constructed in yellow brick and a striking fusion of 1930s industrial architecture and Aztec temples, it attracted a number of nicknames, including 'Legoland'.

Colin McColl, and his incoming successor, David Spedding, greeted Elizabeth and took the opportunity to brief her on various security matters.[19] As she so often does when touring such buildings, the queen pivoted effortlessly – and slightly disarmingly – from shaking hands and smiling to asking penetrating questions about intelligence and threats.

The queen had long maintained a close relationship with MI6. Her private secretary, Robert Fellowes, apparently communicated regularly with McColl. Every day, McColl would send summaries of intelligence reports to the palace, accompanied by a formal note signed in his traditional green ink.[20] Fellowes' successor as private secretary, Robin Janvrin, was himself reportedly a one-time intelligence officer, reviving the tradition of Charteris and Lascelles in years long past.[21]

Like her predecessors, Elizabeth occasionally met particularly brave intelligence agents from both MI6 and MI5 – those who had secretly, and without public credit, risked their lives for her country. She would later present Oleg Gordievsky, the remarkable agent who had provided such valuable intelligence on the Soviets in the latter Cold War, with a CMG 'for services for the security of the UK'. Coincidentally, Margaret Thatcher had been with the queen at Balmoral when the then chief of MI6, Christopher Curwen, had briefed Thatcher's Foreign Office private secretary, Charles Powell, who in turn immediately flew to Scotland to seek permission for his rescue from Russia back in 1985.[22] The two MI6 officers who physically exfiltrated Gordievsky through Finland were treated to a private audience with the queen, where they told their hair-raising story. Each was awarded a secret OBE – being told that they could not reveal their decoration for ten years.[23]

The empire may have been long gone, but MI6 existed officially and publicly for the first time. Perhaps it was being reinvented as a form of soft power. The vicious war in the former Yugoslavia had shown everyone that Britain had moved from a period of Cold War to 'hot peace' and so the spies were needed now more than ever. By 1995, the budgets of both MI6 and its American sister service, the CIA, were being expanded. The acting head of CIA operations, Jack Devine, visited London to see David Spedding, with whom he had once served secretly in Chile. During the trip, he met the queen. He wondered about how he would be described to Elizabeth in terms of his precise function in the US government. As he approached the queen, she politely asked: 'How are my boys treating you?' Devine took that to mean that she knew exactly who he was. He recalls how he 'then heard a loud squeaking noise coming out of my mouth, saying, "wonderful, wonderful!"' He could not believe how over-excited he had become.[24]

In March 1995, Elizabeth and Philip visited GCHQ headquarters in Cheltenham. Although less well known, this organization was the source of much of the material in her famous red boxes. When asked by a minister what she had made of the employee strike at GCHQ in the 1980s, the queen replied that she was quietly delighted, since it meant her boxes were lighter and so she had less homework to do in the evening.[25] Again, they met its staff in an informal setting and received a briefing on its activities. The visit, coming shortly after similar visits to MI5 and MI6, constituted part of the queen's more public links with the secret services.[26] The trip to GCHQ was, however, potentially more contentious. The service had recently fended off allegations of intercepting private royal communications.

While MI5 and MI6 had already moved into new premises, GCHQ was still a bit of a mess. Straddled across two different sites in the elegant Cotswold spa town of Cheltenham, it was a melange of random structures and 'temporary' buildings that had been there rather too long. It was dominated by a brutalist concrete headquarters constructed in the 1970s, where the queen was received. She was then taken to a curious green computer centre, built in the 1980s, to see some of the mathematical wizardry.

A new GCHQ headquarters concept was already emerging, pioneered by the agency's perceptive director David Omand, and construction began in the late 1990s. This was a vast circular unitary spy hub, at the time the largest building project in Europe, and fitting it out absorbed some fifteen miles of carpet. It was finally opened by the queen herself a few years later. By then, Britain was in a post-9/11 world and spy budgets, trimmed only a decade before, were booming again. The spies were no longer just stepping out, but also stepping up.

IN FACT, SPIES and royals mattered more than ever in the 1990s. The royal visits made to resplendent new secret service headquarters were symbolic of a continued importance of both intelligence and the monarchy. As the Berlin Wall came down and a new world opened up, British diplomats found the royals fabulously useful in establishing a beachhead as they tussled with other countries for new diplomacy and new opportunities in Russia and eastern Europe. The queen in particular offered an advantage that few other countries could match. Patrick Wright, the senior official at the Foreign Office, recalls how important the royal family were in opening up the former eastern bloc. They were not quite a 'weapon', he mused, but they were of 'enormous assistance to us in our foreign policy'.[27]

Fully engaged in this mission, the royals operated like an army battalion. The pathfinder unit was Prince Charles, taking his visits incredibly seriously. If it went well, he would report back and other royals, and then eventually the queen, would follow. To mop up, in her wake, would come perhaps Prince Andrew or Prince Edward and then a host of minor royals.[28]

This format was developed in Hungary, the first place chosen for this soft political offensive. John Birch, the ambassador, recalls that the royal activity kicked off with a visit from the prince and princess of Wales in May 1990. Although their marriage was by now thoroughly 'on the rocks', Birch recalls he 'didn't spot it at all' although on subsequent visits they came separately. They were followed by Prince Andrew, Prince Edward and Prince and Princess Michael of Kent. The most important was a state visit by the queen – her first to any communist country. The Foreign Office knew it carried 'a strong political message'.

Birch was struck by how much the queen knew about eastern Europe. She talked frankly about Romania and 'about the dreadful experience of having Ceausescu to stay'. She also knew all about King Michael, Romania's last monarch, who had come to her wedding in 1947 and all the other ex-royals of the east. Diplomats often noted the contrast with Margaret Thatcher, for despite her legendary capacity for late-night homework, she was much weaker in understanding the countries she visited. Birch observed that perhaps it was 'a comparison one shouldn't make' but nevertheless 'the Queen had the edge'. Years of diligently reading intelligence reports and telegrams from ambassadors was now paying off.[29]

The highlight of the queen's programme of 'Eastpolitik' was her visit to Moscow in October 1994. Officials were anxious about the Russian leader, Boris Yeltsin, who only a year before had been too drunk even to get off his plane when it landed in Ireland at Shannon airport. Would the effusive Russian president bear-hug the queen or perhaps do something worse? He had come to power during a battle around the Russian parliament, in which there had been considerable casualties. Would security be as tight as it had been during the pioneering visits of Prince Philip and Princess Anne in the 1970s?

Brian Fall, the British ambassador in Moscow, already an experienced diplomat and recipient of two knighthoods, realized how important it was to show support for Yeltsin's rather wobbly capitalist democracy. So, over a period of three years, he repeatedly pressed the royal button and conjured up separate visits for Elizabeth, Philip, Charles, Diana and Anne.[30]

Francis Richards, minister at the Moscow embassy, recalls the queen's visit as the most 'extraordinary experience' of his time there. 'It was like watching 1917 in reverse', adding that 'one watched Communist apparatchiks rushing out to buy dinner jackets which hadn't been worn in Moscow since the revolution'. Kremlin guards were dressed up in fantastic Tsarist-era uniforms. Coming out of her visit to the Kremlin, with the sound of the great bells of the Kremlin tolling, the Russians had assembled a remarkable line-up including bishops in their full regalia. There was some tension between the central government and the mayor of Moscow over who was running the show; the latter 'hijacked the programme' so it proceeded in a 'slightly anarchic way'. The queen took it all in her stride.[31]

While on the whole the visit went well, some things went wrong. Embracing the new spirit of openness, the embassy decided to organize a walkabout for the queen around Red Square to meet normal Russians. Unfortunately, the eager security forces had cleared the square. It was deserted. Elizabeth, looking around confused, apparently said: 'Oh.' They walked round the square and eventually managed to meet one or two people separately.[32]

The whole circus then moved down to St Petersburg. Richards, whose next job would be director of GCHQ, recalled that he had great fun here because he was tasked with arranging the programme and that meant he could go everywhere in that great city. First of all, he had a meeting with the local mayor and his entire array of deputies, one of whom was Vladimir Putin.

Putin had finished his KGB career, but because of his intelligence credentials was now the deputy mayor put in charge of security. 'I am afraid I shook his hand – we did have a discussion of security – but I cannot remember anything about him – which perhaps shows he was a fine professional intelligence officer.'[33] Other diplomats recall that while the St Petersburg part of the programme was a bit more 'relaxed', the Russian security apparatus was simultaneously both omnipresent yet difficult to get hold of.[34]

Russian intelligence was discreet, but constant, attentive and friendly. They were determined that nothing would go wrong. Occasionally they would reveal themselves to the queen's entourage. Some of the British team had been designated to capture a few moments of film for inclusion in the queen's Christmas broadcast. They had arranged to film the queen carrying a posy of flowers and pick up the sound via a small high-powered and cordless radio microphone concealed in her bouquet. Her team had ordered the flowers but were slightly surprised when they arrived in a large black limousine escorted by two stern elderly women who did not seem much like florists. The women watched as the royal team arranged the electronic bouquet and then asked in flawless English: 'Is the transmission diversity system on VHF or UHF?' The royals hoped that their hosts were 'impressed by Her Majesty's state-of-the-art bugging techniques'.[35]

The two women were perhaps part of what was once the KGB's legendary 'granny squad'. One of the aspects of Russian tradecraft that the British admired during this period was their decision to dispense with the traditional 'undercover' operative, often an awkward figure of muscular build in jeans, police boots and a leather jacket. By the 1990s, they were more subtle and would often shadow visitors with a group of ladies who were senior in years, but no less effective. A British security official recalls that on one visit, a member of his team had briefly strayed into a local market to buy souvenirs but was relieved of his wallet by a pickpocket. Instantly the Russian female surveillance officer who was quietly shadowing him set upon the thief, subdued him, wordlessly returned the wallet to its owner, smiled politely and then vanished into the crowd. British dignitaries were perhaps never safer than when walking Russia's streets.[36]

WHEREVER THE ROYALS went, the biggest point of tension was motorcades. The security services in each country were so used to a high level of threat against their leaders that their answer was to drive at the greatest possible speed. In advance of each visit, the queen sent out her diplomats who then quietly retrained the locals.

On October 1991, the queen attended the commonwealth heads of government meeting in Zimbabwe. This was a special conference, since the wave of democratic transition was not only sweeping over the eastern bloc but also South Africa and she was able to meet Nelson Mandela. She took the opportunity to visit several other African countries including Namibia. The British high commissioner recalled that because this was the first royal visit they went 'rather over the top' in their preparations in a 'touching way'. They changed the uniform of the army, dressing them in specially designed scarlet coats. More alarmingly, they decided it was a good idea to ring the whole capital with anti-aircraft batteries – from which they had to be gently dissuaded. Such 'precautions' were often more dangerous than the threat they were trying to avert.

Predictably, the main issue was the drive from the airport into the city. Security officials were determined that the queen's motorcade should proceed the same way that those of most African leaders did. Used to being shot at and assaulted by roadside bombs at every turn their answer was to go 'at 100 miles an hour' and to ensure that there was a hefty advance guard of equally fast police cars, with sirens blaring and lights flashing, while 'zig zagging down the middle of the road' to force anybody travelling along the highway in the opposite direction off the road and into a ditch. The high commissioner took polite but elaborate steps to prevent this. He had located a little motor-racing circuit outside of the main town, and together with the president of Namibia, they went out there and personally schooled the cavalcade to go around slowly enough for the queen to see the faces and wave at them. These careful preparations ensured that her short visit was 'indeed a triumph'.[37]

The queen then headed on to Zimbabwe for the commonwealth heads of government meeting. Once again, the local security officials, mostly Soviet-trained, were horrified when the palace insisted that her itinerary be published in the newspapers well ahead of schedule so that if local people wanted to see her, they would know exactly where she was going to be and could line the route, which they did in their thousands. By contrast, President Mugabe's itinerary was always 'a great secret' for security reasons. He used to speed about in an armoured Mercedes, accompanied by a huge convoy including motorcycle outriders going at about sixty or seventy miles an hour. The queen dispensed with outriders as they obscured her from the people who had taken the trouble to come and see her.[38] Even at home, for years, she had been the only royal who refused to be escorted by the white-gloved motorcycle outriders of the Met's special escort group.[39]

Not all royal motorcades went quite so smoothly. Prince Michael of Kent visited St Petersburg in the wake of the queen. He recalled being taken from place to place at horrifying speed. One of the escorting police cars ahead 'shot a red light and drove full tilt into some unfortunate car going across its bows', then just kept going, without bothering to check on the occupants, following what was, by all accounts, standard local procedure. Prince Michael was on his way to an international meeting about road safety standards.[40]

Some of this behaviour may have rubbed off. One day, returning in her modest motorcade through London to Buckingham Palace, the queen found herself inexplicably stuck in traffic. Nothing moved and she waited, finally enquiring what seemed to be the hold-up. Before anyone could answer, there was the wail of police sirens and a long procession of motorcycle outriders came into view followed by a Rolls-Royce travelling at high speed. Her police escort explained apologetically that it was Princess Michael of Kent, known within the royal family as 'Princess Pushy'. All this confirmed the queen's view that there were just too many 'minor royals'.[41]

A lesser risk on these visits, but still alarming, came from 'briefing notes'. All the royals were famously well prepared for their various meetings, dinners and other occasions. They not only displayed a remarkable ability to remember the names of people they had often never met, but miraculously avoided sensitive subjects and committed few diplomatic faux pas, with the exception of Prince Philip who sometimes just could not resist putting his foot in it. This magical ability was possible because, the night before, they received their 'background', often full of gossip about local dignitaries expressed in delightfully droll language. This in turn made the homework for the royals rather more enjoyable, as the briefing notes were often a salacious scandal sheet and a riveting read. In the 1990s, the top billing for bad behaviour were Saudi minor royals, one of whom had reportedly kept some of his staff prisoner in feudal conditions on the top floors of the five-star fortress-like Ramses Hilton hotel in Cairo. Two cooks finally escaped by knotting sheets together and descending more than twenty storeys.[42]

For a hundred years, the royals had enjoyed these digests of diplomatic gossip, often covering the dubious deeds of other royal families: a tasty reward for doing their 'boxes'. However, one of the terrors that all the royal private secretaries faced was if these notes ever got misplaced. The 'incendiary cocktail' of background material was supposed to be kept safely in their private apartments. But sometimes, if the homework had not been completed on time, these 'sensitive documents' were stuffed into royal handbags or pockets for last-minute 'cramming' in the car on the way to the event. Occasionally panic ensued when they were lost. Patrick Jephson, Princess Diana's private secretary, recalls a moment when 'a wad of the typewritten dynamite' was misplaced by the princess on an aircraft. It required the efforts of three police forces to retrieve it safely.[43]

THE SOFT POWER exerted by the royals during this critical period, often at some personal risk, is hard to measure. But no British diplomat disputes its importance. David Dain, the high commissioner in Islamabad, waxes lyrical about the queen's visit to Pakistan in 1997. He regarded it 'as one of the high spots, if not the highest spot in my whole career'. He added that it was difficult to describe the enormous benefit of a state visit to British diplomacy. He took up his post about six months before she arrived and the magical effects of the imminent visit were already visible. In this case the queen's safety was partly in the hands of Pakistan's famously effective Inter-Services Intelligence.

Just as in Sudan years ago, no one wanted to miss the show. All the parties co-operated in a way that was 'quite extraordinary'. Leaders who were previously at 'daggers drawn', people who had probably not been on speaking terms for years, were suddenly in each other's presence because they could not afford not to be seen with the queen. According to Dain, this in turn 'gave us the chance to influence whatever it might be we wanted', ranging from commercial interests to security matters. Britain, of course, had a huge range of interests in Pakistan that stretched back to the creation of the state, presided over by Prince Philip's uncle, Lord Louis Mountbatten, exactly half a century before.[44]

Yet while Britain's three secret services all received approval for shiny new headquarters during the 1990s, its fourth and most secret service, the royal family, lost one of its key facilities, the royal yacht. Its final mission was to transport the last governor of Hong Kong, Chris Patten, and the prince of Wales back from Hong Kong after its handover to the People's Republic of China on 1 July 1997. *Britannia* was decommissioned six months later. The queen, normally famously stoical and unmoved at public events, is reported to have shed a tear at the decommissioning ceremony. The crown was slowly contracting and perhaps the spies did indeed now constitute the last vestige of her empire.

BUGS AND BUGGING

*'There are powers at work in this country about
which we have no knowledge'*

The Queen, 1997[1]

B ACK IN MID-DECEMBER 1936, William Bateman, a loyal member
of King Edward VIII's household, moved a campbed, blankets
and thermos flask into the royal telephone exchange. During the
abdication crisis, Edward talked for hours on the phone each day,
alternating between Wallis, his brother and Downing Street. His
loyal telephonist Bateman was worried that others might overhear
and so he guarded the exchange by day and slept there at night for
ten days. But he could do nothing about others elsewhere on the
line – and as we now know there were many eavesdroppers.[2] Over
half a century later, Princess Diana feared the same: that someone
was out to steal her royal secrets.

Britain has long enjoyed a historical reputation for success with
secret listening, symbolized by Bletchley Park. As we have seen, King
George VI was a regular reader of the intelligence product it provided.
His daughter Elizabeth followed in his footsteps and became a top
customer of its successor organization, GCHQ.

But they were both less familiar with the defensive side of
communications security. Communications protection was essential to stop the enemy listening in on British secrets, including

those of the royal family. Britain was not so good at this and the traditional green scrambler phone that Churchill used to talk to Roosevelt was weak. The Germans could intercept it. Eventually, scientists, with the help of Alan Turing, created a better device called 'Sigsaly', but its machinery was so vast that it could not be accommodated within Whitehall. Instead, the apparatus for these secret transatlantic calls filled the entire basement of Selfridges department store on Oxford Street.[3]

Such elaborate devices were therefore very rare. Whitehall, Westminster and also Buckingham Palace continued to subsist on the old green scrambler phone. In June 1953, when a crisis broke out over the possible marriage of Princess Margaret to the equerry Peter Townsend, Churchill's secretary called Lascelles 'on the scrambler phone' and asked him to come to Chartwell, his home in Kent, for discussions.[4]

By contrast, in October 1955, Margaret telephoned the queen who was away at the Castle of Mey on the north coast of Scotland where there was no scrambler. While Margaret talked to her sister about Townsend, the conversation was highly constrained 'because one feels that so many people are listening in most eagerly'.[5] The main advantage of the scrambler was to prevent telephonists at multiple exchanges from earwigging on conversations, but they could not protect against anything other than the amateur eavesdropper.

The queen's biggest problem was Britain's network of outdated local exchanges staffed by bored telephonists hungry for gossip. In August 1965, reports surfaced that telephone exchange operators had been giggling about things they had heard over the queen's private phone line during the recent Badminton Horse Trials. Local telephonists at Chippenham in Wiltshire had been earwigging on calls made not only by the queen and her children but also Princess Margaret. One operator admitted that such calls 'are very popular for tapping', adding that 'we consider them to be "juicy conversation"'. The claims appeared first in sleepy weekly local paper the *Wiltshire Echo*, but soon made the front page of the *Daily Express* and then international papers.[6] Tony Benn, the Labour minister in charge of telephones as postmaster general, was normally keen to believe every report of bugging and wiretapping. He constantly worried about the secret state and surveillance. On this occasion, the royal dimension left him embarrassed and rather eager to dismiss this one as a 'silly season' story.[7]

MODERN BRITISH COMMUNICATIONS security was a nightmare. During the early 1950s, officials discovered that even the best communications equipment 'leaked' a plain-text version of their message at a distance up to two hundred yards. Even worse, in the 1960s, miniature transistors raised the threat of the 'micro-bug', hidden in walls and doors, even bedrooms – unconnected to any phone. All this prompted Britain to create, and then expand, a new body tasked solely with communications security. At the top of their list for protection was the monarch.[8]

By the 1960s, Britain's plans for a secure speech network for Whitehall and Westminster represented nothing less than a map of the secret state, connecting Downing Street, the Cabinet Office, MI5, MI6, GCHQ, Britain's V-bomber strike force – and of course the queen. This meant the secret network for crisis consultation had to be extended to obscure places including prime ministers on holiday and remote royal palaces.

Unfortunately, this was often more ambition than reality. Elizabeth still had an old-model humble green scrambler phone. Highly secure speech was a huge technical challenge because of the need to encypher and decypher in real time as someone spoke. Moreover, normal telephone lines did not offer enough bandwidth to send the data backwards and forwards. The possibility of secure speech over ordinary telephone lines to rural places like Sandringham only became possible in the late 1970s, and even then, the costs were eye-wateringly high. Viable systems eventually started to be rolled out, but these were restricted to Elizabeth and her private secretary who had access to serious government secrets. Key areas of Buckingham Palace were also swept for bugs by the same team that protected Downing Street.[9]

By 1981, secure speech was at last plentiful and becoming relatively cheap. Britain boasted a family of secure phones codenamed Melody that were capable of using the public phone network. There was even a lightweight version that could be carried in a discreet attaché case codenamed Brahms.[10]

Unfortunately, the rest of the royal family and their residences were still unprotected. In hindsight, this was a mistake given the changes that had swept over the royal family in the 1980s, including the arrival of a new member – Princess Diana – and the frenzy of public interest.

As early as 1981, officials were clearly worried that Charles and Diana were targets. Foreign Office officials compiled ominous files entitled 'Prince of Wales: telephone tapping'.[11] And with Diana came new enemies, not just the traditional anarchists, spies and maniacs who had tried to assassinate royal families for more than a hundred years, but also an aggressive and intrusive press. It was sometimes hard to tell the difference. In 1986, Princess Margaret told a friend: 'Journalists have learned how to pick up police messages on the wireless at Balmoral, so they always know where to follow us. We regard them as our enemies.'[12]

Even the best security devices only worked when used by both speakers at either end of the line. Private secretaries who often had a diplomatic or intelligence background used them professionally, but in practice the royals themselves rarely accessed them. By the late 1980s, the higher echelons of society were addicted to their mobile phones, which at that time were easy to intercept. This left the entire royal family vulnerable to both phone interception and bugging with microphones. Moreover, their own personal security discipline was lamentably weak. All this pointed to future trouble.

ALTHOUGH PRINCESS DIANA was part of the British nobility and spent her early years close to the royal family, living in Park House on the Sandringham estate, things changed quickly once she met Charles.

Diana was the youngest daughter of John Spencer, an earl who had once been equerry to the young Queen Elizabeth, and Frances Shand Kydd, born on the royal estate in Sandringham to a mother who had served as a lady in waiting to Queen Elizabeth, the Queen Mother. In 1967, when Diana was only seven years old, her parents divorced and her relationship with her new stepmother was turbulent. Conscious of being less academically gifted than her brother, she focused on music, dance and sports. After attending a number of fee-paying schools, then a finishing school in Switzerland, she moved to London, where she lived with friends and worked in a kindergarten. Happily, she became what was then called a 'Sloane Ranger', indeed to some extent she epitomized the phenomenon and its fashions, yet at the same time she enjoyed a degree of invisibility.[13]

In 1981, she shot into the public eye. Aged twenty-one, she became engaged to Prince Charles, the heir to the throne, after a brief and secretive courtship. Their wedding in July of the same year was a fairy-tale event. The public lapped it up, bringing the monarchy an extraordinary new level of popularity, approval and international press interest. Diana, now princess of Wales, seemed to have achieved the impossible, providing the royal family with not only freshness and modernity but also a sense of old-style romance and magic. For those obsessed with dynasties, she followed this with further success, quickly producing two sons, Prince William in 1982 and Prince Harry in 1984. Much had happened in just a few short years.

However, the behaviour of the press was already bad and deteriorating. Even in the 1970s, the media had mostly remained quite respectful of the royal family. Indeed, it was perhaps one of the last areas of journalistic self-restraint. But that did not mean the press were happy. For decades, the royal press office had been under the command of the notorious Commander Richard Colville, who thought the best place for energetic journalists was 'a dungeon in the tower'.[14]

By the 1980s, even with the more accommodating Michael Shea as the palace press secretary, reporters and a new breed of paparazzi were increasingly prepared to break the rules. And there was now an additional factor giving this activity more purpose and resource – the rise of media mogul Rupert Murdoch. An Australian and a republican who loathed the royal family, he had a personal interest in bad behaviour towards the royals. Not for nothing did *Private Eye* magazine dub him 'The Dirty Digger'. Almost from the moment of Diana's wedding to Charles, he unleashed the hounds. Press attention was not the same as being spied on by government security agencies, but the techniques were increasingly similar and sometimes these worlds merged.

Early on in their marriage, when Charles and Diana were skiing in Switzerland, four balaclava-clad journalists, looking for all the world like the SAS, leapt from a black helicopter onto a snowy mountaintop, and snapped their photos before being whisked away. Even at Balmoral, which Charles regarded as his rural idyll where he could escape from the cares of the world, photographers lurked in the long grass. In August 1982, when pressmen staked out Charles and Diana in the Scottish countryside, they had hoped for pictures of royal kisses. But instead, what they saw was a contemplative prince alone and stretched out on a riverbank engrossed in reading a large tome. The book in question was the memoirs of R.V. Jones, Britain's top wartime defence scientist, entitled *Most Secret War*, which related the origins of electronic espionage.[15] This was an ideal primer for the battle that the royals were about to confront.

Charles and Diana are often perceived as having enjoyed a honeymoon period but by early 1984 things had already fallen apart badly. In April, Roy Strong, a discerning keeper of national collections and an even more diligent diary keeper, noted with some delight that Princess Michael of Kent had come to an event at the V&A Museum and was 'wildly indiscreet'. She explained that the marriage was a catastrophe, droves of the household were leaving and Charles 'had bought Highgrove to be near his former girlfriends'. The princess relayed the detail with relish, adding that the royal family often regarded her as their highest risk factor, but she insisted that 'The time bomb is Diana.'[16]

Sadly, Diana's marriage to Charles was doomed as the couple were fundamentally incompatible: Diana found the reflective and serious Charles stuffy and uncool; Charles found Diana superficial, mercurial, moody and uncommitted to the life of monarchy, which involves countless hours of dutiful drudgery. Both had several extra-marital affairs. Charles maintained a lingering attachment to Camilla Parker Bowles, an old flame whom he had not pursued because of his long absence on naval service, but who had remained a close friend. She was now married to Andrew Parker Bowles, an officer in the Household Cavalry. Diana later had a number of romances, including a long liaison with the army officer James Hewitt who served in the same regiment.

The royal household, led by personal protection officers, accommodated these indiscretions quickly and efficiently. Security and exuberant sexuality sat awkwardly together given that Charles and Diana both always needed to be accompanied. When Charles drove the eleven miles from Highgrove, their country house in Gloucestershire, to visit Camilla at Middlewick House in his Aston Martin, he was always partnered by his Special Branch officer, Colin Trimming.[17] When Diana visited Hewitt at his mother's cottage in the West Country, her security officer slept downstairs on the sofa while the couple were upstairs.[18]

More remarkably, the London residences of James Hewitt and Camilla Parker Bowles were literally opposite each other in Clareville Grove in South Kensington, next to the headquarters of the Palestine Liberation Organization. Camilla had an eccentric affection for doing her household chores in the nude and one day Hewitt glanced across the road to see her in a state of undress. Her husband, Andrew Parker Bowles, was his commanding officer.

Although not close friends they would regularly greet each other with a polite 'good morning'.[19] This curious menage was sustained for some years, but was fundamentally unstable. The royal couple separated in 1992, although the breakdown of their marriage had long been suspected by the press. They finally divorced in 1996, only a year before Diana died in Paris.

Their various love affairs contributed directly to a deterioration in their security. In the 1980s and early 1990s, the intrusiveness of the press extended to the suborning of members of the royal staff, often for considerable sums of money. The media even planted moles among the staff inside Buckingham Palace. Famously, the palace press secretary, Michael Shea, once triumphantly told *The Sun* that he had finally identified the newspaper's informant, but *The Sun* scoffed that this was unlikely: there were 'eleven of them'.[20] This was annoying to the royals, even in terms of everyday life, but it made conducting illicit romantic liaisons excruciatingly difficult. For this reason, both Charles and Diana became intensely secretive and at times tried to evade their own security.

Diana was the worst. Even early in her marriage, she became rather good at giving her own security the slip. Like a human intelligence operative, she knew how to elude her tail. This caused periodic panics when royal flunkies realized that Diana had evaded her security yet again and slid out to go shopping down the King's Road protected only by a pair of stylish sunglasses.[21] Initially, when meeting James Hewitt in Devon, she would ask to be dropped off for the weekend and then disappear alone. Her police protection officers were loyal and discreet, but simultaneously horrified, since they knew that if anything happened to her, their necks would be on the chopping block. Fortunately, Hewitt was more sensible than Diana and he was soon co-opted by the protection officers who found him to be very diligent about security.[22]

If they were initially secretive, by the early 1990s Charles and Diana had become embittered practitioners of exposure. In 1991, Diana collaborated with the journalist Andrew Morton on an explosive book, *Diana: Her True Story*, which revealed not only the depth of the marital difficulties but also her suicidal unhappiness. When the book came out the following year, many condemned it as malicious fiction, but Diana had not only been happy to take questions from Morton but had also arranged for a secret courier, in spy parlance a 'cut-out', to transport tape-recorded replies back to him by motorbike courier.[23] Remarkably, Diana even deceived Patrick Jephson about both her co-operation with Morton and also her extremely frank BBC interview with Martin Bashir, the so-called *Panorama* plot, a few years later.[24] But she did not outwit the capable Cabinet secretary, Robin Butler, who was 'one step ahead' and used his friendship with Fellowes to warn the queen. Butler always travelled the short distance to the palace on his rusty bicycle, thereby deliberately avoiding the beady eyes of the press.[25]

Britain's most experienced Cabinet secretary was ahead of the curve. More than a decade before the Leveson Inquiry into the culture, practices and ethics of the British press, he had realized just what a serious menace some journalists had become. At various times during the 1990s, he assisted the palace by working with others in Downing Street to identify especially dangerous leakers who were close to the royals. Butler thought that Fellowes was doing a difficult job, explaining to his colleagues that he 'was a personal friend and he wanted to help him'.[26]

Even now, the queen and the duke of Edinburgh tried to promote a reconciliation. But their efforts were met by a bombshell. In August 1992, audio tapes emerged of private conversations between Princess Diana and James Gilbey, a childhood friend who owned a Lotus car dealership and was heir to the Gilbey's Gin fortune. The recordings were highly personal and deeply embarrassing, most famously for Gilbey's constant use of 'Squidge' or 'Squidgy' as a pet name for the princess. Diana, who was staying at Sandringham, spoke of her depression, the awkwardness of family meals and the detached way the queen mother looked at her with a 'sort of interest and pity'. Her life was a soap opera; she was trapped in a claustrophobic marriage.[27]

In November, these were followed by leaked 'Camillagate' tapes, intercepted intimate exchanges between Charles and Camilla Parker Bowles. Charles, with all the entitled arrogance of an heir to the throne, famously declared: 'Your greatest achievement is to love me.' The tabloids lingered over every cringe-inducing detail. John Major, the prime minister, found that his regular Tuesday meetings with the queen increasingly resembled a joint confessional. While he and Elizabeth spoke alone for around an hour and a half, their respective private secretaries would sit downstairs drinking sherry – there was much to discuss.[28] In December 1992, Major announced the 'amicable separation' of Charles and Diana to the House of Commons.

'SQUIDGYGATE' WAS PROBABLY the low point of the queen's infamous *annus horribilis*. Much of the royal family were at Balmoral when the story broke. It was one among many sensational royal revelations published within quick succession, including the duchess of York's predilection for having her toes sucked and, shortly afterwards, 'Camillagate'. The queen simply would not discuss the sordid stories within the family. 'What do you all do?' a friend of Princess Margaret asked shortly afterwards. Margaret replied that 'we all had to come down to breakfast anyway', but no one mentioned it at all. They were perhaps the only family in the whole country who kept off the subject that morning.[29]

The 'Squidgygate' tapes were supposedly intercepted accidentally by amateurs armed only with a cheap scanner and a sense of mischief. Early mobile phones were 'analogue' and laughably easy to intercept so, at first glance, Charles and Diana seemed foolish to have used them for such a private purpose. Their police security, including the loyal Ken Wharfe, 'consistently' warned them against using these phones and asked them to use coded language and nicknames if they did – this advice was mostly disregarded.[30]

But who had made the tapes? Who had intercepted the calls, listening in on Diana? Amid fevered speculation, some were already pointing the finger towards the intelligence agencies, still struggling for a role in the post-Cold War world.

Answers soon began to emerge. Supposedly, in the first weeks of 1990, Cyril Reenan, a retired bank manager, parked outside Didcot railway station not far from his house in Abingdon, a quiet town in Oxfordshire, to meet two journalists from *The Sun*. In his spare time, Reenan was an amateur eavesdropper who used a radio scanner to listen in to all types of radio transmissions, including mobile phones, for his private amusement. In his home, he had arranged an old 1960s-style reel to reel tape recorder next to his scanner to capture anything interesting that he overheard. What he believed he had captured was an extremely intimate conversation between Diana and James Gilbey. He was frightened by what he had recorded and had now decided to hand the tape over to *The Sun* – he just wanted it to go away. This seems a strange decision, when he could have just destroyed the tape.

Oddly, the tape did not emerge for over two years and was finally published by *The Sun* in August 1992. Gilbey initially insisted the story was false, but the tabloid took the remarkable step of setting up a dedicated phone line that allowed callers to hear the whole tape at a cost of 36 pence per minute. In fact, this was not the whole tape, since even *The Sun* had blushed at certain sections of the recording and had edited out some passages.[31]

Through the early 1990s, interest in the tapes was sustained by the so-called War of the Waleses during which the prince and princess of Wales battled for public sympathy. The most confidential document in this battle was the list of forthcoming engagements, so highly prized by journalists, protestors, obsessives and terrorists alike that the royal household referred to it as 'Mole News'. Patrick Jephson recalls that it 'practically lost its original innocent purpose as a simple planning aid and became instead just another piece in the board game of misinformation in the intelligence war between them'.[32] No prisoners were taken in this struggle and Diana routinely referred to Camilla as 'The Rottweiler'.[33] In her off-the-record briefings to the press she called Buckingham Palace the 'leper colony' – designating the queen mother as the 'chief leper'.[34]

This battle included the leaking of material to trusted journalists and finally entire television programmes. Each week the tabloids offered new revelations, including accounts of depression and failed suicide attempts. Increasing attention was given to Charles's long-standing relationship with Camilla, which many journalists had known about, but was only now in the public domain.

The growing public interest prompted the *Sunday Times* to ask a company of surveillance specialists called Audiotel International to revisit and analyse the Diana tape obtained by *The Sun*. They quickly realized that this was not a conversation that could have been recorded on a simple radio scanner in the manner recounted by Cyril Reenan.

First of all, the tape contained what Audiotel called 'data bursts' or 'pips', which were indicators used for charging the call. This seemingly innocuous fact was important since these 'pips' are not broadcast over the radio system that carries mobile telephone calls and instead are filtered out at the local exchange. This, and the fact that two other amateur scanners had also recorded the conversation, suggested strongly that the tape had been recorded by professionals in another way and then deliberately re-broadcast, probably repeatedly, whereupon it was picked up by Reenan.

This was a more malicious act. Within a few days, the *Sunday Times* had asked a second set of audio experts retained by Sony International to examine the tape. They agreed that this was not a conversation captured by a scanner, partly because scanners usually capture only one half of a conversation clearly. More importantly, there was a 50 megahertz 'hum' in the background, which they noted was the usual effect of trying to record a telephone conversation via a direct physical tap on a landline.[35]

Given that Gilbey was the one speaking from a mobile telephone, this pointed strongly to the possibility that someone had secretly attached a professional telephone tap to Diana's landline inside Sandringham. Experts insisted that the doctoring of the tape constituted a crude attempt to make a tap on a landline sound as if it was an intercepted mobile telephone call. A little later there was further confirmation when Cellnet, the company that supported Gilbey's mobile phone, revealed that the sensational press stories had triggered an internal investigation as the company initially feared its own security had been breached. It too concluded that this was a professional tap on a landline. Tellingly, all the amateur listeners who intercepted the call on their 'scanners', and there were several, heard it several days after the real call was actually made.[36]

This information was dynamite, since many believed it pointed to involvement by the police or the intelligence services. But the Conservative home secretary, Ken Clarke, categorically dismissed the allegations of intelligence agency participation as 'extremely silly'. Ministers, he insisted, had not authorized such an invasion of royal privacy and wiretapping was so tightly controlled that even if any rogue actors inside the intelligence services wanted to tap royal phones without authorization, they would have found it impossible. Instead, Clarke blamed the press for hacking private communications.[37]

However, the chairman of the Broadcasting Standards Authority, Lord Rees-Mogg, expressed a different view. He wondered whether the tapes were the illicit by-product of a legitimate monitoring operation that was part of the protection of the royal family. He added that once the sensational recording had been made, it was almost inevitable that it would be leaked. The press seized on this suggestion and the story gathered pace. Behind the scenes, Robin Butler, the Cabinet secretary, was infuriated, since this contradicted the assurances of ministers. Confessing himself 'very disappointed', Butler had since 'spoken to Lord Rees-Mogg, who had refrained from further comment'.[38]

At first glance, Rees-Mogg's suggestion seemed absurd, but few members of the public were aware of the intense anxiety about the threat from the IRA. In fact, the police and security services had taken elaborate measures to protect prominent people, including senior officials, after the assassination of the MP Ian Gow by the IRA in 1990. This included setting up a new central unit focused on personal security. Fantastically complex monitoring equipment and alarms had been installed in the homes of VIPs by a veritable army of technicians, some of whom were from the police and security services and some of whom were contract workers. The same was true of the royal palaces and in practice this surge of technical protection had provided opportunities for freelance activity.[39]

Moreover, with the end of the Cold War, the world was positively crawling with redundant intelligence officers of every hue, offering their services for a fee. In Russia, many former KGB officers drifted off into private security work or organized crime – the two spheres overlapped to an alarming degree. Other parts of the world saw former Guards officers setting up private military companies that were active in Africa and which would later become prominent in the Middle East after the invasion of Kuwait.[40] In Britain too, the long years of the Cold War, together with an extended struggle against organizations like the IRA, had meant that even routine army engineers were trained in the dark arts of telephone interception and bugging. Their services were now available for hire. By the early 1990s, this was having its impact on public life in Britain, largely through the growing use of freelance interception and other forms of privatized intelligence gathering by tabloid journalists. One of the top targets of this new privatized activity was the royal family.

QUEEN ELIZABETH QUICKLY recognized the implications for the security of royal communications and was particularly perturbed by the scandal.[41] The days of Queen Victoria learning how to use intercepted letters to deceive opponents were long gone. Her private secretary, Robert Fellowes, himself married to Diana's sister Jane, thought 'it was unlikely that the security services would be involved in this action'. Even with the Soviet threat no longer preoccupying them, he assumed 'they had much more important things to do than bugging private conversations of the Royal Family'. Nonetheless, he sought reassurance from the prime minister that the bugging was 'not official'.[42]

On 19 January 1993, John Major offered exactly that: 'there is no substance to rumours about the involvement of the security and intelligence agencies in interception of the communications of the Royal Family'.[43]

Official denials continued to come thick and fast. The director of GCHQ, John Adye, told John Bingham, the interception of communications commissioner, that 'GCHQ categorically denies any involvement in intercepting, recording or disclosing telephone calls involving the royal family'.[44] In his annual report for 1993, Bingham, part of the legal oversight mechanism for GCHQ, concluded that 'from time to time, stories are published describing interceptions said to have been carried out by GCHQ or by what are usually called MI5 or MI6. Such stories are, in my experience, without exception false.' Likewise, the commissioner for the security service, Lord Justice Stuart-Smith, stated that, in his opinion, MI5 operations involving illegally installed bugging devices 'are not undertaken'.[45]

But the queen was not satisfied and wanted some sort of inquiry.[46] She was not in a constitutional position to order one – and it was not her style – but it became clear that the main thinking in the palace, according to Fellowes, was 'that this had happened and what action should be taken to ensure that it did not happen again'.[47] Kenneth Scott, a cheery and experienced former diplomat who had become her deputy private secretary a couple of years before, fought the queen's corner on a proper investigation.

As a result, Scott met the Cabinet secretary, Robin Butler, on 21 January 1993. Joining them were Clive Whitmore, the top civil servant at the Home Office, Stella Rimington, the director general of MI5, and a senior member of MI6. They were clearly in favour of an investigation and discussed whether it should be done by MI5 or the police. Scott chipped in that Charles had 'a preference for an interview conducted by the security service rather than the police'. Both Charles and Diana may have begun to have worries about their police protection teams and now confronted the dilemma of which arm of the state they distrusted least.[48]

But Scott came up against Ken Clarke who, as home secretary, presided over both the police and MI5. He thought the press simply had no interest in the truth and that they might interpret an investigation as evidence that ministers secretly believed that intelligence involvement 'was a real possibility'. He therefore told officials that an inquiry by MI5 was pointless as 'the press would not accept the line that the very fact that the inquiry was being undertaken by the security service was a clear indication that the government was confident that the security and intelligence agencies had not been involved in some way in the interception of the conversations'.[49]

Privately, Clarke was reluctant for other reasons. He was highly experienced and slightly cynical about the possibility of introspecting into the security services. He observed later that, despite his best efforts: 'I never made as much progress as I intended in establishing proper accountability for their more unconventional activities.'[50] He was also following the old Whitehall rule: never launch an inquiry unless you know in advance what it might uncover. He worried about what it might unearth and he did not want to give further ammunition to another spate of 'Squidgygate' stories.[51]

Robert Fellowes accepted Clarke's decision – he had little choice – but did not disguise his disappointment. As a consolation he did, however, receive an 'expert opinion' from GCHQ about whether an amateur or professional had been behind the interception – just to put the queen's mind at rest. Some technical advice, Fellowes noted, would also help the palace to better understand the 'real risks of using mobile phones' and 'whether it may or may not be necessary to have all Royal residences comprehensively swept for bugging devices'.[52]

The head of GCHQ, John Adye, agreed to answer Fellowes' questions.[53] Intriguingly, his experts, whom, he pointed out, did not have access to the tapes, nevertheless broadly agreed with the Audiotel analysis commissioned by the *Sunday Times*.[54] They also concluded that 'people intent on recording private conversations between members of the Royal Family and their friends would be able to do so on a regular basis in a rural area by equipping a vehicle with a scanning receiver within a few kilometres of the portable hand or car phone in use'. Diana's recorded conversations 'would have been vulnerable to such a technique'. Adye pointed to a second possibility as well: 'illegal interference with fixed telephone lines'. Unprotected premises in rural locations, he told Fellowes, 'would be more accessible to this form of tampering', and both the alleged incidents could have occurred in this way.[55]

Adye thought this was possibly a criminal activity – in other words freelance bugging by an illegal agent. He may have been right, since evidence was later found of physical interference on a line at Sandringham. However, this in turn raises the awkward issue of how such individuals gained physical access to some of the most sensitive areas of the royal palaces. The most likely explanation remains a rogue individual working in a security capacity or maybe in a more mundane capacity who enjoyed legitimate access to Sandringham.[56]

But Adye was perhaps not telling the whole story. Reportedly, an internal investigation at GCHQ had found a potential disgruntled individual who was a suspect, but 'there was not enough evidence for a prosecution'.[57] Ken Wharfe, Diana's protection officer, also asserts that a full investigation by the internal security services 'identified all those involved', but he has refused to be more specific.[58] In April 1993, Stella Rimington was considering a wider MI5 investigation into the whole issue of royal security in conjunction with the palace.[59]

To some extent the impression that all this left was more important than the reality. What mattered was that some members of the royal household and even some police protection officers became privately convinced that a small special unit had been monitoring the movements and the communications of the royals.[60]

GCHQ FAILED TO provide the direct answers desired by the palace. Nonetheless, Fellowes found these equivocal responses 'reassuring' in their own way. He thanked Adye for GCHQ's opinion, conceding that he 'never believed there was any possibility of a definitive answer emerging'. The security services regularly swept particular rooms inside Buckingham Palace where Elizabeth and her private secretaries conducted state business, and indeed the office used by Fellowes, but he would now assure Charles and Diana that the security services would 'undertake sweeping' of their 'telephone equipment speedily and efficiently' as well. What he left unsaid was that much of the problem was not technical but human: the royals continued to take unnecessary risks on the phone.[61]

Diana complained to David Meynell, head of the royal protection unit, that her phone was being tapped, perhaps in 1992 or 1993.[62] Meynell insists that a team checked her apartment and car afterwards. This was somewhat odd, though, because the police unit used was a search assistance team, more used to looking for caches of drugs, and not the sorts of electronic specialists normally used by the intelligence and security services to sweep places like 10 Downing Street. Perhaps Diana was being humoured or was now regarded as a lower priority.[63]

Because of her growing distrust of the authorities, Diana turned to private advice in the form of Grahame Harding, the owner of an electronics and security company. Harding had served in the Royal Signals before setting up a company offering protection to merchant banks. He was recommended by Sarah, duchess of York, who had also been plagued by unwanted press attention. He first visited her main residence, Kensington Palace, in 1994. Harding recalled: 'The Princess of Wales told me that she was concerned that people were listening in to her conversations and that there were listening devices in her apartments including her bedroom.'[64]

Harding reassured her that her new mobile phone was digital and these were very hard to listen in to. Thereafter, she spoke to her friends quite freely on her mobile, but would rarely use her home telephone. Over the two years or so that he provided the princess with her mobile phones, she asked him to change the number on numerous occasions, once after only three weeks. Worries also extended to the mobile phone companies. Eventually, Harding suggested obtaining a mobile phone in his name so that he could give her the phone but the billing would be sent to him and she could pay the bills through him. She agreed and he opened a mobile telephone account for her.[65]

Diana also worried about audio bugs inside Kensington Palace. These did not need to be connected to telephones. She considered it 'a matter of routine that members of government and the Royal family are monitored'. She assumed that 'the powers' were discreetly at work throughout her time as a member of the royal family. This clearly impacted upon her mental health because, as her butler, Paul Burrell, recalls: 'if there was one thing about life at Kensington palace that the princess loathed it was the inescapable feeling of being listened to or watched'. This had a deleterious effect since she did not trust the police, seeing them as a tool of the state. In fact, she had 'a deep-seated suspicion about anything and everything to do with the state'. And this had long-term consequences as 'It was one of the reasons why she shed her police protection.'[66]

Diana's physical investigations of her own environment underline how seriously she took all this. Burrell recalls their efforts to probe apartments eight and nine at Kensington Palace:

> Once, both of us moved all the furniture to one side in her sitting room, rolled up an Aztec-style rug, the blue fitted carpeted and its underlay. Then, we prised up the floorboards with screwdrivers. She was convinced there were listening devices

in the palace but we found nothing. She worried about devices being placed in plug sockets, light switches or lamps. Some will dismiss this kind of worrying as outright paranoia... But... she was acting on sound information received from someone who had worked for the British intelligence services; a man whose expertise, advice and friendship the princess came to rely on.[67]

The princess was learning more and more about modern surveillance. Experts told her that that this did not require a device to be planted inside her apartments. New techniques were so hi-tech that she could be eavesdropped on by a van parked outside. Possible mediums included mirrors to bounce back conversation. 'As a result, she took down a round convex mirror that hung above the marble fireplace opposite the window in her sitting room.' This was not paranoia, instead it was professional surveillance advice.[68]

Who exactly did Diana think was listening? She spoke of 'dark forces', but other than worrying about the existence of listening devices, she never told Harding precisely whom she suspected of spying on her. Harding tried to reassure her, explaining that listening devices in real life, unlike those depicted on television, were more difficult to use than many understood and that their batteries were prone to fail very quickly. To reassure her, he conducted a limited sweep of the palace but he used 'equipment that was not very sophisticated and would only locate the normal or basic type of listening devices'. Over the next two years, Harding conducted several sweeps of her apartments but did not have people in his organization who were experts in physical searches.[69]

On one occasion Harding thought he found something. In 1994, soon after Diana started using his services, his equipment detected an electronic signal, which indicated that 'a possible bugging device may have been present behind a wall in her bedroom'. Diana was present and watched eagerly, but whatever was on the other side of the wall was not part of her apartments. He was therefore unable to investigate further as he did not have access. There was no evidence of disturbance to the wall or fixtures. When he came back a few days later, the signal had gone. He conceded that it could have been innocent electronic equipment in the next room. He conducted three or four further searches over the next few weeks.[70]

DID THE WESTERN intelligence agencies have intercepts on Diana? The US National Security Agency (NSA), the world's most powerful intelligence collector and the American equivalent of GCHQ, was adamant that it did not target her. The director of policy at the NSA, Louis Giles, stated: 'I can categorically confirm that NSA did not target Princess Diana nor collect any of her communications.' But he did concede that NSA documents, acquired from intelligence gathering of international communications, contained some references to Diana.[71]

Remarkably, the US government had a big file on Diana. This amounted to a dossier of over a thousand pages, including thirty-nine documents from the NSA, some of which were transcriptions of telephone calls. Although these are still classified, most of the material likely related to her work overseas in the cause of arms control and campaigning against the arms trade rather than the Americans actively spying on Diana. The intelligence was therefore incidental collection, acquired through channels – unrelated to the royal family – which the NSA routinely monitored.[72]

Although we think of listening agencies like GCHQ and the NSA being focused on 'big' enemies like China and Russia, in fact, at this time, most of their intelligence came from listening to smaller countries, especially those in the global south. For more than thirty years, and as late as 2000, the world's most popular and trusted manufacturer of diplomatic cypher equipment, Crypto AG in Switzerland, sold phoney machines with deliberately weakened security to over a hundred countries around the world. Therefore, countries like the USA, Britain, Germany and Sweden could read most of their diplomatic traffic. The communications of developing countries like Saudi Arabia, Iran, Brazil and Indonesia were an open book. Many of these diplomatic messages were about the various royal families and their personal interactions.[73]

In March 1993, Diana visited Nepal, before travelling to Zimbabwe the following year. In 1995, she travelled to Moscow, a trip where bugging and counter-bugging must have been high on the agenda, and then, under the alias 'K. Stafford', to Argentina. The latter invitation bore the fingerprints of President Carlos Menem and was the most high-profile British visit since the Falklands War. Just months before her death, she even visited a minefield in Angola. British diplomats were particularly concerned for her safety and lobbied against the trip. The Ministry of Defence was opposed too, not least because Diana was advocating a ban on landmines of which the UK still had its own stores. A defence minister was even more obstructive: 'we do not need a loose cannon like her'.[74] Partly for reasons of defence policy, American intelligence would have been monitoring many of these places.

The respected lawyer and investigative journalist Gerald Posner later explained that his sources inside the NSA not only confirmed all this for him, but actually played him several sample tapes to verify it. This included an interception of Diana speaking to her friend, the wife of the Brazilian ambassador in Washington. The conversations were not about great matters of state, but subjects such as hairstyles. Nonetheless, it confirmed the vast hoovering of diplomatic chatter which meant that the NSA and others collected much material on royals, even if they claimed they were not expressly targeting them.[75]

The NSA eventually admitted that it had 124 pages relating to Diana.[76] Senator George Mitchell, the widely esteemed majority leader of the United States Senate, who had received several awards for his involvement in the peace talks in Northern Ireland, was eventually allowed to inspect the documents as an independent inter-mediary and confirmed there was nothing suspicious about them.[77] A further review was conducted by the CIA inspector general, who stated that the CIA's files yielded no suspicious information either, but confirmed that they also had paperwork on the princess.[78]

This raises the intriguing question of who else saw this US intelligence. For decades, British politicians and policymakers have praised the Anglo-American intelligence special relationship and emphasized the remarkable sharing of what they collect. Were these files kept by the NSA and the CIA available to their British counterparts?

What we know for sure is that the most active 'spies' watching the royals in the 1990s were the press. Even in a prephone hacking age, phone scanners had not only been used to intercept conversations between Charles and Camilla Parker Bowles and between Diana and James Gilbey, but also to follow the various police protection teams. According to an unnamed former *News of the World* reporter, these were a 'vital tool in knowing about the movements of the royals', allowing the photographers to track the conversations of royal protection officers and find out where Diana would be.[79] At this time the press had become truly obsessed with Diana and her ostracizing from the royal family, the fallout of her separation from Prince Charles. Diana was right to conclude that the police, with their poor communications security, were unwittingly assisting the press in their pursuit of her. This pursuit would end in Paris in the summer of 1997.

THE DIANA CONSPIRACY

'I think he was bumped off'

Princess Diana, 1987[1]

'I DO THINGS DIFFERENTLY,' Princess Diana once commented, 'because I don't go by a rule book... albeit that's got me into trouble... Some don't like that,' she added defiantly, 'but that's the way I am.'[2]

This was perhaps her most profound self-reflection. Her independent spirit, which grew over the years, was one of her most attractive qualities, bringing originality and freshness to everything she did. But it also made her marriage to Prince Charles, her protocol-ridden life within the royal family, and above all her own royal duties onerous. She found the intersection of the public and private especially overbearing; and responded by disregarding the impediment of ever-present security.

Royal protection, far too amateurish in the 1970s, had intensified and become increasingly oppressive during the 1980s. As we have seen, security threats to royals and indeed all VIPs ramped up remarkably from the death of Mountbatten in 1979. In 1984, the Brighton bomb came within a whisker of killing the prime minister. Not only was the IRA attacking mainland Britain, but organizations like the Palestine Liberation Organization had taken their struggle to the streets of London, killing ambassadors and former foreign prime ministers. MPs who stepped up as Cabinet ministers recall with horror how their houses were transformed into fortresses and how teams of policemen camped out around the clock in their kitchens, with machine guns piled up alongside the crockery on the table.[3]

Royals, and Diana in particular, required protection from the press too. Tired of being muzzled by the palace's distinctly unco-operative approach, a new brand of paparazzi was now prepared to break the rules. The press who followed Diana were known as the 'royal rat-pack' and were a self-confessed nasty bunch. As Ken Wharfe has observed, they were organized, well funded and increasingly equipped with electronic scanners and other devices that would not have disgraced the average spy. A motley crew, often sunburnt from many hours on stakeouts, their ample bellies festooned with binoculars, they were an elite force of sorts. Wharfe recalls that Prince Charles once vehemently told veteran *Sun* reporter Harry Arnold that they were all 'scum'. Arnold replied, politely and respectfully: 'We may be scum, sir, but we are la crème de la scum.'[4]

In terms of tradecraft and surveillance expertise, this was actually a rather astute observation. At this time MI6 boasted several crack units who provided special skills on covert operations. One was the so-called 'increment', a force of SAS and Special Boat Service veterans who assisted with paramilitary activities and provided protection when operating in dangerous areas like Eritrea. The other was UKN, an elite group of pilots, safe-crackers, scientists and other specialists who could be called on at a moment's notice to perform exotic tasks. UKN boasted the world's top long-range photographer, and, predictably perhaps, his day job was working as a royal paparazzo.[5]

It is often remarked that, from birth, Diana seemed to have the perfect training for the peculiar life led by the royal family. Growing up close to royalty, she was certainly familiar with the norms of the British upper classes. But Britain's run-of-the-mill nobility are remarkably free from these extreme pressures. Diana initially found royal security shocking and difficult to deal with. On the night of her wedding, the Special Branch officer guarding her warned ominously:

'I just want you to know that this is your last night of freedom ever in the rest of life, so make the most of it.'[6] Once married, she took more risks. She took yet more still following her separation from Charles in 1992.

Of course, the queen and other members of her family also took startling security risks, indeed perhaps were even literally in the line of fire, in the course of their duties. But this was done in a calculated way, and with great consultation and planning, working together with security teams behind the scenes. Perhaps the only person who was as cavalier with their security as Diana was Mountbatten, and that did not end well.

AFTER HER SEPARATION, Diana, still the princess of Wales, remained a royal and continued to live in an apartment on the north side of Kensington Palace. She continued to wear jewellery that she had received during her marriage and could still use the air transport of the British royal family and government. But in late 1993, very much against advice, she dropped most of her police protection, hoping for more privacy.[7] Hitherto, the Met's specialist SO14 unit had provided protection round the clock. Now she was given protection only when on an official visit or on a trip where her sons accompanied her.[8]

There were also changes in her private life. For over a year, between early 1996 and June 1997, Diana dated the British-Pakistani heart surgeon Hasnat Khan, often described as 'the love of her life' by her confidants. In the summer of 1996, she visited Lahore where, in secret, she met his family. Khan was intensely private, and their relationship was conducted in great secrecy, with Diana deceiving members of the press who questioned her about it. They broke up the following summer, partly because Khan found the press intrusion impossible to deal with — but also because Diana's family disapproved of a relationship with a Muslim man. Diana stopped talking to her mother for a while as a result.[9]

On the rebound, in July 1997, Diana began a relationship with Dodi Fayed, son of the Egyptian tycoon and flamboyant owner of Harrods, Mohamed Al-Fayed. That summer, security and intrusion again became important forces in her life. She had considered taking her sons on a holiday to the Hamptons on Long Island, New York, but security officials advised against it. After deciding against a trip to Thailand as too risky, she accepted Fayed's invitation to join his family in the Mediterranean, where his compound, yacht and large security detail would keep her safe from prying eyes.

On 31 August, two months after beginning their liaison, they died together in Paris. The couple had decided, at short notice, to make the trip to France. Previously, Diana had spent some time on holiday with her close friend Rosa Monckton.[10] Then, on 30 August, she and Dodi flew from Sardinia, arriving at Villa Windsor, Edward VIII's old house in the Bois de Boulogne now owned by Al-Fayed. At 4.30 in the afternoon, Diana, Dodi and their security guard, Trevor Rees-Jones, an ex-soldier who was employed by Al-Fayed's team, were driven to the Ritz hotel. They tried to go out for dinner but eventually retreated to their suite because of the attentions of the paparazzi – the French press being especially notorious and persistent. Just after midnight, they decided to move again, this time to Dodi's own apartment not far away in Rue Arsène Houssaye, close to the Arc de Triomphe.[11] Pursued once more by merciless paparazzi, their car collided with a pillar in the Pont de l'Alma tunnel while travelling at speeds of up to a hundred miles per hour. Only Rees-Jones survived.

This shattering event, over in seconds, triggered three painstaking inquiries or inquests that lasted for over a decade. In September 1997, the French appointed an examining magistrate, Judge Hervé Stéphan, to look into the case. Taking two years, he eventually found there was insufficient evidence against the paparazzi, who were being investigated for involuntary manslaughter, or indeed anyone else. He declared that Diana's death was a simple accident. But not everyone agreed. Mohamed Al-Fayed in particular loudly asserted foul play by the British government.

For this reason, in January 2004, John Stevens, previously commissioner of the Metropolitan Police, began a more thorough investigation known as Operation Paget, drawing on many of the leads opened by the French. Perhaps Britain's most experienced and independent senior police investigator, he was the ideal person to conduct such an inquiry. His conclusions were more sophisticated, asserting that a combination of factors caused the fatal accident, including the condition of her driver, his speeding, the pursuit by the paparazzi and the fact that the passengers were not wearing seatbelts.

Although explicitly ruling out any conspiracy theories, accusations of the hidden hand continued to swirl. Therefore, in an unprecedented decision, a third major inquiry was ordered under Justice Scott Baker, which reached broadly the same conclusion. But in the course of all this digging, the inquiries uncovered many fascinating facts about the interaction of spies, security and royals.

MORE THAN A third of British people believe that Diana's death was 'not an accident' – in other words an assassination plot. Despite the exhaustive inquiries that took evidence from hundreds of people, including the then chiefs of MI6 and GCHQ, many still point the finger at 'dark forces': a conspiracy between the royal family, supposedly spearheaded by Prince Philip, and his friends in British intelligence.[12]

The primary reason behind this is simple human psychology. Unexpected and catastrophic events cause panic in the public mind. They challenge people's desire for clear, rational and ordered explanations. As Diana's favoured biographer, Andrew Morton, neatly put it, people need big explanations for big events.[13] The messy and sporadic reality of a globalized world is disquieting and feeds these tendencies.

Moreover, the exhaustive inquiries, designed to reduce public anxiety, inevitably turned up a bewildering number of puzzling, idiosyncratic and even suspicious-looking 'facts'. These mostly occurred because governments are unwieldy bureaucracies and make mistakes. As any police officer will confirm, eyewitnesses rarely agree on a single account of any event and so there are bound to be curious discrepancies in the narrative. This seeming lack of congruity only feeds the public appetite for a 'hidden hand' explanation. Fundamentally, human beings often prefer a dark conspiratorial account that offers an image of strong central control to the option of accepting that history is often the result of coincidences, mistakes and accidents. In the world of conspiracy, at least someone, however malevolent, is holding the metaphorical steering wheel.

Yet, at a higher level, the secret state does have something to answer for. Governments – and even the royal family – have engaged in real plots in the past. Given that MI6 and other secret units almost certainly participated in the assassination of Rasputin, considered the assassination of Hitler and discussed, attempted or encouraged others to kill Rommel, Mussolini, President Nasser of Egypt and Prime Minister Lumumba of Congo – then why not others? Even the urbane David Owen, foreign secretary in Harold Wilson's Labour government, speaking on Radio 4's *PM* programme, admitted that he had proposed assassinating Idi Amin. Knowledge of some genuine covert actions, however embryonic, spawns the reasonable assumption that there have been others.[14]

In other words, real conspiracies have an additional cost; a sort of postmodern 'blowback' that often takes the form of public paranoia. This is most visible in the Middle East and Asia, for centuries the stage of imperial meddling and intrigue where every British consulate, however minor, had its own secret service funds. Anxiety about the western hidden hand became so great that in India during the 1970s even natural events like monsoons and crop failures were attributed to the work of MI6, the CIA or the KGB. It is no surprise that the first people to assert that Diana was killed by MI6 were Gaddafi's Libya and Saddam Hussein's Iraq. An account of MI6 and the Diana conspiracy, written by Al-Fayed, became a sensational overnight bestseller in Egypt.[15]

The Middle Eastern media piled in behind. The Iraqi government news agency, headed by Saddam's son Uday, announced that 'Diana was liquidated by the British secret service' because she 'dabbled in politics'. In Libya, Colonel Gaddafi stayed close to the Al-Fayed line, insisting that the crash had been a plot by the British and French secret services working together to prevent a member of the royal family marrying an Arab. This drew a formal protest from the Foreign Office.[16] They knew that although these were wild allegations, they might well inspire a revenge attack by some fringe group. The queen asked whether, as a result, Islamic groups were now more of a threat to her than the IRA.[17]

Al-Fayed made matters far worse. Grief-stricken, he offered $20 million for information about the 'killing' of Dodi and Diana and attracted precisely the wrong sort of attention. Oswald Le Winter stepped forward, claiming to be a former CIA operative with access to key documents on the events in Paris and offered to hand them over in return for the full reward. He claimed these American messages showed that MI6 had contacted the CIA for help with the 'assassination'. Although shying away from carrying out the deed themselves, the CIA then supposedly put MI6 in touch with an Israeli Mossad-affiliated hit squad operating out of Switzerland.[18] Le Winter was a well-known fabricator who had already done time in jail for drug-related crimes. He frequently tried to make money out of intelligence-related sensations and would end up imprisoned for fraud by a Swiss judge.[19]

Nevertheless, Al-Fayed continued to insist that his son and Diana were assassinated by MI6 on the orders of Prince Philip. He believed that she was pregnant with Dodi's child and that the royal family 'could not accept that an Egyptian Muslim could eventually be the stepfather of the future King of England'. Therefore, he continued, the British intelligence and security services 'covertly obtained the information concerning pregnancy and engagement, with or without the co-operation of overseas agencies, precipitating the need to put into operation a plan to murder them'. An establishment cover-up then prevented the conspiracy from coming to light.[20]

Al-Fayed leapt to this conclusion within days – even hours – of the crash. Conducting his own inquiries, he asked his head of security, John McNamara, a former detective chief inspector from the Met, to arrange meetings with some of the leading paparazzi, including Darryn Lyons, often considered to be one of the leading exponents of this arcane art. Lyons met Al-Fayed on the top floor of Harrods. As he entered the office, the tycoon rose and greeted him warmly, before asking straight out: 'Do you think those bastards killed my son? Because I think those bastards killed my son.' Lyons, knowing he meant the royal family and MI6, tried to be both sympathetic and noncommittal, but recalls: 'I was with him for forty-five minutes and most of the conversation seemed to be him convincing himself that something had been done to the couple... it was very hard to get a word in.'[21]

Yet not all the accusers who supported the Al-Fayed view are fraudsters, fantasists or writers of dubious footnote-free 'true crime'. McNamara, admittedly an employee of Al-Fayed, but also a senior ex-policeman, agreed that it 'was an assassination' and the paparazzi were used to cover this up.[22] Michael Mansfield QC, who represented Al-Fayed in the Scott Baker inquest, is a most distinguished barrister and perhaps Britain's best-known human rights lawyer, having represented the Birmingham Six and the family of Jean Charles de Menezes. From the outset he 'felt very strongly there was more to this case than a mere accident'.[23] But what was the substance of their case?

The prosecution's star witness was Richard Tomlinson, an MI6 officer who had served during the 1990s. A New Zealander, he had grown up in Britain and, showing an early talent for science, won a scholarship to Cambridge University to study maths and physics in 1981. Affable, widely liked by his peers and seeming to fit the profile for an intelligence officer, he nevertheless failed MI6 selection after university and worked for a consultancy in the City. Finding his desk job financially rewarding but unsatisfying, Tomlinson joined the Territorial Army in September 1989 and, after passing selection, served as a reservist with the SAS in the Artists Rifles, and then 23 SAS, qualifying as a military parachutist and radio operator. Ten years after his first efforts, entering through a side-door, he finally arrived in his desired profession as an intelligence officer in MI6 on 23 September 1991.

If Tomlinson is to be believed, he was the best recruit in his batch, sailing through the 'Iconic' course at MI6's quirky training establishment, Fort Monckton near Portsmouth. He quickly took up a position in the 'Soviet' department, at an exciting time when the former Soviet Union was haemorrhaging secrets. From March 1992 until September 1993, he then worked in the eastern European department, before being posted to Sarajevo for six months as the MI6 representative during the break-up of Yugoslavia. He was a targeting officer, with a mission to identify potential informants and gather intelligence. Moving again, from 1994 to 1995, Tomlinson worked in the counter-proliferation department, supposedly infiltrating a network of arms dealers.[24]

On 22 May 1995, Tomlinson was suddenly dismissed. This should not have been entirely a surprise to him, since his probationary period had been extended again and again beyond the standard six-month duration, due to a line manager's doubts about his personality. Tomlinson claimed that he had become depressed following the death of his long-term girlfriend from cancer and that he had suffered from post-traumatic stress after witnessing violence in Sarajevo. Admittedly, MI6 was famously poor at supporting its own officers with either physical or mental health problems, displaying 'a sink or swim' mentality towards troubled officers.[25]

Tomlinson tried to challenge the decision, but his efforts were quickly quashed by the foreign secretary. Angry and disillusioned, he then went abroad to write a tell-all book detailing his five years in MI6. Panicking, the service initially tried to buy him off by arranging interesting jobs, including a desirable position with a Formula One team. It did not work and, in 1997, MI6 lost patience. Tomlinson was imprisoned under the Official Secrets Act; authorities seized his manuscript. He served six months before leaving the country once more, finally publishing his book in 2001, which focused on MI6's supposed 'licence to kill'.[26]

After the death of Diana, Tomlinson quickly stepped forward. He dramatically claimed that MI6 had considered assassinating Slobodan Milosevic, the president of Serbia, by staging a car crash in a tunnel using a powerful strobe light to blind the driver, later adding that this was a mainstream assassination technique and had even been covered as part of his training. The similarities with Diana's death were striking and, Tomlinson suggested, MI6 may have killed her in the same way.

Tomlinson claimed that when a friend showed him the assassination plan for Milosevic, he first 'checked the date on the top left-hand corner' to establish that it was not April Fools' Day. He then read the two-page memo. The first page was a justification for the assassination, citing Milosevic's secret support for Radovan Karadzic and his genocidal plans for the Albanian population of Kosovo. The second page outlined the possibilities for actual assassination.

According to Tomlinson, MI6 proposed three alternative plans for implementation and considered the advantages of each. The first was to use a joint MI6/special forces unit to train and equip a dissident local paramilitary faction to assassinate Milosevic in Serbia. The advantage of this plan was its deniability, but, on the downside, proxies were notoriously difficult to control. The second plan was to use a UK special forces team to infiltrate Serbia and kill the president themselves with a bomb or a sniper ambush. This option came with a higher chance of success but would not have been deniable if it went wrong. The third was to arrange a car accident to kill him, possibly while he was attending peace talks in Geneva. MI6 supposedly proposed using a bright flashing strobe gun to disorient Milosevic's chauffeur while the cavalcade passed through a tunnel.[27]

Shocked by the 'audacity and ruthlessness' of the plan, Tomlinson responded: 'You're off your trolley.' He advised his colleague that the very mention of such a plan would damage his career and impact his reputation with senior officers. But his friend replied confidently,

'What do you know?' as if Tomlinson was an innocent schoolboy 'learning for the first time the facts of life'.[28]

Despite senior MI6 officers pleading implausibly poor memories, documents and witnesses finally surfaced during the various Diana inquiries to show that assassination was indeed discussed. An MI6 officer working on the Balkans had frustratedly argued that Cold War 'spy games' were a million miles from this 'bloody civil war in the centre of Europe, where tens of thousands of innocent people are being killed'. He suggested using either dissidents or special forces to assassinate a radical Serbian leader, albeit not Milosevic. The MI6 officer in charge of the region rejected the plan outright. 'The whole idea of SIS [MI6] being involved in targeted assassination,' he spluttered, 'is repugnant to the ethos of the service and certainly repugnant to me personally.'[29] The Diana inquiry heard that, while the plan existed, it was eventually 'deleted and shredded'.[30]

At first glance, Tomlinson's testimony seems compelling. It bore an uncanny resemblance to events in Paris; and an MI6 officer did propose an assassination in the Balkans, partly corroborating him. There were problems, though, including his assertion that this was some sort of mainstream assassination technique, but which left him shocked when actually proposed. The biggest problem was that Tomlinson seemed to have changed his story. In the version of his memoir seized by police before the death of Diana, he offered only the first assassination option, but in the versions and testimony after her assassination there were suddenly three.[31] Over the years, he added that he thought MI6 was monitoring Diana before her death and that her driver on the night she died, Henri Paul, might have been an MI6 informant.[32] But Tomlinson undermined his testimony by making other errors, mis-identifying Sherard Cowper-Coles, the embassy's political counsellor, as head of the MI6 Paris station.[33] Whatever the nature of his allegations, the investigative work of John Stevens had effectively busted Tomlinson as a reliable witness.[34]

SHERARD COWPER-COLES RECALLS that the conspiracy theorists 'crawled out of the swamp' following Diana's death. In fact, the timeline began rather earlier.[35] The most remarkable star witness affirming the assassination conspiracy was Diana herself. Since 1987, she had repeatedly claimed that people in the 'Establishment' were out to kill her. During the mid-1980s, she had become rather close to one of her police protection officers, Barry Mannakee, and for this reason, in 1986, he was moved to diplomatic rather than royal protection. Shortly afterwards he died in a motorcycle accident. Riding pillion with a friend, they collided with a car coming out of a junction.[36] Diana told several close friends that he had been 'bumped off'.[37]

Such paranoia was understandable. Both Charles and Diana lived for years with the constant threat of assassination and had adapted their life accordingly. When they travelled abroad, they were accompanied by three metal cases that contained extra supplies of their blood in case of an accident or 'a terrorist outrage'. They were marked with the label 'Vital: Keep at Room Temperature' and so one of the key jobs of the secretaries was to make sure the air conditioning did not malfunction, allowing the royal blood to go off.[38] Diana was a regular on the police gun range at Lippins Hill in Loughton in Essex where the police did their firearms training. On one occasion she brought William and Harry with her, who both revelled in firing a .38 Smith & Wesson revolver, under the close supervision of a police instructor.[39]

Suspicion gradually turned to paranoia after the 'Squidgygate' episode. Her private secretary, Patrick Jephson, remembers that her anxiety about security had now 'reached new heights'. 'She saw plots everywhere,' he explained, and 'was obsessed with the thought that she was being bugged.' Still living in Kensington Palace, Diana received the full counter-surveillance protection extended to other royals – yet she increasingly suspected these very same people of being the culprits. When asked about these allegations, Jephson expressed 'polite mystification', adding that 'exasperation would have been nearer the mark'. After all, 'none of these hidden micro-phones had actually been discovered'.[40] The Conservative minister and friend of Prince Charles, Nicholas Soames, accused Diana of being in 'the advanced stages of paranoia'. A junior member of the royal household decoded this, remarking that my 'super-sized friend' is 'saying that she is completely mad'.[41] John Major apparently had to slap him down for the remark.[42]

On one occasion, Diana pulled up a carpet in an upstairs room at Kensington Palace, to show Jephson what she believed was evidence of bugging: fresh sawdust and disturbed planks. 'She pointed silently at the sawdust, and nodded significantly.' Jephson tried to reassure her that this was simply the result of the safety work and rewiring of all the royal palaces, following the 1992 fire at Windsor Castle, but Diana, gesturing for him to be silent, was unconvinced.[43] The episode is remarkably similar to those recounted by friends of Prime Minister Harold Wilson when he became beset by similar anxieties in 1974. He would remove pictures in Downing Street and point ominously to metal brackets, or insist on talking in the gents' toilet with the taps running.[44]

By 1995, Diana was voicing her fears with increasing frequency. Her solicitor, Lord Mishcon, recalled her predicting that 'efforts would be made if not to get rid of her (be it by some accident in her car such as a pre-prepared brake failure or whatever)... at least to see that she was so injured or damaged as to be declared "unbalanced"'.[45] This scenario was something she also discussed with her inner circle of friends. Typically, she told one confidant, Roberto Devorik:

> I am a threat in their eyes. They only use me when they need me for official functions and then they drop me again in the darkness... they are not going to kill me by poisoning me or in a big plane where others will get hurt. They will either do it when I am on a small plane, in a car when I am driving or in a helicopter. The only time I really feel safe is when I

am in the USA. Everybody in America likes me. I am very
popular there. The 'Establishment' doesn't like me and there is
no 'Establishment' there.[46]

Diana's butler, Paul Burrell, claimed she wrote a similar note in
1996, and, although the date is disputed, this is merely one among
many examples.[47]

Diana believed that her fears reflected her real experience. In
1995, she was driving through London alone and without bodyguards in her distinctive green Audi A4 Cabriolet. As she made her
way towards a junction, the traffic lights turned red and she braked.
Nothing happened. The car kept rolling forward but mercifully
there was no collision. When she finally came to a stop she jumped
out in a state of distress and flagged down a taxi. She returned to
Kensington Palace and rang a close friend insisting that someone
had tampered with her brakes. Mechanics blamed the brake failure
on normal wear and tear and lack of maintenance.[48]

This was supposedly not the only incident involving dodgy
brakes. Rita Rogers, one of Diana's 'psychics' and spiritual healers,
warned the princess of a premonition that someone had tampered
with her brakes. When Diana duly checked them, she indeed found
a problem.[49] Whether or not Rogers really did have a premonition is
immaterial, the important point is that Diana discussed her worries
about her brakes with psychics and friends, but not her driver and
security staff. She became increasingly suspicious of those who were
designated to protect her.

These views were encouraged by the growing army of therapists,
psychics and astrologers whom she had mustered by 1995. Jephson
laments that some had become 'highly influential and coloured her
thinking with unpredictable results'. They frequently predicted the
death of Charles in a helicopter crash. This had 'a destructive effect
on the princess's own judgement' and even encouraged a 'blind
belief in her own intuition' that became a substitute for reasoned
analysis or basic common sense. Meetings with these people took

up a remarkable amount of her time. Although restrained and polite in his language, this astute observer was convinced that collectively they 'fed the paranoia that never lurked far below the well-groomed surface'.[50]

For much of this time, the policeman in charge of her security was the kind and long-suffering Ken Wharfe. He was gradually transforming from personal protection officer into a kind of pest control officer focused on the press, especially the foreign press; one of his main roles was to scout out holiday sanctuaries where the princess and her children could escape 'prying eyes'.[51]

Sadly, his superiors criticized him for this, insisting that his role was 'not that of a press officer but a protection officer'. But Wharfe was more sophisticated and understood that the boundary between security and other kinds of intrusion was increasingly fuzzy. He recalled that he and his three assistants were up against the 'crack troops of the world's press', adding that even General Custer 'had better odds' of success than them. On Diana's foreign travels, Wharfe struck deals to try to keep the hordes away, appreciating full well the extent to which the press posed an indirect threat to her safety and even her mental health.

In the winter of 1993, in Lech in Austria, she evaded her own protection team by making a night-time leap into deep snow off a first-floor balcony in her hotel and then going for a walk. Wharfe later asked her: 'Ma'am, what were you thinking?' Their relationship of mutual trust was coming to an end. He left her service and thereafter she dispensed with routine police protection, a dangerous strategy indeed.

Somewhat later, Diana had a frank conversation with David Meynell, the senior police officer who ran SO14, the Metropolitan Police unit presiding over all VIP protection in Britain. She explained that while 'she had a lot of enemies', she also 'had a lot of friends, some in places of knowledge'. She had used these high-level contacts to probe what was really going on and to ask some questions. According to Meynell,

She could not name them because they could lose their jobs but she had been told that without any doubt five people from an organisation had been assigned full time to 'oversee' her activities, including listening to her private phone conversations and from the same source she knew that two people from the same organisation performed a similar function in respect of parliament.

In other words, Diana suspected that a small deep-state unit was engaged in political surveillance, probably unknown to routine members of MI5, MI6 or GCHQ. Meynell replied that this was a 'very serious matter', but that he insisted he had seen no evidence of it.[52]

The late-night jump off the balcony into the snow in December signified Diana's desperate bid for freedom. At 11.20 on the morning of 13 December 1993, Meynell came to Kensington Palace for a formal meeting about Diana's security protection, already knowing her general intentions. He warned her that quite apart from the press, SO14 had 'on record the details of some 3,000 individuals who have various fixations about the Royal Family' and who 'would not be put off'. It was a list of royal obsessives and maniacs long maintained by the police and the Home Office. But the princess was 'very determined' that there be no interference with her plans.[53] Indeed, Meynell recalled that the princess 'was quite gleeful about it'.[54]

The police gradually – and reluctantly – withdrew her protection over the following year. David Veness, one of the most senior officers in the Metropolitan Police, observed that it was 'unwise'. He later recalled that the police gave Diana 'unequivocal' advice against seeking any changes at all to her security measures both in person and through her own advisers. 'She was however adamant and insisted that her wishes prevail.' The views of the Met were supported by MI5, who had 'primary responsibility for assessment of threats to the Royal Family'. Worried officials from MI5, the Met

and the Foreign Office met to discuss and indeed lament the implications of her request, but ultimately could do nothing about it.[55] In
February 1994, the home secretary, Michael Howard, asked to be
'absolved of all responsibility', and threatened to involve the prime
minister. Thereafter, she received police protection only when on
official duties or when travelling with her sons.[56]

Diana took this distinctly odd decision because she now associated
everyone in an official role, no matter how kind and well meaning,
with a gargantuan plot. She became not only the subject of conspiracy theories but ultimately had succumbed to them herself. Family,
friends, protectors, detractors, paparazzi, protection officers, private
security and secret service all overlapped in what was an increasingly
claustrophobic world. One cannot help feel that her fears of secret
service, however misplaced, had tipped her over the edge and accordingly, when she arrived in Paris in August 1997, she had lacked the
support of the Met's highly professional and kindly protection teams.

Patrick Jephson speaks eloquently of this bizarre decision. He
admired her police protection officers working their weekly shifts.
They were seasoned by years of policing in the capital and honed
by periodic 'training with the SAS'. Jephson rated them as 'loyal,
discreet, wise and brave' and he remains mystified by her decision to
dispense with their protection and replace it with the 'well-meaning
amateurishness of hired substitutes'.[57]

The BBC stoked her paranoia further before the bombshell
Panorama interview in November 1995. Diana wanted to give her
side of the story and in a remarkably candid performance told her
interviewer, Martin Bashir, about her self-harm and mental health
struggles. She uttered the infamous line: 'there were three of us in
this marriage'. Twenty-three million people tuned in. Shortly afterwards, apparently the queen angrily called it a 'frightful thing to do,
frightful thing my daughter-in-law did'.[58]

The landmark interview raised all sorts of questions about why
Diana had agreed to be so open. In early 1995, Bashir had begun
working on a story about the royal family. 'Well placed sources'

suggested to him that Charles and Diana were being closely scrutinized – 'possibly even bugged'. He needed more information and
access to Diana herself, eventually meeting the princess through her
brother, Earl Spencer. Spencer later claimed that Bashir had intentionally duped him and Diana by playing on her fears of espionage.
Bashir had allegedly used fake bank statements intended to suggest
senior courtiers and security staff were being paid to spy on her. The
BBC later admitted that Bashir did ask a designer to mock up at
least one of these documents, and an independent inquiry found it
highly likely he had fabricated others, but Bashir insisted that they
had played no role in securing the interview.

Bashir told Diana explicitly that he was interested in the campaign
against her; he made it clear he wanted to discuss this in an interview. In response, she said she thought someone was bugging and
following her.[59] The eventual interview evolved from this conspiratorial starting point and his actions were deeply unethical.

The BBC later acknowledged that Bashir had made notes on
the subject of MI5 surveillance, but he had no documentary proof.
Nonetheless, unsubstantiated rumours soon swirled in the press that
she had given the interview because Bashir had evidence that MI5
was spying on her.[60] It all added to the princess's claustrophobic
paranoia. She could trust very few people.

WHEN DIANA APPEARED in Paris, she was not entirely without
cover. The Al-Fayeds had a large private security team numbering
some forty people, often with guns. Indeed, it would not be an
exaggeration to say that the Egyptian magnate boasted a veritable
private army. Because of his long-running feud with a business
rival, Tiny Rowland, his teams reportedly had long been engaged
in the covert filming and recording of his own employees. Former
policemen were employed by both sides in this famously bitter
business battle. There also seem to have been extensive telephone

monitoring operations in some of his key hotels, including the Ritz in Paris. Diana had perhaps stepped out of one panopticon into another.[61]

In Paris, Henri Paul, acting head of security at the Ritz, oversaw her safety and also served as her driver during the fateful pursuit through the tunnel. Accompanying them was the bodyguard and former soldier, Trevor Rees-Jones. Paul himself moved in the world of intelligence and has been the subject of endless speculation.

Henri Paul, a forty-one-year-old Frenchman who cultivated an action man reputation, was clearly known to several intelligence agencies. He was in regular contact with the Direction Général de la Sécurité Extérieure (DGSE), the French equivalent of MI6. He also had informal relations with the Direction de la Surveillance du Territoire (DST), which is the equivalent of MI5. His personal notebooks contained the names and telephone numbers of two people next to the letters 'DST'.[62] According to an American law enforcement official and an American intelligence agent, Paul spent the last several hours before the crash 'with a security officer from the DGSE'.[63] On this occasion, he was paid 12,560 francs, over £1,000, and still had the money on him when he died.[64]

Such arrangements were common, even routine, among security staffers at premier international hotels. Sometimes they had to manage delicate situations such as weapons on the premises or incidents involving high-profile international guests. Indeed, earlier that year, he had dealt smoothly with the death of the elderly US ambassador in the hotel pool.[65] Less formally, he was perhaps a useful informant for French intelligence given the number of influential guests, especially from the Arab world, who stayed at the hotel. Paul relished this work rather more than most and was a spy by any other name. His girlfriend recalled that for this reason he was unpopular with his colleagues but was able to provide 'satisfaction to his superiors', namely the hotel manager and Al-Fayed. He was nicknamed 'the Ferret' by his colleagues because he was always 'sticking his nose in everywhere'.[66]

Meanwhile, Paul's passion was recreational flying, something hard to do on his salary of about £40,000 a year. But his freelance security work for both secret services and visiting VIPs brought him a healthy additional income. He had deposited around £43,000 into his accounts in the last eight months of his life. Some have attempted to dismiss these payments as mere 'tips', but they perhaps point to rather more substantial spy work.[67]

Either way, Paul worked harder for himself than for his superiors and presided over a ramshackle security system. He was not a professional driver, and was supposed to use professional chauffeurs for VIPs, but he meekly complied when Dodi ordered him to drive on the fateful night. Worst of all, he was probably under the influence of both alcohol and prescription drugs when he drove the car.[68]

The manner of their departure from the hotel also broke with convention. One of the golden rules of convoy protection is to have a team of cars. But the party of several cars had not left the Ritz together; instead Dodi hatched an ill-considered 'decoy plan' that involved vehicles leaving from both the front and rear of the hotel. This left him and Diana exposed in a single vehicle without a backup car.[69] Rees-Jones, the bodyguard, had misgivings: 'I was not happy, as Dodi was splitting the two security officers up, but I toed the line.'[70]

More remarkably, neither John McNamara, the head of Al-Fayed's security organization in London, nor anyone in his team initially had any idea that Dodi and Diana had even gone to Paris.[71] By contrast, the paparazzi were expecting them. Unlike the security officials, they had paid sources inside air traffic control and so knew the celebrity couple were coming even before they touched down in France.[72] In 1997, the voracious press even paid one unnamed bodyguard £30,000 just for revealing Diana's location.[73]

Diana was a major media industry that generated unimaginable wealth for certain journalists and transformed the profession, but not for the better. Darryn Lyons confessed that after she died, 'the paparazzi world went into meltdown'. The leaders of the pack tried diversifying into extreme sports, animal shots, or 'anything we could pull in just to keep the till ringing'. Others simply panicked and wondered 'what the hell they were going to do now'. They had travelled the world in Diana's wake, often on lavish expenses. After her death, Lyons spoke the truth in rather cold words, observing that their 'gravy train had just been derailed in a truly spectacular fashion'.[74]

It was now the turn of the paparazzi themselves to come in for some unwelcome attention. Lyons received photographs of the crash scene on his computer just hours after Diana's death. Someone then burgled his offices at around 11 p.m. that night. The home of another photographer, Lionel Cherruault, was also broken into on the same night. Cherruault was informed by the crime investigation officer that it had been 'no ordinary burglary': the intruders gained entry seamlessly.[75] They seemed to have knowledge of the premises and only took selected items. Cherruault asked him: 'Do you mean the grey men, MI5, MI6, whatever?' The officer replied: 'Well, you can call them what you wish; local henchmen,' adding, 'You would be surprised what kind of people they use.' The policeman's main intent was to reassure him that because this was a professional government job their lives had not been in danger.[76] The photographer felt that the clear implication by the police was that the burglary had been carried out by the security services.

Oddly, one of Diana's closer personal associations with the security services is rarely mentioned. One of her dearest and most loyal friends was Rosa Monckton; together they often undertook charity work supporting vulnerable children. Monckton was in almost daily contact with Diana in the days before she set off for her last holiday on the Al-Fayed yacht before travelling to Paris. She was anxious about her friend's relationship with Dodi. In the week before her departure, Diana arranged for her mobile to be allocated a new number that 'only a handful of people would know'.[77] Rosa Monckton would have been one.

Rosa's youngest brother, Anthony, was a long-serving and distinguished MI6 officer who arrived in the former Yugoslavia in the early 1990s and had sometimes worked alongside Tomlinson.

A decade later he was still there, based in the British embassy in Belgrade and engaged in the tricky business of bringing war criminals before the tribunal in The Hague. In February 2004, he was horrified when he was 'outed' in a memoir by Zoran Mijatovic, the former deputy chief of the Serbian intelligence service. Exposed, he feared that he might now be targeted by Milosevic supporters and grew a beard to change his appearance. He fled, never having netted his greatest prize, General Ratko Mladic.[78] Al-Fayed suggested that Rosa was reporting on Diana to MI6, indeed he even asserted that she had befriended the princess precisely for this purpose, but there is absolutely no evidence to suggest this.[79]

Instead, it is more likely that the relationship was the other way around: perhaps Rosa and her brother were among the helpful friends in high places of whom Diana asked questions back in 1993 when she feared the activities of the supposed deep state. Wisely, Rosa had warned Diana to stay away from Al-Fayed, insisting that he was 'the man who put lots of cash in 25 brown envelopes and bribed MPs'.[80]

Fascinatingly, Rosa and Anthony were the grandchildren of Walter Monckton, the lawyer and later Cabinet minister who had remained a loyal friend to Edward VIII throughout the abdication and beyond. Walter Monckton had often travelled to Paris to advise him, staying at what subsequently became Al-Fayed's Villa Windsor in the Bois de Boulogne – Diana's first stop on her fateful visit to Paris in August 1997.[81]

DIANA HAD ASSERTED that she would be killed by the 'men in grey suits'. There was no doubt that during the early 1990s many in the establishment believed she represented an existential threat to the British monarchy. 'Squidgygate', 'Camillagate' and finally the 1995 BBC *Panorama* interview with Martin Bashir were all shocking. Prince Philip railed about this frequently, but then his temper was short, and he railed against a long list of people. In private he was always kind to the princess. More importantly, these episodes took their toll on both Charles and Diana.

Diana's death in Paris was unlikely to have been an assassination for one simple reason. Diana and Dodi chose to go to Paris at short notice and on a whim. This makes the existence of a state plot highly unlikely, since secret services are ultimately government bureaucracies and a deliberate death takes months to arrange. Equally importantly, unlike the French, Russians and Americans, British intelligence has no established track record of assassination and no 'licence to kill'. Covert actions are very rarely independent initiatives by spies known in the trade as 'rogue elephants'. The more serious the action, the more likely it is the decision makes its way circuitously and ponderously to the very top. Even if MI6 were in the assassination business, it would not have acted without prime ministerial approval and Tony Blair, a new, young and idealistic leader, would hardly have authorized the assassination of a popular princess only months into office.

In any country, once a 'hit' is approved, teams of assassins, backed by further supporters, are despatched. After months of planning, the CIA sent a team of a dozen simply to kidnap one person from Italy in 2003. Similarly, when Israel killed a leading member of Hezbollah in Dubai in 2010, it sent no fewer than twenty assassins, some disguised as tennis players. A large British assassination team operating in Paris that night would not have stayed untraceable, let alone plausibly deniable, for long.

The fact that Lord Stevens was chosen to head the British police inquiry also lends confidence. He had previously led an investigation into collusion between British security forces and loyalist paramilitaries in Northern Ireland and believed that simple statements by the security services that 'they have no involvement in illegal activities such as assassinations, is not credible. In other words, Stevens, perhaps more than any other such figure, was likely to keep an open mind and probe the evidence. He was certain that she was not assassinated.[82]

Although Diana's fears of the secret state, expressed with increasing frankness in the years before she died, overlap with Al-Fayed's allegations in some respects, in other important ways they do not. Fayed insisted that Diana was effectively killed on the orders of the duke of Edinburgh. But Hasnat Khan, the quiet, kind and intelligent doctor, who was perhaps closest to Diana in the year before she died, recalls, 'although she did not like the Duke of Edinburgh, she never expressed any fear of him'.[83] While Diana was not the victim of a conspiracy, she was effectively the victim of *conspiracy theory* and it was her fears of 'dark forces' that persuaded her to withdraw her police protection, against even the pleading of the home secretary. Had that been in place in Paris she would have been professionally cared for and would not have died on the last day of August 1997.

Patrick Jephson recalls with emotion her decision to 'dispense with her bodyguards'. Her team of police officers long afterwards retained a deep emotional loyalty to their 'wayward charge'. Ever watchful and professional to the end, he met them after her death and encountered the profound distress that they expressed, noting that she had died in circumstances which they would never have allowed to develop given their years of careful training.[84]

Meanwhile, Michael Mansfield, who acted for Al-Fayed in the Scott Baker inquiry, and penned his own account in 2009 after all the inquiries had finished, presents us with almost nothing. Instead, his essay on the Diana episode, entitled 'Big Brother', is a rhetorical *tour d'horizon* of the British secret state from George Orwell to omnipresent CCTV. Every historic skeleton in the cupboard of MI5 and MI6 is rattled, but he has surprisingly few things to say about the case itself. This notably laconic treatment of the key issues by a skilled advocate is all but a frank admission that he and his team had little to go on.[85]

More facts continue to emerge and they do not reflect well on the case for prosecution. In 2017, investigators showed that the car involved in the fatal crash enjoyed a remarkable 'first life'. It had been bought new and then stolen two years before the death of the princess by an escaped prisoner who took it on a joyride in the countryside near Paris. It was found destroyed in a field near Charles de Gaulle airport after rolling over several times. As a result, it was subsequently classified as a total loss and the owner reimbursed in full by the insurer. Yet a company, Etoile Limousine, which rented out cars with drivers and worked in part for the Ritz in Paris, bought the rebuilt car from a Mercedes dealer. It was soon clear that it had stability problems. A former driver complained that it was unpredictable if driven faster than sixty kilometres per hour.[86] As more details appear from the car to allegations against Bashir, one thing is for certain: the controversial case continues to fascinate.

THE SECRET ROYALS

IN SPRING 2019, a new recruit showed up for work at MI6. The thirty-six-year-old balding father of three looked rather nondescript. Each day he passed through the 'circlelock' security doors backlit with softly glowing aqua-blue glass. He ate in the canteen and, like many of his colleagues, was known only by his forename: 'Will'.

Prince William spent most of his time at MI6 based in its iconic 'ziggurat' headquarters at Vauxhall Cross. Here, he learnt about tradecraft: how intelligence officers recruit and nurture foreign agents. He noted how MI6 monitors risks to national security, to the economy, and, particularly close to his heart, to military effectiveness. He also gained a rare insight into covert action, learning about how intelligence can identify and exploit opportunities to shape events overseas.

The next week, William transferred across the river to MI5. He worked with covert counter-terrorism teams as they conducted surveillance, potentially even including riding in undercover vehicles, and sitting alongside intelligence analysts.

He spent the third week at GCHQ's impressive base in Cheltenham. Often described as 'the Doughnut', it rather more resembles a vast silver flying saucer. Each day he commuted to work from Prince Charles's Highgrove estate a few miles to the south. Again, he saw a range of intelligence activities, including how cutting-edge technology monitors targets and, through online covert action, disrupts threats. GCHQ's head of counter-terrorism operations praised William for comfortably holding his own among highly trained intelligence officers and analysts.

William attended security briefings with senior officials to discuss threats facing Britain. Learning how intelligence agencies monitor the threat from extremists, especially those returning from Syria, he was exposed to the full range of counter-terrorism operations, including those launched against Islamic State, the far right and the Real IRA. Some activities targeted Russia. He even got into the field during practice operations.

At the end of his assignment, William expressed a deep interest in security and defence and, like other royals before him, felt that intelligence gave him an insight into the threat to Britain and the British people. He said that 'spending time inside our security and intelligence agencies, understanding more about the vital contribution they make to our national security, was a truly humbling experience'.

'These agencies,' he continued, 'are full of people from everyday backgrounds doing the most extraordinary work to keep us safe. They work in secret, often not even able to tell their family and friends about the work they do or the stresses they face. They are driven by an unrivalled patriotism and dedication to upholding the values of this country. We all owe them deep gratitude for the difficult and dangerous work they do.'[1]

WILLIAM WAS TOO polite to say which service he preferred, but each royal has their favourite. Queen Elizabeth seems to have a soft spot for GCHQ. For fifty years, the successors of Bletchley Park have kept her 'boxes' packed with the most remarkable secrets. In more recent years GCHQ has taken on another role that is perhaps even more important – the defence of 'cyberspace'. Responsibility for the security of the internet is a job that could have reasonably ended up in the in-tray of any one of a dozen government departments, but few had the depth of technical expertise. In the end, the GCHQ defensive team that had built the queen's scrambler phones in the 1980s then became responsible for the defence of banks and ATMs in the 1990s, and finally took over the defence of 'everything' as Britain rushed towards e-government in the twenty-first century. GCHQ now has the tricky job of keeping the internet flowing safely.

On 17 February 2017, the queen visited Britain's first 'open' secret building. GCHQ's striking new National Cyber Security Centre in London's Victoria is the first secret service headquarters that anyone can visit – at least on the ground floor. She expounded the growing importance of the internet not only for government, but the every-day lives of her subjects. She was shown a book of secret cyphers used by her father, King George VI, to communicate during the war. Robert Hannigan, the director of GCHQ, responded warmly and recalled: 'During the War, King George VI, who was a regular reader of Bletchley's intelligence reports, was told that our math-ematicians and engineers were building Colossus, the world's first digital computer.' He explained that this breakthrough was to have consequences well beyond the vital job of codebreaking, ushering in the era of digital information and computing power. He character-ized the sixty-five years of the queen's reign as the 'new Machine Age' and added that now she had a new branch of secret service that was designed to defend it.[2]

The queen herself is a titan whose era has spanned the most exciting decades of secret history. She is able to look back as well as forward, and so in 2019, she commemorated GCHQ's centenary by unveil-ing a green plaque at Watergate House, near Charing Cross station, the birthplace of the organization. The Government Code & Cypher School (GC&CS), as it was known at the time, was established on 1 November 1919 as a peacetime cryptanalytic unit made up of staff from the Admiralty's Room 40 and the War Office's MI1(b).

For generations, the royal family have shown a close interest in intelligence. As the secret world gradually becomes less secretive and more bureaucratic, the relationship with the monarchy is becoming more formal and public. The queen is at its centre.

WHEN PRINCE PHILIP died in 2021, the intelligence services were quick to pay tribute. The chief of MI6, Richard Moore, described Philip as a 'true friend of the Service' and recalled that Philip had visited the agency on numerous occasions. 'Always his sharp mind, experience gained from active service and knowledge of global affairs shone through.' Philip 'called it as he saw it with directness and wit. Visits were never dull.'[3]

Philip had served as royal colonel of the Intelligence Corps. According to Tom Tugendhat, a soldier turned Conservative politician, Philip was both entertaining and diligent in this role, 'always astute in keeping an eye on what the Corps was up to'. One colleague apparently asked him why the unit had never been made the Royal Intelligence Corps. His answer was simple: 'Because you bastards aren't gentlemen.'[4]

Like his father, Prince Charles, the colonel in chief of the Parachute Regiment, is particularly interested in action. In 2019, the heir to the throne followed in his mother's footsteps and met Bond actor Daniel Craig on the set of the twenty-fifth 007 film. They 'bonded' over a display of eight classic 1960s Aston Martin DB5s. Surrounded by stars, Charles joked: 'The cars are the interesting thing here, much more interesting.' He joined Naomie Harris, who plays Moneypenny, and Ralph Fiennes, who plays 'M', along with director Cary Fukunaga in M's office. After watching some rushes from the film, Charles went to see the set of Q's workshop. But the media were not allowed to follow and see the gadgets because of the strict secrecy surrounding 'Bond 25'.

'Q' did not realize that Charles could have given them all a few tips. In the spy world life often imitates art and vice versa.[5] He is the patron of the intelligence agencies and, as such, regularly engages with real intelligence officers. On a visit to GCHQ in 2019, at which he received 'top secret briefings', Charles praised their 'utterly essential work'. 'Few people in this country,' he told the intelligence officers, 'will ever know just how great a debt we all owe you.'[6] He has visited GCHQ headquarters at least three times, including shortly after 9/11, as well as a secret GCHQ base in Scarborough; and has met the head of GCHQ in Clarence House, the prince's London residence.

The number of visits is remarkable. He has also visited MI5's Thames House at least three times, including the week following the attempted assassination of former Soviet spy Sergei Skripal in Salisbury and the day after Britain accused Russia of his attempted murder. Charles also met directors general Jonathan Evans and Andrew Parker at Clarence House. In July 2020, he received the new MI5 director general, Kenneth McCallum, the youngest in its history.

Charles has visited MI6 headquarters three times as well, most recently in October 2021. He has also met MI6 chiefs at Clarence House. In the late summer of 2014, he hosted John Sawers in the aftermath of an incredibly busy few weeks for MI6, with intelligence grappling with Russian covert operations in Ukraine, the Syrian civil war, Iranian nuclear negotiations and the rise of ISIS. They must have had plenty to discuss.

On top of these visits, Charles hosts regular awards ceremonies at Clarence House and St James's Palace. The ceremonies – perhaps the most exclusive in the UK – are where he hands out secret commendations for intelligence officers known as the Prince of Wales's Intelligence Community Awards. These are the espionage equivalent of the Victoria Cross and are allocated for the most special kinds of service.

THE ARMS TRADE is a shady and often unspoken area where royals, the secret services and the SAS come together. The SAS role in masterminding royal protection formed an important nexus with arms sales. Sultans and sheiks from Bahrain to Brunei queued up to have their bodyguards or special forces advised by the men in black balaclavas. Intelligence has long been used in support of British-based private commerce, providing intelligence on the negotiating positions of rival manufacturers. Britain's intelligence services are often presented to the public in terms of counter-terrorism or warning mechanisms like the Joint Intelligence Committee. Lurking underneath are a range of parallel practices that are often informal. The royals interact with this more hidden world.[7]

The member of the royal family closest to this curious world was Prince Andrew. More than anyone else, he had enjoyed a serious and successful military career of twenty-two years, serving as a helicopter pilot in the Falklands War. This gave him an insight into the world of military technology, including both advanced naval ships and aviation. When he left the navy and became an ambassador for British trade, military technology was always high on his list of priorities for promotion.

In late October 2008, the American ambassador to Kyrgyzstan, Tatiana Gfoeller, was offered a surprising glimpse of this activity. Her British opposite number in Bishkek, the new nation's capital, invited her to a large business lunch at which she was the only participant from outside Britain or the commonwealth. She reported back to Washington on Andrew's comments, which she found 'astonishingly candid', adding that the discussion at times verged on 'the rude'. As Andrew fielded questions, he was reportedly 'super-engaged' and then, addressing the ambassador directly, stated frankly that Britain was 'back in the thick of playing the Great Game'. Now rather animated, he added cheekily: 'and this time we aim to win!'[8]

Andrew next turned his fire on the Serious Fraud Office. He ripped into its investigators, who had had the 'idiocy' of almost scuttling the al-Yamama arms deal with Saudi Arabia, reportedly worth some £40 billion. The ambassador explained to Washington that the prince 'was referencing an investigation, subsequently closed, into alleged kickbacks a senior Saudi royal had received in exchange for the multi-year, lucrative BAE Systems contract to provide equipment and training to Saudi security forces'. Andrew then went on to attack 'those (expletive) journalists', especially from the *Guardian*, 'who poke their noses everywhere' and made it harder for British businessmen to do business. 'His mother's subjects seated around the table roared their approval.'[9]

Andrew's salty comments surfaced shortly afterwards when the ambassador's cable was released by WikiLeaks. But the security services' fears over him have now shifted to blackmail vulnerabilities. Andrew's friendship with the late billionaire paedophile Jeffrey Epstein came under close scrutiny following a disastrous interview he gave to the BBC in 2019. He strenuously denies knowledge of, or involvement in, Epstein's activities. His friendship, however, has created a potential counter-intelligence risk.

MI6 apparently feared that Russia could link Andrew to the abuse, thereby creating a blackmail – or 'leverage' – possibility. *The Times* reported that MI6 was concerned about a former Florida policeman who had access to the investigation, and claimed to have confidential documents, but who then moved to Russia where he made contact with a senior Russian government official sometimes referred to as a mentor to President Vladimir Putin. According to a 'western intelligence source', this information on the Epstein case 'would have been of great interest to Russian intelligence'.[10] Security officials have since carefully reviewed the security of the prince's internet and phone connections in case of bugging.[11]

PERHAPS THE MOST ambiguous relationship has been with the silent sentinels of Special Branch, who protected the royals around the world for over a hundred years. The royals created problems for their bodyguards, but also feared that the police reported on them. King Edward VIII is the most notorious example and there is no doubt that his secret policemen protected him but also spied on him – something he knew full well – making for a very special relationship.

The queen created all sorts of problems for her silent sentinels by insisting on being accessible and visible even in an era of rising international terrorism. Locking herself away would cause the crown to wither and die. Secret intelligence and advance warning proved vital in achieving this.

Gradually, as times changed and threats increased, security became more oppressive. For Princess Diana it was too much. Engulfed in a claustrophobic world and increasingly concerned, she first evaded her security and then shed it altogether.

Diana's youngest son, Prince Harry, tried to scale back his own royal duties in 2020. His wife is Meghan Markle, duchess of Sussex, an articulate and outspoken American actor whom many hoped would bring new dynamism and diversity to the institution. Unfortunately, things soon deteriorated. The press persistently attacked her for the most bizarre things: eating avocados, opening car doors wrongly and even caressing her pregnant stomach. Meghan told friends not to worry: the palace would protect her.

Soon, though, like Diana, she did not feel safe. She faced a constant barrage of press attention – as well as issues of race and social media trolling with which Diana did not have to contend. She became lonely and depressed. When pregnant, she learnt that her child would not receive security. Amid all the clickbait and paparazzi, she found that particularly difficult to accept. She felt trapped.[12]

In late 2019, she and Harry left the UK and moved to Canada. They claim that the royal family quickly cut off their security. Harry felt neither secure nor safe, especially as the newspapers revealed their location. He protested that even though his status may have changed, the threat to his safety had not. London prevaricated before agreeing that the latest intelligence did in fact show that the threat had not changed. However, he was no longer a working member of the royal family and so his security would be cut. Harry was shocked: 'I never thought that I would have my security removed, because I was born into this position. I inherited the risk.'[13]

Meghan wrote letters to the palace pleading: 'Please keep my husband safe. I see the death threats. I see the racist propaganda. Please keep him safe. Please don't pull his security and announce to the world when he and we are most vulnerable.'[14]

The following March, days after the first coronavirus lockdown, they moved to Los Angeles. They initially had to rely on private security provided by the media mogul Tyler Perry. As they settled in California, Harry and Meghan claimed they then had to sign lucrative contracts with Netflix and Spotify simply to afford security.[15] It was a remarkable situation: two of the most famous people on the planet, a target for a long list of terrorists and maniacs, apparently denied security. It is also a stark contrast to many of Harry's relatives. Queen Victoria, King Edward VIII, Queen Elizabeth II and even his own mother had resisted security. Harry wanted more. Times had certainly changed.

MONARCHS REQUIRE INTELLIGENCE to perform their duties. They enjoy the constitutional right to offer comments, encouragement and, most importantly, warning. In 1986, the queen's private secretary insisted that doing so actually constituted a duty rather than a mere right, thereby allowing the monarch a more active role. A 2011 Cabinet Office manual extended these rights or duties to include advising and being informed. Although the monarch must remain above party politics or risk undermining confidence in the office, she can express opinions on policy to the prime minister in an entirely confidential manner.[16] Prime Minister David Cameron recalled that the queen asked 'incredibly perceptive' questions;[17] a view shared by senior intelligence officials. She could only do this if she was well briefed and had a full picture of what was going on, including classified material. This is a classic example of intelligence as a form of power.[18]

The relationship between spies and royals raises a crucial question in liberal democracies: to whom are intelligence officers ultimately loyal? The government or the crown? After all, officially speaking, MI6 officers are not civil servants, they are 'crown servants'. The military historian Ian Beckett claims that, for many military officers, the crown represents a higher form of authority than the government of the day. Being servants, first and foremost, of the crown – albeit of the symbol rather than the individual monarch – allows the military to distance itself from the squalid nature of politics.[19] A similar idea extends to the intelligence services. This is not an abstract constitutional conundrum. It manifested itself most prominently and awkwardly in 1936 when the prime minister asked intelligence officers to spy on the king. It also manifested itself in 1974 when rumours emerged about intelligence officers, loyal to the crown, agitating against the prime minister, Harold Wilson, ironically the queen's favourite premier.

In this murky world, one thing is certain. Acquired over decades of reading classified intelligence, Queen Elizabeth II knows more state secrets than anyone alive. She probably knows more state secrets than anyone in history. Famously discreet, she will take them to her grave. How she used that information – and how future monarchs will do so – raises important questions about the role of the crown in British politics. There is so much about the secret royals and their influence that we do not yet know.

In June 1985, two of Britain's longest-serving members of parliament, Julian Amery and Tony Benn, found themselves together after a meeting of the Commons Select Committee of Privileges. Amery had long been close to MI6 and was a life-long enthusiast for covert action. Benn was one of parliament's most avid observers of the secret state. Both denizens of Westminster for decades, they chatted amiably for half an hour and conversation gradually turned to the underlying nature of power in Britain. Amery declared: 'Oh, we're not a democracy... We're a constitutional monarchy.' He explained that it was a 'collective monarchy' which consisted of officials and permanent secretaries, while elected ministers could only shift policy slightly, and 'only if that is acceptable to the collective Crown'. Benn was rather shocked and told him he should say it publicly. Amery replied that he did so and 'often'. Amery, expressing surprise, then turned and asked his friend: 'Surely, you knew it all along?'[20]

A NOTE ON METHODS

'Has sufficient time elapsed for part of the truth to be publicly told? My answer is obviously an unequivocal "No".'

Tommy Lascelles, 1967[1]

O N 2 JANUARY 1984, Kenneth Rose, a superb writer and doyen of royal biographers, lunched with Princess Margaret. The princess told him 'how busy she has been for the past week or two destroying much of the Queen Mother's old correspondence and the battered attaché cases in which it has been kept'. Rose was quite aghast at this 'terrible news', yet Margaret gushed on enthusiastically: 'I have already filled two big sacks and the servants are so pleased at my cleaning up the mess.' This was not a momentary whim, but an organized programme of destruction: three years later she was still at it. These included letters from Princess Diana to the queen mother.[2]

David Griffin, her chauffeur, was her accomplice in this historical crime. Overseen by the princess, who had pulled on an outsize pair of yellow rubber gloves, he had set up a royal incinerator in a dustbin outside the garage at Kensington Palace where Margaret had an apartment. 'The smoke was so thick it made her eyes water and she had to leave,' recalls Griffin. They returned repeatedly to Clarence House afterwards to collect more letters and papers – and burned them all. He saw Diana's name on a few, and even her crest and handwriting, and there were lots of others, from decades earlier, addressed to the king and queen. 'The Princess never said why she was doing it, but she was very determined that they should all be destroyed, thousands of them. I remember thinking we were putting a match to history.'[3]

Margaret's behaviour is symptomatic of a royal determination to rule not only the present but also the past. Anthony Blunt's famous 'raiding expeditions' to the Continent in the company of the Windsor librarian, in search of archives, paintings and jewels, were in fact routine. There is even a prime ministerial file about this in the National Archives entitled 'Royal Family: Duke of Windsor's papers: allegations... that they were stolen by secret agents'. Inevitably, the file is closed.[4]

Mountbatten was sent on a similar expedition to Paris and reportedly 'stole some of the Duke of Windsor papers during a visit in his declining years'.[5] This seems an absurd suggestion, but Rose's wonderful diaries again shine a brief but illuminating light. All of a sudden in 1972, as Edward faltered, there seems to have been a sudden charm offensive. Martin Charteris described 'a rather macabre tea party' when the queen visited the duchess in Paris. There was happy conversation in the drawing room while the duke lay dying upstairs. Charteris added with satisfaction that 'all his papers are now safely in England'. There was a follow-up manoeuvre, at the duke's funeral at Windsor, when Mountbatten and Prince Philip persuaded the duchess 'to part with the rest'. Within a day of her return to Paris, a truck drew up in the Bois de Boulogne 'and whisked them away'.[6]

The removal of the duke's papers was controversial and the reverberations of this eventually reached Downing Street. Nick Sanders, Margaret Thatcher's private secretary, wrote forcefully to deny the allegations that the papers were stolen by 'the Queen's Secret Agents from the House of the Duchess of Windsor' while she was in London 'as the guest of Her Majesty for the Duke's funeral'. He insisted that these papers were taken to Windsor 'with the full knowledge and consent of the duchess of Windsor'.[7] This explanation is most likely correct.

What documents are we missing here? Fortunately, one winsome figure, the writer and biographer James Pope-Hennessy, cast his eyes on some of these papers in Paris in 1957. He recalls that after a hearty breakfast he 'settled down to 1936' and found the papers 'irresistible', adding that if this explosive material was ever published it would offer a 'complete picture of the Abdication chaos'. They include 'grave letters from ministers', 'brilliant' letters from Churchill, 'screeches' from Lady Oxford, fascinating notes from Diana Cooper and 'bleak letters from Queen Mary' all crowded together. This is the wonderful documentation that the history police have suppressed.[8]

It is not just the big fish that are caught in the net. Small fish are also hunted down. In 2007, William Tallon, steward and member of the queen mother's staff at Clarence House, died in his Duchy of Cornwall apartment in Kennington, where his body lay undiscovered for some time. The 'authorities' then quickly arrived and cleaned out his private papers, including 'self-pitying letters from Prince Charles'.[9]

All this material makes its way to the vast archive at Windsor Castle. This is clearly a special archive with peculiar rules and even those who preside over it do not always know what lies inside. There are arcane levels of clearance and access. Tommy Lascelles was perhaps one of the most trusted royal servants and so was put in charge of this historical treasure house. Yet even he recalls a moment of jealousy when Harold Nicolson, official biographer of George V, was 'shown everything', adding that this included intimate letters 'which I, though Keeper of the Archives, had never seen'.[10]

Even the loss of the smallest morsel is cause for panic. Prince Charles was not only bullied at Gordonstoun but also stolen from mercilessly by the other boys. Anything with his signature was valuable, even name tags that had been ripped from his vest and pants fetched half a crown with eager local dealers. Panic set in when his English language exercise book was taken, in which he had expounded all sorts of things, including 'theories on corrupt governments' – it had last been seen lying on the prince's desk. Although initially sold for only seven shillings and sixpence, it was soon in London changing hands for thousands of pounds. 'Finally, by a clever trick of deception it was retrieved by Special Branch and returned to the parents of the rightful owner.'[11]

The Royal Archives are also vast because they are fed by the government machine. Much goes in, but little comes out. Diplomats all around the world are encouraged to report to the royals about royals. Warwick Morris, a lowly third secretary in Paris in the early 1970s, recalls that there was much to tell. Many French people were fascinated by the British royal family, having done away with their own in the revolution. Certain French newspapers and magazines like *France Dimanche* and *Paris Match*, as well as the more sensational ones, featured articles every week about the royals. 'These included outrageous and fictitious ones, like the whole Everton football team having been in Princess Anne's bedroom at Buckingham Palace, or the Queen Mother being dead and having a living double.' The British embassy used to send a selection of 'these scurrilous stories' to Buckingham Palace from time to time. Never having got any reaction, they eventually wrote proposing to stop. Suddenly a reply came: 'No, please don't. The Family derives huge entertainment and amusement from what you send. Keep them coming!'[12]

As we have seen, in so many ways, the intelligence services and the royal family have much in common. They are small, secretive and highly mythologized with a band of loyal devotees at their centre. They both know many secrets and, through their various channels, thrive on the gathering of information – although they have not always shared it with each other. Both have even intervened secretly in the affairs of other states.

Both control and curate their own histories carefully; both are exempt from freedom of information requests. Historians have to wait a long time for intelligence files to make their way to the National Archives – but at least some do eventually arrive. The royal family, by contrast, are the real enemies of history. There is no area where restrictions and redactions are so severe.

Like MI6, they are also engaged in positive information control. For more than half a century, Britain's secret intelligence service has not only assisted the right defectors to pen their memoirs, but has also opened the door of its archives to favoured historians.[13] The Royal

Archives at Windsor, especially files covering more recent decades, operate in exactly the same way. Cameras are forbidden. Even then, historical supplicants obediently have to sign a form promising to let the palace see how they will use the material in advance of publication. They sometimes ask for quotes to be removed from a manuscript.[14] Favoured historians are given access to more recent documents, such as King George VI's rather boring diaries, creating an incentive to write yet more sycophantic biographies. The rest languish on ancient history or hunt for scraps.

Where is the scrap-heap? In west London, alongside the Royal Botanic Gardens at Kew, the National Archives are a barren waste-land of royal history. What the historian most wants to see is the minutes of meetings between monarchs and prime ministers, but they do not exist here – and even if they did, historians would not be allowed to read them. The 'files' on Harold Macmillan's weekly audiences with the queen, for example, just catalogue dull correspondence about scheduling and whether the prime minister could wear a certain suit. Even so, many of these are closed.

The only record of these meetings depended on drink. No one else sits in on the prime minister's weekly audience with the queen, each Tuesday afternoon. Clearly, the queen's private secretary would like to attend. So, down the years the gambit was to offer the various prime ministers a drink afterwards and try to debrief them. Martin Charteris found Jim Callaghan very frustrating as he would not play the game. Callaghan recalls that he wanted a drink but 'deliberately refused to talk to Martin about our audiences, which I regarded as confidential between the queen and her PM'. It was not all about spies and secrets – often the queen would talk about family matters and clearly found the confidential setting therapeutic.[15] Where prime ministers played the private secretaries' game, a partial record may exist in the Windsor archives.

On the rare occasion when a good file on the royals makes its way to the archives it can be clawed back. In 2018, Professor Philip Murphy, director of the Institute of Commonwealth Studies and one of Britain's most skilful royal researchers, found a file about the royal yacht. Murphy's discovery was a classic example of historical sleuthing, for instead of heading for the highlights of Cabinet Office files, he had doggedly pursued a trail into obscure Welsh Office material. Here he found a gem.

What he was able to demonstrate was that in the 1990s, when the queen was crying public tears for the retirement of the royal yacht *Britannia*, she was privately lobbying for a brand-new vessel. The file contained a delicately worded letter from her deputy private secretary, Kenneth Scott. He explained that she was 'deeply interested in the subject' and would 'naturally very much welcome' a replacement for the twenty-first century. The *Britannia* is now berthed in Edinburgh and visited by hundreds of thousands of tourists each year. But Prince Philip wanted it broken up and the familiar fittings that he loved installed in a new vessel. When this story emerged in *The Times*, there was trouble. The palace rang the Cabinet Office and stamped its foot, so in no time at all the history police were on their way to Kew. The file has now been withdrawn and the catalogue says: 'This record is closed whilst access is under review.'[16]

The relative absence of royal records even prompted one enterprising historian to create his own. Martin Allen wrote three books about the Nazis based partly on forged documents, including one entitled *Hidden Agenda: How the Duke of Windsor Betrayed the Allies*. This triggered a police investigation and the National Archives eventually uncovered the full scale of the deception. It unearthed some twenty-nine faked documents, planted in a dozen separate files at some point between 2000 and 2005, which were used to bolster Allen's specious arguments.[17] Top journalist and historian Max Hastings observed that it was hard to conceive of actions 'more damaging to the cause of preserving the nation's heritage, than wilfully forging documents designed to alter our historical record'.[18]

What about interviews? In writing this book, we have mostly tended to stay away from the temptations of oral evidence. All stories grow with the telling, but royal stories grow faster. Nevertheless, these testimonies are fascinating, and we are always interested in stories about 'the files'. With MI6, it is tales of jewellery thefts on behalf of the crown or top agents being smuggled into the palace to meet a monarch as a special treat. With MI5 it is normally stories about the surveillance of the royals themselves. A number of knowledgeable figures in MI5 have asserted that dossiers on the duke and duchess of Windsor did exist and were kept out of the main registry as they were 'too hot'. Instead, they were kept in a separate safe in the director general's office. This was largely because Edward was thought to be too close to Ribbentrop. We are assured that these files, if they existed, are now long gone.[19]

The phenomenon of the 'special' office safe is fascinating – every government department has one. Sherard Cowper-Coles, one of Britain's most distinguished diplomats, who served as ambassador in war-torn Kabul, offers us a rare glimpse of such a fascinating facility. When serving as private secretary in the office of the most senior diplomat in the Foreign Office, he recalls that in the corner sat 'an ancient safe' that was 'about the size of a washing machine'. It did not contain big national secrets in the sense of material with wonderfully high classifications, or compartmentalized stuff from secret agents. Instead, it held material that was 'too sensitive' to be placed in the main Foreign Office file registry. What did its 'explosive contents' consist of? It was a selection of delicious scandal: mole-hunting in MI6, secret payments to foreign rulers and, of course, complaints from ambassadors 'about the behaviour of members of the royal family visiting their parish'.[20] For decades, the misdeeds of Britain's royals and foreign monarchs alike were a rich source of dinner table stories in all government departments.[21]

Even fictitious files have their uses. The infamous 'China Dossier' on Mrs Simpson is a case in point. Our conclusions are that this almost certainly did not exist and no one ever laid eyes on it. But by 1951, the Windsors' circle, including Churchill, were being told of the China Dossier. Kenneth de Courcy, a close friend of Edward, concludes, probably rightly, that this 'file' was used repeatedly to deflate continued supporters of Edward and Wallis. Jock Colville insisted that, despite his many years alternating between Downing Street and the palace, he had 'never heard' of the dossier.[22]

No less than in the spy world, the story of the Windsors is often a wilderness of mirrors. Despite these impediments, we have painstakingly pieced together fragments scattered across thousands of files and personal accounts. Memoirs are a potentially useful source; people love to write about their encounters with royalty. Yet these too are censored. The queen's comment about assassinating a Middle Eastern leader was mysteriously airbrushed from Evelyn Shuckburgh's published diaries about the Suez Crisis. Alexander Cadogan's famous wartime published diaries are strangely thin on references to royals. Nomadic historians have to travel far and wide to forage in the hand-written originals.

Writing intelligence history is difficult; writing contemporary royal history, using primary source material, is more difficult still. As the intelligence services become more open, though, so too has their relationship with the royal family. But beyond the much-publicized royal tours of shiny new intelligence headquarters, a deeper and far more clandestine relationship binds these two powerful institutions together. Like the intelligence services, the crown has its secrets. Neither wants them to be told.

Are the royal family the antichrists of history? Perhaps not entirely so. It is certainly reported that the queen does not like books about the royal family. She has often refused to say anything to official royal biographers, indeed even figures as loyal as Philip Ziegler have been blanked. Yet there is one book about the royal family that Elizabeth likes – her own. Apparently, she keeps a meticulous diary. Historians can only dream of the wonderful secrets it contains. One day perhaps we will read it…

ACKNOWLEDGEMENTS

WRITING ABOUT SPIES is challenging; writing about royals is more difficult; and writing about spies and royals has sometimes seemed impossible. But the intellectual journey has been fascinating, not least because of what it has taught us about efforts to control and shape the past. Research for this book began back in 2015 and took us well beyond our comfort zone. It was made more difficult by the Covid-19 'lockdown' in 2020–21, which even hampered access to books in our own university offices. Every successful raid on a body of records depends on good intelligence and so often we have benefited from the thorough reconnaissance of others. Therefore, more than with our previous books, we have depended on the kindness of friends and invaluable assistance from many people over many years, and we are very pleased to be able to thank them here. Any errors of fact or interpretation, of course, remain our own. Please do write to us with comments and corrections at r.j.aldrich@warwick.ac.uk or rory.cormac@nottingham.ac.uk.

A wide circle of friends and colleagues have encouraged, warned, advised and consulted us. We would particularly like to thank Christopher Andrew, Sally Bedell Smith, Huw Bennett, Gill Bennett, Mark Bishop, Piers Brendon, Jock Bruce, Ed Burke, Gordon Corera, Oliver Daddow, Philip Davies, Annabelle de Heus, Stephen Dorril, Rob Dover, Peter Dunn, Huw Dylan, Tom Eason, David Easter, John Ferris, Tom Frew, Jamie Gaskarth, Jules Gaspard, Liam Gearon, David Gioe, Anthony Glees, Susan Glen, Michael Goodman, Andrew Hammond, Jonathan Haslam, Max Hastings, Peter Hennessy, Michael Herman, Lewis Herrington,

Davinia Hoggarth, Mark Hollingsworth, Gerry Hughes, Peter Jackson, Rhodri Jeffreys-Jones, Clive Jones, Matthew Jones, Athina Karatzogianni, John Kasuku, Sheila Kerr, Anthony King, Dan Larson, Paul Lashmar, Thomas Leahy, Magda Long, W. Scott Lucas, Paul McGarr, Paul Maddrell, Victor Madeira, Tom Maguire, Peter Martland, Spencer Mawby, Paul Mercer, Chris Moran, Philip Murphy, David Omand, Mark Phythian, David Porter, Tilman Remme, Dina Rezk, Lee Richards, Daniela Richterova, David Schaefer, Ann Sebba, Zakia Shiraz, Michael Smith, David Stafford, Mark Stout, Phil Tinline, Karina Urbach, Damien Van Puyvelde, Kate Vigurs, Calder Walton, Wesley K. Wark, Michael Warner, Cees Wiebes, Simon Willmetts, Nikita Wolf and John Young. In particular, Mike Kenner and Philip Murphy both read sections of this book for us, providing helpful corrections and feedback.

Despite the unfortunate disruptions to travel in 2020–21, our research took us to fabulous places, from the Hoover Institute in California to the Resistance Museum in Oslo. We are grateful to them all, but in particular to the help and support of archivists and librarians on both sides of the Atlantic. These include, in the UK, the National Archives, Churchill College Cambridge, the Cadbury Research Library at Birmingham University, the Bodleian Library, the British Library, Cambridge University Library, the Churchill Archives, the House of Lords Library, National Archives II, the Royal Archives and King's College London. We are especially grateful to Anthea Boylston and Celia Catchpole for allowing us to quote from the Seabury Ashmead-Bartlett Papers. We are grateful to 'the permission of Her Majesty the Queen' for allowing us to quote from the Royal Archives. In the US, we are grateful to staff at the National Archives and Records Administration, the presidential libraries, Library of Congress, Georgetown University and the National Security Archive.

The universities of Warwick and Nottingham have provided stimulating environments in which to conduct this research over the years, including generous periods of study leave. Warwick's unique undergraduate research programme provided us with two wonderful researchers, Bryan Hughes and Kiran Heer Kaur, who assisted our work at the National Archives in Kew. Nottingham kindly funded a fact-checker and we are very grateful to Charley Ferris for carrying out this work. We are also grateful to Anastasia Zabludovskaya for translating documents. Colleagues have been incredibly support-ive, including through times of personal difficulty (special thanks to George Christou, David Gill, Chris Moran, Nikki Muckle and Andrew Mumford). Our wonderful postdoctoral researchers and postgraduate students at both universities have provided constant encouragement and criticism. Our respective secret intelligence modules provided tough but constructive testing grounds for many a royal anecdote.

A few individuals deserve special thanks and some sadly are no longer with us. Matthew Aid, Ralph Erskine, Julian Lewis, Bradley F. Smith and David Stafford collectively and long ago pioneered the lateral research techniques we use today and which will be deployed by our research students tomorrow. Michael Herman developed the idea of 'intelligence power' which informs this study. Oddly, one of the most helpful authors is someone we have never met. The wonderful works of Kenneth Rose were often our unseen companion, and his diaries, beautifully edited by D.R. Thorpe, illuminated our path. Other important figures, including Hugo Vickers and Duff Hart-Davies, have contributed meticulously edited volumes of diaries and papers that have proved similarly vital.

This book would not have happened without Paul Elston, who spotted the potential in a couple of pages about King Edward VIII in our previous book, *The Black Door*. A visionary director, he tenaciously turned it into a highly successful two-part television documentary on the Windsors for Channel 4. This then evolved into two further documentaries on royals and intelligence, and we are particularly grateful to Paul and his very professional team for continually pushing us on, and to Channel 4 for placing their faith in us and allowing us to showcase deep archival research. Helen Ford at Warwick Modern Records Centre has generously provided us with the university equivalent of Pinewood Studios on the fringes of Coventry. We are grateful to our literary agents, Andrew Lownie in the UK, together with Martin Redfern and a tremendous group at Northbank Talent for North America. Likewise, we are grateful to James Nightingale and his colleagues at Atlantic for developing the idea and publishing the book. Tamsin Shelton provided a thorough copyedit, for which we are also most grateful.

Above all, we once again owe an enormous debt to our families. Rory's family has doubled in size since this project began. Finlay and Genevieve have provided ample distractions, and a growing interest in inappropriate royal bedtime stories, especially the investiture of Prince Charles and the kidnap of Princess Anne. This book, and indeed much else, would not be here without Joanne. Thank you. It should also be noted that Christy Cormac, who is fed up with Joanne receiving acknowledgements in book after book, is a 'hero'. Richard is grateful to Harrie, Tom and Nick for enduring endless anecdotes about the antics of royal dogs of every shape and size, especially the royal labrador that was taught 'basic French' at Sandringham before being gifted to the French president. Libby has tolerated Richard's inexplicable passion for Princess Margaret with commendable good humour and quiet bemusement. As always, she has offered boundless love and encouragement despite the late nights, turning to the grey light of dawn, as the book drew to its conclusion.

ENDNOTES

Introduction

1. Fleming, *On Her Majesty's Secret Service*.
2. Hennessy, *Establishment and Meritocracy*, p.17.

Chapter 1

1. Elizabeth, letter to the King of Sweden, 1561, in Lane, *The Sayings of Queen Elizabeth*, p.128.
2. Fischlin, 'Political Allegory', pp.175–7.
3. Strong, *The Cult of Elizabeth*, pp.52, 156; Graziani, 'The "Rainbow Portrait"', pp.247–59.
4. Christopher Andrew's study of *The Secret World* is the most masterly exploration of this long global history.
5. Budiansky, *Her Majesty's Spymaster*, p.v.
6. Ash, *Power, knowledge, and expertise in Elizabethan England*, pp.12–24.
7. Potter, *Foreign Intelligence and Information in Elizabethan England*, p.vi.
8. King, 'Queen Elizabeth I', pp.34–7.
9. Alford, *The Watchers*, p.13. In fact, the most proto-modern system was in Italy, see Iordanou, *Venice's Secret Service*.
10. Read, 'Walsingham and Burghley in Queen Elizabeth's Privy Council', pp.34–42.
11. Tu, 'The Pursuit of God's Glory', pp.2–3.
12. TNA, SP 12/48/61, Walsingham to Cecil, 20/12/68.
13. Hutchinson, *Elizabeth's Spy Master*, pp.3–5.
14. Ibid., p.22.
15. Haynes, *Invisible Powers*, p.157.
16. Hutchinson, *Elizabeth's Spy Master*, pp.54–5.
17. Tu, 'The Pursuit of God's Glory', p.89.
18. Budiansky, *Her Majesty's Spymaster*, p.78.
19. Jenkins, *Elizabeth the Great*, pp.176–7.
20. ODNB: L. E. Hunt, 'Roberto di Ridolfi'.
21. Alford, *Burghley*, p.168; Cooper, *The Queen's Agent*, pp.58–9.
22. Cooper, *The Queen's Agent*, p.95.
23. Alford, *The Watchers*, pp.206, 262, 268, 298.
24. Ibid., pp.12–14.
25. Rose, 'Rebellion, Spymasters and Spies', p.44.
26. Tu, 'The Pursuit of God's Glory', p.54.
27. Pollitt, 'The Abduction of Doctor John Story', pp.131–2.
28. Ibid., p.131.
29. Trim, 'The secret war of Elizabeth I', pp.194–6.
30. Doran, *Elizabeth I and Foreign Policy*, p.35; Trim, 'The secret war of Elizabeth I', pp.194–6.
31. Fritschy, 'A "financial revolution" reconsidered', pp.60, 67; Doran, *Elizabeth I and Foreign Policy*, pp.37, 41; Adams, '"The Service I

am here for'", pp.217–38; Adams, 'Signs of Intelligence', pp.1–18.

32. Trim, 'The secret war of Elizabeth I', pp.194–6.

33. Doran, *Elizabeth I and Foreign Policy*, p.35.

34. Tu, 'The Pursuit of God's Glory', p.174; Haynes, *Walsingham*, pp.170–71; Alford, *The Watchers*, p.243.

35. Cooper, *The Queen's Agent*, p.104.

36. Hicks, 'The Strange Case of Dr. William Parry', pp.342–62.

37. Tu, 'The Pursuit of God's Glory', p.155.

38. Alford, *The Watchers*, pp.214–30; Haynes, *Walsingham*, pp.181–4.

39. Calendar of State Papers: The Scottish Series in relation to Mary, Scot, 8, 10.

40. Hutchinson, *Elizabeth's Spy Master*, p.181.

41. Leimon and Parker, 'Treason and Plot in Elizabethan Diplomacy', pp.1148–58; Tu, *The Politics of Intelligence*, pp.63–98.

42. Leimon and Parker, 'Treason and Plot in Elizabethan Diplomacy', pp.134–6.

43. Tu, 'The Pursuit of God's Glory', pp.115–16; Matthews, *The Spanish Armada*, pp.33–41.

44. Tu, 'The Pursuit of God's Glory', pp.93–4.

45. Hutchinson, *Elizabeth's Spy Master*, pp.99–101.

46. Alford, *The Watchers*, p.235.

47. Rankin, 'Richard Topcliffe and the Book Culture', pp.492–7.

48. Hutchinson, *Elizabeth's Spy Master*, pp.75–9. Also ODNB: William Richardson, 'Topcliffe, Richard (1531–1604)'.

49. Hutchinson, *Elizabeth's Spy Master*, p.101.

50. Andrew, *The Secret World*, pp.188–90.

51. Sherman, 'Research Intelligence in Early Modern England', p.98.

Chapter 2

1. Thackeray, *The Four Georges*, p.75.

2. Pady and Kline, 'Finger Counting', p.440.

3. Chiasson-Taylor, 'Musicians and intelligence operations', pp.7–19.

4. Andrew, *The Secret World*, pp.191–3.

5. Travers, *The Gunpowder Plot*, pp.2–14.

6. ODNB: King James VI and I.

7. Andrew, *The Secret World*, p.195.

8. Stewart, *The Cradle King*, pp.264–79.

9. Bellany and Cogswell, *The Murder of King James I*, pp.321–43.

10. Ibid., pp.283–303.

11. Wooley, *The King's Assassin*, pp.139–141.

12. Bellany and Cogswell, *The Murder of King James I*, pp.193–8.

13. Stewart, *The Cradle King*, pp.264–8.

14. Bellany and Cogswell, *The Murder of King James I*, pp.363–5, 414–38.

15. Purkiss, *The English Civil War*, pp.561–70.

16. Cogswell, 'The Politics of Propaganda', pp.187–215.

17. Smith, *Royalist Agents*, p.7.

18. Fissel, *The Bishops' Wars*, pp.56–78.

19. Wallis's Autobiography (1697). See also Scriba, 'The Autobiography of John Wallis', pp.17–21.

20. Wallis's Autobiography (1697).

21. Andrew, *The Secret World*, pp.220–2.

22. Smith, *Royalist Agents*, p.244.

23. Andrew, *The Secret World*, p.231.

24. Trevor Timpson, 'How a king's judges were hunted down', BBC News, 9 March 2012.

25. Ibid.

26. Twigge, *Codebreakers*, pp. 10–11; Andrew, *The Secret World*, pp.237–41.

27. ODNB: King Charles II.

28. See Raymond, *Pamphlets and Pamphleteering in Early Modern Britain*.

29. Walker, 'The Popish Plot and the Construction of Panic in Seventeenth-Century Media', pp.112–38; Andrew, *The Secret World*, pp.237–41.

30. Harris, *Revolution*, pp.23–66.

31. Sowerby, *Making Toleration*, *passim*; Pincus, *1688: The First Modern Revolution*, *passim*.

32. Kahn, *The Codebreakers*, p.168; Andrew, *The Secret World*, pp.249–58.

33. Andrew, *The Secret World*, pp.271.

34. Kahn, *Codebreakers*, pp.172–86.

35. Black, 'British intelligence and the mid-eighteenth-century crisis', pp.213–6.

36. Ibid.

37. Andrew, *The Secret World*, p.299.

38. Arthur MacNalty, 'Edward Bancroft MRD FRS and the War of American Independence', Reprinted from the Proceedings of the Royal Society of Medicine, Section of the History of Medicine (June 1944), p.11; Daigler, 'In Defense of John Honeyman', p.88.

39. Skocpol, *States and Revolutions*, pp.54–7.

40. Andrew, *The Secret World*, pp.303–21.

41. Harrison, *The Second Coming*, pp.77–8.

42. *Times*, 16 May 1800, p. 2.

43. Moran, 'The origin of insanity as a special verdict', pp.489–94.

44. Ibid., p.507.

45. Ibid., pp.487–519.

Chapter 3

1. Hibbert, *Queen Victoria*, p.424.

2. Porter, *Plots and Paranoia*, pp.83–4; Andrew, *Secret Service*, pp.5, 6.

3. Porter, *Plots and Paranoia*, p.81.

4. St Aubyn, *Queen Victoria*, p.236; Marshal, *Victoria*, p.103.

5. Queen Victoria's Journals 22/12/51.

6. Leopold to Victoria, 24/7/37, Benson and Esher (eds), *The Letters of Queen Victoria*, vol. 1, p.113.

7. Leopold to Victoria, 9/10/37, Benson and Esher (eds), *The Letters of Queen Victoria*, vol. 1, p.120.

8. Queen Victoria's Journals 5/3/39.

9. Weintraub, *Victoria*, pp.144, 156–7, 170.

10. Sinclair, *The Other Victoria*, p.75.

11. Ibid., pp.20–21.

12. Hibbert, *Queen Victoria*, p.196.

13. Queen Victoria's Journals 10/6/40.

14. Ibid.

15. Murphy, *Shooting Victoria*, p.55.

16. Queen Victoria's Journals 10/6/40; Hibbert, *Queen Victoria*, p.421.

17. Murphy, *Shooting Victoria*, pp.59–60.

18. Queen Victoria's Journals 10/6/40, 11/6/40, 12/6/40.

19. Ibid., 15/6/40.

20. Guizot, *An Embassy to The Court of St. James's*, p.117.

21. Ibid., pp.5–6.

22. Ibid., p.37.

23. Queen Victoria's Journals 12/6/40, 15/6/40, 11/7/40.

24. Murphy, *Shooting Victoria*, pp.4–5.

25. Ibid., pp.44, 126.

26. Griffin, 'Detective Policing', p.232.

27. St Aubyn, *Queen Victoria*, p.162.
28. Thomson, *The Story of Scotland Yard*, p.105.
29. St Aubyn, *Queen Victoria*, p.162.
30. Murphy, *Shooting Victoria*, p.180.
31. Queen Victoria's Journals 1/7/42.
32. Murphy, *Shooting Victoria*, pp.54–64.
33. Lacey, *Royal*, p.19.
34. Victoria to Leopold, 31/5/42, Benson and Esher (eds), *The Letters of Queen Victoria*, vol. 1, p.499.
35. Queen Victoria's Journals 30/5/42, 31/5/42.
36. Moran, 'The punitive uses of the insanity defense', p.171.
37. Queen Victoria's Journals 1/7/42.
38. Ibid., 3/7/42.
39. Rivington Holmes, *Queen Victoria*, p.58.
40. St Aubyn, *Queen Victoria*, p.163.
41. Griffin, 'Detective Policing', pp.226, 292, 311.
42. Judith Flanders, 'The creation of the police and the rise of detective fiction', British Library, 15 May 2014; Worthington, *The Rise of the Detective*, pp.3–75.
43. Black, 'The Victorian Information Society', pp.53–90.
44. Lyon, *Electronic Eye*, p.14.
45. Queen Victoria's Journals 20/1/43.
46. Ibid., 21/1/43.
47. Peel to Victoria, 25/1/43, Benson and Esher (eds), *The Letters of Queen Victoria*, vol. 1, p.572.
48. Darryl Chamberlain, 'Charlton history: The man who took a bullet for the PM', *Charlton Champion*, 16/8/11.
49. Queen Victoria's Journals 5/3/43.
50. Rix, 'Towards a More Just Insanity Defence', pp.44–52.
51. Murphy, *Shooting Victoria*, p.225.
52. Peel to Victoria, 27/3/43, Benson and Esher (eds), *The Letters of Queen Victoria*, vol. 1, pp.591–2.
53. Campbell, *Fenian Fire*, p.10.
54. Murphy, *Shooting Victoria*, p.275.
55. Queen Victoria's Journals 20/5/49.
56. Ibid., 27/6/50.
57. St Aubyn, *Queen Victoria*, p.164.
58. Smith, 'British Post Office Espionage', pp.189–99.
59. Porter, *Plots and Paranoia*, pp.77–8.
60. Moran, *Classified*, p.27.
61. Vincent, 'Surveillance, Privacy and History', pp.1–3.
62. Queen Victoria's Journals 4/4/38, 11/5/38, 1/1/39.
63. Ibid., 1/1/39, 2/9/40, 29/12/40.
64. Ibid., 3/1/39.
65. Ibid., 5/10/38.
66. Ibid., 6/10/38.
67. Ibid., 30/9/38.
68. Ibid., 11/11/38.
69. Ibid., 3/5/39.
70. Sinclair, *The Other Victoria*, p.55.
71. Queen Victoria's Journals 25/6/44.
72. Vincent, 'Surveillance, Privacy and History', pp.1–3.
73. Porter, *Plots and Paranoia*, pp.77–8.
74. Cobain, *The History Thieves*, p.45.
75. Andrew, *The Secret World*, pp.381–3.
76. Queen Victoria's Journals 1/3/45.
77. Ibid., 6/3/53.
78. Ibid., 1/12/55.
79. Ibid., 23/4/64.
80. Porter, *The Refugee Question in Mid-Victorian Politics*, pp.1–11, 201–28.
81. Kemp, *Bombs, Bullets and Bread*, p.51.
82. Griffin, 'Detective Policing', pp.294–5.
83. Ibid., pp.299–300.
84. Griffin, 'Detective Policing', p.301; Porter, *The Refugee Question in Mid-Victorian Politics*, pp.149–52.
85. Griffin, 'Detective Policing', p.304.

86. Queen Victoria's Journals 2/4/48, 4/4/48.
87. Brown, *Palmerston and the Politics of Foreign Policy*, p.90.
88. Queen Victoria's Journals 22/1/49.
89. Ibid., 24/1/49.
90. Ibid., 22/1/49; Victoria to Russell, 22/1/49, Benson and Esher (eds), *The Letters of Queen Victoria*, vol. 2, p.251. See also Brown, *Palmerston and the Politics of Foreign Policy*, p.90.
91. Queen Victoria's Journals 24/1/49.
92. Chamberlain, *Pax Britannica?*, p.96.
93. Marshall, *Victoria*, p.107
94. Porter, *Plots and Paranoia*, p.91.
95. Ibid., p.88.
96. Queen Victoria's Journals 1–2/5/51.
97. Ibid., 14/10/51, 23/10/51.
98. Ibid., 28/10/51, 31/10/51.
99. Ibid., 2/11/51.
100. Albert to Duke Ernst II, Duke of Saxe-Coburg-Gotha, 29/12/51, Bolitho (ed.), *The Prince Consort to His Brother*, p.126.
101. Queen Victoria's Journals 22/4/53.
102. Ibid., 26/5/50.
103. Leopold to Victoria, 3/6/53, Benson and Esher (eds), *The Letters of Queen Victoria*, vol. 2, p.544.
104. Queen Victoria's Journals 13/10/48; Marshall, *Victoria*, p.107.
105. Ibid., 13/10/48.
106. Leopold to Victoria, 3/6/53, Benson and Esher (eds), *The Letters of Queen Victoria*, vol. 2, p.544.
107. Queen Victoria's Journals 26/2/53.
108. Marshall, *Victoria*, pp.104, 106.
109. Queen Victoria's Journals 22/12/51.
110. Ibid., 3/3/52.
111. Ibid., 18/3/53.
112. Ibid., 15/1/58.
113. Porter, *Plots and Paranoia*, pp.91–92; St Aubyn, *Queen Victoria*, p.304.
114. Queen Victoria's Journals 20/2/58, 28/2/58.
115. Ibid., 28/1/58.
116. Porter, *Plots and Paranoia*, p.92.
117. Marshall, *Victoria*, p.117.
118. Queen Victoria's Journals 20/2/58.
119. Ibid., 19/2/58.
120. Malmesbury to Victoria, 7/3/58, Benson and Esher (eds), *The Letters of Queen Victoria*, vol. 3 p.346.

Chapter 4

1. Queen Victoria's Journals 28/4/66.
2. Ibid., 7/8/53.
3. Victoria to Clarendon, 24/53, Benson and Esher (eds), *The Letters of Queen Victoria*, vol. 2, p.549.
4. Weintraub, *Victoria*, pp.235–6.
5. Queen Victoria's Journals 9/10/53.
6. Andrew, *Secret Service*, pp.8–9; Wade, *Spies in the Empire*, p.69.
7. Hibbert, *Queen Victoria*, p.222; Weintraub, *Victoria*, pp.232–4.
8. Queen Victoria's Journals 4/1/54.
9. Ibid., 9/1/54.
10. Weintraub, *Victoria*, p.235.
11. Queen Victoria's Journals 21/1/54, 23/1/54.
12. Weintraub, *Uncrowned King*, pp.296–8. See also Weintraub, *Victoria*, pp.232–4.
13. Hibbert, *Queen Victoria*, p.223.

14. Weintraub, *Uncrowned King*, pp.6–18.
15. Andrew, *The Secret World*, p.402.
16. Quoted in Hibbert, *Queen Victoria*, p.224.
17. Andrew, *The Secret World*, p.402.
18. Judd, *The Crimean War*, p.95.
19. Weintraub, *Victoria*, p.242.
20. Queen Victoria's Journals 29/3/54.
21. Harris, *British Military Intelligence in the Crimean War*, pp.234–58.
22. Queen Victoria's Journals 2/8/54.
23. ODNB: Cattley, Charles Robert.
24. Andrew, *The Secret World*, pp.404–5; ODNB: Cattley, Charles Robert.
25. Queen Victoria's Journals 27/7/55; Harris, *British Military Intelligence in the Crimean War*, p.69.
26. Victoria to Panmure, 30/7/55, Benson and Esher (eds), *The Letters of Queen Victoria*, vol. 3, p.170.
27. Bartley, *Queen Victoria*, pp.145–75.
28. Hibbert, *Queen Victoria*, p.225.
29. Queen Victoria's Journals 18/4/55.
30. Weintraub, *Victoria*, p.246.
31. Panmure to Simpson, 12/9/55, Benson and Esher (eds), *The Letters of Queen Victoria*, vol. 3, p.181.
32. Queen Victoria's Journals 17/1/56.
33. Weintraub, *Victoria*, p.255.
34. Queen Victoria's Journals 27/2/56.
35. Ibid., 30/3/56.
36. Rath, *The Crimean War*, pp.194–6.
37. Weintraub, *Uncrowned King*, pp.314–6, 325.
38. Queen Victoria's Journals 13/3/54.
39. Sinclair, *The Other Victoria*, pp.50–52.
40. Pakula, *An Uncommon Woman*, p.106.
41. Ibid., p.197.
42. Ibid., pp.354–5.
43. Kollander, 'Empress Frederick', p.53.
44. Sinclair, *The Other Victoria*, pp.82–7.
45. Vicky to Victoria, 8/6/63, Buckle (ed.), *The Letters of Queen Victoria, 1862–1878*, vol. 1, p.87.
46. Vicky to Victoria, 21/6/63, ibid., p.92.
47. Hardie, *Political Influence of Queen Victoria*, p.146; Victoria to Vicky, 27/1/64, Buckle (ed.), The *Letters of Queen Victoria, 1862–1878*, vol. 1, p.153; Victoria to Granville, 27/1/64, Bourne, *The Foreign Policy of Victorian England*, p.373.
48. Mosse, 'Queen Victoria and Her Ministers in the Schleswig-Holstein Crisis', p.273.
49. For examples see Queen Victoria's Journals 8/2/64, 11/2/64.
50. Sinclair, *The Other Victoria*, p.93.
51. Andrew, *Secret Service*, p.4.
52. Casey, *The Double Life of Laurence Oliphant*, p.88.
53. Queen Victoria's Journals 28/2/64.
54. Vicky to Victoria, 13/4/64, Buckle (ed.), *The Letters of Queen Victoria, 1862–1878*, vol. 1, pp.170–71.
55. Victoria to Russell, 19/4/64, ibid., vol. 1, p.174.
56. Vicky to Victoria, 26/5/64, Ponsonby (ed.), *Letters of Empress Frederick*, pp.54–5.
57. Queen Victoria's Journals 20/6/64.
58. Mosse, 'Queen Victoria and Her Ministers in the Schleswig-Holstein Crisis', pp.263–77.
59. Ibid., pp.278–9.
60. Hardie, *The Political Influence of Queen Victoria*, pp.152, 157.
61. Steinberg, *Bismarck*, p.430.
62. Mosse, 'The Crown and Foreign Policy', p.206.
63. Sinclair, *The Other Victoria*, pp.106–7.
64. Mosse, 'The Crown and Foreign Policy', p.214.

65. Duchess of Coburg to Victoria, 28/3/66, Buckle (ed.), *The Letters of Queen Victoria, 1862–1878*, vol. 1, p.812.

66. Sinclair, *The Other Victoria*, pp.106–7.

67. Ibid., p.107; Vicky to Victoria, 20/3/66, Buckle (ed.), *The Letters of Queen Victoria, 1862–1878*, vol. 1, p.305.

68. Sinclair, *The Other Victoria*, pp.106–7.

69. Queen Victoria's Journals 4/2/63.

70. Mosse, 'The Crown and Foreign Policy', p.212.

71. Sinclair, *The Other Victoria*, pp.108–9.

72. Queen Victoria's Journals 9/4/66.

73. Loftus to Grey, 14/4/66, Buckle (ed.), *The Letters of Queen Victoria, 1862–1878*, vol. 2, p.318.

74. Queen Victoria's Journals 1–2/4/66, 8/4/66, 18/4/66, 23/4/66; Sinclair, *The Other Victoria*, pp.108–9.

75. Queen Victoria's Journals 28/4/66.

76. Ibid., 23/4/66.

77. Ibid., 15/5/66.

78. Otte, *The Foreign Office Mind*, p.37.

79. Mosse, 'The Crown and Foreign Policy', pp.208–9, 215–6, 222.

80. Victoria to Stanley, 7/8/66, Buckle (ed.), *The Letters of Queen Victoria, 1862–1878*, vol. 2, p.364.

81. Otte, *The Foreign Office Mind*, p.39.

82. Sinclair, *The Other Victoria*, p.129.

83. Howard, *The Franco-Prussian War*, p.50.

84. Vicky to Victoria, 12/3/70, Buckle (ed.), *The Letters of Queen Victoria, 1862–1878*, vol. 2, p.10; Millman, *British Policy and the Coming of the Franco-Prussian War*, p.170.

85. Pakula, *An Uncommon Woman*, p.266.

86. Memorandum by Crown Prince of Prussia (undated, July 1870), Buckle (ed.), *The Letters of Queen Victoria, 1862–1878*, vol. 2 p.10.

87. Queen Victoria's Journals 13/7/70.

88. Millman, *British Policy and the Franco-Prussian War*, p.190.

89. Sinclair, *The Other Victoria*, pp.140–43; Howard, *The Franco-Prussian War*, p.53.

90. Pakula, *An Uncommon Woman*, p.269.

91. Bourne, *The Foreign Policy of Victorian England*, p.120.

92. Queen Victoria's Journals 15/7/70, 10/7/70.

93. Clarendon to Victoria, 31/3/66, Buckle (ed.), *The Letters of Queen Victoria, 1862–1878*, vol. 1, p.314.

94. Granville to Victoria, 15/7/70, ibid., vol. 2, p.35.

95. Vicky to Victoria, 18/7/70, ibid., p.43.

96. Millman, *British Policy and the Franco-Prussian War*, p.201.

97. Ibid.; Seton-Watson, *Britain in Europe*, p.32.

98. Queen Victoria's Journals 26/7/70.

99. Millman, *British Policy and the Franco-Prussian War*, p.202.

100. Pakula, *An Uncommon Woman*, p.271.

101. Ponsonby to Victoria, 12/10/70, Buckle (ed.), *The Letters of Queen Victoria, 1862–1878*, vol. 2, p.75; Hardie, *Political Influence of Queen Victoria*, p.158.

102. Sinclair, *The Other Victoria*, p.147.

103. Queen Victoria's Journals 31/7/70.

104. Sinclair, *The Other Victoria*, pp.150–1.

105. Evans, *Memoirs*, pp.169–98.
106. Queen Victoria's Journals 23/9/70.
107. Burgoyne to Ponsonby, 15/9/70, Buckle (ed.), *The Letters of Queen Victoria, 1862–1878*, vol. 2, pp.68–70; see also Evans, *Memoirs*.
108. Burgoyne to Ponsonby, 15/9/70, ibid., pp.68–70; Queen Victoria's Journals 23/9/70.
109. Burgoyne to Ponsonby, 15/9/70, Buckle (ed.), *The Letters of Queen Victoria, 1862–1878*, vol. 2, pp.68–70.
110. Queen Victoria's Journals 14/8/84.
111. Ibid., 30/1/90.
112. Sinclair, *The Other Victoria*, p.168.
113. St Aubyn, *Queen Victoria*, p.462.
114. Erickson, *Her Little Majesty*, p.153.
115. Sinclair, *The Other Victoria*, p.202.
116. Pakula, *An Uncommon Woman*, p.398, see also pp.390–91.
117. Hibbert, *Queen Victoria*, p.389.
118. Sinclair, *The Other Victoria*, pp.220–21.
119. Pakula, *An Uncommon Woman*, p.599.
120. Vicky to Victoria, 24/8/89, Ponsonby (ed.), *Letters of the Empress Frederick*, pp.384–5.
121. Cathcart, *Anne and the Princesses Royal*, p.88.
122. Clay, *King, Kaiser, Tsar*, p.79.

Chapter 5

1. Queen Victoria's Journal 21/1/93.
2. Wade, *Spies in the Empire*, pp.2–15.
3. Farwell, *Queen Victoria's Little Wars*, p.1.
4. Andrew, *The Secret World*, pp.407–10.
5. Weintraub, *Queen Victoria*, p.258; Queen Victoria's Journal 1/7/57.
6. Andrew, *Secret Service*, p.5.
7. ODNB: Macnaghten, William.

8. Sale, *A Journal of the Disasters in Afghanistan*, pp.154–6.
9. Queen Victoria's Journal 10/3/42, 11/3/42.
10. Cowles, *The Romanovs*; Van der Kiste, *John Alfred*; VIC/MAIN/H/41 131 Ponsonby to HM 19/1/74; Queen Victoria's Journal 13/3/81.
11. RA VIC/MAIN/H/42, 82. HM to Lord Derby 11/6/77 and 83. Derby to HM 12/6/77.
12. Victoria to Romanian ambassador 3/3/79, available at https://www.raabcollection.com/queen-victoria-autograph/queen-victoria-signed-height-victorian-diplomacy-during-great-game-queen
13. RA VIC/MAIN/H/46 103. Sir Frank Lascelles to HM 30/1/95. His observations, addressed directly to the queen, can be found in TNA FO800/17.
14. Andrew, *Secret Service*, p.11.
15. See, for example, Queen Victoria's Journal 15/12/91.
16. Ferris, *Intelligence and Strategy*, p.15.
17. Barry, *War for the East*, p.116.
18. Ferris, 'Lord Salisbury', p.25.
19. Ibid., p.9.
20. Ibid., p.24.
21. Burnaby, Frederick Gustavus, IMDB.
22. Hopkirk, *The Great Game*, pp.376–7.
23. Ibid., pp.378–9.
24. Ponsonby (ed.), Henry Ponsonby, pp.170–71.
25. ODNB: Burnaby, Frederick.
26. Hibbert, *Queen Victoria*, p.362.
27. Ponsonby, untitled memorandum, 8/7/76; Disraeli to Victoria, 14/7/76, Buckle (ed.), *The Letters of Queen Victoria, 1862–1878*, vol. 2, pp.470–72.

28. Victoria, untitled memorandum, 7/9/77, Buckle (ed.), *The Letters of Queen Victoria, 1862–1878*, vol. 2, p.567; see also Hardie, *Political Influence of Queen Victoria*, p.161.

29. Quoted in Hibbert, *Queen Victoria*, p.362.

30. Weintraub, *Queen Victoria*, p.422.

31. Isba, *Gladstone and Women*, pp.171–3; see also Baylen, 'Madame Olga Novikov', pp.255–71.

32. Weintraub, *Queen Victoria*, p.424.

33. Hopkirk, *The Great Game*, pp.378–9.

34. Ponsonby, 30/8/77, Ponsonby (ed.), *Henry Ponsonby*, pp.165–6.

35. Hibbert, *Queen Victoria*, p.36; Hopkirk, *The Great Game*, pp.378–9.

36. Disraeli to Victoria, 2/5/77, Buckle (ed.), *The Letters of Queen Victoria, 1862–1878*, vol. 2, p.535; Victoria to Derby, 8/6/77, Derby to Victoria, 11/6/77, ibid., pp.539–41.

37. Prince of Wales to Victoria, 1/8/77, ibid., p.559.

38. Wellesley to Victoria, 30/8/77, ibid., pp.565–6.

39. Hardie, *Political Influence of Queen Victoria*, p.162.

40. Queen Victoria's Journal 8/8/77.

41. Ibid., 29/7/77, 30/7/77.

42. Charmley and Davey, 'The Invisible Politician', p.28.

43. Bourne, *The Foreign Policy of Victorian England*, p.131.

44. Weintraub, *Queen Victoria*, p.428.

45. Charmley and Davey, 'The Invisible Politician', pp.30–32.

46. Ponsonby, 16/8/77, Ponsonby (ed.), *Henry Ponsonby*, p.164.

47. Charmley and Davey, 'The Invisible Politician', pp.30–32.

48. Hibbert, *Queen Victoria*, p.363.

49. Thanks to Barbara Emerson for pointing this out.

50. Ferris, 'Lord Salisbury', p.24.

51. Barry, *The War for the East*, pp.114–17; Wellesley, *Recollections of a Soldier-Diplomat*, pp.133–47.

52. Ferris, 'Lord Salisbury', p.24.

53. Queen Victoria's Journal 12/2/78.

54. Ibid., 15/2/78.

55. Ibid., 20/2/78.

56. Ibid., 21/3/78.

57. Hopkirk, *The Great Game*, p.380.

58. Ibid., pp.380–81.

59. Queen Victoria's Journal 15/9/78, 19/9/78, 12/10/78, 24/10/78.

60. Ibid., 14/9/78.

61. Johnson, *Spying for Empire*, p.146.

62. Queen Victoria's Journal 19/8/78.

63. Ibid., 14/9/78.

64. Hopkirk, *The Great Game*, p.386.

65. Queen Victoria's Journal 6/9/79.

66. Victoria to Disraeli, 6/9/79, Buckle (ed.), *The Letters of Queen Victoria, 1862–1878*, vol. 3, p.42.

67. Victoria to Ponsonby, 30/5/82, ibid., p.301.

68. Northbrook to Victoria, 3/7/82, ibid., pp.304–5.

69. Weintraub, *Queen Victoria*, p.453; Farwell, *Queen Victoria's Little Wars*, p.254.

70. Queen Victoria's Journal 11/8/82.

71. Victoria to Granville, 26/7/82, Buckle (ed.), *The Letters of Queen Victoria, 1862–1878*, vol. 3, p.313.

72. Farwell, *Queen Victoria's Little Wars*, pp.253–69.

73. ODNB: Wolseley, Garnet.

74. ODNB: Alison, Sir Archibald.

75. Queen Victoria's Journal 31/8/82, Buckle (ed.), *The Letters of Queen Victoria, 1862–1885*, vol. 3, p.322.

76. Childers to Victoria, 6/8/82, ibid., p.322.

77. Ponsonby to Wolseley, 25/8/82, Ponsonby (ed.), *Henry Ponsonby*, p.224.

78. Queen Victoria's Journal 11/9/82; Farwell, *Queen Victoria's Little Wars*, pp.253–69.

79. Victoria to Gladstone, 21/9/82, Buckle (ed.), *The Letters of Queen Victoria, 1862–1878*, vol. 3, p.338.

80. Fielding, 'Major General Sir Alexander Bruce Tulloch', http://www.mhhv.org.au/?p=3495

81. Wade, *Spies in the Empire*, pp.116–18.

82. Queen Victoria's Journal 11/12/82.

83. RA VIC/MAIN/H/45 20, Ponsonby to Lord Granville and Lord Kimberley, 17/3/85.

84. Farwell, *Queen Victoria's Little Wars*, p.316.

85. RA VIC/MAIN/Q/21 633, Ponsonby to Granville 15/6/82.

86. RA VIC/MAIN/Q/21 633, Granville to HM 28/7/82.

87. Andrew, *Secret Service*, pp.5–6.

88. Frankland, *Witness of a Century*, pp.198–203; ODNB: Wolseley, Garnet.

89. Queen Victoria's Journal 22/8/86.

90. Ibid., 22–24/8/86.

91. Ibid., 27/8–1/9/86.

92. Ibid., 1/9/86.

93. Rekun, *How Russia Lost Bulgaria*, p.117.

94. Queen Victoria's Journal 2/9/86. The government entered a secret agreement with Reuters in 1894, paying £500 from the secret service fund for access to confidential reports. See West, *A–Z of British Intelligence*, p.447.

95. Queen Victoria's Journal 4/9/86.

96. Jelavich, *Tsarist Russia and Balkan Nationalism*, pp. 233–56.

97. Basu, *Victoria and Abdul*, pp.57–9.

98. Hibbert, *Queen Victoria*, pp.447–8; Taylor, *Empress*, p.254; Basu, *Victoria and Abdul*, p.188.

99. Basu, *Victoria and Abdul*, pp.284, 203.

100. Hibbert, *Queen Victoria*, pp.447–8; Taylor, *Empress*, p.254; Basu, *Victoria and Abdul*, p.188.

101. Quoted in Hibbert, *Queen Victoria*, p.449.

102. Basu, *Victoria and Abdul*, pp.191, 224, 227.

103. Baird, *Victoria*, pp.454–5.

104. Miles, *Empress*, p.253; Basu, *Victoria and Abdul*, pp.209–10.

105. Taylor, *Empress*, p.253.

106. Ibid., pp.256–7.

107. Salisbury to Victoria, 16/10/95, Buckle (ed.), *The Letters of Queen Victoria*, series 3, vol. 2, p.567.

108. Baird, *Victoria*, p.456.

109. Taylor, *Empress*, pp.256–7.

110. Reid, *Ask Sir James*, pp.151–5.

111. Hibbert, *Queen Victoria*, pp.451–3; Datta Ray, 'The Queen and Karim', 27/10/17 https://openthemagazine.com/essay/the-queen-karim/

112. Baird, *Victoria*, p.455.

113. Basu, *Victoria and Abdul*, p.228.

114. Taylor, *Empress*, p.254.

115. Ben Leach, 'The lost diary of Queen Victoria's final companion', *Telegraph*, 26 February 2011.

Chapter 6

1. Salisbury to Victoria, 20/10/98, Buckle (ed.), *The Letters of Queen Victoria*, series 3, vol. 3, pp.294–5.

2. Yarmolinsky, *Road to Revolution*, pp.272–87; Radzinsky, *Alexander II*, pp.417–19.

3. Yarmolinsky, *Road to Revolution*, pp.286–87, Radzinsky, *Alexander II*, pp.414–5.

4. Ponsonby (ed.), *Henry Ponsonby*, p.389.

5. Hughes, 'British Opinion and Russian Terrorism in the 1880s', p.261.

6. RA VIC/MAIN/H/43 74. Duke of Edinburgh to HM 21/3/81.

7. RA VIC/MAIN/H/44 7. Translation of Grand Duke of Hesse to HM 4/4/81.

8. Queen Victoria's Journal 1/4/81.

9. RA VIC/MAIN/H/44 23. H Ponsonby to HM 11/4/81; 24. QV to Ponsonby 11/4/81.

10. Porter, *Plots and Paranoia*, p.102.

11. RA VIC/MAIN/H/44 27. Ponsonby to Granville 12/4/81.

12. Queen Victoria's Journal 30/3/81.

13. Wilson and Adams, *Special Branch*, pp.40–41; see also RA VIC/MAIN/H/43.

14. RA VIC/MAIN/H/43 107. Ponsonby to Granville 27/3/81.

15. RA VIC/MAIN/H/43 108. Granville to Ponsonby 30/3/81.

16. Murphy, *Shooting Victoria*, pp.463–7.

17. St Aubyn, *Queen Victoria*, p.373.

18. Queen Victoria's Journal 4/3/68.

19. Campbell, *Fenian Fire*, p.11.

20. Andrew, *Secret Service*, p.17.

21. Ponsonby to Victoria, 16/3/83, Buckle (ed.), *The Letters of Queen Victoria*, series 2, vol. 3, pp.416–7.

22. Harcourt to Victoria, 17/3/83, Buckle (ed.), *The Letters of Queen Victoria*, series 2, vol. 3, p.417.

23. For example see Queen Victoria's Journal 13/10/83.

24. Campbell, *Fenian Fire*, p.11.

25. Queen Victoria's Journal 14/10/84.

26. Wilson and Adams, *Special Branch*, p.74.

27. Harcourt to Ponsonby, 18/6/82, Ponsonby (ed.), *Henry Ponsonby*, pp.270–71.

28. Campbell, *Fenian Fire*, p.11.

29. Harcourt to Victoria, 29/2/84, Buckle (ed.), *The Letters of Queen Victoria*, series 2, vol. 3, pp.480–81.

30. Andrew, *Secret Service*, p.18.

31. Harcourt to Victoria, 29/2/84, Buckle (ed.), *The Letters of Queen Victoria*, series 2, vol. 3, pp.481.

32. Porter, *Plots and Paranoia*, pp.108–9.

33. Victoria to Gladstone, 4/5/82, Buckle (ed.), *The Letters of Queen Victoria*, series 2, vol. 3, p.281.

34. Victoria to Granville, 7/5/82, Buckle(ed.), *The Letters of Queen Victoria*, series 2, vol. 3, p.285.

35. Wilson and Adams, *Special Branch*, pp.21–22; Queen Victoria's Journal 13/4/83.

36. Wilson and Adams, *Special Branch*, p.22.

37. Owen McGee, 'Francis Frederick McGee', Dictionary of Irish Biography.

38. Campbell, *Fenian Fire*, pp.176–7, 293.

39. Ibid., pp. 360, 378, 234; Kenna, 'The Victorian War on Terror'.

40. Victoria to Harcourt, 18/2/83, Buckle (ed.), *The Letters of Queen Victoria*, series 2, vol. 3, p.411.

41. Hibbert, *Queen Victoria*, p.380.

42. Murphy, *Shooting Victoria*, p.495.

43. Andrew, *Secret Service*, p.19; Wilson and Adams, *Special Branch*, p.36.

44. Kenna, 'The Victorian War on Terror'.

45. Campbell, *Fenian Fire*, pp.240–1.

46. Queen Victoria's Journal 21/6/87.

47. Murphy, *Shooting Victoria*, p.499.

48. Campbell, *Fenian Fire*, pp.295, 300.

49. Wilson and Adams, *Special Branch*, p.36.

50. Queen Victoria's Journal 19/6/87.

51. Ibid., 28/6/82.

52. Jensen, 'The International Campaign against Anarchist Terrorism', pp.91, 95.

53. Andrew, *Secret Service*, pp.19–20; Jensen, 'The International Campaign against Anarchist Terrorism', p.93.

54. Asquith to Victoria, 22/2/84, Buckle (ed.), *The Letters of Queen Victoria*, series 3, vol. 3, pp.360–61.

55. Queen Victoria's Journal 17/2/94.

56. Ibid., 25/6/94.

57. Victoria to Rosebery, 13/7/94, Rosebery to Victoria, 13/7/94, Buckle (ed.), *The Letters of Queen Victoria*, series 3, vol. 2, pp.414–5; Collyer, 'Secret Agents', p.287.

58. Ibid.

59. Queen Victoria's Journal 11/9/98.

60. Ibid., 23/9/98.

61. Jensen, 'The International Anti-Anarchist Conference and the Origins of Interpol', pp.325–6.

62. Salisbury to Victoria, 20/10/98, Buckle (ed.), *The Letters of Queen Victoria*, series 3, vol. 3, pp.294–5.

63. Jensen, 'The Battle against Anarchist Terrorism', pp.151–152.

64. Jensen, 'The International Anti-Anarchist Conference and the Origins of Interpol', pp.327–8; Deflem, 'Wild Beasts Without Nationality', pp.275–81.

65. Jensen, 'The International Campaign Against Anarchist Terrorism', p.329; How, *The Life of Sir Howard Vincent*, pp.303–12.

66. Wilson and Adams, *Special Branch*, pp. 55–73; Murphy, *Shooting Victoria*, p.497.

67. Queen Victoria's Journal 6/2/86.

Chapter 7

1. Quoted in Markovich, *British Perceptions of Serbia and the Balkans*, p.76.

2. Magnus, *King Edward the Seventh*, p.81.

3. Granville to Ponsonby, 26/12/71, Ponsonby (ed.), *Henry Ponsonby*, p.102.

4. Cave Brown, 'C', p.15; Dorril, *MI6*, p.3.

5. Hibbert, *Edward VII*, pp.235–6; Andrew, *The Secret World*, p.434.

6. Geraghty, *The Bullet-Catchers*, p.51.

7. Hibbert, *Edward VII*, p.127.

8. St Aubyn, *Edward VII*, pp.153–4.

9. St Aubyn, *Edward VII*, p.198.

10. Frankland, *Witness of a Century*, pp.185–6;

11. Ponsonby (ed.), *Henry Ponsonby*, p.104; Magnus, *King Edward the Seventh*, p.167.

12. Magnus, *King Edward the Seventh*, pp.177, 190; St Aubyn, *Edward VII*, p.204.

13. Ponsonby (ed.), *Henry Ponsonby*, p.104.

14. Magnus, *King Edward the Seventh*, p.237; St Aubyn, *Edward VII*, pp.204, 205.

15. McLean, *Royalty and Diplomacy in Europe*, pp.182–3; Hibbert, *Edward VII*, p.248; Ridley, *Bertie*, p.474; Magnus, *King Edward the Seventh*, p.307; Sinclair, *The Other Victoria*, pp.4, 247.

16. Lee, *King Edward VII*, pp.76–7, 81; Heffer, *Power and Place*, pp.118–20.

17. Moran, *Classified*, p.39.

18. Ibid., p.39.

19. Lee, *King Edward VII*, pp.88–9; on the peace negotiations see Judd and Sturridge, *The Boer War*, pp.269–280.

20. St Aubyn, *Edward VII*, p.459; ODNB: Brett, Reginald Baliol, second Viscount Esher; Lee, *King Edward VII*, p.92; Heffer, *Power and Place*, p.121.

21. Frankland, *Witness of a Century*, pp.229–31; ODNB: Brett,

Reginald Baliol, second Viscount Esher.

22. Esher to Edward, 1/11/02, Brett (ed.), *Journals and Letters of Reginald Viscount Esher*, vol. 1, p.360.

23. Esher to Edward, 30/4/03, ibid., p.399.

24. Esher to Edward, 11/3/03, ibid., pp.387-8; Fergusson, *British Military Intelligence*, p.118.

25. St Aubyn, *Edward VII*, pp.462, 465.

26. Black, 'The Victorian Information Society', pp.95-104.

27. Fergusson, *British Military Intelligence*, pp.119-20; Davies, *Intelligence and Government in Britain and the United States*, pp.77-8; Kennedy, 'Great Britain Beyond 1914', p.176.

28. Heffer, *Power and Place*, p.131; Magnus, *King Edward the Seventh*, p.277; Hibbert, *Edward VII*, pp.208-9; McLean, *Royalty and Diplomacy in Europe*, p.181.

29. Fromkin, *The King and the Cowboy*, p.117; MacMillan, *The War that Ended Peace*, pp.114-15; St Aubyn, *Edward VII*, p.311; Hibbert, *Edward VII*, pp.207-8; Heffer, *Power and Place*, p.131.

30. St Aubyn, *Edward VII*, pp.321-2; Ponsonby, *Recollections of Three Reigns*, p.154.

31. St Aubyn, *Edward VII*, p.321.

32. McLean, *Royalty and Diplomacy in Europe*, p.144; St Aubyn, *Edward VII*, p.321.

33. Ponsonby, *Recollections of Three Reigns*, p.169; McLean, *Royalty and Diplomacy in Europe*, p.145; Glencross, *The State Visits of Edward VII*, p.100.

34. Glencross, *The State Visits of Edward VII*, p.72.

35. See Glencross, *The State Visits of Edward VII*; Ridley, *Bertie*, p.380.

36. St Aubyn, *Edward VII*, p.335.

37. McLean, *Royalty and Diplomacy in Europe*, p.150.

38. Verrier, *Through the Looking Glass*, p.19; Hopkirk, *The Great Game*, pp.507-9, 517.

39. Soroka, *Britain, Russia and the Road to the First World War*, p.80.

40. Seligman, 'Prince Louis of Battenberg', p.168.

41. McLean, *Royalty and Diplomacy in Europe*, pp.159-60.

42. Quoted in Lee, *King Edward VII*, p.355.

43. McLean, *Royalty and Diplomacy in Europe*, p.157; Heffer, *Power and Place*, p.241

44. RA: VIC/MAIN/X/20 Cecil Spring Rice to Knollys 31/10/05; Ridley, *Bertie*, p.399.

45. ODNB: Wallace, Sir Donald Mackenzie.

46. St Aubyn, *Edward VII*, p.357.

47. Kaiser Wilhelm to Tsar Nicholas, 22/8/05, *Between Two Emperors*, p.219.

48. Ibid.

49. Reynolds, *Summits*, p.23.

50. FO800/103 Grey to Knollys, 28/3/06.

51. MacMillan, *The War that Ended Peace*, pp.114-15.

52. Glencross, *The State Visits of Edward VII*, p.171.

53. Ponsonby, *Recollections of Three Reigns*, p.195.

54. McLean, *Royalty and Diplomacy in Europe*, p.167; Heffer, *Power and Place*, p.255.

55. McKee, 'British Perceptions', p.231; Andrew and Green, *Stars and Spies*, pp.166-7.

56. Andrew, *Secret Service*, p.6.

57. Lee, *King Edward VII*, pp.235, 350.

58. Ridley, *Bertie*, p.432.

59. Lee, *King Edward VII*, pp.321–5, 544; Salmon, *Scandinavia and the Great Powers*, pp.61, 69.

60. Lee, *King Edward VII*, pp.129–30.

61. RA: VIC/MAIN/X/21 35, 37, 38 Correspondence between Sir A. Davidson and Foreign Office, 22–23/9/06.

62. St Aubyn, *Edward VII*, p.437.

63. MacMillan, *The War that Ended Peace*, p.113.

64. St Aubyn, *Edward VII*, p.44; Heffer, *Power and Place*, p.256.

65. Seligmann, *Spies in Uniform*, p.223; Heffer, *Power and Place*, pp.256–7.

66. MacMillan, *The War that Ended Peace*, pp.111–12.

67. Andrew, *Secret Service*, p.49.

68. St Aubyn, *Edward VII*, p.349; Ponsonby, *Recollections of Three Reigns*, p.248.

69. Ponsonby, *Recollections of Three Reigns*, p.248.

70. St Aubyn, *Edward VII*, p.349.

71. Ibid., p.343.

72. Lee, *King Edward VII*, p.678.

73. Quoted in Heffer, *Power and Place*, p.270.

74. Lee, *King Edward VII*, p.681.

75. Ibid.

76. Ridley, *Bertie*, p.432.

77. Heffer, *Power and Place*, p.271.

78. Kennedy, 'Great Britain Beyond 1914', pp.179–80, 183.

79. Jeffery, *MI6*, pp.3, 5; Andrew, *Defence of the Realm*, pp.6–7.

80. Esher journals, 30/3/09, Brett (ed.), *Journals and Letters of Reginald Viscount Esher*, vol. 2, p.379.

81. Andrew, *Defence of the Realm*, pp.18–19.

82. St Aubyn, *Edward VII*, p.376.

83. McLean, *Royalty and Diplomacy in Europe*, p.174.

84. Humphries, 'Perfectly Secret and Perfectly Democratic', pp.1156–79.

85. Higgins, 'How Was Haldane Able to Transform the Army?', p.21; MacMillan, *The War that Ended Peace*, pp.114–15.

86. Jeffery, *MI6*, pp.6–7.

87. Magnus, *King Edward the Seventh*, p.277.

88. Ponsonby, *Recollections of Three Reigns*, p.127.

89. McLean, *Royalty and Diplomacy in Europe*, p.177.

90. Ibid., pp.181–2.

91. FO800/103 Edward to Grey, 1/9/09; See also RA: VIC/MAIN/X/23 9 Edward to Grey 28/8/09, 10. Lt-Col F Ponsonby to Sir F Elliot 10/8/09, 15. Sir F Elliot (Athens) to Davidson 2/10/09 16, Edward to Elliot 5/10/09, and 17. Elliot to Ponsonby 19/10/09.

92. Geraghty, *The Bullet-Catchers*, p.53.

93. Porter, *Plots and Paranoia*, p.128; Crowdy, *The Enemy Within*, pp.202–3.

Chapter 8

1. Rose, *George V*, p.165.

2. Sanabria, *Republicanism and Anticlerical Nationalism in Spain*, pp.101–22.

3. George V, diary, 31/5/06, RA, quoted in Rose, *George V*, p.68.

4. Sinclair, *Two Georges*, pp.67–71.

5. 'When Dublin did a roaring trade in lions', *Irish Times*, 09/6/16.

6. McLean, *Royalty and Diplomacy in Europe*, p.192.

7. Rose, *George V*, p.167.

8. Navy List, Royal Naval College Greenwich, here Mansfield Cumming is listed by his previous

name 'Mansfield G Smith', 311, Jeffery, *MI6*, p.9.

9. Judd, *Quest for 'C'*, pp.17–18.

10. Mensdorff to Aehrenthal, 02/9/10, quoted in Rose, *George V*, p.165.

11. 'When Dublin did a roaring trade in lions', *Irish Times*, 09/6/16.

12. Judd, *The Quest for C*, p.239.

13. McLean, *Royalty and Diplomacy in Europe*, pp.192–4.

14. Lady Wigram diary 1926, quoted in Rose, *George V*, p.166.

15. King George V to Nicky, Marlborough House, 24/1/10, Maylunas and Mironenko, *A Lifelong Passion*, p.329.

16. King George V to Nicky, Marlborough House, 14/5/10, ibid., p.329.

17. King George V to Nicky, Buckingham Palace, 02/3/11, ibid., p.342.

18. Beckett, 'November 1913'.

19. Sulzberger, *The Fall of Eagles*, pp.202–3.

20. Hastings, *Catastrophe*, p.xxix.

21. Otte, *The Foreign Office Mind*, p.461; Clay, *King, Kaiser, Tsar*, p.309.

22. RA: GV/PRIV/GVD/1914, 01/8/14, quoted in Heffer, *Staring at God*, p.61.

23. Nicholas to King George V (via Buchanan), 02/8/14, Maylunas and Mironenko, *A Lifelong Passion*, pp.146–7.

24. Clay, *King, Kaiser, Tsar*, p.313.

25. Heffer, *Staring at God*, pp.68–9, 74, 87.

26. Boghardt, *Spies of the Kaiser*, pp.62–3; Andrew, *The Defence of the Realm*, pp.50, 52.

27. Seymour, *Noble Endeavours*, pp.168–79; Clay, *King, Kaiser, Tsar*, p.307.

28. Lambton, *The Mountbattens*, p.215.

29. Asquith to Venetia Stanley, 24/10/14, Brock and Brock (eds), *Asquith Letters*, p.285.

30. Heffer, *Staring at God*, p.432.

31. Rose, *George V*, p.174.

32. Bennett, *Churchill's Man of Mystery*, p.27.

33. ODNB: Wigram, Clive; Rose, *George V*, p.227.

34. Douglas-Home and Kelly (eds), *Dignified and Efficient*, p.40.

35. Ibid., p.43.

36. Glencross, 'A Cause of Tension?', p.160; Douglas-Home and Kelly, *Dignified and Efficient*, p.43.

37. Churchill, *In the Eye of the Storm*, pp.150–51.

38. Ibid., p.52.

39. Matthew Glencross, 'A Cause of Tension? The Leadership of King George V: Visiting the Western Front', Glencross and Rowbotham (eds), *Monarch and the Great War*, p.160; Douglas-Home and Kelly, *Dignified and Efficient*, p.43.

40. Churchill, *In the Eye of the Storm*, p.140; Douglas-Home and Kelly, *Dignified and Efficient*, p.46.

41. Diary entries for 14/3/16 and 19/5/16. Seabury Ashmead-Bartlett Papers, Privately held. We are grateful to Anthea Boylston and Celia Catchpole for permission to publish and to Jock Bruce for sharing the information with us.

42. Churchill, *In the Eye of the Storm*, pp.105–7, 181.

43. Ibid., pp.73, 7, 181.

44. Ibid., p.94–5.

45. Ferris, *Behind the Enigma*, pp.29–63; Stout, 'World War I', pp.378–94; Warner, *Rise and Fall*, pp.79–130.

46. Georgie to Nicky, 8 August 1915, Maylunas and Mironenko, *A Lifelong Passion*, p.432.

47. Ibid.
48. Ania Vyrubova, memoirs, ibid., p.513.
49. Buchanan, *My Mission to Russia*, pp.43–9.
50. RA: PS/GV/Q 1550/313 (draft) in Clay, *King, Kaiser, Tsar*, p.328.
51. RA: PS/GV/Q 1550/314 in ibid.
52. Mikhailovich, *Once a Grand Duke*, p.185.
53. Diary entry, 22/11/16, Stevenson, *Lloyd George: A Diary*, p.127.
54. Jeffery, *MI6*, pp.103–06.
55. Tom Kington, 'Recruited by MI5: the name's Mussolini. Benito Mussolini', *Guardian*, 13/10/09.
56. Milton, *Russian Roulette*, p.14.
57. Cullen, *Rasputin*, p.15; Hoare, *The Fourth Seal*, pp.67–8.
58. Ruud and Stepanov, *Fontanka 16*, pp.293–4.
59. Grand Duchess Xenia, diary, 25 & 26/1/12, Moscow State Archives, Maylunas and Mironenko, *A Lifelong Passion*, p.329.
60. NA FO 371/2093, Sir George Buchanan to Lord Grey, 14/5/14.
61. Carter, *Three Emperors*, p.411.
62. Ruud and Stepanov, *Fontanka 16*, pp.298–9.
63. Cook, *To Kill Rasputin*, pp.2–12; Smith, *Six*, pp.198–205.
64. Yusupov, memoirs, in Maylunas and Mironenko, *A Lifelong Passion*, p.385.
65. Sebag Montefiore, *Romanovs*, p.606.
66. Police Department Report, 'Rasputin', 18 February 1913, Moscow State Archives, Maylunas and Mironenko, *A Lifelong Passion*, p.353.
67. Milton, *Russian Roulette*, pp.17–18.
68. Ruud and Stepanov, *Fontanka 16*, p.312.
69. Milton, *Russian Roulette*, pp.24–5.
70. Judd, *Quest for C*, pp.432–3.
71. Youssoupoff, *Rasputin, passim*; Cullen, *Rasputin*, p.17.
72. Fuhrmann, *Rasputin*, pp.230–31.
73. Ibid., pp.606, 612; Smith, *Six*, p.205.
74. Mikailovich, *Once a Grand Duke*, p.279.
75. Buchanan, *My Mission to Russia*, pp.47–51.
76. Jeffery, *MI6*, pp.106–7.
77. Judd, *Quest for C*, p.436; Smith, *Six*, p.206.
78. Cullen, *Rasputin*, p.193.
79. McKee, 'British Perceptions of Tsar Nicholas II and Empress Alexandra Fedorovna 1894–1918', p.282.
80. Jeffery, *MI6*, pp.106–7.
81. PS/PSO/GV/C/Q/722/37 Sir John Hanbury-Williams (head of British military mission to high command of the Russian armed forces) to Arthur Bigge 7/1/17.
82. Clay, *King, Kaiser, Tsar*, p.333.
83. Cambridge University Library, Hardinge Papers, vol. 23, Sir George Buchanan to Sir Charles Hardinge, 20/1/17.
84. William Le Queux, *Rasputin, The Rascal Monk*, p.69; William Le Queux, *The Minister of Evil: The Secret History of Rasputin's Betrayal of Russia*, p.26.
85. Cook, *The Murder of the Romanovs*, p.62.
86. Yusupov, memoirs, Maylunas and Mironenko, *A Lifelong Passion*, p.353.

Chapter 9

1. RA: GV/GVD/1918 28 July 1918 in Clay, *King, Kaiser, Tsar*, p.345.
2. George, diary, 28/2/17, Maylunas and Mironenko, *A Lifelong Passion*, p.541.
3. George, diary, 02/3/17, ibid., p.546.
4. Hall, *To Free the Romanovs*, pp.48–9.

5. Journal No.1 of the Sitting of the provisional Government on the deportation of the Tsar's family and member of the imperial family abroad, 2 March 1917, Moscow State Archives, Maylunas and Mironenko, *A Lifelong Passion*, p.544.

6. FO 371/2998, 19/3/17.

7. Hanbury-Williams, *Emperor Nicholas II*, pp.169–70.

8. McKee, 'British Perceptions of Tsar Nicholas II', p.305.

9. Rappaport, *The Race to Save the Romanovs*, pp.55, 66.

10. Lord Stamfordham, note of meeting at Buckingham Palace, 9/3/17 (22 March), Maylunas and Mironenko, *A Lifelong Passion*, pp. 559–60. See also Rose, *George V*, p.211.

11. FO 371/3008.

12. RA: 22/4/17, PS/PSO/GV/C/1067/M/29, Heffer, *Staring at God*, p.587.

13. RA: PS/PSO/GV/C/M/1067/29 Stamfordham, 22/3/17.

14. Cf. Chapter 18.

15. Nicky, diary, 23/3/17, Tsarkoe Selo, Moscow State Archives, Maylunas and Mironenko, *A Lifelong Passion*, p.567.

16. Rappaport, *The Race to Save the Romanovs*, p.81.

17. Prochaska, 'George V and Republicanism', pp.32–3.

18. Entry for 23/1/77, Thorpe (ed.), *Who's In, Who's Out*, p.539; RA: PS/PSO/GV/C/1067/M/26, cited in Heffer, *Staring at God*, p.588.

19. RA: PS/PSO/GV/C/M/1067/39 Stamfordham to Balfour (FS), 30/3/17.

20. Prochaska, 'George V and Republicanism', pp.33–7.

21. RA: PS/PSO/GV/C/M/1067/26 Harry Verney (MP and 4th baronet) to Stamfordham, 21/3/17.

22. RA: PS/PSO/GV/C/M/1067/44 Balfour to Stamfordham, 2/4/17.

23. RA: PS/PSO/GV/C/M/1067/51 Stamfordham to Balfour, 6/4/17.

24. RA: PS/PSO/GV/C/M/1067/52 Stamfordham to Balfour, 6/4/17.

25. Prochaska, 'George V and Republicanism', p.30.

26. RA: PS/PSO/GV/C/M/1067/61 Stamfordham minute, 10/4/17.

27. Bennett, *Churchill's Man of Mystery*, p.27.

28. RA: PS/PSO/GV/C/M/1067/63 telegram from Buchanan, Petrograd, 15/4/17.

29. Cook, *The Murder of the Romanovs*, p.90.

30. FO 800/205, Balfour to Buchanan, 18/4/17, Balfour Papers.

31. FO 800/78, Sir Charles Hardinge to Sir Francis Lascelles, 17/4/17.

32. FO 800/205 23/4/17.

33. Hamilton, 'Addressing the Past', pp.117–18.

34. Markov, *Tsaritsa*, pp.79–89.

35. Mikailovich, *The Grand Duke*, p.334.

36. Kettle, *Russia and the Allies*, vol. 1, p.168.

37. West, *MI6*, pp.13–15.

38. Milton, *Russian Roulette*, pp.57–9, 73.

39. Heffer, *Staring at God*, pp.591–6.

40. Rappaport, *Four Sisters*, pp.329–38.

41. Day, *Trotsky's Favourite Spy*, p.48; HO 144/2158 Chicherin file, 1917.

42. CAB 23/4/295, 10/12/17.

43. Nansen, *Through Siberia the Land of the Future*, pp.132–49; McKee, 'British Perceptions', pp.315–16.

44. Hoare to Nansen, 28/11/21, File 8, Russian refugees, Constantinople,

1920–1924, Templewood papers, Cambridge University Library; Summers and Mangold, *File on the Tsar*, pp.249–52.

45. Rappaport, *The Race to Save the Romanovs*, pp.204–8.

46. Gilliard, *Thirteen years at the Russian Court*, p.256.

47. Cook, *The Murder of the Romanovs*, p.152.

48. John Crossland, 'British Spies in Plot to Save the Tsar', *Sunday Times*, 15/10/06.

49. Urbach, *Go-Betweens for Hitler*, p.335.

50. FO 371/3329/93852.

51. McGuire Mohr, *The Czech and Slovak Legion*, p.65; Pipes, *Russian Revolution*, p.640.

52. Lockhart, *Memoirs of a British Agent*, p.317.

53. Smith, *Six*, pp.228–31.

54. Jeffery, *MI6*, pp.134, 137.

55. Lockhart, *Memoirs of a British Agent*, p.323.

56. Reilly, *The Adventures of Britain's Master Spy*, pp.42–6.

57. Ibid.

58. Lockhart, *Memoirs of a British Agent*, p.317.

59. West, *MI6*, pp.16–17.

60. Hall, *To Free the Romanovs*, pp.152–3.

61. Radzinsky, *The Last Tsar*, pp.239–41.

62. Ibid., pp.341–3.

63. Kate Baklitskaya, 'Go East, Royal dog fled from Siberia into British exile, living in shadow of Windsor Castle', *Siberian Times*, 21/1/14.

64. FO 800/205, FORSINT the Intelligence co-ordinator for all British forces and Missions in Russia and Siberia, 28/8/18.

65. Hall, *To Free the Romanovs*, pp.183–5.

66. PS/PSO/GV/C/M/1344A/31 Stamfordham to Milner 1/9/18.

67. Hall, *To Free the Romanovs*, pp.183–5.

68. Ibid., pp.186–7.

69. FO 371/3977, Sir Basil Thomson, Director of Intelligence, 3/7/20, file 983, paper 208702; see also PRO 30/26/144.

70. FO 800/205, Sir Arthur Balfour to Lord Stamfordham, 23/7/18.

71. George, diary, 25/7/18, Maylunas and Mironenko, *A Lifelong Passion*, p.640.

72. Rappaport, *The Race to Save the Romanovs*, pp.268–9.

73. Rose, *King George V*, p.243.

74. Day, *Trotsky's Favourite Spy*, p.86.

75. Rappaport, *The Race to Save the Romanovs*, pp.272, 278.

76. Cook, *The Murder of the Romanovs*, p.175.

77. Rose, *King George V*, p.385.

78. Schabas, *The Trial of the Kaiser*, pp.13–56.

79. Lea and Alderson, 'The Attempt to Capture the Kaiser', pp.222–61.

80. Ibid.

81. Lea and Alderson, 'The Attempt to Capture the Kaiser', pp.222–61.

82. Schabas, *The Trial of the K*, pp.223–32.

83. Ibid.

84. West, *MI6*, pp.18–19; Judd, *Quest for C*, p.435.

85. Agar, *Baltic Episode*, p.215.

86. Linklater, *Compton Mackenzie*, pp.145–72.

87. Smith, *Six*, pp.168–86.

88. Frankland, *Witness of a Century*, pp.238–9.

89. Prochaska, 'George V and Republicanism', p.49.

90. Churchill, *In the Eye of the Storm*, p.225.

91. Rose, *King George V*, p.334.

92. Andrew, *Defend the Realm*, p.149.
93. Rose, *King George V*, p.336.
94. Bennett, *The Zinoviev Letter*, pp.1–4.
95. Prochaska, 'George V and Republicanism', p.42.
96. Hemming, '*M*': *Maxwell Knight*, p.77.
97. Entry for 27/11/34, Gorodetsky (ed.), *The Maisky Diary*, pp.18–21.

Chapter 10

1. Edward VIII, *A King's Story*, p.362.
2. RA, M.2472, quoted in Nicolson, *George V*, p.668.
3. Nicolson, *George V*, p.668.
4. Ibid., pp.661–3.
5. Nicolson, *George V*, pp.665–6; Rose, *King George V*, pp.386–8.
6. Rose, *King George V*, p.388.
7. Robert W. Smith, 'A brilliant history of the ultimate spy', *Chicago Sun – Times*, 31/1/88; Cave Brown, *Menzies*, pp.151–2.
8. Entry for 29/1/36, Gorodetsky (ed.), *The Maisky Diary*, pp.64–5.
9. Ziegler, *King Edward VIII*, pp.54–5, 59.
10. Rose, *The Prince, the Princess and the Perfect Murder*, pp.55–6.
11. Ibid., pp.72–5, 129.
12. Lord Norfolk, interviewed for *Spying on the Royals*, Channel 4, broadcast 2/4/17 and 9/4/17.
13. Rose, *The Prince, the Princess and the Perfect Murder*, p.312.
14. Bland, *Modern Women on Trial*, pp.142–3.
15. Rose, *The Prince, the Princess and the Perfect Murder*, pp.172–84.
16. Ziegler, *King Edward VIII*, p.165.
17. Sebba, *That Woman*, pp.75–96.
18. Lord Wigram, interviewed for *Spying on the Royals*, Channel 4, broadcast 2/4/17 and 9/4/17.
19. 'The Windsor Woods', *Illustrated London News*, 18/3/33.
20. HO 38/151, Trotter (St James's Palace) to Carter (Met), 24/5/24 & 10/6/24.
21. MEPO 10/35, Canning report, n.d.
22. Ibid., Canning to Game 25/6/35.
23. Ibid., Canning report, n.d.
24. Ibid.
25. Larman, *The Crown in Crisis*, p.46.
26. Entry for 16/6/35, Heffer (ed.), *Henry 'Chips' Channon*, p.435.
27. Much is made of this story but it is unlikely – see, for example, Morton, *17 Carnations*, pp. 54–8.
28. MEPO 10/35, Canning to Game (Met), 3/7/35.
29. Ziegler, *King Edward VIII*, p.269.
30. Entry for 27/11/69, Thorpe (ed.), *Who's In, Who's Out*, p.384.
31. Entry for 26/11/69, ibid., p.383; entry for 1/11/72, ibid., p.466.
32. Young (ed.), *The Diaries of Sir Robert Bruce Lockhart*, p.263.
33. MEPO 3/1713, 'George Andrew McMahon: attempt on the life of H.M. King Edward VIII at Constitution Hill'.
34. Parris, *The Man in the Brown Suit*, pp.129–30.
35. 'Edward's would-be killer leaves a trail of doubt', *Melbourne Age*, 7/1/03.
36. Dalya Alberge, 'British state "covered up plot to assassinate King Edward VIII"', *Guardian*, 28/6/20.
37. Andrew Cook, *The Guardian*, 3/1/03.
38. The most cogent analysis is offered in Larman, *The Crown in Crisis*, pp.50–71.
39. Dalya Alberge, 'British state "covered up plot to assassinate

King Edward VIII'", *Guardian*, 28/6/20.

40. Wilson and Adams, *Special Branch*, pp.70–71.

41. See, for example, entry for 1/1/41, West (ed.), *Liddell Diaries*, vol. 1, p.119.

42. Entry for 13/4/35, Heffer (ed.), *Henry 'Chips' Channon*, p.413.

43. Entry for 5/3/43, Hart-Davis (ed.), *King's Counsellor*, p.108.

44. Thornton, *Royal Feud*, pp.93, 99; Milne, *Nicolson*, pp.86–7.

45. Ziegler, *King Edward VIII*, p.273.

46. Beaken, *Cosmo Lang*, pp.87–109.

47. Robert Beaken, 'How to topple a king', *Church Times*, 19/10/12. See also Beaken, *Cosmo Lang*.

48. Norwich (ed.), *The Duff Cooper Diaries*, pp.230–1.

49. MSS., Cadogan diary, 1936, CCC.

50. Howarth, *George VI*, p.61.

51. Entry for June 1953, Colville, *Fringes of Power*, p.717.

52. Pope-Hennessy, *The Quest for Queen Mary*, p.200.

53. Robert Beaken, 'How to topple a king', *Church Times*, 19/10/12.

54. *Spying on the Royals*, Channel 4, broadcast 2/4/17 and 9/4/17.

55. Phillips, *The King Who Had to Go*, pp.124–40.

56. Cannadine, *In Churchill's Shadow*, p.64

57. Memo to Gardiner, 5/12/36, CAB 301/101.

58. Elliot, *Gentleman Spymaster*, pp.84–6.

59. Faber, *Speaking for England*, p.275.

60. Ibid.

61. Pope-Hennessy, *The Quest for Queen Mary*, p.200.

62. Entry for 28/12/36, Ball (ed.), *Headlam Diaries*, p.105.

63. Cadbury, *Princes at War*, pp.3–4.

64. Dorril, *Blackshirt*, p.406.

65. Windsor, *A King's Story*, pp.409–11.

66. Entry for 26/1/77, Thorpe (ed.), *Who's In, Who's Out*, p.540.

67. Entry for Spring 1937, Buckle (ed.), *Self Portrait with Friends*, p.52.

68. Ziegler, *Mountbatten*, p.680.

69. Entry for Spring 1937, Buckle (ed.), *Self Portrait with Friends*, p.52.

70. Lewis Clark, 'Diplomacy as a Career: Hard Work, Hardship, and Happy Times', (United States Foreign Service Officer, 1926–1958) ADST Oral History Collection https://adst.org/wp-content/uploads/2013/12/Clark-Lewis-memoir.pdf. See also Morton, *Wallis in Love*, p.221.

71. 'The Abdication Crisis', pp.48–9, BBK/G/6/10, Beaverbrook papers.

72. Martin, *The Woman He Loved*, pp.168–9. Martin spoke to Brownlow at length for this book. We are indebted to Mark Hollingsworth for this reference.

73. Larman, *Crown in Crisis*, pp.151–2.

74. Entry for 12/3/37, Gorodetsky (ed). *The Maisky Diary*, pp.74–5.

75. Ibid.

76. Roberts, *Sunshine and Shadow*, pp.378–9.

77. Graeme Strachan, 'Museum to shine a light on the "guardian shadow" of the King who signed away the crown', *The Courier*, 6/9/18.

78. MEPO 3/558, memo 'SD Inspector Storrier', 22/11/33.

79. MEPO 3/558, Memo by DAC1 (Supt A), 'Royalty', 26/PTN/109 (A-2) 27/9/34. Edward's previous long-serving detective, Len Burt, had become ill.

80. MEPO 3/558, Aird (St James's Palace) to Laurie, 17/1/34.

81. MEPO 3/558, Aird (St James's Palace) to Trenchard (Met), 26/9/34.

82. MEPO 3/558, Division A Memo, 'Division Sub-Inspector Storrier', n.d. 1934.

83. MEPO 10/35, Storrier (Schloss Wasserleonburg) to Game (Met), 18/6/37, fol.90.

84. Ibid., Storrier (Schloss Enzesfeld) to Game (Met), 18/6/37.

85. Ibid., 'Admettre au Chateau Personnes Suivantes', 1937.

86. CRES 35/417, E.H. Savill, memo. 'Fort Belverdere – Carctaker', 22/9/37, E6633.

87. MEPO 10/35, fol.80–87, Storrier to London, 7/6/37.

88. MEPO 10/35, fol.93, Storrier (Schloss Wasserleonburg) to Game (Met), 1/7/37.

89. Ibid., fol./99, Storrier (Schloss Wasserleonburg) to Game (Met), 30/8/37.

90. Norwich (ed.), *The Duff Cooper Diaries*, p.231.

91. FO 1093/23, Appendix to Report 166 'Rogers, Herman L.'

92. MEPO 10/35, fol.99, Storrier (Schloss Wasserleonburg) to Game, 30/8/37.

93. FO 954/33, win/37/32.

94. Ibid., Forbes to London, 'This letter which I have typed myself will not be put in the Chancellery archives'.

95. Cadbury, *Princes at War*, pp.49–66. See also Morton, *Wallis in Love*, p.251.

96. FO 954/33, Berlin (Phipps) to London, 6/10/37.

97. Ibid., British Embassy, Berlin. 13/10/37; ibid., Foreign Office telegram No.178 of 6/10/37.

98. MEPO 10/35, Canning to Game (Met), 15/11/37.

99. Ziegler, *King Edward VIII*, p.393.

100. FO 954/33, British Embassy Berlin to Secretary of State, 17/10/37.

101. MEPO 10/35, fol.99, Storrier (Paris) to Game, 19/12/37.

102. KV 2/1272, Prost (ADB3) to Capt. Anthony Blunt MI5 (B1b) 3/6/42.

103. Linklater, *Compton Mackenzie*, pp.253–4; Andrew, *Secret Service*, pp.351–2.

104. KV 2/1271, *The Sunday Dispatch*, 17 July 1938.

105. Linklater, *Compton Mackenzie*, pp.280–1.

106. Mackenzie, *The Windsor Tapestry*, pp.139, 160, 213–4, 459.

107. KV2/1271, MI5 minute, 10/8/38.

108. KV 2/1271, P.F.41196, 'Compton Mackenzie', 6/9/34.

109. KV 2/1272, Prost (ADB3) to Capt. Anthony Blunt, MI5 (B1b), 3/6/42.

110. Sitwell, *Rat Week*, pp.15, 16, 37, 67.

111. See, for example, KV 2/1271, P.F. 41196 (Intercepted) Mackenzie to Pollitt (CPGB) 17/11/36.

112. Linklater, *Compton Mackenzie*, pp.280–83.

113. MEPO 10/35, Storrier (Paris) to Game, 26/1/38.

114. CRES 35/417, Stock (Crown Lands) to Savill (Crown Estates), 5/4/38.

115. Bloch, *The Secret File*, p.116.

116. MEPO 3/567, Game to Monckton 4/4/39; ibid., Monkton to Game, 6/4/39.

117. Ibid. Monckton to Game (Met), 13/4/39.

Chapter 11

1. Stohrer, German Ambassador to Spain to German Foreign Ministry, 23 July 1940, No.211 DGFP, D, X, pp.276–7.
2. Howarth, *George VI*, p.84.
3. Shawcross, *Queen Elizabeth the Queen Mother*, p.440.
4. Weisbrode, *Churchill and the King*, p.54.
5. CAD: NC/7/3/26-65, George to Chamberlain, 16/9/38.
6. CAD: NC/7/3/26-65, PM to Palace, 23/9/38.
7. Shawcross, *Queen Elizabeth the Queen Mother*, p.441.
8. Howarth, *George VI*, p.84; Chamberlain papers, Dep 57, F 157, BUL.
9. Shawcross, *Queen Elizabeth the Queen Mother*, p.443.
10. Entry for 18/12/38, Gorodetsky (ed.), *The Maisky Diary*, pp.150–51.
11. CAD: NC/7/3/26-65, George to Chamberlain, 19/1/39
12. Ibid., George to Chamberlain, 18/3/39.
13. Petropoulos, *Royals and the Reich*, pp.200–21.
14. Chamberlain papers, Dep 57, F 157, BUL.
15. Howarth, *George VI*, pp.104–5.
16. CAB21/4552, Hastings to Hardinge, 25/7/39.
17. CRES 35/417, Sir Vernon Kell (Room 4327) to Stokes (Crown Lands), 21/9/39.
18. Paget, *Second to None*, p. 488; Stewart, *The King's Private Army*, pp.47, 54.
19. Rhodes, *The Final Curtsey*, p.68.
20. Howarth, *George VI*, pp.112–3.
21. Shawcross, *Queen Elizabeth the Queen Mother*, pp.508–9.
22. McKinstry, *Operation Sealion*, pp.229–32.
23. For a sceptical critique see Stewart, *The King's Private Army*, pp.111–19.
24. Entry for 31/5/40, Pimlott, *The Second World Diary of Hugh Dalton*, p.31. See also entry for 27/7/40, Dilks (ed.), *Cadogan Diaries*, p.317.
25. Entry for 6/8/40, Smith (ed.), *Hostage to Fortune*, p.457. See also Churchill to King, 15/5/45, Langworth (ed.), *Churchill by Himself*, p.84.
26. Manchester, *The Last Lion*, p.64.
27. Rhodes, *The Final Curtsey*, p.69.
28. Entry for 10/7/40, Nicolson (ed.), *Nicolson Diaries*, p.100.
29. Costello, *Ten Days to Destiny*, pp.47–8.
30. Gillman and Gillman, *'Collar the Lot!'*, p.112.
31. Ibid.; CAB 67/6, WPG (40) 131, Anderson memo.
32. Ziegler, *Edward VIII*, pp.402–3.
33. Shawcross, *Queen Elizabeth the Queen Mother*, pp.494–5.
34. Entry for 21/3/71, Thorpe (ed.), *Who's In, Who's Out*, p.456.
35. Bloch, *The Secret File*, pp.147–9.
36. MEPO 3/567, Hardinge (Buckingham Palace) to Game, 8/5/40. They rented this until 1949, then moved to 85 rue de la Faisanderie in Paris.
37. MEPO 3/567, Game (Met) to Phillips, 27/5/40.
38. Ibid., Phillips to Game, 5/6/40; Game to Phillips, 8/6/40.
39. Ibid., Phillips to Game, 5/6/40; Game to Phillips, 8/6/40.
40. Thornton, *Royal Feud*, p.201.
41. Ziegler, *King Edward VIII*, p.417.
42. Morton, *Wallis in Love*, p.263.
43. FOI FBI EDWARD VIII P1-5, Memo to Director of FBI, 13/9/40.

44. Ibid.
45. FOI FBI EDWARD VIII P55, Memo to the Director, 2/5/41.
46. FO 800/326/183, Halifax to Consulates, 19/6/40.
47. Day, *Franco's Friends*, pp.171, 182.
48. Entry for 20/5/40, Dilks (ed.), *Cadogan Diaries*, p.287.
49. Entry for 21/5/40, ibid., p.288.
50. Burns, *Papa Spy*, pp.119–30
51. FO 800/327, Hoare to FO, 20/6/40.
52. Christy, *Price of Power*, 235; Glass, *Americans in Paris*, pp.197–98.
53. RG 319/E134B/B14 X 8062007: CIC file, 'Bedaux, Charles Eugene'.
54. Thornton, *Royal Feud*, p.142.
55. FRUS 1940, III, Weddell to SoS, 2 July 1940.
56. Cadbury, *Princes at War*, p.174.
57. Ibid.
58. Entry for 26/7/40, Dilks (ed.), *Cadogan Diaries*, p.317.
59. Whiting, *The Kents*, pp.96–9.
60. Von Zech-Burkersroda to Weizacker, 27/1/40, *Documents on German Foreign Policy*, 1918–1945: series D (1937–45) Vol. VIII, The War Years Sept 4, 1939 – March 18, 1940, p.713.
61. John Curry, 'The Security Service: The Problems and Organisational Adjustments, 1908–1945' (March 1946), Pt II: The Nazi Threat, KV 4/1, p.86.
62. Dorrill, *Blackshirt*, pp.406–7.
63. Hauner, *India in Axis Strategy*, p.139.
64. FO 1093/23, C/5023, MI6 to Cadogan 26/9/40, enclosing MI6 report from Lisbon. Three days later Churchill noted 'seen' on the document.
65. Bloch, *Operation Willi*, pp.75–77.
66. FO 1093/23, Eccles (SOE) to Jebb SOE HQ (Baker Street), 4/7/40.
67. Ibid., mins by Cadogan 6/7/40 and Halifax 7/7/40.
68. Burns, *Papa Spy*, pp.119–30.
69. FO 1093/23, Menzies to Cadogan, 19/7/40, C/4720, seen by Halifax.
70. Ibid., Morton to Churchill, 4/8/40.
71. West, *Cold War Spymaster*, pp.2–10; KV 4/446, entry for 24/8/45, Guy Liddell Diary.
72. Cadbury, *Princes at War*, pp.174–6.
73. Ibid., pp.174–7.
74. FO 1093/23, MI6 to Cadogan, 7/7/40, C/4633, and Cadogan minute, 7/7/40.
75. Cadbury, *Princes at War*, pp.199–215.
76. Bloch, *Operation Willi*, pp.171–98.
77. Hoyningen-Huene to Ribbentrop, 2/8/40, nos.276–7, DGFP, D, X, pp.397–40. Also Cadbury, *Princes at War*, pp.154–5.
78. Ibid.; Sweet, 'The Windsor File', p.266.
79. FO 1093/23, Sir W. Selby, Lisbon, Cypher No.460, 22/7/40.
80. Costello, *Ten Days to Destiny*, pp.370–71.
81. CO 967/122, extract of a letter from Monckton, 8/8/40 to PM.
82. Ibid.
83. CO 967/122, Note for SoS for Foreign Affairs, 23/7/40, (DSCN7057-9).
84. Schellenberg, *Memoirs*, pp.139–46.
85. West, *Cold War Spymaster*, p.5.
86. Ziegler, *King Edward VIII*, p.431.
87. West, *Cold War Spymaster*, pp.1–12.
88. Hoyningen-Huene to Ribbentrop, 15/8/40, No.884, DGFP X.
89. FO 371/26542, C4216/324/16.
90. FO 371/24408, Mallet to Cadogan, 7/9/40, C/1973.

91. Costello, *Ten Days to Destiny*, pp.402–3.
92. Entry for 28/12/42, Hart-Davis (ed.), *King's Counsellor*, pp.87–8.
93. Bloch, *The Secret File*, p.165.

Chapter 12

1. Hyde, *Secret Intelligence Agent*, pp.119–20.
2. Lownie, *John Buchan*, pp.186–212, 241–72.
3. Bousfield and Toffoli, *Royal Spring*, pp.12–36.
4. Jaime Fuller, 'That Time FDR Served Hot Dogs to the King', 2/11/14, *Washington Post*.
5. NARA: RG59, Counsellor of embassy (London) to secretary of state (DC), 18/6/39, P294, #41, Great Britain, June 1939.
6. Bradford, *George VI*, p.281.
7. Jeffery, *MI6*, p.441; Hyde, *Secret Intelligence Agent*, p.135.
8. Undated memo, CIA file, Box 107, Cuneo Papers, Franklin D. Roosevelt Library.
9. Mahl, *Desperate Deception*, pp.21–2.
10. Ibid., pp.442–5; Stafford, *Station X*, pp.25–9.
11. Dunlop, *Donovan*, pp.209–10. See also Soley, *Radio Warfare*, p.50.
12. Dunlop, *Donovan*, pp.209–10.
13. Mahl, *Desperate Deception*, Cull, *Selling War*, pp.57–100.
14. Dahl, *Desperate Delusions*, pp.54–106.
15. Rankin, *Defending the Rock*, pp.89–102.
16. Hyde, *Secret Intelligence Agent*, p.68.
17. D/L to B, 12/7/40, enclosing Section IX Sub-section D/L, Censorship: Revised Budget, Montgomery Hyde papers, 3/11, CCC.

18. Ibid.
19. Rankin, *Defending the Rock*, pp.89–102.
20. Hyde, *Secret Intelligence Agent*, pp.98–99, 108.
21. Private information.
22. Lloyd to Duke of Windsor, 29/7/40, CHAR/20/9a/105, Churchill papers, CCC.
23. Hyde, *Secret Intelligence Agent*, pp.61–2.
24. CO 967/122, Edward to Lord Lloyd, 12/10/40.
25. Ibid., Monckton to Thomas, 11/10/40.
26. Ibid., Monckton to Churchill, 8/8/40.
27. Entry for 9/11/40, Pimlott (ed.), *Second World War Diary of Hugh Dalton*, p.98.
28. CO 967/122, Lothian to Cadogan, 4/9/40, 4424.
29. Thomson to Montgomery Hyde, 22/4/41, enclosing Halifax to Duke of Windsor, 21/4/41, Montgomery Hyde papers, 3/11, CCC.
30. Hyde, *Secret Intelligence Agent*, pp.73–5.
31. FO 371/24249, Halifax to Lothian, 9/40, A4271/G; WSC min 3 Oct 1940.
32. Ibid., Lothian to Halifax, 11/10/40 2269, A4271/G.
33. Ibid., NNNS 8/10/40 (intelligence), fo 362.
34. FO 371/24263, FO to Marquess of Lothian, 29/11/40, A 4887/4887/45.
35. Ibid., Butler (Washington) to FO, 22/11/40, A 4887/4887/45.
36. FO 371/26191, British consulate Jacksonville, Florida, to London, 20/12/40, enclosing 'Report on visit of the Duke and Duchess of Windsor to Miami, 10–17/12/40'.

37. Roosevelt to Lothian, 30/11/40, Box 34, PSF files, Franklin D. Roosevelt Library. See also Lothian to Roosevelt, 29/11/40, ibid.

38. Roosevelt (ed.), *F. D. R., His Personal Letters*, Vol. 4, p.1086.

39. Roosevelt to George VI, 22/11/40, PSF Box 34, Franklin D. Roosevelt Library.

40. Howarth, *George VI*, p.113.

41. 'Report on the Co-ordination of Security Intelligence in the West Indies and Caribbean Area' by Captain H Montgomery Hyde, 3/4/41, HYDE 3/13, CCC.

42. FO 1093/24, Governor to Vernon Kell (Director MI5), 18/10/39.

43. KV 4/185, Entry for 29/2/40, Guy Liddell Diary.

44. Entry for 17/1/41, Guy Liddell Diary, ibid.

45. FO 1093/24, Governor to duke, 11/12/40, 13131/39/40.

46. Hoover to Berle, 8/3/40, FBI file Wenner-Gren, FBI FOIA number 1485731-000.

47. FO 1093/24, Alec Hardinge (Buckingham Palace) to Cadogan, 14/12/40.

48. FO 1093/24, Min. to Cadogan, 1/1/41, Cadogan min., 1/1/41; 'C' to Hopkinson, 3 January 1941.

49. CO 967/125, PM to Duke of Windsor (To be decyphered by HRH's personal secretary) Private and Personal, 17/3/41.

50. FO 371/26191, Mail intercept, 3/5/41, to CO/FO/MI5, Frazier Jelke to Reginald Baxter, 14/4/41, A3509/165/45.

51. Hyde, *Secret Intelligence Agent*, p.63.

52. FBI FOIA EDWARD VIII P28.

53. FO 1093/23, 'C' to Hopkinson, enclosing censorship interception on Jelke, 12/4/41.

54. Adolfe Berle memo to SoS, 5/9/41, Berle papers, 0308, Franklin D. Roosevelt Library.

55. FBI EDWARD VIII P89 My dear Attorney General, 14/4/41.

56. FBI EDWARD VIII P19 Memo to Foxworth, 18/4/41.

57. FBI EDWARD VIII P18 19/4/41 Time: 9.10AM

58. Ibid.

59. Hyde, *Secret Intelligence Agent*, p.83.

60. FO 371/26191, Interview with Fulton Oursler, 16/5/41, *Liberty*, and *Sunday Dispatch*. Carried in the European press on 9 May. Berne to FO, 12/5/41, A3505/165/45.

61. Ibid., Minute to D Scott, 14/5/41; Eden minute, 15/5/41, ibid.

62. CO 967/125, Moyne to Davidson, 31/3/41.

63. 'Report on the Co-ordination of Security Intelligence in the West Indies and Caribbean Area' by Captain H Montgomery Hyde, 3/4/41, HYDE 3/13, CCC.

64. Hyde, *Secret Intelligence Agent*, pp.119–20.

65. 'Report on the Co-ordination of Security Intelligence in the West Indies and Caribbean Area' by Captain H Montgomery Hyde, 3/4/41, HYDE 3/13, CCC.

66. Memo Nassau B.W.I. 10/8/41, HYDE 3/13, CCC.. This MI6 document was initially marked Closed until 2042. 'Withold Sensitive HRH D.O.W.'

67. Hyde, *Secret Intelligence Agent*, pp.119–20.

68. Ziegler, *King Edward VIII*, p.478.

69. 'Report on the Co-ordination of Security Intelligence in the West Indies and Caribbean Area' by Captain H Montgomery Hyde, 3/4/41, HYDE 3/13, CCC.

70. Memo Nassau B.W.I. 10/8/41.
71. Hyde, *Secret Intelligence Agent*, pp.119–20.
72. Ziegler, *King Edward VIII*, p.477.
73. Churchill, *The Second World War*, vol. 3, pp.540–41.
74. Shawcross, *Queen Elizabeth the Queen Mother*, p.794; Rose, *King, Queens and Courtiers*, p.105.
75. Rhodes, *The Final Curtsey*, pp.76–89.
76. Ibid., pp.77–90.
77. Entry for 07/2/41, Pimlott (ed.), *The Second World War Diary of Hugh Dalton*, p.154.
78. Jackson, *SOE's Balls of Steel*, p.179.
79. Entry for 30/3/41, Pimlott (ed.), *The Second World War Diary of Hugh Dalton*, p. 179.
80. Entry for 13/8/42, Hart-Davis (ed.), *King's Counsellor*, pp.45–6.
81. http://clutch.open.ac.uk/schools/emerson00/pwe_page2.html, accessed 17/5/20, 'WWII Secret Activities Around Milton Keynes', a remarkable website created by a team of parents who have or had children attending Emerson Valley Combined School, Milton Keynes.
82. Howarth, *George VI*, p.138; entries for 04/2/42 and 04/3/42, Pimlott (ed.), *Second World War Diaries of Hugh Dalton*, pp.361, 388.
83. Entry for QM, conversations with Eric Anderson, 1994–5, RA/QEQM/ADD/MISC, Shawcross, *Queen Elizabeth the Queen Mother*, p.559.
84. King diary, 3/11/42, RAG VI/PRIV/DIARY, quoted in Shawcross, *Queen Elizabeth the Queen Mother*, p.559.
85. Entry for QM, conversations with Eric Anderson, 1994–5, RA/QEQM/ADD/MISC, Shawcross,

Queen Elizabeth the Queen Mother, p.560.

Chapter 13

1. CAB 127/30, Lascelles to Ismay, 28/7/43.
2. Christopher H. Sterling, 'Getting There: Churchill's Wartime Journeys', https://winstonchurchill.org/publications/finest-hour/finest-hour-148/getting-there-churchills-wartime-journeys/
3. AIR 8/775, Portal (CAS) to Churchill, 'Operation Loader', 11/6/43; Bridges (Cabinet Secretary), 'LOADER: Cover for General Lion's absence from the UK', 11/6/43, ibid.
4. PREM 3/497/3, Churchill to Bridges, 8/6/43, C 12/3.
5. Entry for 2–4/6/43, Diary of John Mitchell, MISC 59, CCC, pp.14–17.
6. Entry for 2/6/43, Payn and Morley (eds), *The Diaries of Noël Coward*, p.21.
7. AIR 8/775, Hollis (Secretary War Cabinet) to Macfarlane, 'LOADER', 11/6/43.
8. Ibid., Portal (CAS) to Churchill, 'Operation Loader', 11/6/43.
9. Churchill to George VI, 16/6/42, AP/19/1, Avon Papers, BUL.
10. Bradford, *George VI*, pp.467–9; Macmillan, *War Diaries*, p.120.
11. ODNB: Hardinge, Alexander.
12. Wales, 'The "Massingham" Mission', pp.42–65.
13. Wilkinson, *Foreign Fields*, p.131.
14. Ibid.
15. Dodds-Parker, *Setting Europe Ablaze*, pp.130–1.
16. Brooks Richards, *Secret Flotillas*, p.276.
17. Brooks Richards, Reel 9, Oral

History Collection, Imperial War Museum.

18. Ibid.

19. AIR 8/775, Portal (CAS) to Churchill, 15/6/43.

20. Bennett, Ralph, *Intelligence Investigations*, pp. 74–112.

21. Churchill to Alexander, 11/4/43, CHAR 20/109/114, Churchill Papers, CCC.

22. Castillo, *The Maltese Cross*, p.211. See also Macmillan, *War Diaries*, p.124c.

23. Walton, *Empire of Secrets*, p.41.

24. West, *Double Cross in Cairo*, p.104c.

25. CAB 127/30, Lascelles to Ismay, 28/7/43.

26. Major Kempholme, *The History of RAF Station Tempsford*, unpublished.

27. O'Conner, *The Tempsford Academy*, pp.88–91.

28. Wheeler-Bennett, *George VI*, p.595.

29. Entry for 1/3/45, Hart-Davis (ed.), *King's Counsellor*, p.298.

30. Shawcross, *Queen Elizabeth the Queen Mother*, p.555.

31. Ibid., p.571.

32. Entries for October 1943 and January 1944, Hart-Davis (ed.), *King's Counsellor*, pp.170, 194.

33. Entry for 3/3/44, ibid., p.204.

34. Howard, *British Intelligence in the Second World War, Volume 5*, pp.110–21.

35. Wheatley, *The Time has Come*, p.670; Morley, *Noël Coward*, p.73.

36. Hesketh, *Fortitude*, pp.261–7.

37. Rankin, *A Genius for Deception*, p.399.

38. Hesketh, *Fortitude*, p.274; see also KV 4/194-5.

39. *The King Who Fooled Hitler*, Channel 4, broadcast 5/5/19.

40. Entry for 18/4/44, Hart-Davis (ed.), *King's Counsellor*, p.214.

41. 'The King Takes Leave of His Fleet', *Daily Mail*, 15/5/44.

42. *The King Who Fooled Hitler*, Channel 4, broadcast 5/5/19.

43. Entry for 31/5/44, Hart-Davis (ed.), *King's Counsellor*, pp.225.

44. Stafford, *Ten Days to D-Day*, p.123c.

45. Entry for 6/5/44, Hart-Davis (ed.), *King's Counsellor*, pp.230–1.

46. Entry for 14/6/44, ibid., p.233.

47. CAB 120/16, Lascelles to Wilson, 20/7/44.

48. Ibid., Churchill to George VI, T.1486/4, 24/7/44.

49. CAB 127/30, George VI to General Maitland Wilson, 4/8/44.

50. FO 954/14A/214, Eden to Churchill, 12/7/44, PM 44/518.

51. Ibid., Churchill to Lascelles, 2/7/44, It/44/163.

52. Entry for 29/3/41, Pimlott, *The Second World War Diary of Hugh Dalton*, p.179.

53. Foot, *Resistance: European Resistance to Nazism*, pp.317–18.

54. Entry for 4/12/41, Pimlott (ed.), *Second World War Diaries of Hugh Dalton*, p.330.

55. Entry for 30/9/42, ibid., p.499.

56. Entry for 4/5/44, Hart-Davis (ed.), *King's Counsellor*, p.217.

57. The full story is in HS 6/216: 'PATRON mission: proposed exfiltration by sea of Prince Charles, brother of King Leopold'.

58. FO 954/26B/467, Lascelles to Lawford (FO), 27/9/44, SU/44/190.

59. HS 2/34, Major Gen. Whiteley (SHAEF), to Brig E.W. Mockler-Ferryman, 'King of Denmark', 18/9/44.

60. FO 371/43130, min. by Warner of conversation with Mockler-Ferryman, 'Possible evacuation from Denmark of King Christian', 30/11/44, N7664/3781/15. Also Eden minute, 16/6/44, ibid.

61. The Annual Obituary, Roland Turner, St Martin's, 1982, p.466; see also entry for 16/1/45, Hart-Davis (ed.), King's Counsellor, p.289.

62. HS 2/34, Mieville (Buckingham Palace) to Wilson (SOE), 8/1/45; see also Tillotson, SOE and the Resistance, p.68.

63. Tillotson, SOE and The Resistance, p.73.

64. Entry for 30/3/41, Pimlott, The Second World Diary of Hugh Dalton, p.179.

65. Hart-Davis (ed.), King's Counsellor, pp.286-7.

66. Iatrides, Revolt in Athens, pp.213-14.

67. PREM 3/339/8, Bridges to Rowan, 10/10/44.

68. Ibid., Montgomery to Churchill, T.1901A/4, 6/10/44.

69. Entry for 2/1/44, Pimlott, The Second World War Diary of Hugh Dalton, p.693.

70. Entries for 16-21/6/44, Hart-Davis (ed.), King's Counsellor, pp.235, 238.

71. FO 1093/247, Cadogan to Halifax, August 1942.

72. PREM 3/339/8, King to Churchill, 5/10/44.

73. Entry for 26/9/43, Hart-Davis (ed.), King's Counsellor, pp.165.

74. Entry for 19/7/44, ibid., p.246.

75. Pincher, Dangerous to Know: A Life, p.168.

76. Entry for 7/2/45, Hart-Davis (ed.), King's Counsellor, p.293.

77. Wilkinson and Astley, Gubbins & SOE, p.192.

78. This episode is documented at length in HS 7/49.

79. Rigden, How to Be a Spy, pp.20-22.

80. Entry for 1/3/45, Hart-Davis (ed.), King's Counsellor, p.298.

81. Entry for 4/5/44, ibid., p.217.

82. Entry for 7/2/45, ibid., p.293.

83. CAB 127/40, Lascelles to Ismay, 5 April 1945.

84. Entry for 25/7/46, Hart-Davis (ed.), King's Counsellor, p.341.

85. CAB 127/31, Zuletta minute 25/7/46 on Ismay to Lascelles, 23/7/46. The paper in question was TWC (46) 15 (Revise), 'Future Developments in Weapons and Methods of War'.

Chapter 14

1. Bradford, George VI, p.500.

2. Pimlott, The Queen, p.79.

3. Bertrand, Enigma, p. 256. See also Cave Brown, 'C', p.671.

4. Turing, Alan M. Turing: Centenary Edition, p.156.

5. Harper, Capturing Enigma, p.26.

6. The importance of this report was first recognized in Lewis, Changing Direction, pp.310-32.

7. O'Reagan, Taking Nazi Technology, pp.1-14.

8. FO 1093/23, Herman Rodgers, appendix to report 166., n.d.

9. Private information.

10. FO 954/33A/13357, Washington to London, 12/6/43.

11. CAB 127/30, Lascelles to Ismay, 15/5/45.

12. Ibid., Morgan (SHAEF) to Ismay, 5/6/45.

13. NC7/3/36, King George VI to Chamberlain, 3/7/39, Chamberlain papers, BUL.

14. Petropolous, *Royals and the Reich*, pp.190–91.

15. CAB 127/40, Morgan (SHAEF) to Ismay, 5/6/45.

16. Entry for 12/8/45 and 15/8/45, Hart-Davis (ed.), *King's Counsellor*, pp.351–2.

17. Entry for 11/10/45, ibid., pp. 360–61.

18. Entries for 5/10/45 and 9/11/45, ibid., pp.356, 367.

19. Bloch, *The Secret File*, p.34.

20. Entry for 14/5/45, Hart-Davis (ed.), *King's Counsellor*, pp.324–5.

21. Guide to the Lady Leonie Leslie Papers 1902–1935, The University of Chicago Library, https://www.lib.uchicago.edu/e/scrc/findingaids/view.php?eadid=ICU.SPCL.LESLIE

22. Rose, *Elusive Rothschild*, pp.233–4.

23. Ibid., pp.233–4.

24. Haslam, *Near and Distant Neighbours*, p.151.

25. Carter, *Anthony Blunt*, p.303.

26. FO 371/65327, Turner to PUS, 9/1/46, C240/240/182G.

27. Ibid., Playfair to Ritchie, OF.46/20/8, 19/1/46.

28. Ibid., Lascelles to Street, 29/2/46. Renamed 'Rommel', the horse was sent by Windsor to be coached in ceremonial duties, but proved to be too high spirited and was put down in 1947.

29. Ibid., Playfair to Ritchie, 25/1/46.

30. Ibid., Street to Lascelles, 15/1/46; Lascelles to Street, 17/1/46, ibid.

31. Ibid., Templer to Playfair, DCOS (X)/DO/TS/800, 2/3/46.

32. Ibid., Blunt to Playfair 4/3/46.

33. Ibid., Playfair to Templer, 5/3/46.

34. ODNB: Ismay, Hastings.

35. CAB 127/30, Lascelles to Jacob, 25/7/45; Ismay to Eisenhower, 25/7/45, ibid.

36. Petropoulos, *Royals and the Reich*, p.338.

37. CAB 127/30, Lascelles to Ismay, 8/8/45; Ismay to Eisenhower, 8/8/45, ibid.

38. Poland Perry, *The Queen, Her Lover and the Most Notorious Spy in History*, pp.1–14.

39. Petropoulos, *Royals and the Reich*, p.338: Carter, *Anthony Blunt*, p.312.

40. CAD: NC7/3/36, King George VI to Chamberlain, 3/7/39. See also Carter, *Anthony Blunt*, p.312.

41. Cadbury, *Princes at War*, p.323; Petropoulos, *Royals and the Reich*, pp.199–204.

42. Petropoulos, *Royals and the Reich*, pp.339–40; Carter, *Anthony Blunt*, p.315.

43. Bradford, *George VI*, p.565.

44. Rose, *Elusive Rothschild*, pp.235–6.

45. FO 371/49012, Hoyer Millar min. to ps, 5/12/45, Z13431/3172/G4.

46. CAB 127/31, Lascelles (Sandringham) to Ismay, 19/1/46.

47. Ziegler, *King Edward VIII*, pp.494, 503–6, 514.

48. Ibid., p.512.

49. MEPO 2/9149, 'Robbery at "Ednam", Sunningdale, Surrey, 16 Oct 1946, of valuable jewellery, property of the Duke and Duchess of Windsor'. See also Peter Day, 'The Duchess and the thief who would not confess', *Telegraph*, 27/12/03.

50. CAB 127/31, Lascelles to Hollis, 16/1/47.

51. Aldrich, *Intelligence and the War Against Japan*, pp.385–7.

52. West, *Cold War Spymaster*, pp.1–2.

53. Ibid, p.1; Sweet, 'The Windsor File', pp.263–5.

54. Entry for 12/8/45, Hart-Davis (ed.), *King's Counsellor*, p.351.

55. KV4/466, entry for 25/8/45, Guy Liddell Diary.

56. Bradford, *George VI*, p.563; Petropoulos, *Royals and the Reich*, p.341.

57. Costello, *Mask of Treachery*, pp.455-6; Bloch, *Operation Willi*, p.230.

58. Sweet, 'The Windsor File', pp.263-8.

59. Kent, 'Editing Diplomatic Documents', p.474.

60. Young (ed.), *Diaries of Sir Robert Bruce Lockhart*, vol. 2, p.572.

61. Sweet, 'The Windsor File', p.270.

62. Davies, *MI6 and the Machinery of Spying*, p.180.

63. Ziegler, *King Edward VIII*, p.269.

64. Sweet, 'The Windsor File', p.270.

65. Entries for 11-12/8/53, Colville, *The Fringes of Power*, p.675.

66. Sweet, 'The Windsor File', pp.270-76.

67. Ibid., pp.272-5.

68. Ibid., p.278.

69. Kent, 'Editing Diplomatic Documents', p.475.

70. Eckert, *The Struggle For the Files*, pp.177, 182-6, 197.

71. *DGFP*, D10, p.188.

72. HW 3/29, Special Order by Edward Travis, 7/5/45; Central Office note 195, 27/4/45, ibid.

73. CAB 76/36, COS (45) 187th mtg, Confidential Annexe.

74. FO 371/39171, Cavendish Bentinck min., 15 July 1944, C9682/9386/18.

75. Murphy, 'By invitation only', pp.245-65.

76. Aldrich, *Hidden Hand*, p.4.

77. Reynolds, *In Command of History*, pp.159-63.

78. Moran, *Classified*, p.4.

79. Aldrich, *Hidden Hand*, pp.4-7; Aldrich, 'Policing the Past', pp.922-53.

80. Curry, 'History of the Security Service', KV 4/1-3.

81. West (ed.), *British Security Co-ordination*, passim.

82. DEFE 28/1, Directorate of Forward Plans: terms of reference, 1950.

83. Aldrich, 'Policing the Past', pp.922-53.

84. Lascelles note, 9/12/50, Masterman papers, Worcester College, Oxford.

85. Lascelles to Masterman, 9/12/50, ibid.

86. Masterman to Lascelles, 4/10/51, ibid.

87. Lascelles to Masterman, 6/10/51, ibid.

88. Andrew, *Defence of the Realm*, p.836.

89. Masterman to Lascelles, 2/4/52, Worcester College, Oxford.

90. Lascelles to Masterman, 4/4/52, ibid. The receipt read 'Book returned April 22nd 1952, J.C.M.', ibid.

91. Dick White (MI6) to Masterman, 5/10/67, ibid.; Furnival-Jones (MI5) to Masterman 1/12/67, ibid.

92. Moran, *Classified*, pp.271-3.

93. Andrew, *Defence of the Realm*, p.836.

Chapter 15

1. Corera, *The Art of Betrayal*, pp.140, 153-4.

2. MEPO 3/1872, Chief Superintendent Osborne, 'Buckingham Palace – Police Protection', 19/10/50. The main files on this theft remain closed, see MEPO 2/9151, 'Burglary at

Buckingham Palace committed by Douglas Monro on night of 12–13 Oct 1950'; MEPO 2/8912, 'Unauthorised entry into Buckingham Palace 5–6 July 1951: new security arrangements'.

3. Ibid.
4. MEPO 3/1872, AC 'A' minute 27/10/50.
5. Bedell Smith, *Elizabeth the Queen*, p.3.
6. Hennessy, *The Hidden Wiring*, pp.47–8.
7. Murphy, *Monarchy and the End of Empire*, p.11.
8. PREM 8/1271, Brook to Attlee, 14/6/50.
9. Bradford, *Her Life in Our Times*, p.66.
10. Cohen, *Palestine and the Great Powers, 1945–1948*, p.94. See also Charteris, 'A Year as an Intelligence Officer in Palestine', pp.17–20.
11. Noreen Taylor, 'Saying What Everyone Thinks', *Spectator*, 7/1/95, p.14.
12. PREM 8/1271, Downing Street, 'Note for File', 26/6/50.
13. Chris Ship, 'Queen Marks GCHQ Centenary and Recalls Getting "Cross" With Scrambler Phone', *ITV News*, 14/2/19.
14. GCHQ codebook, tweeted by the Royal Family to mark the centenary of GCHQ, 14/2/2019.
15. Pimlott, *The Queen*, pp.79–91.
16. Entry for 23/8/44, Evans (ed.), *The Killearn Diaries, 1934–1946*, pp.311–12. See also Pimlott, *The Queen*, pp.96–7.
17. CAB 127/30, McEwan to Lascelles, 14/8/45.
18. Eade, *Young Prince Philip*, p.102.
19. Davies, *Queen Elizabeth*, p.84.

20. Ibid., p.86.
21. 'The romances of young Prince Philip', *Telegraph*, 10/10/17.
22. Bradford, *George VI*, p.420.
23. Ibid.; Seward, *The Queen and Di*, p.93. See also Pimlott, *The Queen*, p.93.
24. Petropoulos, *Royals and the Reich*, p.95.
25. *Prince Philip: The Plot to Make a King*, Channel 4, broadcast 26/7/15.
26. Heald, *The Duke*, p.93.
27. Eade, *Young Prince Philip*, p.194.
28. KV 4/469, Guy Liddell diary entry for 17/11/47.
29. CAB 195/5/66, Cabinet Secretary's note on CM(88)47, 17/11/47.
30. KV 4/469, Guy Liddell diary entry for 17/11/47.
31. KV 2/1864 Dick White, untitled note, 24/11/47.
32. Eade, *Young Prince Philip*, p.202.
33. CAB 195/5/66, Cabinet Secretary's note on CM (88)47, 17/11/47.
34. KV 4/469, Guy Liddell diary entry for 17/11/47.
35. Hansard HC Deb 27/11/47 vol 444 cc2117–8.
36. MEPO 2/7967, Commander A, 'Royal Wedding – Security', 18/11/47.
37. Ibid., Deputy Commander 1, 'Royal Wedding', 28/11/47.
38. Ibid., St James's Palace to Commissioner of Police, 21/11/47; Chuter Ede to Commissioner of Police, 24/11/47.
39. Cantarini, *Savoy Was My Oyster*, pp.87–8.
40. Morley, *Our Man in Mexico*, pp.39–41.
41. Grose, *Allen Dulles*, p.500.

42. Morley, 'The Spy Who Loved Him', *Washington Post*, 17/3/96, https://www.washingtonpost.com/archive/lifestyle/1996/03/17/the-spy-who-loved-him/91843a35-2027-486c-874c-b67a51cce9f6/?noredirect=on&utm_term=.af71dd0e658e

43. CREST: Walter Reid (Deputy Director CIA), 'Attendance at Ceremonies in Honor of their Royal Highnesses the Princess Elizabeth, Duchess of Edinburgh and the Duke of Edinburgh', 29/10/51, https://www.cia.gov/library/readingroom/docs/CIA-RDP81-00728R000100110007-5.pdf

44. Aldrich and Cormac, *The Black Door*, pp.109–10.

45. Shlaim, 'A Totalitarian Concept of History', pp.52–5.

46. Corera, *The Art of Betrayal*, p.61.

47. Bethell, *The Albanian Operation of the CIA and MI6*, p.158; Smiley, *Albanian Assignment*, p.166.

48. CREST, CIA, 'Monthly Project Status Report for Month of January 1952', https://www.cia.gov/library/readingroom/docs/OBOPUS%20BGFIEND%20%20%20VOL.%2020%20%20%20%28BGFIEND%20OPERATIONS%29_0044.pdf; CIA, Chief SE to [redacted], 'Reorganization of Athens BGFIEND P/W Effort', 9 December 1952, https://www.cia.gov/library/readingroom/docs/OBOPUS%20BFIEND%20%20%20VOL.%2023%20%20(BGFIEND%20OPERATIONS)_0086.pdf

49. Rhodes, *The Final Curtsey*, pp.71.

50. Entry for 10/8/51, Catterall (ed.), *Macmillan Diaries, Vol. I*, pp.94–5.

51. Bethell, *The Albanian Operation*, p.64; Lulushi, *Operation Valuable Fiend*, p.79.

52. Bethell, *The Albanian Operation*, p.158.

53. Nicholas Best, 'The day Princess Elizabeth became Queen', *Guardian*, 8/1/12.

54. Ibid. See also Bennet, *Fighting the Mau Mau*, pp.23, 135–8, 235–9..

55. Franklin, *A Pied Cloak*, pp.95–8, also private information.

56. Hardman, *Queen of the World*, p.128.

57. Henderson, *Man Hunt in Kenya*, p.15.

58. Ibid., p.237.

59. Ian Henderson, Obituary, *Telegraph*, 22/4/13.

60. Entry for Spring 1967, Vickers (ed.), *Beaton in the Sixties*, p.167.

61. Private information.

62. Aldrich, *Hidden Hand*, p.646.

63. Young, 'Talking to Tito', pp.31–41.

64. Harrison, 'The Duke and the Dictator', p.222.

65. Ibid., p.224.

66. PREM 11/578, FO report to Churchill, March 1953.

67. Harrison, 'The Duke and the Dictator', p.224.

68. Ibid., pp.227–29.

69. KV 4/475, Guy Liddell diary entries for 13/3/53 and 14/3/53.

70. Ibid., entry for 14/3/53.

71. CAD: Shuckburgh Diary, MS191/1/2/2, 16/3/53.

72. Jagger, *Escorting the Monarch*, pp.2–4.

73. TNA, FO 371/102184, Minutes of 11/12/52.

74. 'Stalin's Plan to Assassinate Tito', *Cold War International History Project Bulletin*, No.10, p.137. This was found by the Russian military historian Dmitrii Volkogonov

(1928–95) in the Presidential Archive of the Russian Federation in Moscow.

75. Ibid. See also AP, 'Soviet Plan to Assassinate Tito', *Los Angeles Times*, 12/6/93.

76. Barnett, *Tito*, p.92.

77. Harrison, 'The Duke and the Dictator', pp.227–9.

78. CAD: Shuckburgh Diary, MS191/1/2/2, 10/3/53.

79. FO 371/112726, Foreign Office, 'Submission to the Queen on Proposed Secret Talks Between the UK, US and the Yugoslav Governments on Trieste', 6 January 1054; CAD: Shuckburgh Diary, MS191/1/2/2, 8 October 1953.

80. Bedel Smith, *Elizabeth the Queen*, p.8.

81. Ibid., p.93; Bradford, *Elizabeth*, p.229.

Chapter 16

1. Graham Turner, 'The real Elizabeth II: part two', *Telegraph*, 09/1/02.

2. Shawcross, *Queen and Country*, p.15.

3. KV 4/474, Guy Liddell diary entry, 6/2/52.

4. See, for example, Edward, La Croe, Cap d' Antibes, to de Courcy, 28/8/48, File 11, Box 5, de Courcy papers, Hoover Institute.

5. Christopher Wilson, 'Revealed: The Duke and Duchess of Windsor's Secret Plot to Deny the Queen the Throne', *Daily Telegraph*, 22/11/09.

6. De Courcy to Wallis, Ritz Hotel, Paris, 13/5/49, File 11, Box 5, de Courcy papers, Hoover Institute.

7. De Courcy to Blum, 19/4/79, ibid.

8. Quoted in Lownie, *The Mountbattens*, p.257.

9. Ibid., p.258.

10. KV 4/474, Guy Liddell diary entry, 28/2/52.

11. Ibid., diary entry, 5/3/52.

12. Colville, *The Fringes of Power*, pp.640–41.

13. Pimlott, *The Queen*, p.184; Lownie, *The Mountbattens*, p.257.

14. Murphy, *Monarchy and the End of Empire*, pp.54–9.

15. Colville, *The Fringes of Power*, p.327.

16. Ibid.

17. KV 4/475, Guy Liddell diary entries, 15/3/53 and 18/3/53.

18. Ibid., diary entries, 15/3/53 and 18/3/53.

19. MEPO 4/140, Commissioner's Office, 'Coronation of Her Majesty Queen Elizabeth II', May 1953.

20. CAD: Shuckburgh Diary, MS191/1/2/2, 5/6/53.

21. Bedell Smith, *Elizabeth the Queen*, pp.71–2.

22. Hennessy, *Secret State*, p.5.

23. CAB 181/7, Precedent Book: Part V Relations with Buckingham Palace', n.d.

24. Bedell Smith, *Elizabeth the Queen*, pp.71–2.

25. Hardman, *Her Majesty*, p.156.

26. PREM 11/753, Kirkpatrick to Colville, 25/5/54.

27. Ibid., Queen Mother to Churchill, 10/6/54.

28. Ibid., Kirkpatrick to Colville, 25/5/54.

29. Ibid., Churchill to Queen Mother, 4/6/54.

30. Ibid., Colville to Churchill, 2/6/54.

31. PREM 11/752, Colville to Kirkpatrick, 4/6/54; Prince Philip to Churchill, 10/6/54.

32. Bedell Smith, *Elizabeth the Queen*, p.72.
33. Hennessy, *The Hidden Wiring*, p.65.
34. Ibid., pp.65, 69; Bedell Smith, *Elizabeth the Queen*, p.67.
35. Bedell Smith, *Elizabeth the Queen*, p.108.
36. Bradford, *Her Life in Our Times*, p.66.
37. Aldrich and Cormac, *The Black Door*, p.188.
38. Entries for 12/4/56 and 24/4/56, Thorpe (ed.), *Who's In, Who's Out*, pp.76, 80.
39. Ibid., p.83; Williams (ed.), *The Diary of Hugh Gaitskell*, pp.509–15.
40. Davenport-Hines, *Enemies Within*, p.484.
41. Kapitonova, 'Visit of Soviet leaders', pp.148–9.
42. FO 371/122824, anon FO, 'Decisions taken at PM's Meeting on 28/3 on arrangements for Soviet leaders' visit', 29/3/56.
43. Khrushchev, *Khrushchev Remembers*, p.406.
44. Bradford, *Her Life in Our Times*, p.100.
45. Kapitonova, 'Visit of Soviet leaders', p.143.
46. Khrushchev, *Khrushchev Remembers*, p.406.
47. Lownie, *The Mountbattens*, p.275.
48. Khrushchev, *Khrushchev Remembers*, p.407.
49. FRUS: President's Trip to Europe, 29/8/59, Memorandum of Conversation, FRUS, 1958–1960, Western Europe, Vol VII, Pt 2, p.856.
50. CREST: CIA, LCCASSOCK Review, 19/10/56.
51. FO 371/122392, Brimelow, 'Message from Marshal Voroshilov to the Queen about Hungary', 15/11/56.
52. Békés, 'President Kliment Voroshilov's Telegram to Queen Elizabeth', p.128.
53. FO 371/122392, Brimelow, 'Message from Marshal Voroshilov to the Queen about Hungary', 15/11/56.
54. Ibid., Hibbert, 'Message about Hungary from Marshal Voroshilov to the Queen', 15/11/56.
55. FO 371/122394, Reilly to Beith, 19/11/56.
56. Corera, *The Art of Betrayal*, pp.140, 153–4.
57. Duns, *Dead Drop*, p.64.
58. Summers and Dorril, *The Secret Worlds of Stephen Ward*, pp.290–92.
59. Davies, *Queen Elizabeth*, pp.129–30.
60. Ibid.
61. Lacey, *Royal*, p.208.
62. Quoted in Heald, *The Duke*, p.129.
63. Seward, *The Queen and Di*, pp.92–3.
64. Ibid., p.93.
65. PREM 11/991, Millard to Stark, 15/12/55; Stark to Millard, 13/12/55.
66. Davenport-Hines, *An English Affair*, p.276.
67. Quoted in Pimlott, *The Queen*, p.320.
68. Summers and Dorril, *The Secret Worlds of Stephen Ward*, pp.xiv, 20, 103, 290.
69. Keeler, *Secrets and Lies*, p.38.
70. Ibid.
71. Private information.
72. Keeler foreword in Ivanov, *The Naked Spy*, p.7.
73. Andrew, *Defence of the Realm*, pp.495–6.
74. Ivanov, *The Naked Spy*, pp.29–32.
75. Ibid., pp.92–3; Davenport-Hines, *An English Affair*, pp.105–6.

76. Ivanov, *The Naked Spy*, pp.92–3.
77. Ibid.
78. Botham, *Margaret*, p.75.
79. Keeler, *Secrets and Lies*, pp.40–41.
80. Summers and Dorril, *The Secret Worlds of Stephen Ward*, p.293.
81. FOI, Hoover the Legal Attache London, 11/6/63.
82. FOI, Hoover Director FBI to Attorney General, 18/6/63.
83. Summers and Dorril, *Secret Worlds of Stephen Ward*, p.329.
84. Ivanov, *The Naked Spy*, p.53.
85. Ibid., pp.92–3.
86. Summers and Dorril, *The Secret Worlds of Stephen Ward*, p.329.
87. Jason Lewis and Kim Willsher, 'The KGB's Spy at the Palace', *Mail on Sunday*, 20/2/00.
88. Davenport-Hines, *An English Affair*, pp.262–3.
89. Clive Irving, 'What Netflix's The Crown Leaves Out', *Daily Beast*, 6/1/18.
90. The letter, dated 5 March 1960, was published by the *Mirror* in January 1999 much to the royal family's consternation. See Nic North, 'The Elizabeth and Margaret Letters: Spies in Secret of Royal Lovers', *Daily Mirror*, 20/1/99, p.13.
91. Bradford, *Elizabeth*, p.307.
92. Crossman in Davenport-Hines, *An English Affair*, p.294.
93. Aldrich and Cormac, *The Black Door*, p.230.
94. Bedell Smith, *Elizabeth the Queen*, p.123.
95. Pimlott, *The Queen*, p.320.
96. Davenport-Hines, *An English Affair*, p.344.
97. Pincher, *Dangerous to Know*, p.168.
98. Haslam, *Near and Distant Neighbours*, p.151.
99. Carter, *Anthony Blunt*, p.376.
100. ODNB: Blunt, Anthony Frederick.
101. KV 2/4115, Reed, notes on 'I/L from Burgess to his Mother', 30/4/56.
102. Entry for 12/2/01, Thorpe (ed.), *Who Wins, Who Loses*, pp.350–51.
103. Carter, *Anthony Blunt*, p.449.
104. http://www.ealingtoday.co.uk/default.asp?section=info&page=eapoundprofumo001.htm
105. Lownie, *Stalin's Englishman*, pp.247–50.
106. KV 4/474, Guy Liddell diary entry, 12/6/51.
107. Ibid., Guy Liddell diary entry, 13/7/51.
108. Ibid.
109. PREM 16/2230, 'Sir Anthony Blunt', attached to Hunt to Thatcher, 20/12/78; PREM 19/120, Note of Possible Supplementaries and Suggested Answers, 1979.
110. PREM 16/2230, 'Sir Anthony Blunt', attached to Hunt to Thatcher, 20/12/78.
111. Modin, *My Five Cambridge Friends*, p.180.
112. PREM 19/120, untitled chronology of the Blunt case, undated, filed in inside cover.
113. Thatcher, Hansard, 21/11/79, paras 405–6.
114. Ibid., 21/11/79, paras 405–6.
115. PREM 16/2230, Hunt to Wilson, 'Sir Anthony Blunt', 3/7/74.
116. Wright, *Spycatcher*, p.223. She also apparently told a friend of the investigative journalist Chapman Pincher that she had been well briefed of the affair while working her gundogs at a shoot lunch at Broadlands. Pincher, *Treachery*, p.515.

117. Thatcher, Hansard, 21/11/79, paras 405–6.

118. Andrew, *Defence of the Realm*, p.706.

119. PREM 19/120, Armstrong to No.10, 'Blunt', 20/11/79; notes for Thatcher's speech attached to Armstrong to Whitmore, 18/11/79.

120. Andrew, *Defence of the Realm*, p.706.

121. PREM 19/120, *Private Eye* no.467, 9/11/79.

122. Davenport-Hines, *Enemies Within*, p.514; Moore, *Thatcher, Vol. 1*, p.484.

123. PREM 19/120, Armstrong to Thatcher, 20/11/79.

124. Bower, *The Perfect English Spy*, pp.324–6.

125. PREM 19/120, notes for Thatcher's speech attached to Armstrong to Whitmore, 18/11/79.

126. Pimlott, *The Queen*, p.337.

127. PREM 16/2230, Hunt to Wilson, 'Sir Anthony Blunt', 3/7/74.

128. Ibid., Hunt to Wilson, 'Sir Anthony Blunt', 3/7/74.

129. PREM 19/120, MI5, 'Investigation of Russian Penetration of the Secret Services', annexe to Hunt to Prime Minister, 29/5/79.

130. PREM 16/2230, 'Sir Anthony Blunt', attached to Hunt to Thatcher, 20/12/78.

131. PREM 19/120, anon. 'Background' undated.

132. PREM 16/2230, 'Sir Anthony Blunt', attached to Hunt to Thatcher, 20/12/78.

133. Ibid., John Hunt, 'Sir Anthony Blunt', 20/12/78.

134. Carter, *Anthony Blunt,* p.449.

135. Heald, *The Duke*, p.108.

136. Carter, *Anthony Blunt,* p.449.

137. Ibid.

138. PREM 19/120, 'Interview with Anthony Blunt by Christopher Morris', 20/11/79.

139. Entry for 21/9/77, Donoughue, *Downing Street Diary: Volume Two*, p.238. Donoughue renders the name 'Beevers' in his diary.

140. Ibid. See also Christopher Hitchens, 'The Crown and the Mole', *LA Times*, 21/4/21.

141. Entry for 7/11/77, ibid. p.259. See also Purvis, 'When spooks pulled strings', pp.62–7.

142. PREM 16/2230, 'Note for the Record, 21/6/77.

143. Ibid., John Hunt, 'Sir Anthony Blunt', 20/12/78; ibid., Hunt to Cartledge (No.10), 'Sir Anthony Blunt', 17/12/78.

144. Ibid., John Hunt, 'Sir Anthony Blunt', 20/12/78.

145. Ibid., Hunt to Callaghan, 16/1/79.

146. PREM 19/120, Armstrong to Whitmore, 16/11/79.

147. Ibid., Armstrong to Whitmore, 16/11/79.

148. PREM 16/2230, Hunt to Callaghan, 16/1/79.

149. Ibid., John Hunt, 'Blunt and the Palace', December 78.

150. Carter, *Anthony Blunt*, p.484; https://www.bbc.co.uk/news/uk-24803131

151. PREM 19/120, Armstrong to Whitmore, 14/11/79.

152. Ibid., Anon. 'Blunt and the Palace', annexe to Hunt to Prime Minister, 29/7/79.

153. Entry for 14/11/89, Benn, *The End of an Era: Diaries 1980–1990*, pp.580–81.

154. PREM 19/120, Lankester to Whitmore, 18/11/79.

155. PREM 19/3942, Thatcher to Leadbitter, 11/12/79.

156. PREM 19/120, Anthony Blunt statement, November 1959.
157. Carter, *Anthony Blunt,* p.486.
158. Diary entry 18/7/64, Jebb (ed.), *The Diaries of Cynthia Gladwyn,* p.309.
159. Moore, *Thatcher, Vol. 1,* p.485.
160. Entry for 28/11/79, Strong, *Splendours and Miseries,* p.385.
161. Entry for 8/11/83, ibid., p.541.
162. Entry for 6/11/81, ibid., pp.420–21.
163. Entry for 8/2/57, Catterall (ed.), *Macmillan Diaries, Vol. II,* p.3.
164. Entry for 10/10/67, Crossman, *Crossman Diaries,* p.342.
165. PREM 11/3280, Macmillan to Queen, 'Laos', 27/3/61.
166. Bedell Smith, *Elizabeth the Queen,* pp.122–3.
167. PREM 11/3480, Macmillan to Queen, 23/12/59.
168. Entry for April 1968, Vickers (ed.), *Beaton in the Sixties,* pp.230–31.
169. Ziegler, *Wilson,* p.215.
170. Entry for 21/9/63, Catterall (ed.), *Macmillan Diaries, Vol. II,* pp.596–7.
171. Davenport-Hines, *An English Affair,* pp.269–70.

Chapter 17

1. WO 32/21796, Blackner, 'Operation Instruction: The Protection of the Royal Family in an Emergency (Plan Synchronise)', December 1968.
2. Ruane, *Churchill and the Bomb,* pp.32, 137; entry for 2/8/45, Hart-Davis (ed.), *King's Counsellor,* pp.347–8.
3. Entries for 2/8/45 and 9/8/45, Hart-Davis (ed.), *King's Counsellor,* pp.348, 350.
4. Ibid.

5. Szasz, *British Scientists and the Manhattan Project,* pp.16–31; Cathcart, *Test of Greatness,* pp.99–107.
6. Twigge and Scott, *Planning Armageddon,* pp.3–57.
7. Entries for 2/8/45, and 9/8/45, Hart-David (ed.), *King's Counsellor,* pp.348, 350.
8. Pimlott, *Queen,* p.81.
9. Ziegler, *Mountbatten,* pp.298–9.
10. Ruane, *Churchill and the Bomb,* pp.xii–xiii.
11. Dylan, 'Operation TIGRESS', p.4.
12. Ibid., pp.3–4.
13. Ibid., pp. 9–10; 'The Duke Sees Atom Engine', *Daily Mail,* 27/3/52, p.3.
14. Dylan, 'Operation TIGRESS', pp. 9–10.
15. Ibid.
16. Ibid.; Hennessy, *The Prime Minister,* p.202.
17. *Times,* Court Circular, 27/5/52, p.8.
18. 'The Duke Sees Secret Weapons', *Daily Mail,* 8/11/52, p.3.
19. Dylan, 'Operation TIGRESS', p.13.
20. Ibid., p.15; Andrew and Mitrokhin, *The Mitrokhin Archive,* p.519.
21. Gill, *Britain and the Bomb,* p.24.
22. CAD: Shuckburgh Diary, MS191/1/2/2, 19/1/53.
23. CAD: Shuckburgh Diary, MS191/1/2/3, 11/5/54.
24. Gill, *Britain and the Bomb,* pp.24–5.
25. PREM 11/747, Churchill to Queen, 16/7/54.
26. Ibid.
27. PREM 11/747, Colville to Adeane, 16/12/54.
28. CAB 129/72, Churchill, 'Notes on Tube Alloys, 1954', C(54)390, December 1954.

29. Goodman, *Spying on the Nuclear Bear*, p.27.

30. Susie Boniface, 'Prince Philip almost landed on site of nuke tests just weeks after last A-bomb blast', *Mirror*, 2/7/18. See also AIR 20/11598; AIR 20/10434.

31. Quoted in Hogg, *British Nuclear Culture*, p.144.

32. Entry for 17/10/59, Ziegler (ed.), *From Shore to Shore*, pp.28–9.

33. Ibid.

34. Entry for 5–6/10/59, ibid.

35. Horne, *Macmillan*, pp.168–70.

36. PREM 11/3510, Macmillan to Queen, 17/11/61.

37. Ibid., Macmillan to Queen, 16/6/1960; Hennessy, *Cabinets and the Bomb*, pp.20–22.

38. Entry for 22/10/62, Catterall (ed.), *Macmillan Diaries Vol. II*, p.508.

39. James Tull, interviewed by Raymond Ewing, *Association for Diplomatic Studies and Training Oral Histories*, 31/5/01.

40. Raj and Young (eds), *Ambassador to Sixties London*, pp.64, 127, 427.

41. DNSA: Cuban Missile Crisis, David Bruce Diaries, 23/10/1962.

42. Ibid.

43. Ferris, *Behind the Enigma*, pp.532–6.

44. Wilson, *Britain on the Brink*, p.152.

45. Ibid., pp.152–3.

46. Philip shared his interest in UFOs with Mountbatten and Bernhard of the Netherlands, see entry for 10/7/77, Ziegler (ed.), *From Shore to Shore*, pp.369–70.

47. The papers of Sir Peter Scott, held in Cambridge, show that the queen was interested in the phenomenon too, but had already rebuffed requests to name the monster, if it were to be found, in her honour. Charteris warned that it would require 'absolutely irrefutable evidence' because 'it would be most regrettable to connect Her Majesty in any way with something which ultimately turned out to be a hoax'. Reported in Selina Sykes, 'How the Loch Ness Monster was Nearly Named After the Queen', *Express*, 5/9/15.

48. David Clarke, *Britain's X-traordinary Files*, Bloomsbury, pp.188–9.

49. Wilson, *Launch Pad UK*, pp.161–2.

50. Ibid.; Scott, 'Intelligence and the Risk of Nuclear War', pp.31–2.

51. Horne, *Macmillan, Vol. 2 1957–1986*, p.385.

52. Quoted in Hennessy, *Cabinet and the Bomb*, p.142.

53. PREM 11/4437, Macmillan to Queen, 22/12/62.

54. Hennessy, *Cabinet and the Bomb*, p.147.

55. FRUS: State Department, 'Memorandum of Conversation: Skybolt', 19/12/62 doc no. 402 in FRUS 1961–63 vol. XIII, 'Western Europe and Canada'.

56. PREM 11/4437, Macmillan to Queen, 22/12/62.

57. DEFE 28/140, NATO Defense College, 'Address delivered on 14 December 1964 by His Royal Highness The Prince Philip, Duke of Edinburgh', 14/12/64. We are grateful to Lee Richards for sharing this file.

58. Ibid.

59. DEFE 28/140, Wild, untitled memo, 5/11/65. We are grateful to Lee Richards for sharing this file.

60. DEFE 28/140, NATO Defense College, 'Address delivered on 14 December 1964 by His Royal

Highness The Prince Philip, Duke of Edinburgh', 14/12/64.

61. Ibid.

62. Hennessy, *The Prime Minister*, pp.124, 134.

63. Ibid., p.134; DEFE 13/321, Trend to Thorneycroft, 21/5/63.

64. Hennessy, *The Secret State*, pp.xxiii–xxiv.

65. CAB 21/5655, McIndoe to Mitchell, 'Transition to War – Information to be Passed to the Queen', 9/3/65.

66. Hennessy, 'Inescapable, Necessary and Lunatic', pp.212–16.

67. Twigge and Scott, *Planning Armageddon*, pp.62–89.

68. Hennessy, *The Secret State*, pp.191–2.

69. Thanks to Mike Kenner for pointing this out.

70. Snippet from CAB 21/4135. Document released through FOI request submitted by Mike Kenner. We are grateful to him for sharing it.

71. Thanks to Mike Kenner for pointing this out.

72. Entry for 19/5/86, Strong, *Splendours and Miseries*, p.614.

73. Laurie, *Beneath the City Streets*, pp.218–20.

74. Hennessy, *The Secret State*, pp.191–2.

75. WO 32/21796, Director of Army Staff Duties, 'Protection of Royal Family in an Emergency', 13/7/64; Director of Army Staff Duties, 'Operation Instruction: The Protection of the Royal Family in an Emergency (Plan Candid)', 13/7/64.

76. Hennessy, *The Secret State* (revised ed.), pp.293, 295.

77. Stewart, *The King's Private Army*, pp.120–22.

78. Hennessy, *The Secret State*, pp.155–6.

79. WO 32/21796, Brind, MOD, 'Protection of the Royal Family in War', 28/8/64. Thanks to Mike Kenner.

80. WO 32/21796, Blackner, 'Operation Instruction: The Protection of the Royal Family in an Emergency (Plan Synchronise)', December 1968.

81. Home Defence Committee, 'Peacetime Preparations at, and Covert Stories for, PYTHON Sites', HDC(MG)15, 23/3/67. Document released through FOI request submitted by Mike Kenner. We are grateful to him for sharing it.

82. Emergency Services and Defence Division, 'Machinery of Government in War – HDC(67)5, note to Mr Engholm, Annex A: Function of PYTHON Groups', 6/11/67. Document released through FOI request submitted by Mike Kenner. We are grateful to him for sharing it.

83. Home Defence Committee, 'Python Planning – HM Ships, Note by the Ministry of Defence (Navy Department)', HDC(MG)(67)14, 23/3/67. Document released through FOI request submitted by Mike Kenner. We are grateful to him for sharing it.

84. WO 32/21796, Blackner, 'Operation Instruction: The Protection of the Royal Family in an Emergency (Plan Synchronise)', December 1968.

Chapter 18

1. CAD: MS 191/1/2/4, Shuckburgh Diary, 7/7/55.

2. Cannadine, *The Pleasures of the Past*, p.67.
3. See Murphy, *The Empire's New Clothes*.
4. Louis, *The British Empire in the Middle East*, pp.i–xx.
5. Balfour-Paul, 'Britain's Informal Empire in the Middle East', pp.490–98.
6. Marr, *The Diamond Queen*, p.143.
7. Milani, *The Shah*, p.85.
8. FO 371/86726, E8126/100/G, Lascelles to Henniker, 21/6/48; FO 371/68730, E11183/1006/34/G, The Flag Officer commanding, HMS Tebbus to C IN C Home Fleet, 27/7/48. See also Townsend, *Time and Chance*, pp.133–4.
9. FRUS: US ambassador to the UK to Secretary of State, 5/8/48 (1948, The Near East, South Asia and Africa v/1 doc.122).
10. FO 371/91522, minute by Bevin, 19/1/51.
11. Cormac, *Disrupt and Deny*, pp.94–6.
12. LHCMA: Woodhouse 8/1, Woodhouse, 'Iran 1950–3', 16/8/76, p.2.
13. Rahnema, *Behind the 1953 Coup in Iran*, p.xx.
14. Louis, 'Britain and the Overthrow of the Mosaddeq Government', p.168.
15. Rahnema, *Behind the 1953 Coup in Iran*, p.xxi; Louis, 'Britain and the Overthrow of the Mosaddeq Government', p.167.
16. FRUS: Telegram from the US Embassy in Iran to the Department of State, 28/2/53 (1952–1954, Iran, 1951–1954 doc.166).
17. NARA: US embassy, London to State Department, RG 59, Central Files 1950–1954, 788.11/2–2753, telegram 4844 to Tehran, 27/2/53.
18. FRUS: Telegram from the US Embassy in Iran to the Department of State, 28/2/53.
19. Ibid.
20. Ibid.
21. *The Queen and the Coup*, Channel 4, broadcast 14/6/20.
22. Ibid.
23. Cormac, *Disrupt and Deny*, p.95.
24. Rahnema, *Behind the 1953 Coup in Iran*, p.39.
25. Bayandor, *Iran and the CIA*, pp.76–7; Rahnema, *Behind the 1953 Coup in Iran*, pp.xxi, 50–51.
26. Rahnema, *Behind the 1953 Coup in Iran*, p.xxii; Louis, 'Britain and the Overthrow of the Mosaddeq Government', p.168.
27. FO 371/104659, EP1943/1/G, Makins (Washington) to London No.1085, 21/5/53.
28. Ibid., Churchill to Strang, 22/5/53, M.151/53.
29. Aldrich and Cormac, *The Black Door*, p.177.
30. Vanessa Thorpe, 'Documentary reveals evidence confirming a British spy's role in restoring the Shah in 1953', *Guardian*, 02/8/20.
31. Bayandor, *Iran and the CIA*, p.78; Rahnema, *Behind the 1953 Coup in Iran*, p.38.
32. NARA: US embassy Iran to Department of State, RG 59, Central Files 1950–1954, 788.11/8-2353, telegram 462, 23/8/53, quoted in FRUS: US ambassador to UK to Department of State, 25/8/53, (Iran, 1952–1954 doc.356).
33. FO 371/104659, EP1943/8, Falla min. 'Message to the Persian Government', 21/8/53.

34. Ibid., EP1943/8, Montague Brown min., 24/8/53.

35. FRUS: US ambassador to UK to Department of State, 25/8/53, (Iran, 1952–1954 doc.356).

36. FO 371/110092, EP 1941/G/1, Eden minute 20/1/54 on Tehran to London, 18/1/54.

37. Ibid., EP 1941/4, Wiggin to HE 19/3/54; Stewart minute, 26/3/54, ibid.

38. Entry for 18/2/55, Nicolson, The Later Years, p.276.

39. FO 371/110092, EP 1941/8a, Churchill to Kirkpatrick, 22/8/54. M.141./54.

40. Milani, The Shah, pp.199–201, 363.

41. Entry for 11 September 1973, Alikhani, The Shah and I, pp.316–17.

42. Scott Cooper, The Fall of Heaven, p.29.

43. Aldrich and Cormac, The Black Door, pp.268.

44. FO 371/ 114868, EP 1941/51/G, Bailey (Washington) to Fry, 3/3/55.

45. FO 371/140872, EP1941/4/1G, Harrison to London, 'The Shah's Matrimonial Affairs', 13/10/59, Personal and Very Confidential.

46. FO 371/140872, EP 1941/1/G, West memo, 'The Shah's Prospective Fiancé', 28/10/59.

47. Entry for 15 June 1974, Alikhani, The Shah and I, pp.375–6.

48. Murphy, Monarchy and the End of Empire, p.60.

49. ASIO Monthly Summary, Bulletin nos. 1, 2, 4 and attachment, A11438, NAA. See also Pfennigwerth, A Man of Intelligence, p.252.

50. Crockett, Evatt, pp.238–41.

51. Murphy, Monarchy and the End of Empire, pp.62–5; Bradford, Queen Elizabeth, p.90.

52. Mawby, 'The Clandestine Defence of Empire', pp.105–30.

53. Bill Wickham, 'The Royal Visit: Aden 1954', Overseas Service Pensioners' Association Journal, No. 97 (2009), accessed via https://www.britishempire.co.uk/article/adenroyalvisit.htm

54. Wickham, 'The Royal Visit'.

55. Ibid.

56. Hashimoto, Twilight of the British Empire, p.57.

57. Jevon, Glubb Pasha and the Arab Legion, pp.224–5.

58. CAD: MS 191/1/2/4, Shuckburgh Diary, 7/7/55.

59. Ibid.

60. Ibid.

61. Hashimoto, Twilight of the British Empire, p.155.

62. Ashton, King Hussein of Jordan, pp.49–56.

63. Ibid., p.52.

64. Ibid., pp.65–6.

65. Jones, 'The "preferred plan"', pp.401–15.

66. CAB 128/30, Cabinet Minutes, CM24(56), 21/3/56.

67. Quoted in Rathmell, Secret War in the Middle East, p.118.

68. Kyle, Suez, p.145.

69. Ibid., pp.145–6.

70. Hennessy, The Prime Minister, pp.228, 231, 232.

71. Pearson, Sir Anthony Eden and the Suez Crisis, pp.156–7; Hennessy, The Prime Minister, p.221.

72. Smith, 'Resignation of a First Sea Lord', p.115.

73. Ibid., pp.108, 115.

74. Ibid., pp.111, 115; Murphy, Monarchy and the End of Empire, p.67.

75. Murphy, *Monarchy and the End of Empire*, p.67.
76. Smith, 'Resignation of a First Sea Lord', p.124.
77. Hennessy, *The Prime Minister*, pp.223–4.
78. Ibid., p.223.
79. Pimlott, *The Queen*, p.253.
80. Murphy, *Monarchy and the End of Empire*, pp.68–9.
81. Hennessy, *The Prime Minister*, p.223.
82. Murphy, *Monarchy and the End of Empire*, pp.68–9.
83. Pimlott, *The Queen*, p.253.
84. Ibid., p.255.
85. Ibid., pp.253–5.
86. Moran, 'Concealing Collusion', p.364.
87. Murphy, *Monarchy and the End of Empire*, p.67.
88. Ibid., pp.67–8; Hennessy, *The Prime Minister*, p.218; Pimlott, *The Queen*, p.254.
89. Murphy, *Monarchy and the End of Empire*, p.69.
90. PREM 11/1163, 'Bulletin for Her Majesty the Queen for the 24 hours ending 6am 1st November 1956'.
91. Ibid., 'Bulletin for HM the Queen for the period 24 hours ending 7am 5th November 1956'.
92. Aldrich and Cormac, *The Black Door*, pp.194–202; Aldrich, *GCHQ*, p.149; William Clark, interviewed on BBC One's *An Ocean Apart*, Part 5, 'If You Don't Like Our Peaches, Quit Shaking Our Tree', 1988.
93. FRUS: Telegram from the US embassy in the UK to the Department of State, 12/11/56 (Suez Crisis vol. XVI doc.571).
94. Bedell Smith, *Elizabeth the Queen*, p.116.
95. PREM 11/1163, 'Bulletin No.20 for Her Majesty the Queen for the 24 hours ending 7am 21st November 1956'.
96. Ibid., 'Bulletin No.16 for Her Majesty the Queen for the 24 hours ending 7am 15th November 1956'.
97. Ibid., 'Bulletin for Her Majesty the Queen for the 24 hours ending 7am 10 November 1956'; 'Bulletin No.19 for Her Majesty the Queen for the 24 hours ending 7am 20th November 1956'.
98. Ibid., 'Bulletin No.21 for Her Majesty the Queen for the 24 hours ending 7am 22nd November 1956'.
99. PREM 11/1163, Adeane to Gibbons, 22/11/56; Gibbons to Richmond, 23/11/56.
100. Ibid., Colonial Secretary to Jamaica, 2/12/56.
101. CAD: AP23/2/18B, Elizabeth to Eden, 16/1/57.
102. Ibid.
103. Pimlott, *The Queen*, p.256.
104. Thorpe, *Eden*, pp.586, 589.
105. Entry for 30/1/62, Thorpe (ed.), *Who's In, Who's Out*, pp.208–9.
106. Lycett, *The Life of Ian Fleming*, p.205.
107. Pearson, *The Ultimate Family*, pp.144–5.
108. Lacey, *Monarchy*, p.206.
109. Pearson, *The Ultimate Family*, pp.182–3, see also Pearson, *The Life of Ian Fleming*.
110. Macintyre, *For Your Eyes Only*, p.88.
111. McCrisken and Moran, 'James Bond, Ian Fleming and intelligence', pp.804–10; Stillman, 'Two of the MADdest scientists', pp.487–94.
112. British Pathé, King Faisal Visits Britain, 1956, 19/7/56.

113. Karam, 'Missing Revolution', pp.693–709.
114. FO 371/134262, Wright to Hoyer Millar, 21/4/58.
115. Ibid.
116. Ibid., Hoyer Millar to Adeane, 30/4/58.
117. Ibid., Adeane to Hoyer Millar, 2/5/58.
118. Hashimoto, *Twilight of the British Empire*, pp.152, 154–5; Karam, 'Missing Revolution', pp. 693–709.
119. FO 371/133139, 103//58, Baghdad to London, 21 August 1958, No.135.
120. Hashimoto, *Twilight of the British Empire*, p.155.
121. Wright, *Behind Diplomatic Lines*, p.4.
122. Ashton, '"Great New Venture?"', pp.59–89.

Chapter 19

1. PREM 13/3427, Philip to Wilson, 25/11/64.
2. Lacey, *Royal*, p.199.
3. PREM 11/3507, Bligh to Macmillan, 21/12/60.
4. Ibid., Bligh to Macmillan, 14/3/61; ibid., Mills to Bligh, 6/3/61.
5. Ibid., Adeane to Bligh, 20/12/60.
6. Ibid., Keeble (Accra) to Clutterbuck (CRO), 21/2/61; ibid., Clutterbuck to Accra, 16/2/61.
7. Ibid., Mills to De Zulueta, 3/3/61; Andrew, *Defence of the Realm*, p.454; Walton, *Empire of Secrets*, p.230.
8. PREM 11/3508, Bligh to Macmillan, 'The Queen's Visit to Ghana', 1/1/61.
9. Ibid., Adeane to Bligh, 10/7/61.
10. Ibid., MI5, 'Queen's Visit to

Ghana: Assessment of Risk to her Majesty's Personal Safety', 30/10/61.
11. Ibid.
12. Ibid.
13. Ibid., Adeane to Bligh, 10/9/61 (and Macmillan's handwritten response).
14. Ibid., Clutterbuck to Accra, 21/10/61.
15. Ibid.
16. Ibid., Accra to CRO, 31/10/61.
17. Entry for 2/11/61, Catterall (ed.), *Macmillan Diaries, Vol. II*, p.424.
18. PREM 11/3508, Prime Minister to Karachi, Colombo, Kuala Lumpur, Lagos, Nicosia, Washington, 7/11/61.
19. Ibid., Macmillan to Sandys, undated, early November 1961.
20. Ibid., Bligh, 'Note for the Record, 6/11/61.
21. Ibid.
22. PREM 11/3510, Macmillan to Queen, 3/11/61.
23. Pimlott, *The Queen*, p.307.
24. PREM 11/3508, Sandys to Cabinet and Adeane, 7/11/51.
25. CAB 195/20/4197, Cabinet secretary's record, 'Ghana: Queens Visit', CC60(61), 8/11/61.
26. CAB 128/35/60, Cabinet Minutes, CC60(61), 8/11/61; PREM 11/3508, Sandys to Cabinet and Adeane, 7/7/51.
27. PREM 11/3508, Accra to CRO, no.1394, 8/11/61; Accra to CRO, no.1393 8/11/61; Accra to CRO, no.1389, 7/11/61.
28. PREM 11/3508, Macmillan to Sandys, 7/11/61; CAB 195/20/4197, Cabinet secretary's record, 'Ghana: Queens Visit', CC60(61), 8/11/61; CAB 128/35/60, Cabinet Minutes, CC60(61), 8/11/61.

29. Quoted in Bedell Smith, *Elizabeth the Queen*, p.158.
30. PREM 11/3510, Macmillan to Queen, 17/11/61.
31. Pimlott, *The Queen*, p.307.
32. PREM 11/3509, Acting British High Commissioner to the Secretary of State for Commonwealth Relations, Ghana: The Royal Visit, 29/12/61.
33. Quoted in Bedell Smith, *Elizabeth the Queen*, p.159.
34. Nkrumah to Johnson, 26/2/64, NSC file, Special Head of State Correspondence File, Box 19, LBJ library, Austin, Texas.
35. BDOHP: Stephen Miles interview, pp.20–21.
36. BDOHP: John Edmonds interview, pp.15–17.
37. BDOHP: Sir Anthony Parsons interview, p.7.
38. Ibid., p.9.
39. FO 371/178822, Foreign Office to Sudan, telegram 773, 16/11/64 and Foreign Office to Khartoum, telegram 778, 17/11/64.
40. Ibid., Khartoum to Foreign Office, No. 613, 17/11/64.
41. BDOHP: Parsons interview, p.9.
42. FO 371/178822, Scrivener to Scott, 9/12/64, du Boulay to Parsons, 4/12/64.
43. Ibid., note to PUS, Harrison and Scrivener, 22/12/64.
44. Ibid., Scott to Scrivener, 17/12/64.
45. Ibid., Scrivener to Scott, 9/12/64, du Boulay to Parsons, 4/12/64.
46. Ibid., Scrivener, 'The Queen's Visit to Sudan', 21/12/64.
47. BDOHP: Parsons interview, p.9.
48. Ibid.
49. Judd (ed.), *A British Tale*, p.212.
50. BDOHP: Edmonds interview, pp.15–17.
51. Judd (ed.), *A British Tale*, p.220.
52. https://blogs.fcdo.gov.uk/petertibber/2015/02/22/50th-anniversary-of-the-state-visit-of-queen-elizabeth-to-sudan/
53. BDOHP: Parsons interview, p.9.
54. CIA, President's Daily Brief, 8/2/65, FOIA: CIA-RDP79T00936A003400430001-2.
55. BDOHP: Parsons interview, p.9.
56. Murphy, 'By invitation only', pp.245–65.
57. Ibid.; Aubourg, 'Organizing Atlanticism', pp. 92–105; Aldrich, 'OSS, CIA and European unity', pp.184–227; Wilford, 'CIA plot, socialist conspiracy, or new world order?', pp.70–82.
58. Scott-Smith, 'The Congress for Cultural Freedom', pp.437–55.
59. Mountbatten papers, MB1/J105, Meeting between PM, SoS Defence and CDS, 10/6/65.
60. Dylan, *Defence Intelligence*, p.200.
61. Jackson, Bramall and Bramall, *The Chiefs*, pp.328–58.
62. Murphy, 'By invitation only', pp.245–65.
63. Ibid.
64. Murphy, *Monarchy and the End of Empire*, pp.100–02.
65. 'Duke's Advice on Rhodesia Problem', *Times*, 3/7/65, p.8.
66. 'Peer Joins Row over the Duke', *Daily Mirror*, 5/7/65, p.1.
67. PREM 13/570, King to Wilson, 13/7/65.
68. Beesley, *The Official History of the Cabinet Secretaries*, p.320.
69. Murphy, *Monarchy and the End of Empire*, pp.100–2; Pimlott, *The Queen*, p.350.
70. Murphy, *Monarchy and the End of Empire*, pp.100–3.
71. CAB 301/535, O'Neill to Wilson, 1/10/66.
72. Ibid.

73. Murphy, *Monarchy and the End of Empire*, p.103.

74. CAB 301/535, O'Neill to Wilson, 3/1/67.

75. Ibid., Palliser to Mackilligin, 13/1/67.

76. Murphy, *Monarchy and the End of Empire*, p.105.

77. Flower, *Serving Secretly*, p.10.

78. Ibid., pp.11, 14–15.

79. 'Rhodesia Defies Queen's Reprieve', *New York Times*, 6/3/68.

80. Flower, *Serving Secretly*, p.88.

81. Murphy, *Monarchy and the End of Empire*, p.106.

82. Shawcross, *Queen Elizabeth: The Queen Mother*, p.760.

Chapter 20

1. FCO 8/3644, Miers, 'The Shah', 8/2/80.

2. FO 372/8184, Adeane to Gore-Booth, 23/5/66.

3. Entry for 20/5/66, Benn, *Out of the Wilderness*, p.414.

4. CAD AP23/12/2, Eden to Queen, 27/7/65

5. Manchester, *The Arms of Krupp*, pp.10–12.

6. FO 371/189311, Roberts to A Campbell (FO), 6/6/66.

7. Ibid., Roberts to FO, 'Duke of Edinburgh's Visit', 20/6/66.

8. See FCO 21/923-5.

9. FO 372/8184, Gore-Booth to Adeane, 20/5/66.

10. Ibid.

11. FO 371/152126, PUSC, 'Steering Committee: United Kingdom Policy in Latin America', SC(60)7(2nd Revise), 20/5/60.

12. Ibid.

13. FO1110/1615, Glass, 'Latin American Tour', 6/5/63.

14. Hardman, *Queen of the World*, p.508.

15. FCO 26/55, Minter to Shakespeare, 'The British Monarchy Today: Latin American Portuguese Edition', 13/8/68.

16. FCO 26/55, Information Policy Department, 'Publicity for the State Visit to Brazil and Chile between 1 and 18 November 1968', undated.

17. FCO 7/1145, Mason to Diggins, cc Charteris, 'State Visit to Chile', 15/10/68.

18. FCO 168/3069, Allott to Dyer, 11/9/68.

19. FCO 168/3560, Allott, 'Brief for Call by Sir David Hunt', 3/9/69.

20. FCO 95/419, quoted in John McEvoy and Daniel Hunt, 'Britain and Brazil's Dictatorship', *Brasilwire* (2020), https://www.brasilwire.com/britain-brazil-dictatorship/

21. Senate Select Committee on Intelligence Activities, Staff report, Covert Action in Chile, 1963–73, III: 10, Gerald Ford Library.

22. FCO 168/3069, IRD, 'Chile: IRD Annual Report – April 1968', April 1968.

23. USDDO: State Dept., 'Queen Elizabeth's Visit to Chile Discussed', 13/11/68.

24. Ibid.

25. FCO168/674, SPA in Chile.

26. FCO 168/3069, IRD, 'Chile: IRD Annual Report – April 1968', April 1968.00

27. PREM 13/2358, Foreign Office, 'State Visit to Brazil and Chile', 13/9/68.

28. FCO 7/1145, Mason, 'The State Visit of Her Majesty the Queen and His Royal Highness the

Duke of Edinburgh to Chile, 11–18 November, 1968', 3/12/68.

29. FO 371/1182764, NSIO5I/109, Bridges to Wright, 2/8/65.

30. PREM 13/2352, 'record of conversation between the prime minister and Mr Kosygin over lunch at No 10 Downing Street on 10 February 1967'.

31. PREM 13/2352, Gore-Booth to Sutherland, 10/2/67.

32. Wilson, *The Labour Government*, p.353.

33. PREM 13/2352, Gore-Booth to Sutherland, 10/2/67; Adeane to Gore-Booth, 6/2/67.

34. Ibid., Morphett to Palliser, 12/1/68.

35. PREM 13/2352, Morphett to Palliser, 12/1/68.

36. Bower, *The Perfect English Spy*, p.350.

37. Platt, 'The Soviet Imprisonment of Gerald Brooke and Subsequent Exchange for the Krogers, 1965–1969', pp.193–212.

38. PREM 13/2352, handwritten note for prime minister, 19/1/68.

39. Ibid., Adeane to Halls, 2/2/68.

40. Ibid., Halls to Adeane, 30/1/68; Adeane to Halls, 2/2/68.

41. Platt, 'The Soviet Imprisonment of Gerald Brooke and Subsequent Exchange for the Krogers, 1965–1969', pp.193–212.

42. Walden, *Lucky George*, p.142.

43. FCO 57/195, Mayall to FO Security Department, 20/5/70.

44. Ibid., Holmer to Mayall, 21/5/70.

45. Ibid., Mayall to Leigh 21/5/70.

46. CIA, 'Eastern European Intelligencer', 26/10/72. CREST: CIA-RDP79B00864A0012000 20039-5.

47. FCO 28/2111, Waldon to Bullard, 'Royal Visits to the USSR',

48. Ibid., 'Possible Visit to USSR by Princess Anne', 11/12/72.

49. Ibid., Westwood, 'Possible Visit of the Duke of Edinburgh to the USSR', 16/10/72

50. Cowan, *A Spy's Wife*, p.102.

51. FCO 28/2111, Walden to Bullard, 'Royal Visits to Soviet Union', 26/6/72.

52. Ibid., Walden to Scott, 'Duke of Edinburgh's Visit to the Soviet Union', 20/6/72.

53. Ibid.

54. FCO 57/539, Walden to Bullard, 'Duke of Edinburgh's Visit to the Soviet Union', 1/3/73.

55. FCO 28/2111, Walden, 'Possible Visit by Prince Philip to the Soviet Union', 17/5/72.

56. FCO 57/543, Mayall to Willett, 19/7/72.

57. FCO 28/2111, Walden, 'Possible Visit by Prince Philip to the Soviet Union', 17/5/72.

58. FCO 57/539 Handwritten note, Greenhill, 22/1/73.

59. FCO 57/543, Willett to Mayall, 5/7/72.

60. FCO 57/539, Willett to Curle, 11/4/73.

61. FCO 57/540, Willett to Killick, 31/7/73.

62. Ibid., Killick to Willett, 2/8/73.

63. FCO 57/542, Cartledge to Bullard, 30/7/73.

64. FCO 57/540, Curle to Willett, 17/7/73.

65. Ibid., Westood, handwritten note, 6/7/73; FCO 57/541, Bullard to Cartledge, 22/6/73.

66. FCO 57/542, Cartledge to Bullard, 30/7/73.

67. FCO 57/540, Curle, untitled note, 31/7/73.

17/5/72; Killick to Bullard, 6/12/72.

68. Ibid., Killick to FCO, 30/7/73.
69. Nicholson, *Activities Incompatible*, pp.55–6.
70. FCO 57/541, Douglas-Home to Killick, 7/8/73; Killick to FCO, 9/8/73.
71. Ibid., Bullard to Cartledge, 22/6/73.
72. Ibid., Douglas-Home to Killick, 7/8/73; Killick to FCO, 9/8/73.
73. Ibid., 'Protocol and Conference Department', briefing pack, 28/8/73.
74. Vice-chairman of national security commission under Council of Ministers of Ukrainian SSR, 'NATIONAL SECURITY COMMISSION CENTRAL COMMISSION OF THE UKRAINIAN COMMUNIST PARTY: Announcement', 31/8/73 (KGB document found in the Ukrainian archives and shared on Twitter by @kgb_files. Translated by Anastasia Zabludovskaya.
75. Alan Travis, 'The Duke, the Spies, and the KGB: How Cold War Plotting Entangled Royal Visit', *Guardian*, 26/4/04.
76. FCO 57/542, Killick, 'Visit of HRH The Duke of Edinburgh to the Soviet Union', 2/10/73.
77. Ibid.
78. Vice-chairman of national security commission under Council of Ministers of Ukrainian SSR, 'Announcement', 4/8973 (KGB document found in the Ukrainian archives and shared on Twitter by @kgb_files. Translated by Anastasia Zabludovskaya.
79. BDOHP: Sir Curtis Keeble interview, p.94.
80. NAA: AA1984/609 part II, 'The CIA and Whitlam's Dismissal', *Australian Financial Review*, 5/12/75; Kerr to Charteris, 5/12/75.
81. NAA: AA1984/609 part I, Kerr to Charteris, 12/9/75.
82. Ibid., Charteris to Kerr, 2/10/75.
83. NAA: AA1984/609 part II, Charteris to Kerr, 4/11/75.
84. Ibid., Kerr to Charteris, 11/11/75 and Charteris to Kerr, 17/11/75.
85. NAA: AA1984/609 part III, Kerr to Charteris, 10/6/76.
86. Ibid., Charteris to Kerr, 16/10/76.
87. NAA: AA1984/609 part IV, Kerr to Charteris, 10/6/76 including attachment: ASIO report 'Australian League of Rights', 8/6/76.
88. Entry for 15/3/76, Donoughue, *Downing Street Diary*, pp.697.
89. Pimlott, *The Queen*, p.430.
90. Entry for 15/3/76, Donoughue, *Downing Street Diary*, pp.697.
91. Ibid. See also entry for 19/1/76, p.634.
92. Aldrich and Cormac, *The Black Door*, pp.327–8.
93. Haines, *Glimmers of Twilight*, p.129.
94. Murphy, *Monarchy and the End of Empire*, p.132.
95. Entry for 17/7/75, Thorpe, (ed.), *Who's In, Who's Out*, p.504.
96. BDOHP: Colin Munro interview, pp.8–9.
97. BDOHP: Sir James Hennessy interview, pp.8–15.
98. Kyemba, *State of Blood*, p.77.
99. We are grateful to Spencer Mawby for sharing the files on this episode with us. CAB 128/61, CM(77) 21st mtg, Confidential Annex, minute 2, 26/5/77.
100. *The Times*, 1 June 1977. Courtesy of Spencer Mawby. See also

Murphy, *Monarchy and the End of Empire*, p.135.

101. FCO 68/714, Sinclair minute, 17/3/77, Memo on CHOGM: President Amin's Attendance by Duff, 25/3/77; FCO 31/2157, Rowlands to Secretary of State (ud); FCO 31/2159, Memo on President Amin and the Commonwealth Heads of Government Meeting by Hunt (ud). Courtesy of Spencer Mawby.

102. FCO 73/358, Record of Private Conversation with Munyua Waiyaki by Owen, 22/6/77. Courtesy of Spencer Mawby.

103. Hardman, *Queen of the World*, pp.83–5.

104. Charles Harrison, former editor of the *Uganda Argus*, provided the fullest account of these events in *The Times*. See *The Times*, 21/6/77, p.1, 22/6/77, p.1, 23/6/77, p.10, 24/6/77, p.6, 25/6/77, p.5. See also *Los Angeles Times*, 23/6/77, B10, 26/6/77, A22; *New York Times*, 21/6/77, p.3. See also Reid, *A History of Modern Uganda*, pp.61–2. Courtesy of Spencer Mawby.

105. Hardman, *Queen of the World*, pp.84–5.

106. FCO 8/2522, Parsons to London, 06/10/75.

107. FCO 8/1887, Special Branch memo, 'Visit of HM the Queen and the Shah to Ascot', 15/6/72.

108. FCO 8/1886, Memo to Smith, 'Shah's Visit', 12/6/72.

109. FCO 8/1887 'Meeting at the Iranian embassy to consider the security plan for the Shah's visit', 19/6/72.

110. Ibid., Armstrong note, 19/6/72.

111. Ibid., Charteris to Downing Street, 21/6/72.

112. Ibid., Armstrong to Charteris, 16/6/72.

113. Ibid., Memo to Smith 'Tehran telegram 549: Shah's visit', 19/6/72.

114. BDOHP: Sir Peter Ramsbotham interview, p.38.

115. FCO 8/2077, Grattan to MDR, 'The Queen's Return Flight from Australia' 11/10/73.

116. Ibid., 'Some points made by the Shah in private meeting with the Queen on 23 October 1973 at Teheran'.

117. Entry for 23/10/73, Alikhani (ed)., *The Shah and I*, p.329.

118. FCO 8/2179, Craig minute, 15/10/74.

119. FCO 8/2179, Wright to Campbell, attaching 'Royal Visits between Iran and the UK', 29/5/74.

120. FCO 8/2289, Thompson report, 12/8/74.

121. FCO 8/2523, Parsons to Lucas, 'Royal Visits', 28/5/75.

122. FCO 8/2522: Parsons to Callaghan, 30/4/75.

123. Entry for 14/12/78, Radji, *In the Service of the Peacock Throne*, p.285.

124. Cormac, *Disrupt and Deny*, p.216.

125. Cooper, *The Fall of Heaven*, pp.468–79.

126. Walden, *Lucky George*, pp.182–3.

127. PREM 16/2131, Owen to Cartledge, 8/1/79.

128. AAD: US Embassy Rabat to US Secretary of State, 'President Carter's Messages on his Middle East Trip', 14/3/79, doc. 1979RABAT01698.

129. Ibid.

130. PREM 16/2131, Chilcot to Cartledge, 14/2/79; Cartledge to Lever, 15/2/79, 19/2/79.

131. HO 287/2826, Owen quoted in Lever to Cartledge 'the Shah of Iran', 21/2/79.
132. Palmer, *The Queen and Mrs Thatcher*, p.76.
133. FCO 8/3392, Lever to Cartledge, 21/5/79.
134. AAD: US Embassy Rabat to US Secretary of State, 'President Carter's Messages on his Middle East Trip', 14/3/79, doc. 1979RABAT01698.
135. Henderson, *Mandarin*, p.272.
136. Shawcross, *The Shah's Last Ride*, p.287.
137. Weiner, *Legacy of Ashes*, p.274.
138. FCO 8/3644, Miers, 'The Shah', 8/2/80.
139. PREM 19/2577, Thatcher to Margaret, 9/1/80.
140. Ibid., Margaret to Thatcher, 7/2/80.
141. FCO8/3644, Walden to Adeane, 18/7/80; Miers to Private Secretary, 18/7/80.
142. Cooper, *The Fall of Heaven*, p.495.
143. Entry for 30/1/73, Alikhani (ed.), *The Shah and I*, p.283; entry for 14/07/74, ibid., p.380. See also entry for 8/8/78, Radji, *In the Service of the Peacock Throne*, p.213.
144. FCO 8/3644, Lever, 'Ex King Constantine', 6/8/80; Miers, 'Admission of Empress Farah to Britain', 17/9/80.
145. FCO 8/3644, Humfrey to Miers, 11/8/80.
146. Ibid., Roberts to FCO, 19/8/80.
147. Ibid., Lamport to Beckett, 20/10/80; Humfrey to Miers, 15/10/80.
148. Cormac, *Disrupt and Deny*, p.217.
149. FCO 8/3644: Miers to Weir, 29/10/80; FCO 8/3645, Weir to Heseltine, 29/12/80.
150. HO 287/2826, Amery to Carrington, 22/12/81; Snuffbox to Home Office, Jan 83.
151. National Security Archive: 'Cold War: Politburo discussion of MT-Gorbachev meeting', 13/4/89.

Chapter 21

1. Princess Anne interview, *Parkinson*, BBC, 1980.
2. PREM 13/1772, Forster to Halls, 10/3/67; Foreign Office to Bangkok, no.238, 14/3/67; New Delhi to Commonwealth Office, no.533, 14/3/67; note for the record, 10/3/67.
3. PREM 19/916, Bridge Inquiry into the activities of Commander Trestrail, 24/11/82.
4. Geraghty, *The Bullet-Catchers*, pp.56, 64.
5. Connor, *Ghost Force*, pp.153–4.
6. Entry for 4/11/68, Vickers (ed.), *Beaton in the Sixties*, p.275.
7. Dimbleby, *Prince of Wales*, p.131.
8. Varney, *Bodyguard to Prince Charles*, p.124.
9. Ibid., p.126.
10. Ibid., p.127.
11. Ibid., p.128.
12. Ibid.
13. Brooke, *Terrorism and Nationalism in the United Kingdom*, p.49.
14. Thomas, *John Jenkins: The Reluctant Revolutionary?*, pp.10–24.
15. PREM 13/2903, Trend to Wilson, 28/2/68.
16. PREM 13/2903, Callaghan to Wilson, 'Wales: Security', 12/2/69; Brooke, *Terrorism and Nationalism in the United Kingdom*, p.49.
17. E. Crump, 'The bizarre plots to stop Prince Charles' investiture using "kamikaze dogs" and

manure', *The Daily Post*, 1/7/19; Obituary, 'Dennis Coslett, Dashing commandant of the Free Wales Army', *Independent*, 10/10/11.

18. PREM 13/2903, Callaghan to Wilson, 14/4/69.

19. Ibid.

20. PREM 13/2903, No.10 to Cubbon, 16/4/69.

21. Bedell Smith, *Prince Charles*, p.40.

22. PREM 13/2903, Callaghan to Wilson, 'Wales: Security', 12/2/69; ibid., Cubbon to Wilson, 'Investiture of the Prince of Wales', 14/2/69.

23. Ibid., No.10 to Wilson, 1/3/68.

24. Kandiah et al., 'The Ultimate Windsor Ceremonials: Coronations and Investitures', p.81.

25. Thomas, *Hands off Wales*, pp.114–15.

26. Bradford, *Elizabeth*, pp.349–51; De Courcy, *Snowdon*, p.191.

27. PREM 13/2903, Halls to Cubbon, 25/6/67; Jagger, *Escorting the Monarch*, pp.43–5.

28. Eryl Crump, 'The bizarre plots to stop Prince Charles' investiture using "kamikaze dogs" and manure', *Daily Post*, 1/7/19.

29. Entry for 26 April 1969, Williams (ed.), *The Richard Burton Diaries*, pp.272–3.

30. De Courcy, *Snowdon*, p.186.

31. Entry for 2/7/69, Ziegler (ed.), *From Shore to Shore*, p.183.

32. PREM 13/2903, Callaghan to Wilson, 14/4/69.

33. Ibid., Halls to Cubbon, 27/6/69.

34. Entry for 11/7/69, Benn, *Office Without Power, Diaries 1968–72*, p.191.

35. PREM 13/2903, Cubbon to Halls, 26/6/69.

36. Ibid., Maybe to Halls, 27/6/69.

37. Ibid., Cubbon to Halls, 26/6/69.

38. Andrew and Mitrokhin, *The Mitrokhin Archive*, pp.491–2.

39. Brooke, *Terrorism and Nationalism in the United Kingdom*, p.50.

40. Dimbleby, *The Prince of Wales*, p.162.

41. Hardman, *Her Majesty*, p.58.

42. Entry for 2/7/69, Ziegler (ed.), *From Shore to Shore*, p.183.

43. Jagger, *Escorting the Monarch*, pp.43–5; Alwyn Turner, 'Meanwhile Back on Planet Earth', *BBC History Magazine*, August 2019, p.33.

44. Pimlott, *The Queen*, p.390.

45. Bedell Smith, *Prince Charles*, p.40.

46. Hardman, *Her Majesty*, p.59.

47. Crump, 'The bizarre plots to stop Prince Charles' investiture…', *Daily Post*, 1/7/19.

48. 'Governor of Bermuda and Aide are Assassinated', *New York Times*, 12/3/73, p.1, https://www.nytimes.com/1973/03/12/archives/governor-of-bermuda-and-aide-are-assassinated-acting-governor-sworn.html?

49. Hodgson, *Charles*, pp.21–2.

50. FCO 63/1074, Leather to FCO, 9/7/73.

51. Ibid., Philip, 'The Prince of Wales', 24/7/73.

52. Ibid., Bridges to Acland, 23/7/75.

53. FCO 65/1074, Watson, 'Visit to Bermuda by the Prince of Wales'.

54. Holden, *Charles at 50*, p.104.

55. DPP 2/5401, 'Brief for the Prosecution: Note', April 1974.

56. DPP 2/5403, Statement of Witness: J Beaton, 28/3/74.

57. Ibid., Statement of Witness: A Callender, 21/3/74.

58. Ibid., Statement of Witness: J Beaton, 28/3/74.

59. PREM 16/268, Armstrong to Wilson, 21/3/74.

60. DPP 2/5403, Statement of Witness: J Beaton, 28/3/74; DPP/2/5402, Collective account of Princess Anne and Captain Mark Philips, 21/3/74.

61. Princess Anne interview, *Parkinson*, BBC, 1980.

62. Ibid; Jagger, *Escorting the Monarch*, pp.54–5.

63. HO 287/2287/2, Deputy Assistant Commissioner, untitled report on the arrest of Ian Ball, 21/3/74.

64. Mark, *In the Office of Constable*, p.166.

65. 'Princess Anne kidnap medal fetches £50,000 at auction', *Guardian*, 4/3/20.

66. Wilson scribbled note on PREM 16/268, Armstrong to Wilson, 21/3/74.

67. PREM 16/268, Wilson to Miller, 26/3/74.

68. Prince of Wales, Naval Journal, 20/3/74, Dimbleby, *Prince of Wales*, p.255.

69. PREM 16/268, Armstrong to Charteris, 21/3/74.

70. HO 287/2287/2, 'Random demand for £3 million addressed to HM The Queen', n.d.

71. Ibid.

72. Ibid., Deputy Assistant Commissioner, untitled report on the arrest of Ian Ball, 21/3/74.

73. Jagger, *Escorting the Monarch*, pp.54–6.

74. HO 287/2287/1, 'Personal Protection', 28/3/74.

75. Aldrich and Herrington, 'Secrets, Hostages and Ransoms', pp.738–44.

76. PREM 16/640, to 'state visit' Galsworthy to Carlisle 4/3/74 (Lord Bridges to see).

77. HO 287/2287/1, Gerrard to Hilary, 5/4/74.

78. Ibid., Met Police, 'Royalty Protection', 22/3/74.

79. HO 287/2287/1, Met Police, 'Royalty Protection', 22/3/74.

80. Ibid., 'Personal Protection', 28/3/74.

81. Ibid.

82. Jagger, *Escorting the Monarch*, pp.54–5.

83. HO 287/2287/1, 'Personal Protection', 28/3/74; Geraghty, *The Bullet-Catchers*, pp.81–3.

84. Entry for 21/3/74, Ziegler (ed.), *From Shore to Shore*, p.290.

85. HO 287/2287/1, 'Personal Protection', 28/3/74.

86. Geraghty, *The Bullet-Catchers*, p.83.

87. Fremont-Barnes and Winner, *Who Dares Wins*, pp.8, 11; Asher, *The Regiment*, p.399.

88. Geraghty, *The Bullet-Catchers*, pp.83–4.

89. Asher, *The Regiment*, p.423.

90. PREM 19/916, Bridge Inquiry into the activities of Commander Trestrail, 24/11/82.

91. HO 287/2287/1, memo. A Department Metropolitan Police, 22/3/74.

92. Evans, *On Her Majesty's Service*, pp.48–9. Glocks came in 1994.

93. Chris Hastings, 'Crazed gunman who tried to kidnap Princess Anne', *Daily Mail*, 22/11/04; Clare Dyer, 'Hunger Strike by man held for bid to kidnap Princess', *Guardian*, 17/6/02.

94. Seward, *Queen's Speech*, p.114.

95. CJ 4/1518, Stephens, 'Call out of UDR for 6–15 August', 1/8/77.

96. See FCO 23/197, Carter to Vining, Feb. 1968.

97. CJ 4/1527, Charteris to Cooper, 12/11/75.

98. R. W. Apple Jr., 'Northern Ireland, Awaiting Jubilee Visit by the Queen, Erupts in Violence Fatal to Two', *New York Times*, 10/8/77.

99. CJ 4/1519, Marsh to Waterfield, 'Queen's Silver Jubilee: Visit to Northern Ireland 10/11 August 1977', 11/10/76.

100. Ibid., Waterfield, 'Jubilee – Queen's Visit to Northern Ireland – Meeting at Buckingham Palace 19 January: Note for File', 19/1/77.

101. Ibid.

102. Pimlott, *The Queen*, p.449.

103. CJ 4/1521, Silver Jubilee – Operational and Planning Committee, 'Appreciation of the Options for an outline programme for HM The Queen's visit to Northern Ireland in August 1977', February 1977.

104. CJ 4/1518, 'A Military Assessment of the Threat and of Tasks for the Army during the Visit of HM The Queen to Northern Ireland 10 and 11 Aug 77', 11/7/77.

105. Ibid., 'Op Inheritor – Threat Assessment', 12/7/77.

106. Geraghty, *The Bullet Catchers*, p.86.

107. CJ 4/1519, Waterfield, 'Jubilee Visit Planning: Note for the File', 23/12/76.

108. Geraghty, *The Bullet-Catchers*, pp.84–8.

109. CJ 4/1518, Mason, 'The Queen's Jubilee Visit to Northern Ireland 10 and 11 August', 19/7/77.

110. Seward, *Queen's Speech*, p.114.

111. CJ 4/1518, Ramsay to Stowe, 'The Queen's Jubilee Visit to Northern Ireland', 28/7/77.

112. Ibid., Waterfield, 'Jubilee Visit – PR etc', 8/7/77.

113. Ibid., Charteris to Cubbon, 13/7/77.

114. Hardman, *Her Majesty*, p.62.

115. CJ 4/1521, Silver Jubilee – Operational and Planning Committee, 'Appreciation of the Options for an outline programme for HM The Queen's visit to Northern Ireland in August 1977', February 1977.

116. CJ 4/1518, 'Op Inheritor – Threat Assessment', 12/7/77.

117. Ibid., Ramsay to Stowe, 'Incident at the New University of Ulster', 29/7/77.

118. Loughlin, *The British Monarchy and Ireland*, pp.370–71.

119. Geraghty, *The Bullet-Catchers*, pp.84–8.

120. Hardman, *Her Majesty*, p.57.

121. David McKittrick, 'Northern Ireland: Memories of 1977 and a "Terribly Tense" Royal Visitor', *Independent*, 28/6/12.

122. CJ 4/1518, Charteris to Cubbon, draft speech, 28/7/77.

123. Geraghty, *The Bullet-Catchers*, pp.84–8.

124. McKittrick, 'Northern Ireland: Memories of 1977…', *Independent*, 28/6/12.

125. Pimlott, *The Queen*, p.449.

126. Loughlin, *The British Monarchy and Ireland*, pp.371, 374.

127. Entry for 25–28/10/76, Henderson, *Mandarin*, pp.129–31.

Chapter 22

1. Prince Charles, diary, 27/8/79, Dimbleby, *The Prince of Wales*, p.324.

2. Murphy, *Monarchy and the End of Empire*, pp.140–41.

3. Carrington, *Reflect on Things Past*, pp.295–6; Ingram, 'Thatcher and Ramphal', pp.781–3.

4. Hardman, *Queen of the World,* p.315.

5. Ibid., pp.308–9.

6. Ibid., p.331.

7. Pimlot, *The Queen,* p.467.

8. Murphy, *Monarchy and the End of Empire,* pp.140–41.

9. Pimlott, *The Queen,* p.467.

10. Murphy, *Monarchy and the End of Empire,* p.141.

11. Taylor, *Brits,* p.221.

12. Broadlands Archive, S19, Mountbatten to the Queen, 25/8/71, Ziegler, *Mountbatten,* p.697.

13. Entry for 16/5/78, Ziegler (ed.), *From Shore to Shore,* pp.379–80.

14. Lownie, *The Mountbattens,* p.338.

15. Ibid., p.340.

16. Pearce, *Spymaster,* p.13.

17. Lownie, *The Mountbattens,* p.340.

18. Bowyer-Bell, *The Secret Army,* p.451

19. Lownie, *The Mountbattens,* p.341.

20. Bowyer-Bell, *The Secret Army,* p.451

21. Entry for 28/12/87, Thorpe (ed.), *Who Loses, Who Wins,* p.168.

22. Ziegler, *Mountbatten,* p.699.

23. Ibid.

24. Bradford, *Elizabeth,* p.427; Bedell Smith, *Elizabeth the Queen,* pp.295–6.

25. Cormac, *Disrupt and Deny,* pp.165–6.

26. Shawcross, *Queen Elizabeth, The Queen Mother,* p.855; English, *Armed Struggle,* p.220.

27. Bradford, *Elizabeth,* p.427; Bedell Smith, *Elizabeth the Queen,* pp.295–6.

28. Warwick, *Princess Margaret,* p.16.

29. Entry for 4/7/81, Henderson, *Mandarin,* p.404.

30. FCO 87/842, Haydon, 'Murder of Lord Mountbatten on 27 August 1979: Implications, 26/9/79. Evidence that despatch was shared with palace at Free-Gore to Newington, 24/10/79.

31. Moore, *Margaret Thatcher, Vol. 1,* p.482.

32. Lacey, *Royal,* p.260.

33. Hardman, *Her Majesty,* p.60.

34. HO 287/2842, Andrew to Chilcot, 'Protection of VIPs', 12/9/79.

35. Ibid., McNee to Moore, 10/9/79.

36. Ibid., McNee to Moore, 10/9/79; Andrew to Chilcot, 'Protection of VIPs', 12/9/79; Dawson to Phillips, 8/11/79.

37. Ibid., Chilcot to Andrew, 'Protection of VIPs', 12/9/79; McNee to Moore, 10/9/79.

38. DEFE 68/749, Home Office to Chief Officers of Police, 'Protection of Members of the Royal Family, Ministers and Other Public Servants', 7/7/81.

39. Ibid.

40. Erickson, *Lilibet,* p.253.

41. Andrew, *Defence of the Realm,* p.694.

42. Ibid., p.695.

43. Ibid., pp.695–6.

44. Blair, *Policing Controversy,* pp.78–9.

45. Bedel Smith, *Elizabeth the Queen*; Pimlott, *The Queen,* p.476.

46. Eleanor Ainge Roy, '"Damn…I missed" The Incredible Story of the Day the Queen was Nearly Shot', *Guardian,* 13/1/18, https://www.theguardian.com/uk-news/2018/jan/13/queen-elizabeth-assassination-attempt-new-zealand-1981; Hamish McNeilly, 'Declassified intelligence Service Documents Confirm New Zealand Assassination Attempt on Queen

Elizabeth II', *Stuff*, 1/3/18, https://www.stuff.co.nz/national/crime/101794948/the-snowman-and-the-queen-declassified-nz-intelligence-service-documents-confirm-assassination-attempt-on-queen

47. Geraghty, *The Bullet-Catchers*, p.99.
48. BDOHP: Oliver Miles interview, p.68.
49. Ibid., pp.68–9.
50. Geraghty, *The Bullet-Catchers*, pp.62–3.
51. 'Text of Scotland Yard's Report on July 9 Intrusion into Buckingham Palace', *New York Times*, 22/7/82; Pimlott, *The Queen*, p.491.
52. Keay, *Royal Pursuit*, p.199.
53. Entry for 26/7/82, Henderson, *Mandarin*, p.484.
54. PREM 19/916, Bridge Inquiry into the activities of Commander Trestrail, 24/11/82.
55. Ibid., 'Briefing for Prime Minister's Questions on Thursday 25 November 1982'.
56. Ibid., 'Question and Answer Brief for Responding to Enquiries on the Publication of Lord Bridge's Report', n.d. 1982.
57. PREM 19/916, 'Bridge Inquiry into the activities of Commander Trestrail', 24/11/82.
58. Ibid.
59. Ibid.
60. McNee, *McNee's Law*, pp.220–21.
61. Ibid., p.215.
62. Ibid., pp. 216–17.
63. William Whitelaw, 'Buckingham Palace (Security)', 21/7/82, Hansard column 397–8.
64. HO 287/3110, meeting 'The Law of Trespass', 4/10/82.
65. Geraghty, *The Bullet-Catchers*, p.96.
66. William Whitelaw, Buckingham Palace (Security), 21/7/82,

Hansard column 397–8.
67. HO 287/3216, Royal security: assessments of risk to the Royal Family from psychiatric patients 1982 Jan 01–1983 Dec 31.
68. Keay, *Royal Pursuit*, p.204.
69. CAB 128/74, Cabinet Conclusions, CC(82) 38th Conclusions, 15/7/82; PREM 19/916, 'Briefing for Prime Minister's Questions on Thursday 25 November 1982'; William Whitelaw, Buckingham Palace (Security), 21/7/82, Hansard column 397–8.
70. Seward, *The Queen's Speech*, p.127.
71. Adam Helliker, 'The Queen Reveals the Worst Day of Her Life, *Express*, 30/9/18.
72. O'Callaghan, *The Informer*, pp.197–210.
73. Ian Gallagher, 'Duran Duran Drummer Tells how IRA Nearly Killed His Band', *Mail on Sunday*, 26/7/15, https://www.dailymail.co.uk/news/article-3174722/Duran-Duran-drummer-tells-IRA-nearly-killed-band-Princess-Diana-Prince-Charles-gelignite-concert-bomb-plot.html
74. Hoey, *Not in Front of the Corgis*, pp.168–9.
75. Davies, *Queen Elizabeth II*, pp.314–15.
76. Connor, *Ghost Force*, pp.315–16.
77. Ibid., pp.315–17.
78. Campbell, *The Iron Lady*, p.361.
79. PREM 19/1120, Thatcher minute on Woodfield to Butler, 17.6.83, PUL/L/1474/MR.
80. Firmin, *The Regiment*, pp.246–8.
81. Ibid.
82. Ibid.; Newsinger, *Dangerous Men*; Vincen, *Thatcher's Britain*, p.94; Rhodes, *The Final Curtsey*, p.110.
83. PREM 19/1698, Acland to du

Boulay, 'Protection of British VIPs on Visits Abroad', 1/12/81.

84. De la Billière, *Looking for Trouble*, p.353.

85. FCO 57/533, Bolland to Buckingham Palace, 'Duke of Edinburgh's Visit: Evxinograd', 13/9/73.

86. Global Terrorism Database.

87. Thatcher Archives: THCR6/1/2/6, Thatcher Engagement Diary, 21/3/84; De la Billière, *Looking for Trouble*, p.353.

88. Thatcher Archives: THCR 3/1/36/f152, Thatcher to Hussein, 23/3/84.

89. CIA, 'National Intelligence Daily', 26/3/84. CREST: CIA-RDP87T00970R000200010059-6.

90. BDOHP: Sir John Leahy interview, pp.31–2.

91. Thatcher Archives: THCR 6/1/2/6, Thatcher's Engagement Diary, 24/3/84; De la Billière, *Looking for Trouble*, p.353–4.

92. Ashton, 'Love's Labours Lost', p.667.

93. Thatcher Archives: THCR6/1/2/6, Thatcher Engagement Diary, 21/3/84; De la Billière, *Looking for Trouble*, pp.353–4.

94. AP, 'Elizabeth in Jordan Under Tight Guard', *New York Times*, 27/3/84, p.3.

95. CIA, National Intelligence Daily, 26/3/84. CREST: CIA-RDP87 T00970R000200010059-6.

96. AP, 'Elizabeth in Jordan Under Tight Guard', *New York Times*, 27/3/84, p.3.

97. Quoted in Ashton, 'Love's Labours Lost', p.654.

98. Moore, *Margaret Thatcher, Vol. 2*, p.141.

99. David Connett, 'British Defence Equipment "Diverted to Iraq"', *Independent*, 22/6/93, https://www.independent.co.uk/news/uk/british-defence-equipment-diverted-to-iraq-thatcher-given-detailed-reports-about-arms-deals-inquiry-1493048.html

100. R.W. Apple Jr, 'Queen Embroiled in Mideast Dispute', *New York Times*, 3/4/84, p.11.

101. 'Background information and recommended talking points for President Ronald Reagan's 6/4–6/10 visit to Great Britain', n.d., USDDO.

102. US embassy, Doha, to Secretary of State, 'United States Support for Camp David', 27/9/78, Doc No. 1978DOHA01309.

103. Paul Anastasi, 'British Diplomat is Shot to Death in Athens', *New York Times*, 29/3/84.

104. BDOHP: Sir Peregrine Rhodes interview, pp.40–45.

105. SoS to Algeria, 'Abu Nidal Terrorist group', 6/12/85, https://wikileaks.org/plusd/cables/85STATE371963_a.html

106. Geraghty, *The Bullet-Catchers*, pp.104, 106.

107. Delffs, *The Faith of Queen Elizabeth, passim*.

108. Hardman, *Queen of the World*, p.60.

109. Geraghty, *The Bullet-Catchers* p.436.

110. Ibid., p.107.

111. David Blunkett, Buckingham Palace (Security Breach), 13/9/04, Hansard column 1089.

112. Hardman, *Queen of the World*, p.44.

Chapter 23

1. '"Thank you" Queen Elizabeth tells Britain's spies', Reuters, 25/2/20.

2. Hardman, *Queen of the World*.

3. Pimlott, *The Queen*, p.538; Urban, *UK Eyes Alpha*, p.180.

4. Douglas Hurd quoted in entry for 21/11/90, Benn, *The End of an Era: Diaries 1980–1990*, pp.612–13.

5. Healey, *The Queen's House*, p.358. See also Glenn Frankel, 'British Debate Consequences of Heath's Visit to Baghdad', *Washington Post*, 23/10/90.

6. 'The Queen Learns how to Pick Pockets', Charles Greville, *Daily Mirror*, 18/5/67, MEPO 2/11005; Scotland Yard, 'Royal Visit to New Scotland Yard', 16/5/67.

7. Ibid.; ibid.

8. Scotland Yard, 'Royal Visit to New Scotland Yard', 16/5/67.

9. Andrew, *Defence of the Realm*, p.555.

10. Ibid. pp.555–6.

11. https://api.parliament.uk/ historic-hansard/commons/1988/ nov/22/queens-speech

12. Rimington, *Open Secret*, p.250.

13. Andrew, *Defence of the Realm*, p.767.

14. Peter Archer, 'Prince Meets Spycatchers', Press Association, 7/7/95.

15. 'Court Circular', *The Times* 28/1/98.

16. Adams, *The New Spies*, pp.105.

17. Dorril, *The Silent Conspiracy*, p.424.

18. Adams, *The New Spies*, pp.88–9.

19. 'Queen Visits MI6', *The Times*, 15/7/94.

20. Richard Norton-Taylor, 'Secrets of the Crown', *Guardian*, 3/1/90; Richard Norton-Taylor, 'The Spies who've Moved Upmarket', *Guardian*, 16/7/94.

21. According to the *Sunday Times*, Peter Millar, 'Cheerful Charlie,' *Sunday Times*, 9/11/97.

22. Obituary: Christopher Curwen, https://oldshirburnian.org.uk/ obituaries/curwen- christopher-c-43-47/

23. Cowper-Cowles, *Ever the Diplomat*, p.92.

24. Devine, *Good Hunting*, p.221.

25. Entry for 8/5/79, Benn (ed.), *Conflicts of Interest*, p.499. Private information.

26. Michael Harvey, 'Queen to Visit GCHQ', Press Association, 25/1/95.

27. BDOHP: Patrick Wright interview.

28. Hardman, *The Queen of the World*, pp.443, 488–9.

29. BDOHP: Sir John Birch interview, pp.42–3.

30. Hardman, *Queen of the World*, pp.443–4.

31. BDOHP: Sir Francis Richards interview, p.16.

32. BDOHP: Sir Charles Crawford interview, p.29.

33. BDOHP: Richards interview, p.17.

34. BDOHP: Crawford interview, p.29.

35. Lacey, *Monarchy*, p.340.

36. Private information.

37. BDOHP: Richards interview, p.12.

38. BDOHP: Kieran Prendergast interview, pp.46–7.

39. Jagger, *Escorting the Monarch*, pp.96–7.

40. HRH Prince Michael of Kent, 'Foreword' in Jagger, *Escorting the Monarch*, p.xvii.

41. Lacey, *Monarchy*, pp.396–7. Private information.

42. Wynn, *Pyramids and Nightclubs*, pp.121–86.

43. Jephson, *Shadows of a Princess*, p.314.

44. BDOHP: Sir David Dain interview, p.22.

Chapter 24

1. Stevens, *The Operation Paget inquiry report*, p.818.
2. Pasternak, *The American Duchess*, p.155; Healey, *The Queen's House*, p.278.
3. Boone and Peterson, *SIGSALY–the start of the digital revolution*, pp.8–11.
4. Shawcross, *Queen Elizabeth: The Queen Mother*, p.684.
5. Ibid., p.698.
6. 'British Checking Reports Queen has eavesdroppers', *Baltimore Morning Sun*, 20/8/65.
7. Entry 1/9/65, Benn, *Out of the Wilderness*, p.314.
8. Aldrich, *GCHQ*, pp.191–217.
9. Ibid.
10. CAB 134/4572, CESG, 'Secure Telephone Equipments (An Introduction to Melody)', April 1981.
11. FCO 57/963, 'Prince of Wales: telephone tapping', TXR 394/1, 1981. The file is still closed.
12. Entry for 11 May 1986, Thorpe (ed.), *Who Loses, Who Wins*, p.138.
13. Bradford, *Diana*, pp.14–54.
14. Lacey, *Monarchy*, p.206; Talbot, 'Into the Nineties', p.229.
15. Keay, *Royal Pursuit*, pp.42, 217, 231.
16. Entry for 24/4/84, Strong, *Splendours and Miseries*, pp.556–7.
17. Burrell, *A Royal Duty*, p.126.
18. Entry for April 2008, Goodall, *The Palace Diaries*, pp.314–5.
19. Entry for March 1989, ibid., pp.90–92.
20. Keay, *Royal Pursuit*, p.89.
21. Burgess, *Behind Palace Doors*, p.220.

22. Wharfe, *Closely Guarded Secret*, pp.39–45.
23. Peck, 'Drawing back the curtain', p.86.
24. Jephson, *Shadows of a Princess*, p.357.
25. Jago, *Robin Butler*, pp.131–2, 217.
26. Entry for 9/9/97, Campbell, *Power to the People*, pp.144–6.
27. Pimlott, *The Queen*, p.555.
28. Seldon, *John Major*, p.347.
29. Pimlott, *The Queen*, p.556.
30. Wharfe, *Guarding Diana*, p.203.
31. S. Boggan, 'Bugging: Can You Hear Me Darling?', *Independent on Sunday*, 17/1/93.
32. Jephson, *Shadows of a Princess*, p.67.
33. Wharfe, *Guarding Diana*, pp.168–9.
34. Clayton and Craig, *Diana*, pp.248–9.
35. Aldrich, *GCHQ*, pp.479–81.
36. Ibid., pp.479–82.
37. Ibid., pp.479–83.
38. Note for the record, 'Possible investigation into alleged interception of the communications of the royal family', ref AO93/192 21/1/93, INQ0060696-8. Scott Baker.
39. CM 44/34, Butler (Cab Sec) to Whitmore (HO), 'Review of Security Arrangements for Public Figures', AO90/2395, 12.10.90; Home Office, 'Review of Security Arrangements for Public Figures', section on 'Technical Protection', pp.30–41, Sept. 1990, ibid.
40. Blackhall, *Simon Mann*, pp.13–55; Spicer, *An Unorthodox Soldier*, pp.12–44.
41. Aldrich, *GCHQ*, pp.481–2.
42. Fellowes evidence 12/2/08 paras 10.11. Scott Baker.

43. Fellowes evidence 12/2/08 para 10. Scott Baker.

44. Adye (D/GCHQ) to Ringshaw-Dowle, D/9874DQ/3000/9, 5/2/92, INQ0061065. Scott Baker.

45. https://www.standard.co.uk/news/queens-fury-at-squidgygate-tape-palace-ordered-inquiry-over-the-leaked-call-between-diana-and-her-7300801.html

46. Aldrich, *GCHQ*, pp.481–2.

47. Fellowes evidence, 12/2/08, para 9. Scott Baker.

48. Note for the record, 'Possible investigation into alleged interception of the communications of the royal family', ref AO93/192 21/1/93, INQ0060696-8. Scott Baker.

49. Whitmore to Butler, 22/1/93, 21/1/93, INQ0060700. Scott Baker. Also Sir John Adye (GCHQ) testimony, morning 28/5/08, 28 Scott Baker.

50. Clarke, *Kind of Blue*, pp. 282–3, 295–9. Intriguingly, his memoirs omit this episode entirely.

51. Aldrich, *GCHQ*, pp.481–2; Fellowes evidence 12/2/08 20–22. Scott Baker.

52. Fellowes evidence 12/2/08 22–23. See also Fellowes to Whitmore, 26/1/93, INQ0060702. Scott Baker.

53. Fellowes evidence 12/2/08 24. Scott Baker.

54. Sir John Adye, (GCHQ) testimony, morning, 28/5/08, 28, Scott Baker.

55. Fellowes evidence 12/2/08 27–8. Scott Baker.

56. N. Allen and G. Rayner, 'Diana's Squidgygate tapes "leaked by GCHQ"', *Telegraph*, 10/1/08.

57. Adams, *The New Spies*, pp.112–13. See also Bower, *Rebel Prince*, p.10.

58. Wharfe, *Diana: Closely Guarded Secret*, pp.174–5.

59. Note for the Record, Ref. A093/1455, 28.4.43. INQ0061066. Scott Baker.

60. Wharfe, *Diana: Closely Guarded Secret*, pp.174–5.

61. Fellowes to Adye (GCHQ), 24/3/93, INQ0060729. Scott Baker.

62. Meynell at Scott Baker 0058847.

63. Ibid.

64. Stevens, *The Operation Paget inquiry report*, p.119.

65. Ibid., p.120.

66. Burrell, *A Royal Duty*, pp.319–20.

67. Ibid., pp.320–21.

68. Ibid., pp.321.

69. Stevens, *The Operation Paget inquiry report*, p.119.

70. Ibid., p.120.

71. Ibid., p.735.

72. Aldrich, *GCHQ*, p.483.

73. Dover, Aldrich, 'Cryptography and the Global South'.

74. Hardman, *Queen of the World*, pp.515–22.

75. Al-Fayed v. CIA US District Court, D. Columbia, 31/8/00, Case Number 1:00CV02092, paras 61–8.

76. Stevens, *The Operation Paget inquiry report*, p.733.

77. Ibid.

78. Ibid., p.734.

79. Hanning, *The News Machine*, pp.37–8.

Chapter 25

1. Stevens, *The Operation Paget inquiry report*, p.132 and NBC broadcast.

2. Interview with Martin Bashir on

Panorama, BBC, broadcast on 20/11/95.

3. Waldegrave, *A Different Kind of Weather*, p.396.

4. Wharfe, *Guarding Diana*, p.68.

5. Tomlinson, *The Big Breach*, pp.51–3, 98.

6. Peck, 'Drawing back the curtain', p.86.

7. Stevens, *The Operation Paget inquiry report*, p.6.

8. Ibid. pp.6–7.

9. Hasnat Ahmad Khan testimony, para.85, lines 17–19, Morning, 3/3/08, Scott Baker.

10. Clayton and Craig, *Diana*, p.337.

11. Stevens, *The Operation Paget inquiry report*, pp.7–8.

12. William Jordan, '38% of Brits think Princess Diana's death "NOT an accident"', YouGov, 17/9/13.

13. 'Dewsbury-born author Andrew Morton explores Royal family conspiracy theory', *Dewsbury Reporter*, 3/5/15.

14. 'UK considered killing Idi Amin', BBC News website, 16/8/03.

15. Zonis and Joseph, 'Conspiracy thinking in the Middle East', pp.443–59.

16. Cohen, *Diana, Death of a Goddess*, p.110.

17. Junor, *Charles*, p.29.

18. Al-Fayed v. CIA US District Court, D. Columbia, 31/8/00, Case Number 1:00CV02092.

19. Vernon Loeb and Bill Miller, 'Tinker, Tailor, Poet, Spy?', *Washington Post*, 15/2/01; Al-Fayed v. CIA US District Court, D. Columbia, 31/8/00, Case Number 1:00CV02092.

20. Stevens, *The Operation Paget inquiry report*, p.5.

21. Lyons, *Mr Paparazzi*, pp.250–51.

22. McNamara interview in Stevens, *The Operation Paget inquiry report*, p.676.

23. Laura Harding, 'Diana death "linked to arms trade" says QC', *Independent*, 31/5/10.

24. Tomlinson, *The Big Breach*, pp.81–174.

25. Anthea Temple, 'The Spy Who Loved Me', *Guardian*, 02/11/02.

26. Antony Barnett, 'Jackie Stewart teamed up with MI6 renegade', *Observer*, 27/8/20; Tomlinson, *The Big Breach*, pp.153–5, 207–10, 269–71.

27. Stevens, *The Operation Paget inquiry report*, p.759.

28. Ibid., pp.759–60.

29. Cormac, *Disrupt and Deny*, p.246.

30. Testimony of 'Witness F' (MI6), para 1–2, 28/2/08, Scott Baker.

31. Stevens, *The Operation Paget inquiry report*, p.755.

32. Tomlinson affidavit to French judges' investigation, 1997.

33. Cowper-Coles, *Ever the Diplomat*, p.184.

34. Stevens, *The Operation Paget inquiry report*, p.772.

35. Cowper-Coles, *Ever the Diplomat*, p.184.

36. William Langley, 'The Mannakee file', *Telegraph*, 12/12/04.

37. Stevens, *The Operation Paget inquiry report*, p.130.

38. Goodall, *The Palace Diaries*, pp.154.

39. Wharfe, *Diana: Closely Guarded Secret*, pp.32–3.

40. Jephson, *Shadows of a Princess*, p.371.

41. Entry for November 1995, Goodall, *The Palace Diaries*, pp.208–9.

42. Seldon, *John Major*, p.619.

43. Ibid.

44. Aldrich and Cormac, *The Black Door*, pp.307–19.

45. Inquest document INQ0006335, Scott Baker.

46. Stevens, *The Operation Paget inquiry report*, p.108.

47. Mansfield, *Memoirs of a Radical Lawyer*, pp.328–9.

48. Simmons, *Diana: The Last Word*, pp.244–6.

49. Stevens, *The Operation Paget inquiry report*, p.106.

50. Jephson, *Shadows of a Princess*, pp.120, 423. See also Burrell, *A Royal Duty*, p.xiii.

51. Wharfe, *Guarding Diana*, pp.23, 66–7, 218–19, 246.

52. Meynell (Met) memo, 'Meeting with HRH Princess of Wales 1045am on 18 October 1994', 18/10/1994, INQ0058848, Scott Baker.

53. DAC Meynell (Met) memo, 'Meeting on 13 December with Princess of Wales at Kensington Palace, 11.20am', 14/12/93, INQ0058863, Scott Baker.

54. DAC Meynell (Met), evidence, para 46, line 19, Morning 04/03/08, Scott Baker.

55. Sir David Veness, Former Assistant Commissioner, Metropolitan Police Service, Statement 227, cited in Stevens, *The Operation Paget inquiry report*, p.802.

56. RDPD (Met) memo, 'Security of HRH Princess of Wales, 1/2/94, INQ0058850, Scott Baker.

57. Jephson, *Shadows of a Princess*, p.298.

58. Sir Richard Eyre, interview in *Diana: The Interview That Shocked The World*, Channel 5, broadcast on 11/10/20.

59. FOI: John Birt's Office (BBC), 'Chronology', 23/11/95; FOI:

60. FOI: Alison Jackson (BBC) to Richard Peel (BBC), 'MI5', 4/12/95.

61. Bower, *Fayed*, pp.192, 236, 262, 288, 332, 337, 368–9, 408–9.

62. French Dossier D975-D985 and D990-D1006, cited in Stevens, *The Operation Paget inquiry report*, p.160.

63. Al-Fayed v. CIA US District Court, D. Columbia, 31/8/00, Case Number 1:00CV02092, paras 61–8.

64. Stevens, *The Operation Paget inquiry report*, p.736.

65. Elizabeth Owen, 'U.S. Ambassador Pamela Harriman Dies', *Time Magazine*, 5/2/97.

66. French Dossier D2208-D2213, cited in Stevens, *The Operation Paget inquiry report*, p.160.

67. Stevens, *The Operation Paget inquiry report*, p.774.

68. Interview with Hocquet, cited in ibid., p.159.

69. Interview with Moodie, cited in ibid., p.223.

70. Interview with Rees-Jones, cited in ibid., p.230.

71. Interview with McNamara, cited in ibid., p.623.

72. Stevens, *The Operation Paget inquiry report*, p.618.

73. Leveson Inquiry, afternoon hearing, 29/11/11, p.73 (lines 2022), available at: http://www.levesoninquiry.org.uk/wpcontent/uploads/2011/11/TranscriptofAfternoonHearing29November2011.pdf.

74. Lyons, *Mr Paparazzi*, pp.266–7.

75. Stevens, *The Operation Paget inquiry report*, p.746.

76. Lionel Cherruault testimony, para

BBC 'Statement to the Board of Governors', n.d.

23 lines 8–12, 03.03.08, Scott Baker.

77. Burrell, *A Royal Duty*, pp.xi–xiii.

78. Ian Traynor, 'MI6 involved in Balkan spy plot', *Guardian*, 27/8/04; Tom Walker & Michael Ivanovic, 'Vengeful Serbs betray top MI6 man', *Sunday Times*, 15/8/04.

79. Evidence, para 110, lines 19–25, Afternoon, 13/12/08, Scott Baker.

80. Testimony of Rosa Monckton, para 111, lines 2–10, & para 131, lines 24–5, 13/12/07, Scott Baker.

81. Tom Walker and Milorad Ivanovic, 'Vengeful Serbs betray top MI6 man', *Sunday Times*, 16/08/04.

82. Stevens, *The Operation Paget inquiry report*, p.745.

83. Hasnat Ahmad Khan testimony, para.86, lines 1–2, Morning, 03/03/08, Scott Baker.

84. Jephson, *Shadows of a Princess*, p.482.

85. Mansfield, *Memoirs of a Radical Lawyer*, pp.324–35.

86. Cecilia Rodriguez, 'Princess Diana: Secrets That Never End About Her Death', *Forbes*, 20/6/17; Rostain, Mouron and Caradech, *Qui a tué Lady Di?*, pp.12–35.

Conclusion

1. Roya Nikkah and Richard Kerbaj, 'MI6 Placement Gives Prince a Licence to Will', *Sunday Times*, p.5 7/4/19; BBC, 'Prince William Works with Security Agencies on Attachment', BBC News website, 7/4/19, https://www.bbc.co.uk/news/uk-47842097

2. Robert Hannigan, 'GCHQ Director's speech at the launch of the NCSC', 13/2/17, https://www.ncsc.gov.uk/news/gchq-directors-speech-launch-ncsc-2

3. Richard Moore, 'A Tribute to His Royal Highness The Duke of Edinburgh, 1921–2021', MI6 website, 9/4/21.

4. Tugendhat, Hansard, cm60, 12/4/21.

5. McCrisken and Moran, 'James Bond, Ian Fleming and intelligence,' pp.804–21; Zegart, *Spies, Lies, and Algorithms*, pp.16–44.

6. 'Prince Charles Praises "Utterly Essential" GCHQ Work', BBC News website, 12/7/19, https://www.bbc.co.uk/news/uk-england-gloucestershire-48969333

7. Dover, *For Queen and Company*, p.683.

8. US State Department cable, Tatiana Gfoeller (Bishkek) to Washington, 29/10/08, https://wikileaks.org/plusd/cables/08BISHKEK1095_a.html

9. David Leigh, Heather Brooke and Rob Evans, 'WikiLeaks cables: "Rude" Prince Andrew shocks US ambassador', *Guardian*, 29/11/10.

10. Tom Harper, 'MI6 Fears Russia Can Link Prince Andrew to the Jeffrey Epstein Abuse Scandal', *The Times*, 21/9/19.

11. Anon, *Private Eye*, no.1527, 31/7/20, p.13.

12. *Oprah with Meghan and Harry*, CBS, 2021.

13. Prince Harry, interviewed in ibid.

14. Meghan Markle, interviewed in ibid.

15. *Oprah with Meghan and Harry*, CBS, 2021.

16. Anne Twomey, 'From Bagehot to Brexit: The Monarch's Rights to be Consulted, to Encourage and to Warn,' *The Round Table*, 107:4, (2018), pp.417–28, 422–4.

17. *The Times*, 'Palace Anger Mounts as Cameron Spills Secrets', 20/9/19, p.1.

18. Herman, *Intelligence Power in Peace and War*, *passim*.

19. Beckett, 'Royalty and the Army in the Twentieth Century', p.110.

20. Entry for 4/6/85, Benn, *The End of an Era: Diaries 1980–1990*, p.410.

Ruling the Past

1. Lascelles to Nigel Nicolson, Jan 1967, Hart-Davis (ed.), *Kings Counsellor*, pp.420–21.

2. Entry for 2/1/84, Thorpe (ed.), *Who Wins, Who Loses*, p.248; entry for 3/5/87, ibid., p.298.

3. Richard Kay and Geoffrey Levy, 'Mystery of royal love letters burnt by the Queen's sister', *Daily Mail*, 14/3/16.

4. PREM 19/355, 'Royal Family. Duke of Windsor's papers: allegations by Duc de Grantmesnil that they were stolen by secret agents', 1979 May 10–1980 Jun 18. Closed.

5. Entry for 6/12/80, Thorpe (ed.), *Who Wins, Who Loses*, p.29.; entry for 21/1/83, ibid., pp.68–9.

6. Entry for 5/2/76, ibid., p.516.

7. Sanders (Downing Street) to de Courcy, 17/4/79, File 11, Box 5, de Courcy papers, Hoover Institute.

8. Pope-Hennessy, *The Quest for Queen Mary*, p.293.

9. Entry for 1/12/07, Thorpe (ed.), *Who Wins, Who Loses*, p.415.

10. Lascelles to Nigel Nicolson, Jan 1967, Hart-Davis (ed.), *King's Counsellor*, pp.420–21.

11. Bellisario, *To Tread on Royal Toes*, p.128.

12. BDOHP, Warwick Morris interview, p.5.

13. Gordon Brook-Shepherd was one of many: see his account of early KGB defectors called *The Storm Petrels: The First Soviet Defectors, 1928–38* (Collins, 1977).

14. See, for example, Heald, *Princess Margaret*, p.318.

15. Entry for 20/9/83, Thorpe (ed.), *Who Wins, Who Loses*, p.84.

16. Valentine Low, 'Queen's request for new Royal Yacht Britannia removed from public scrutiny', *The Times*, 30/1/19.

17. Paul Lewis, 'The 29 fakes behind a rewriting of history', *Guardian*, 05/05/08.

18. Ben Fenton, 'Himmler forgeries in National Archives case will stay unsolved', *Financial Times*, 3/5/08.

19. Private information.

20. Cowper-Coles, *Ever the Diplomat*, pp.89–90.

21. See, for example, DPP 2/10544 (Prince Faisal of Saudi Arabia): procuring the execution of a valuable security by deception and conspiracy to defraud between 22 April 1987 and 11 April 1989 in various locations. Convicted 1988 Jan 01–1994 Dec 31. Closed.

22. Colville to de Courcy, 4/1/99, ibid.

BIBLIOGRAPHY

THERE HAVE BEEN many books on British intelligence over the last hundred years and even more on the royals. We have only referenced those that we have used extensively or quoted. All books referred to in the Bibliography are published in London unless otherwise stated. All references to primary documents in the endnotes are to the UK National Archives at Kew unless otherwise stated.

Private Papers

Max Beaverbrook papers, Houses of Parliament Archives
Adolf Berle papers, Franklin D. Roosevelt Library, New York
Alexander Cadogan papers, Churchill College Cambridge (CCC)
John Colville papers, Churchill College Cambridge
Neville Chamberlain papers, Birmingham University Archives
Winston Churchill papers, Churchill College Cambridge
Kenneth de Courcy papers, Hoover Institute, Stanford University
Ernest Cuneo Papers, Franklin D. Roosevelt Library, New York
Oliver Harvey papers, British Museum
John Masterman papers, Worcester College Oxford
John Mitchell papers, Churchill College Cambridge
H. Montgomery Hyde papers, Churchill College Cambridge
Lord Louis Mountbatten papers, Hartley Library, Southampton University
Harold Nicolson papers, Yale University Library
President Secretaries Files, Franklin D. Roosevelt Library, New York
President Secretaries Files, Lyndon B. Johnson Library, University of Texas at Austin
Queen Victoria's Journals, Royal Archives, Windsor Castle
Templewood papers, Cambridge University Library

Oral History Projects

British Diplomatic Oral History Project (BDOHP), Churchill Archives, Churchill College Cambridge
Foreign Affairs Oral History Project, Special Collections, Lauinger Library, Georgetown University
Suez Oral History Project, Liddell Hart Centre for Military Archives (LHCMA), King's College London

Inquiries and Inquests

Lord Justice Scott Baker Inquests into the deaths of Diana, Princess of Wales and Dodi Al-Fayed. https://webarchive.nationalarchives.gov.uk/20090607230333/http://www.scottbaker-inquests.gov.uk/index.htm

Lord Chilcot: The Iraq Inquiry https://webarchive.nationalarchives.gov.uk/20171123123237/http://www.iraqinquiry.org.uk/

Memoirs, Diaries, Published Documents and Reports

Agar, Augustus, *Baltic Episode* (Washington: Naval Institute Press, 1963)

Alikhani, Alinaghi (ed.), *The Shah and I: The Confidential Diary of Iran's Royal Court – Asadollah Alam* (NY: St Martin's Press, 1991)

Bellisario, Ray, *To Tread on Royal Toes* (Impulse Books, 1972)

Benn, Tony, *The Benn Diaries, 1940–1990* (Arrow, 1995)

Benn, Tony, *Out of the Wilderness: Diaries 1963–1967* (Hutchinson, 1987)

Benn, Tony, *Office Without Power: Diaries 1968–1972* (Hutchinson, 1988)

Benn, Tony, *Conflicts of Interest: Diaries 1977–1980* (Hutchinson, 1990)

Benn, Tony, *The End of an Era: Diaries 1980–1990* (Hutchinson, 1992)

Benson, A.C. and Viscount Esher (eds), *The Letters of Queen Victoria, Vols 1–3* (John Murray, 1908)

Blair, Ian, *Policing Controversy* (Profile, 2009)

Bolitho, Hector (ed.), *The Prince Consort to His Brother: Two Hundred New Letters* (Cobden-Sanderson, 1933)

Brett, Maurice, V. (ed.), *Journals and Letters of Reginald Viscount Esher*, vols 1–2 (Ivor Nicholson and Watson, 1934)

Brock, M., and Brock, E. (eds), *H. H. Asquith Letters to Venetia Stanley* (Oxford: Oxford University Press, 2014)

Buchanan, G., *My Mission to Russia and Other Diplomatic Memories, Vols 1–2* (Boston: Little, Brown, 1923)

Buckle, George (ed.), *The Letters of Queen Victoria, 1862–1878*, series 2, vols 1–3, (John Murray, 1926)

Buckle, George, (ed.), *The Letters of Queen Victoria, 1886–1901*, series 3, vols 1–3 (John Murray, 1932)

Buckle, Richard, (ed.), *Self Portrait with Friends: The Selected Diaries of Cecil Beaton, 1926–1974* (Weidenfeld & Nicolson, 1979)

Burgess, Colin, *Behind Palace Doors: My Service as the Queen Mother's Equerry* (Blake, 2007)

Burrell, Paul, *A Royal Duty* (Michael Joseph, 2003)

Campbell, Alastair, *The Alastair Campbell Diaries: Power and the People, 1997–1999, Vol. 2* (Hutchinson, 2011)

Cantarini, Paolo, *Savoy Was My Oyster* (Robert Hale, 1976)

Carrington, Lord, *Reflect on Things Past – The Memoirs of Lord Carrington* (Collins, 1988)

Catterall, Peter (ed.), *The Macmillan Diaries, Vol. I: The Cabinet Years, 1950–1957* (Pan, 2004)

Catterall, Peter (ed.), *The Macmillan Diaries, Vol. II: Prime Minister and After, 1957–1966* (Pan, 2011)

Charteris, M.M.C., 'A Year as an Intelligence Officer in Palestine', *Middle East Society Journal*, 1 (1946), pp.17–20

Churchill, Winston S., *The Second World War: The Grand Alliance*, vol. 3 (Boston: Houghton Mifflin, 1950)

Clarke, Ken, *Kind of Blue: A Political Memoir* (Macmillan, 2017)

Colville, John, *The Fringes of Power: Downing Street Diaries Vol. 2, 1941–April 1955* (Sceptre, 1987)

Cowan, Janice, *A Spy's Wife: The Moscow Memoirs of a Canadian who Witnessed the End of the Cold War* (Toronto: Lorimer, 2006)

Crossman, Richard, *The Crossman Diaries: Selections from the Diaries of a Cabinet Minister, 1964–1970* (Jonathan Cape, 1979)

De la Billière, Peter, *Looking for Trouble: SAS to Gulf Command* (HarperCollins, 1995)

Dilks, David (ed.), *The Diaries of Sir Alexander Cadogan, 1938–1945* (Cassell, 1971)

Dodds-Parker, Douglas, *Setting Europe Ablaze: Some Account of Ungentlemanly Warfare* (Springwood Books, 1984)

Donoughue, Bernard, *Downing Street Diary: With James Callaghan in No.10* (Cape, 2008)

Duke of Windsor, *A King's Story: The Memoirs of H.R.H. the Duke of Windsor* (Cassell, 1951)

Evans, Ron, *On Her Majesty's Service: My Incredible Life in the World's Most Dangerous Close Protection Squad* (Blake, 2008)

Evans, Trevor (ed.), *The Killearn Diaries, 1934–1946: The Diplomatic and Personal Record of Lord Killearn (Sir Miles Lampson), High Commissioner and Ambassador, Egypt* (Sidgwick and Jackson, 1972)

Flower, Ken, *Serving Secretly: An Intelligence Chief on Record* (John Murray, 1987)

Franklin, Derek, *A Pied Cloak: Memoirs of a Colonial Police Officer* (Janus, 1996)

Gilliard, Peter, *Thirteen Years at the Russian Court (A Personal Record of the Last Years and Death of the Czar Nicholas II and His Family)* (NY: Doran, 1923)

Goodall, Sarah, *The Palace Diaries: the True Story of Life at the Palace by Prince Charles' Secretary* (Dynasty, 2006)

Gorodetsky, Gabriel (ed.), *The Maisky Diaries: Red Ambassador to the Court of St James's, 1932–1943* (New Haven: Yale University Press, 2015)

Guizot, F., *An Embassy to The Court of St. James's in 1840* (Bentley, 1862)

Haines, Joe, *Glimmers of Twilight: Harold Wilson in Decline* (Politico's, 2003)

Hart-Davis, Duff, *In Royal Service* (Hamish Hamilton, 1979)

Hart-Davis, Duff (ed.), *King's Counsellor: Abdication and War: The Diaries of Sir Alan Lascelles* (Weidenfeld & Nicolson, 2006)

Heffer, Simon (ed.), *Henry Chips Channon: The Diaries, Vol. 1, 1918–38* (Hutchinson, 2001)

Henderson, Ian, *Man Hunt in Kenya* (NY: Doubleday, 1958)

Henderson, N., *Mandarin: the Diaries of an Ambassador, 1969–81* (Weidenfeld & Nicolson, 1994)

Hoare, Samuel, *The Fourth Seal: The End of a Russian Chapter* (Heinemann, 1930)

Hyde, H. Montgomery, *Secret Intelligence Agent* (Constable, 1982)

Ivanov, Yevgeny, *The Naked Spy* (Blake, 1994)

Jebb, Miles (ed.), *The Diaries of Cynthia Gladwyn* (Constable, 1995)

Jephson, Patrick, *Shadows of a Princess: Diana, Princess of Wales 1987–1996* (Collins, 2000)

Judd, Denis (ed.), *A British Tale of Indian and Foreign Service: The Memoirs of Sir Ian Scott* (Radcliffe Press, 1999)

Kaiser Wilhelm and Tsar Nicholas, *Between Two Emperors: The Willy-Nicky Telegrams and Letters, 1894–1914* (A&F Reprints, 2017)

Keeler, Christine, and Thompson, Douglas, *Secrets and Lies* (John Blake, 2012)

Kelly, Angela, *The Other Side of the Coin: The Queen, the Dresser and the Wardrobe* (Collins, 2019)

Khrushchev, Nikita, *Khrushchev Remembers* (Book Club Associates, 1971)

Langworth, Richard, *Churchill by Himself: The Definitive Collection of Quotations by Winston Churchill* (Public Affairs, 2008)

Lockhart, R.B., *Memoirs of a British Agent* (Macmillan 1932)

Lyons, Darryn, *Mr Paparazzi: My Life as the World's Most Outrageous Celebrity Photographer* (John Blake, 2010)

Macmillan, Harold, *Pointing the Way, 1959–61* (Macmillan, 1972)

Macmillan, Harold, *War Diaries* (Macmillan, 1984)

Mansfield, Michael, *Memoirs of a Radical Lawyer* (Bloomsbury, 2009)

Marcus, Leah S., Mueller, Janel, and Rose, Mary Beth (eds), *Elizabeth I: Collected Works* (Chicago: University of Chicago Press, 2000)

Mark, Sir Robert, *In the Office of Constable: An Autobiography* (Collins, 1978)

Markov, Sergei Vladimirovich, Flint, Frank Stuart, and Tait, Dorothy Fraser, *How We Tried to Save the Tsaritsa... Translated by F.S. Flint and D.F. Tait.* (NY: G.P. Putnam's Sons, 1929)

Maylunas, Andrei, and Mironenko, Sergei, *A Lifelong Passion: Nicholas and Alexandra: Their Own Story* (NY: Diane Publishing, 2005)

McNee, Sir David, *McNee's Law* (Collins, 1983)

Mikhailovich, Alexander, *Once a Grand Duke* (Cassell, 1932)

Modin, Yuri, *My Five Cambridge Friends* (Headline, 1994)

Nansen, Fridtjof, *Through Siberia, the Land of the Future* (NY: Stokes, 1914)

Nicholson, Martin, *Activities Incompatible: Memoirs of a Kremlinologist and a Family Man, 1963–1971* (self-published, 2013)

Nicolson, Harold, *The Later Years: 1945–1962* (Atheneum, 1966)

Nicolson, Nigel (ed.), *The Harold Nicolson Diaries: 1907–1963* (Weidenfeld & Nicolson, 2004)

O'Callaghan, Sean, *The Informer: The Real Life Story of One Man's War against Terrorism* (Bantam, 1999)

Payn, Graham, and Morley, Sheridan (eds), *The Noël Coward Diaries* (Macmillan, 1982)

Pimlott, Ben (ed.), *The Second World War Diary of Hugh Dalton* (Cape, 1986)

Pincher, Chapman, *Dangerous to Know: A Life* (Biteback, 2014)

Ponsonby, Arthur (ed.), *Henry Ponsonby: Queen Victoria's Private Secretary, His Life in Letters* (Macmillan, 1942)

Ponsonby, Frederick (ed.), *Letters of the Empress Frederick* (Macmillan, 1928)

Ponsonby, Frederick, *Recollections of Three Reigns* (Eyre and Spottiswoode, 1951)

Potter, David (ed.), *Foreign Intelligence and Information in Elizabethan England*: Volume 25 (Cambridge: Cambridge University Press, 2004)

Archer, John M., *Sovereignty and Intelligence: Spying and Court Culture in the English Renaissance* (Stanford: Stanford University Press, 1993)

Ash, Eric H., *Power, Knowledge, and Expertise in Elizabethan England* (Baltimore: Johns Hopkins University Press, 2004)

Asher, Michael, *The Regiment: The Real Story of the SAS* (Penguin, 2008)

Ashton, Nigel, *King Hussein of Jordan: A Political Life* (New Haven: Yale University Press, 2008)

Ayling, Stanley, *George the Third* (Collins, 1972)

Baird, Julia, *Victoria: The Queen: An Intimate Biography of the Woman Who Ruled an Empire* (Random House, 2016)

Ball, Simon, *Secret History: Writing the Rise of Britain's Intelligence Services* (Montreal: McGill-Queen's University Press, 2020)

Barnett, Neil, *Tito* (Haus, 2006)

Bartley, Paula, *Queen Victoria* (Routledge, 2016)

Basu, Shrabani, *Victoria and Abdul: The True Story of the Queen's Closest Confidant* (Stroud: The History Press, 2010)

Bayandor, Darioush, *Iran and the CIA: The Fall of Mosaddeq Revisited* (Basingstoke: Palgrave Macmillan, 2010)

Beaken, Robert, *Cosmo Lang: Archbishop in War and Crisis* (IB Tauris, 2012)

Bedell Smith, Sally, *Elizabeth the Queen: The Woman. The Family. The Life* (Penguin, 2012)

Bedell Smith, Sally, *Prince Charles: The Passions and Paradoxes of an Improbable Life* (Random House, 2017)

Beesley, Ian, *The Official History of the Cabinet Secretaries* (Routledge, 2018)

Bellany, Alastair, and Cogswell, Thomas, *The Murder of King James I* (New Haven: Yale University Press, 2015)

Bennett, Gill, *Churchill's Man of Mystery: Desmond Morton and the World of Intelligence* (Routledge, 2006)

Bennett, Gill, *The Zinoviev Letter: The Conspiracy that Never Dies* (Oxford: Oxford University Press, 2018)

Bennett, Huw, *Fighting the Mau Mau: The British Army and Counter-Insurgency in the Kenya Emergency* (Cambridge: Cambridge University Press, 2012)

Bennett, Ralph, *Intelligence Investigations: How Ultra Changed History* (Frank Cass, 1996)

Bertrand, Gustave, *Enigma ou la plus grande énigme de la guerre 1939–1945* (Paris: Plon, 1973)

Bethell, Nicholas, *The Albanian Operation of the CIA and MI6, 1949–1953: Conversations with Participants in a Venture Betrayed* (McFarland, 2016)

Blackhall, Sue, *Simon Mann: The Real Story* (Pen & Sword, 2011)

Bland, Lucy, *Modern Women on Trial: Sexual Transgression in the Age of the Flapper* (Manchester: Manchester University Press, 2013)

Bloch, Michael, *Operation Willi: The Nazi Plot to Kidnap the Duke of Windsor, July 1940* (Weidenfeld & Nicolson, 1986)

Bloch, Michael, *The Secret File of the Duke of Windsor* (Bantam, 1988)

Boghardt, Thomas, *Spies of the Kaiser: German Covert Operations in Britain during the First World War Era* (Palgrave, 2004)

Boone, J. V., and Peterson, R. R., *SIGSALY – the start of the digital revolution* (National Security Agency, 2009)

Bossy, John, *Giordano Bruno and the Embassy Affair* (Vintage, 1991)

Bossy, John, *Under the Molehill: An Elizabethan Spy Story* (New Haven: Yale University Press, 2001)

Botham, Noel, *Margaret: The Last Real Princess* (John Blake, 2002)

Bourne, Kenneth, *The Foreign Policy of Victorian England, 1830–1902* (Oxford: Clarendon Press, 1970)

Bousfield, Arthur, and Toffoli, Garry, *Royal Spring: The Royal Tour of 1939 and the Queen Mother in Canada* (Toronto: Dundurn Press, 1989)

Bower, Tom, *The Perfect English Spy: Sir Dick White and the Secret War, 1935–90* (NY: St Martin's Press, 1995)

Bower, Tom, *The Rebel Prince; the Power, Passion and Defiance of Prince Charles* (Collins, 2018)

Bower, Tom, *Fayed: The Unauthorised Biography* (Macmillan, 1999)

Bowyer-Bell, J., *The Secret Army: The IRA* (Transaction, 1997)

Bradford, Sarah, *Diana* (Penguin, 2006)

Bradford, Sarah, *George VI: The Dutiful King* (Penguin, 2013)

Bradford, Sarah, *Queen Elizabeth: Her Life in our Times* (Penguin, 2012)

Brewer, Susan, *To Win the Peace: British Propaganda in the United States during World War II* (NY: Cornell University Press, 1997)

Brooke, John, *King George III* (Constable, 1972)

Brooke, Nick, *Terrorism and Nationalism in the United Kingdom: The Absence of Noise* (Palgrave, 2018)

Brook-Shepherd, Gordon, *Iron Maze: The Western secret services and the Bolsheviks* (Pan Macmillan, 1999)

Brown, David, *Palmerston and the Politics of Foreign Policy, 1846–55* (Manchester: Manchester University Press, 2002)

Budiansky, Stephen, *Her Majesty's Spymaster: Elizabeth I, Sir Francis Walsingham, and the Birth of Modern Espionage* (Plume, 2005)

Burk, Kathleen, *Old World, New World: The Story of Britain and America* (Grove, 2007)

Burns, Jimmy, *Papa Spy: A True Story of Love, Wartime Espionage in Madrid, and the Treachery of the Cambridge Spies* (Bloomsbury, 2009)

Cadbury, Deborah, *Princes at War: The British Royal Family's Private Battle in the Second World War* (Bloomsbury, 2016)

Campbell, Christy, *Fenian Fire: The British Government Plot to Assassinate Queen Victoria* (Collins, 2011)

Campbell, John, *Margaret Thatcher: The Iron Lady* (Vintage, 2007)

Carter, Miranda, *Anthony Blunt: His Lives* (Pan, 2002)

Carter, Miranda, *The Three Emperors: Three Cousins, Three Empires and the Road to World War One* (Penguin, 2010)

Cannadine, David, *The Pleasures of the Past* (Fontana, 1990)

Casey, Bart, *The Double Life of Laurence Oliphant: Victorian Pilgrim and Prophet* (Post Hill Press, 2015)

Castillo, Dennis Angelo, *The Maltese Cross: A Strategic History of Malta* (Greenwood, 2006)

Cathcart, Brian, *Test of Greatness: Britain's Struggle for the Atom Bomb* (John Murray, 1994)

Cathcart, Helen, *Anne and the Princesses Royal* (W.H. Allen, 1973)

Cave Brown, Anthony, *'C': The Secret Life of Sir Stewart Menzies, Spymaster to Winston Churchill* (NY: Macmillan, 1987)

Chamberlain, Muriel, *Pax Britannica? British Foreign Policy 1789–1914* (Routledge, 1989)

Christy, Jim, *The Price of Power: A Biography of Charles Eugène Bedaux* (Toronto: Doubleday, 1984)

Churchill, Alexandra, *In the Eye of the Storm: George V and the Great War* (Warwick: Helion, 2018)

Clarke, David, *Britain's X-traordinary Files* (Bloomsbury, 2014)

Clay, Catrine, *King, Kaiser, Tsar: Three Royal Cousins Who Led the World to War* (NY: Walker, 2007)

Clayton, Tim, and Craig, Phil, *Diana: The Story of a Princess* (Hodder & Stoughton, 2001)

Cobain, Ian, *The History Thieves: Secrets, Lies and the Shaping of a Modern Nation* (Portobello, 2016)

Cohen, David, *Diana, Death of a Goddess* (Century, 2004)

Cohen, Michael J., *Palestine and the Great Powers, 1945–1948* (Princeton: Princeton University Press, 1982)

Conant, Jennet, *The Irregulars: Roald Dahl and the British Spy Ring in Wartime Washington* (Simon & Schuster, 2008)

Connor, Ken, *Ghost Force: The Secret History of the SAS* (Cassell, 1998)

Cook, Andrew, *The Murder of the Romanovs* (Stroud: Amberley, 2010)

Cook, Andrew, *To Kill Rasputin: The Life and Death of Grigori Rasputin* (Stroud: The History Press, 2006)

Cooper, John, *The Queen's Agent: Francis Walsingham at the Court of Elizabeth I* (NY: Pegasus Books, 2012)

Corera, Gordon, *The Art of Betrayal: Life and Death in the British Secret Service* (Weidenfeld & Nicolson, 2011)

Cormac, Rory, *Confronting the Colonies: British Intelligence and Counterinsurgency* (NY: Oxford University Press, 2013)

Cormac, Rory, *Disrupt and Deny: Spies, Special Forces and the Secret Pursuit of British Foreign Policy* (Oxford: Oxford University Press, 2018)

Costello, John, *Ten Days to Destiny, The Secret Story of the Hess Peace Initiative and British Efforts to Strike a Deal with Hitler* (NY: Morrow, 1991)

Cowles, Virginia, *The Romanovs* (Harper & Ross, 1971)

Cowper-Coles, Sherard, *Ever the Diplomat: Confessions of a Foreign Office Mandarin* (Collins, 2012)

Crockett, Peter, *Evatt: A Life* (Oxford: Oxford University Press, 1993)

Crowdy, Terry, *The Enemy Within: A History of Spies, Spymasters and Espionage* (Oxford: Osprey, 2008)

Cull, Nicholas, *Selling War: The British Propaganda Campaign against American 'Neutrality' in World War II* (Oxford: Oxford University Press, 1996)

Cullen, Richard, *Rasputin: The Role of Britain's Secret Service in His Torture and Murder* (Dialogue, 2010)

Culme, John, and Rayner, Nicholas, *Jewels of the Duchess of Windsor* (NY: Vendome Press, 1987)

Curry, John Court, *The Security Service 1908–1945: The Official History* (Public Record Office, 1999)

Davenport-Hines, Richard, *An English Affair: Sex, Class and Power in the Age of Profumo* (Collins, 2013)

Davenport-Hines, Richard, *Enemies Within: Communists, the Cambridge Spies and the Making of Modern Britain* (Collins, 2018)

Davies, Nicholas, *Queen Elizabeth II: A Woman who is not Amused* (NY: Birch Lane, 1994)

Davies, Philip, *MI6 and the Machinery of Spying* (Frank Cass, 2004)

Davies, Philip, *Intelligence and Government in Britain and the United States, Vol. 2: Evolution of the UK Intelligence Community* (Santa Barbara, CA: Praeger, 2012)

Day, Peter, *Trotsky's Favourite Spy: The Life of George Alexander Hill* (Biteback, 2017)

Day, Peter, *Franco's Friends: How British Intelligence Helped Bring Franco to Power in Spain* (Biteback, 2011)

De Courcy, Anne, *Snowdon: The Biography* (Weidenfeld & Nicolson, 2008)

Delffs, Dudley, *The Faith of Queen Elizabeth: The Poise, Grace, and Quiet Strength behind the Crown* (Zondervan, 2019)

Dimbleby, Jonathan, *The Prince of Wales* (Little, Brown, 1994)

Docherty, Gerry, and MacGregor, James, *Hidden History: The Secret Origins of the First World War* (Edinburgh: Mainstream, 2013)

Doran, Susan, *Elizabeth I and Foreign Policy, 1558–1603* (Routledge, 2002)

Dorril, Stephen, *Blackshirt: Sir Oswald Mosley and British Fascism* (Viking, 2006)

Dorril, Stephen, *MI6: Fifty Years of Special Operations* (Fourth Estate, 2000)

Dorril, Stephen, *The Silent Conspiracy: Inside the Intelligence Service in the 1990s* (Heinemann, 1993)

Douglas-Home, Charles, and Kelly, Saul (eds), *Dignified and Efficient: The British Monarchy in the Twentieth Century* (Brinkworth: Claridge, 2000)

Dukes, Paul, *Great Men in the Second World War: The Rise and Fall of the Big Three* (Bloomsbury, 2017)

Dunlop, Richard, *Donovan: America's Master Spy* (Delaware: Skyhorse, 2014)

Duns, Jeremy, *Dead Drop: The True Story of Oleg Penkovsky and the Cold War's Most Dangerous Operation* (Simon & Schuster, 2013)

Dylan, Huw, *Defence Intelligence and the Cold War: Britain's Joint Intelligence Bureau 1945–1964* (Oxford: Oxford University Press, 2014)

Eade, Philip, *Young Prince Philip: His Turbulent Early Life* (HarperPress, 2012)

Eckert, Astrid, *The Struggle for the Files: The Western Allies and the Return of German Archives After the Second World War* (Cambridge: Cambridge University Press, 2014)

Edwards, Francis, *Plots and Plotters in the Reign of Elizabeth I* (Portland, OR: Four Court Press, 2002)

Eigen, J.P., *Witnessing Insanity: Madness and Mad-doctors in the English Court* (New Haven: Yale University Press, 1995)

Elliott, Geoffrey, *Gentleman Spymaster: How Lt Col Tommy 'Tar' Robertson Double-crossed the Nazis* (Methuen, 2011)

Elton, Geoffrey, *Policy and Police: The Enforcement of the Reformation in the Age of Thomas Cromwell* (Cambridge: Cambridge University Press, 1985)

English, Richard, *Armed Struggle: The History of the IRA* (Pan, 2004)

Erickson, Caroline, *Her Little Majesty: The Life of Queen Victoria* (Simon & Schuster, 2002)

Erickson, Carolly, *Lilibet: An Intimate Portrait of Elizabeth II* (St Martin's Press, 2005)

Evans, Thomas, *The Memoirs of Dr. Thomas W. Evans: Recollections of The Second French Empire* (Unwin, 1905)

Farwell, Bryan, *Queen Victoria's Little Wars* (NY: W.W. Norton, 1985)

Fergusson, Thomas, *British Military Intelligence 1870–1914: The Development of a Modern Intelligence Organization* (Arms and Armour Press, 1984)

Ferris, John Robert, *Behind the Enigma: The Authorised History of GCHQ Britain's Secret Cyber-Intelligence Agency* (Bloomsbury, 2020)

Ferris, John Robert, *Intelligence and Strategy* (Routledge, 2015)

Ferro, Marc, *Nicholas II: Last of the Tsars* (Oxford: Oxford University Press, 1994)

Fissel, Mark, *The Bishops' Wars: Charles I's Campaigns against Scotland, 1638–1640.* (Cambridge: Cambridge University Press, 1994)

Fleming, Ian, *On Her Majesty's Secret Service* (Jonathan Cape, 1963)

Foot, M.R.D., *Resistance: European Resistance to Nazism, 1940–1945* (NY: McGraw-Hill, 1977)

Frankland, Noble, *Witness of a Century: Life and Times of Prince Arthur, Duke of Connaught* (Shepheard-Walwyn, 1993)

Fremont-Barnes, Gregory, and Winner, Pete, *Who Dares Wins: The SAS and the Iranian Embassy Siege 1980* (Oxford: Osprey, 2009)

Fromkin, David, *The King and the Cowboy: Theodore Roosevelt and Edward VII, Secret Partners* (Penguin, 2008)

Fuhrmann, Joseph T., *Rasputin: The Untold Story* (New Jersey: John Wiley, 2013)

Geraghty, Tony, *The Bullet-Catchers: Bodyguard and the World of Close Protections* (Grafton, 1988)

Gill, David, *Britain and the Bomb: Nuclear Diplomacy, 1964–1970* (Stanford: Stanford University Press, 2013)

Gillman, Peter, and Gillman, Leni, *'Collar the Lot!': How Britain Interned and Expelled Its Wartime Refugees* (Quartet Books, 1980)

Glass, Charles, *Americans in Paris: Life and Death under Nazi Occupation 1940–44* (Collins, 2009)

Glencross, Matthew, *The State Visits of Edward VII: Reinventing Royal Diplomacy for the Twentieth Century* (Palgrave Macmillan, 2015)

Glencross, Matthew, Rowbotham, Judith, and Kandiah Michael D., *The Windsor Dynasty 1910 to the Present: 'Long to Reign Over Us'?* (Palgrave Macmillan, 2016)

Goodman, Michael, *Spying on the Nuclear Bear: Anglo-American Intelligence and the Soviet Bomb* (Stanford: Stanford University Press, 2008)

Gregory, Martyn, *The Diana Conspiracy Exposed* (Olmstead, 2000)

Grose, Peter, *Allen Dulles: Spymaster, The Life and Times of the First Civilian Director of the CIA* (Andre Deutsch, 2006)

Hall, Coryne, *Little Mother of Russia: A Biography of Empress Marie Feodorovna* (Shepheard-Walwyn, 2001)

Hall, Coryne, *To Free the Romanovs: Royal Kinship and Betrayal in Europe, 1917–19* (Stroud: Amberley, 2018)

Hanbury-Williams, Sir John, *Emperor Nicholas II as I Knew Him* (Humphreys, 1922)

Hanning, James (with Mulcaire, Glenn), *The News Machine: Hacking, The Untold Story* (NY: Gibson Square, 2014)

Hardcastle-Taylor, Jeane D., *The Windsors I Knew: An American Private Secretary's Memoir of the Duke and Duchess of Windsor*, edited by Hugo Vickers (privately published, 2018)

Hardie, Frank, *Political Influence of Queen Victoria, 1861–1901* (Frank Cass, 1938)

Hardman, Robert, *Her Majesty: Queen Elizabeth II and her Court* (NY: Pegasus, 2012)

Hardman, Robert, *Our Queen* (Arrow, 2012)

Hardman, Robert, *Queen of the World* (Century, 2018)

Harper, Stephen, *Capturing Enigma: How HMS Petard Seized the German Naval Codes* (Stroud: Sutton, 1999)

Harris, Stephen, *British Military Intelligence in the Crimean War, 1854–56* (Routledge, 2015)

Harris, Tim, *Revolution: The Great Crisis of the British Monarchy, 1685–1720* (Penguin, 2007)

Harrison, J.F.C., *The Second Coming: Popular Millenarianism 1780–1850* (Routledge & Kegan Paul, 1979)

Hashimoto, Chikara, *Twilight of the British Empire: British Intelligence and Counter-Subversion in the Middle East, 1948–63* (Edinburgh: Edinburgh University Press, 2018)

Haslam, Jonathan, *Near and Distant Neighbours: A New History of Soviet Intelligence* (Oxford: Oxford University Press, 2015)

Hastings, Max, *Catastrophe: Europe goes to War 1914* (Collins, 2014)

Hauner, Milan, *India in Axis Strategy* (Berlin: Klett-Cotta, 1982)

Haynes, Alan, *Invisible Powers: The Elizabethan Secret Service 1570–1603* (Stroud: Alan Sutton, 1992)

Haynes, Alan, *Walsingham: Elizabeth's Spymaster and Statesman* (Stroud: Sutton, 2004)

Heald, Tim, *The Duke: A Portrait of Prince Philip* (Hodder & Stoughton, 1991)

Healey, Edna, *The Queen's House: A Social History of Buckingham Palace* (The Royal Collection/Michael Joseph, 1997)

Heffer, Simon, *Power and Place: The Political Consequences of King Edward VII* (Phoenix, 1998)

Heffer, Simon, *Staring at God: Britain in the Great War* (Random, 2019)

Hemming, Henry, *M: Maxwell Knight, MI5's Greatest Spymaster* (Penguin, 2017)

Hennessy, Peter, *Cabinets and the Bomb* (Oxford: British Academy/Oxford University Press, 2007)

Hennessy, Peter, *Having it So Good: Britain in the Fifties* (Penguin, 2006)

Hennessy, Peter, *The Hidden Wiring: Unearthing the British Constitution* (Indigo, 1996)

Hennessy, Peter, *The Prime Minister: The Office and its Holders Since 1945* (Allen Lane, 2001)

Hennessy, Peter, *The Secret State: Whitehall and the Cold War* (Penguin, 2003; rev. edn, 2010)

Herman, Michael, *Intelligence Power in Peace and War* (Cambridge: Cambridge University Press, 1996)

Hesketh, R., *Fortitude: The D-Day Deception Campaign* (NY: Overlook, 2000)

Heuser, Beatrice, *Western 'Containment' Policies in the Cold War: The Yugoslav Case, 1948–53* (Routledge, 1989)

Hibbert, Christopher, *Edward VII: A Portrait* (Allen Lane, 1976)

Hibbert, Christopher, *George III: A Personal History* (Penguin, 1999)

Hibbert, Christopher, *Queen Victoria: A Personal History* (Collins, 2001)

Hodgson, Howard, *Charles: The Man who will be King* (John Blake, 2007)

Hogg, Jonathan, *Britain's Nuclear Culture: Official and Unofficial Narratives in the Long 20th Century* (Bloomsbury Academic, 2016)

Holden, Anthony, *Charles at 50* (Random House, 1998)

Holmes, Richard Rivington, *Queen Victoria* (Boussod, Valadon, 1897)

Hopkirk, Peter, *The Great Game: On Secret Service in High Asia* (John Murray, 2006)

Horne, Alistair, *Macmillan: The Official Biography, Vol. 2 1957–1986* (Macmillan, 1989)

Hoey, Brian, *Not in Front of the Corgis* (Biteback, 2011)

How, F.D., *The Life of Sir Howard Vincent* (Allen, 1912)

Howard, Michael, *British Intelligence in the Second World War, Vol. 5, Strategic Deception* (HMSO, 1990)

Howard, Michael, *The Franco-Prussian War: The German Invasion of France, 1870–71* (Routledge, 2001, 2nd ed.)

Howarth, Patrick, *George VI* (Hutchinson, 1987)

Hutchinson, Robert, *Elizabeth's Spy Master: Francis Walsingham and the Secret War That Saved England* (Weidenfeld & Nicolson, 2006)

Iatrides, John O., *Revolt in Athens: The Greek Communist 'Second Round' 1944–1945* (Princeton: Princeton University Press, 1972)

Iordanou, Ioanna, *Venice's Secret Service: Organizing Intelligence in the Renaissance* (Oxford: Oxford University Press, 2019)

Isba, Anne, *Gladstone and Women* (Continuum, 2006)

Jackson, W.F.G., Bramall, E., and Bramall, B., *Chiefs: Story of the United Kingdom Chiefs of Staff* (Brassey's, 1992)

Jackson, Sophie, *SOE's Balls of Steel: Operation Rubble* (Stroud: The History Press, 2013)

Jagger, Chris, *Escorting the Monarch: We Lead, Others Follow* (Barnsley: Pen & Sword, 2017)

Jago, Michael, *Robin Butler: At the Heart of Power from Heath to Blair* (Biteback, 2017)

Jeffery, Keith, *The Secret History of MI6* (NY: Penguin, 2010)

Jelavich, Charles, *Tsarist Russia and Balkan Nationalism: Russian Influence in the Internal Affairs of Bulgaria and Serbia, 1879–1886* (Berkeley: University of California Press, 1958)

Jenkins, Elizabeth, *Elizabeth the Great* (Coward McCann, 1958)

Jensen, Richard Bach, *The Battle Against Anarchist Terrorism: An International History, 1878–1934* (Cambridge: Cambridge University Press, 2014)

Jevon, Graham, *Glubb Pasha and the Arab Legion: Britain, Jordan and the End of Empire in the Middle East* (Cambridge: Cambridge University Press, 2017)

Johnson, Robert, *Spying for Empire: The Great Game in Central and South Asia, 1757–1947* (Greenhill, 2006)

Judd, Alan, *The Quest for C: Sir Mansfield Cumming and the Founding of the British Secret Service* (Collins, 1999)

Judd, Denis, and Sturridge, Keith, *The Boer War: A History* (NY: I.B. Tauris, 2013)

Judd, Denis, *The Crimean War, 1853–1856* (Hart-Davis, MacGibbon, 1975)

Junor, Penny, *Charles: Victim or Villain?* (Collins, 1998)

Kahn, David, *The Codebreakers: The Story of Secret Writing* (NY: Scribner, 1996)

Kemp, Michael, *Bombs, Bullets and Bread: The Politics of Anarchist Terrorism Worldwide* (Jefferson: McFarland, 2018)

Kettle, Michael, *Russia and the Allies, 1917–1920. Vol. 1, The Allies and the Russian Collapse, March 1917–March 1918* (Minneapolis: University of Minnesota Press, 1981)

Kyemba, Henry, *State of Blood: The Inside Story of Idi Amin* (NY: Putnam, 1977)

Kyle, Keith, *Suez: Britain's End of Empire in the Middle East* (Weidenfeld & Nicolson, 1991)

Lacey, Robert, *Royal: Her Majesty Queen Elizabeth II* (Little, Brown, 2002)

Lambton, Antony, *The Mountbattens: The Battenbergs and Young Mountbatten* (Constable, 1989)

Lane, John, *The Sayings of Queen Elizabeth* (NY: Dodd, Mead, 1923)

Larman, Alexander, *The Crown in Crisis: Countdown to the Abdication* (Weidenfeld & Nicolson, 2020)

Laurie, Peter, *Beneath the City Streets: A Private Inquiry into the Nuclear Preoccupations of Government* (Penguin, 1974)

Le Queux, William, *The Minister of Evil: The Secret History of Rasputin's Betrayal of Russia* (Cassell, 1918)

Le Queux, William, *Rasputin, The Rascal Monk* (Hurst & Blackett, 1917)

Lee, Sidney, *King Edward VII: A Biography*, vol. 2 (Macmillan, 1927)

Lees-Milne, James, *Harold Nicolson, 1930–1968* (Chatto & Windus, 1981)

Lewis, Julian, *Changing Direction: British Military Planning for Post-war Strategic Defence, 1942–47* (Frank Cass, 2000)

Linklater, Andrew, *Compton Mackenzie* (Chatto & Windus, 1987)

Lockyer, Roger, *Buckingham: The Life and Political Career of George Villiers, First Duke of Buckingham 1592–1628* (Routledge, 1981)

Loughlin, James, *The British Monarchy and Ireland: 1800 to the Present* (Cambridge: Cambridge University Press, 2007)

Louis, William Roger, *The British Empire in the Middle East, 1945–1951: Arab Nationalism, the United States, and Postwar Imperialism* (Oxford: Oxford University Press, 1984)

Lownie, Andrew, *John Buchan: The Presbyterian Cavalier* (Constable, 1995)

Lownie, Andrew, *The Mountbattens: Their Lives and Loves* (Blink, 2019)

Lownie, Andrew, *Stalin's Englishman: The Lives of Guy Burgess* (Hodder & Stoughton, 2015)

Lownie, Andrew, *The Traitor King: Scandalous Exile of the Duke and Duchess of Windsor* (Blink, 2021).

Lulushi, Albert, *Operation Valuable Fiend: The CIA's First Paramilitary Strike against the Iron Curtain* (Arcade, 2014)

Lycett, Andrew, *Ian Fleming* (St Martin's, 2013)

Lyon, David, *Electronic Eye: The Rise of the Surveillance Society* (Minneapolis: University of Minnesota Press, 1994)

Macintyre, Ben, *For Your Eyes Only* (Bloomsbury, 2008)

Macintyre, Ben, *The Spy and the Traitor: The Greatest Espionage Story of the Cold War* (Viking, 2018)

Mackenzie, Compton, *The Windsor Tapestry: Being a study of the life, heritage and abdication of HRH The Duke of Windsor* (Rich and Cowan, 1938)

MacMillan, Margaret, *The War that Ended Peace: How Europe Abandoned Peace for the First World War* (Profile, 2013)

Magnus, Philip, *King Edward the Seventh* (John Murray, 1964)

Mahl, Thomas E., *Desperate Deception: British Covert Operations in the United States, 1939–44* (Washington, DC: Brassey's, 1999)

Manchester, William, *The Arms of Krupp: The Rise and Fall of the Industrial Dynasty that Armed Germany at War* (Michael Joseph, 1969)

Manchester, William, *The Last Lion: Winston Spencer Churchill: Defender of the Realm, 1940–1965* (Hachette, 2012)

Markovich, Slobodan G., *British Perceptions of Serbia and the Balkans, 1903–1906* (Paris: Dialogue, 2000)

Marr, Andrew, *The Diamond Queen: Elizabeth II and Her People* (Pan, 2012)

Marshall, Dorothy, *The Life and Times of Victoria* (Weidenfeld & Nicolson, 1972)

Martin, Ralph, G., *The Woman He Loved* (NY: Simon & Schuster, 1974)

Masterman, John, *Double-cross System in the War of 1939 to 1945* (New Haven: Yale University Press, 1972)

Matthews, Rupert, *The Spanish Armada: A Campaign in Context* (Stroud: The History Press, 2009)

Mawby, Spencer, *The End of Empire in Uganda: Decolonization and Institutional Conflict 1945–1979* (Bloomsbury, 2020)

McGuire Mohr, Joan, *The Czech and Slovak Legion in Siberia, 1917–1922* (Toronto: McFarland, 2014)

McKinstry, Leo, *Operation Sealion: How Britain Crushed the German War Machine's Dreams of Invasion in 1940* (John Murray, 2015)

McLean, Roderick R., *Royalty and Diplomacy in Europe, 1890–1914* (Cambridge: Cambridge University Press, 2001)

Milani, Abbas, *The Shah* (Macmillan, 2011)

Millman, Richard, *British Policy and the Coming of the Franco-Prussian War* (Oxford: Clarendon Press, 1965)

Milton, Giles, *Russian Roulette: A Deadly Game: How British Spies Thwarted Lenin's Global Plot* (Hachette, 2013)

Moon, Alan, *Alan Turing and the Enigma Machine* (Lulu, 2014)

Moore, Charles, *Margaret Thatcher: The Authorised Biography, Vol. 1: Not for Turning* (Penguin, 2013)

Moore, Charles, *Margaret Thatcher: The Authorised Biography, Vol. 2: Everything She Wants* (Penguin, 2014)

Moran, Christopher, *Classified: Secrecy and the State in Modern Britain* (Cambridge: Cambridge University Press, 2013)

Morley, Jefferson, *Our Man in Mexico: Winston Scott and the Hidden History of the CIA* (Lawrence: Kansas University Press, 2008)

Morley, Sheridan, *Noël Coward* (Haus, 2005)

Morton, Andrew, *17 Carnations: The Windsors, the Nazis and the Cover-Up* (O'Mara, 2015)

Morton, Andrew, *Diana – Her True Story* (O'Mara, 2017)

Morton, Andrew, *Wallis in Love: The Untold Life of the Duchess of Windsor, the Woman Who Changed the Monarchy* (Hachette, 2018)

Murphy, Paul, *Shooting Victoria: Madness, Mayhem and Modernisation of the Monarchy* (Head of Zeus, 2013)

Murphy, Philip, *The Empire's New Clothes: The Myth of the Commonwealth* (Oxford: Oxford University Press, 2018)

Murphy, Philip, *Monarchy and the End of Empire* (Oxford: Oxford University Press, 2013)

Newsinger, John, *Dangerous Men: The SAS and Popular Culture* (Pluto, 1997)

Nicolson, *George V* (Constable, 1952)

O'Conner, Bernard, *The Tempsford Academy* (privately published, 2010)

O'Reagan, Douglas M., *Taking Nazi Technology: Allied Exploitation of German Science after the Second World War* (Baltimore: Johns Hopkins University Press, 2019)

Otte, Thomas, *The Foreign Office Mind: The Making of British Foreign Policy, 1865–1914* (Cambridge: Cambridge University Press, 2013)

Owen, David, *In Sickness and in Power: Illness in Heads of Government during the Last 100 Years* (NY: Praeger, 2008)

Paget, Julian, *Second to None: The History of the Coldstream Guards, 1650–2000* (Leo Cooper, 2000)

Pakula, Hannah, *An Uncommon Woman: The Empress Frederick – Daughter of Queen Victoria, Wife of the Crown Prince of Prussia, Mother of Kaiser Wilhelm* (NY: Touchstone, 1995)

Palmer, Dean, *The Queen and Mrs Thatcher: An Inconvenient Relationship* (Stroud: The History Press, 2015)

Parris, James, *The Man in the Brown Suit: MI5, Edward VIII and an Irish Assassin* (Stroud: The History Press, 2019)

Pasternak, Anna, *The American Duchess: The Real Wallis Simpson* (NY: Atria, 2019)

Pearce, Martin, *Spymaster: The Life of Britain's Most Decorated Cold War Spy and Head of MI6* (Transworld, 2017)

Pearson, John, *The Ultimate Family: The Making of the Royal House of Windsor* (Bloomsbury, 2013)

Pearson, John, *The Life of Ian Fleming* (Pan, 1967)

Pearson, Jonathan, *Sir Anthony Eden and the Suez Crisis: Reluctant Gamble* (Palgrave Macmillan, 2003)

Perry, Rowland, *The Queen, Her Lover and the Most Notorious Spy in History* (Allen & Unwin, 2015)

Petropoulos, Jonathan, *Royals and the Reich: The Princes von Hessen in Nazi Germany* (Oxford: Oxford University Press, 2009)

Pfennigwerth, Ian, *A Man of Intelligence: The Life of Captain Theodore Eric Nave, Australian Codebreaker Extraordinary* (Sydney: Rosenburg, 2006)

Phillips, Adrian, *The King Who Had to Go: Edward VIII, Mrs Simpson and the Hidden Politics of the Abdication Crisis* (Biteback, 2016)

Pimlott, Ben, *The Queen: A Biography of Elizabeth II* (Collins, 1997)

Pincher, Chapman, *Treachery: Betrayals, Blunders and Cover-Ups: Six Decades of Espionage* (Mainstream, 2012)

Pincus, Steven, *1688: The First Modern Revolution* (New Haven: Yale University Press, 2009)

Pipes, Richard, *Russian Revolution* (NY: Knopf, 2011)

Plowden, Alison, *The Elizabethan Secret Service* (NY: St Martin's Press, 1991)

Pope-Hennessy, James, *The Quest for Queen Mary*, edited by Hugo Vickers (Zuleika, 2018)

Porter, Bernard, *Plots and Paranoia: A History of Political Espionage in Britain, 1790–1988* (Unwin Hyman, 1989)

Porter, Bernard, *The Refugee Question in Mid-Victorian Politics* (Cambridge: Cambridge University Press, 1979)

Purkiss, Diane, *The English Civil War: A People's History* (Harper Press, 2006)

Quintin, Barry, *War in the East: A Military History of the Russo-Turkish War 1877–78* (Solihull: Helion, 2012)

Radzinsky, Edvard, *Alexander II: The Last Great Czar* (NY: Freepress, 2005)

Radzinsky, Edvard, *The Last Tsar: The Life and Death of Nicholas II* (NY: Anchor, 2011)

Rahnema, Ali, *Behind the 1953 Coup in Iran: Thugs, Turncoats, Soldiers and Spooks* (Cambridge: Cambridge University Press, 2016)

Rankin, Nicholas, *Defending the Rock: How Gibraltar Defeated Hitler* (Faber & Faber, 2017)

Rankin, Nicholas, *A Genius for Deception: How Cunning Helped the British Win Two World Wars* (NY: Oxford University Press, 2009)

Rappaport, Helen, *Four Sisters: The Lost Lives of the Daughters of Nicholas and Alexandra* (NY: Macmillan, 2004)

Rappaport, Helen, *The Race to Save the Romanovs: The Truth Behind the Secret Plans to Rescue the Russian Imperial Family* (NY: St Martin's Press, 2018)

Rath, Andrew, *The Crimean War in Imperial Context, 1854–1856* (Palgrave, 2015)

Rathmell, Andrew, *Secret War in the Middle East: The Covert Struggle for Syria, 1949–1961* (I.B. Tauris, 1995)

Raymond, Joad, *Pamphlets and Pamphleteering in Early Modern Britain* (Cambridge: Cambridge University Press, 2003)

Reid, Richard J., *A History of Modern Uganda* (Cambridge: Cambridge University Press, 2017)

Rekun, Mikhail, *How Russia Lost Bulgaria, 1878–1886: Empire Unguided* (Lanham: Lexington Books, 2019)

Reynolds, D., *In Command of History: Churchill Fighting and Writing the Second World War* (Penguin, 2005)

Reynolds, David, *Summits: Six Meetings That Shaped the World* (NY: Basic Books, 2007)

Richards, Brooks, *Secret Flotillas: Clandestine Sea Operations in the Mediterranean*, Vol. II (Cass, 2004)

Ridley, Jane, *Bertie: A Life of Edward VII* (Vintage, 2012)

Rigden, Denis, *How to Be a Spy: The World War II SOE Training Manual* (TNA/Dundurn Group, 2004)

Rose, Andrew, *The Prince, the Princess and the Perfect Murder: An Untold History* (Coronet, 2013)

Rose, Kenneth, *Elusive Rothschild: The Life of Victor, Third Baron* (Weidenfeld & Nicolson, 2003)

Rose, Kenneth, *King George V* (Weidenfeld & Nicolson, 2000)

Rose, Kenneth, *King, Queens and Courtiers* (Weidenfeld & Nicolson, 1985)

Rostain, Pascal, Mouron, Bruno, and Caradec'h, Jean-Michel, *Qui a tué Lady Di?* (Paris: Grasset, 2017)

Ruane, Kevin, *Churchill and the Bomb in War and Cold War* (Bloomsbury Academic, 2016)

Ruud, Charles A., and Stepanov, Sergei A., *Fontanka 16: The Tsars' Secret Police* (Montreal: McGill-Queen's University Press, 1999)

Salmon, Patrick, *Scandinavia and the Great Powers 1890–1940* (Cambridge: Cambridge University Press, 2002)

Sanabria, Enrique A., *Republicanism and Anticlerical Nationalism in Spain* (NY: Palgrave Macmillan, 2009)

Schabas, William A., *The Trial of the Kaiser* (Oxford: Oxford University Press, 2008)

Schoefield, Victoria, *Witness to History: The Life of John Wheeler-Bennett* (New Haven: Yale University Press, 2012)

Scott Cooper, Andrew, *The Fall of Heaven: The Pahlavis and the Final Days of Imperial Iran* (Picador, 2018)

Sebag Montefiore, Simon, *The Romanovs: An Intimate Chronicle of the Russian Royal Family* (Weidenfeld & Nicholson, 2014)

Sebba, Anne, *That Woman: The Life of Wallis Simpson, Duchess of Windsor* (Weidenfeld & Nicolson, 2011)

Seldon, Anthony, *John Major: A Political Life* (Weidenfeld & Nicolson, 1997)

Seligmann, Matthew, *Spies in Uniform: British Military and Naval Intelligence on the Eve of the First World War* (Oxford: Oxford University Press, 2006)

Service, Robert, *Spies and Commissars: Bolshevik Russia and the West* (Macmillan, 2011)

Seton-Watson, R.W., *Britain in Europe 1789 to 1914: A Survey of Foreign Policy* (Cambridge: Cambridge University Press, 1955)

Seward, Ingrid, *The Queen and Di* (Collins, 2000)

Seward, Ingrid, *The Queen's Speech: An Intimate Portrait of the Queen in Her Own Words* (Simon & Schuster, 2015)

Seymour, Miranda, *Noble Endeavours: The Life of Two Countries, England and Germany, in Many Stories* (NY: Simon & Schuster, 2013)

Shawcross, William, *Queen and Country* (BBC, 2002)

Shawcross, William, *Queen Elizabeth The Queen Mother: The Official Biography* (Macmillan, 2009)

Shawcross, William, *The Shah's Last Ride: The Fate of an Ally* (NY: Simon & Schuster, 1997)

Simmons, Simone, *Diana: The Last Word* (St Martin's Press, 2005)

Sinclair, Andrew, *The Other Victoria: The Princess Royal and the Great Game of Europe* (Weidenfeld & Nicholson, 1981)

Sinclair, David, *Two Georges: The Making of the Modern Monarchy* (Hodder & Stoughton, 1988)

Sitwell, Osbert, *Rat Week, An Essay on the Abdication* (Michael Joseph, 1986)

Skocpol, Theda, *States and Revolutions* (Cambridge: Cambridge University Press, 1977)

Small, Hugh, *The Crimean War: Europe's Conflict with Russia* (Stroud: The History Press, 2018)

Smith, Douglas, *Rasputin* (NY: Macmillan, 2016)

Smith, Geoffrey, *Royalist Agents, Conspirators and Spies: Their Role in the British Civil Wars, 1640–1660* (Farnham: Ashgate, 2011)

Smith, Michael, *Six: The Real James Bonds 1909–1939* (Biteback, 2011)

Soley, Lawrence C., *Radio Warfare: OSS and CIA Subversive Propaganda* (NY: Praeger, 1989)

Soroka, Marina, *Britain, Russia and the Road to the First World War: The Fateful Embassy of Benckendorff, Count Aleksandr (1903–1916)* (Routledge: 2011)

Sowerby, Scott, *Making Toleration: The Repealers and the Glorious Revolution* (Cambridge, MA: Harvard University Press, 2013)

St Aubyn, Giles, *Edward VII: Prince and King* (Collins, 1979)

St Aubyn, Giles, *Queen Victoria: A Portrait* (Sinclair-Stevenson, 1991)

Stafford, David, *Ten Days to D-Day* (Little, Brown, 2003)

Stafford, David, *Camp X: SOE and the American Connection* (Viking, 1986)

Steinberg, Jonathan, *Bismarck: A Life* (Oxford: Oxford University Press, 2011)

Stewart, Alan, *The Cradle King: A Life of James VI & I* (Macmillan, 2003)

Stewart, Andrew, *The King's Private Army: Protecting the British Royal Family During the Second World War* (Solihull: Helion, 2015)

Strong, Roy, *The Cult of Elizabeth: Elizabethan Portraiture and Pageantry* (Berkeley: University of California Press, 1986)

Sulzberger, C.L., *The Fall of Eagles* (NY: Crown, 1977)

Summers, Anthony, and Mangold, Tom, *The File on the Tsar* (Gollancz, 1976)

Summers, Anthony, and Dorril, Stephen, *The Secret Worlds of Stephen Ward: Sex, Scandal, and Deadly Secrets in the Profumo Affair* (Headline, 2013)

Szasz, Ferenc Morton, *British Scientists and the Manhattan Project: The Los Alamos Years* (Macmillan, 1992)

Taylor, Miles, *Empress: Queen Victoria and India* (New Haven: Yale University Press, 2018)

Taylor, Peter, *Brits: The War against the IRA* (Bloomsbury, 2002)

Thackeray, William Makepeace, *The Four Georges and the English Humourists of the Eighteenth Century* (Smith, Elder, 1890)

Thomas, Wyn, *Hands off Wales: Nationhood and Militancy* (Gomer, 2013)

Thomas, Wyn, *John Jenkins: The Reluctant Revolutionary?* (Y Lolfa, 2019)

Thomson, Basil, *The Story of Scotland Yard* (Grayson & Grayson, 1935)

Thornton, Michael, *Royal Feud: The Queen Mother and the Duchess of Windsor* (Michael Joseph, 1985)

Thorpe, D.R., *Eden: The Life and Times of Anthony Eden, First Earl of Avon, 1897–1977* (Pimlico, 2004)

Tillotson, Michael, *SOE and the Resistance: As Told in The Times Obituaries* (Continuum, 2001)

Travers, John, *The Gunpowder Plot: Terror in Shakespeare's England* (Stroud: Amberley/TNA, 2019)

Twigge, Stephen, *Codebreakers: Images of the National Archives* (Barnsley: Pen & Sword, 2020)

Twigge, Stephen, and Scott, Len, *Planning Armageddon: Britain, the United States and the Command of Western Nuclear Forces, 1945–1964* (Routledge, 2000)

Turing, Sara, *Alan M. Turing: Centenary Edition* (Cambridge: Cambridge University Press, 2012)

Underdown, David, *Royalist Conspiracy 1649–1660* (New Haven: Yale University Press, 1960)

Urbach, Karina, *Go-Betweens for Hitler* (Oxford: Oxford University Press, 2015)

Urban, Mark, *UK Eyes Alpha: The Inside Story of British Intelligence* (Faber & Faber, 1996)

Van der Kiste, John, *Alfred: Queen Victoria's Second Son* (Fonthill, 2015)

Van der Kiste, John, *Queen Victoria and the European Empires* (Fonthill, 2016)

Vasey, Christopher, *Nazi Intelligence Operations in Non-Occupied Territories: Espionage Efforts in the United States, Britain, South America and Southern Africa* (NY: McFarland, 2016)

Verrier, Anthony, *Through the Looking Glass: British Foreign Policy in an Age of Illusions* (NY: Norton, 1983)

Vinen, Richard, *Thatcher's Britain: The Politics and Social Upheaval of the 1980s* (Simon & Schuster, 2010)

Wade, Stephen, *Spies in the Empire: Victorian Military Intelligence* (Anthem, 2007)

Walton, Calder, *Empire of Secrets: British Intelligence, the Cold War and the Twilight of Empire* (Collins, 2013)

Warner, Michael, *The Rise and Fall of Intelligence: An International Security History* (Washington DC: Georgetown UP, 2014).

Warwick, Christopher, *Princess Margaret: A Life in Contrasts* (Andre Deutsch, 2017)

Weiner, Tim, *Legacy of Ashes: The History of the CIA* (Anchor, 2008)

Weintraub, Stanley, *Uncrowned King: The Life of Prince Albert* (NY: Free Press, 1997)

Weintraub, Stanley, *Victoria* (John Murray, 1996)

Weisbrode, Kenneth, *Churchill and the King: The Wartime Alliance of Winston Churchill and George VI* (Penguin, 2015)

West, Nigel, *The A–Z of British Intelligence* (Plymouth: Scarecrow Press, 2009)

West, Nigel (ed.), *British Security Coordination: The Secret History of British Intelligence in the Americas, 1940–1945* (NY: Fromm, 1999)

West, Nigel, *Cold War Spymaster* (Barnsley: Pen & Sword, 2018)

West, Nigel, *Double Cross in Cairo: The True Story of the Spy Who Turned the Tide of War* (Biteback, 2015)

Wheeler-Bennett, John, *George VI* (Macmillan, 1958)

Whiting, Audrey, *The Kents: A Royal Family* (Hutchinson, 1985)

Wilkinson, Peter, and Bright Astley, Joan, *Gubbins & SOE* (Barnsley: Pen & Sword, 1993)

Wilson, Christopher, *The Windsor Knot: Charles, Camilla and the Legacy of Diana* (Citadel, 2003)

Wilson, Jim, *Britain on the Brink: The Cold War's Most Dangerous Weekend: 27–28 October 1962* (Barnsley: Pen & Sword, 2012)

Wilson, Jim, *Launch Pad UK: Britain and the Cuban Missile Crisis* (Barnsley: Pen & Sword, 2008)

Wilson, Ray, and Adams, Ian, *Special Branch: A History, 1883–2006* (Biteback, 2015)

Wooley, Benjamin, *The King's Assassin: The Secret Plot to Murder King James I* (NY: St Martin's Press, 2018)

Worthington, Heather, *The Rise of the Detective in Early Nineteenth-Century Popular Fiction* (Basingstoke: Palgrave Macmillan, 2005)

Yarmolinsky, Avrahm, *Road to Revolution: A Century of Russian Radicalism* (Princeton: Princeton University Press, 2016)

Zegart, Amy, *Spies, Lies, and Algorithms: The History and Future of American Intelligence* (Princeton: Princeton UP, 2022).

Zielger, Philip, *King Edward VIII: The Official Biography* (Collins, 1990)

Ziegler, Philip, *Mountbatten: The Official Biography* (HarperCollins, 1985)

Ziegler, Philip, *Wilson: The Authorized Life* (Weidenfeld & Nicolson, 1993)

Essays

Adams, Robyn, 'A most secret service: William Herle and the circulation of intelligence', in Robyn Adams and Rosanna Cox (eds), *Diplomacy and Early Modern Culture* (Palgrave Macmillan, 2011): 63–81

Adams, Robyn, '"The Service I am here for": William Herle in the Marshalsea Prison, 1571', *Huntington Library Quarterly*, 72 (2009): 217–38

Adams, Robyn, 'Signs of Intelligence: William Herle's Report of the Dutch Situation, 1573', *Lives and Letters*, 1 (2009): 1–18

Aldrich, Richard, J., 'Policing the Past: Official History, Secrecy and British Intelligence since 1945', *English Historical Review*, 119/483 (2004): 922–53

Aldrich, Richard J., 'OSS, CIA and European unity: The American committee on United Europe, 1948–60', *Diplomacy and Statecraft*, 8/1 (1997): 184–227

Aldrich, Richard J., and Coleman, Michael, 'Britain and the Strategic Air Offensive Against the Soviet Union: The Question of South Asian Air Bases, 1945–9', *History*, 74/242 (1989): 400–26

Aldrich, Richard J. and Herrington, Lewis, 'Secrets, Hostages and Ransoms: British Kidnap Policy in Historical Perspective', *Review of International Studies*, 44/4 (2018): 738–59

Ashton, Nigel, '"Great New Venture"? Anglo-American Cooperation in the Middle East and the Response to the Iraqi Revolution, July 1958', *Diplomacy and Statecraft*, 4/1 (1993): 59–89

Ashton, Nigel, 'Love's Labours Lost: Margaret Thatcher, King Hussein and Anglo-Jordanian Relations, 1979–1990', *Diplomacy and Statecraft*, 22/4 (2011): 651–77

Aubourg, Valerie, 'Organizing Atlanticism: the Bilderberg group and the Atlantic institute, 1952–1963', *Intelligence and National Security*, 18/2 (2003): 92–105

Baker, Helen, 'Monarchy discredited? Reactions to the Khodynka coronation catastrophe of 1896', *Revolutionary Russia*, 16/1 (2003): 1–46

Balfour-Paul, Glen, 'Britain's Informal Empire in the Middle East', in Judith Brown and Wm Roger Louis (eds), *The Oxford History of the British Empire vol. IV: The Twentieth Century* (Oxford: Oxford University Press, 1999): 490–514

Baylen, Joseph O., 'Madame Olga Novikov, Propagandist', *The American Slavic and East European Review*, 10/4 (1951): 255–71

Beckett, Ian F.W., 'Royalty and the Army in the Twentieth Century', in Matthew Glencross, Judith Rowbotham and Michael D. Kandiah, *The Windsor Dynasty 1910 to the Present: 'Long to Reign Over Us'?* (Palgrave Macmillan, 2016): 109–33

Beckett, John, 'November 1913: The Archduke, Nottingham and a Near Miss', The Centre for Hidden Histories: Community, Commemoration and the First World War, http://hiddenhistorieswwi.ac.uk/uncategorized/2014/07/november-1913-the-archduke-nottingham-and-a-near-miss/

Békés, Csaba, 'President Kliment Voroshilov's Telegram to Queen Elizabeth of Great Britain on the Soviet Intervention in Hungary on 4 November 1956', *The Slavonic and East European Review*, 71/1 (1993): 126–29

Black, Alistair, 'Information management in the Intelligence Branch of Britain's War Office, 1873–1914: All information flows toward it, or returns to it, in a form worked up into shape', *Open Information Science*, 4/1 (2020): 91–105

Black, Alistair, 'The Victorian Information Society: Surveillance, Bureaucracy, and Public Librarianship in the 19th Century', *The Information Society*, 17/1 (2001): 53–90

Black, Jeremy, 'British intelligence and the mid-eighteenth-century crisis', *Intelligence and National Security*, 2/2 (1987): 209–29

Charmley, John, and Davey, Jennifer, 'The Invisible Politician: Mary Derby and the Eastern Crisis', in John Fisher and Antony Best (eds), *On the Fringes of Diplomacy: Influences on British Foreign Policy, 1800–1945* (Surrey: Ashgate, 2011)

Cogswell, Thomas, 'The Politics of Propaganda: Charles I and the People in the 1620s', *The Journal of British Studies*, 29/3 (1990): 187–215

Collyer, Michael, 'Secret Agents: Anarchists, Islamists and Responses to Politically Active Refugees in London', *Ethnic and Racial Studies*, 28/2 (2006): 278–303

Cull, Nicholas, 'The Munich Crisis and British Propaganda Policy in the United States', in Igor Lukes and Erik Goldstein (eds), *The Munich Crisis: Prelude to World War II* (Frank Cass, 1999): 217–18

Danchev, Alex, 'On Specialness', *International Affairs*, 72/4 (1996): 737–50

Daigler, Kenneth, 'In Defence of John Honeyman (and George Washington)', *Studies in Intelligence*, 53/4 (2009): 87–9

Deflem, Mathieu, '"Wild Beasts Without Nationality": The Uncertain Origins of Interpol, 1898–1910', in Philip Reichel (ed.), *The Handbook of Transnational Crime and Justice* (Thousand Oaks: Sage Publications, 2005): 275–85

Dover, Robert, 'For queen and company: The role of intelligence in the UK's arms trade', *Political Studies*, 55/4 (2007): 683–708

Dylan, Huw, 'Operation TIGRESS: Deception for Counterintelligence and Britain's 1952 Atomic Test', *Journal of Intelligence History*, 14/1 (2014): 1–15

Ferris, John, 'Lord Salisbury, secret intelligence and British policy toward Russia and Central Asia', in John Ferris, *Intelligence and Strategy, Selected Essays* (Taylor and Francis 2005): 8–44

Fischlin, Daniel, 'Political Allegory, Absolutist Ideology, and the "Rainbow Portrait" of Queen Elizabeth I', *Renaissance Quarterly*, 50/1 (1997): 175–206

Fritschy, Wantje, 'A "financial revolution" reconsidered: public finance in Holland during the Dutch Revolt, 1568–1648', *Economic History Review*, 56/1 (2003): 57–89

Glencross, Matthew, 'A Cause of Tension? The Leadership of King George V: Visiting the Western Front', in Matthew Glencross and Judith Rowbotham (eds), *Monarchies and the Great War* (Palgrave, 2018): 153–89

Graziani, René, 'The "Rainbow Portrait" of Queen Elizabeth I and its Religious Symbolism', *Journal of the Warburg and Courtauld Institutes*, 35/1 (1972): 247–59

Hamilton, Keith, 'Addressing the Past', in C. Baxter, M. Dockrill and K. Hamilton (eds), *Britain in Global Politics Volume 1: From Gladstone to Churchill* (Springer, 2013): 117–18

Harrison, Andrew, 'The Duke and the Dictator: The Royal Role in Marshal Tito's Visit to Britain, March 1953', in Matthew Glencross, Judith Rowbotham and Michael D. Kandiah, *The Windsor Dynasty 1910 to the Present: 'Long to Reign Over Us'?* (Palgrave Macmillan, 2016): 217–37

Hennessy, Peter, '"Inescapable, Necessary and Lunatic": Whitehall's Transition-to-war Planning for the Third World War', *Twentieth Century British History*, 21/2 (2010): 206–24

Hicks, Leo, 'The Strange Case of Dr William Parry: The Career of an Agent-Provocateur', *Studies: An Irish Quarterly Review*, 37/147 (1948): 343–62

Hughes, Michael, 'British Opinion and Russian Terrorism in the 1880s', *European History Quarterly*, 41/2 (2011): 255–77

Humphries, Michael, '"Perfectly Secret and Perfectly Democratic": Lord Esher and the Society of Islanders, 1909–14', *The English Historical Review*, 127/528 (2012): 1156–79

Ingram, David, 'Thatcher and Ramphal: A Long and Turbulent Relationship', *The Round Table*, 97/398 (2008): 781–83

Jensen, Richard Bach, 'The International Anti-Anarchist Conference and the Origins of Interpol', *Journal of Contemporary History*, 16 (1981): 323–47

Jensen, Richard Bach, 'The International Campaign Against Anarchist Terrorism, 1880–1930s', *Terrorism and Political Violence*, 21/1 (2009): 89–109

Jones, Matthew, 'The "preferred plan": the Anglo-American Working Group report on covert action in Syria, 1957', *Intelligence and National Security*, 19/3 (2004): 401–15

Kadish, Sharman, '"Boche, Bolshie and the Jewish Bogey": The Russian revolution and press antisemitism in Britain 1917–21', *Patterns of Prejudice*, 22/4 (1988): 24–39

Kandiah, Michael, *et al.*, 'The Ultimate Windsor Ceremonials: Coronations and Investitures', in Matthew Glencross, Judith Rowbotham and Michael D. Kandiah, *The Windsor Dynasty 1910 to the Present: 'Long to Reign Over Us'?* (Palgrave Macmillan, 2016): 59–86

Kapitonova, Natalia, 'Visit of Soviet leaders Nikita Khrushchev and Nicholas Bulganin to Britain in April 1956', *Cold War History*, 14/1 (2014): 127–52

Kaplan, Roger, 'The Hidden War: British Intelligence Operations during the American Revolution', *William and Mary Quarterly*, 47/1 (1990): 115–38

Karam, Jeffrey, 'Missing Revolution: The American Intelligence Failure in Iraq, 1958', *Intelligence and National Security*, 32/6 (2017): 693–709

Kenna, Shane, 'The Victorian War on Terror', *BBC History Extra (November* 2013)

Kennedy, Paul, 'Great Britain Beyond 1914', in Ernest May (ed.), *Knowing One's Enemies* (Princeton: Princeton University Press, 1986): 172–202

Kent, George O., 'Editing Diplomatic Documents: A Review of Official U.S. and German Document Series', *The American Archivist*, 57 (1994): 462–81

King, John N., 'Queen Elizabeth I: Representations of the Virgin Queen', *Renaissance Quarterly*, 43/1 (1990): 30–74

Kollander, Patricia, 'Empress Frederick: The Last Hope for a Liberal Germany?', *The Historian*, 62/1 (1999): 47–62

Lea, Luke and Alderson, William T., 'The Attempt to Capture the Kaiser', *Tennessee Historical Quarterly*, 20/3 (1961): 222–61

Leimon, Mitchell, and Parker, Geoffrey, 'Treason and Plot in Elizabethan Diplomacy: The "Fame of Sir Edward Stafford" Reconsidered', *English Historical Review*, 111/444 (1996): 1134–58

Louis, Wm Roger, and Robinson, Ronald, 'The Imperialism of Decolonisation', in *Ends of British Imperialism: The Scramble for Empire, Suez and Decolonization: Collected Essays* (I.B. Tauris, 2006): 451–502

Louis, Wm Roger, 'Britain and the Overthrow of the Mosaddeq Government', in M. Gasiorowski and M. Byrne (eds), *Mohammad Mosaddeq and the 1953 Coup in Iran* (Syracuse: Syracuse University Press, 2004): 126–77

Mawby, Spencer, 'The Clandestine Defence of Empire: British Special Operations in Yemen 1951–64', *Intelligence and National Security*, 17/3 (2002): 105–30

McCrisken, Trevor, and Moran, Christopher, 'James Bond, Ian Fleming and intelligence: breaking down the boundary between the "real" and the "imagined"', *Intelligence and National Security*, 33/6 (2018): 804–21

Moran, Christopher, 'Concealing Collusion: The Suez Crisis, Political Memoirs and Official Secrecy', *English Historical Review*, 134/567 (2019): 358–89

Moran, Richard, 'The origin of insanity as a special verdict: the trial for treason of James Hadfield, 1800', *Law and Society Review*, 19/3 (1985): 487–519

Moran, Richard, 'The punitive uses of the insanity defense: The trial for treason of Edward Oxford (1840)', *International Journal of Law and Psychiatry*, 9/2 (1986): 171–90

Mosse, W.E., 'The Crown and Foreign Policy: Queen Victoria and the Austro-Prussian Conflict, March–May 1866', *Cambridge Historical Journal*, 10/2 (1951): 205–23

Mosse, W.E., 'Queen Victoria and Her Ministers in the Schleswig-Holstein Crisis 1863–1864', *English Historical Review*, 78/307 (1963): 263–83

Murphy, Philip, 'By invitation only: Lord Mountbatten, Prince Philip, and the attempt to create a Commonwealth "Bilderberg group", 1964–66', *Journal of Imperial and Commonwealth History*, 33/2 (2005): 245–65

Pady, Donald S., and Kline, Laura S., 'Finger Counting and the Identification of James VI's Secret Agents', *Cryptologia*, 4/3 (1980): 140–49

Platt, Roger, 'The Soviet Imprisonment of Gerald Brooke and Subsequent Exchange for the Krogers, 1965–1969', *Contemporary British History*, 24/2 (2010): 193–21

Pollitt, Ronald, 'The Abduction of Doctor John Story and the Evolution of Elizabethan Intelligence Operations', *The Sixteenth Century Journal*, 14/2 (1983): 131–56

Prochaska, Frank, 'George V and Republicanism, 1917–1919', *Twentieth Century British History*, 10/1 (1999): 27–51

Purvis, Stewart, 'When spooks pulled strings', *British Journalism Review*, 27/1 (2016): 62–7

Rankin, Mark, 'Richard Topcliffe and the Book Culture of the Elizabethan Catholic Underground', *Renaissance Quarterly*, 72/2 (2019): 492–36

Read, Conyers, 'Walsingham and Burghley in Queen Elizabeth's Privy Council', *English Historical Review*, 28 (1913): 34–58

Rix, Keith, 'Towards a more just insanity defence: recovering moral wrongfulness in the M'Naghten Rules', *BJPsych Advances*, 22/1 (2016): 44–52

Scott, Jonathan, '"Good Night Amsterdam". Sir George Downing and Anglo-Dutch Statebuilding', *English Historical Review*, 118/476 (2003): 334–56

Scott, Len, 'Intelligence and the Risk of Nuclear War', in D. Gioe, L. Scott and C. Andrew (eds), *An International History of the Cuban Missile Crisis – A 50 Year Retrospective* (Routledge, 2014)

Scott-Smith, Giles, 'The Congress for Cultural Freedom, the End of Ideology and the 1955 Milan Conference: Defining the Parameters of Discourse', *Journal of Contemporary History*, 37/3 (2002): 437–55

Scriba, Christoph J., 'The Autobiography of John Wallis, F.R.S.', *Notes and Records of the Royal Society of London*, 25/1 (1970): 17–46

Seligmann, Matthew, 'Prince Louis of Battenberg', in Karina Urbach (ed.), *Royal Kinship: Anglo-German Family Networks, 1815–1918* (De Gruyter, 2008)

Sherman, William H., 'Research Intelligence in Early Modern England,' *Studies in Intelligence*, 37/5 (1994): 95–8

Shlaim, Avi, 'A Totalitarian Concept of History', *Middle East Quarterly*, 3/3 (1996): 52–5

Smith, Adrian, 'Resignation of a First Sea Lord: Mountbatten and the 1956 Suez Crisis', *History*, 98/329 (2013): 105–34

Smith, Adrian, 'Rewriting History? Admiral Lord Mountbatten's Efforts to Distance Himself From the 1956 Suez Crisis', *Contemporary British History*, 26/4 (2012): 489–508

Smith, F.B., 'British Post Office Espionage, 1844', *Historical Studies*, 14/54 (1970): 189–203

Squiers, Carol, 'Class Struggle: The invention of paparazzi photography and the death of Diana, Princess of Wales', in Carol Squiers (ed.), *Over Exposed: Essays on Contemporary Photography* (NY: The New Press, 1999): 269–304

Stillman, Grant B., 'Two of the MADdest scientists: where Strangelove Meets Dr. No; or, unexpected roots for Kubrick's cold war classic', *Film History*, 20/4 (2008): 487–500

Stout, Mark, 'World War I and the birth of American intelligence culture', *Intelligence and National Security*, 32/3 (2017): 378–394.

Sweet, Paul R., 'The Windsor File', *The Historian*, 59/ 2 (1997): 263–80

Talbot, George, 'Into the Nineties – The Queen Mother', in Caroline Elliot (ed.), *The BBC Book of Royal Memories, 1947–1990* (BBC Books, 1991): 219–43

Trim, David, 'The secret war of Elizabeth I: England and the Huguenots during the early Wars of Religion, 1562–77', *Proceedings of the Huguenot Society*, XXVII/2 (1999): 182–99

Tu, Hsuan-Ying, 'The Politics of Intelligence Gathering: Sir Edward Stafford's Embassy in France (1583–1590)', *Collectanea of History NCCU*, 18 (2010): 63–98

Vincent, David, 'Surveillance, Privacy and History', *History and Policy* (October 2013)

Wales, T.C., 'The "Massingham" Mission and the secret special relationship', in Neville Wylie (ed.), *The Politics and Strategy of Clandestine War: Special Operations Executive* (Routledge, 2005): 42–65

Walker, Claire, '"Remember Justice Godfrey": The Popish Plot and the Construction of Panic in Seventeenth-Century Media', in David Lemmings and Claire Walker (eds), *Moral Panics, the Media and the Law in Early Modern England* (Palgrave Macmillan, 2009): 117–38

Wilford, Hugh, 'CIA plot, socialist conspiracy, or new world order? The origins of the Bilderberg group, 1952–55', *Diplomacy and Statecraft*, 14/3 (2003): 70–82

Young, John, 'Talking to Tito: The Eden Visit to Yugoslavia, September 1952', *Review of International Studies*, 12/1 (1986): 31–41

Zonis, Marvin, and Joseph, Craig M., 'Conspiracy thinking in the Middle East', *Political Psychology*, 15/3 (1994): 443–59

Theses

Chiasson-Taylor, Rachelle A. M., 'Musicians and intelligence operations, 1570–1612: politics, surveillance, and patronage in the late Tudor and early Stuart years', PhD, McGill University, 2007

Fett, Denice Lyn, 'Information, Intelligence and Negotiation in the West European Diplomatic World, 1558–1588', PhD, The Ohio State University, 2010

Griffin, Rachael, *'Detective Policing and the State in Nineteenth Century England: The Detective Department of the London Metropolitan Police'*, PhD, University of Western Ontario, 2016

Higgins, Simon, 'How Was Haldane Able to Transform the Army? A Historical Assessment Using a Contemporary Change Management Model', PhD, University of Birmingham, 2011

McKee, Claire T., 'British Perceptions of Tsar Nicholas II and Empress Alexandra Fedorovna 1894–1918', PhD, University College London, 2014

Peck, N., 'Drawing back the curtain: a post-Leveson examination of celebrity, privacy and press intrusion', PhD, University of London, 2017

Rose, Helen, 'Rebellion, Spymasters and Spies: The Rise of Intelligence Operations in England, 1569–1585', MA Thesis, Texas Tech University, 2014

Tu, Hsuan-Ying, 'The Pursuit of God's Glory: Francis Walsingham's Espionage in Elizabethan Politics, 1568–1588', PhD, University of York, 2012

Television

D-Day: The King Who Fooled Hitler (C4 documentary, 2019)
Die Royals und die Nazis (ZDF Germany documentary, 2018)
Oprah with Meghan and Harry (CBS, 2021)
Spying on the Royals: Parts One and Two (C4 documentary, 2017)
The Queen and the Coup (C4 documentary, 2020)
The Victorian War on Terror (BBC History Extra, 2013)

INDEX